André Heller

# LUNA LUNA

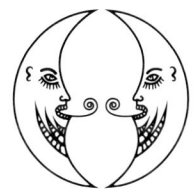

Enabled by Neue Revue

Photo Documentation by
*Sabina Sarnitz*

Essay by
*Hilde Spiel*

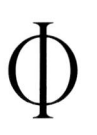

This text was initially published in 1987, coinciding with *Luna Luna*'s debut in Hamburg.

In the decades since, *Luna Luna* has embarked on an unforeseen journey. Instead of the grand global tour first envisioned, *Luna Luna* was sold into obscurity, locked away in forty-four shipping containers, and then rescued thirty-five years later. Now, *Luna Luna* is preparing to tour the world as intended many moons ago, featuring the 1987 collection alongside added amusements by contemporary artists.

Today, we celebrate *Luna Luna*'s origins with a reissue of the original publication, translated from German to English for the first time, including an updated preface by *Luna Luna*'s mastermind, André Heller.

Enjoy the ride.

# André Heller, Vienna, Summer 2022

My life thus far has been a never-ending flight of dreams, filled with wonder and challenges. For the past 75 years, the unimaginable has presented itself to me as a persistent teacher, allowing me to transform myself through learning and helping me to explore uncharted territories on the map of my knowledge.

Time and again, I would set out on expeditions off the beaten track — landscapes, romances, and artistic ventures — so as to fathom my inner self and the world as best I could. As dynamic companions and sources of encouragement, I laid claim to the friendship of numerous deceased individuals who were no longer in a position to fend off my enthusiasm for them. Geniuses as diverse as Schubert, Buster Keaton, Giacometti, Chekhov, Anna Magnani, the Montgolfier brothers, Billie Holiday, Stravinsky, Bill Bojangles, Yma Sumac, Picasso, John Coltrane, and Sergei Diaghilev, to name but a few.

These were the figures I declared to be my private saints as I prayed to them for a blessed existence. And it seems they indeed allowed me, and continue to allow me, to take part in a wealth of adventure. Among the most exciting are the times I have produced something that proves to be an inspiration and a pleasure for people of all ages and levels of education. In my opinion, art is *not* a secret society for a select few: it asks questions and does not shy away from uncomfortable answers.

Art enriches children and adults, Nobel Prize winners and workers alike, offering food for thought and qualities of all kinds, making people laugh or administering a positive shock. The peculiar undertaking that is *Luna Luna* is an expression of this conviction. It is nothing short of a miracle that so many painters, sculptors, poets, and composers tuned to such wildly different keys were willing to pull the same rope at the same time for a mere token sum. The loving gratitude I felt towards these women and men — already immense in 1987 — is infinite today. For when I reflect on the list of names of those gathered for this project, I cannot help but shake my head in disbelief.

For 35 years, the works of *Luna Luna* were buried alive in forty-four shipping containers, and it is thanks to one of the most undoubtedly extraordinary people of our time that this treasure has finally been unearthed: Drake.

I bow down to him and the ever-serene and noble protagonists of his Dream Crew. Without the breathtakingly talented and terrifically persistent Michael Goldberg and my wonderful son Ferdinand, the connection between Drake, *Luna Luna*, and myself would never have come into being; while Daniel McClean and Justin Wills had the talent to master the economic and contractual problems involved in the venture. We, too, owe more to Anthony Gonzales than words can express. Finally, the unique perspective of photographer Sabina Sarnitz made this book possible. May our efforts be rewarded!

# André Heller, Vienna, Summer 1987

*Luna Luna* is an attempt to create a traveling territory of modern art that follows the centuries old principle of the fairground, encouraging people of all ages and educational levels to engage in playful routines. Carousels and swing rides have always been revolving sculptures—but no major artist has ever dedicated themselves to creating one before. The same applies to scary train rides—they have always been a space for images, reliefs, and theatrical machines. With the help of my artist friends, I have resurrected traditional fairground attractions and added some that have never been seen before. As a result, *Luna Luna* has become a collection of surprises—the unprecedented work of more than thirty influential living masters of painting, sculpture, music, and literature. It sets out to offer aesthetic pleasure for the senses. I hope visitors around the world will leave it feeling cheerful and exhilarated as they are reminded of the possibilities of their own creative imagination. I would like to thank *Neue Revue* and Heinrich Bauer Verlag for funding *Luna Luna*.

# The Artists of

Sonia Delaunay

Jörg Immendorff

Wolfgang Herzig

Joseph Beuys

Monika Gilsing

Jim Whiting

Erté

Hans Magnus Enzensberger

Kenny Scharf

André Heller

Jean-Michel Basquiat

# Luna Luna

August Walla

Rebecca Horn

Roland Topor

Gertie Fröhlich

Christian Ludwig Attersee

Peter Pongratz

Keith Haring

Friedensreich Hundertwasser

Daniel Spoerri

Hubert Aratym

George Baselitz

David Hockney

Arik Brauer

Susanne Schmögner

Salvador Dalí

Günter Brus

Patrick Raynaud

Manfred Deix

Jean Tinguely

Roy Lichtenstein

Hermann Nitsch

Philip Glass

# Table

# of Contents

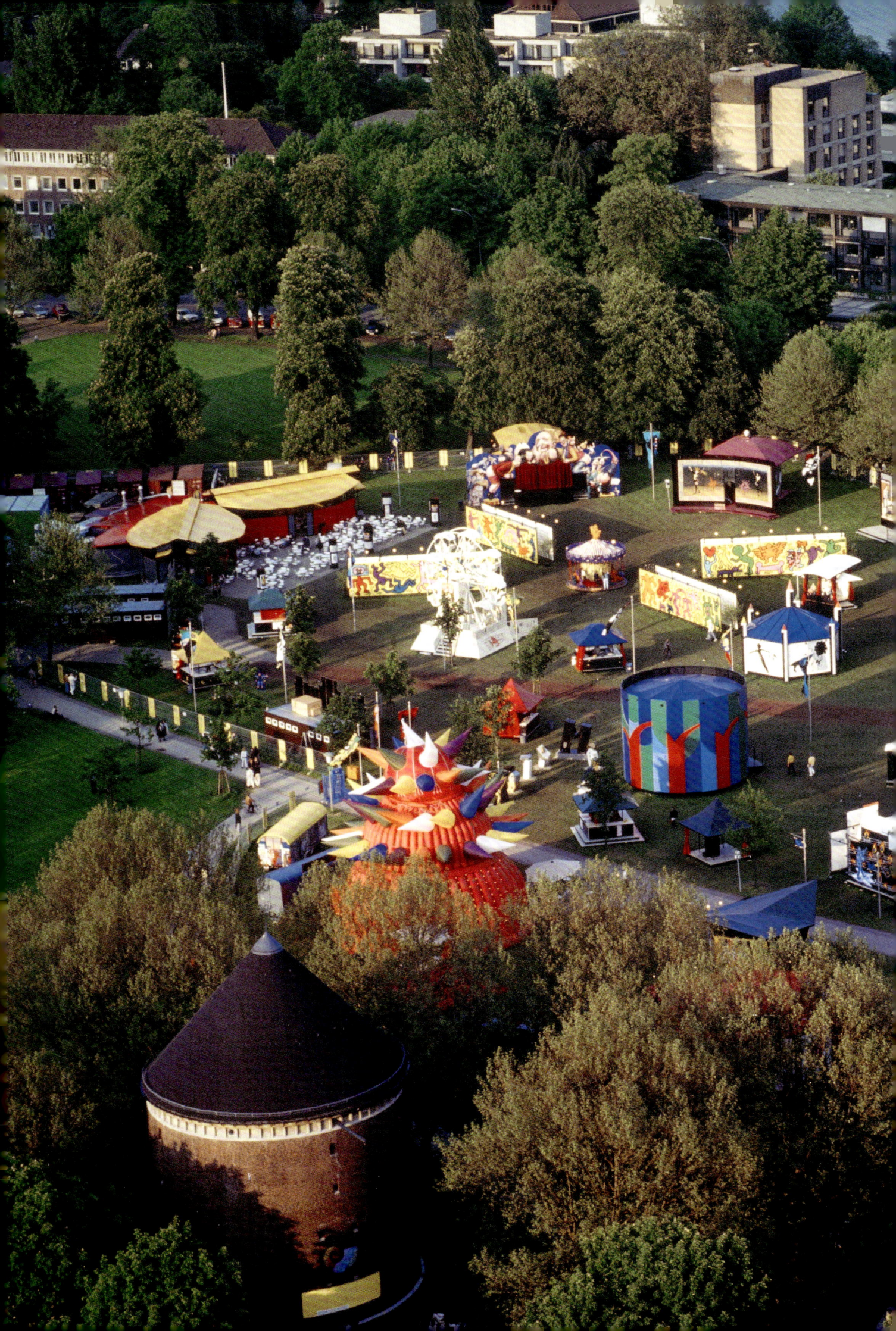

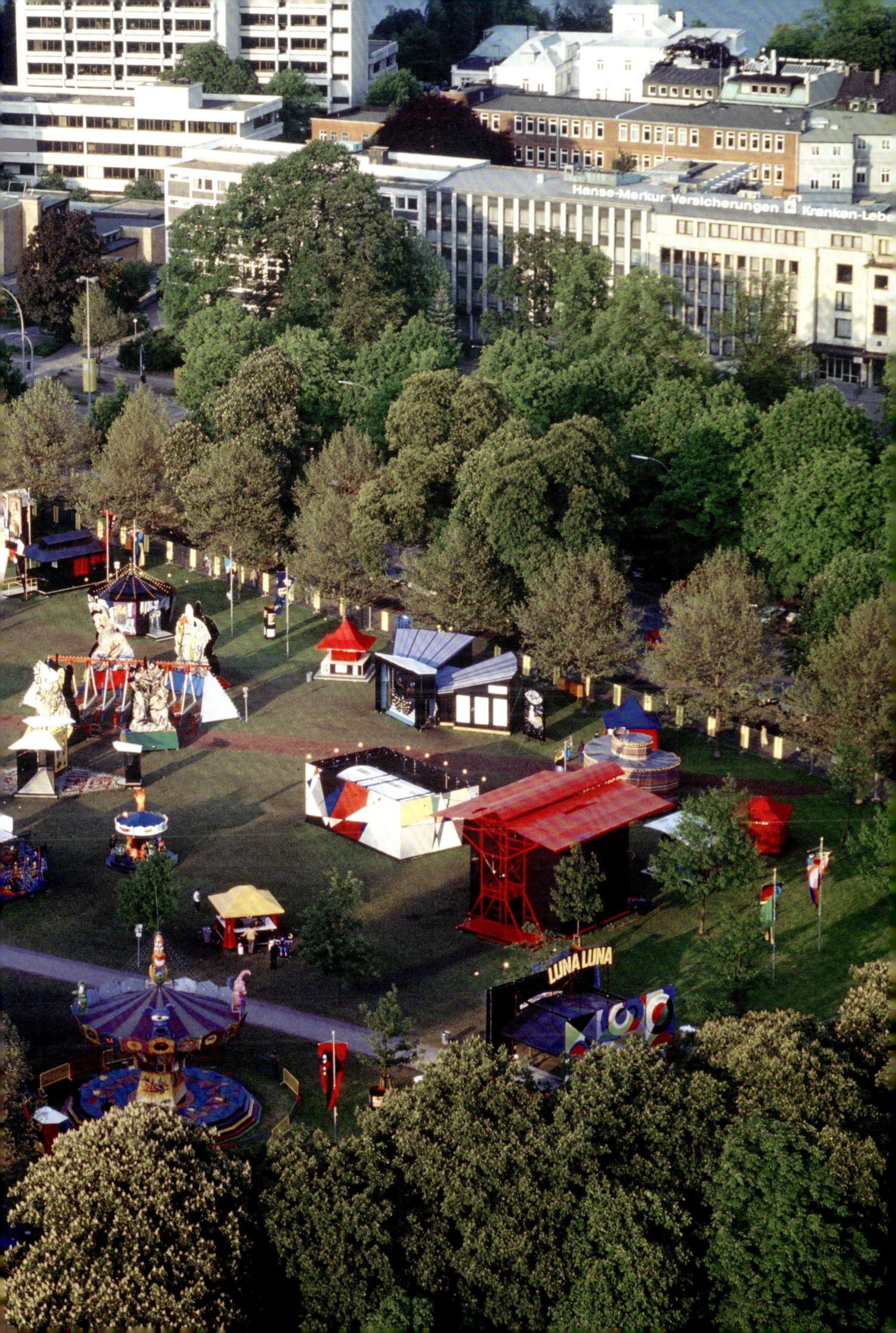

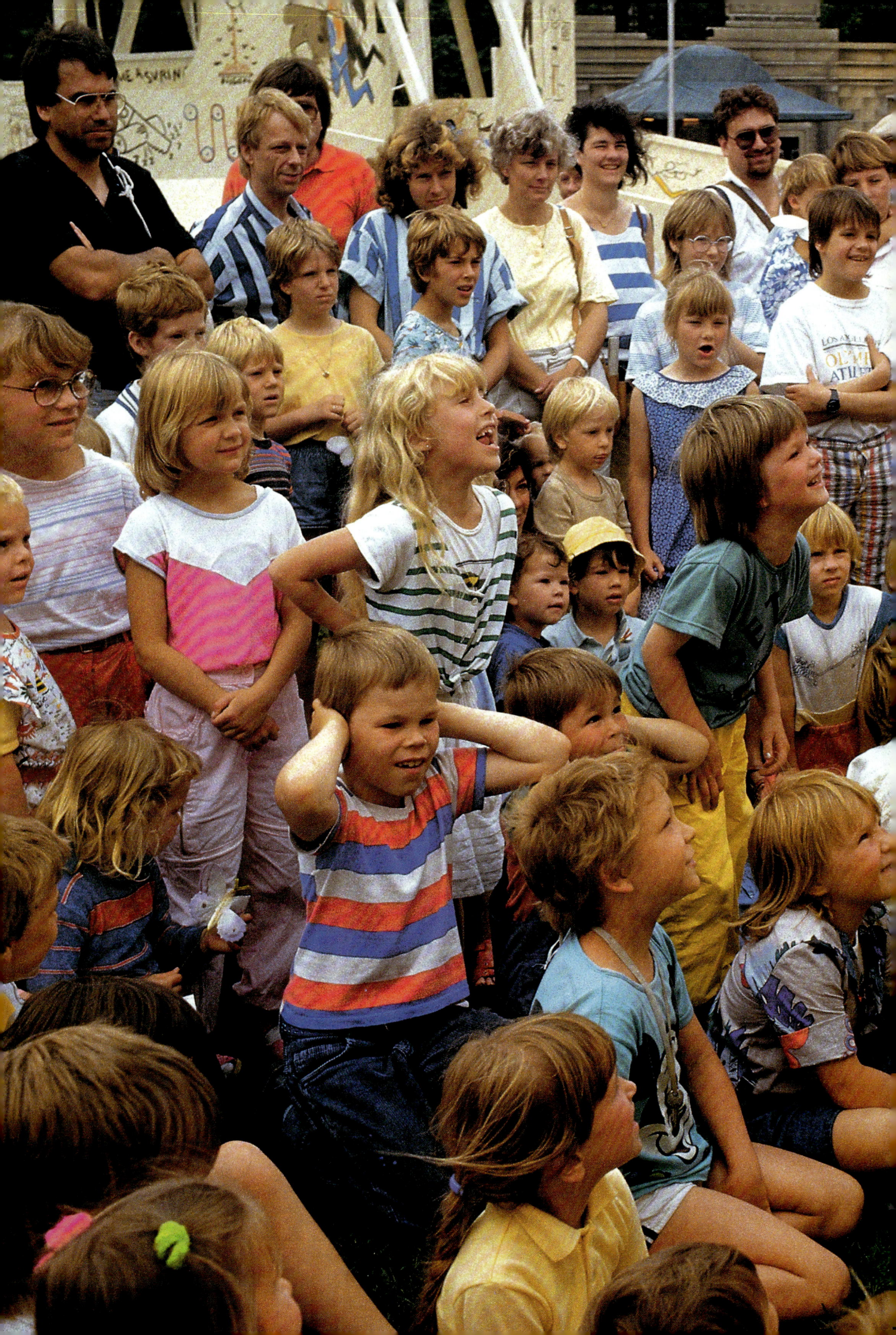

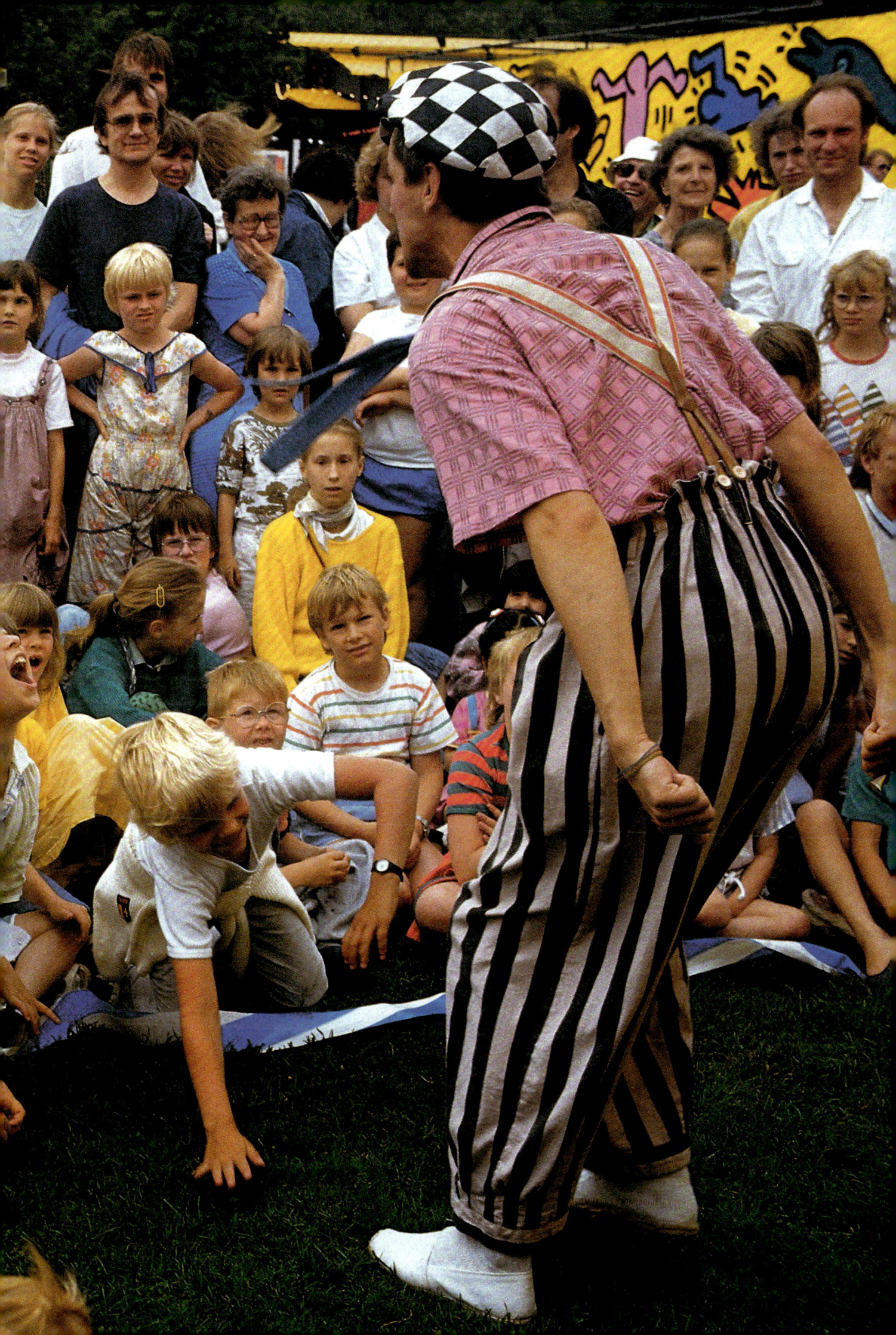

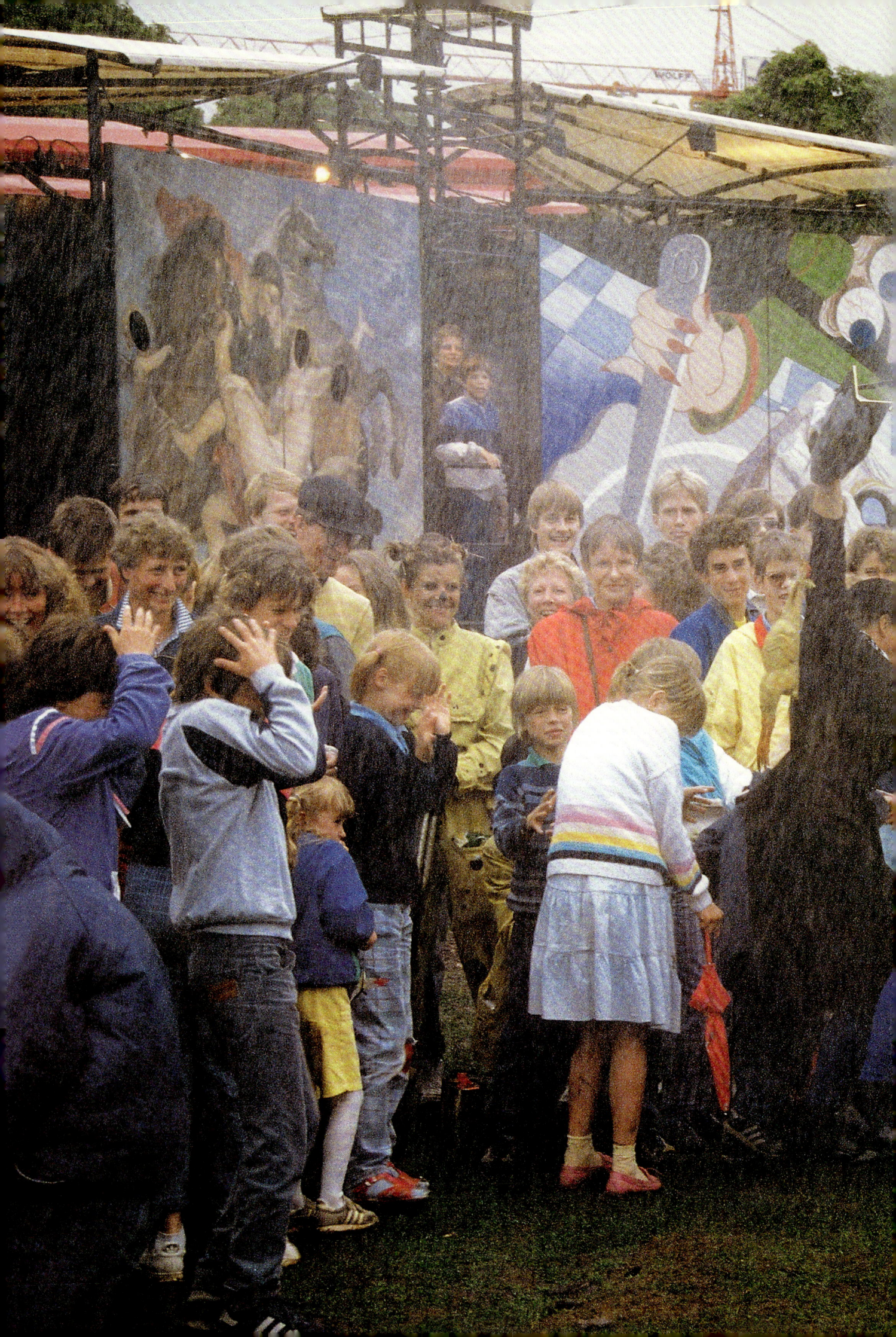

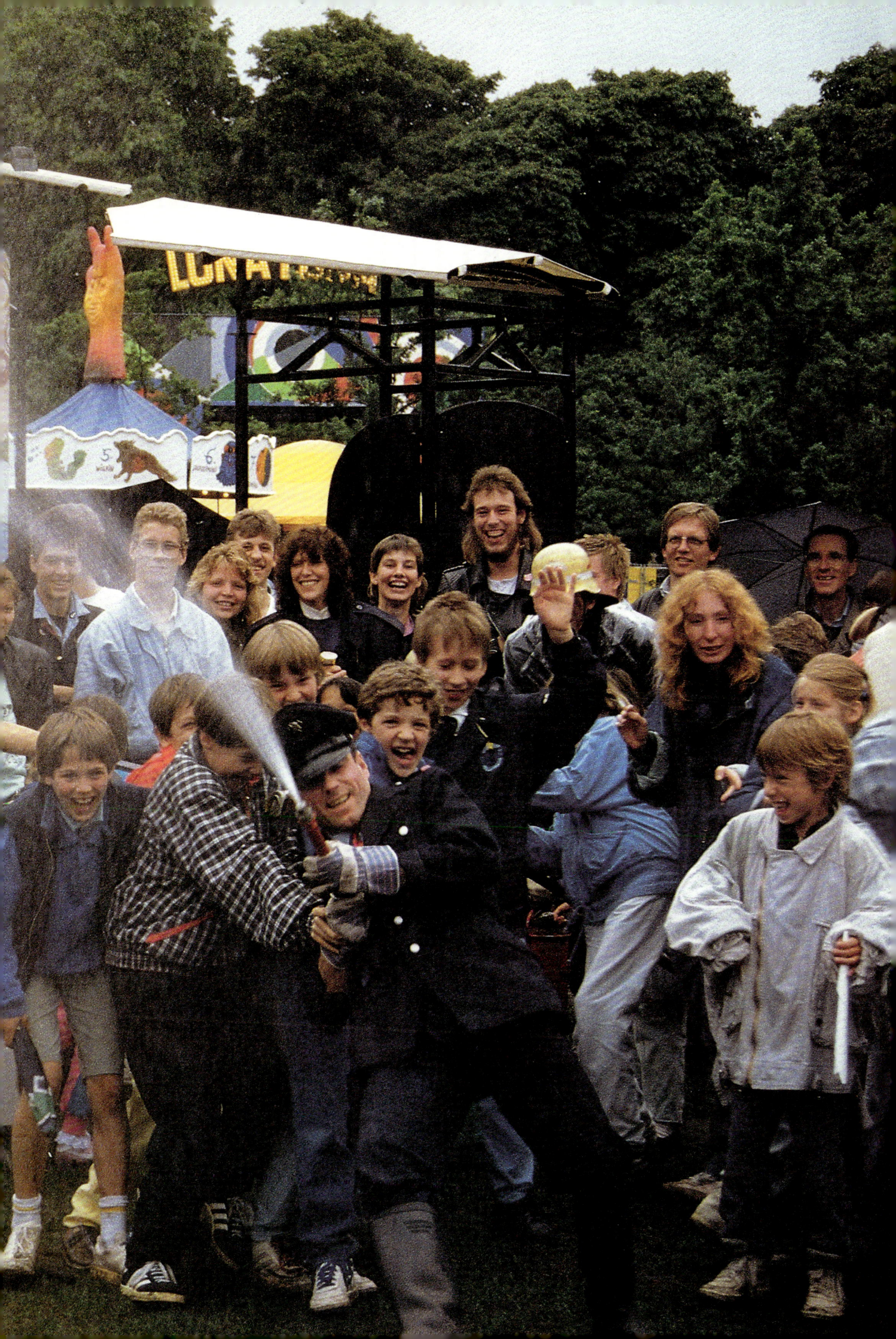

# The Numerous Transformations of André Heller

## Essay by Hilde Spiel

*The artist as demiurge: when did he abandon this aspiration?* To be an architect who designs a counterworld to God's creation is no longer the artist's goal, since imagination has entered the service of technologists and their sidekick—science fiction. The metaphorical flights of fancy of the poet searching for new paradises in space have given way to real-life excursions into the exosphere for the purpose of setting up cosmic experimental stations to prepare for the end of the world.

No wonder that not only poets but also prose writers are now turning their gaze inward, disappointed, fearful, even despairing in the face of an ever-looming present. In fact, it is a wonder that some of them continue to be willing to fight against their own fear and the menace from outside, using the evocative power of reason as well as by drawing on their own inspiration. Countering the appalling possibilities with comforting certainty, standing up to the horror of the war designers with the wishful image of a peaceful visionary that takes shape before the eyes of all of us—this is still a mission the artist can pursue.

André Heller is somebody who does just this. Escaping from reality was never his thing; he always drove away nightmares with daydreams that had the potential to be turned into reality. A hundred years ago, he would have been a Jules Verne, telling of journeys "to the center of the earth," "villages in the skies," and empires "twenty thousand leagues under the sea." A prophetic writer, Jules Verne had people orbiting the earth in 80 days and going to the moon in 97 hours 20 minutes. His once improbable predictions may be long outdated, but we can still admire the audacity of his imagination. André Heller is not inferior to him in this regard. Furthermore, he is able to put his visions into practice.

It is courage, simply courage, that makes this Jules Verne of today a contemporary of the future. He does not merely undertake verbal high jinks, such as "Theatre of Fire," "Flame Reviews," "Pyro-Sculptures," "Signs of the Sky," "Contemplation Monuments," and the naming of his *Circus Roncalli* after a truly noble pope, all this under the title "Trilogy of Possible Miracles"—by now probably a tetralogy, pentalogy, or hexalogy. He has also given them a tangible, visible presence through unique ventures.

He was once compared to the "dreaming boys" of the young Oskar Kokoschka, who described in vivid colors and words their story "under the branches of the dark nut trees around moonlight," who dream on their knees "of unstoppable change" and forgotten cities "in whose closed rooms singing people/hang as if in a birdcage," whose brains have passing thoughts that make them grow "like watchful stones." Kokoschka saw his enlightened youths as "dancers of kings," and Heller, whose imagery sometimes seems to be drawn from the early days of the genius painter, might also bear this presumptuous name.

At that time, André Heller had not produced much more than songs, poems, surreal miniature dramas, and a first book entitled *Die Ernte der Schlaflosigkeit in Wien* ("The Harvest of Insomnia in Vienna"). He was still a poet and music maker, not a magician and master of ceremonies, not an inventor of tremendous spectacles or artistic performances of incomparable perfection, such as his variety show *Flic Flac* or the Chinese acrobatic show *Begnadete Körper* ("Gifted Bodies"). When he set his mind to these, he had other models in mind—respectable ones, but also questionable ones, which will not be concealed here. Heller was undoubtedly inspired by the French cinema pioneer Georges Meliès, the creator of bizarre fairy tales that were as close to the baroque theater of magic as they were to the pictorial worlds of the customs officer Henri Rousseau.

The childlike, sometimes childishly obscene, innocence of the Frenchman can only have been a good influence. Likewise, of Fellini—despite the great moviemaker's fascination with the degeneracies, deformities, and abnormalities of human nature—we can at least concede that he had a basic ethical outlook. However, there are affinities that would be advisable for Heller to avoid. One of them is that of Antonin Artaud and his Theatre of Cruelty.

In Artaud's words, it was his theatre, "that crucible of fire and real flesh in which, anatomically,/through the crushing of bones, limbs, and syllables,/bodies are formed anew,/and where/ physically and through the force of nature/the mythical act of the creation of a body is realized." These are strong words—a breach of taboo, which before 1948, the year of Artaud's death, were excessive and unheard of, and soon to find expression in the magic-cultic, mythical-orgiastic games of the Viennese actionists. Heller, it seems, is not entirely distant from them, and a shiver runs down this eulogist's spine when she hears him speak of "beautiful catastrophes."

In an age that can no longer afford nefarious aestheticisms, Heller should be warned against being seduced by the often-enchanting vocabulary of the immoralists. Charles Baudelaire's *Flowers of Evil* has faded, the challenge *à l'outrance* of the Expressionists has resulted in fascism and Stalinism, and, for good reason, we now even refuse the "sacred" Jean Genet, the altar erected to him by Jean-Paul Sartre. Today, we are forced to confront reality. Moral responsibility, at least inner decency, is also demanded of the followers of arts that feed on the unconscious and the irrational, as well as of the writers of an

*écriture automatique*. But André Heller was well aware of this and ultimately did not get involved in the "beautiful catastrophes" after all.

In the midst of a world that, unlike Voltaire's good soul *Candide*, he by no means considers the "best of all possible worlds," he nevertheless plants his little garden, such as the *Nachdenkmal* ("contemplation monument") in Berlin—the flowers of which admittedly form the words "distrust the idyll"— and creates the most wondrous flying sculptures made of silk, as well as exhilarating humankind in his distress at the mushroom cloud with the most exquisite amusement park: *Luna Luna.* ✺

# "I have no talent for despondency"

# A conversation with André Heller

*How did the desire to make* Luna Luna *materialize?*

No impression in my life to date has been more powerful and influential than the great enchantments of my childhood. I have often mentioned how much a visit to the Rebernigg Circus in 1952 meant to me while living in a gray, bombed-out Vienna, experiencing the Lent processions in the labyrinths of the former imperial park at Schönbrunn, the fireworks to mark the Austrian State Treaty, the triumphal procession of the Pummerin—the great newly cast main bell of St. Stephen's Cathedral—through the country to the capital, the eccentric trick fountains of the prince-archbishops of Salzburg at Hellbrunn, the abnormalities and unique oddities of the Habsburgs' chambers of curiosities, the acclaimed performances by the magician Kalanak, who could turn water into wine and fish into bread as if he were Jesus. I loved Raimund's plays staged in Oskar Kokoschka's sets at the Burgtheater. And the legendary Mozart performances at the State Opera, especially *The Magic Flute*, with melodies that I would sing as a six-year-old before falling asleep, instead of saying prayers.

Solar and lunar eclipses were events that occupied me for months. There are also some drawing books of mine dating back to that time, which I had filled with invented maps, and my grandmother often talked about a fit of rage I had one day, because my family refused to meet my demand to move into the orchid wing of the Schönbrunn Palm House, at least during the winter vacations. It is fascinating what mysterious memories emerge from childhood: slide shows about the stigmata of Therese von Konnersreuth; the magnificent pack ice on the Danube; the shooting stars in the Salzkammergut during the summer months;

the Peruvian-American singer Yma Sumac, who could warble like a nightingale and roar low like a lion; the daredevil equestrian games of the Don Cossacks; the voices of Oskar Werner, Albin Skoda, and Paula Wessely; the ventriloquists, giantesses, trick shooters, and tap-dancing midgets at the Prater in Vienna, a city half destroyed by the war.

As you can see, there is no end to my list. I think it would be easy to demonstrate that I have basically never stopped spinning the web of these childhood myths, a life-saving assertion of the imagination against the sum of what threatens me and causes me despair.

*What is it that threatens you?*

The same as any other human being. The negligence of so many in looking after themselves and this planet. The pathetic babbling of technocrats who believe in progress and are addicted to growth. The alarming gap between knowledge and resulting consequences that can be felt everywhere. But I am also threatened by the chronic humorlessness that is rampant from right to left— especially in Germany—and this panic-stricken fear of sensuality, which causes so many to ultimately block the wellsprings of their imagination and creative resistance. Exuberance, the crossing of boundaries, nonconformism, the notion of being a lone wolf are all considered disreputable in a field where, for example, the absolute majority of all artists belong to some kind of organization dedicated to defending their own territory. Reinforced by my boarding school years, I have always had a physical aversion to "packs." If I fall, then it should preferably be into my own abysses and not into those of strangers.

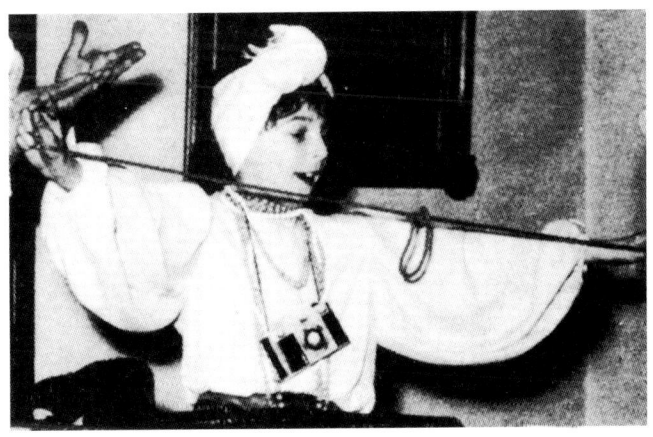

*André Heller in 1953, at the age of six, as a magician*

*What are your guiding principles for life?*

Everyone is well advised to show solidarity with the wise needs of his or her soul and respond to them. I strongly believe that we have come into the world to transform ourselves through learning, in other words, to become more mature, more accurate, more profound, more compassionate, and—let's say it out loud—more loving as we grow older. There is no written law that says you should be a lemming!

*Is this not also the creed of a privileged egomaniac?*

It is precisely because I enjoy so many privileges that I do not have the slightest right to pusillanimity and opportunism. I really can't be harmed by anyone except myself—although I often succeed in doing so in the most disastrous manner. There are moments when I have to laugh out loud, because I have just caught myself in a situation that makes me the ideal target for my ever-vigilant opponents.

*Let's go back to* Luna Luna.

*Luna Luna* is one of the projects that most so-called experts warned me about. They didn't think the artists I wanted would be willing to get involved. First of all, for ideological reasons. An amusement park is, after all, mistakenly regarded as something less serious than, say, an exhibition at the Centre Pompidou [in Paris], and, second, because of the ridiculously low fees I had to offer, which for most people could only be understood as a token amount. I was also warned about the total production costs: people didn't think it was possible to produce 38 artistically designed, containerized buildings,

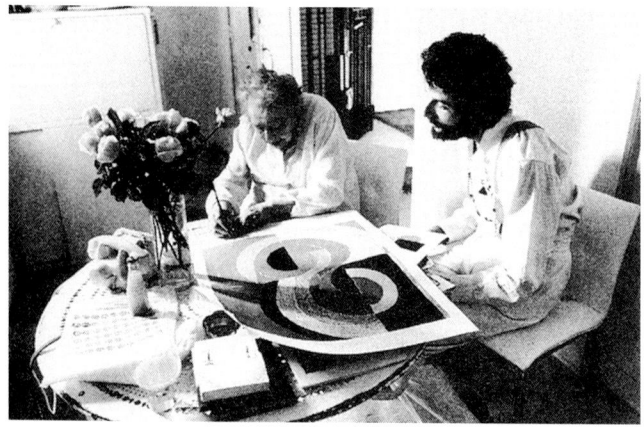

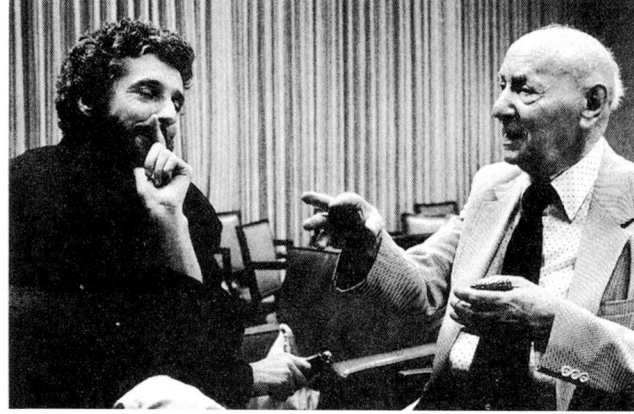

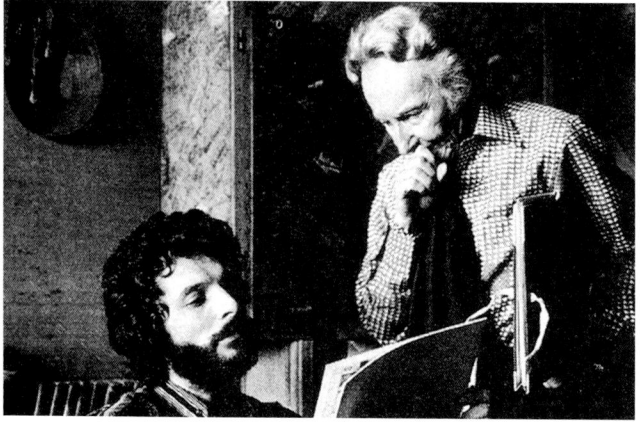

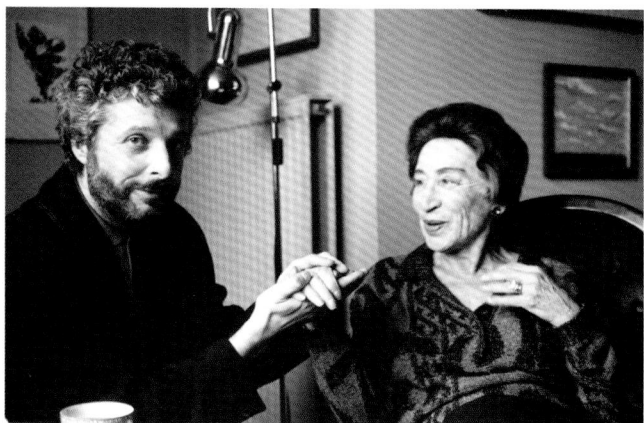

*With Sonia Delaunay in 1976 in her Paris studio—*
*the first meeting with an artist for* Luna Luna

*With Erté in Paris in 1980*

*With Isaac Bashevis Singer in Palm Beach, Florida, in 1986*

*With Hilde Spiel in Vienna in 1987*

the electrification they would require, and all the infrastructure of an amusement park for less than 10 million deutsche mark. Few people know that regular amusement parks cost between 100 and 600 million deutsche mark—and the morbid addiction to electronics makes them more expensive by the day. I'm not a good recipient of warnings: the seemingly impossible has always appealed to me. "Nothing happens unless you do it," as the unpopular saying goes. But I do have some great allies who pull together with me and know how to prevent a collapse in an emergency. The two most important are my friend Stefan Seigner, a brilliant production manager, who in an unselfish, loving manner stands as a shield between me and the endless toil of administration, calculations, meeting deadlines, and organizational plans, and Georg Resetschnig, who since *Flic Flac* has supported all my projects as technical director, artistic adviser, and irreplaceable friend. I believe that if the working atmosphere is not right, all is lost.

*How many employees did you have in total at* Luna Luna?

We had contracted close to two hundred men and women from a wide variety of backgrounds: carpenters, locksmiths, electricians, painters, and welders, as well as precision mechanics, model makers, sculptors, structural engineers, and architects. After all, we had to build a small transportable city that could withstand the onslaught of hundreds of thousands of onlookers.

*So, what did the artists contribute?*

It varied. Each and every one—this was my basic condition—had to design something especially for *Luna Luna*. So, it wasn't possible for

anyone to take something that already existed out of the drawer or rework an old idea a second time. *Luna Luna* had to be distinctive and truly unique. Many, such as Kenny Scharf and Keith Haring, and almost the entire group of Austrian artists, came into our studios to paint the facades, sculptures, and showcases themselves. Others, such as David Hockney and Patrick Raynaud, built and painted meticulous models of their contributions, which were then enlarged and implemented by my collaborators. Roy Lichtenstein, Georg Baselitz, Jean-Michel Basquiat, Jörg Immendorff, [Roland] Topor, and [Daniel] Spoerri also oversaw the implementation of their designs at every key stage, intervening to make corrections whenever necessary. Dalí was ill, so we kept him informed by means of video documentation. Rebecca Horn and Jim Whiting constructed their installations at their own studios in Paris and London. I've already mentioned that I was not in the least able to adequately pay for all these truly great efforts. *Luna Luna* is altogether a wondrous love story that could only come true based on the devoted joy of so many talented people in doing instead of merely talking.

*But there are not only visual artists involved?*

From the beginning, I wanted to create something that could best be described by the much-used word "Gesamtkunstwerk," a combination of painting, sculpture, architecture, music, literature, and theater. I invited musicians, such as Philip Glass, to create compositions for certain objects, and they did so to absolute perfection. Hans Magnus Enzensberger, whom I revere like no other living German poet, wrote the texts for two magic theater spaces I conceived and even recites one of them himself. Isaac

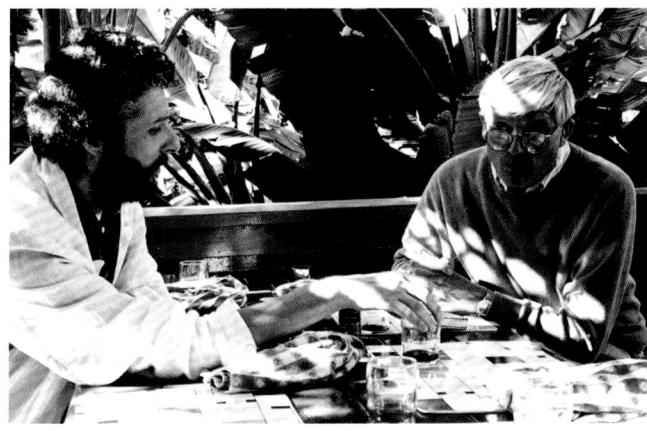

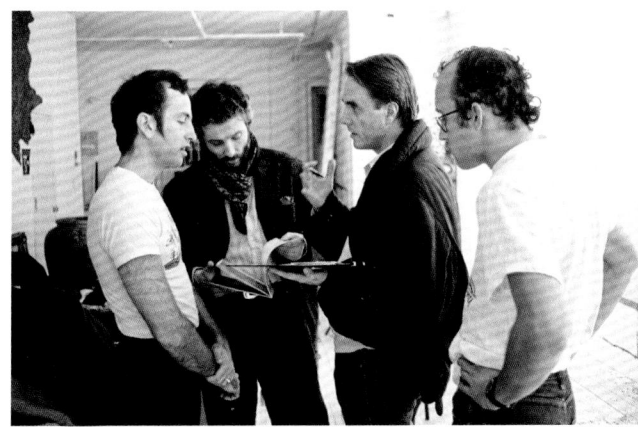

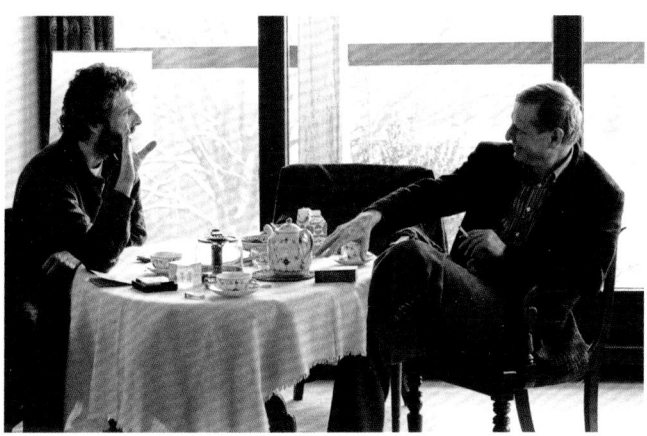

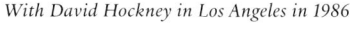

*With David Hockney in Los Angeles in 1986*

*With Hans Magnus Enzensberger in Munich in 1987*

Bashevis Singer sent me an encouraging text for the catalog. And Herbert von Karajan, after a conversation that was very touching for me, agreed to provide waltzes he recorded with the Berlin Philharmonic as music for Hockney's *Enchanted Tree*. I would also have liked to invite a number of movie artists to shoot some shorter works especially for *Luna Luna*, and there were initial plans to do so with Werner Herzog, Alexander Kluge, and [Hans-Jürgen] Syberberg, but ultimately the finances were insufficient to cover this.

*How is it that Sonia Delaunay and Joseph Beuys were involved, although they both died some time ago?*

This takes us to the chronology of the project. My initial plans for the project date back to 1974. Two years later, after my choleric departure from *Roncalli*, there were very advanced negotiations with the Munich Olympiapark Gesellschaft to stage a world exhibition of a fantasy there called *Calafati*. At that time, I had commitments and contributions from Henry Miller, Jean Dubuffet, Takis, Ingmar Bergman—who was to create a children's theater—and some of today's *Luna Luna* participants, including Sonia Delaunay, who was to create a Triumphal Gateway. I knew Beuys from joint political activities and in December 1985, shortly before his death, I asked him to provide me with a handwritten text on creativity and capital for *Luna Luna*. He did so, and his widow later was kind enough to reconfirm his agreement. Incidentally, the Munich *Calafati* project failed in 1977, because of the change of mayor from the SPD to the CDU. Franz Josef Strauß—whom I had called a "statue of un-liberty" on television at the time—put a stop to the project through his infamous minion Peter Gauweiler, with a hair-raising provincial farce.

*Now exactly ten years have passed since the failure of Calafati, and* Luna Luna *is to become a reality! Do you always pursue your plans with such tenacity?*

I knew I would learn a lot through *Luna Luna*. And I could think of no reason why I should have to do without this lesson. It can't be my enemies' business to determine what and how much I change my dreams into reality. As long as I live, I will not give up any essential plan. I have no talent for despondency.

*What criteria did you use to decide which artists to invite?*

I wanted to look for allies who tell stories through work that will open your eyes in every way. I've been working for ten years against the misunderstandings that were brought into the world by *Circus Roncalli* in 1976, the consequences of which can be felt in the most devastating way even in the farthest corners of the theater. Here, I am referring to the abuse of the poetic. A restorative preening that seeks to seal everything and everyone with tinsel and balloons. The *Roncalli* I staged had that only in traces, in the form of brief quotes from childhood. After all, the costumes at that time were designed by Hubert Aratym, someone who had achieved his greatest success in the theater as a set designer for Jean Genet, so his approach was beyond any kind of sugar coating. But the epigones—the "circus journeys to the rainbow," the dream theaters, and such nonsense—did not copy Aratym or the texts written by Chlebnikov and Baudelaire, nor the music composed by Schoenberg and Zappa, nor the anarchic element of the clown numbers elaborated with the help of Pierre Byland, and, above all, nor did my immediate elimination of all animal performances

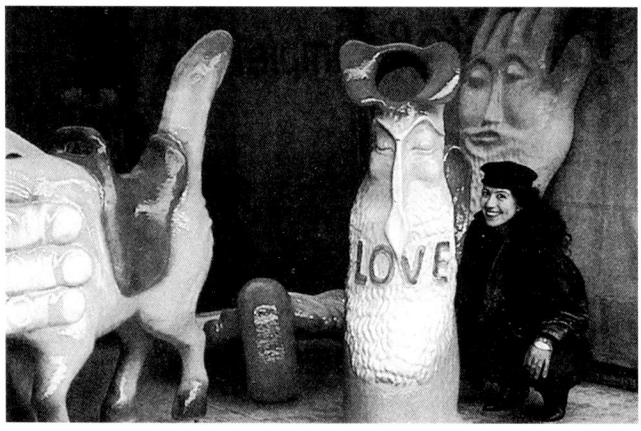

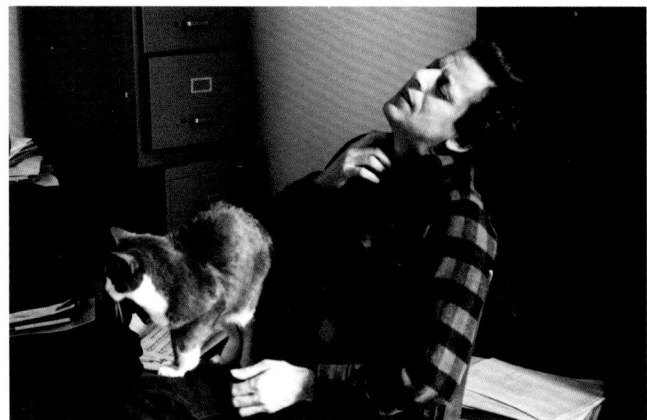

Timna Brauer with carousel sculptures by her father in Vienna in 1987

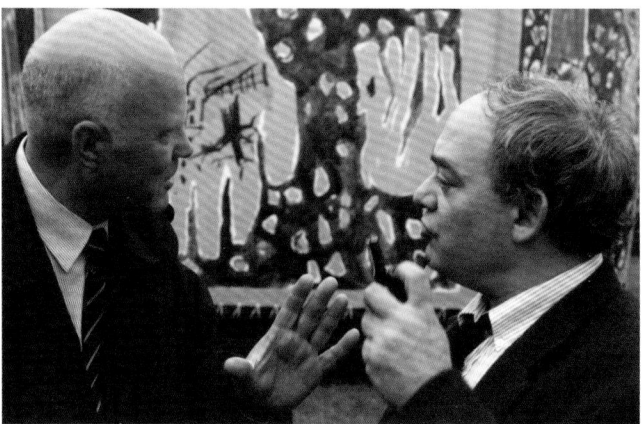

Philip Glass in New York in 1986

Stefan Seigner and Roland Topor in Hamburg in 1987

based on ongoing cruelty, or the detailed justification of this elimination at every performance—which at the time led to heated audience discussions on a daily basis. They merely copied the smell of patchouli, the fairy-tale storytelling, the lighting effects, the androgynous entertainers, multiplying this harmlessness with more of the same to create a wholesome cosmopolitanism that is stranger than strange to me, but which has since become an established success in the Western hemisphere. *Flic Flac, Feuertheater* ("Theatre of Fire"), and *Begnadete Körper* ("Gifted Bodies") all relied on the unwieldy, prickly, irrational element of poetry, and the Berliner Nachdenkmal ("contemplation monument"), composed of forty thousand flowers, contained my thinking, captured in words that were clearly legible for millions of viewers: "Misstraue der Idylle" (Distrust the Idyll). *Luna Luna* tells a story void of nostalgic sentimentality. We're not talking about the supposed beauty of former times here but about what is entirely unglorified in the here and now. We encounter evil images and hauntings along with laughter and ridicule. Sometimes, so-called good taste gets a well-deserved slap in the face; and when Daniel Spoerri designed the toilets in the style of Hitler's Reich Chancellery, setting victory columns with steaming excrement in front of them, I found that a pretty clever idea.

*You said you had an aversion to "packs." Why didn't you design everything yourself for* Luna Luna, *as you do for most of your other projects?*

This is not a pack of mediocre artists, but a collection of highly complex individualists and outsiders who have come together for a single, probably unrepeatable, event, so that children and adults can enjoy a nice, educational treat far removed from the consideration of any contemporary trends. In my opinion, it is something that will remain valid for a very, very long time beyond the moment. I also think it's important that masters, such as Baselitz and Topor, Lichtenstein and Walla, are involved in *Luna Luna* under a common theme, although they represent opposite styles and worlds, thereby disregarding the usual animosities of the art world.

*What is your own personal contribution to* Luna Luna?

I had the idea and, together with Stefan Seigner, the strength—as the Germans say—to pull it off. I came up with the basic form and function of most of the buildings and developed them along with Georg Resetschnig and lead architect Marco Ostertag. I selected and motivated the artists to create the objects and also designed some of them myself, such as the "Dream Station" and the "Wedding Booth." The "Palace of the Winds," with a facade that was designed by Manfred Deix, is an idea that Walter Navratil and myself came up with. Of course, I had to give up a lot of plans due to lack of money, but they have not been abandoned.

*How did the magazine* Neue Revue, *which belongs to the publishing company Heinrich Bauer Verlag, become a sponsor for the project? After all, it's not exactly a corporation one would usually associate with culture?*

The vast majority of truly great projects in the history of art would have remained unrealized without sponsors. This ranges from the Sistine Chapel to Bayreuth to Land Art. Over the centuries, the Catholic Church, emperors and princes, millionaires and industrial

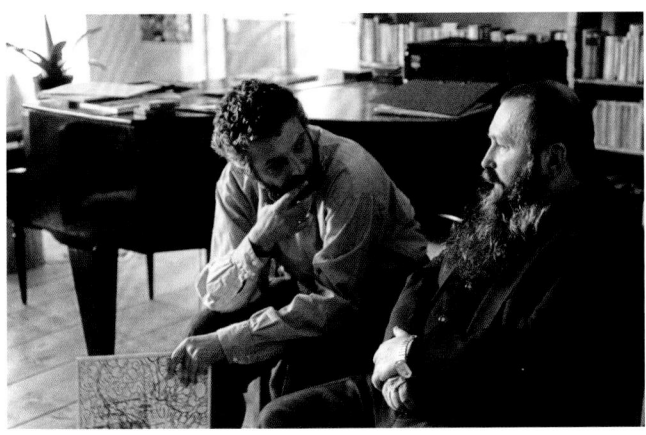

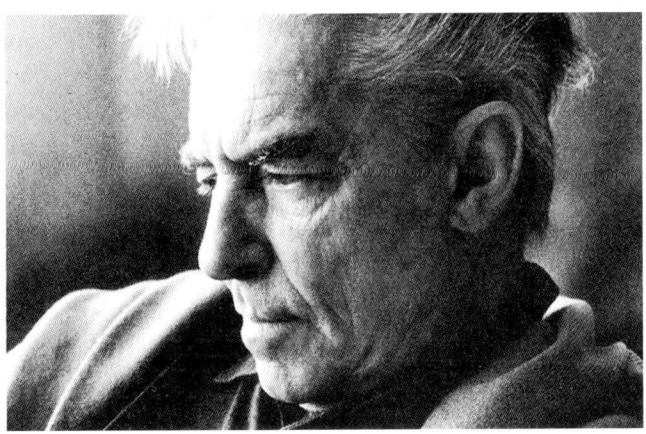

*With Hermann Nitsch in Prinzendorf in 1987*

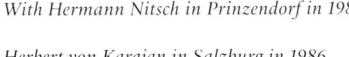

*Herbert von Karajan in Salzburg in 1986*

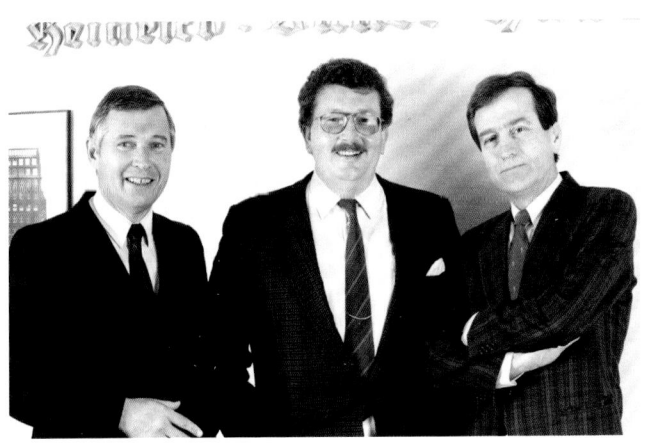

*The two managing directors of Heinrich Bauer Verlag, Gerd Bolls (left) and Dr. Peter  Heidenreich (right), with* Neue Revue *editor-in-chief Richard Mahkorn*

corporations have all acted as sponsors. In the current economic situation, I have long found it unacceptable that, especially in Germany, ninety-five percent of theaters, opera houses, museums, and exhibitions are financed by the state—that is, by the taxpayer—simply because most of those responsible regard themselves as being above negotiating with sponsors—in other words, allowing the name of the enablers to be mentioned for the case of "sacred art." This attitude is wasteful of money, arrogant, and stupid. In the United States and Japan, sponsors are taken for granted, and the media show them the respect they deserve as patrons. Of course, I take a close look at the people who get to support my work. I wouldn't accept a penny from fascists, arms dealers, or Cold War warriors. But the magazine *Neue Revue* has proven to be an interested, passionate partner, which seems to me many times more honorable as a sponsor than, for example, the Vatican—for which half the Louvre produced art.

# The Artists

# and Their Works

Photographer Sabina Sarnitz meticulously documented the creation of *Luna Luna* from October 1985 to June 1987. In the course of all the work processes and adventures involving difficult, sometimes eccentric individuals, she was a constant source of strength and optimism. I have a lot to thank her for.
*André Heller*

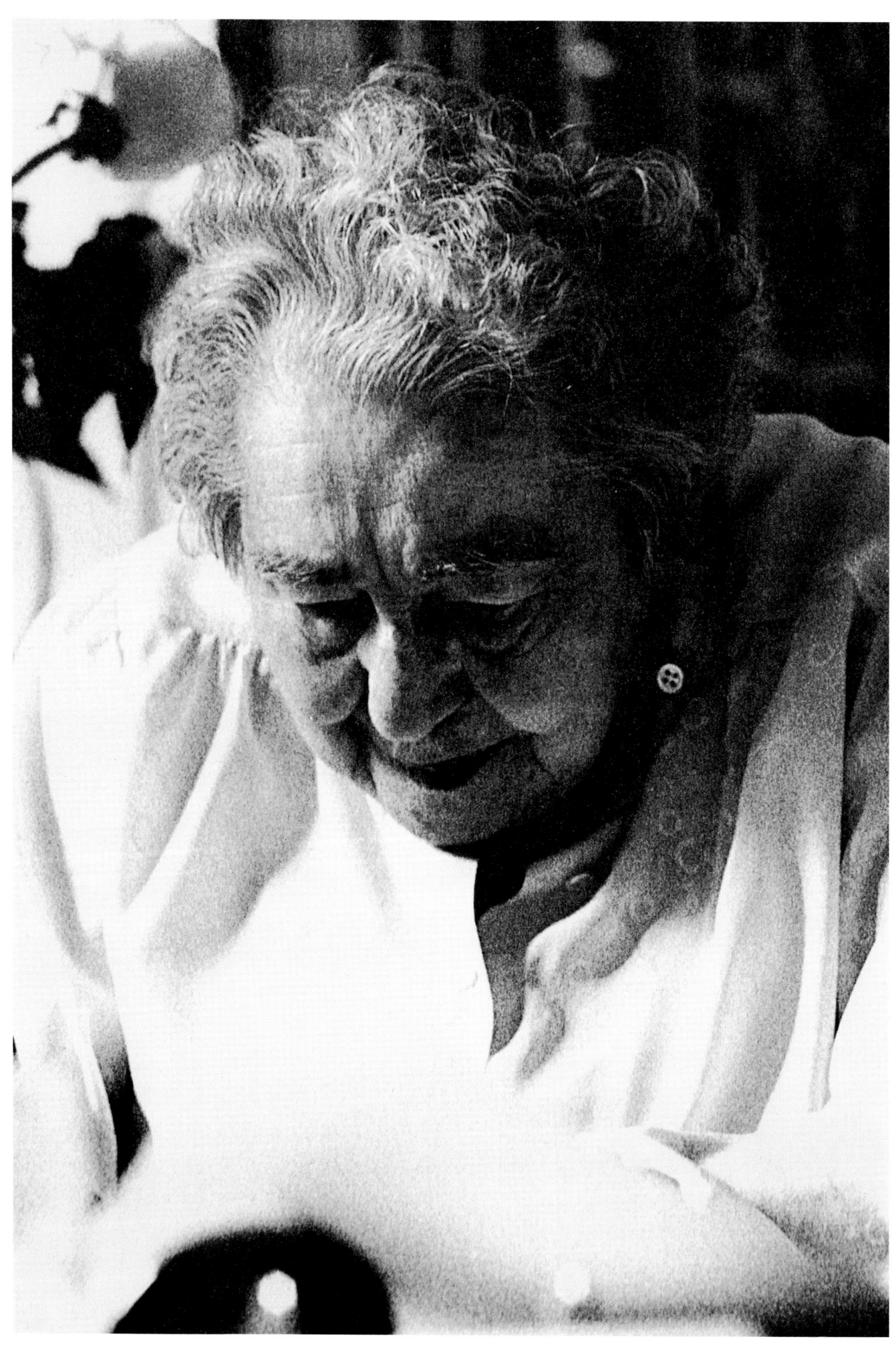

Sonia Delaunay

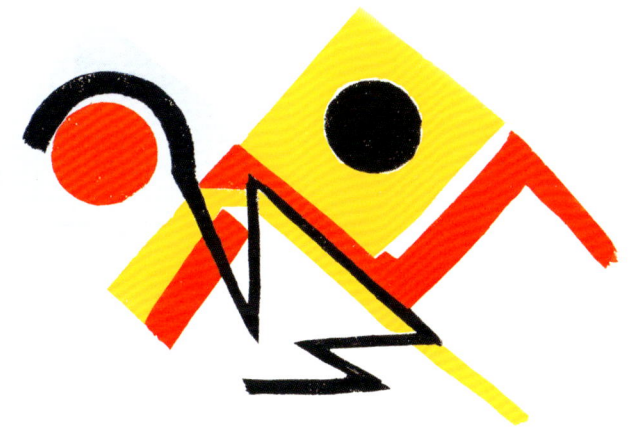

# SONia DELaUNaY

A Monsieur André Heller
Sonia Delaunay cette poésie peinture
et amicalement toute
3-7-77

Sonia Delaunay

Born: November 14, 1885, in Odesa, Ukraine.
Died: December 4, 1979, in Paris.

Painter, illustrator, ceramist, designer,
stage designer.

Sonia Delaunay designed a **triumphal arch**
for *Luna Luna*—the entrance to the Territory
of Surprises.

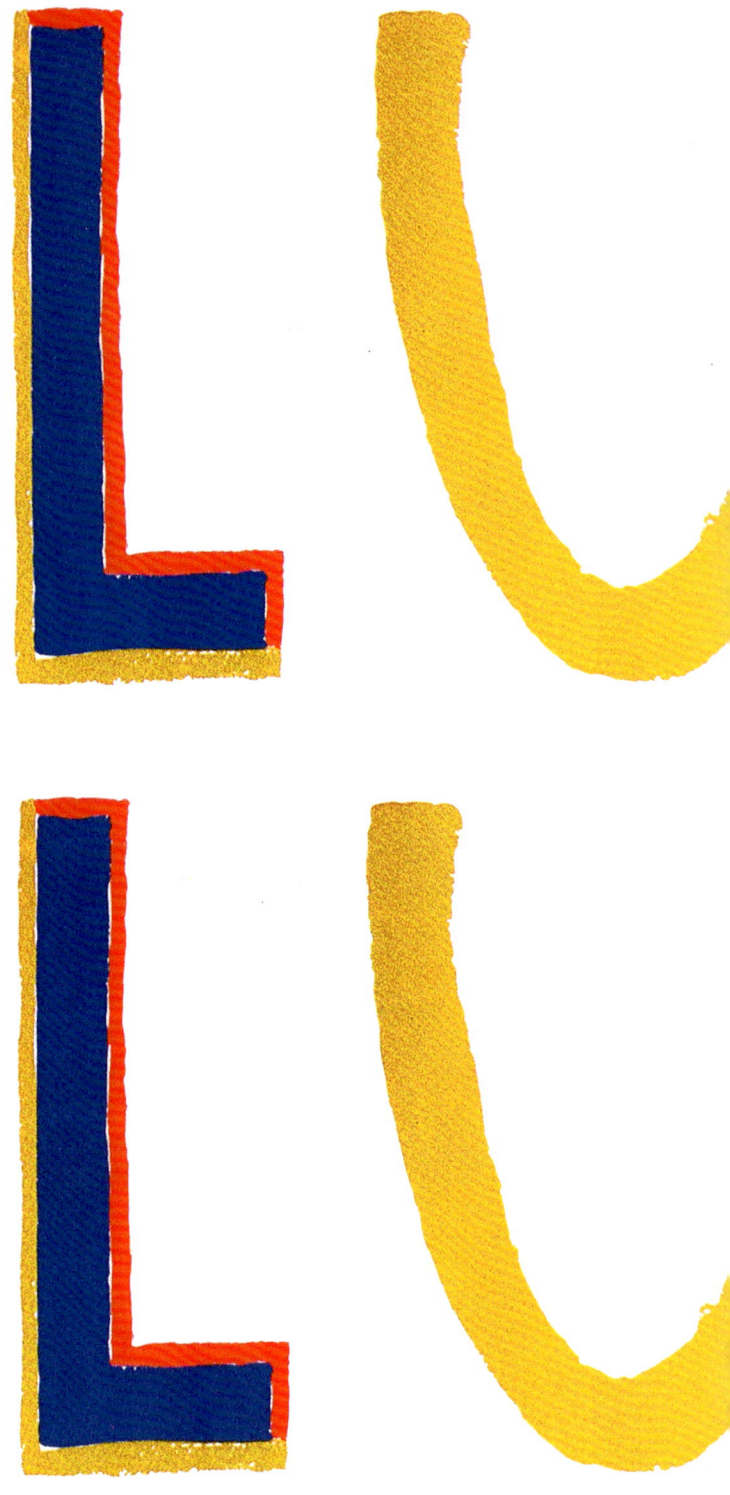

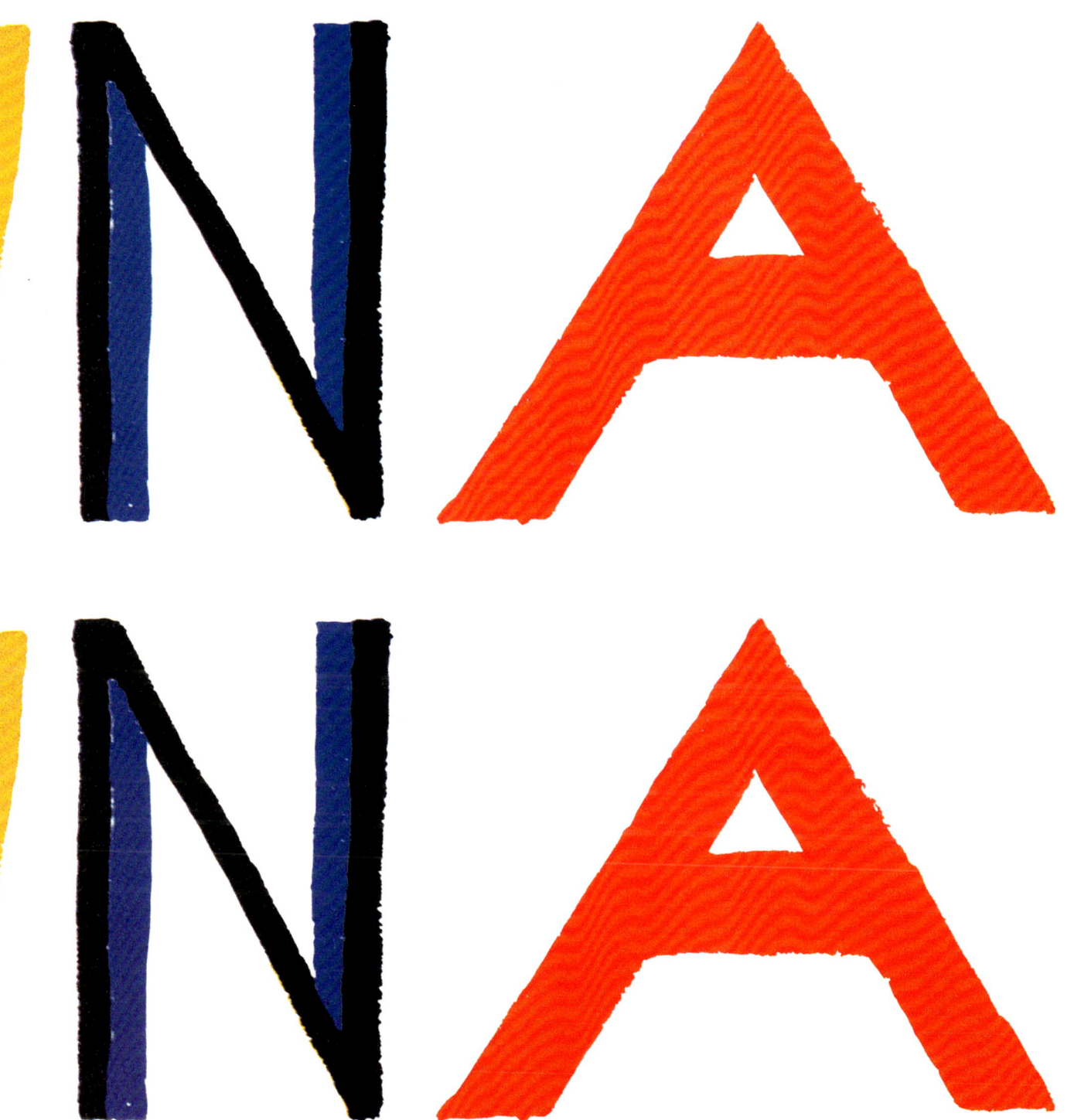

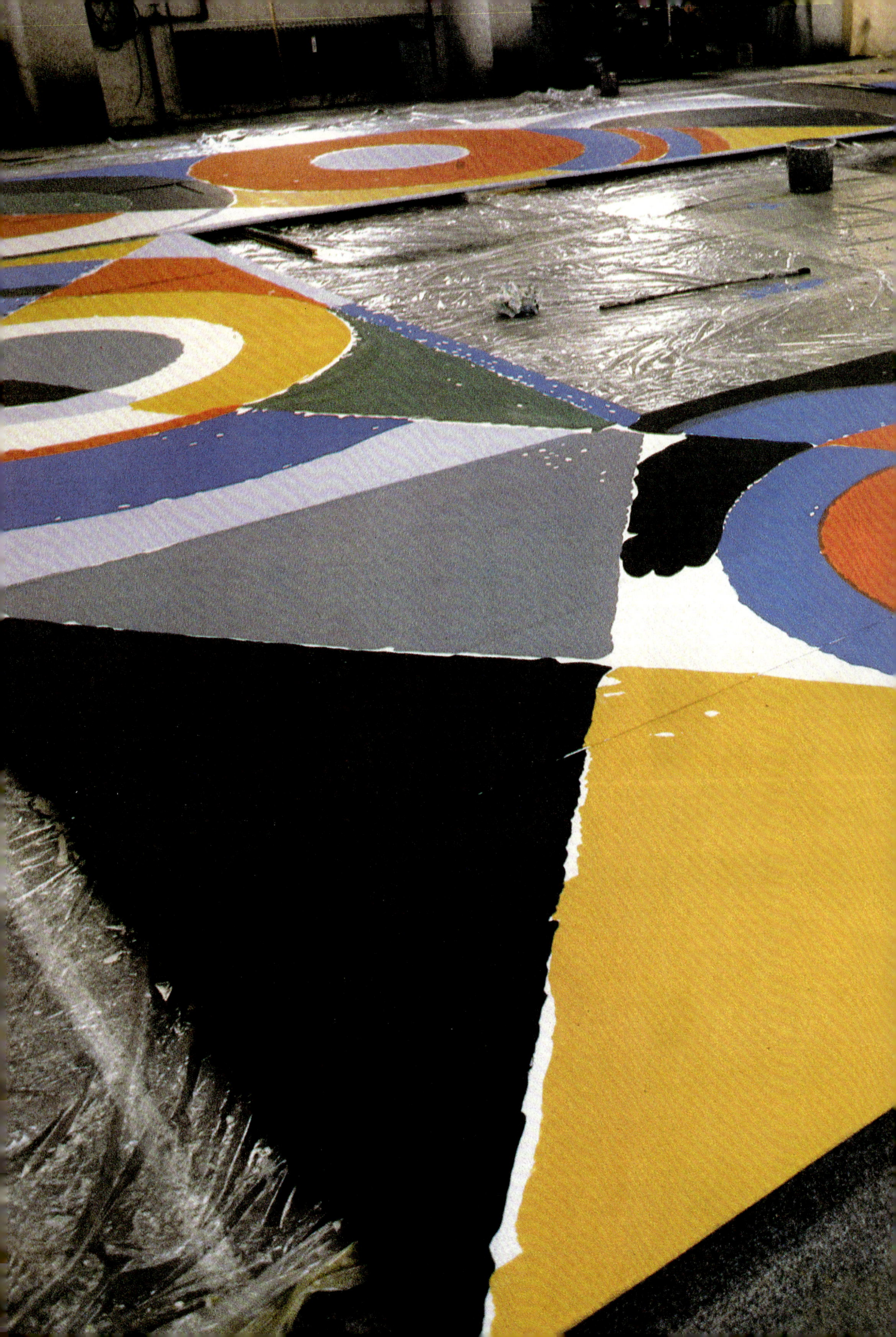

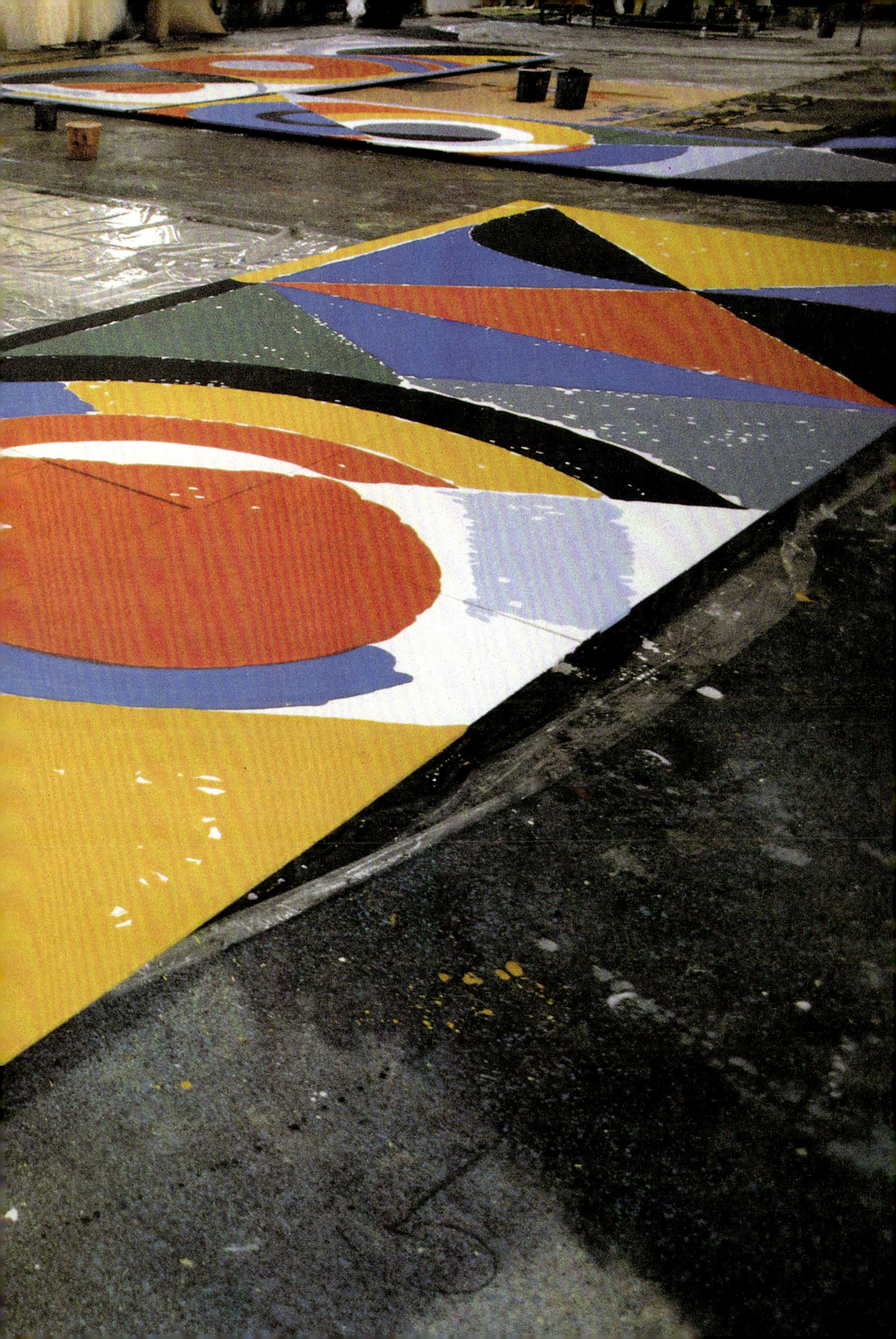

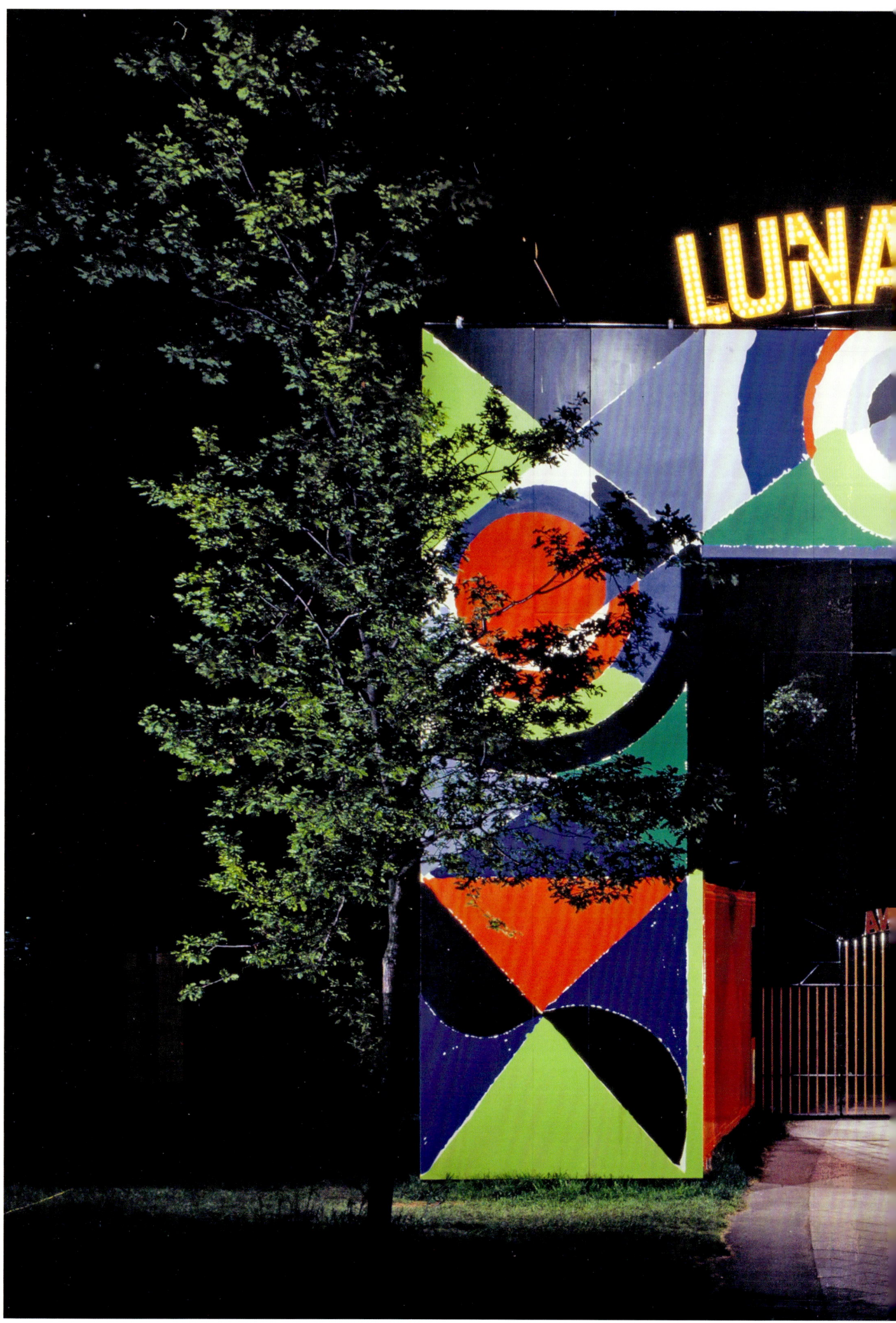

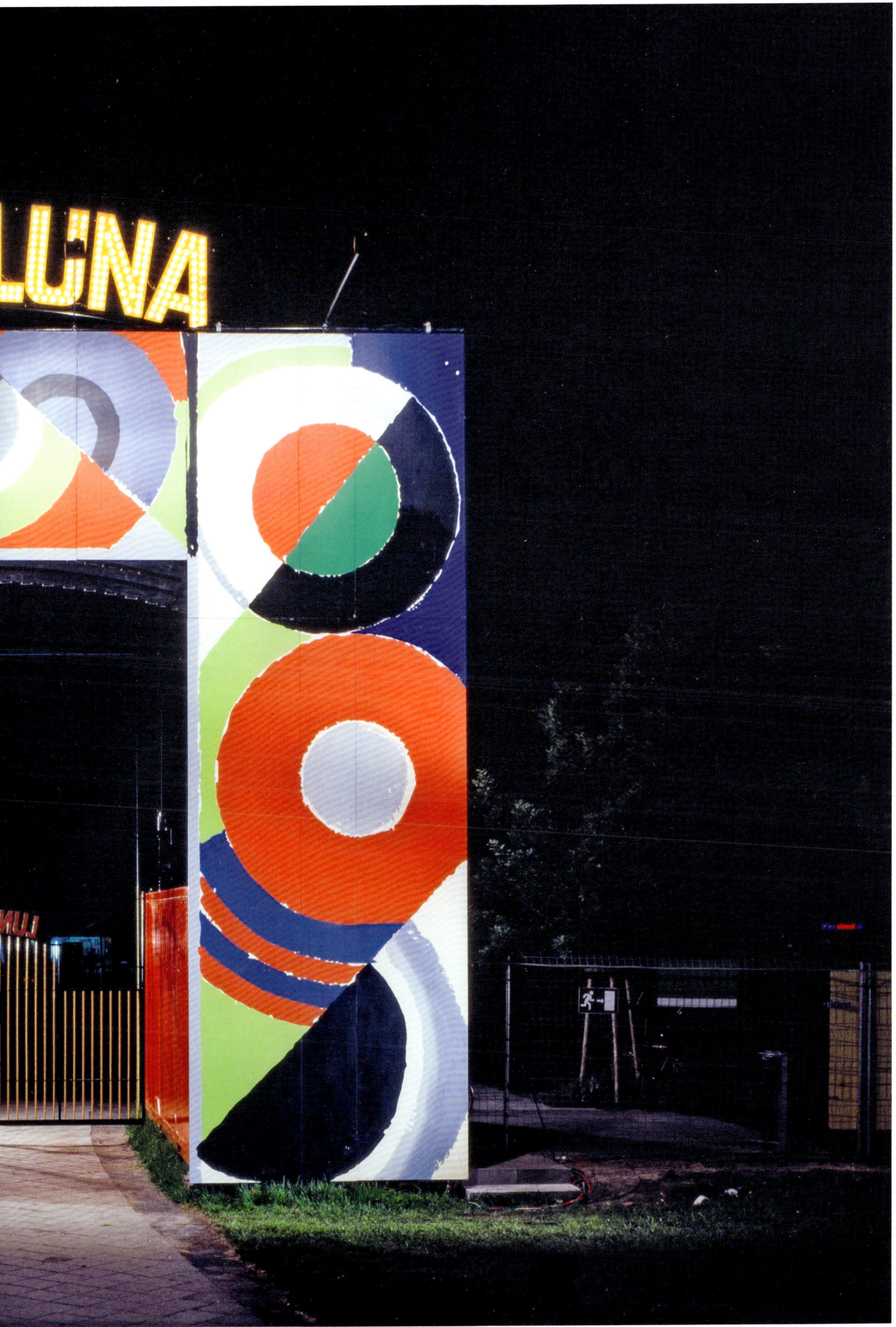

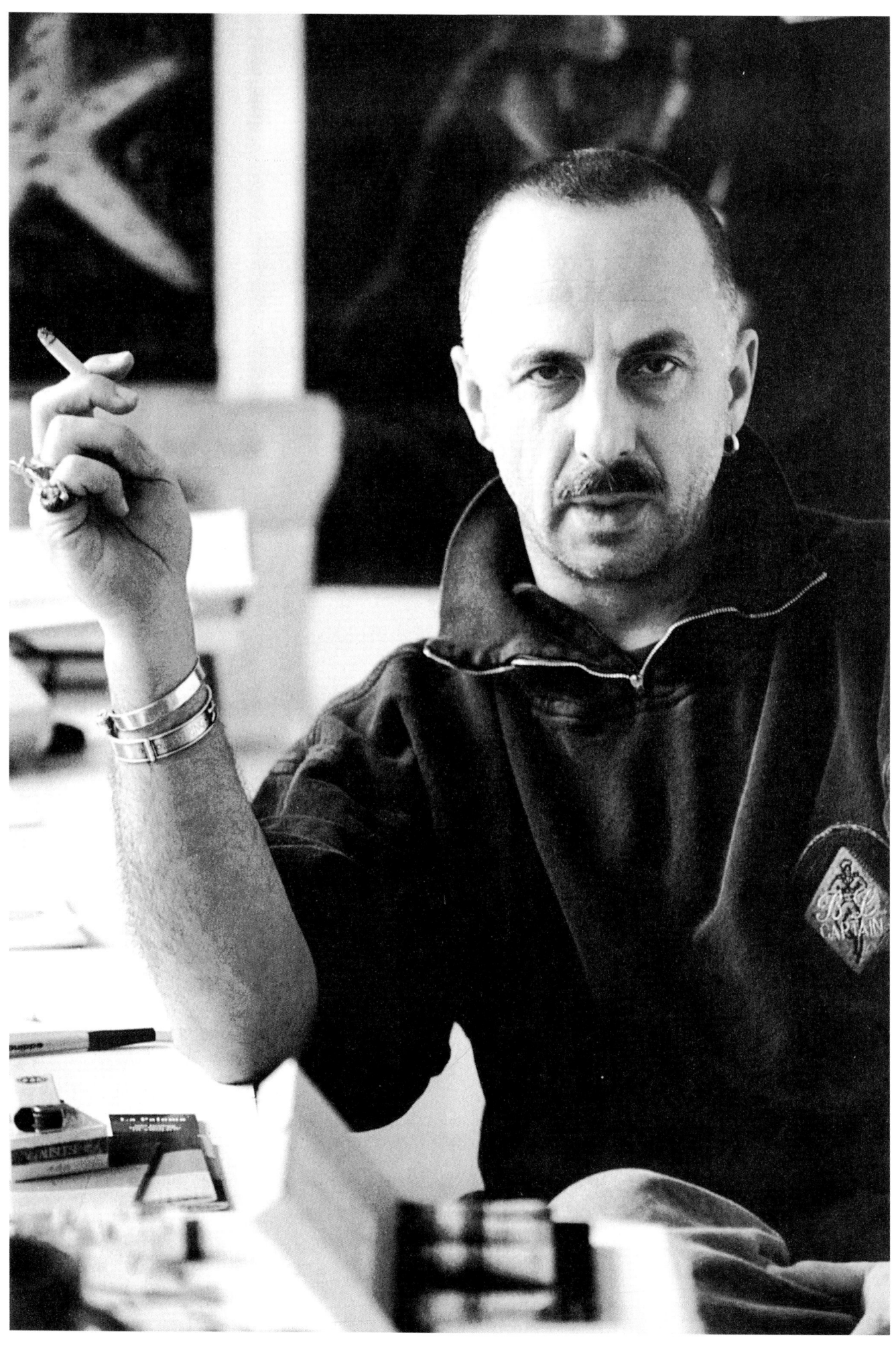

Jörg Immendorff

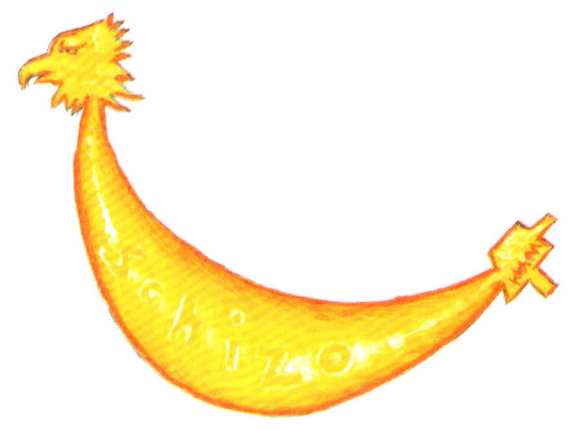

der Bildhauer
im Maler
ist sein bester Feind

———

die Rechnung bringen
die Richtung bringen
die Richtigen bringen

———

der Malerfeind
im Maler
ist sein bester Freund

———

der Frage
wo stehe ich
nachgehend

Immendorff 82

Jörg Immendorff

Born: June 14, 1945, in Bleckede, Lüneburg, GDR
(East Germany).
Died: May 28, 2007, in Düsseldorf.

Painter, illustrator, sculptor.

Jörg Immendorff created **flags**, a **poster**, and a
**shooting gallery** for *Luna Luna*. The walls of the
building tell of nightmares in a divided Germany
and ineradicable impressions of the past.

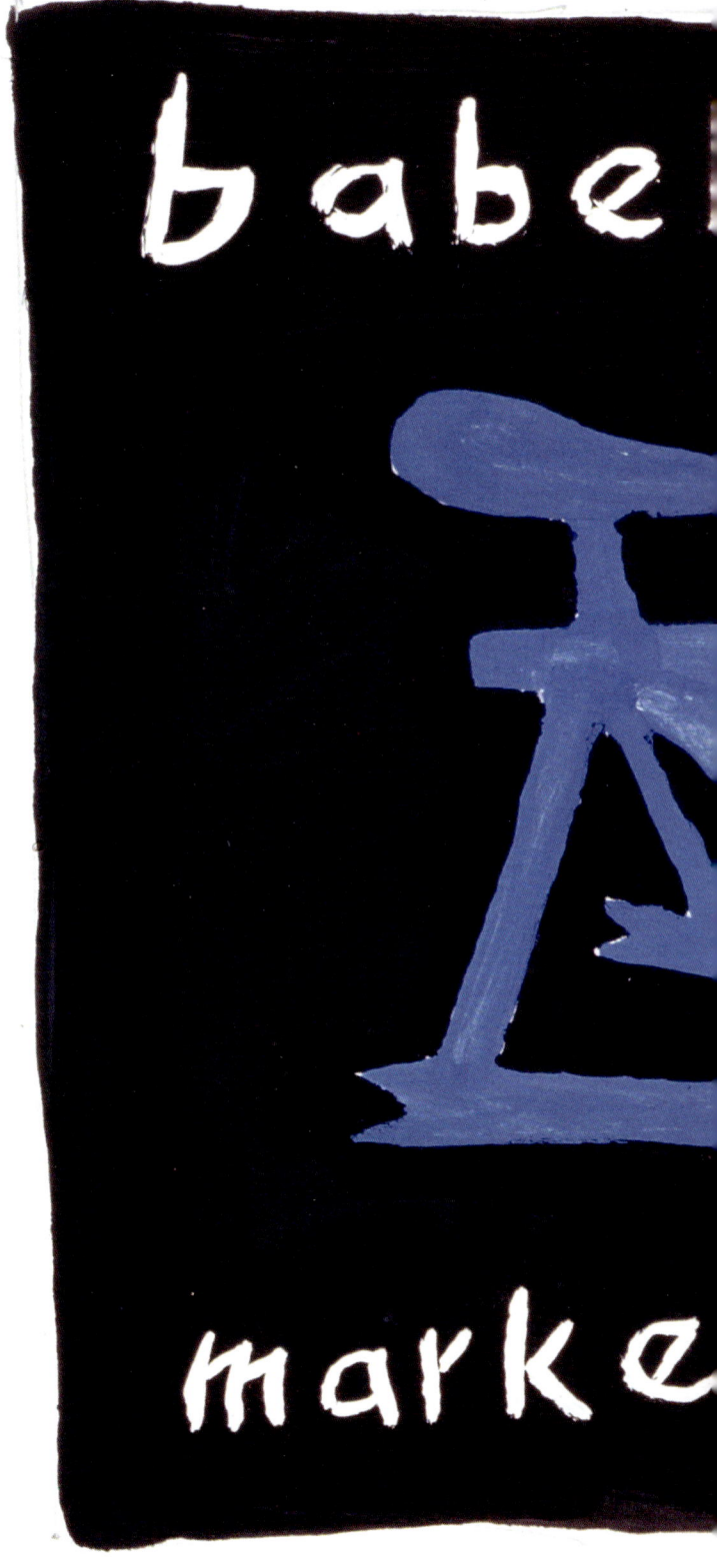

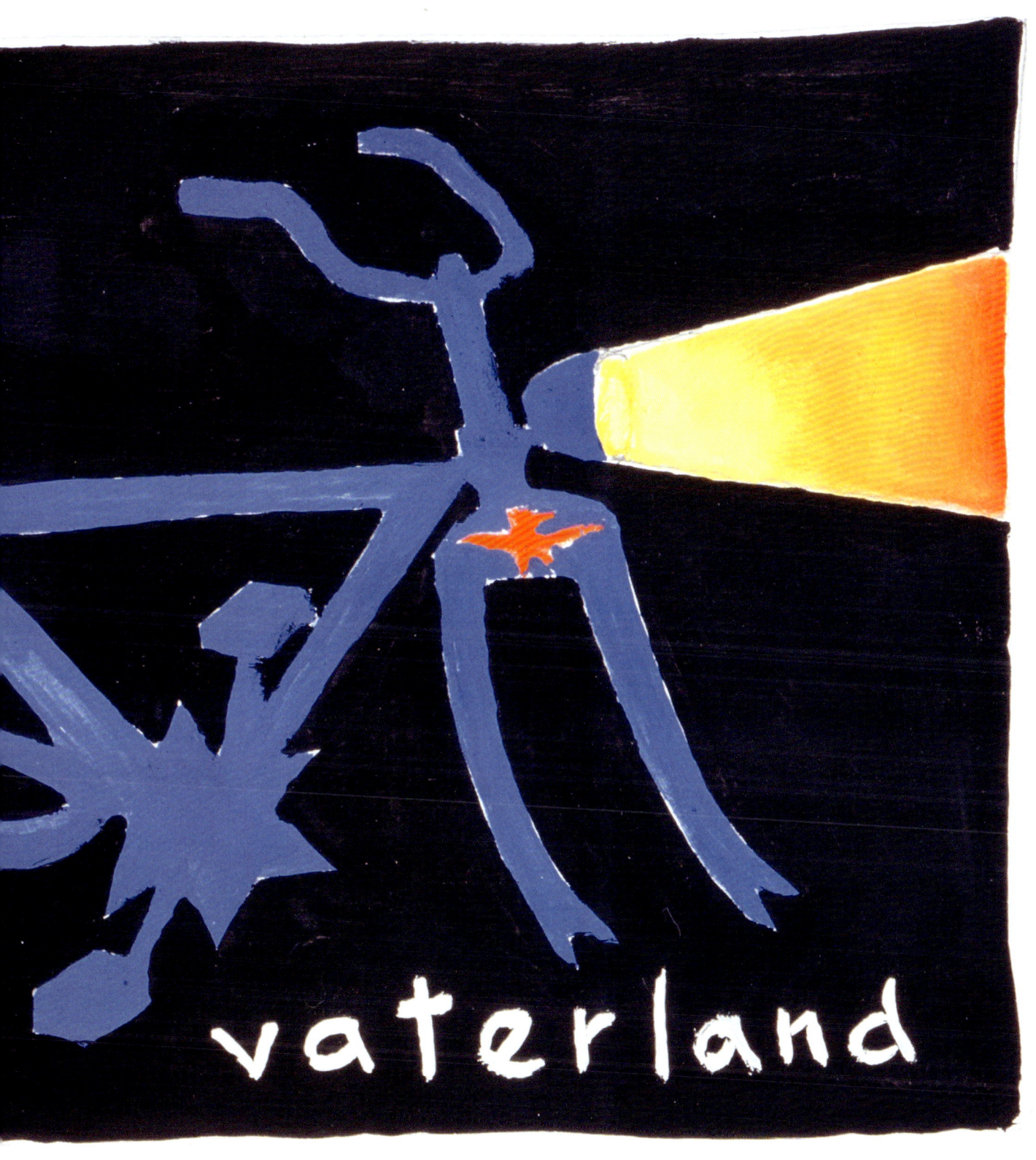

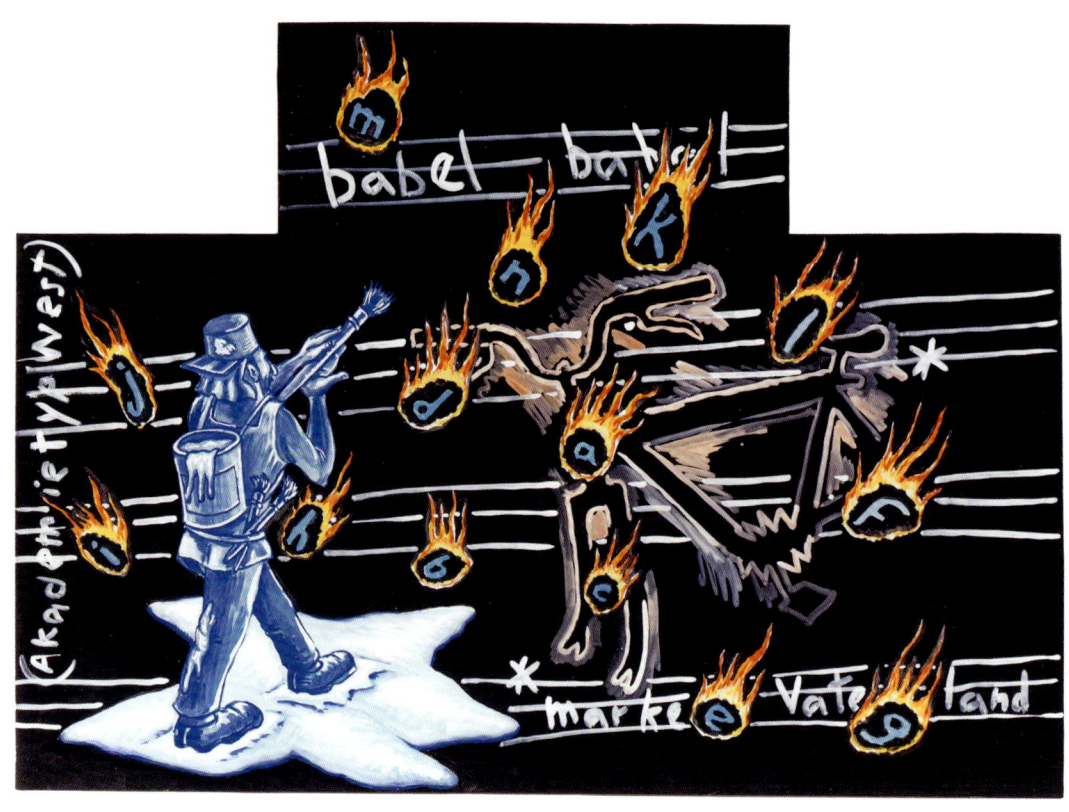

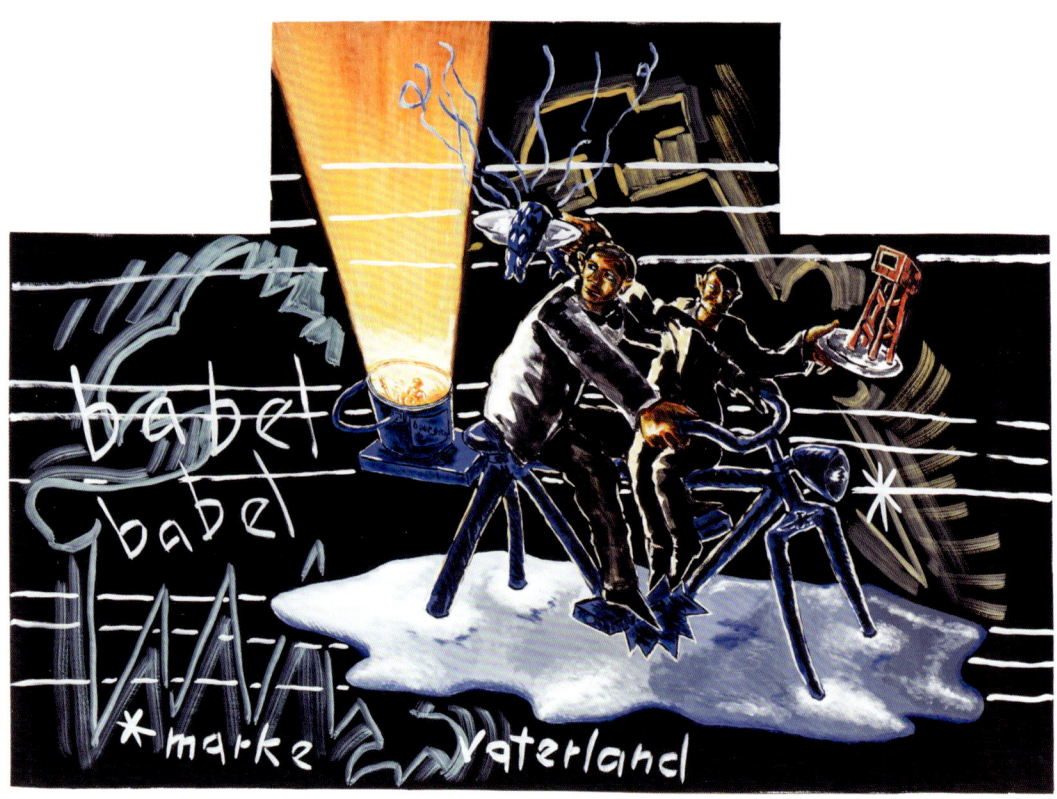

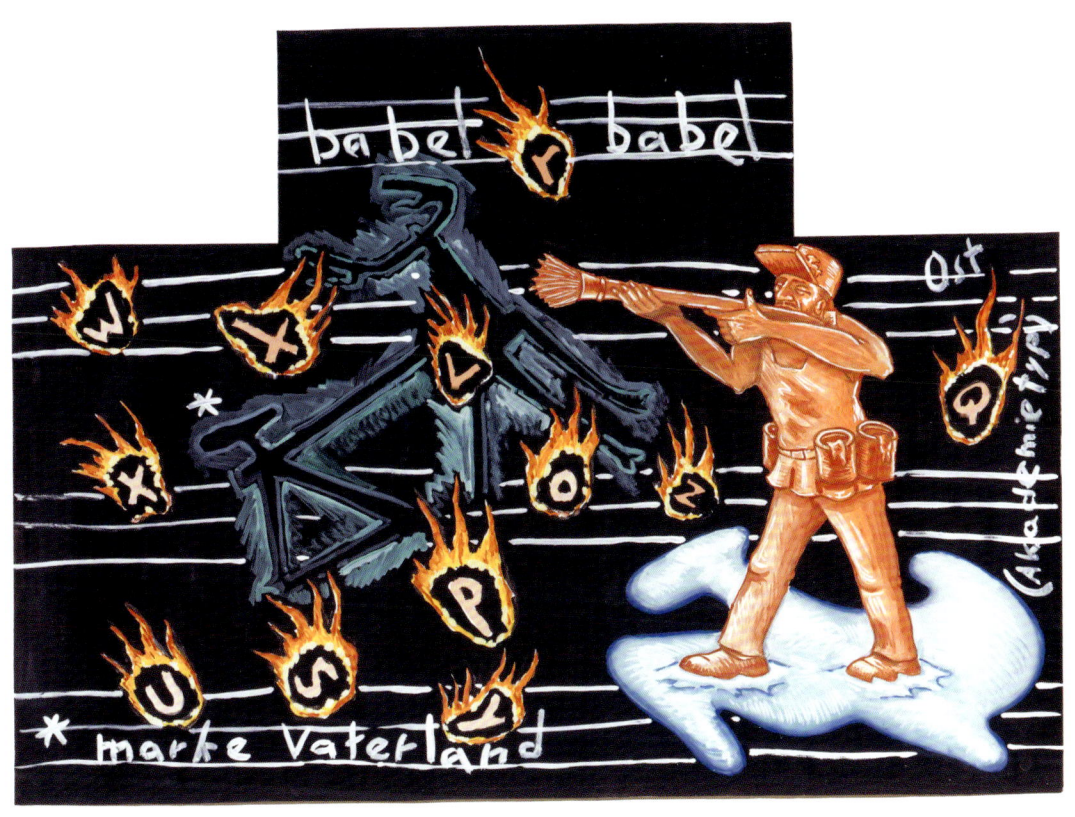

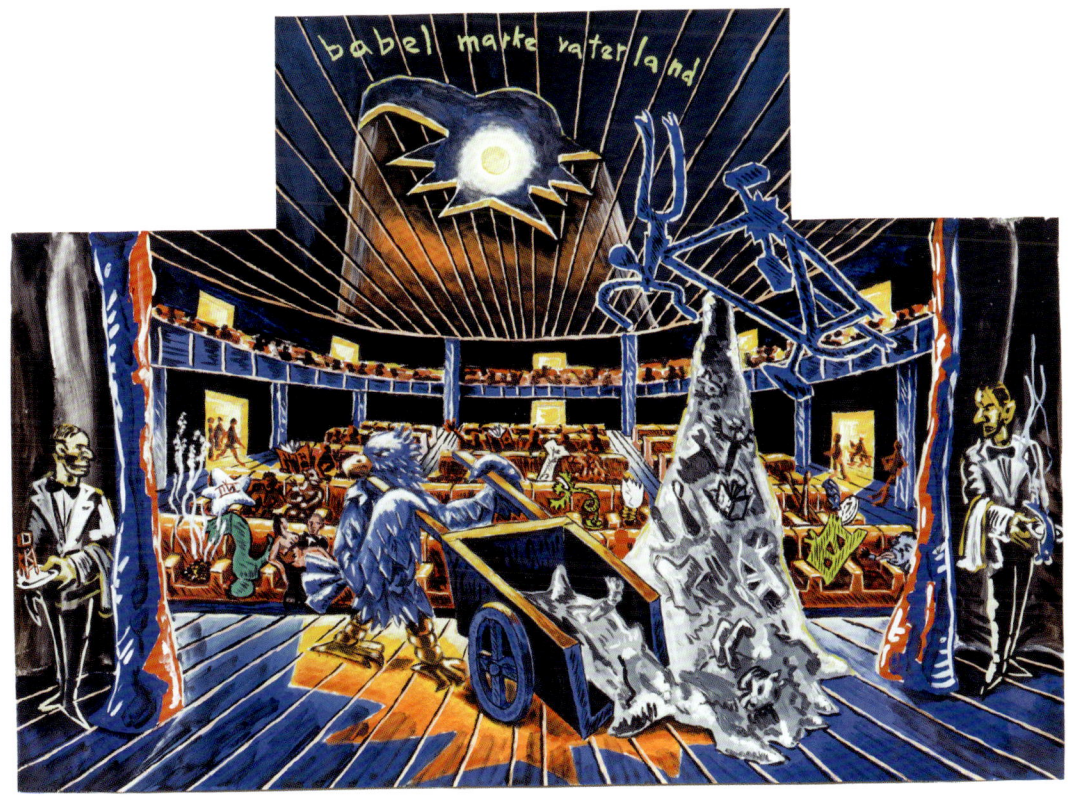

43

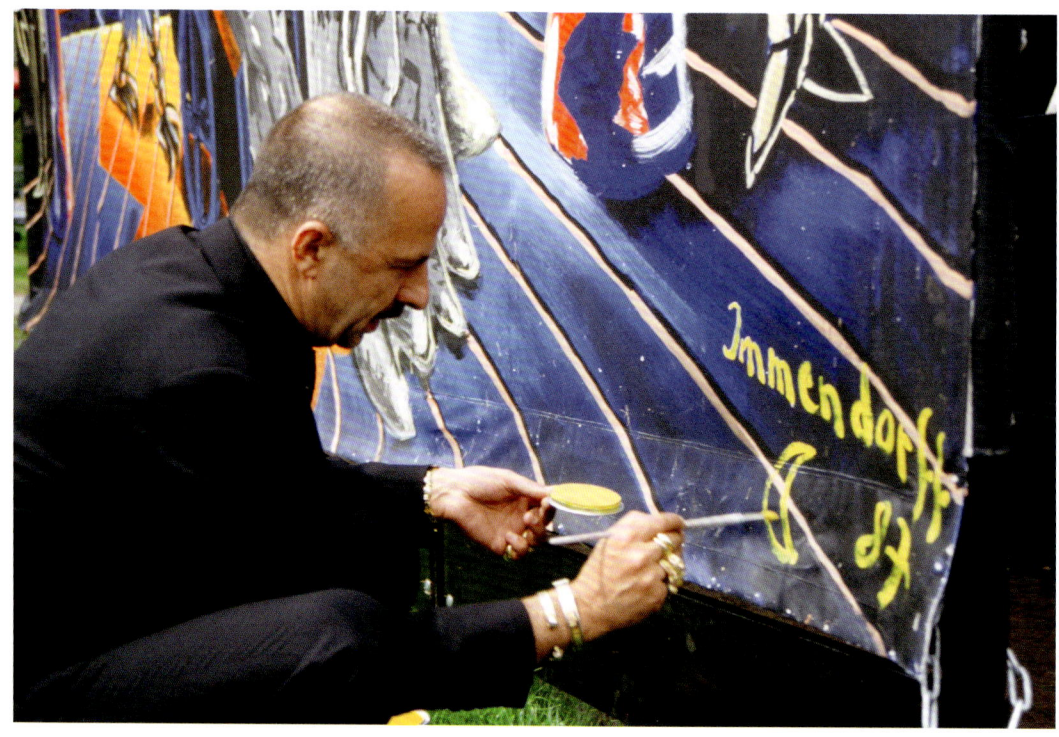

*Jörg Immendorff signing the shooting gallery …*

*… and with the two poster designs*

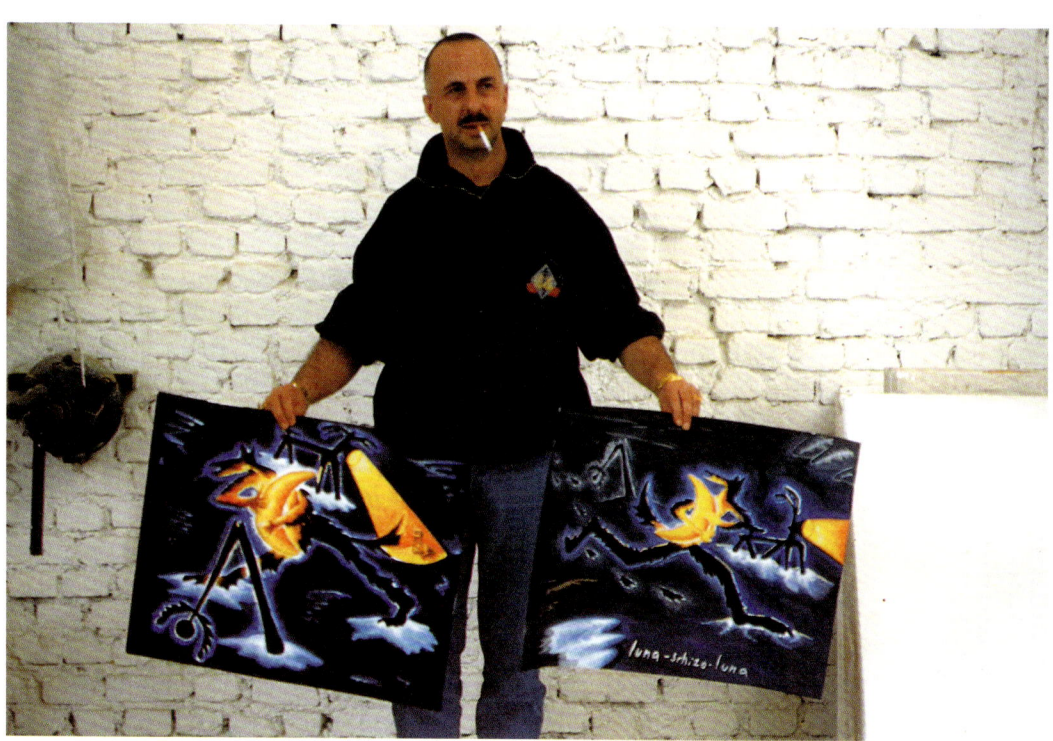

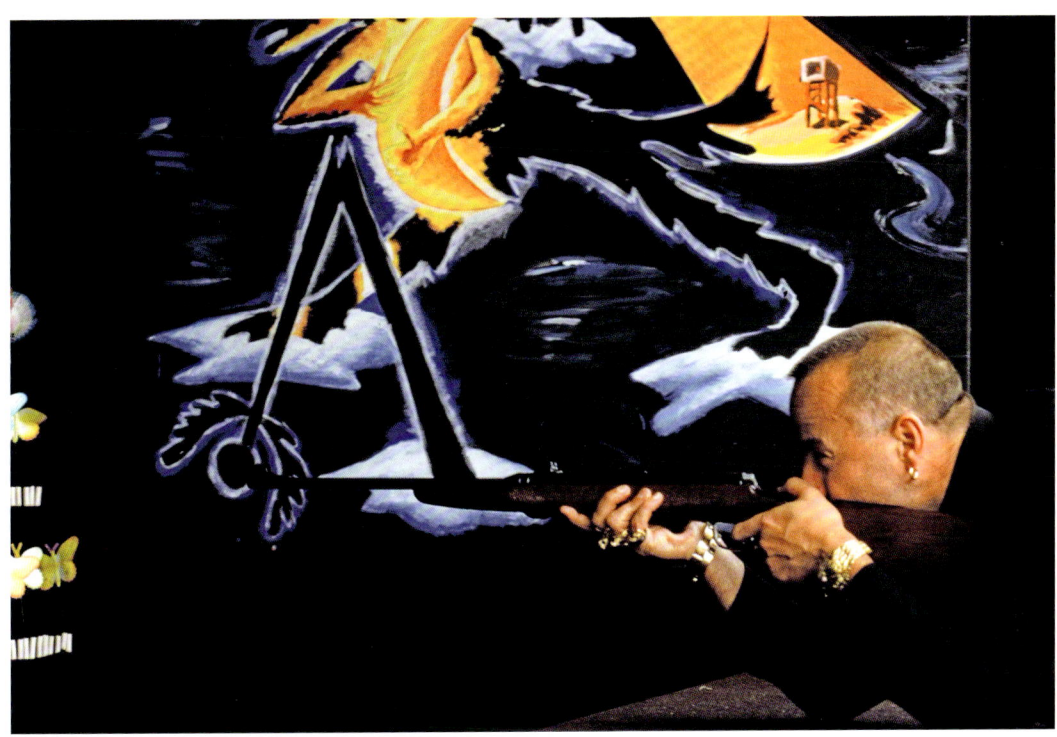

*Taking the first shot in his own shooting gallery*

*View of the Painter's Hall in the Vienna Grain Exchange*

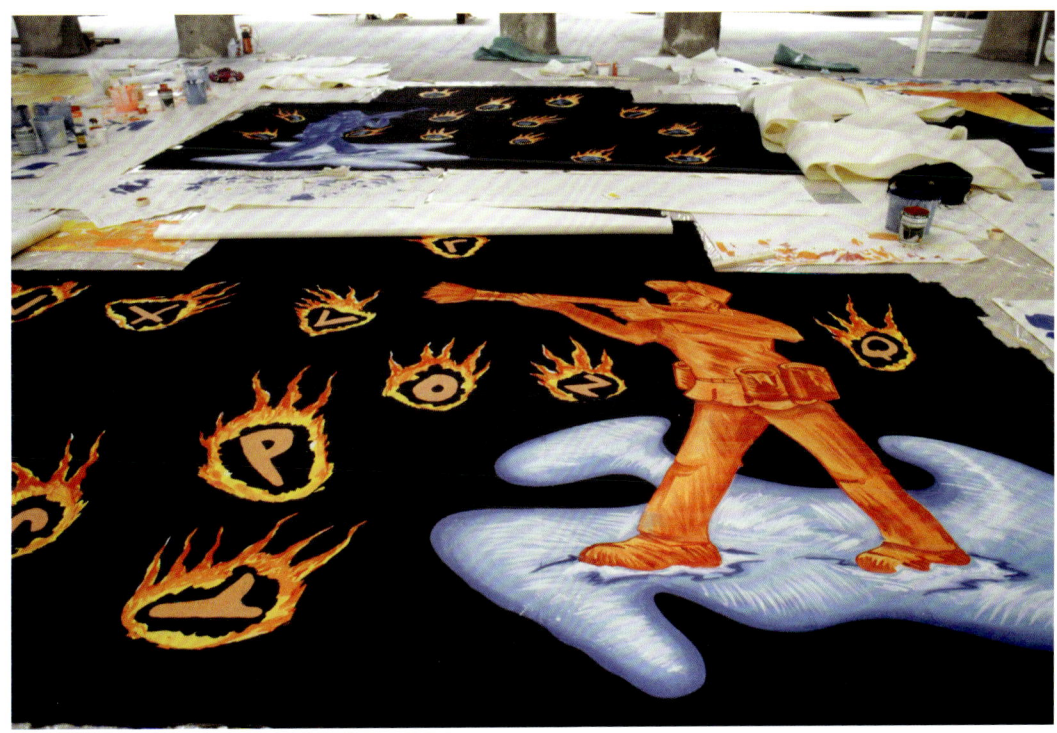

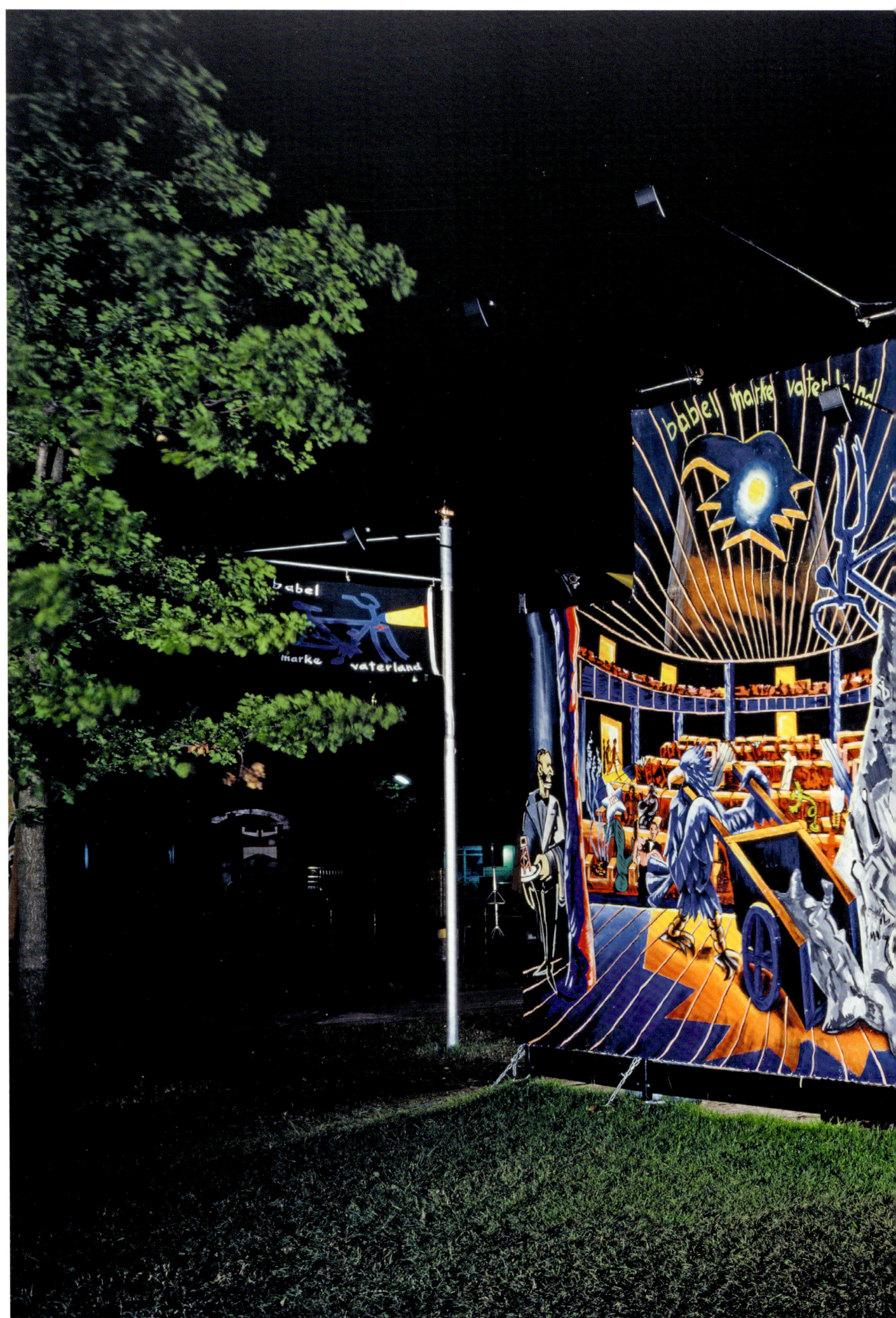

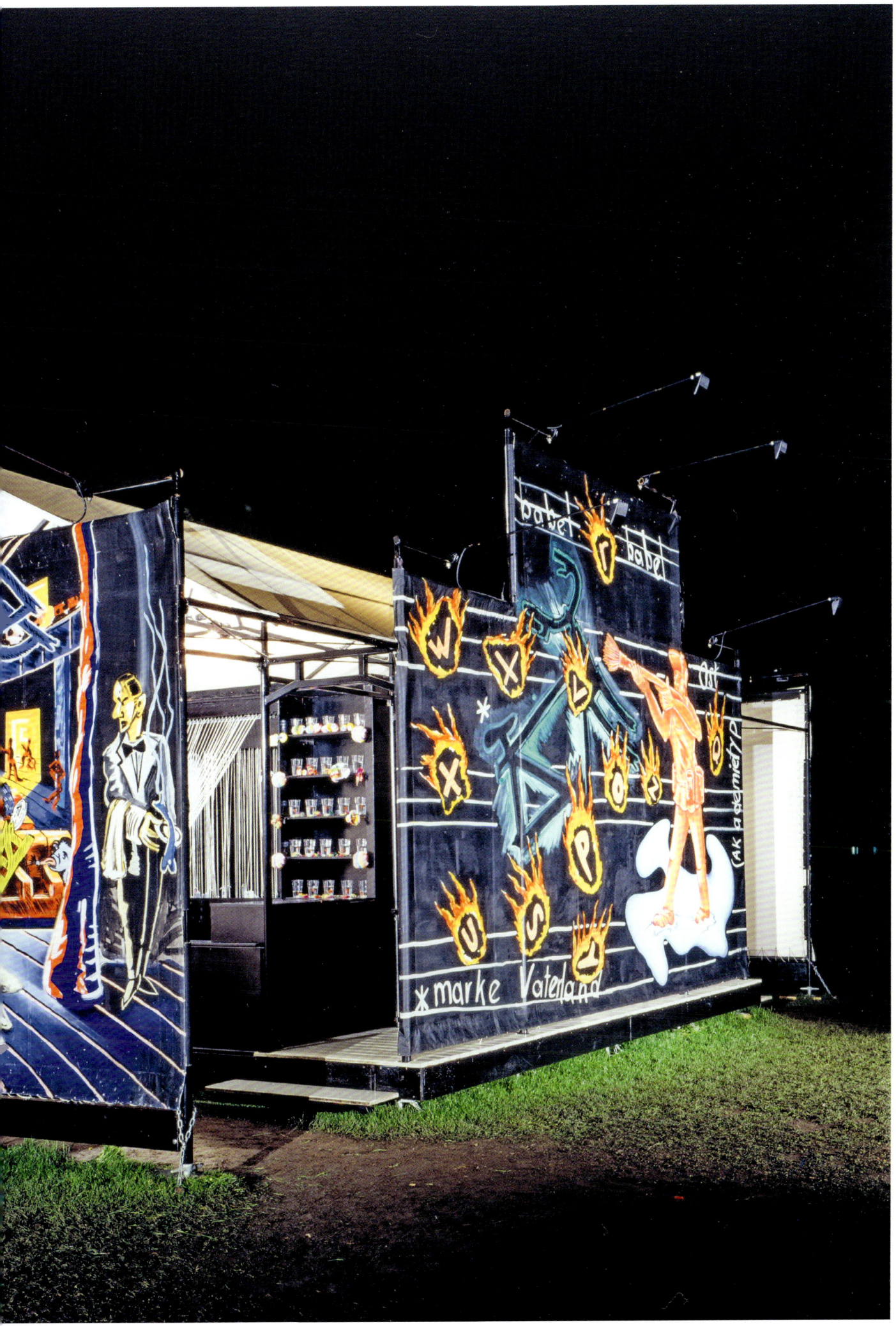

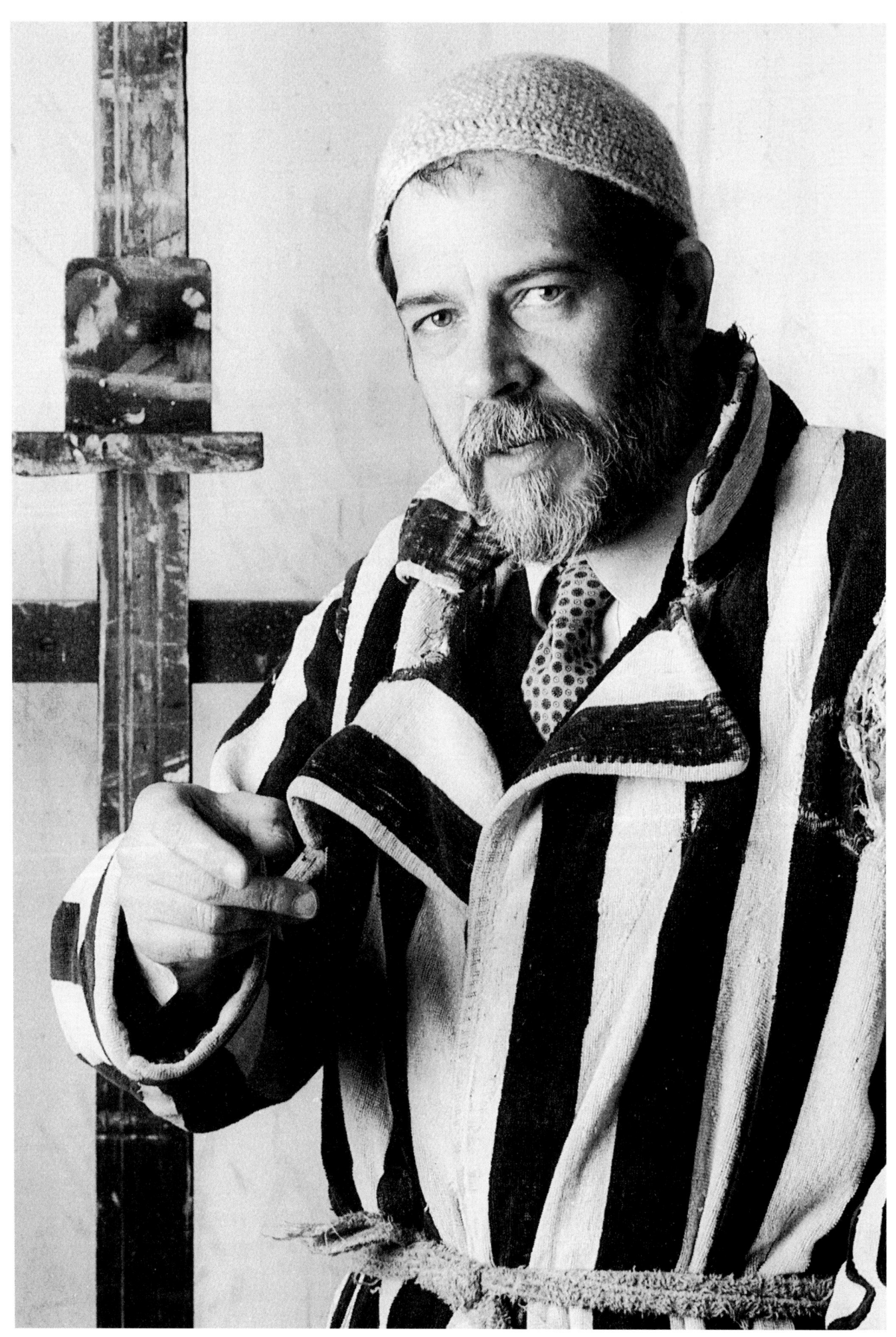

Wolfgang Herzig

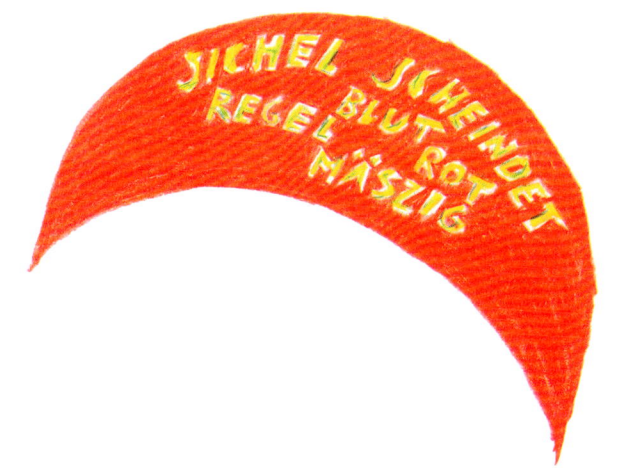

SICHEL SCHEINDET
BLUT ROT
REGEL
MÄSZIG

MOND MOND MOND
MOND MOND MOND
MOND MOND MOND
MOND MOND MOND
MOND MOND MOND
MOND MOND MOND
MOND MOND MOND
MOND MOND MOND
MOND MOND MOND
MOND MOND MOND

Wolfgang Herzig

Born: October 24, 1941, in Judenburg, Austria.

Painter, illustrator.

Wolfgang Herzig designed a **shooting gallery** for
*Luna Luna* in the form of a winged altar.

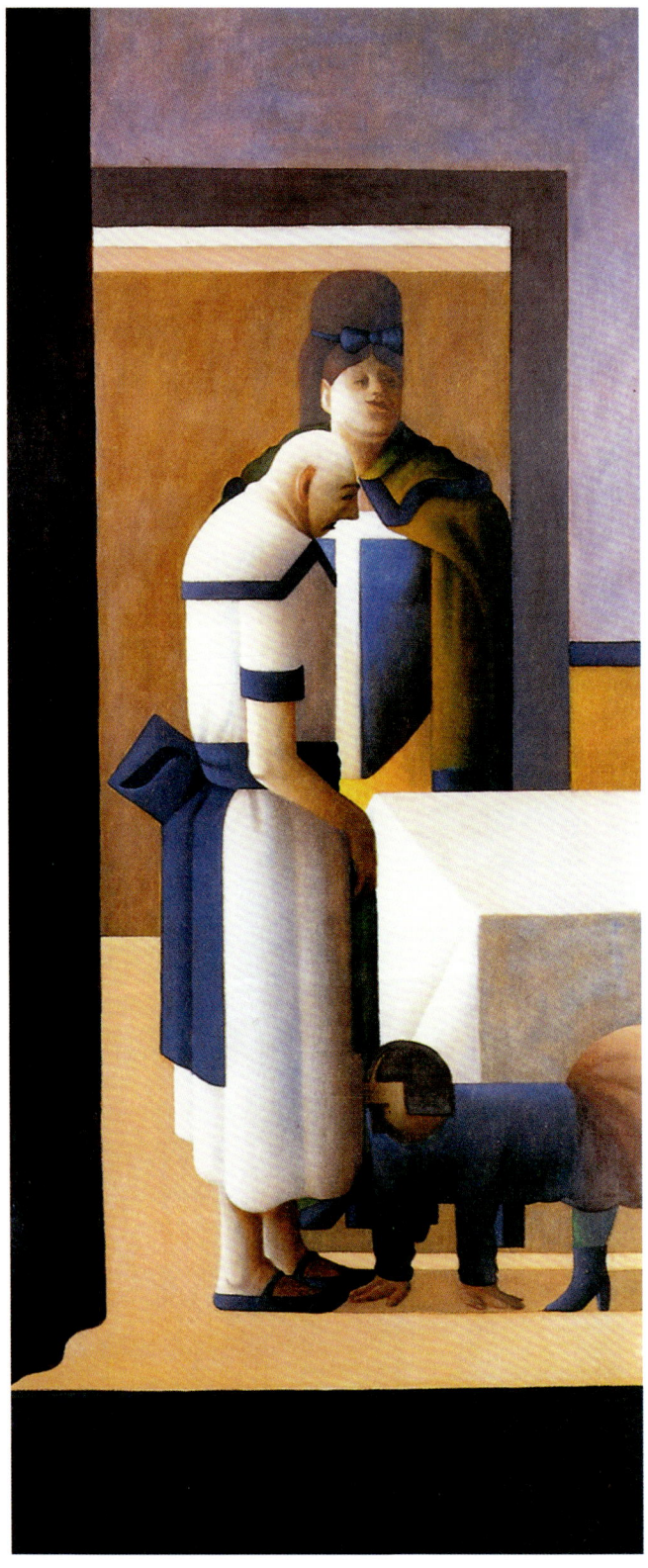

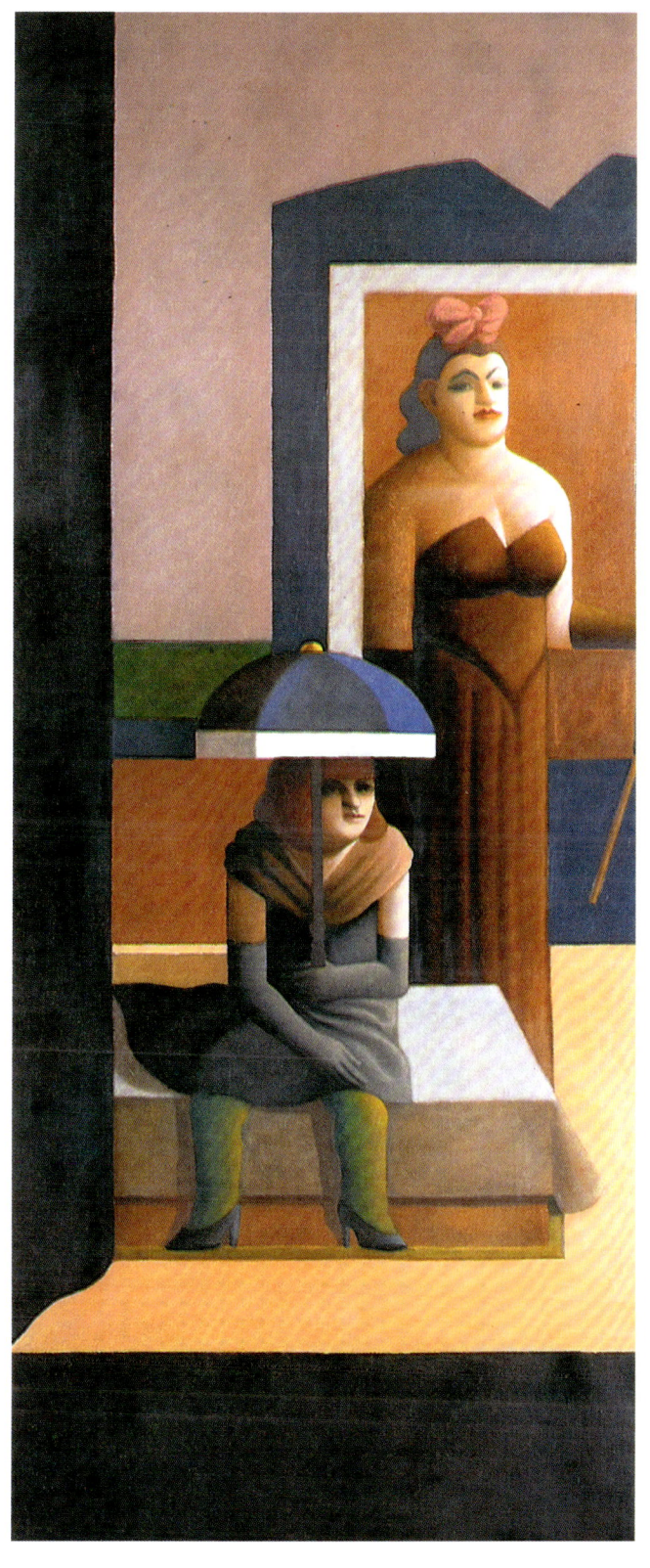
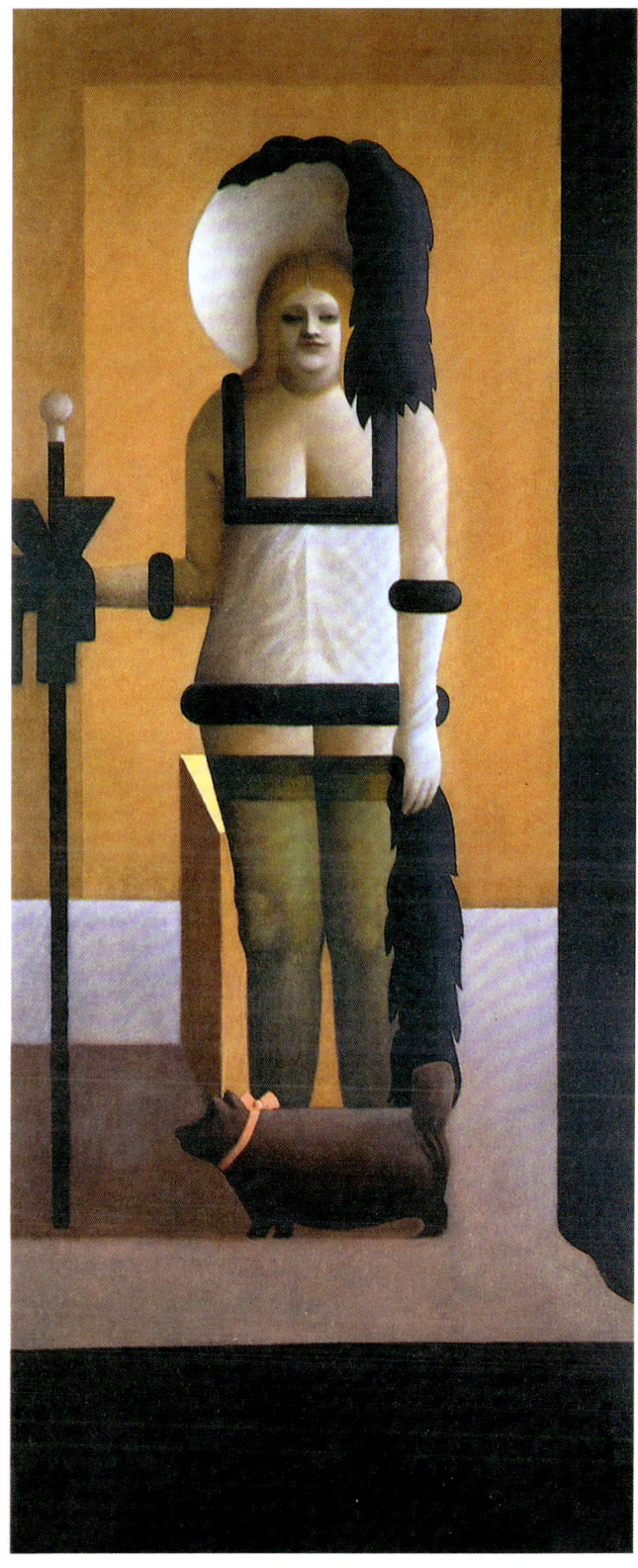

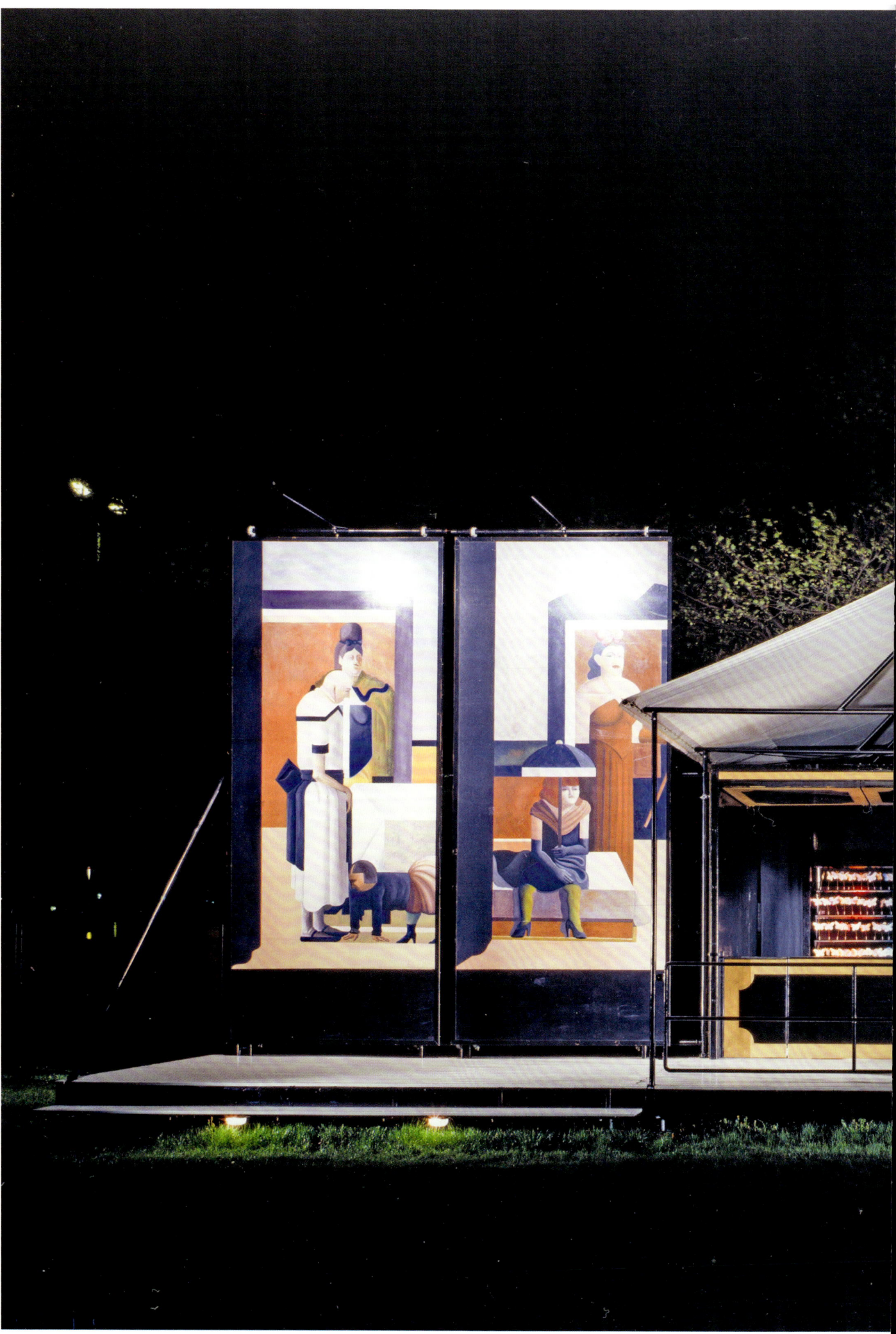

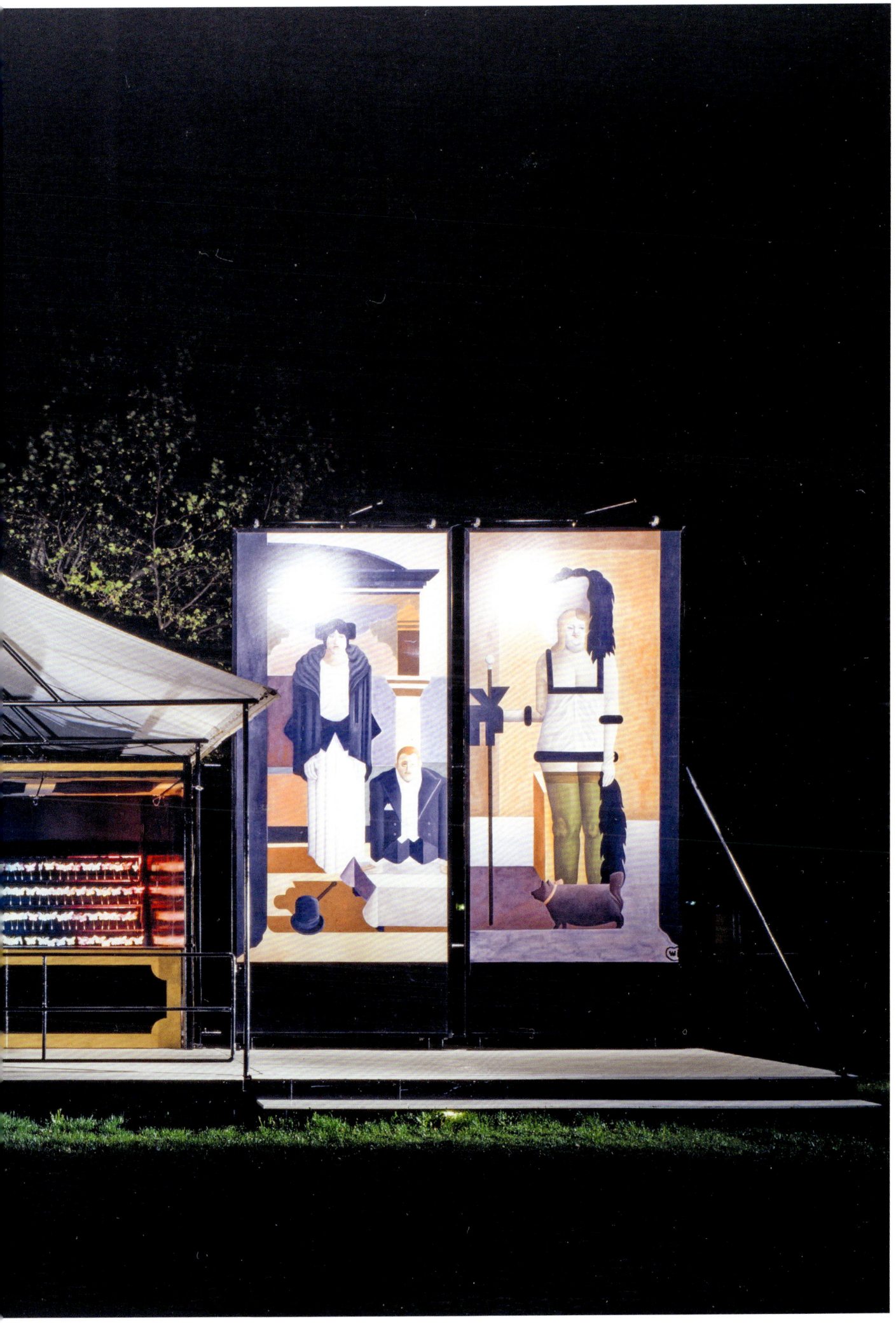

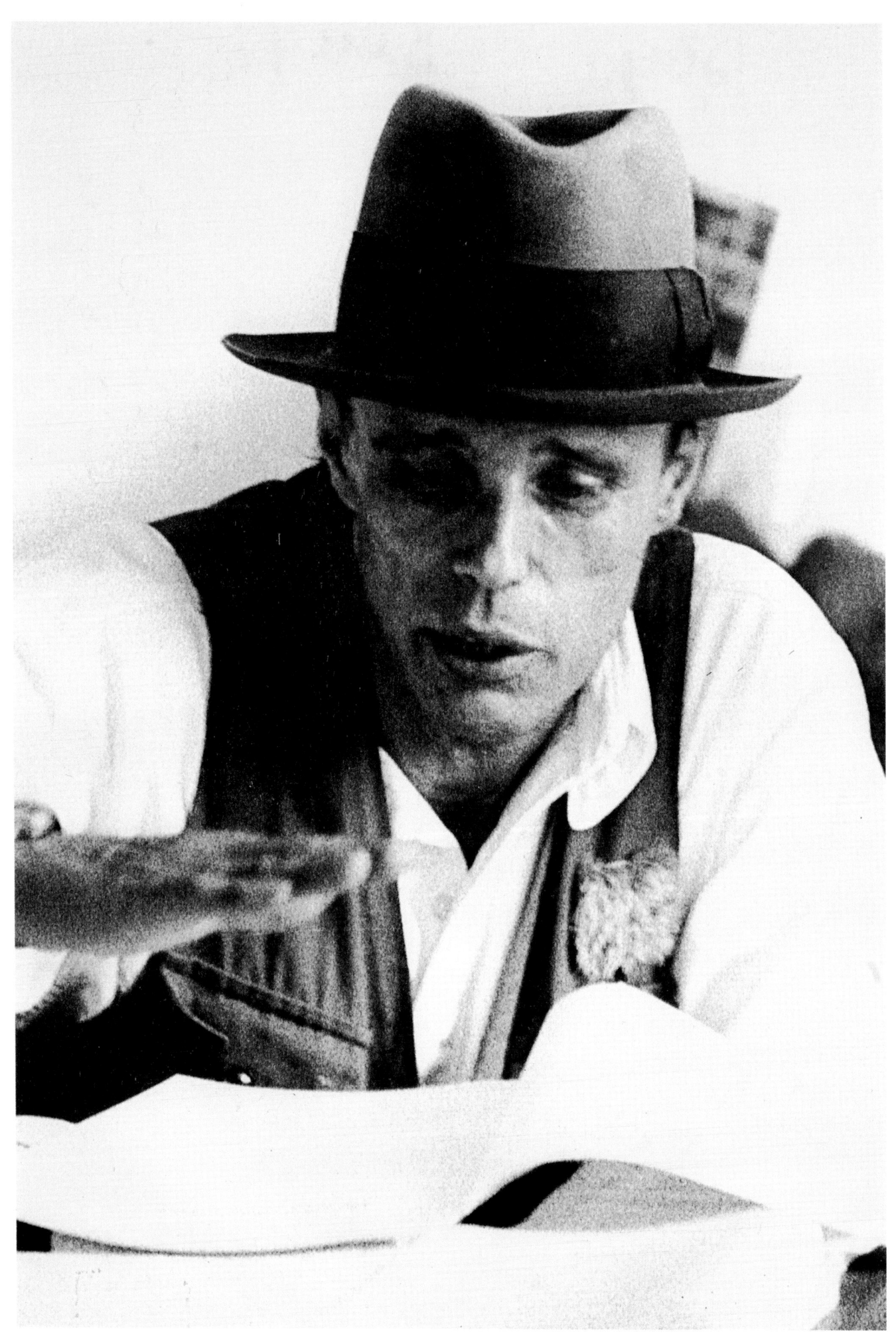

Joseph Beuys

ich bin kein Marxist,
aber ich liebe Marx vielleicht
mehr als viele Marxisten die
nur an ihn glauben.

Die Erkenntnis aus dem
Marx'schen Hebel zu entwickeln,
habe ich mir zur Pflicht
gemacht deshalb in das
DENK-LABOR zu gehen, und was
stelle ich fest!?: Geld ist gar kein
KAPITAL, aber FÄHIGKEIT ist KAPITAL

Ihr Geld als Ware hat also im Produktions-
prozeß der Gesellschaft (Wirtschaft.) nichts
zu suchen, sondern erst als vorstellbar
RECHTSGEBER für die ARBEIT nur an
der Rechtssphäre (demokratisches (Bankwesen)
wirken.
                    Joseph Beuys

Joseph Beuys

Born: May 2, 1921, in Kleve, Germany.
Died: January 23, 1986, in Düsseldorf.

Sculptor, illustrator, action artist, philosopher.

Joseph Beuys provided a **text on capital and creativity** for *Luna Luna*. It is intended to remind viewers of the free raw material of imagination that is inherent in each and every one of us.

# »GELD IST KAPITAL. ABER IST

"Money is not capital at all. However, ability is capital."

# GAR KEIN FÄHIGKEIT KAPITAL. «

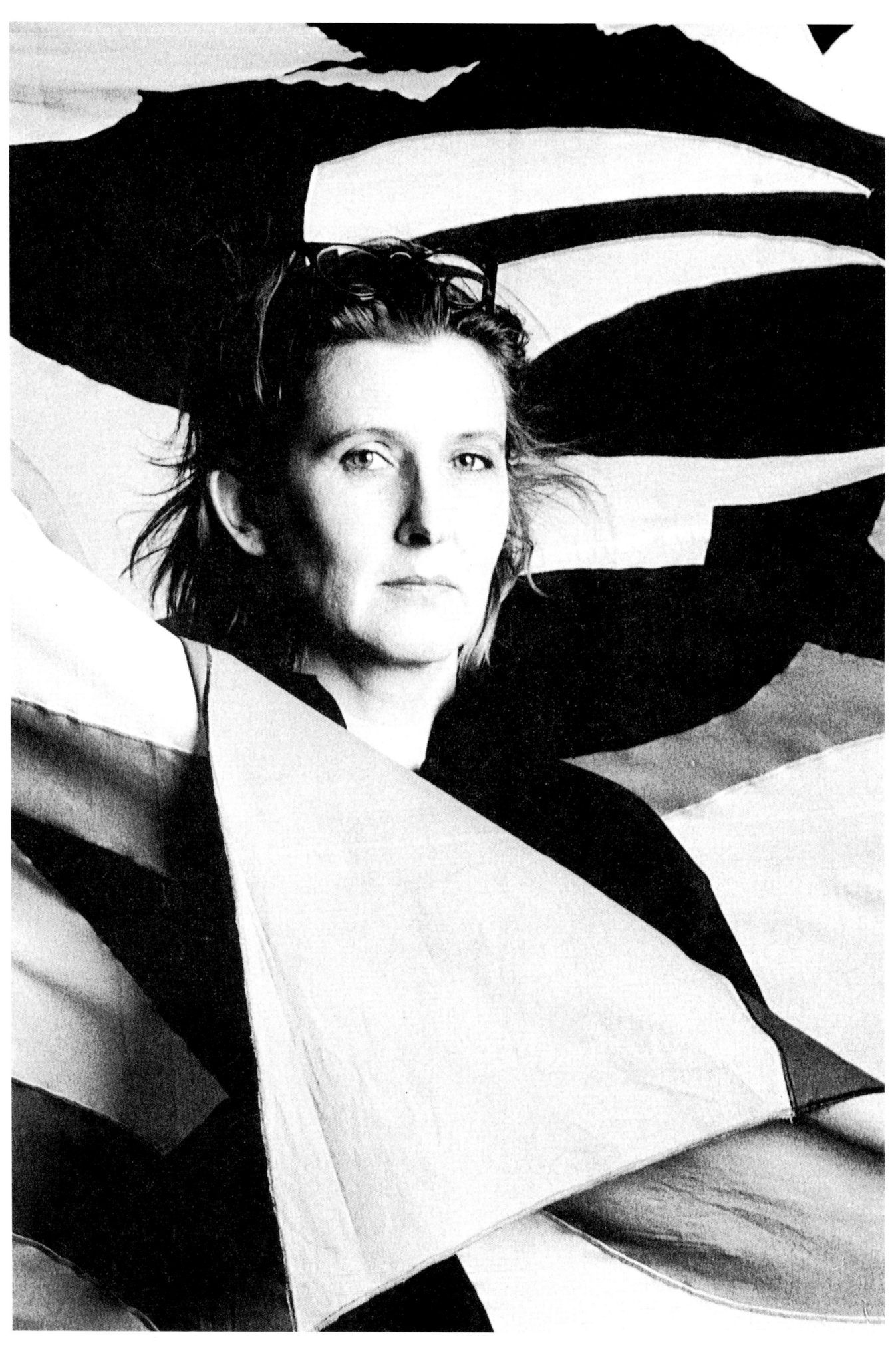

Monika Gilsing

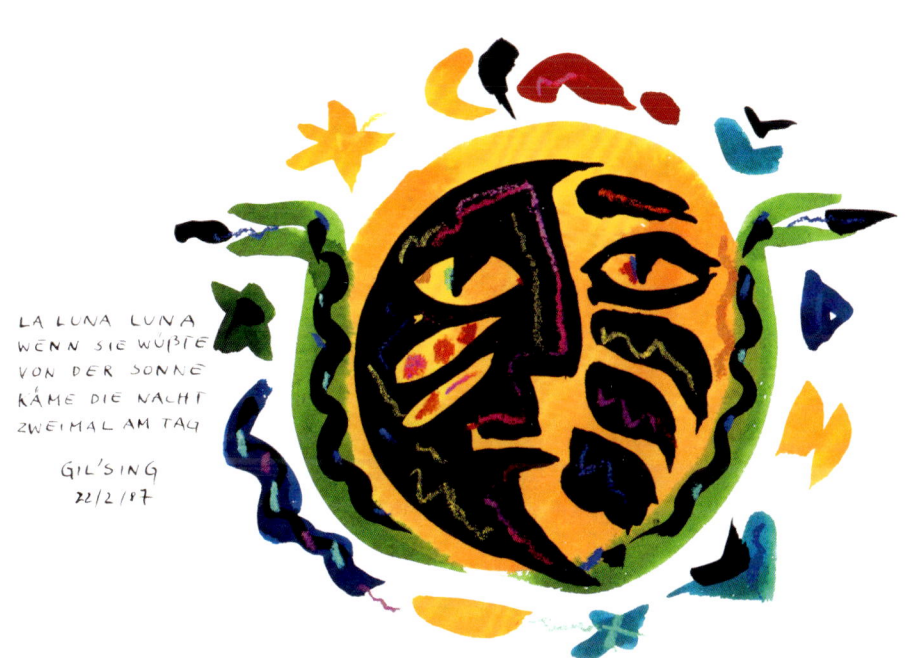

LA LUNA LUNA
WENN SIE WÜßTE
VON DER SONNE
KÄME DIE NACHT
ZWEIMAL AM TAG

GIL'SING
22/2/87

Monika Gilsing

Born: January 22, 1942, in Hamburg, Germany.

Painter, illustrator, photographer, actionist.

Monika Gilsing designed the "Wind Pictures" as **flags** for *Luna Luna*.

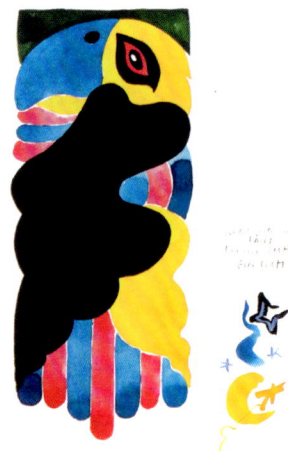
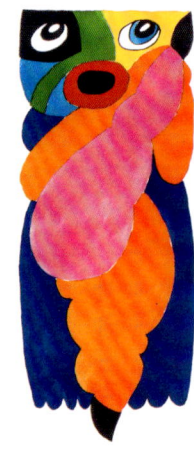

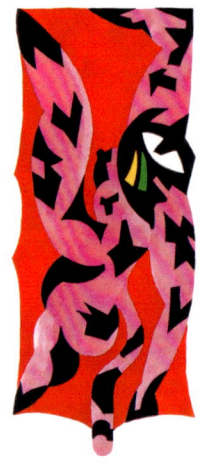
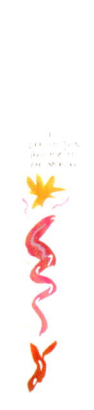
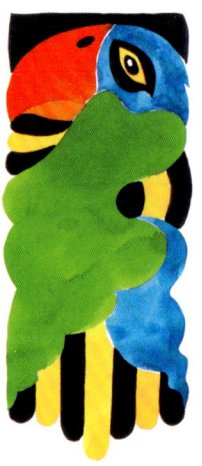
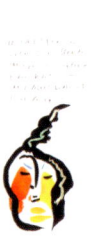

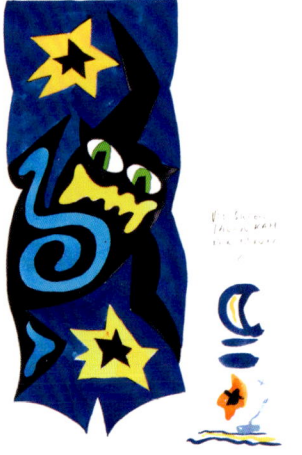
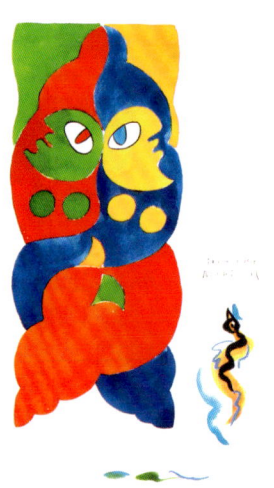

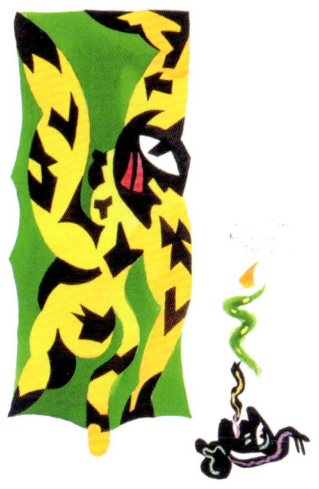
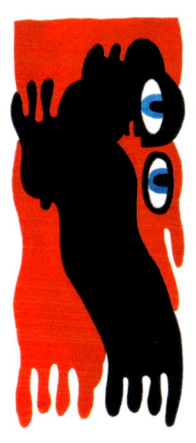

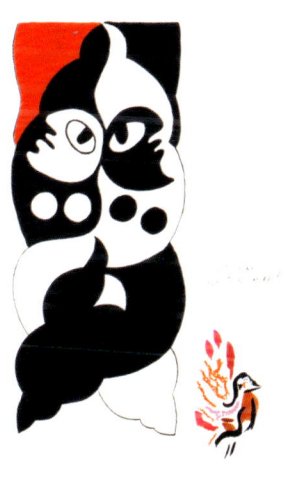
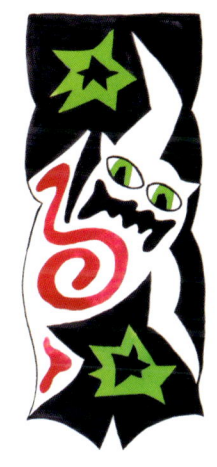
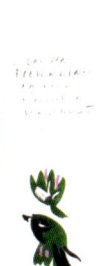
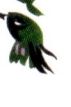
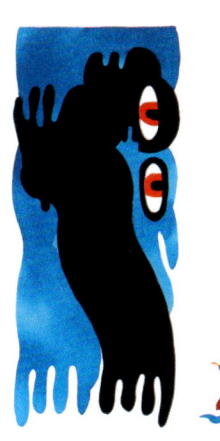

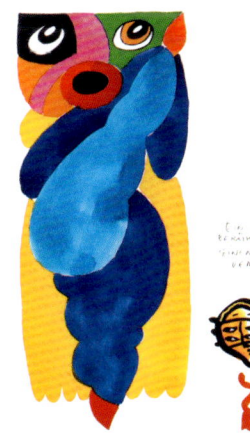

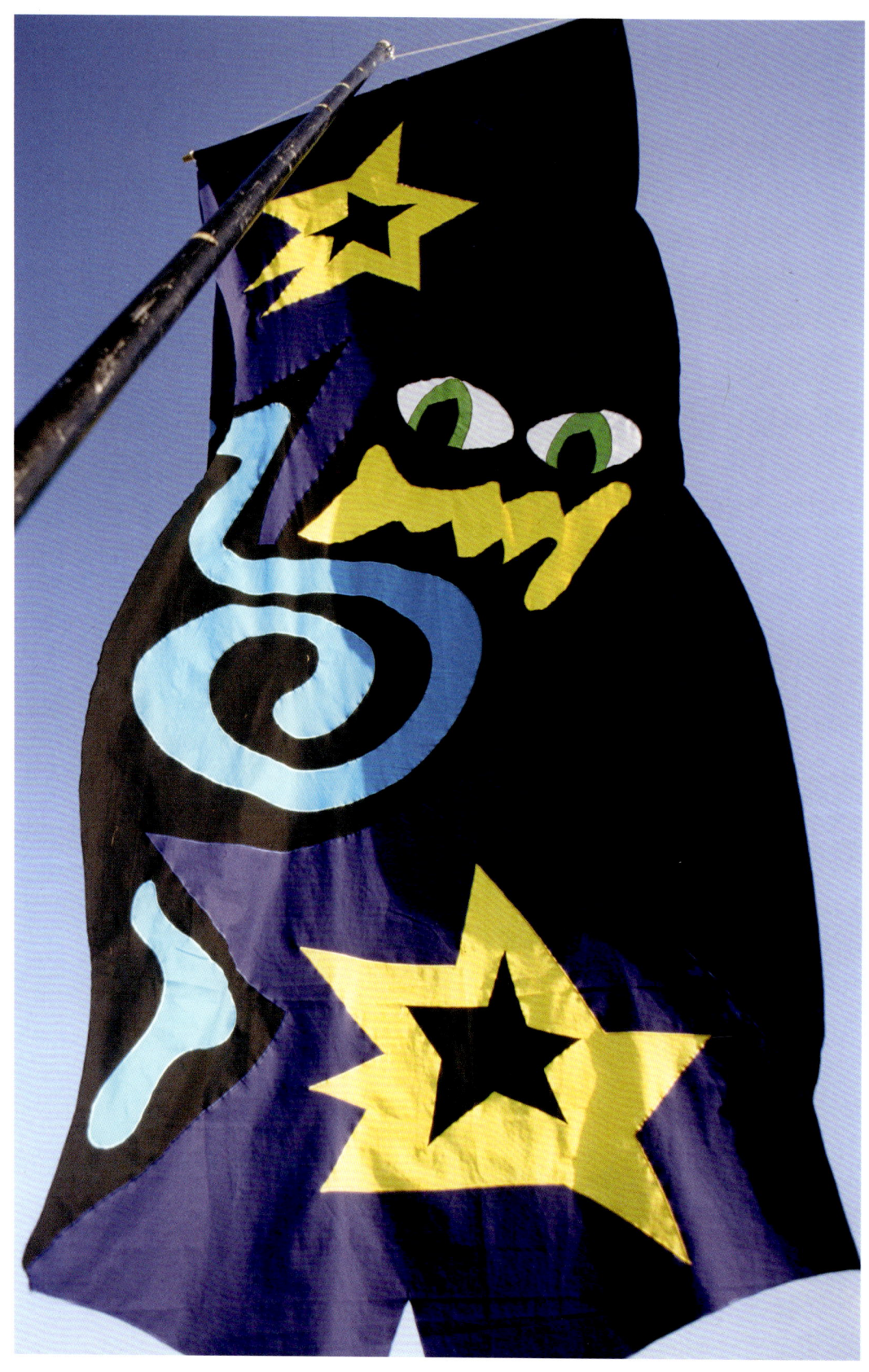

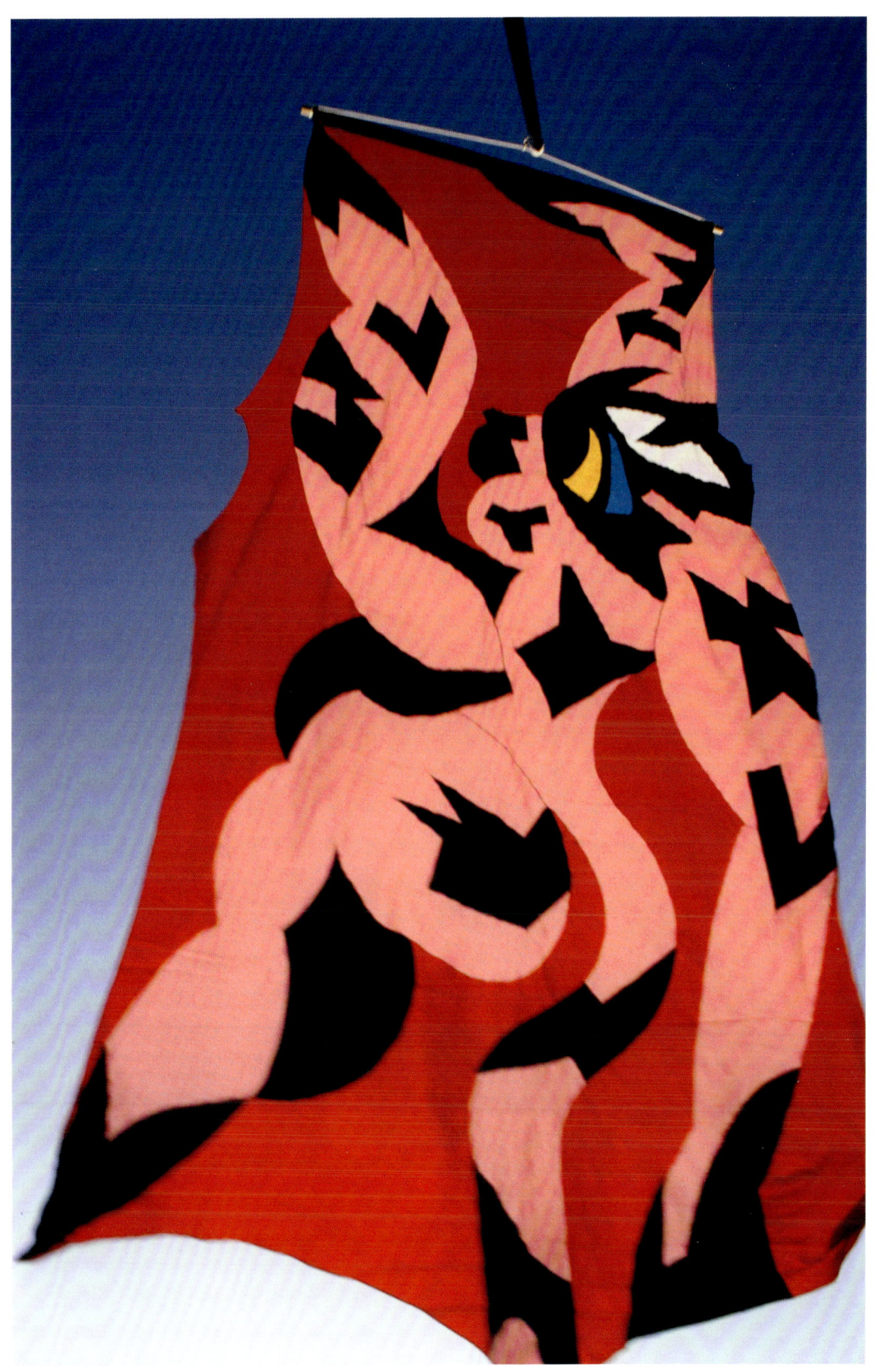

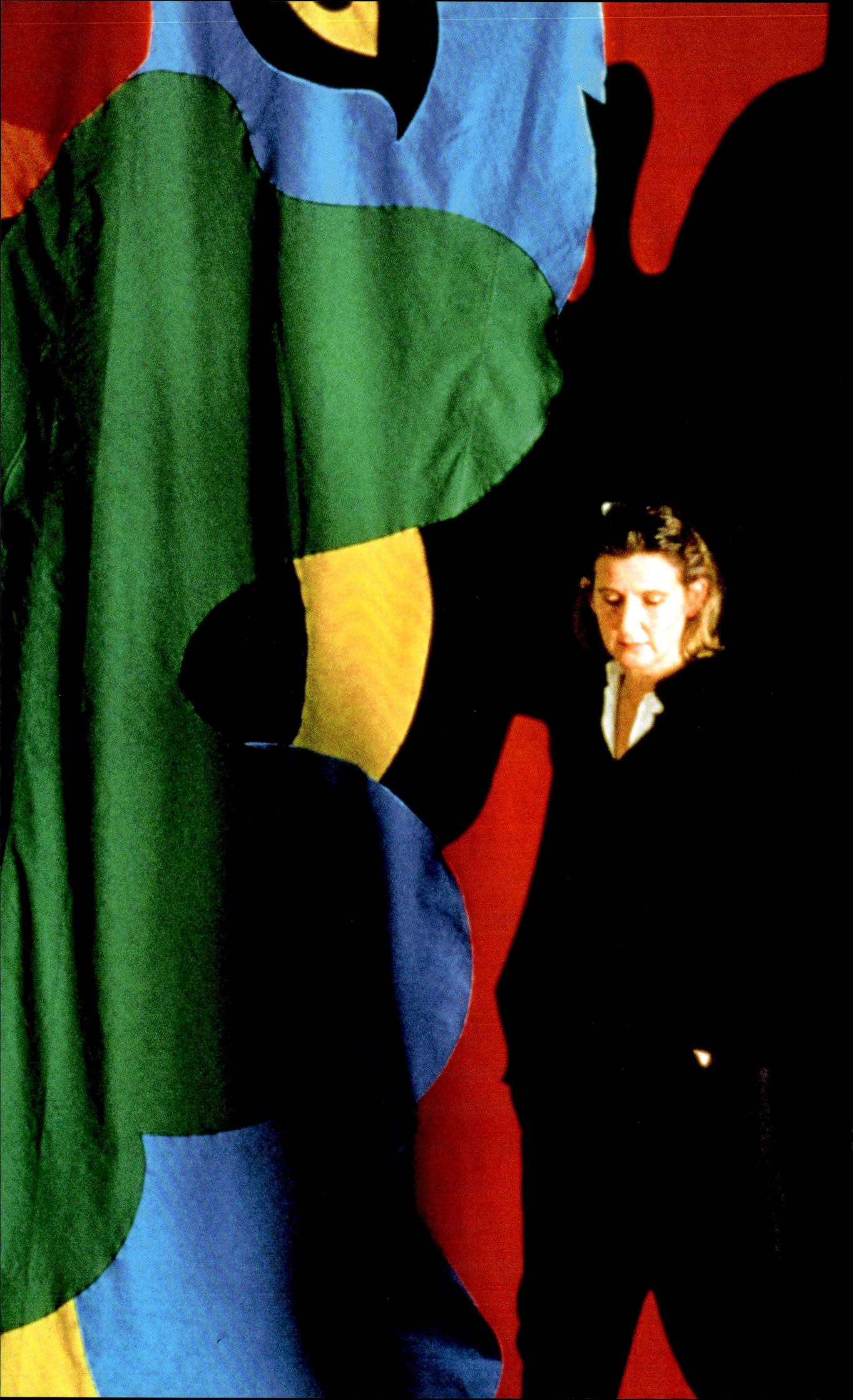

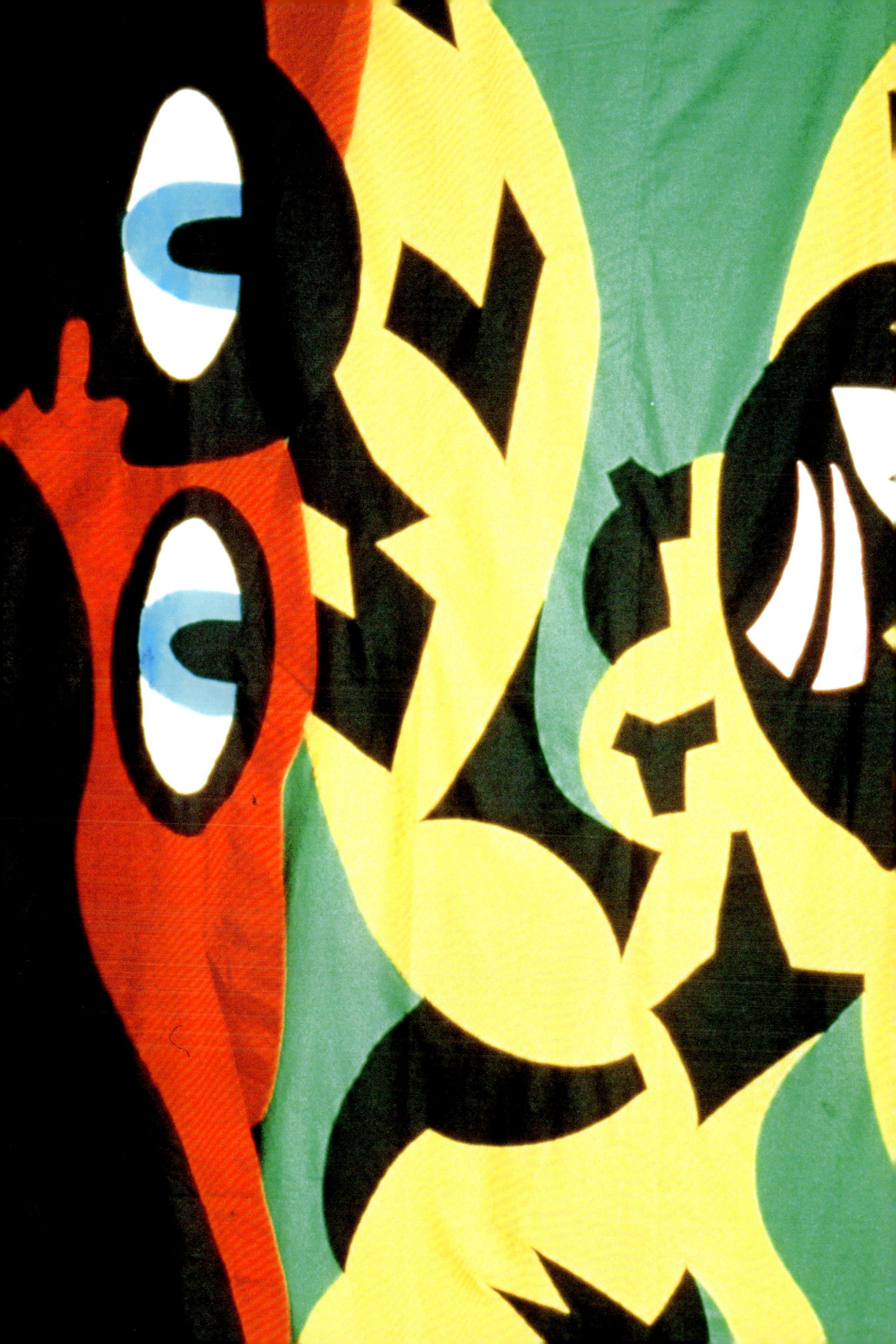

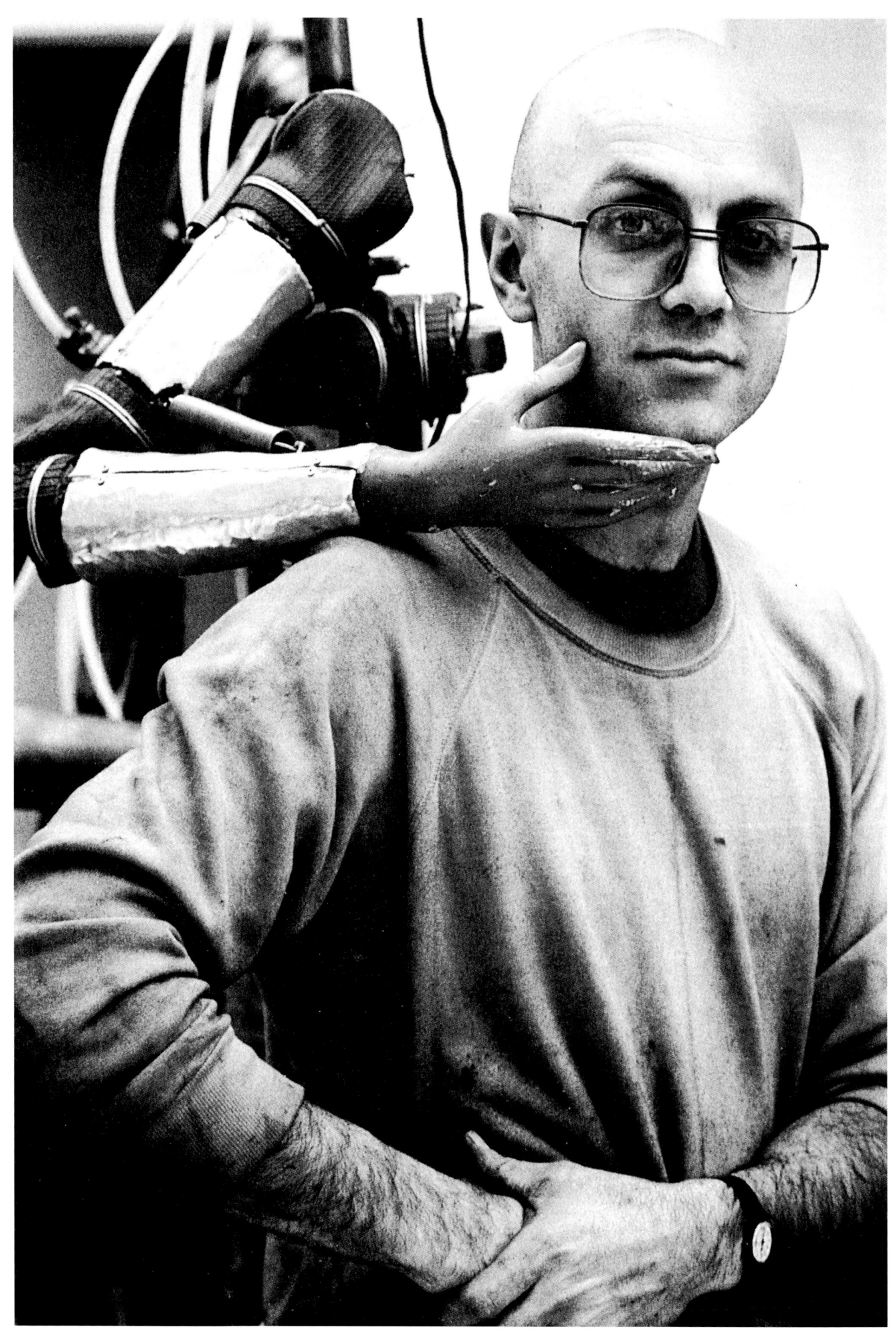

Jim Whiting

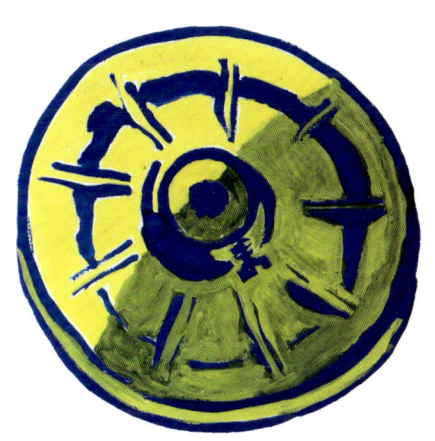

I met a man at Lunaluna. He had no proper head.
It was dark but I noticed a motor inside his neck,
which turned his head from side to side.
He asked me for some old black suits. I didn't
give him any.

Jim Whiting

Born: January 11, 1951, in Paris, France.

Sculptor, inventor, actionist, director of the Mechanical Theatre.

Jim Whiting designed and built the **Mechanical Theater** for *Luna Luna*, a building in which moving, seemingly out-of-control sculptures perform a macabre dance of death to industrial society that believes in progress.

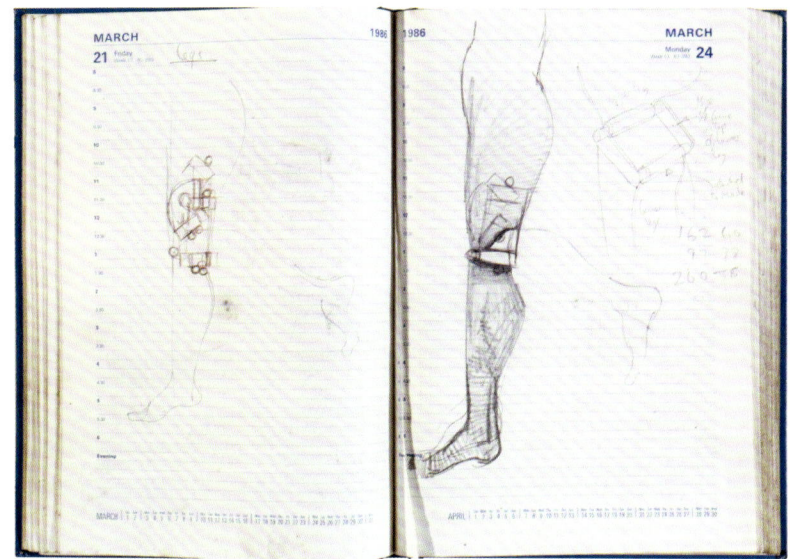

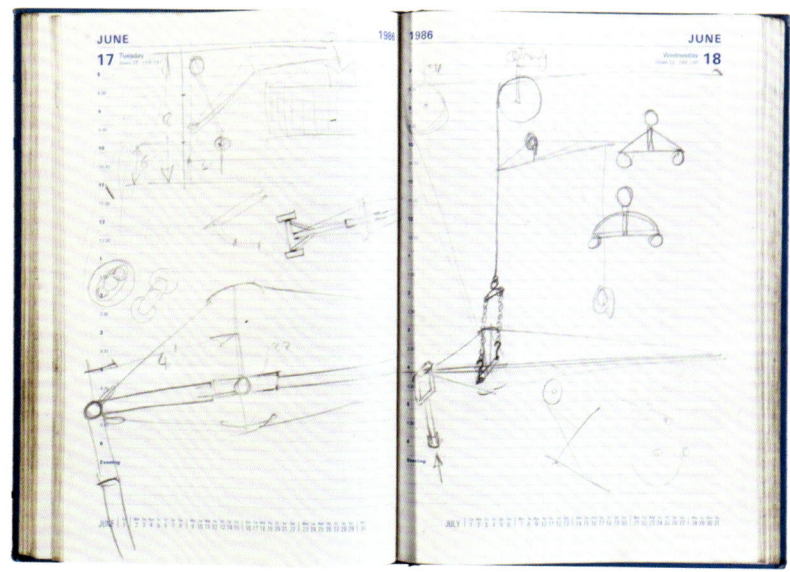

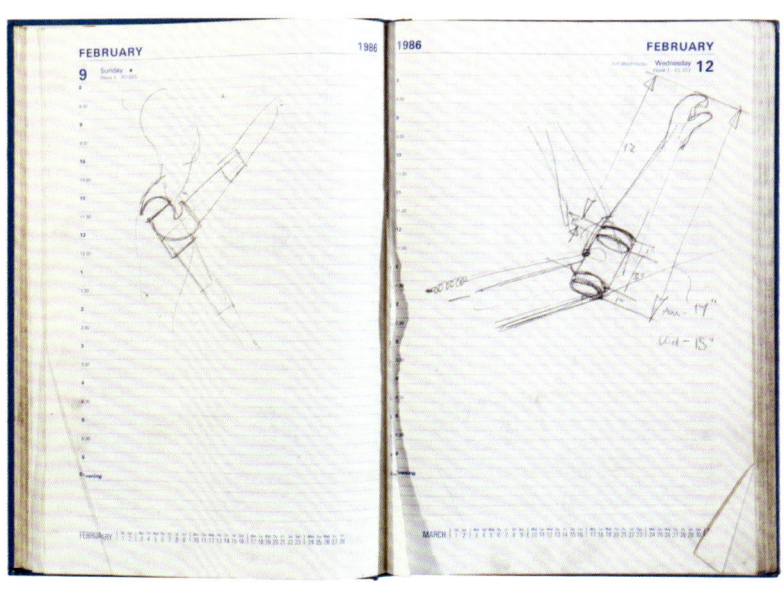

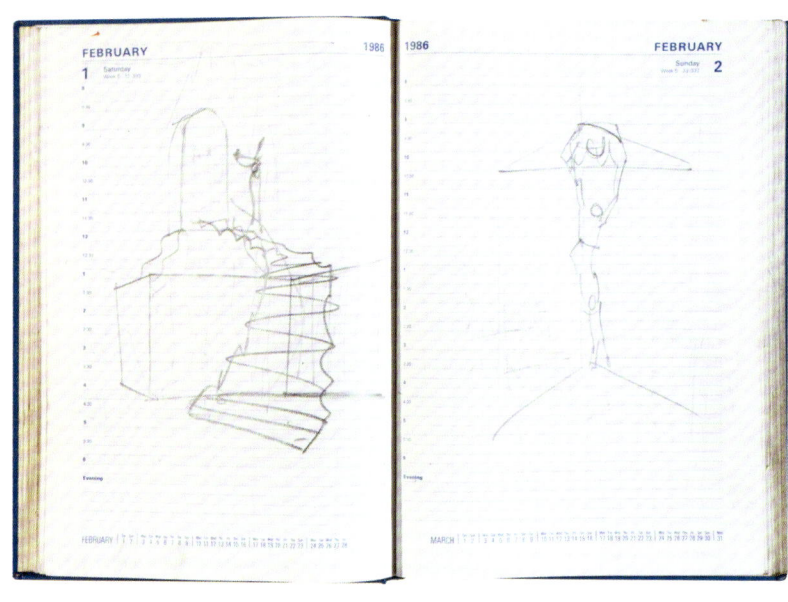

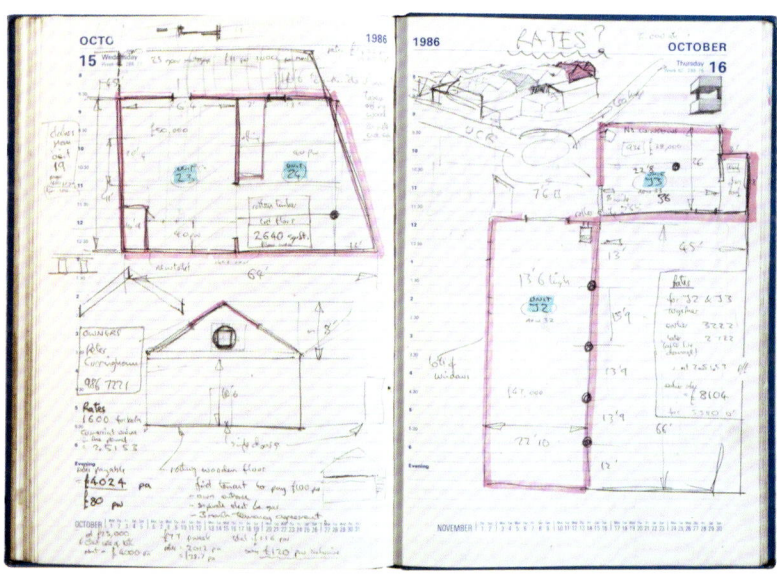

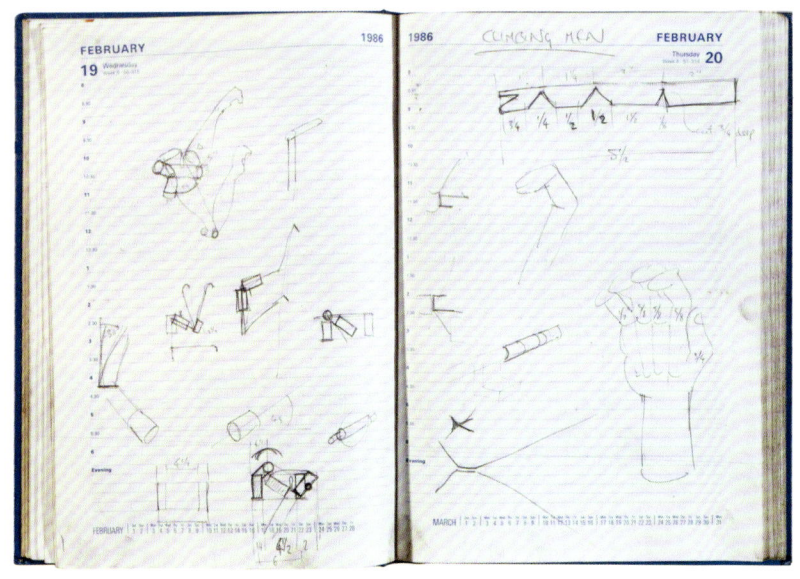

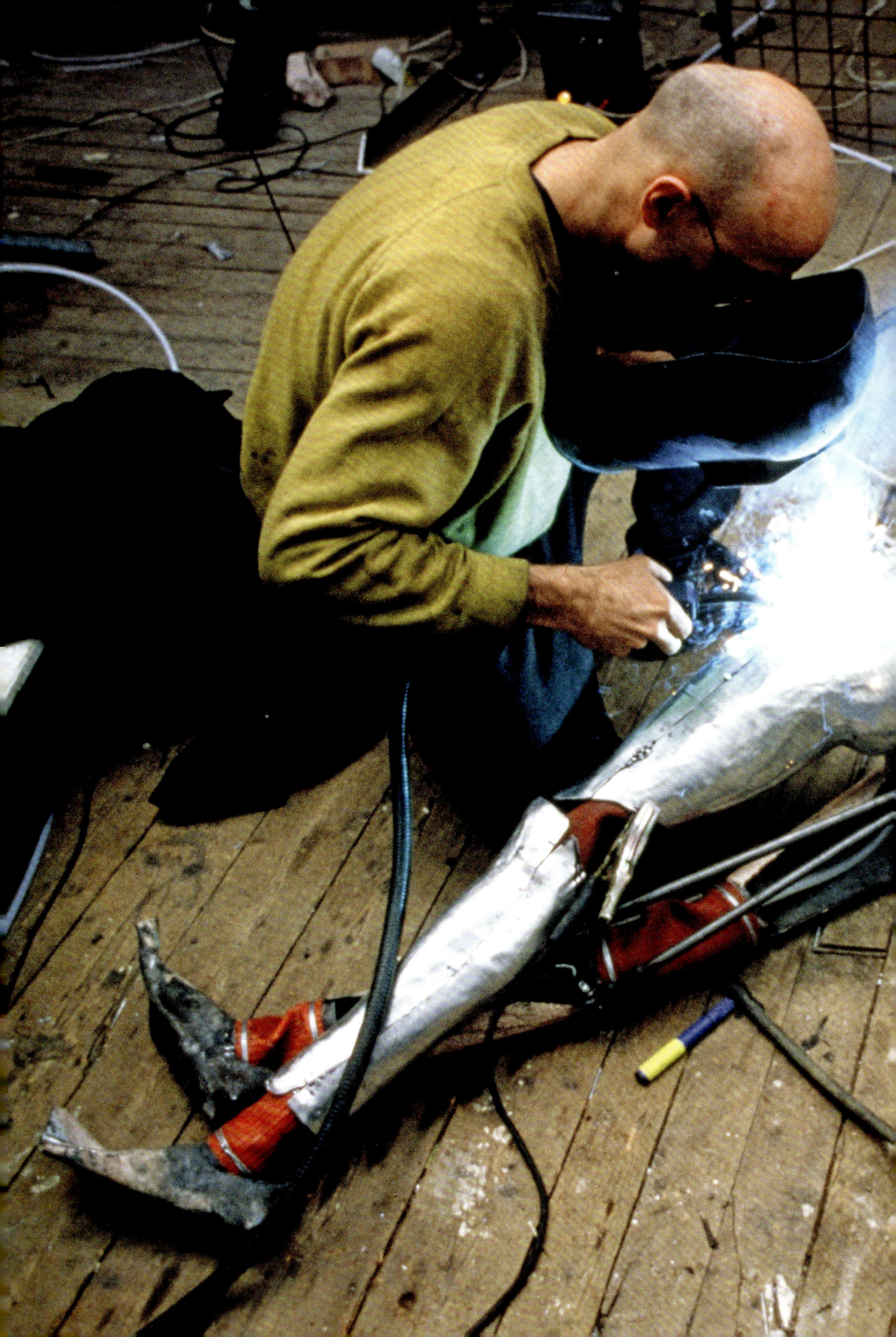

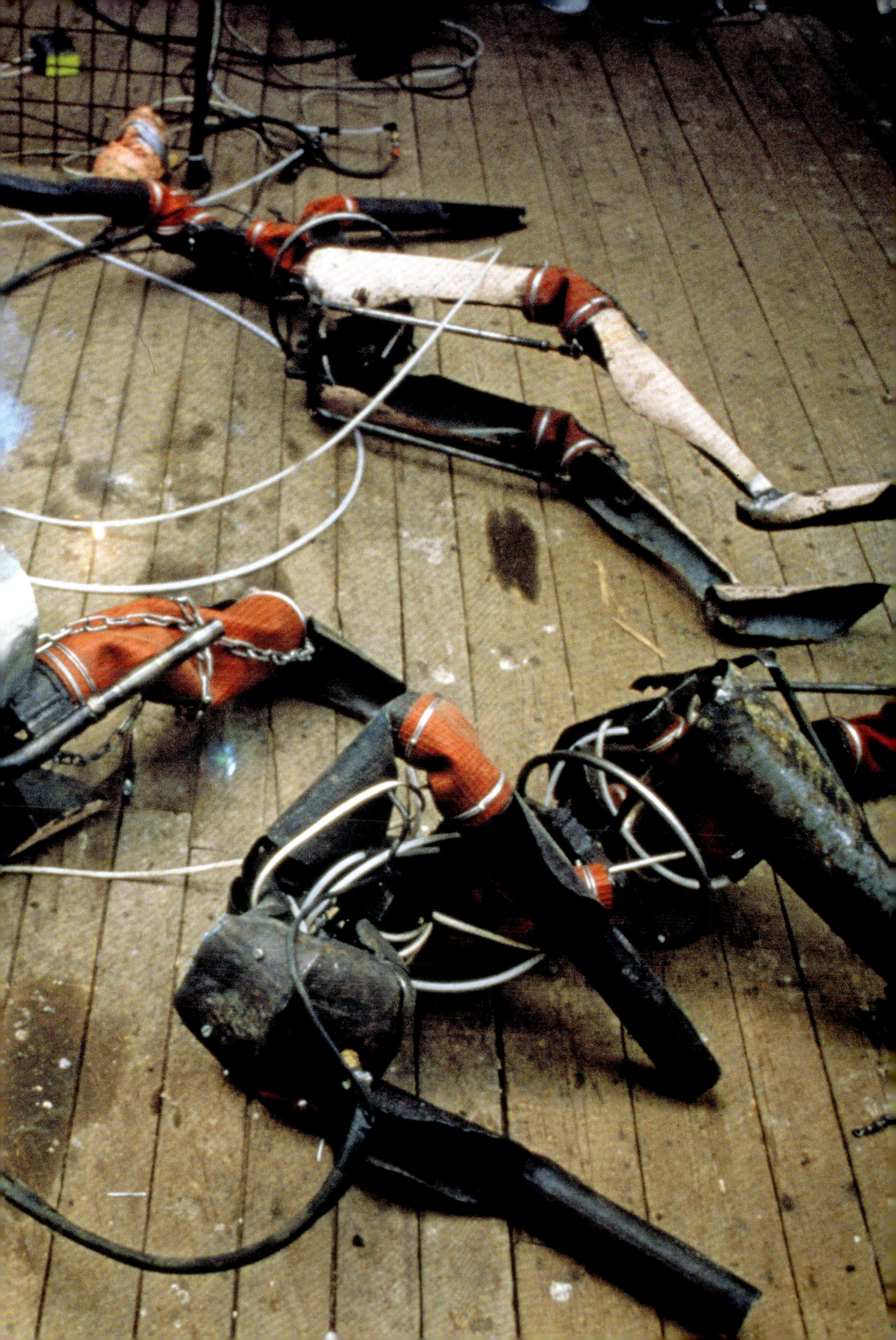

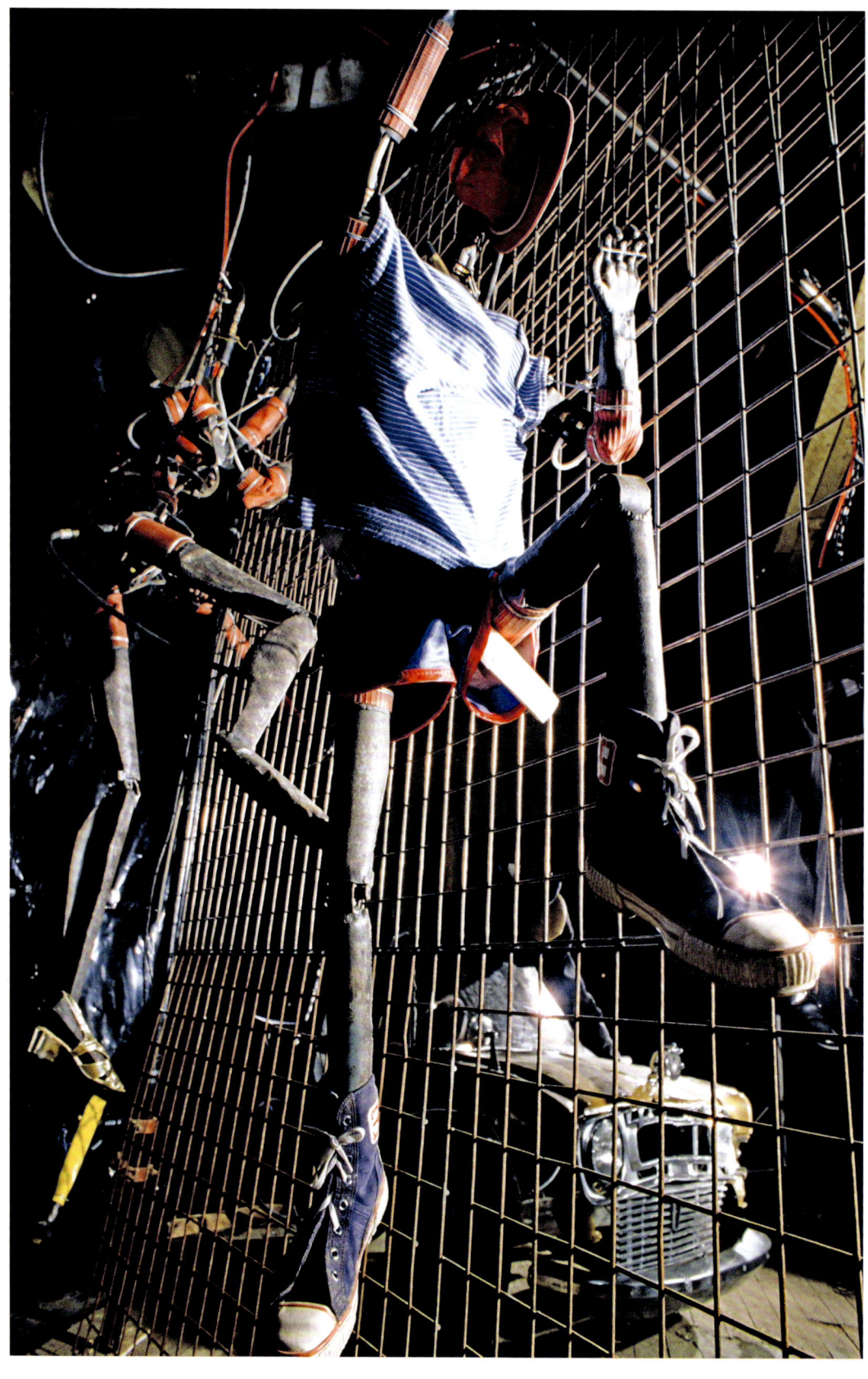

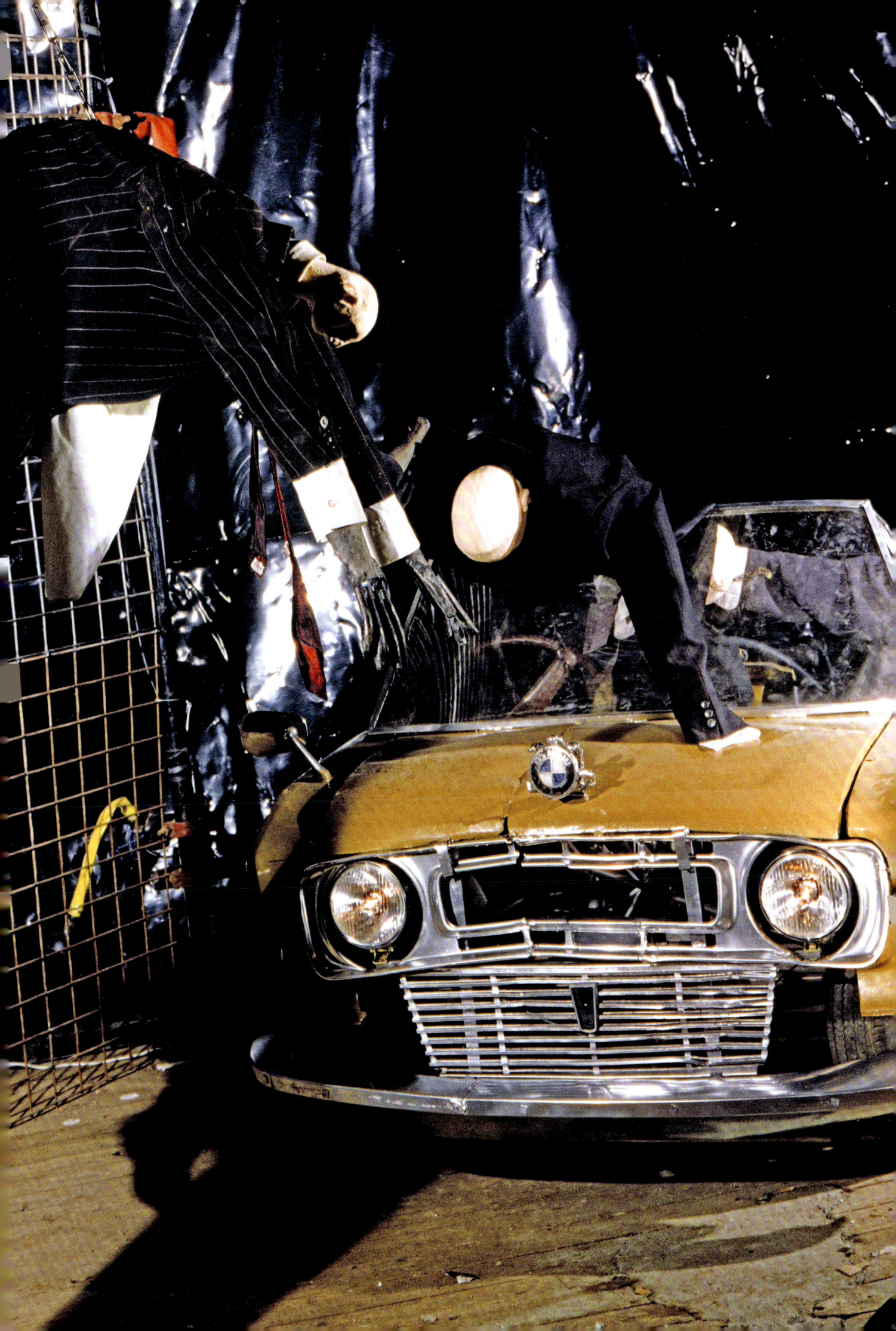

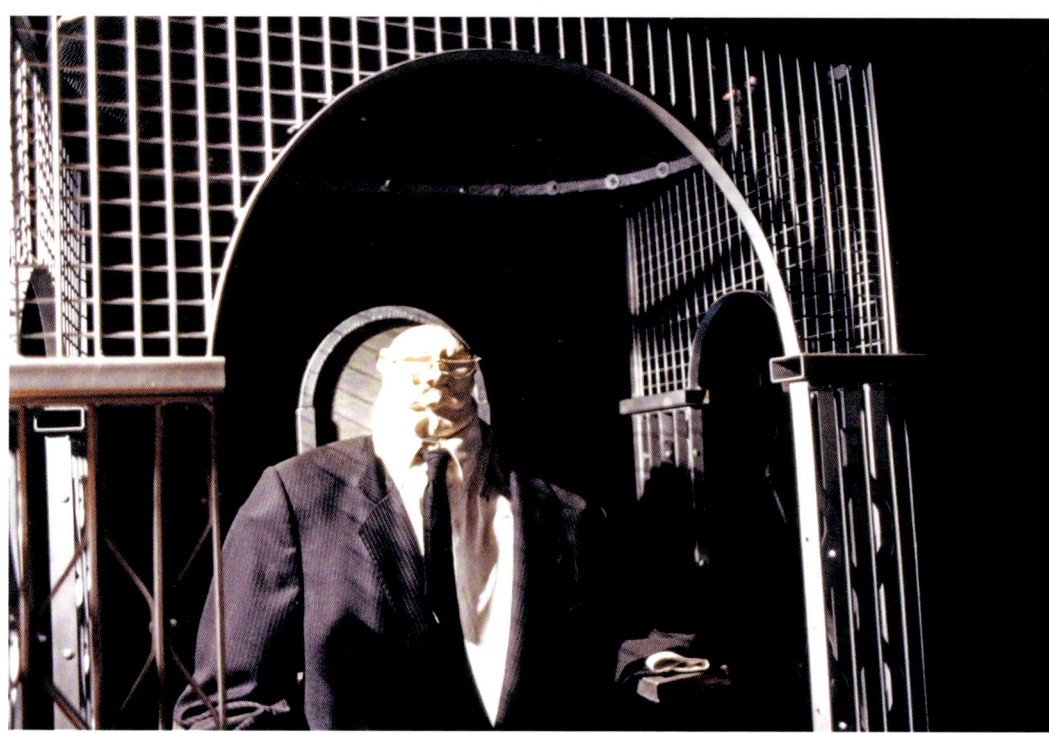

*The holiest of holies of the rejector*

*The hardships of greed*

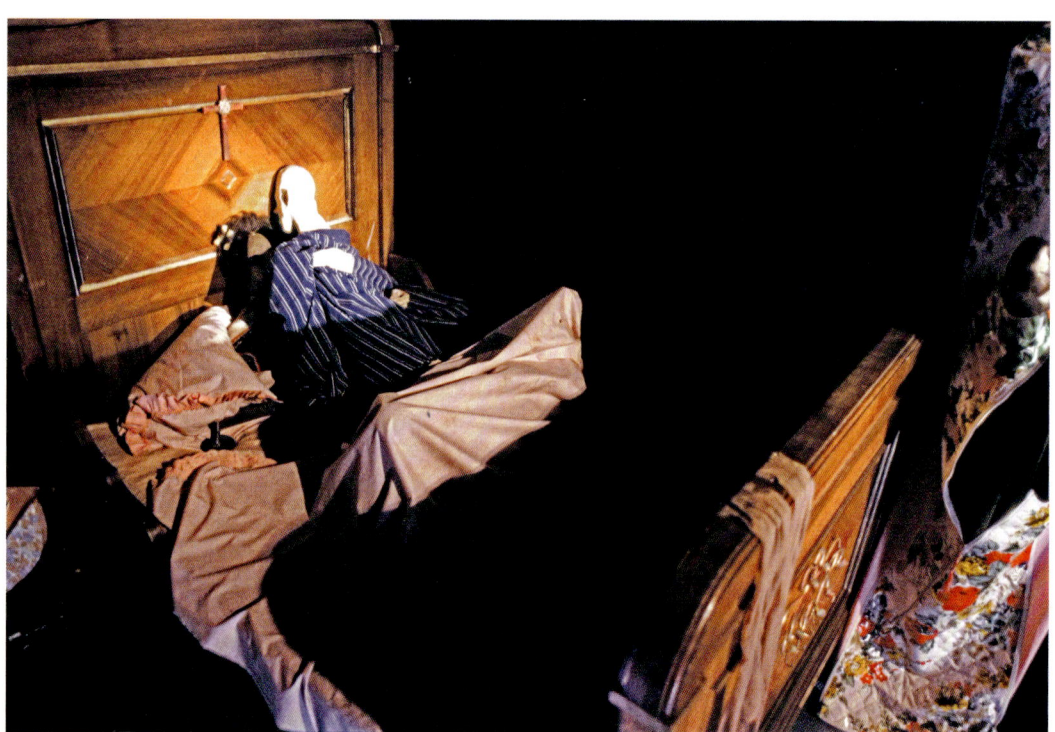

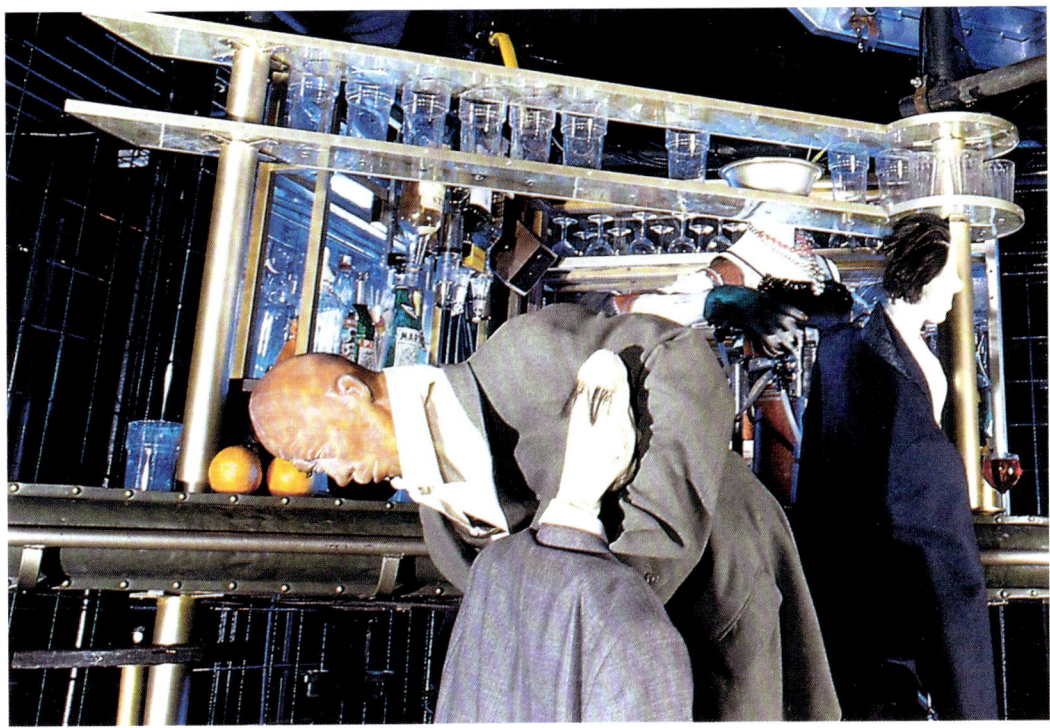

*The horrors of sociability*

*The deadly idyll*

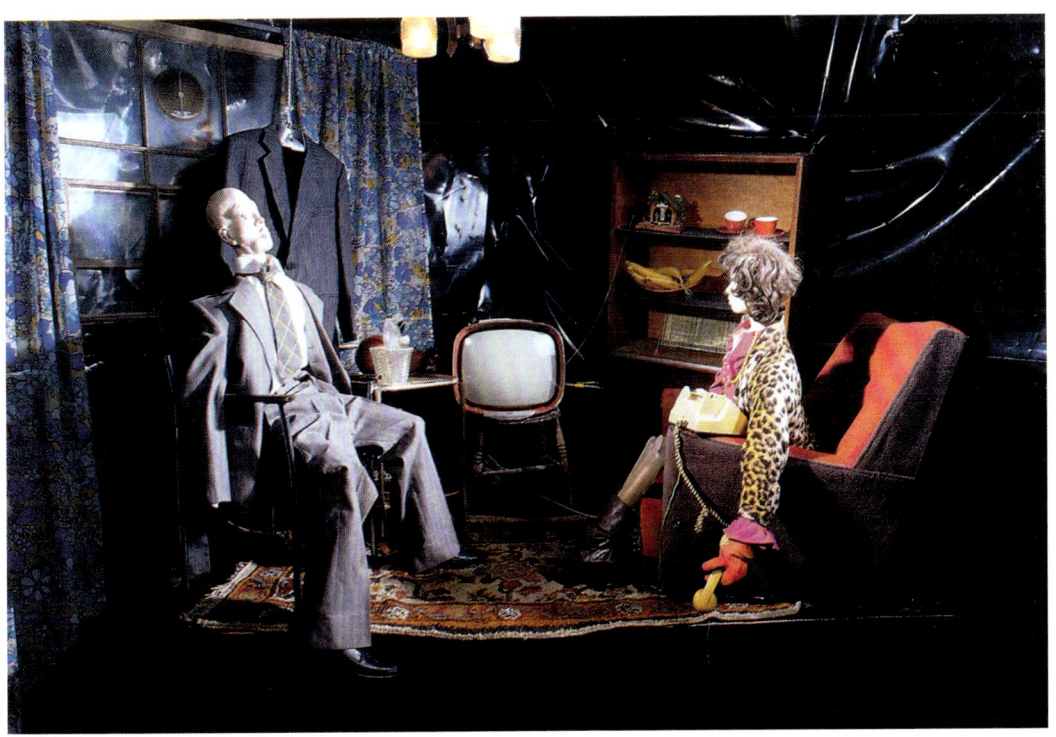

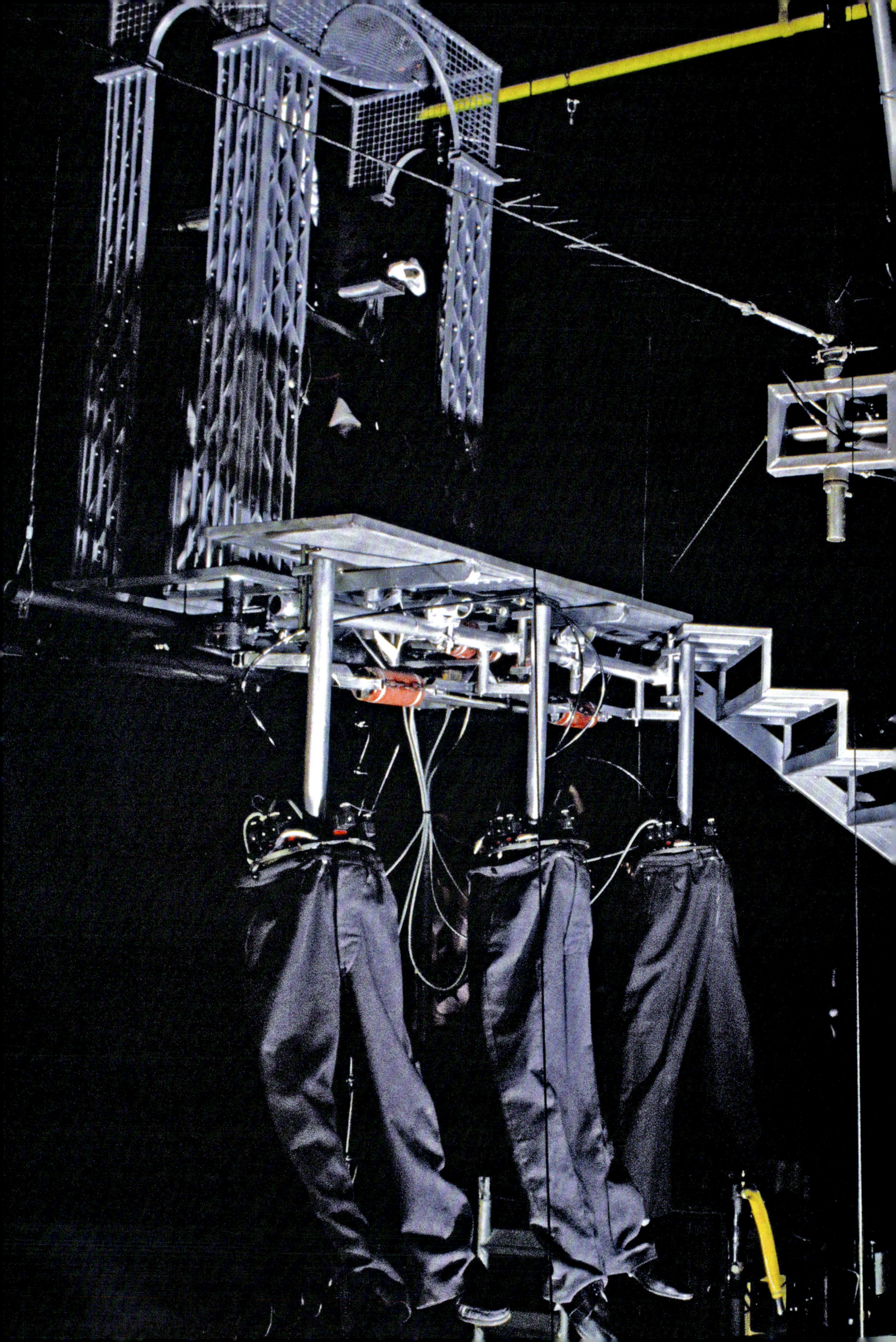

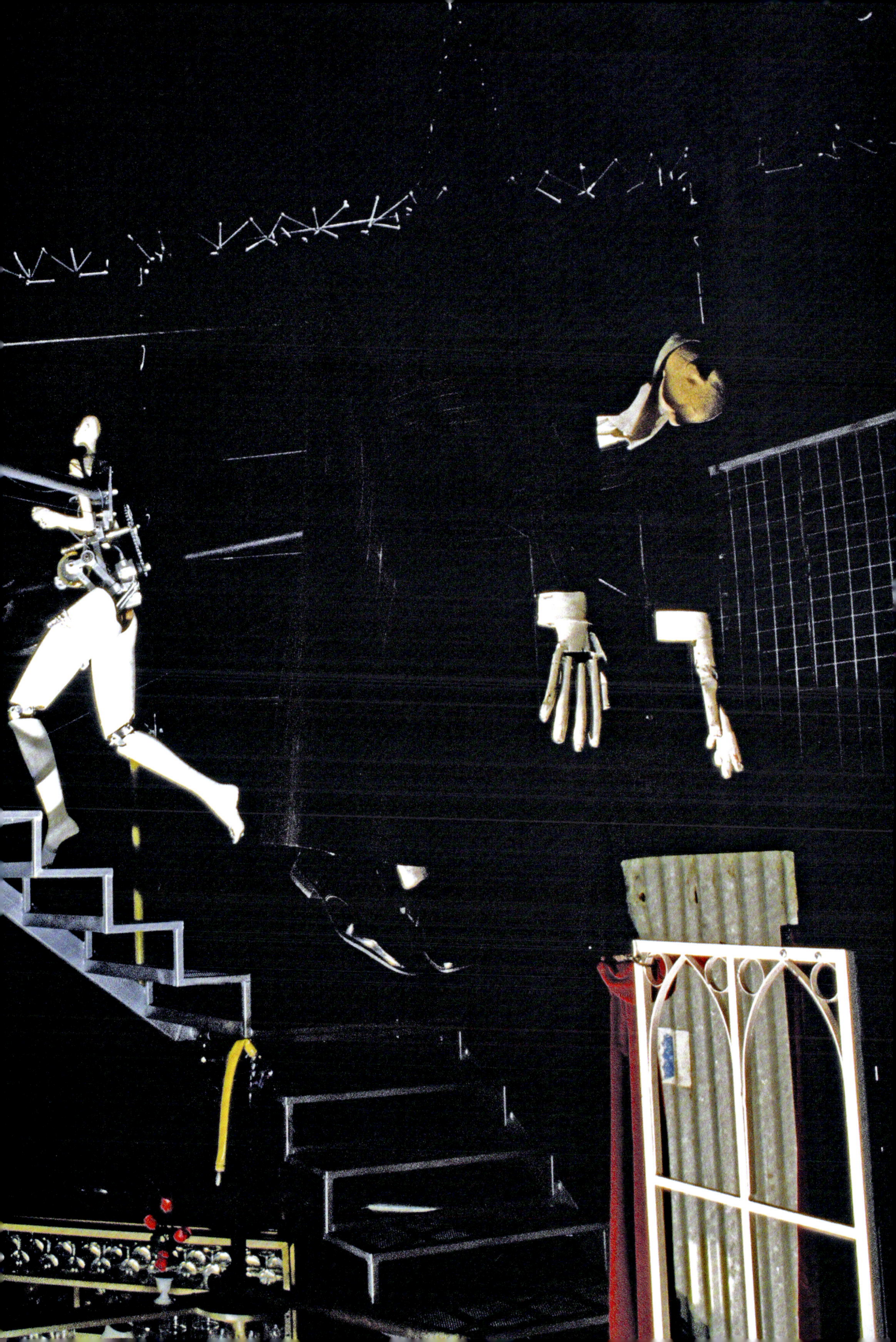

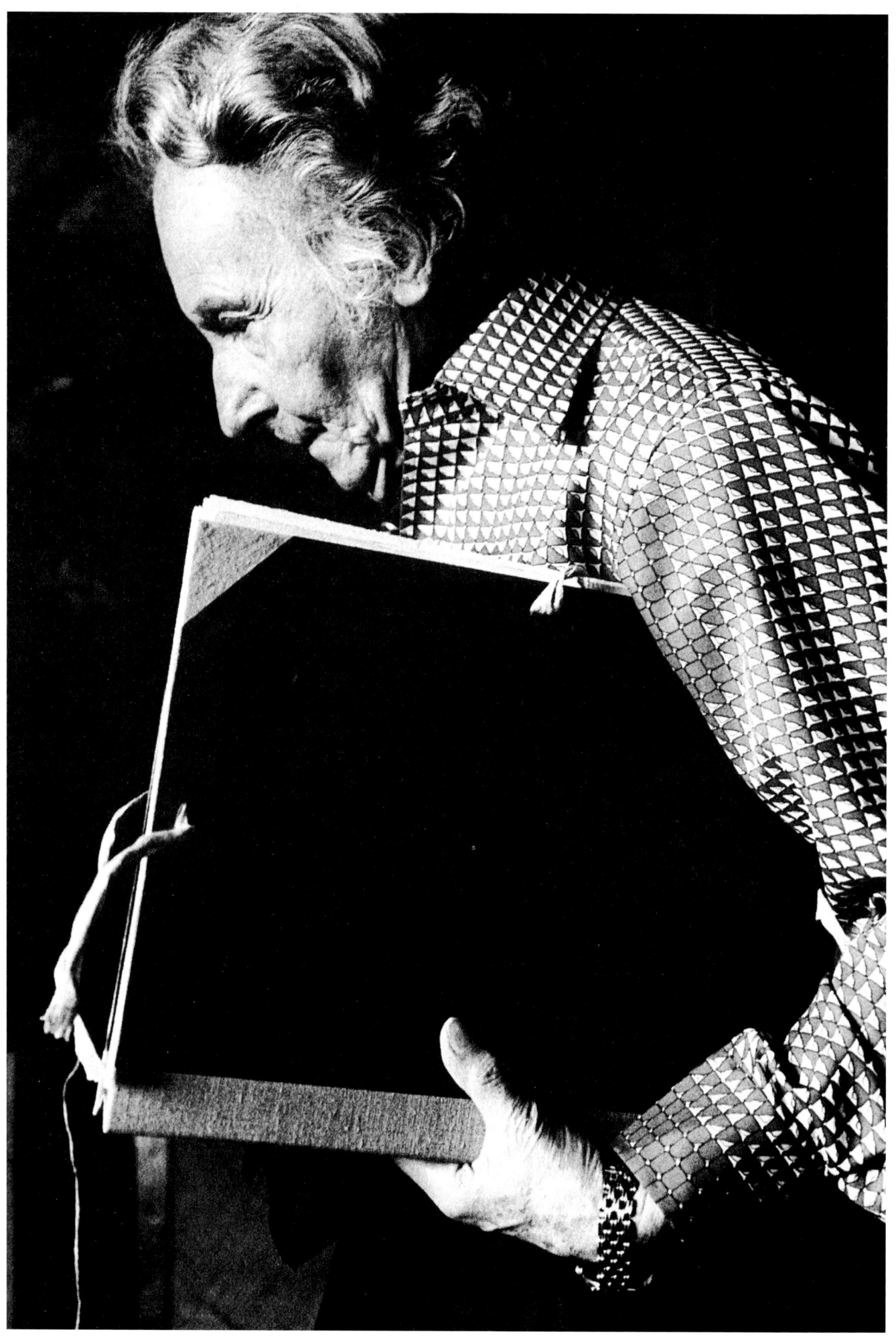

Erté

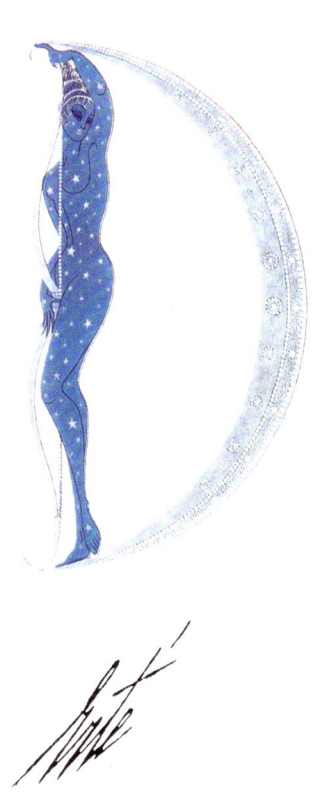

Erté

Born: November 23, 1892, in St. Petersburg, Russia.
Died: April 21, 1990, in Paris.

Illustrator, painter, sculptor, stage designer,
fashion designer.

Erté designed the **Mysterium Cagliostro** for *Luna
Luna*. Inside this building there are two magic
installations by André Heller. The apparitions shown
in these pictures—"The Spider Woman" and "The
Deceived Deceivers"—recite texts written especially
for them by Hans Magnus Enzensberger.

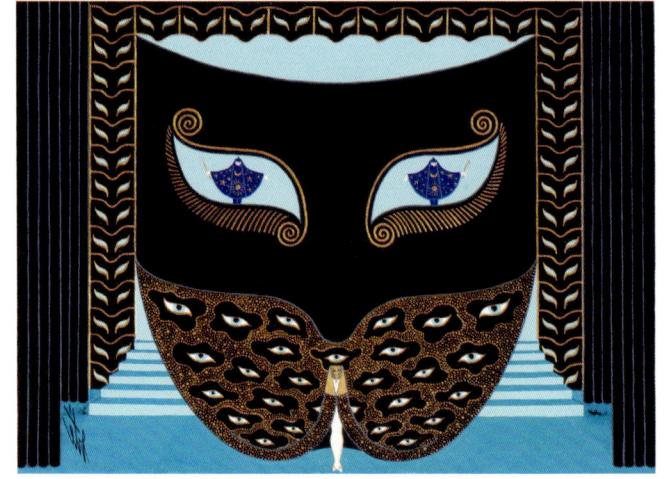

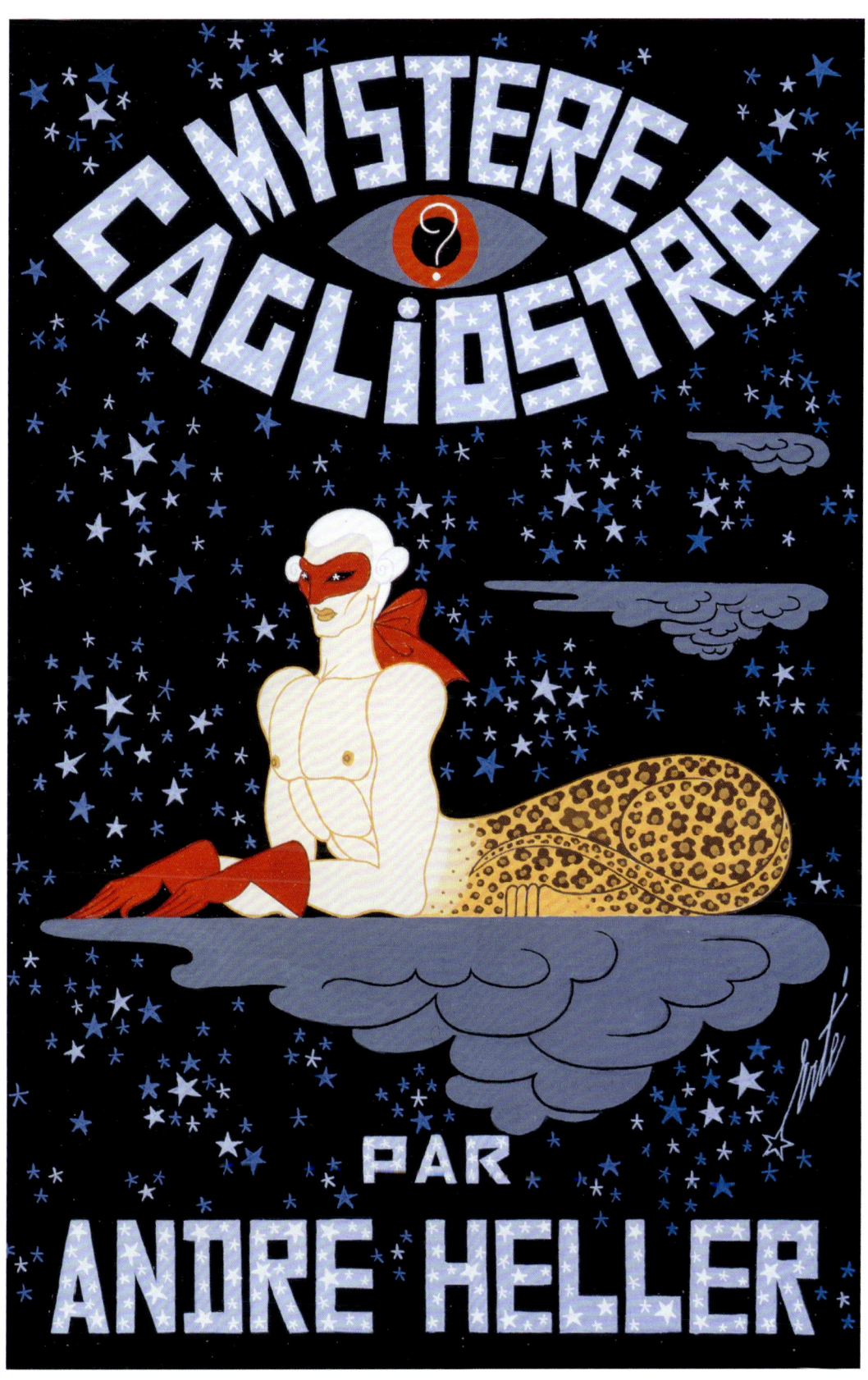

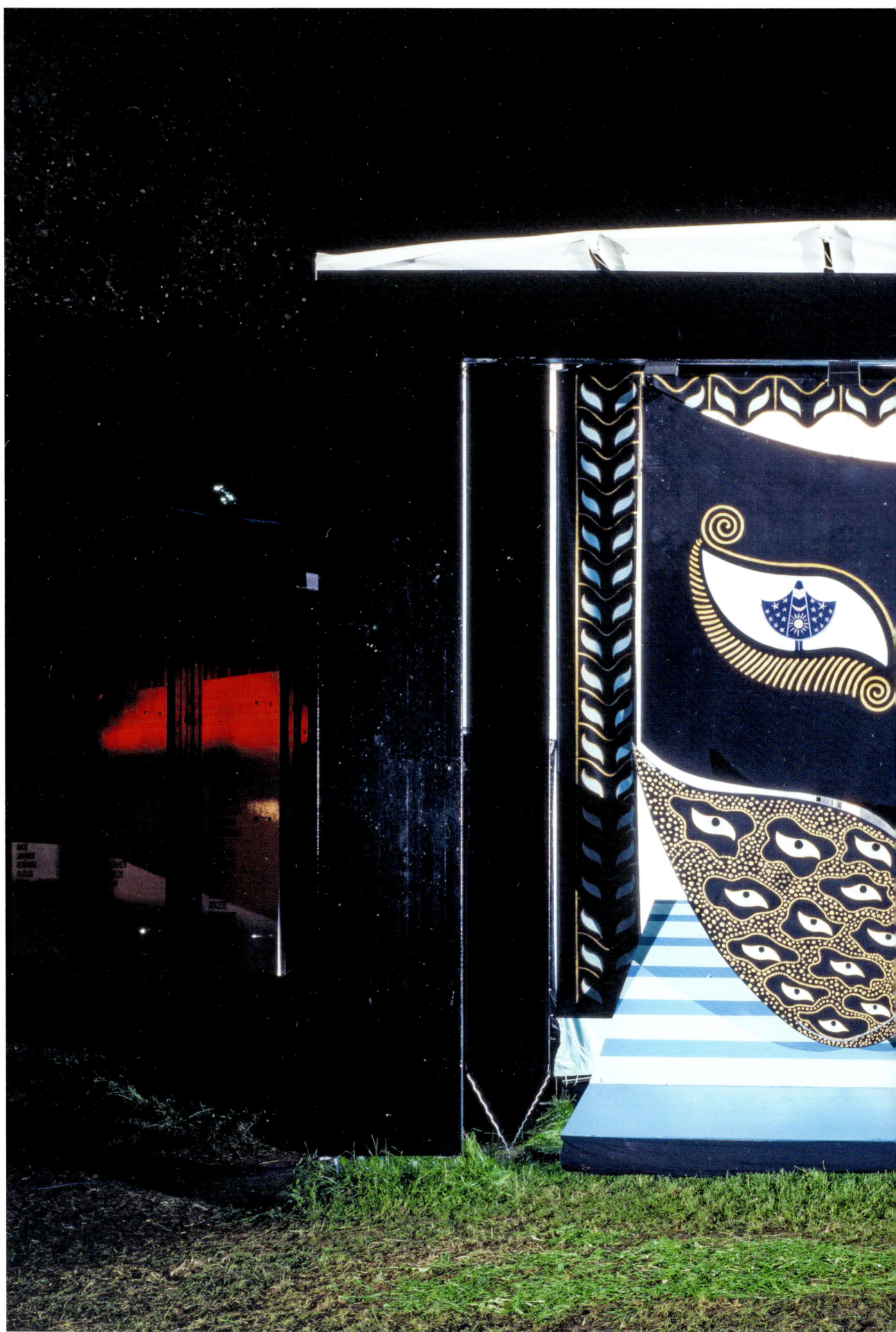

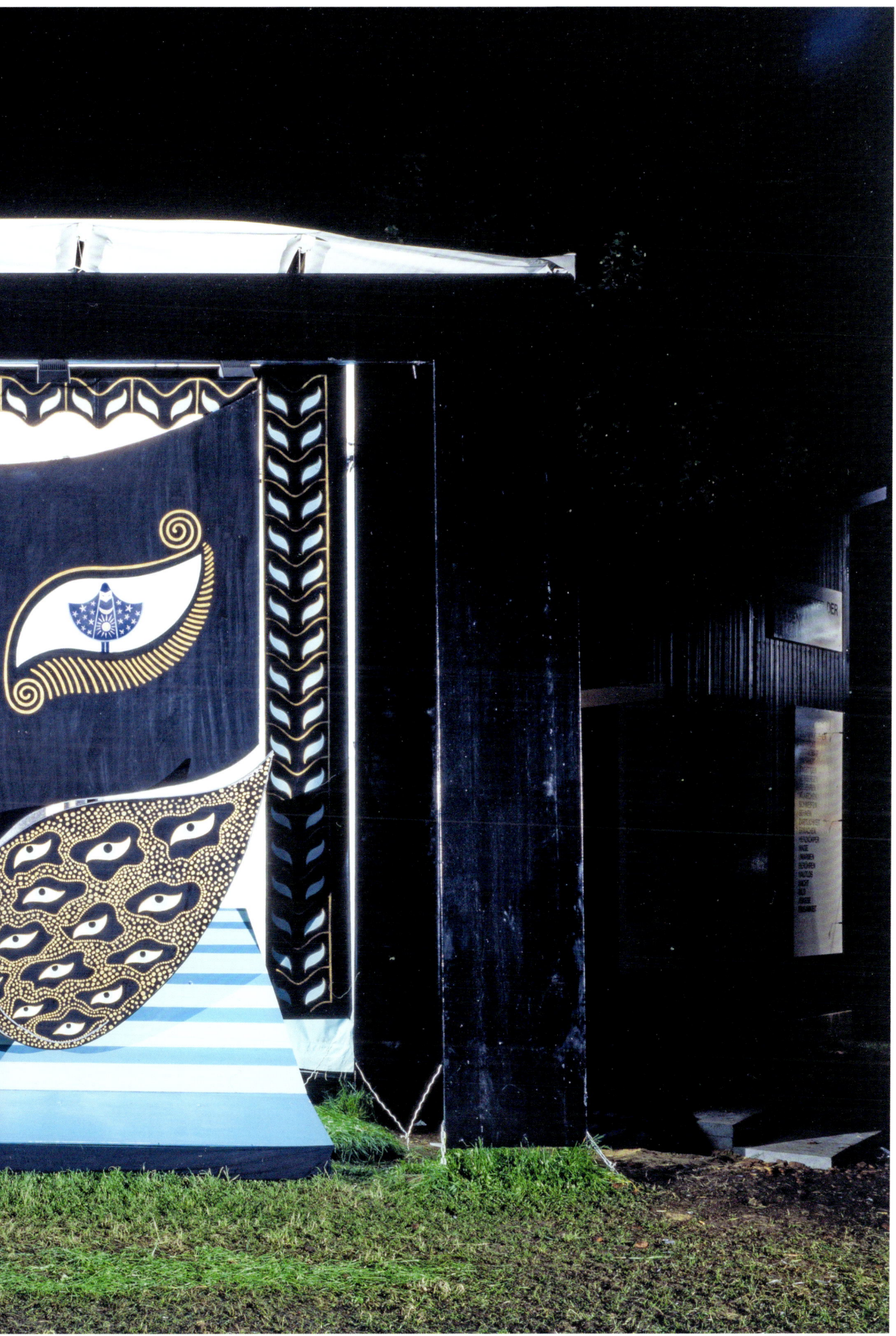

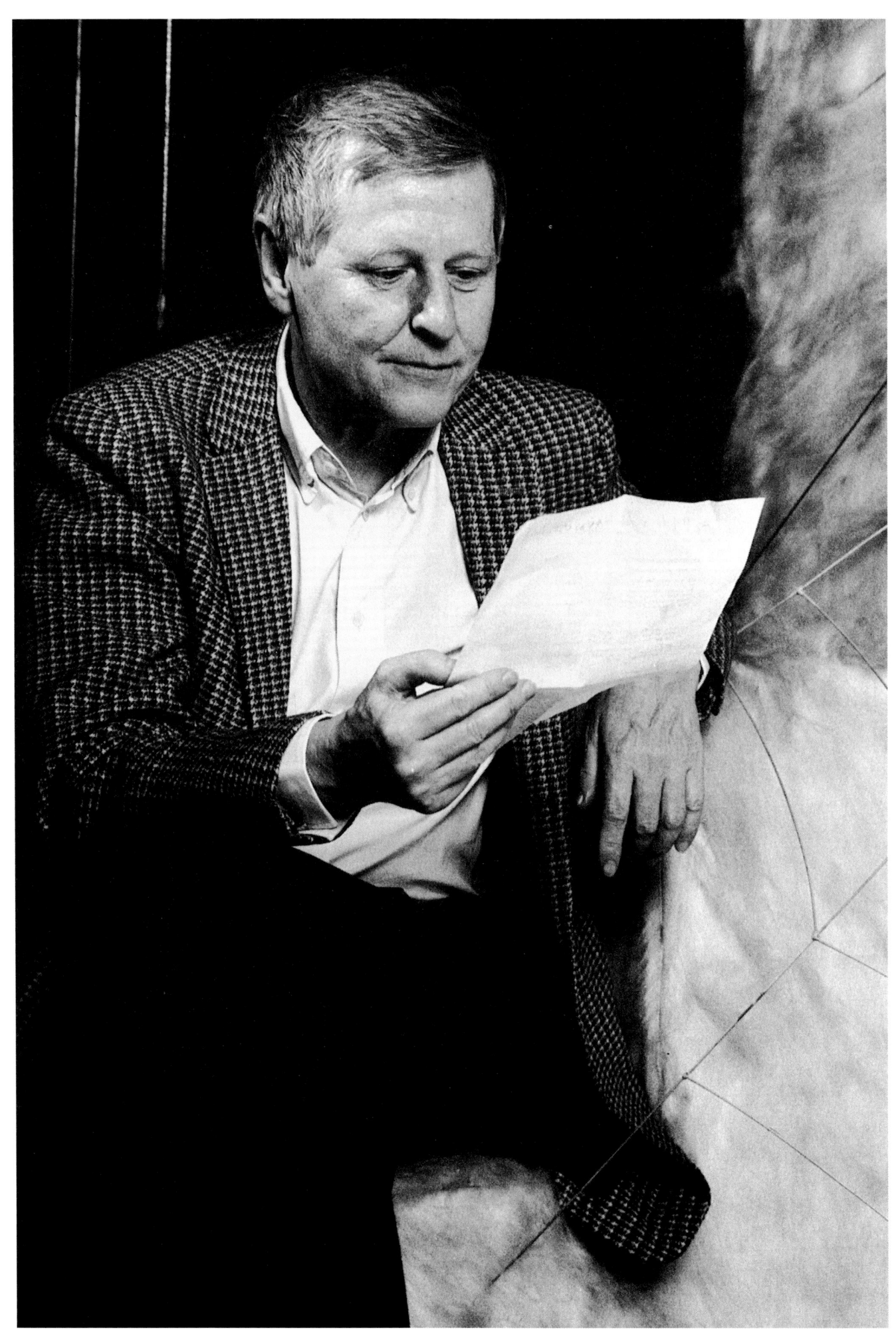

Hans Magnus Enzensberger

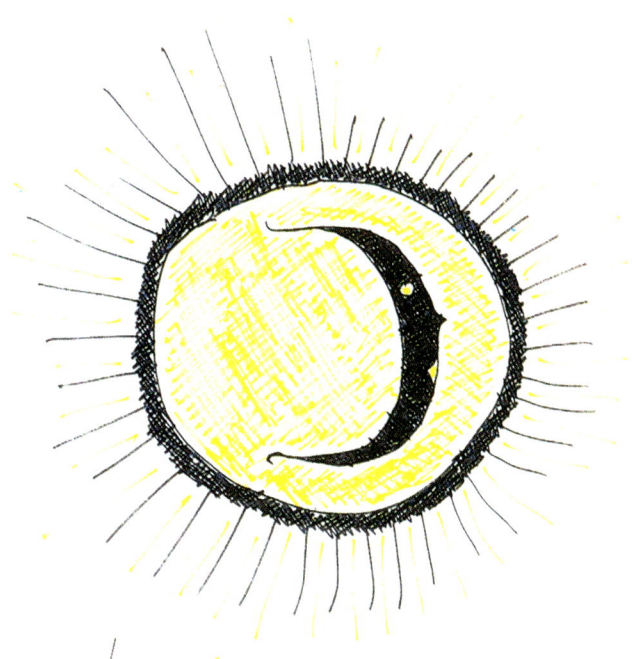

halluzination?

illumination?

, lumenzimm

Hans Magnus Enzensberger

Born: November 11, 1929, in Kaufbeuren, Germany.

Poet, writer.

Hans Magnus Enzensberger wrote **texts** for *Luna Luna* for "The Spider Woman" and "The Deceived Deceivers" in the Mysterium Cagliostro.

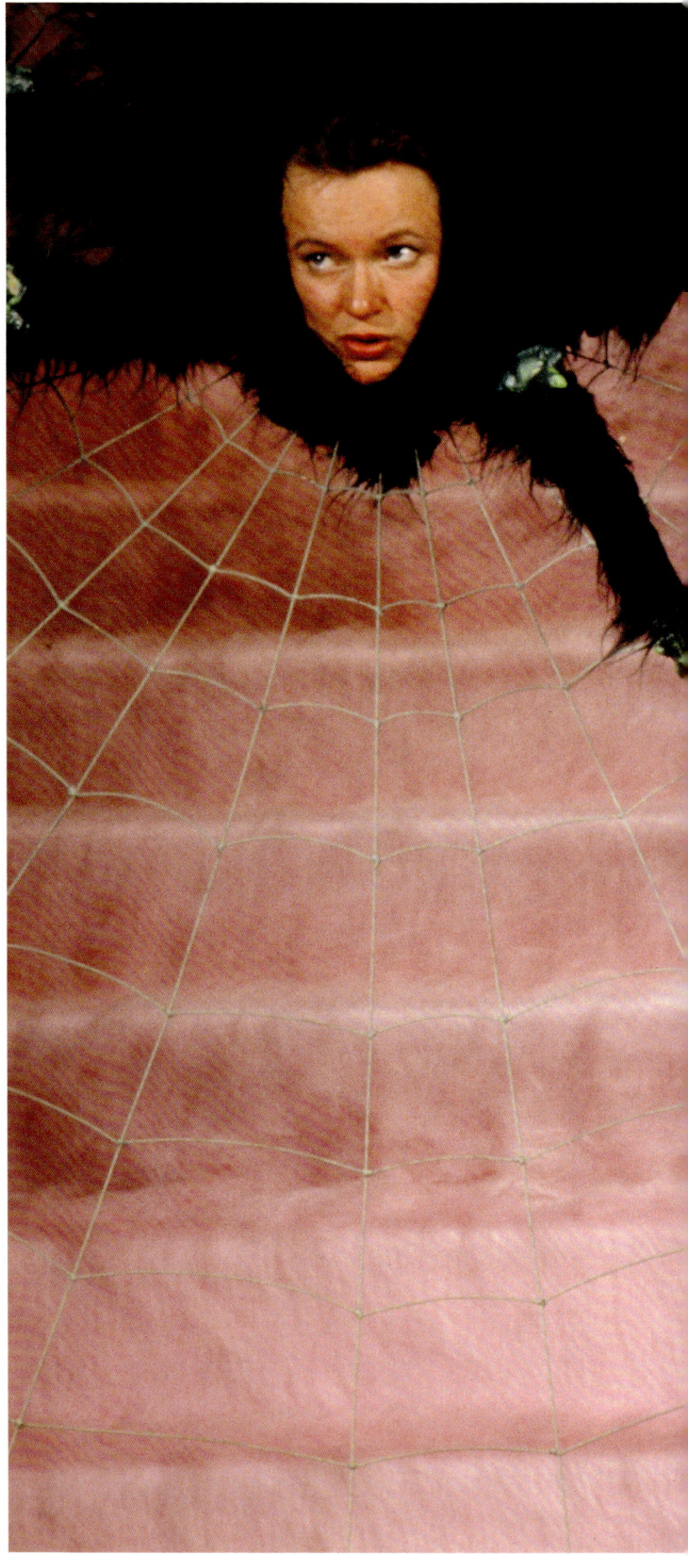

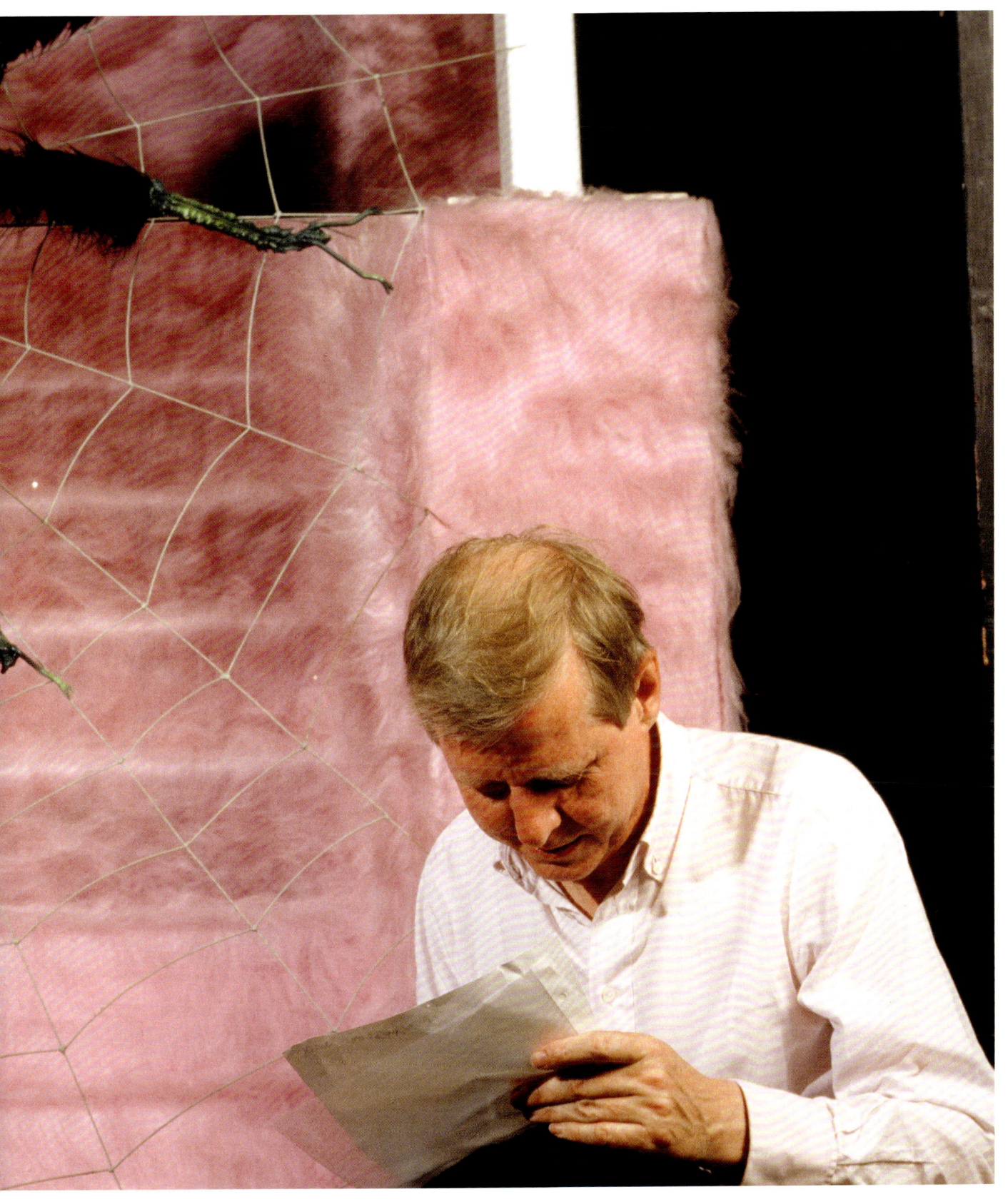

# Eye Test

## Hans Magnus Enzensberger

You say:
I open my eyes and see what is there,
for example, that naked woman on the wall there
or this dull pencil here
or the eye that stares at me incessantly, enough to drive me mad.
I close my eyes and see what is not there.

It's that simple.
You are so easily fooled.

Because in reality, reality is upside down,
your head, too, and the film that runs in your head.

How do you know if the eye is moving and the image is motionless
or if the eye is standing still and the image is moving?

The only certainty is that what has disappeared has not disappeared
and that what is here is not here.

Either you see the cinema or the film,
either the eye or the image.

And that's why you keep staring at that naked woman
that does not move
with eyes wide open, driving you mad,
that woman who is not there,
and you look with closed eyes at these dull spectacles
at that massacre in the cinema,
at these objects dancing in front of you on the table.

It's that simple.
You are so easily fooled.

Or you look into a pair of eyes that mirror your eyes,
which mirror a pair of eyes that you are looking at.

Open your eyes and what appears disappears.
Open your eyes and what has disappeared reappears.

But you can't see it.
You say:                                      etc. ad infinitum

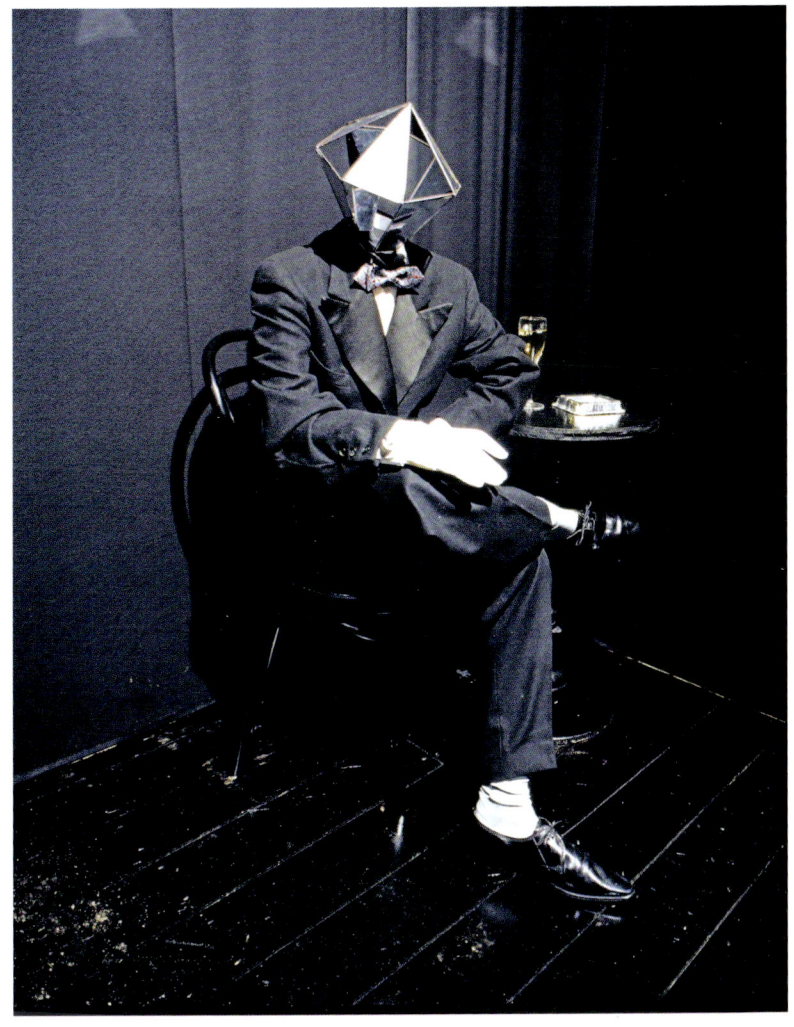

*First image of the*
*"Deceived Deceivers":*

# The
# Diamond
# Rat

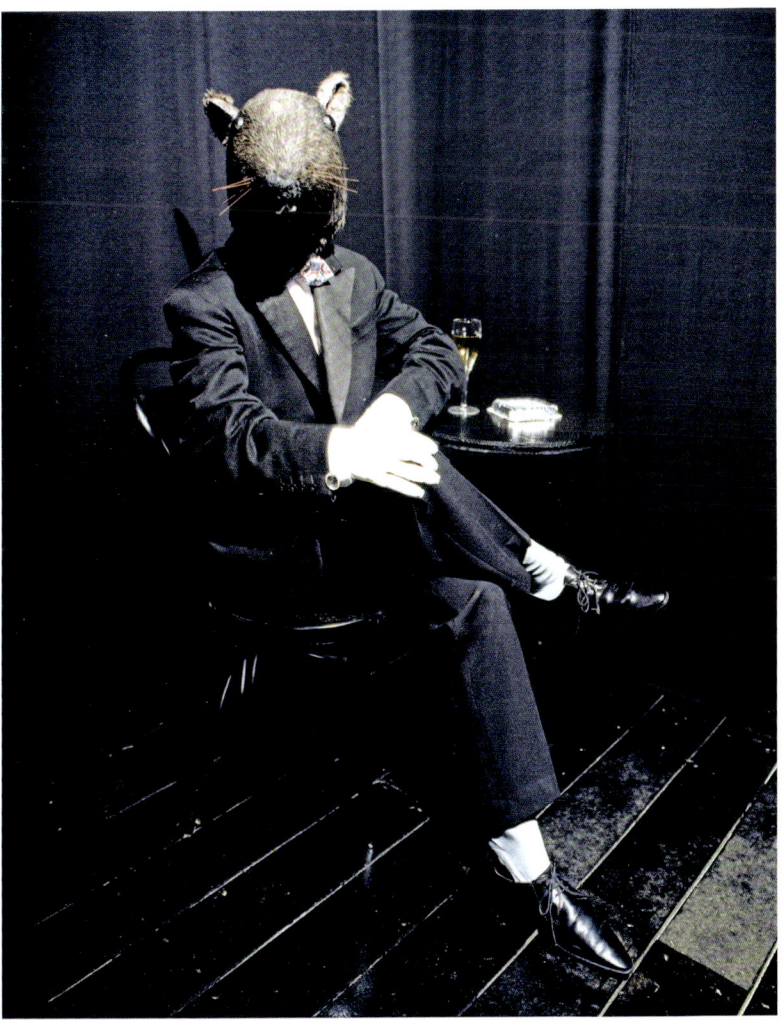

*Second image of the*
*"Deceived Deceivers":*

# The
# Rat
# Diamond

# The Words Spoken by the Spider Woman

## Hans Magnus Enzensberger

Oh, my friend, is nothing moving?
You're staring. You have paid. You are thinking:
Where is that nice cowardly fear
of this animal? And you miss
my black and dreadful face,
my little one,

        krk,

            as it crushes and devours you.

Your blue nerve, still drowsy deep in the sac,
knows nothing of me or of itself—
until you suddenly feel it, the sting
in your brain, the bite like a pinprick—
until a smell in the dark reaches out for you,
puppet, and—

        krk,

            a throb, a crack—

a feeler tugs at the lost string—
What do you want? Disgust? Greed? Fear? Desire?
Electrically wriggling—you want, you may, you must!
I can feel the venom shooting into my mouth,
I'm already there, my feeler is buzzing—
you're panting,

        krk,

            and something sluggishly flows.

The pale dwarf howls blissfully, oozes
and discharges—if that is not love!
And he's still breathing—what an optimist!
His good nerve has discolored.
He smiles quietly. He thinks he's asleep—
he doesn't know,

        krk,

            how little effort is needed to die.

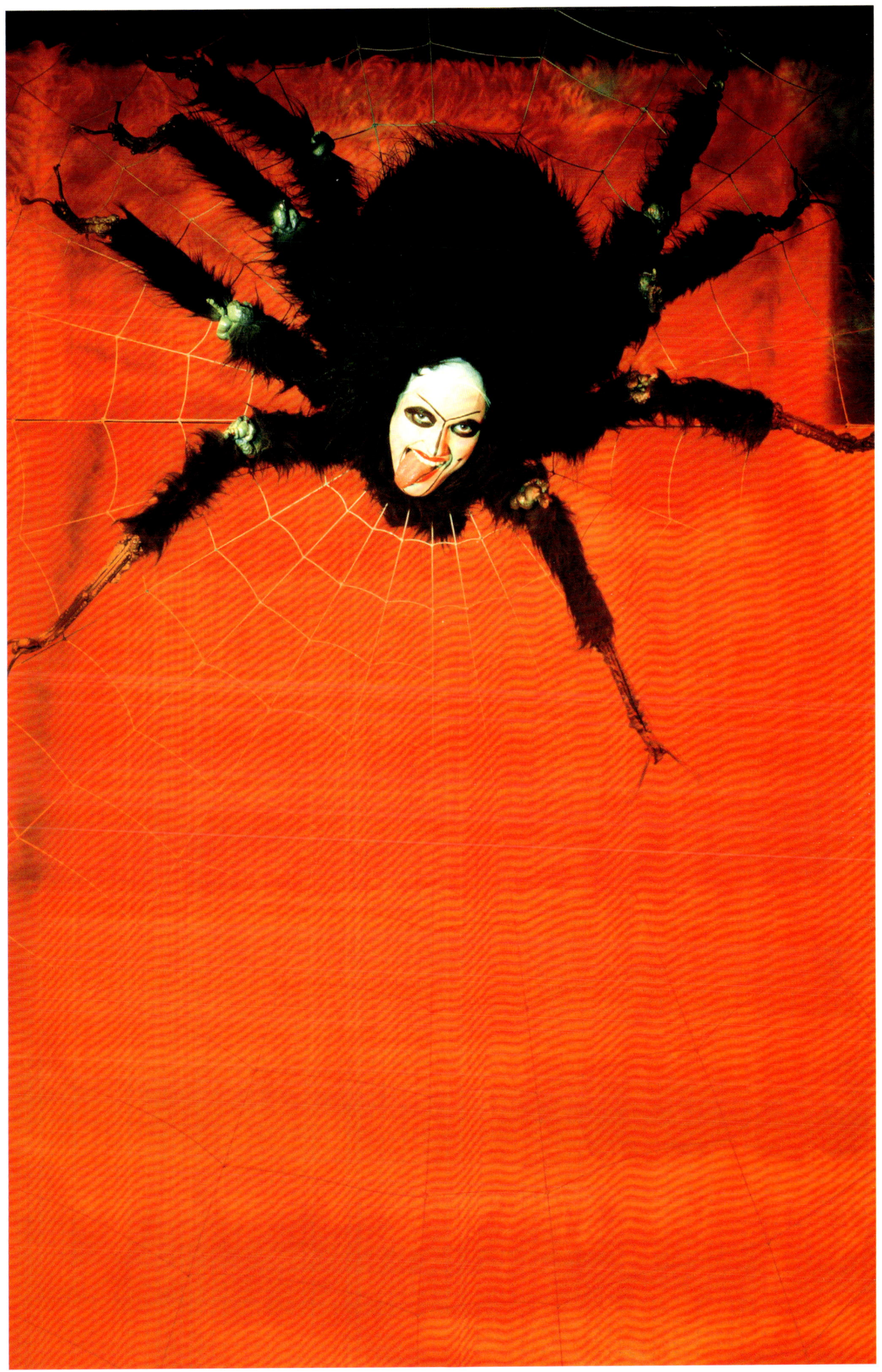

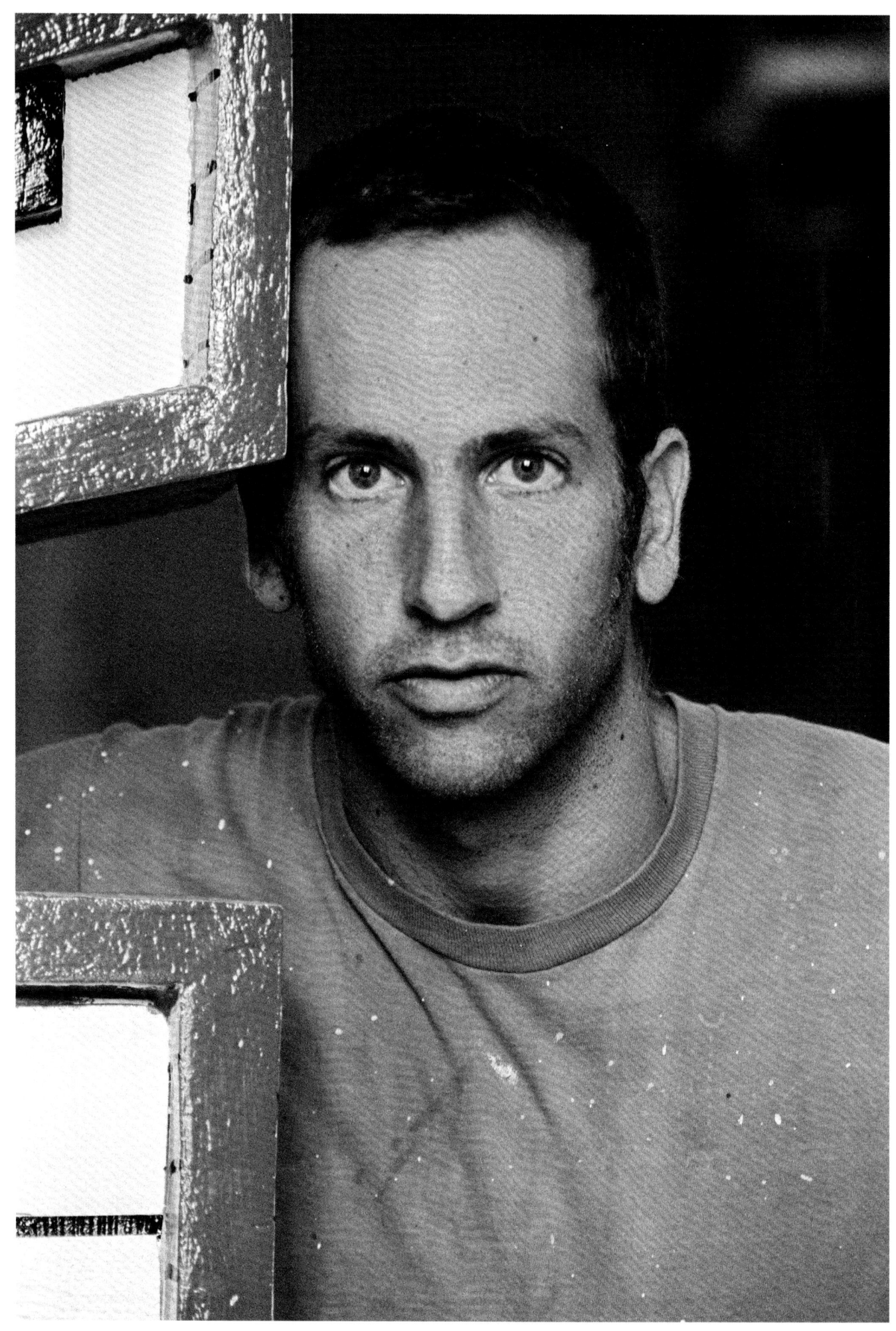

Kenny Scharf

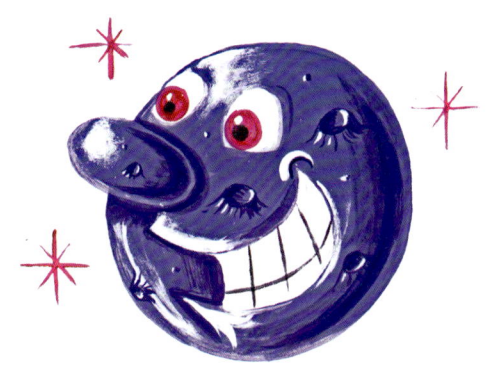

up up in the sky! is it a dream?
No, its Luna Luna!

Kenny Scharf 87

Kenny Scharf

Born: November 23, 1958, in Los Angeles, California.

Painter, illustrator, sculptor.

Kenny Scharf designed a **swing ride** for *Luna Luna*, dedicated to the cosmic spirits of flight; leading toward it is an **Avenue of Sculptures** arranged in perspective.

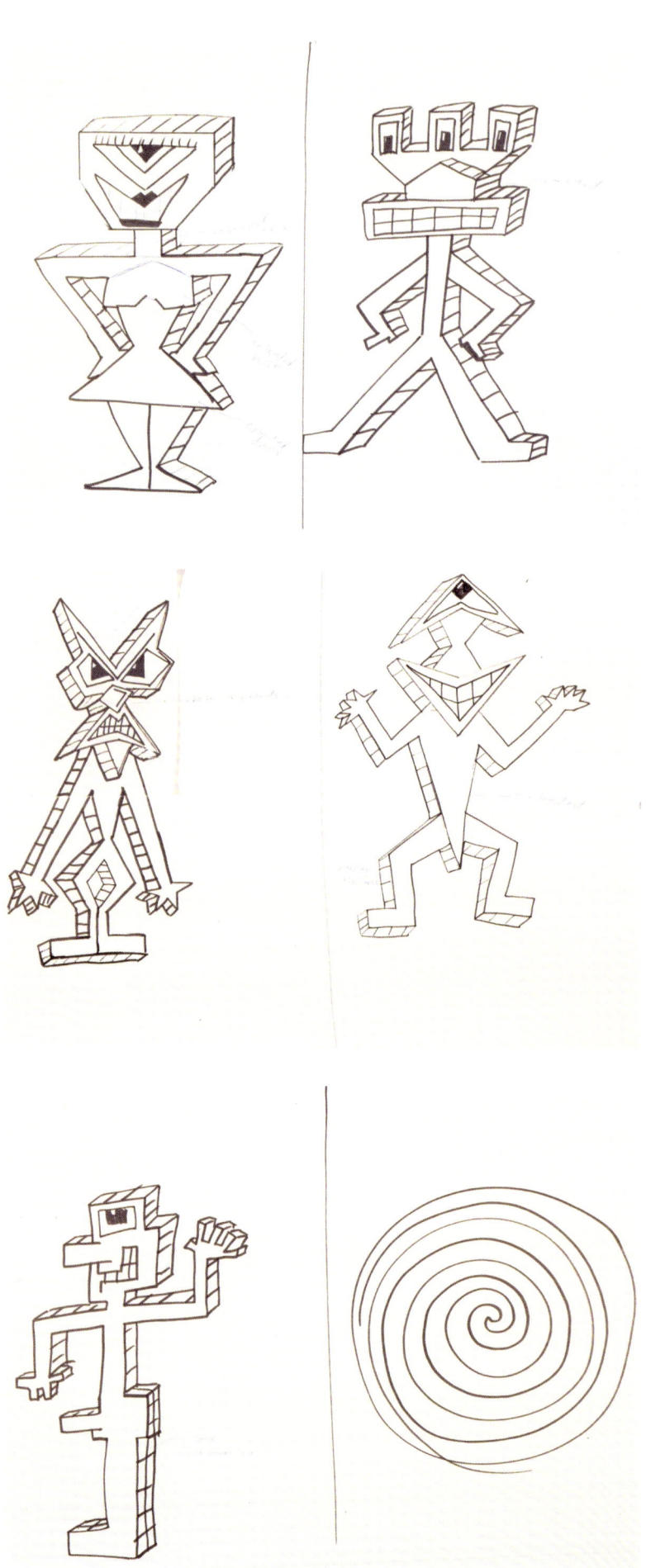

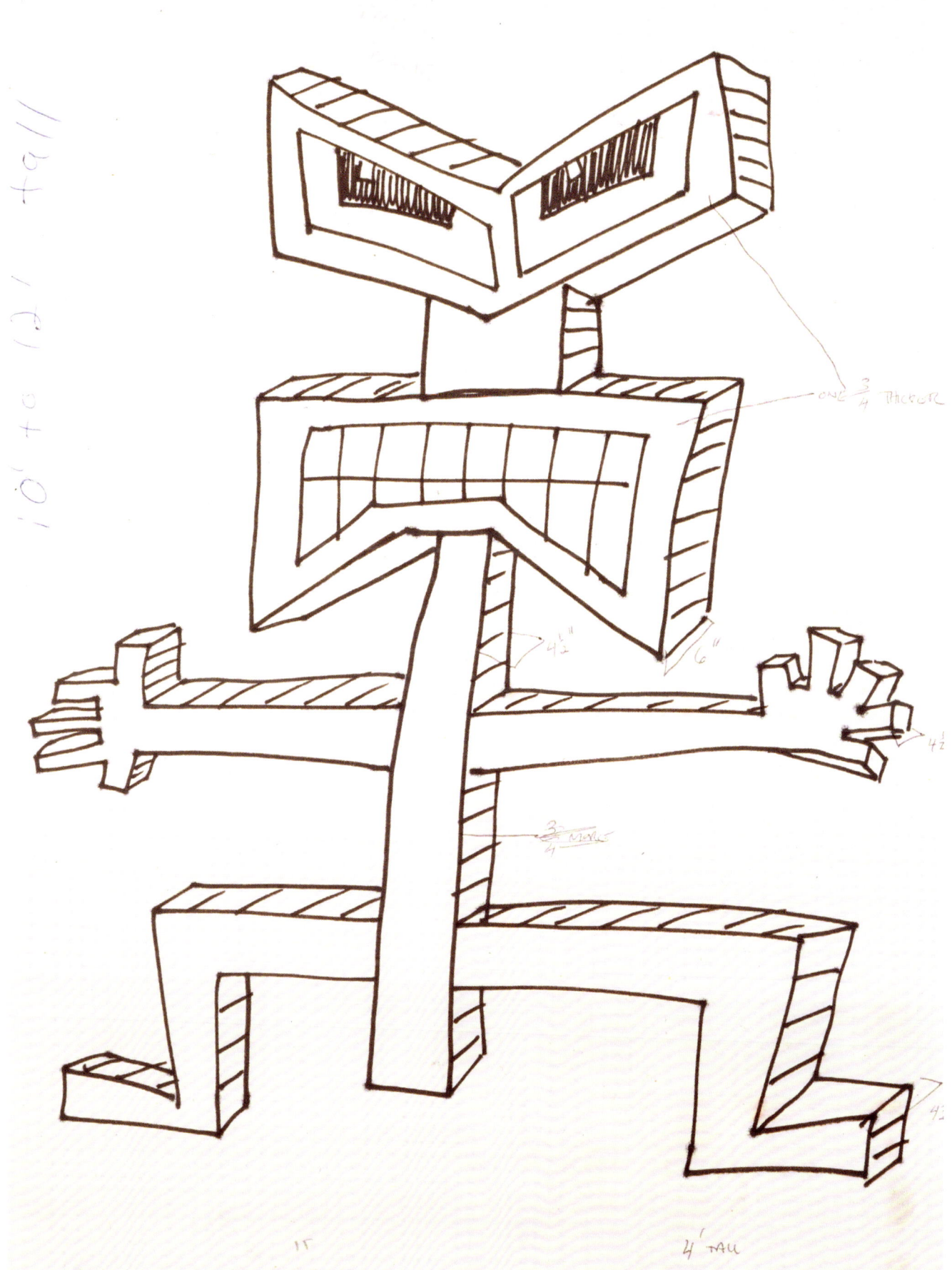

ONE 3/4 THICKOR

4 1/2"

6"

4 1/2

3/4 MORE

10' to 13' tall

15

4' TALL

4

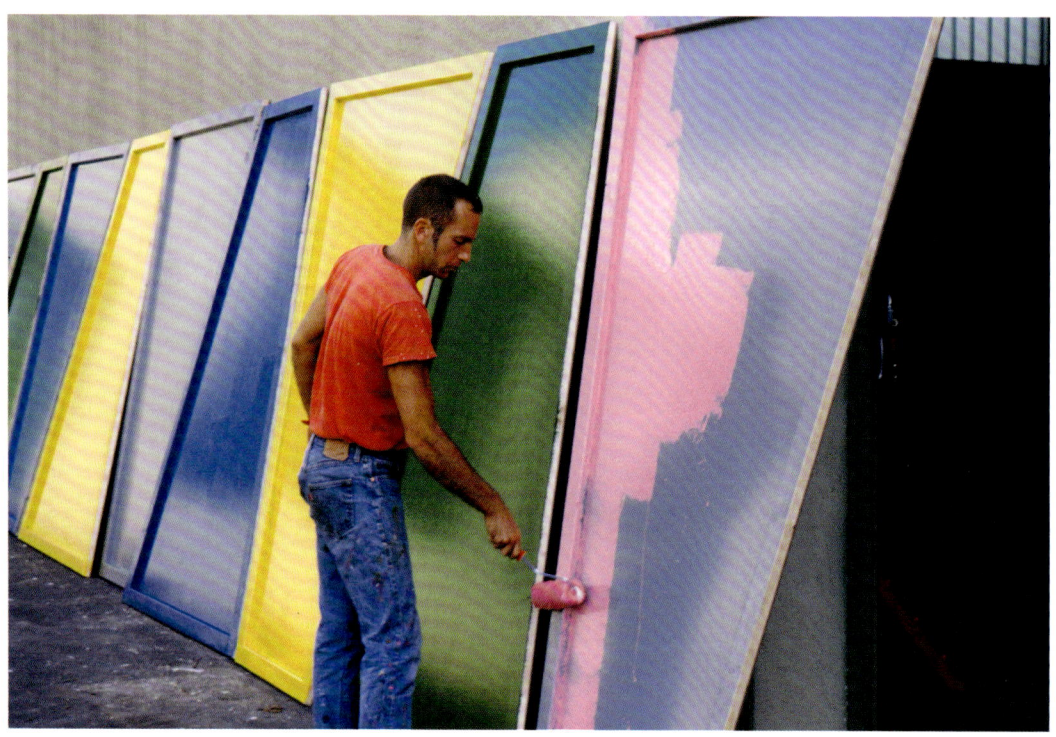

*Kenny Scharf priming parts of the swing ride …*

*… and signing the finished work*

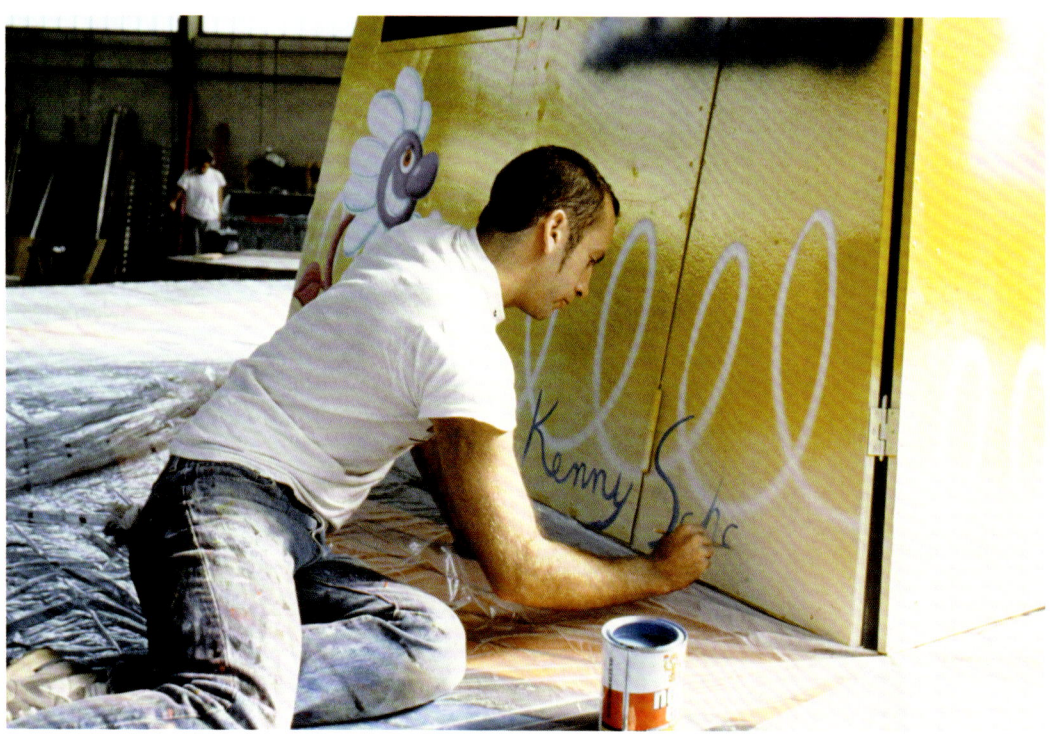

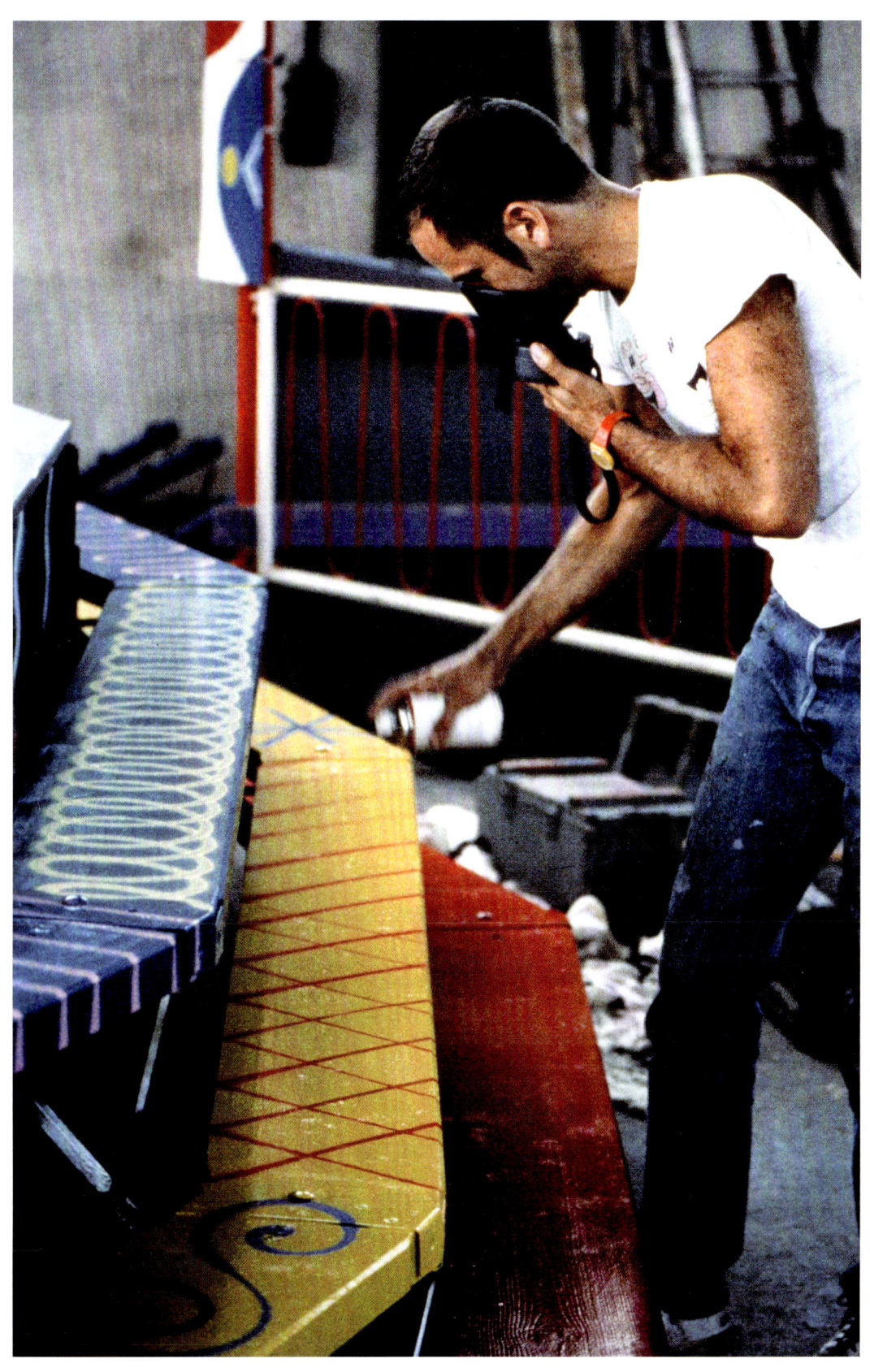

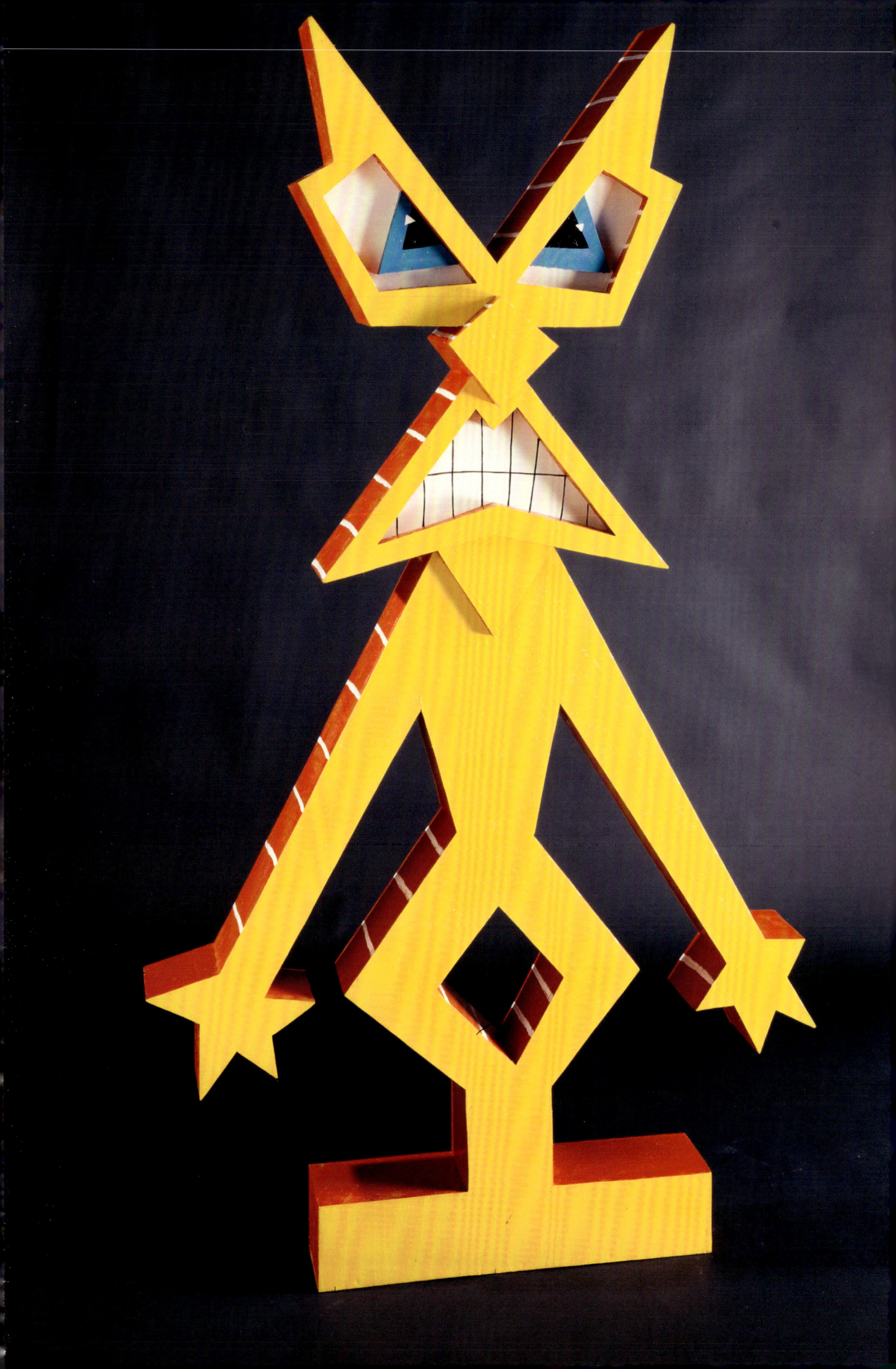

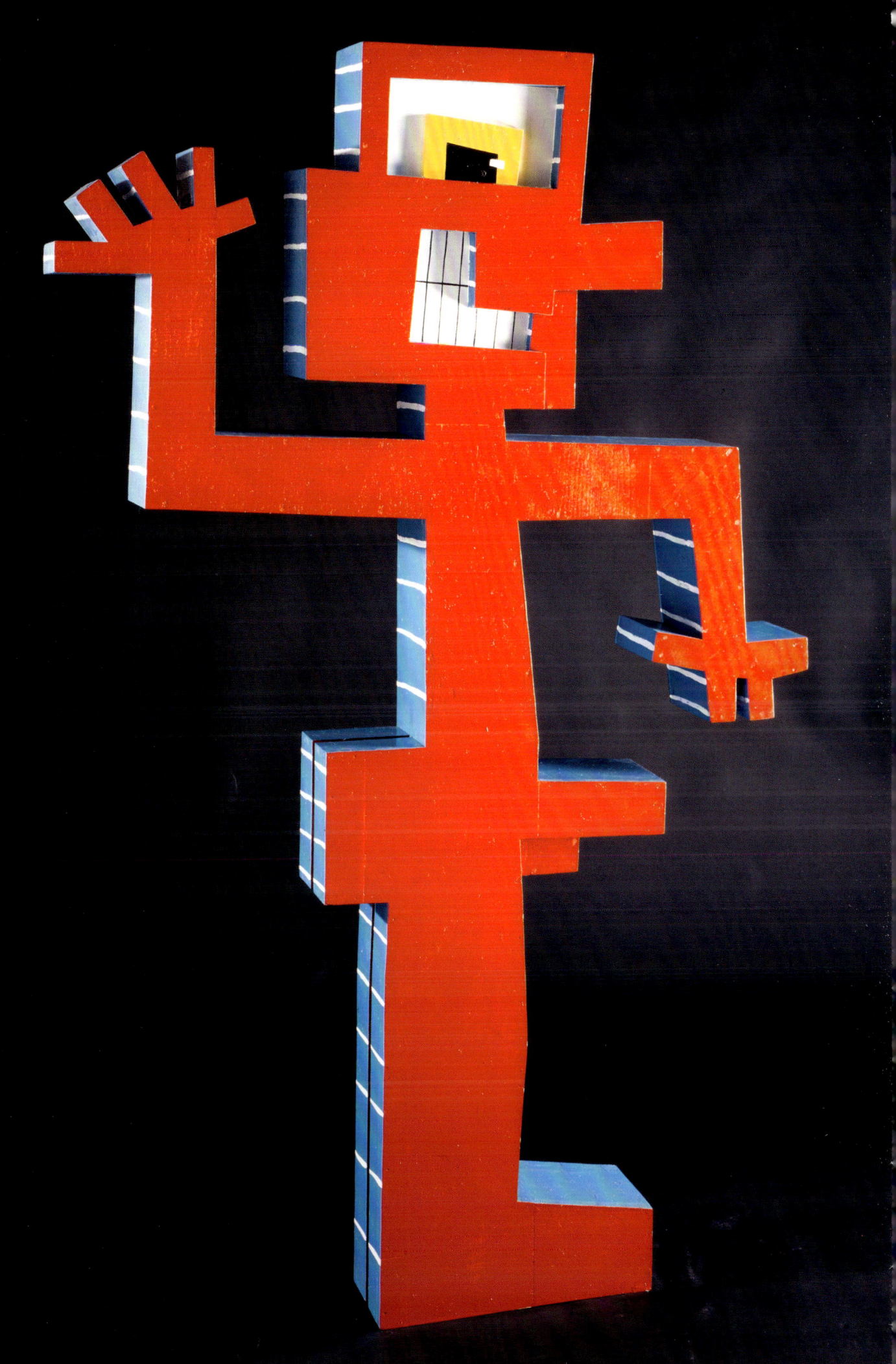

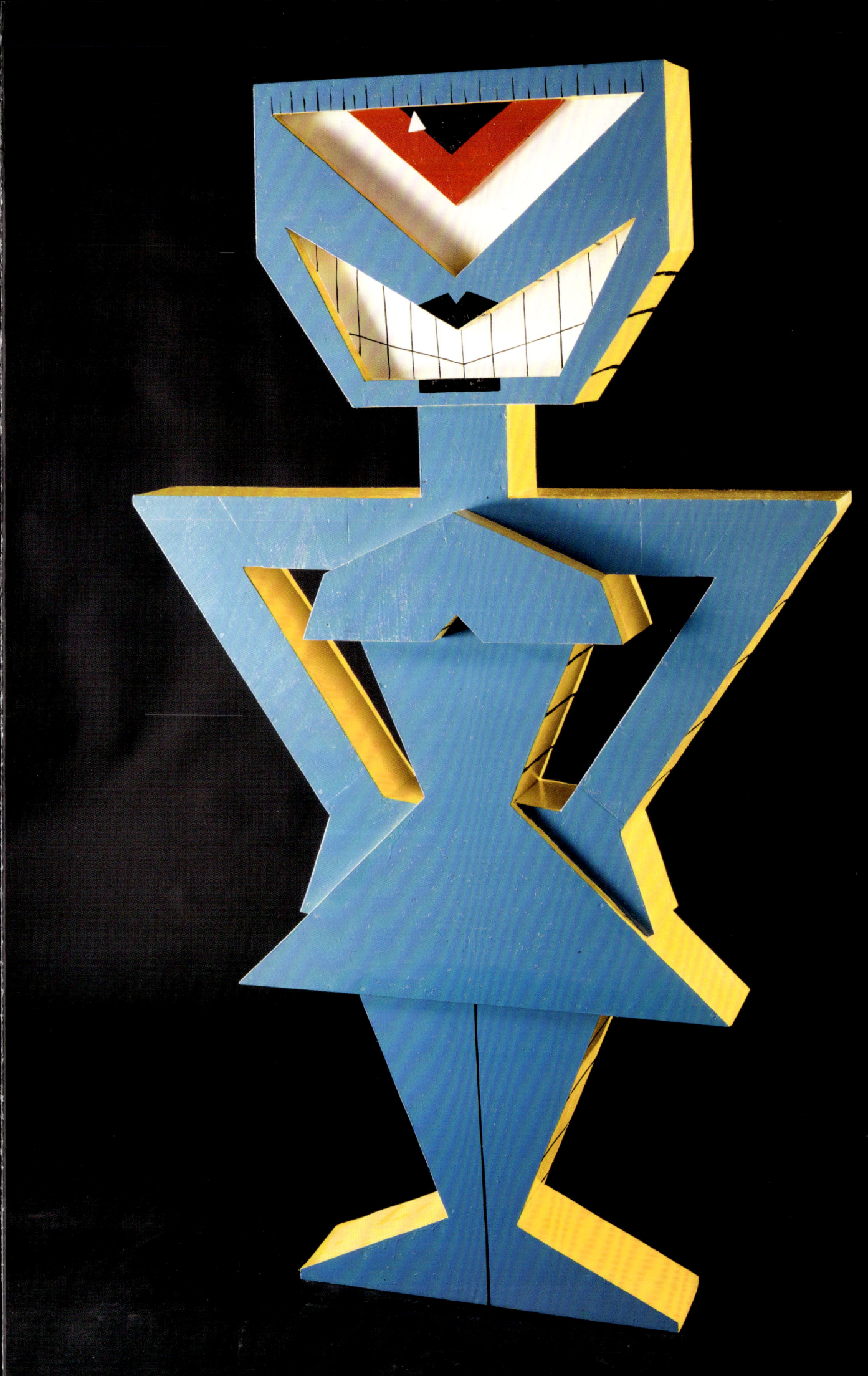

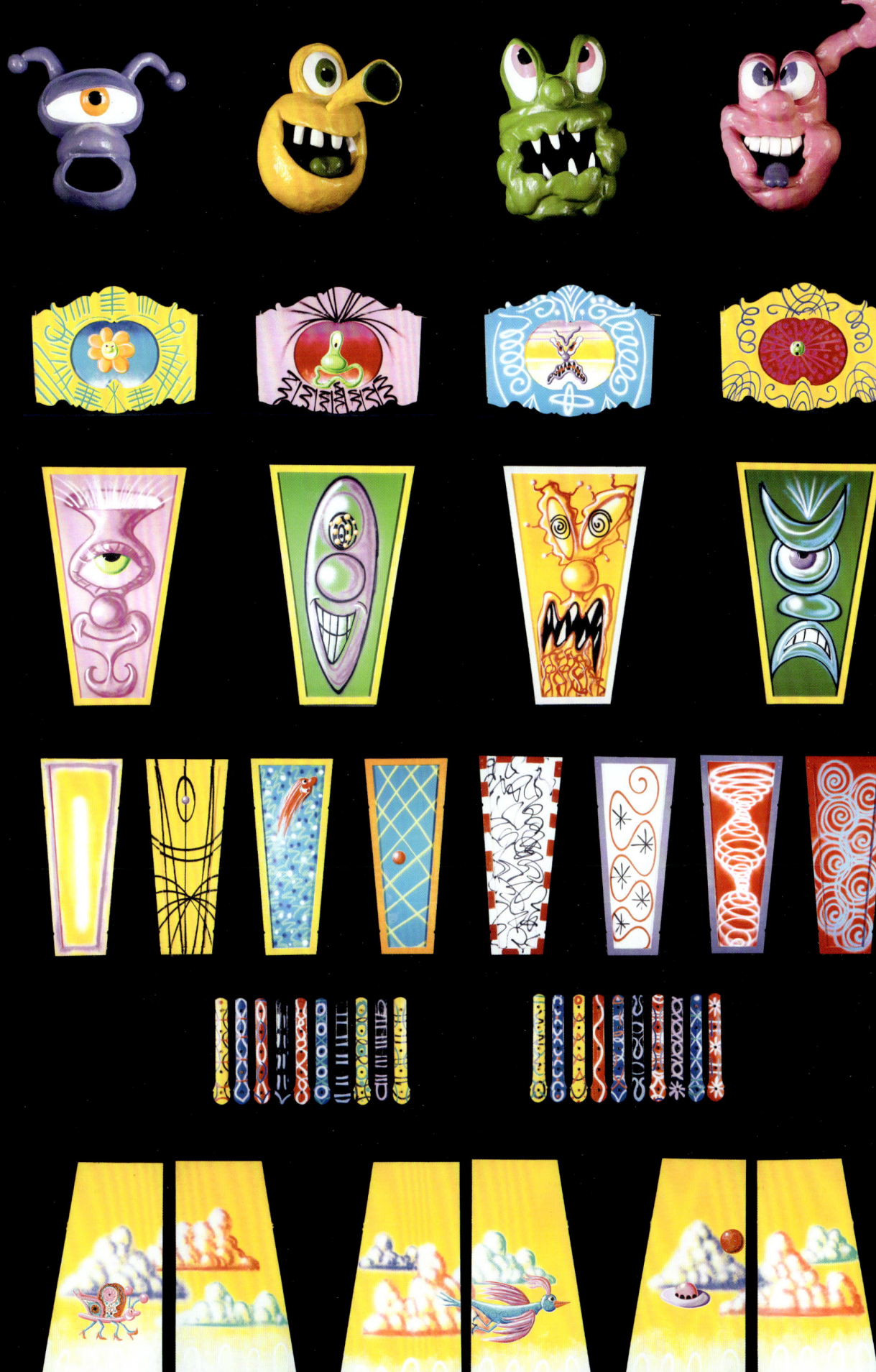

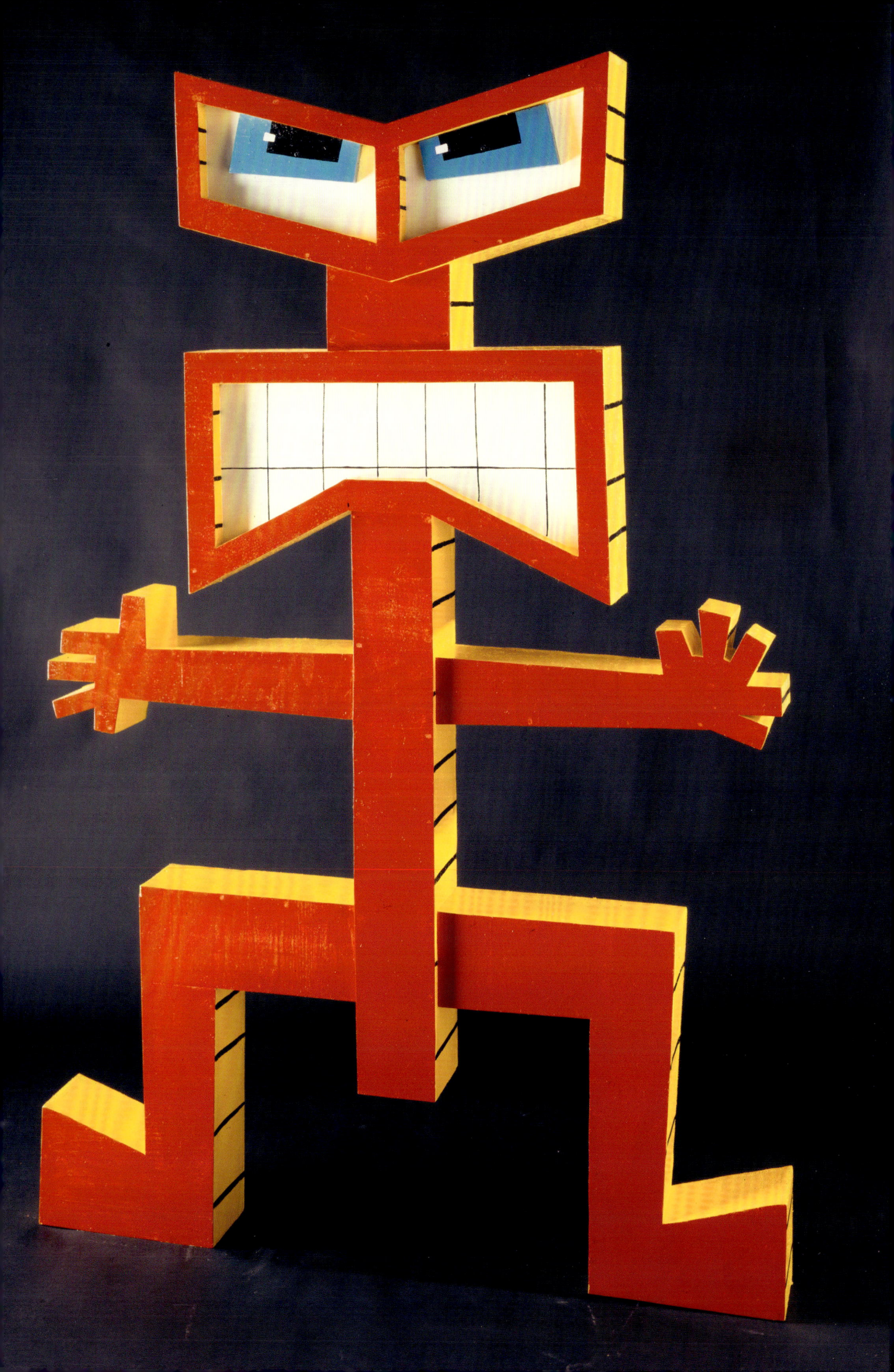

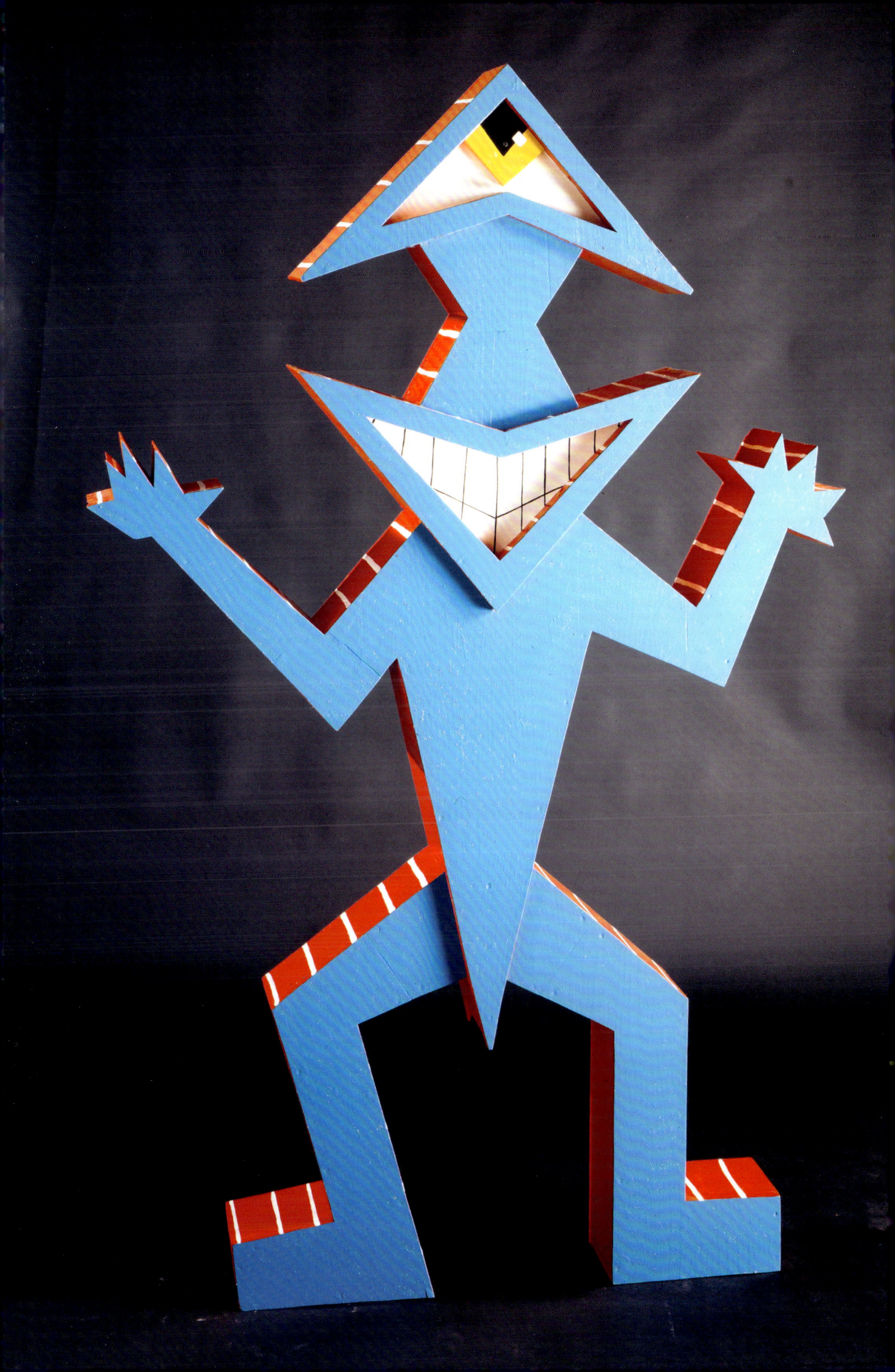

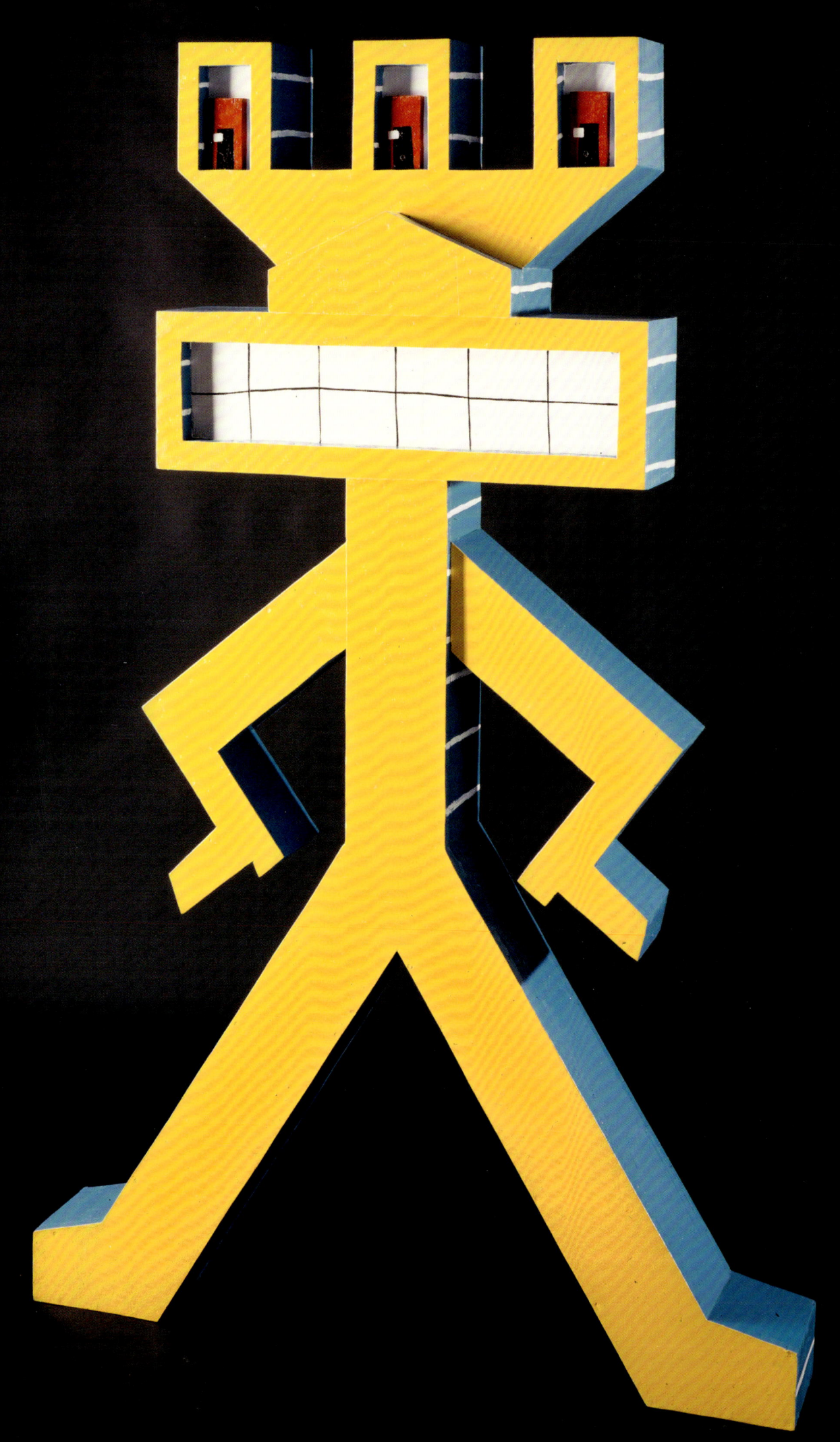

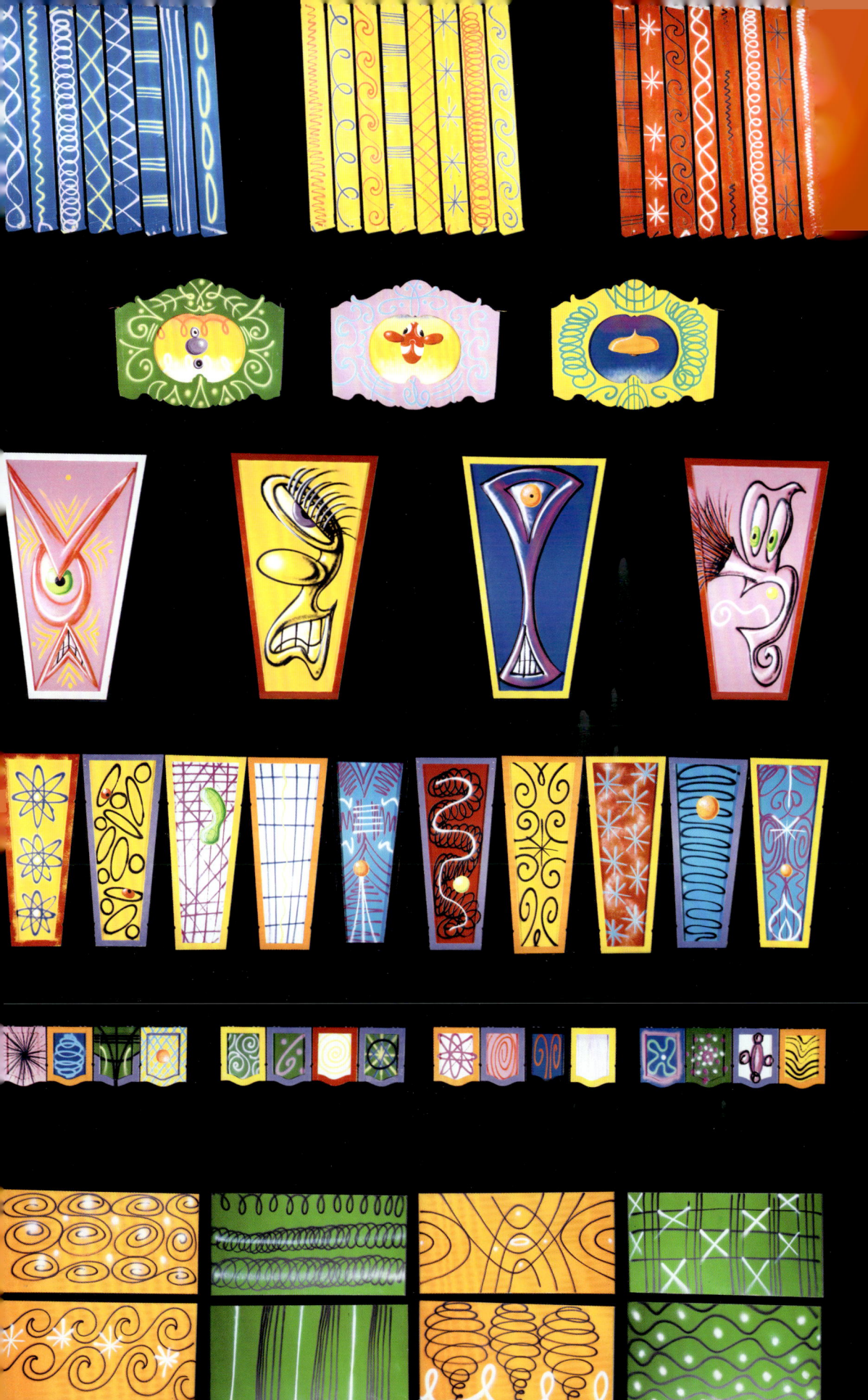

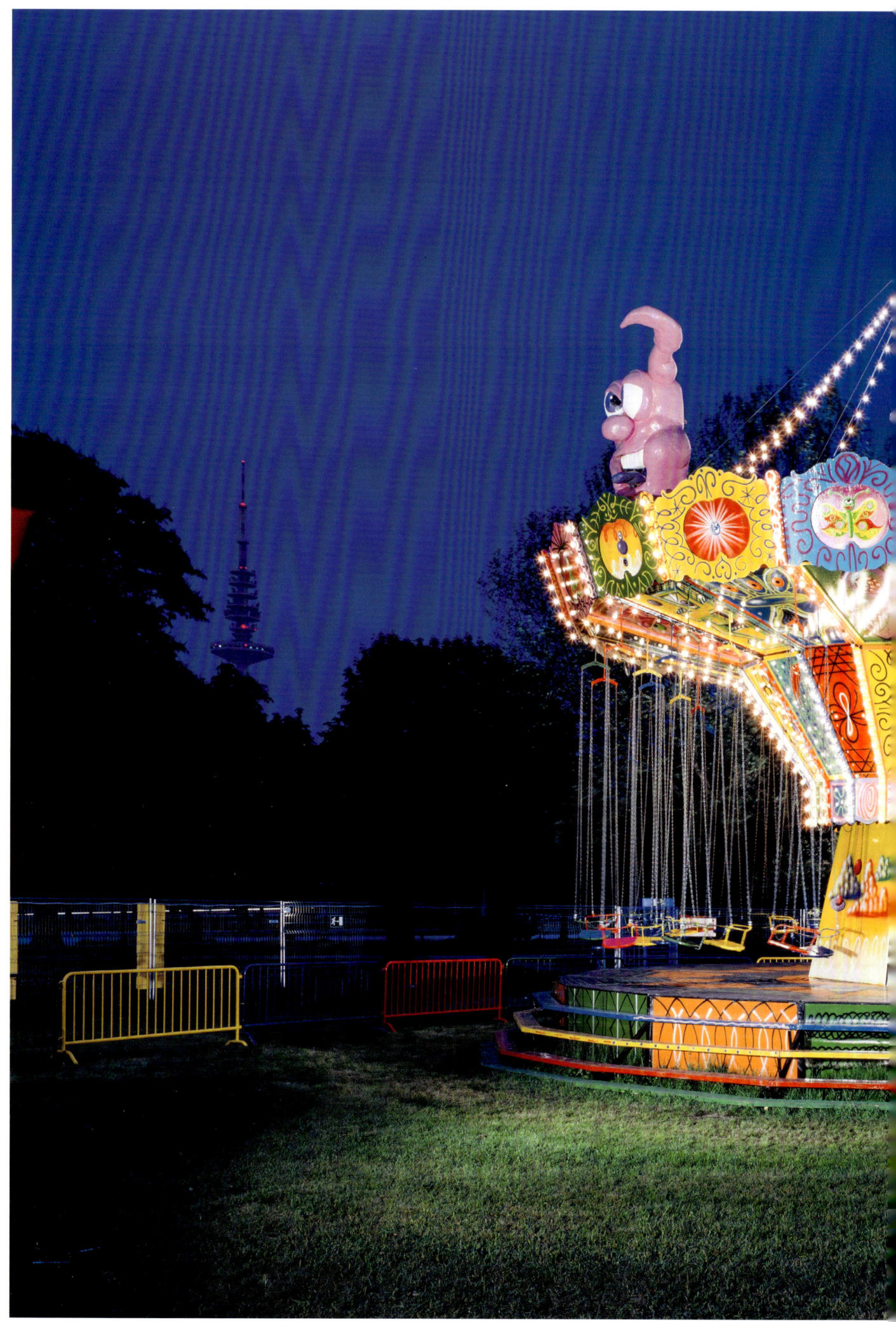

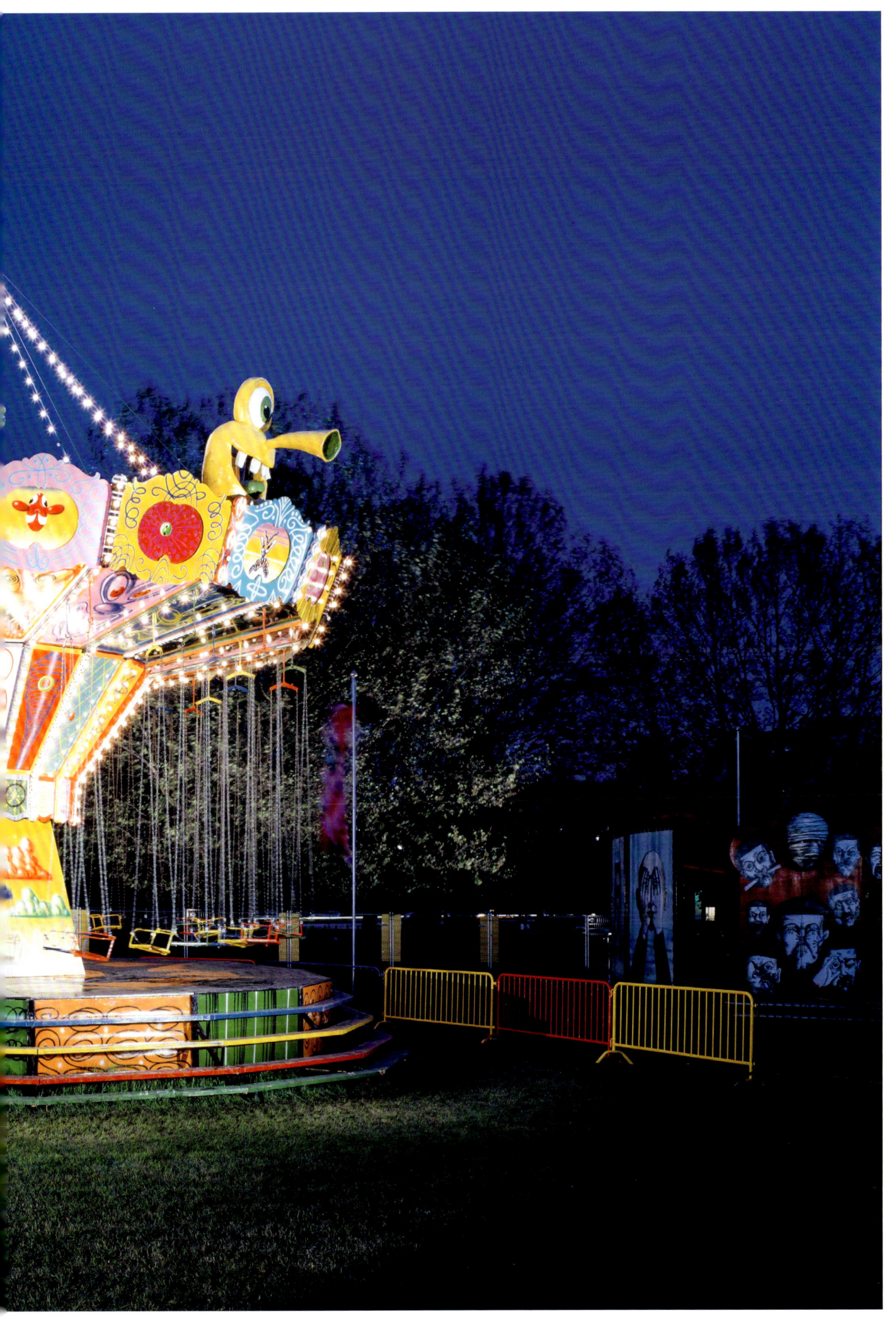

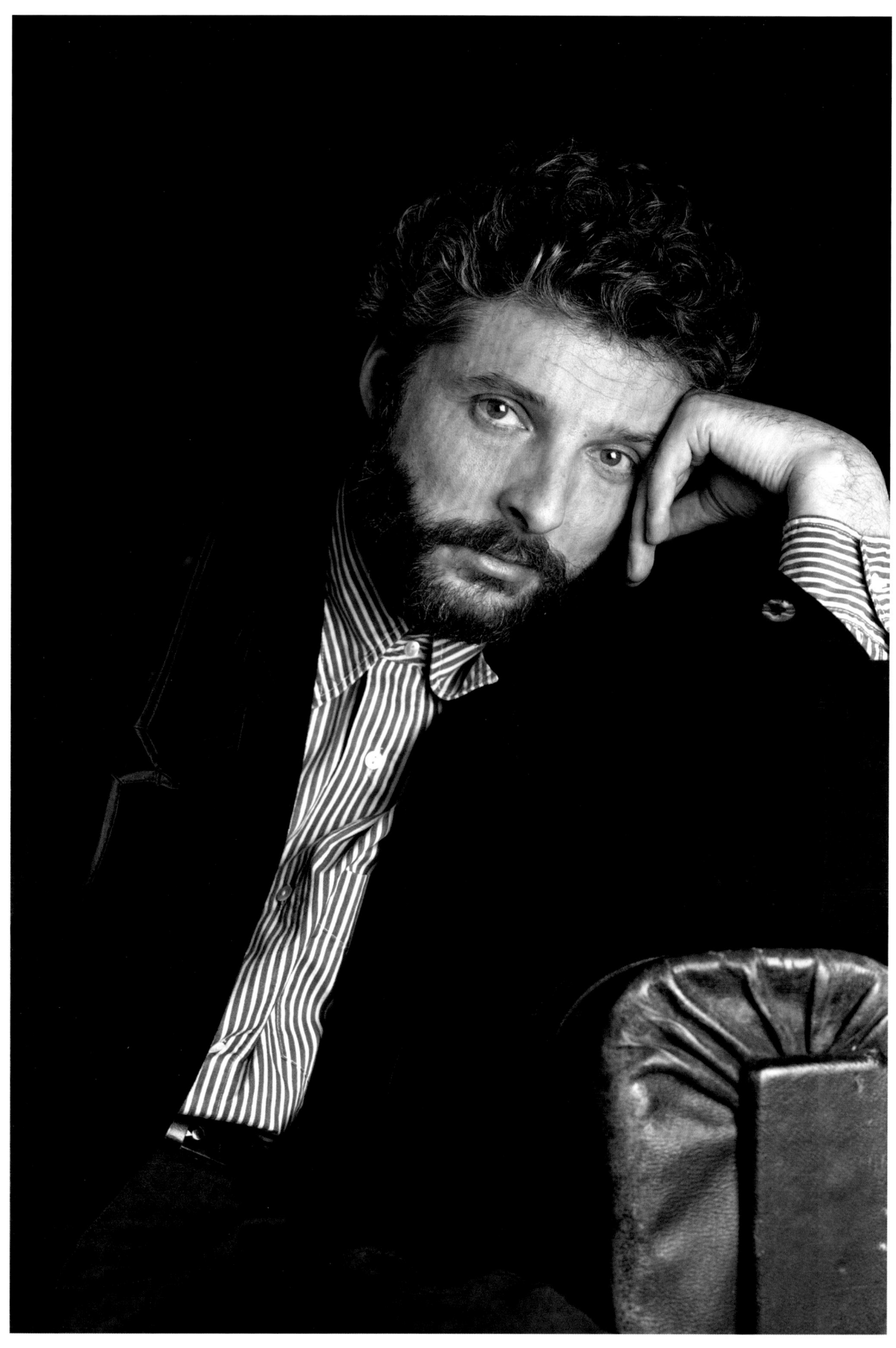

André Heller

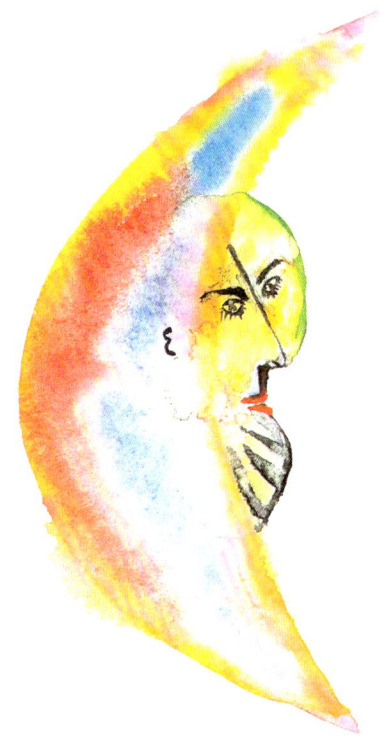

**L**achmeister

**U**rverglücklicher

**N**öte

**A**tlantis.

Heξ—

André Heller

Born: March 22, 1947, in Vienna, Austria.

Actionist, man of letters, inventor, composer, singer, fireworks specialist, illustrator, director, gardener.

André Heller designed the **Wedding House** and the **Dream Station** for *Luna Luna*. In the Wedding House, anyone and everyone can marry what and whom they want. The Dream Station is a sculpture sewn from balloon silk, supported by compressed air, which houses a café.

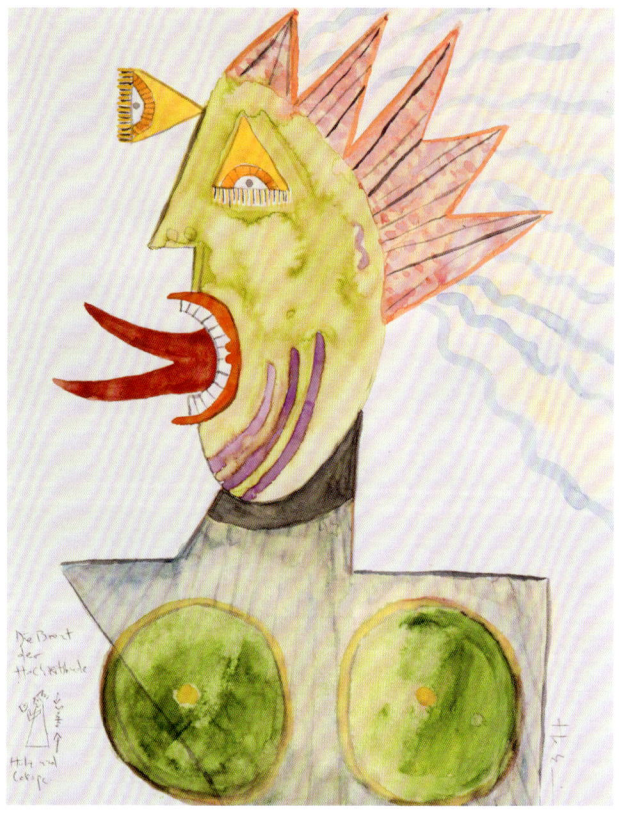

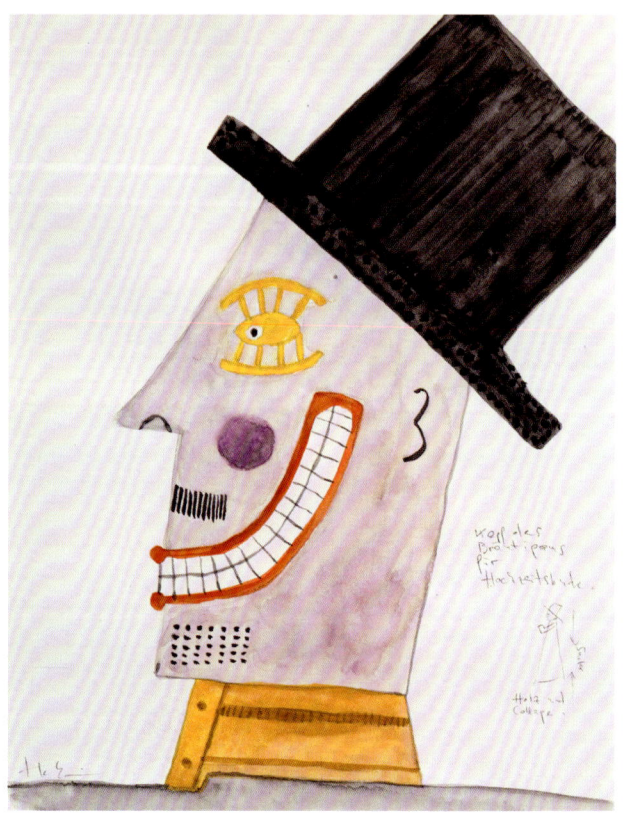

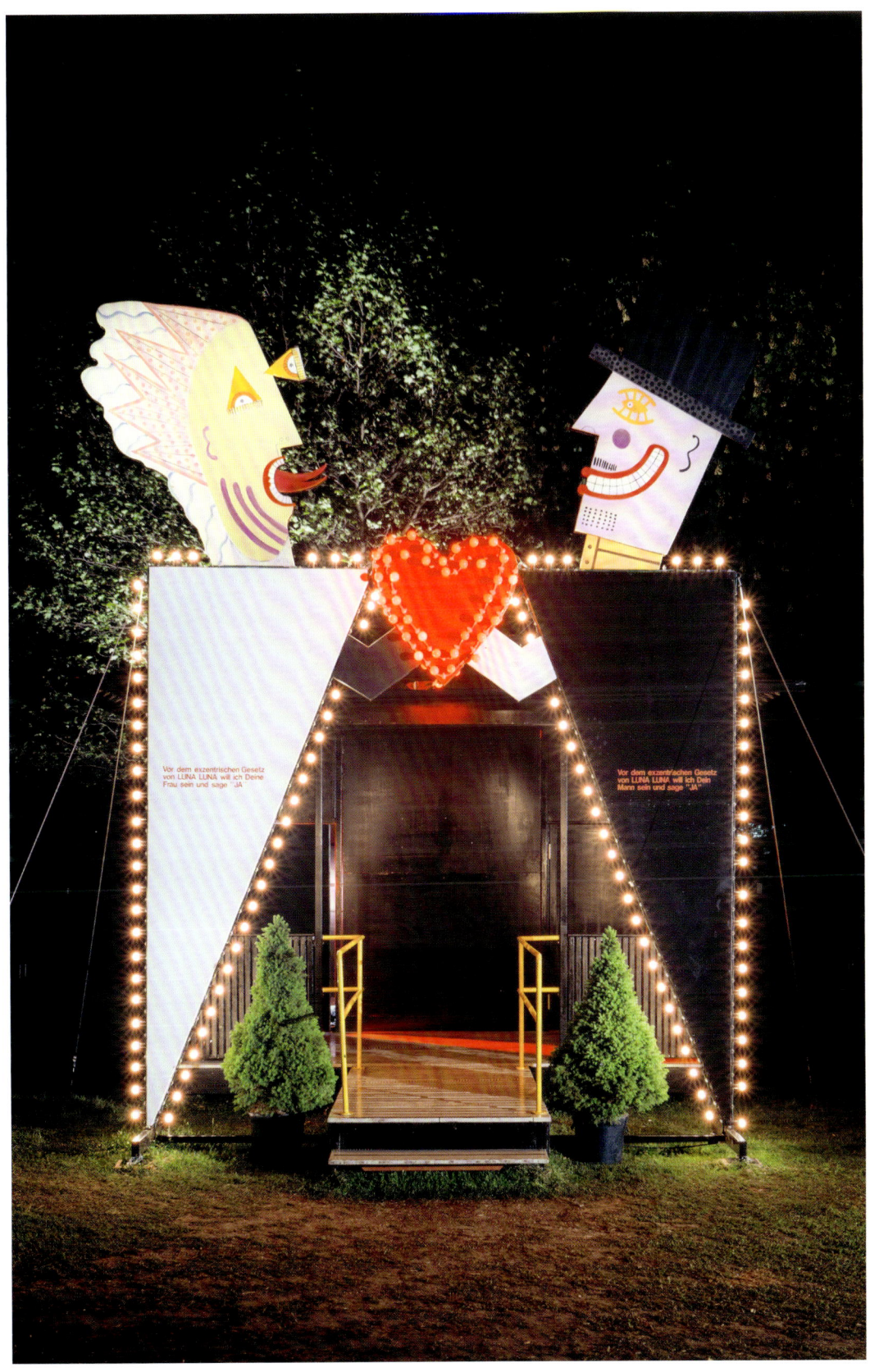

107

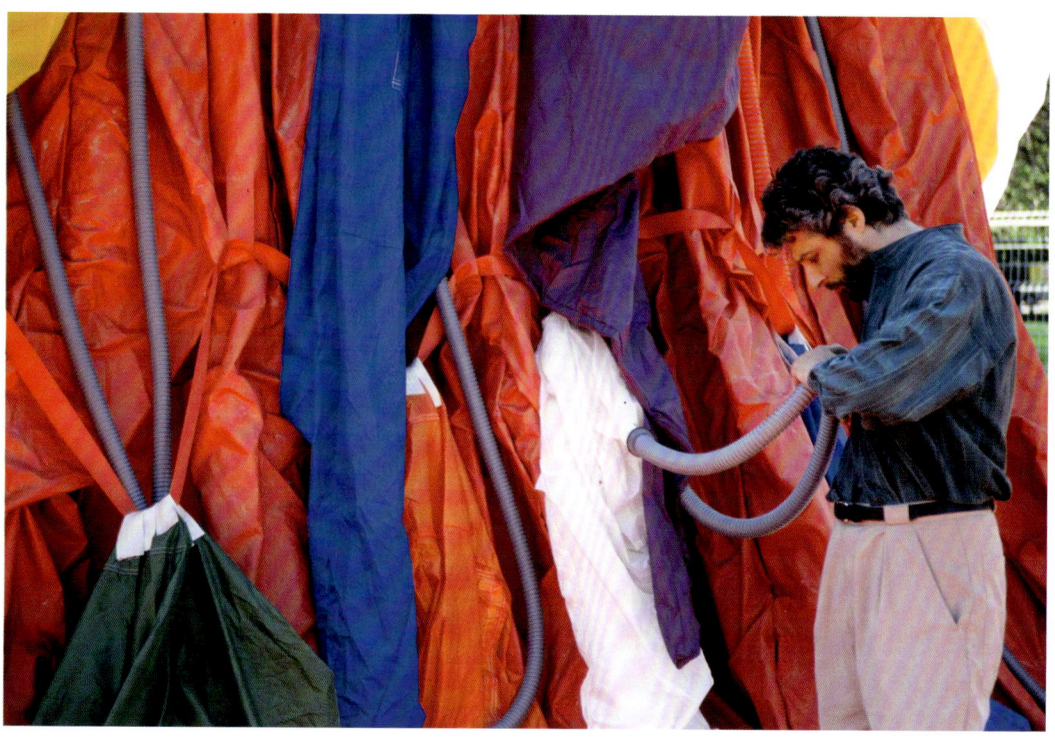

*André Heller assembling the air pumps and conduit hoses needed to inflate the sculpture*

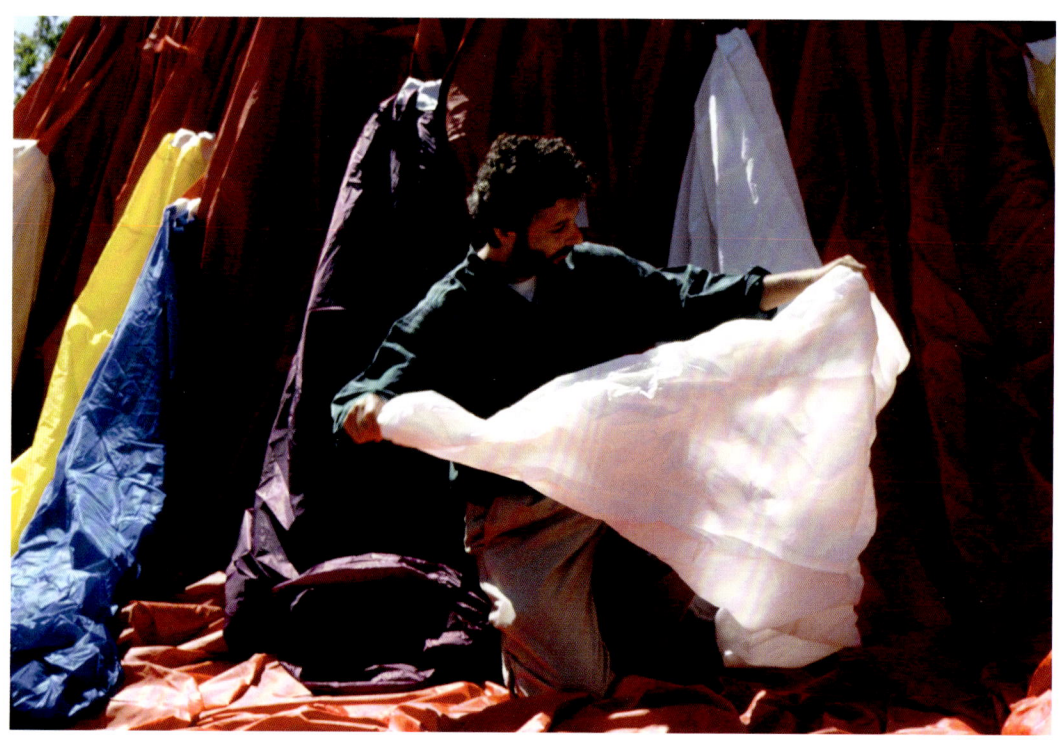

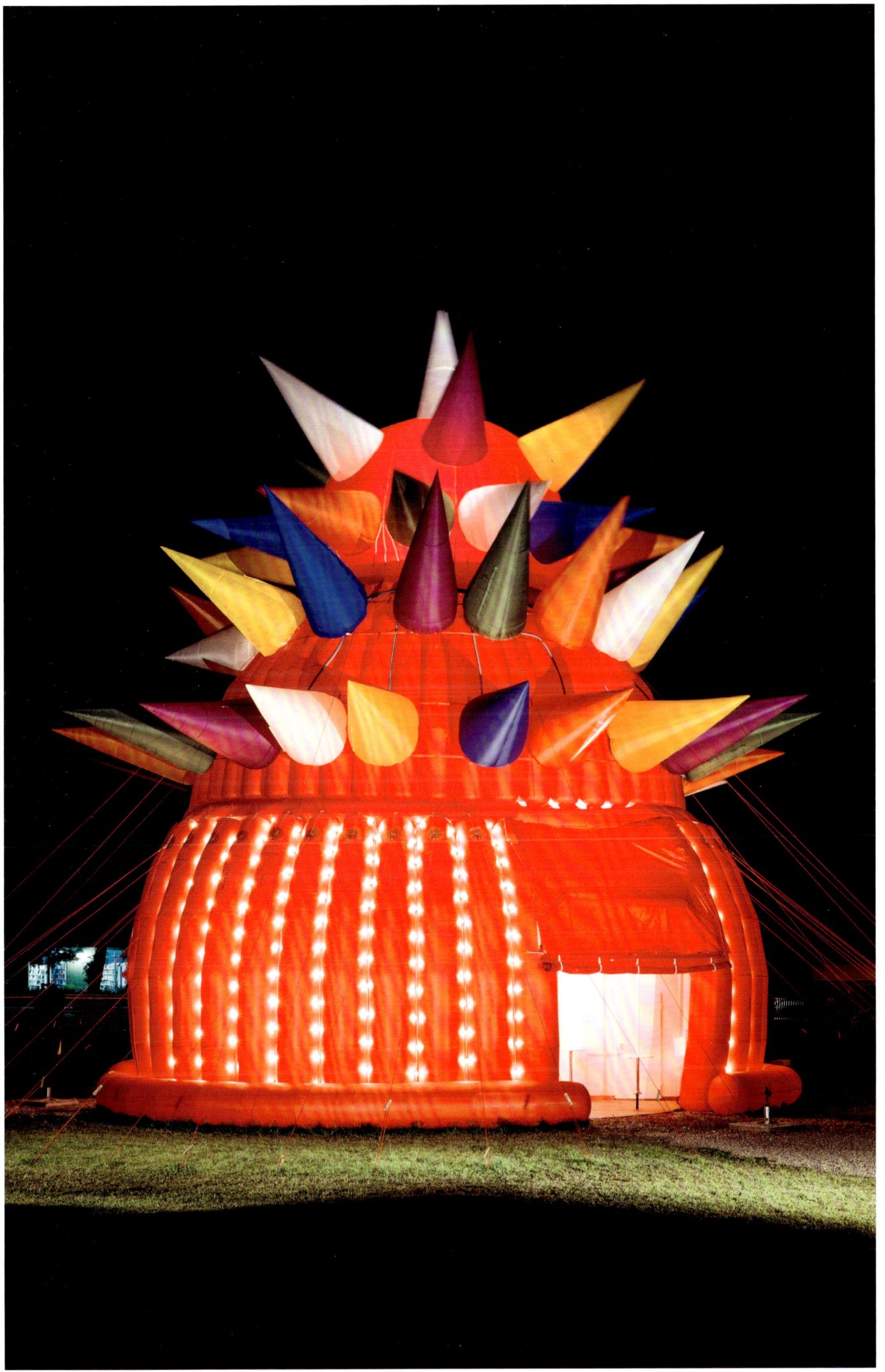

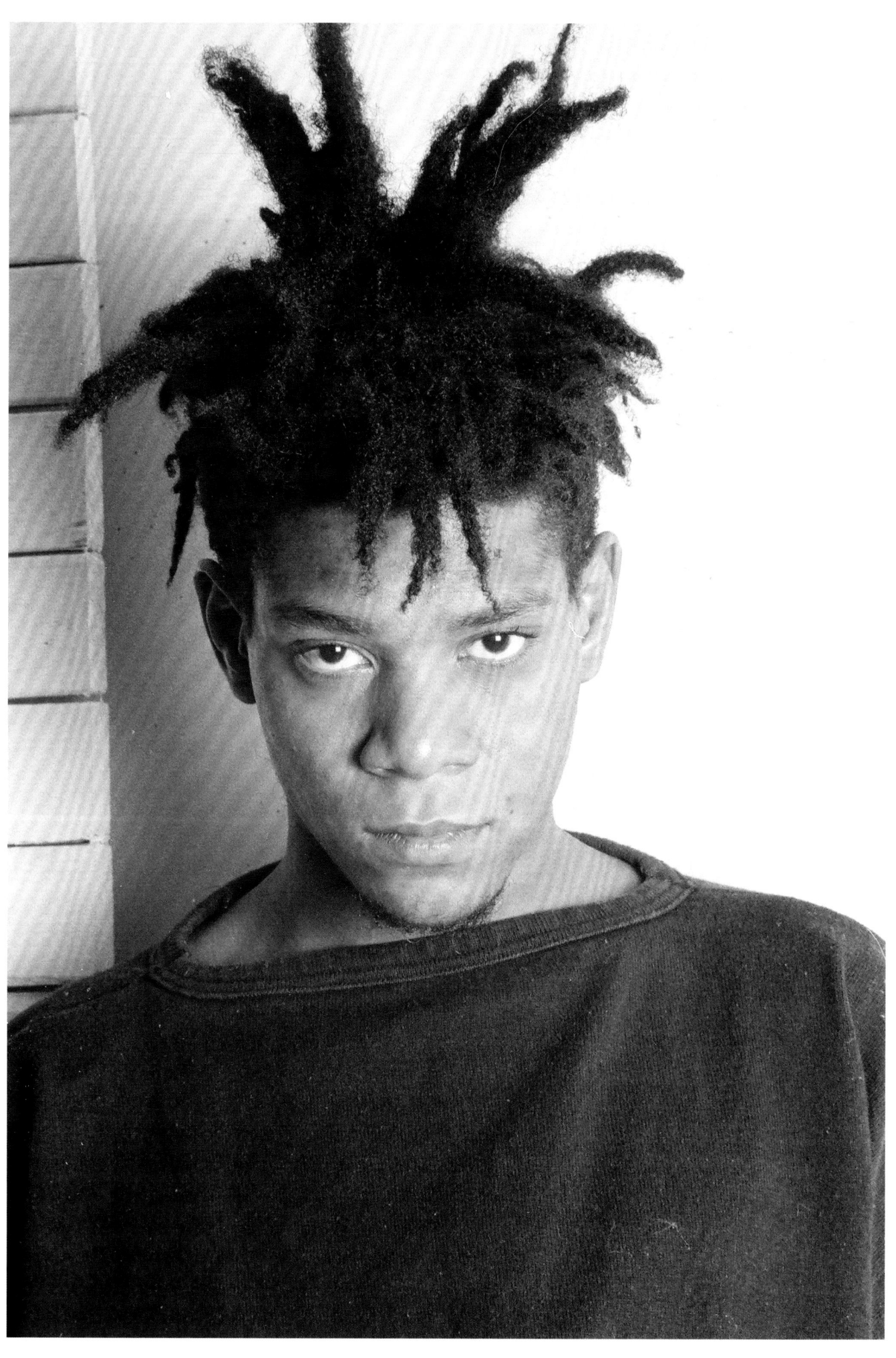

Jean-Michel Basquiat

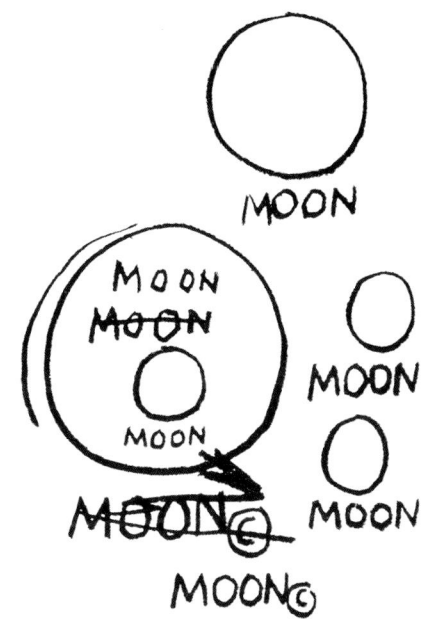

I CAN'T SEE ANYONE
RIGHT NOW —

THIS IS MY SENTANCE

LUNATIC

Jean-Michel Basquiat

Born: December 22, 1960, in New York, New York.
Died: August 12, 1988, in New York, New York.

Painter, illustrator, sculptor.

Jean-Michel Basquiat designed the **Ferris wheel** for
*Luna Luna*. It tells of eclectic myths and daydreams.
The music for it was provided by Miles Davis.

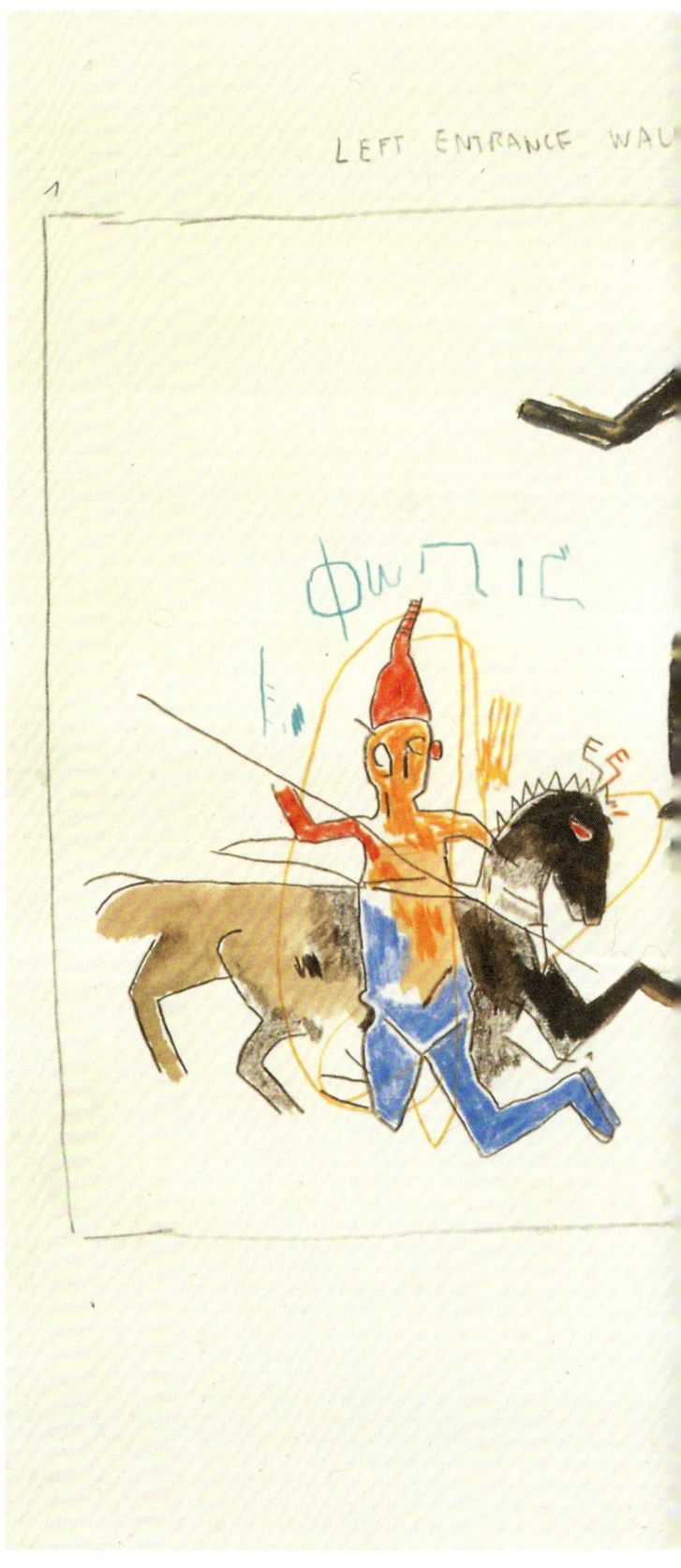

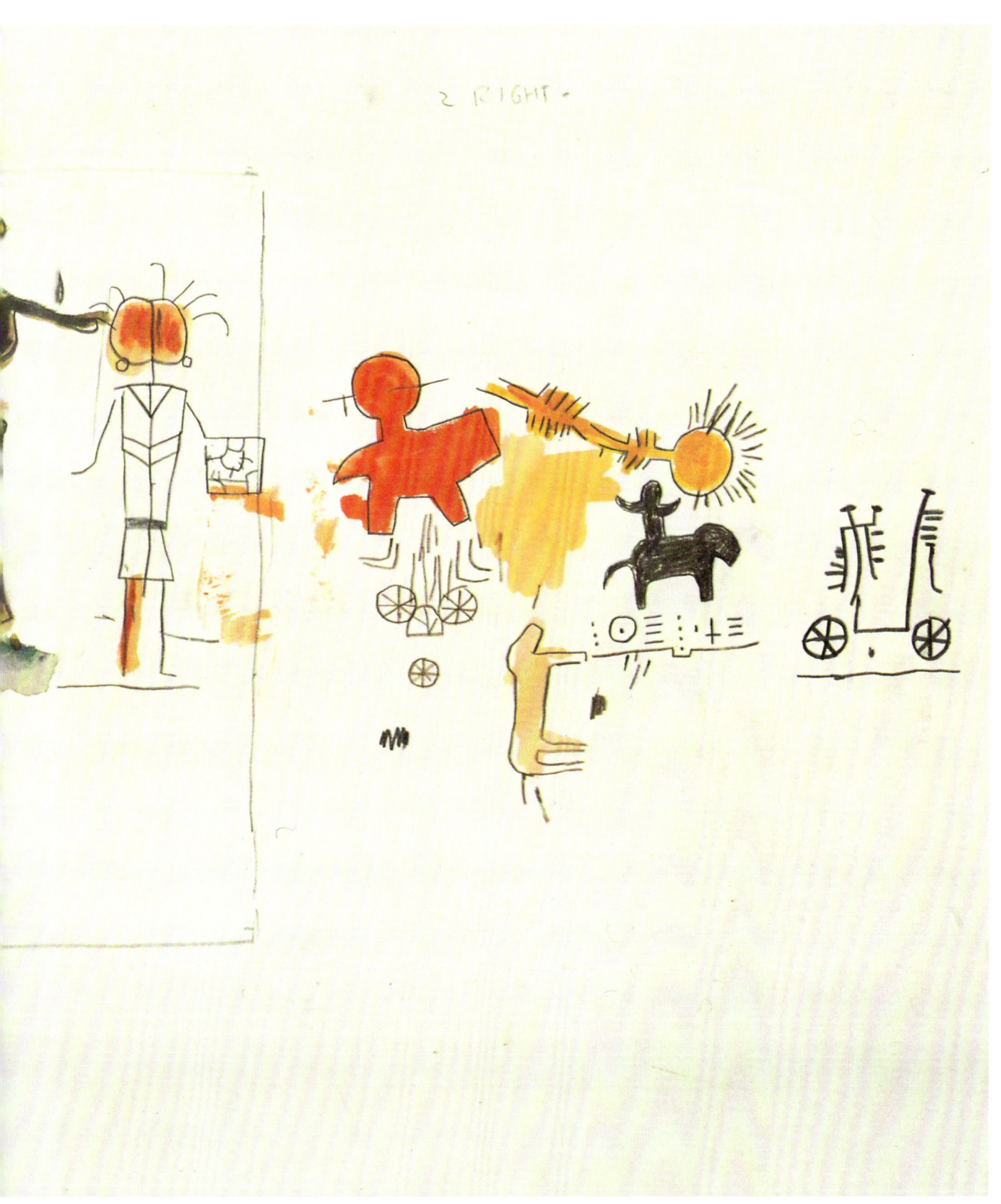

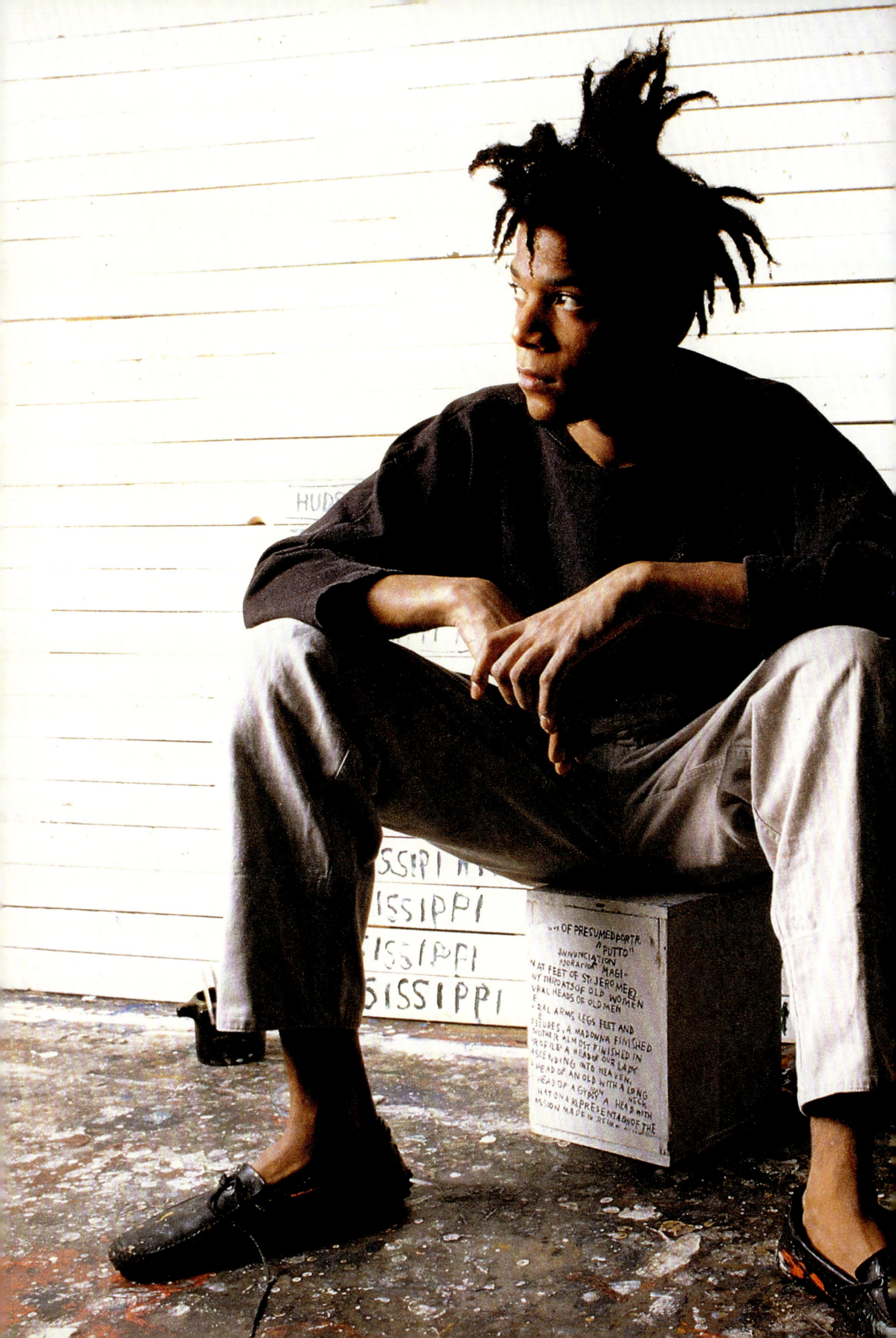

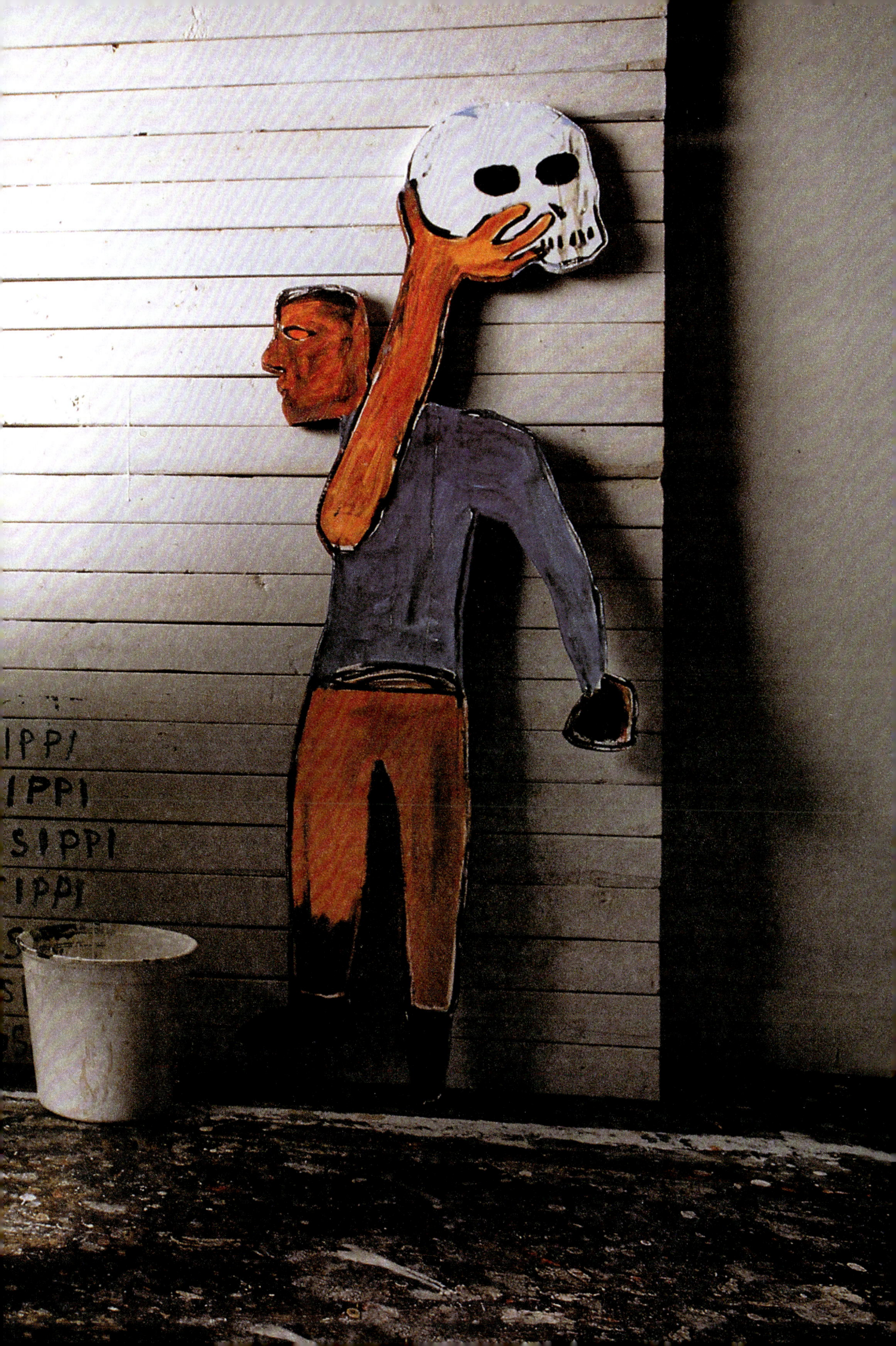

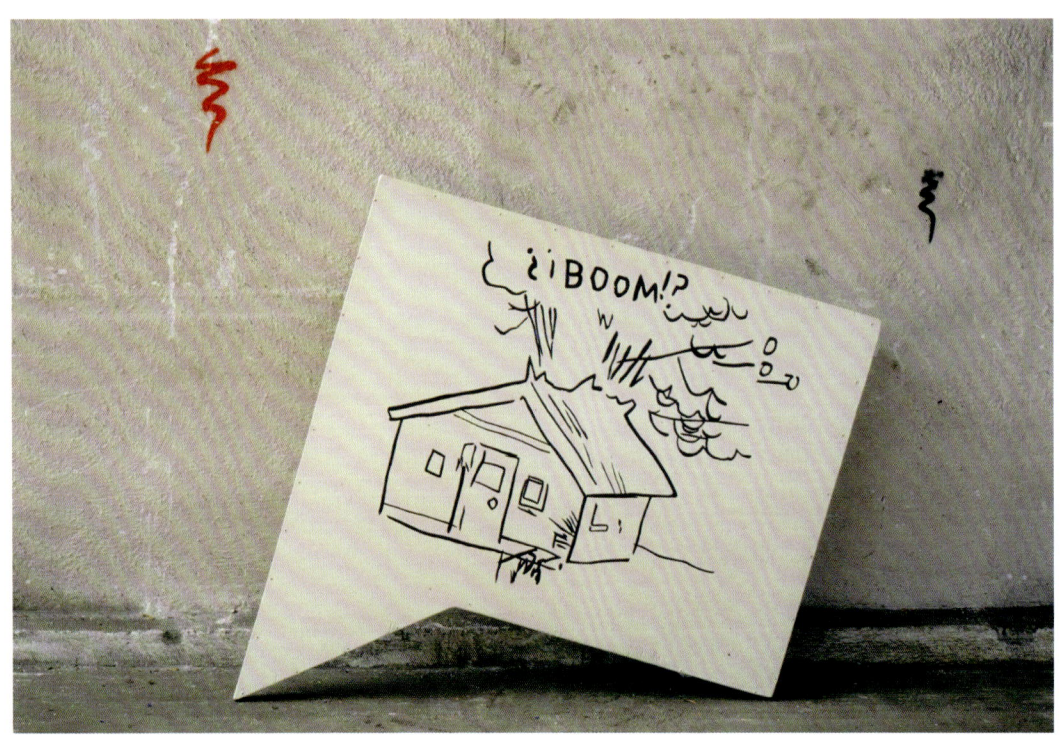

*Drawing for the staircase of the Ferris wheel*

*Detail of the right-hand facade*

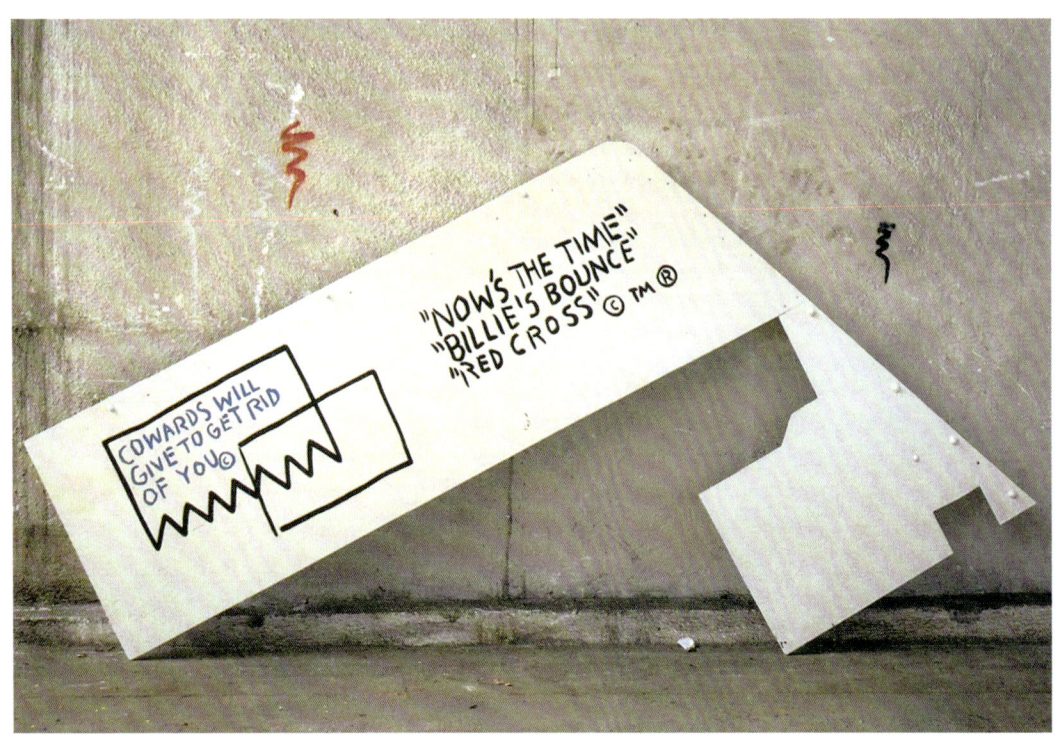

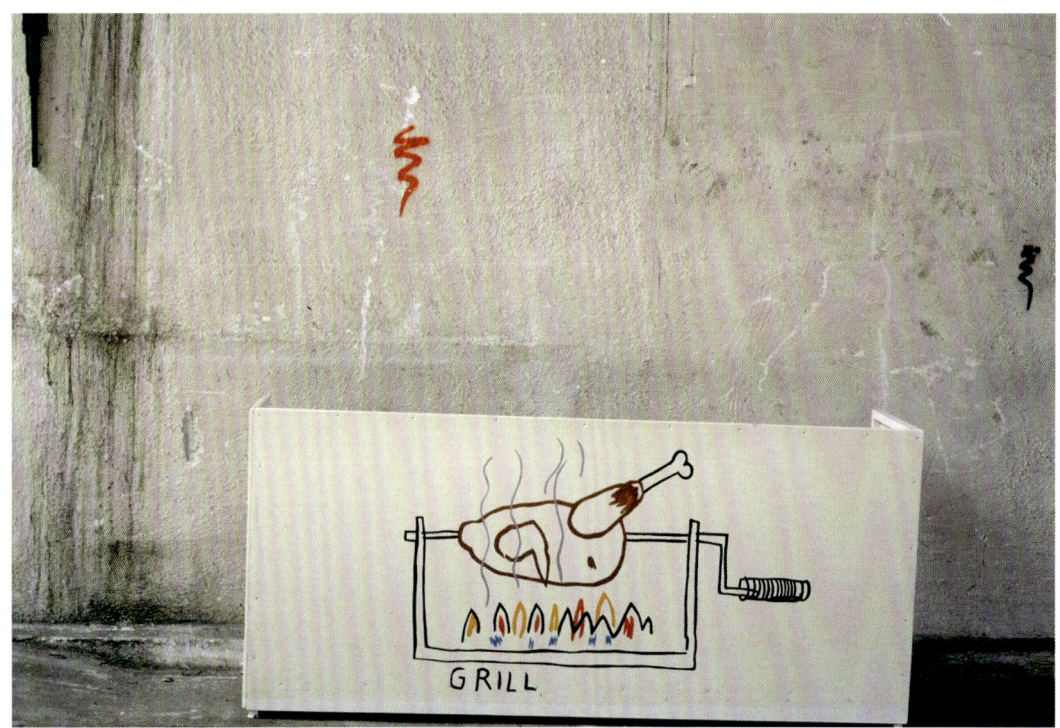

*Detail at the rear right …*

*… and on the left-hand facade*

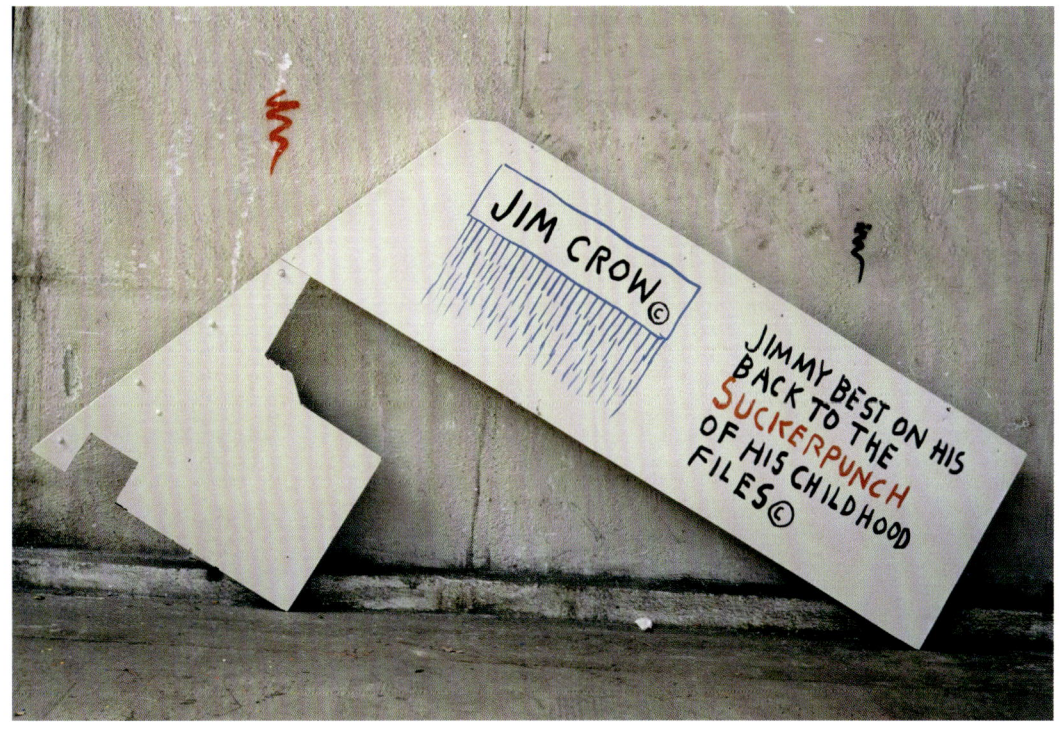

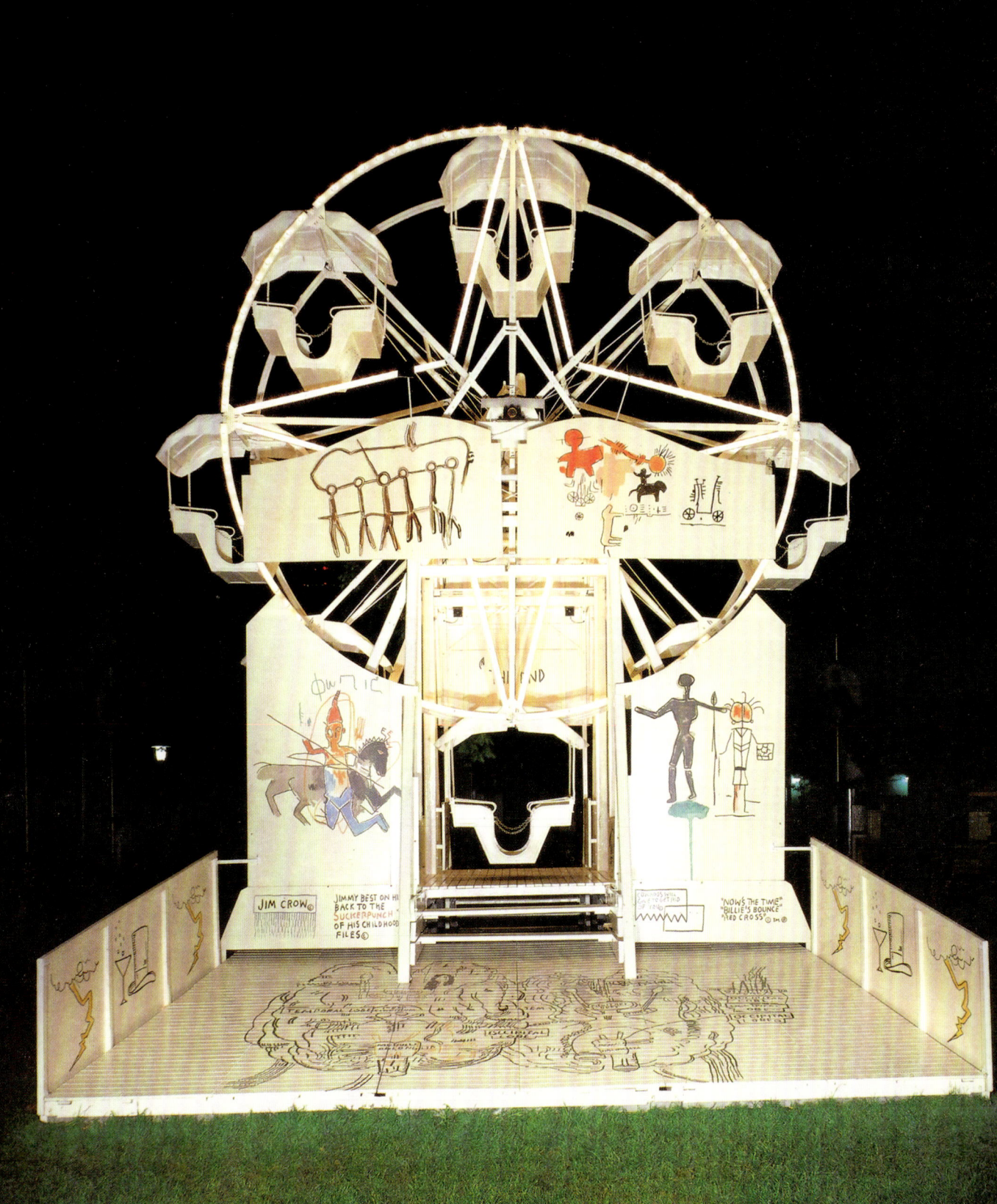

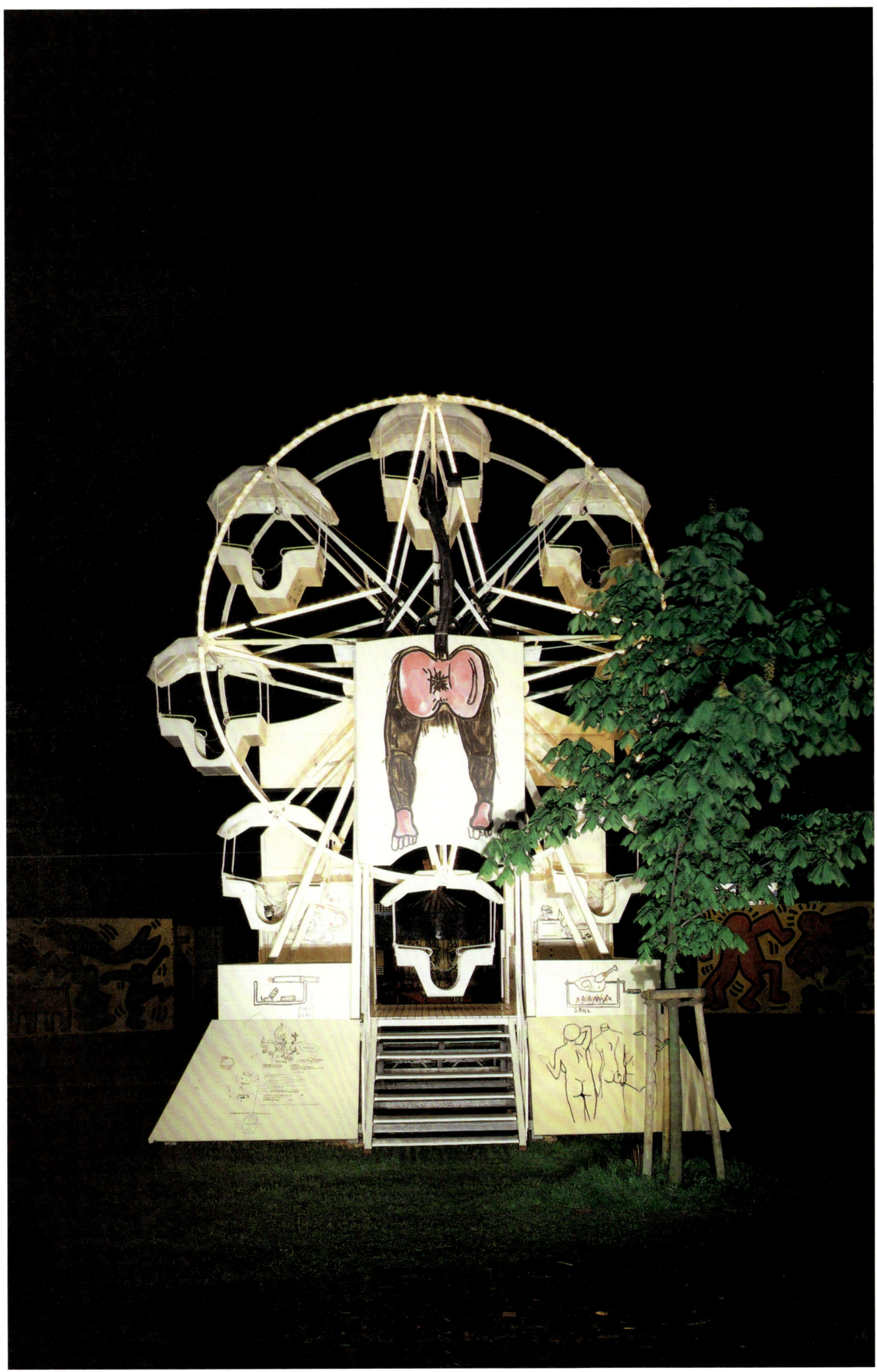

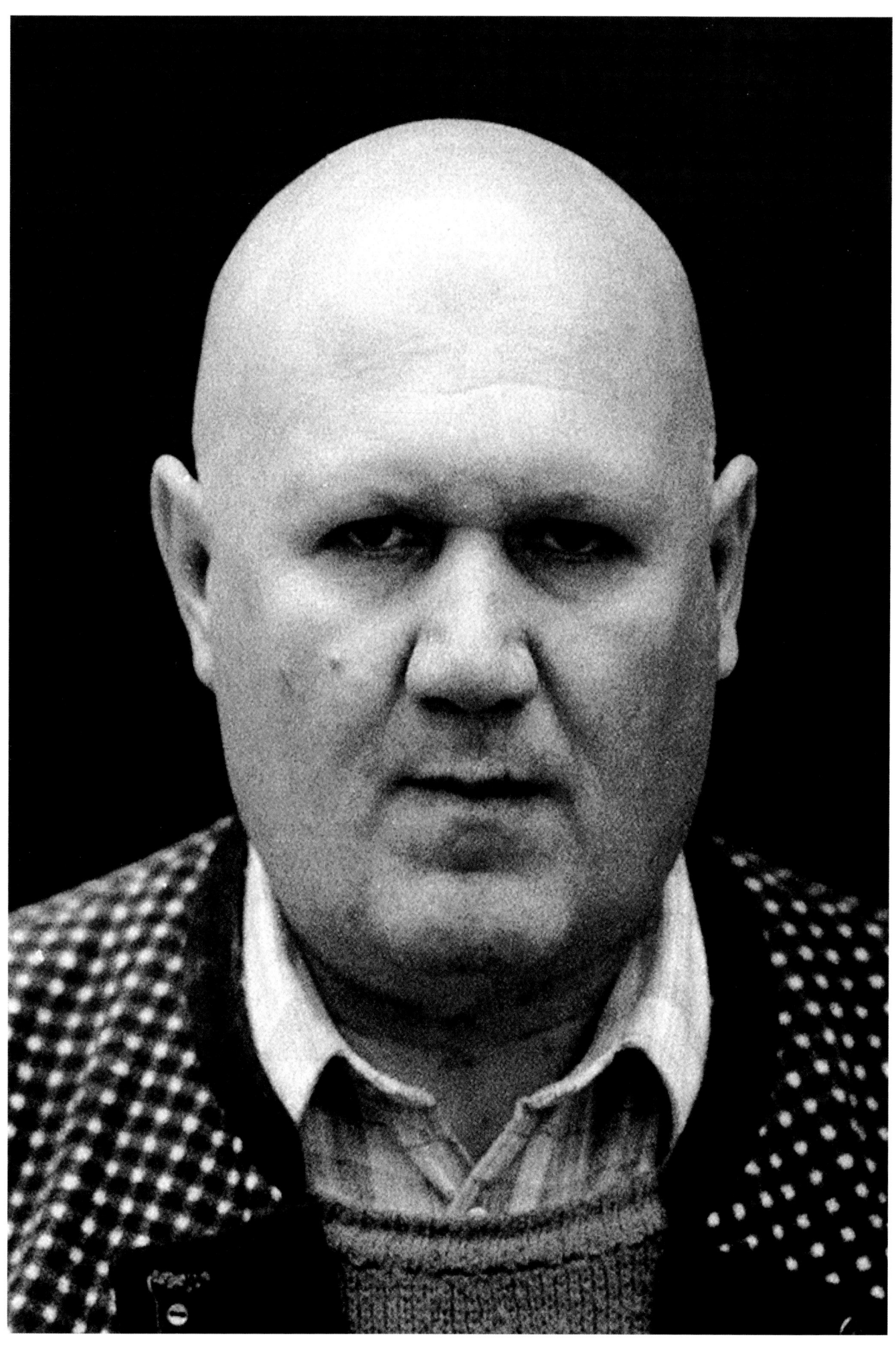

August Walla

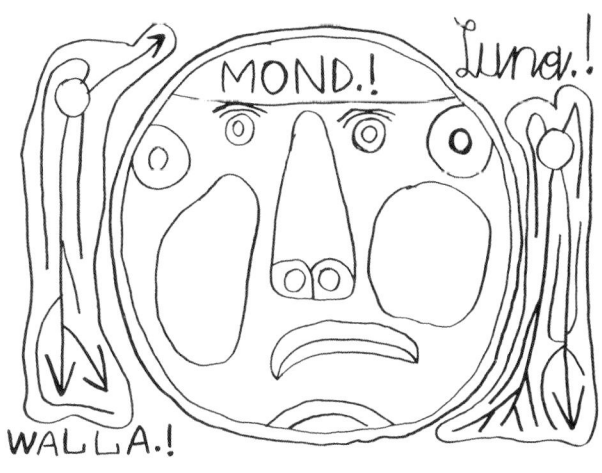

MOND.!

Luna.!

WALLA.!

Luna Luna und August W
alla sind am Abend, im
Mondeslicht sehr freund
lich anzusehn. August
am Felsen, Luna der Mond
in des Himmels Höhen, Lu
na im Meer auch zu sehn.

August Walla

Born: June 22, 1936, in Klosterneuburg, Austria.
Died: July 7, 2001, in Vienna.

Painter, illustrator, sculptor, poet, language inventor, photographer, actionist.

August Walla painted a **Puzzle Wagon** for *Luna Luna* with figures and characters drawn from his private mythology.

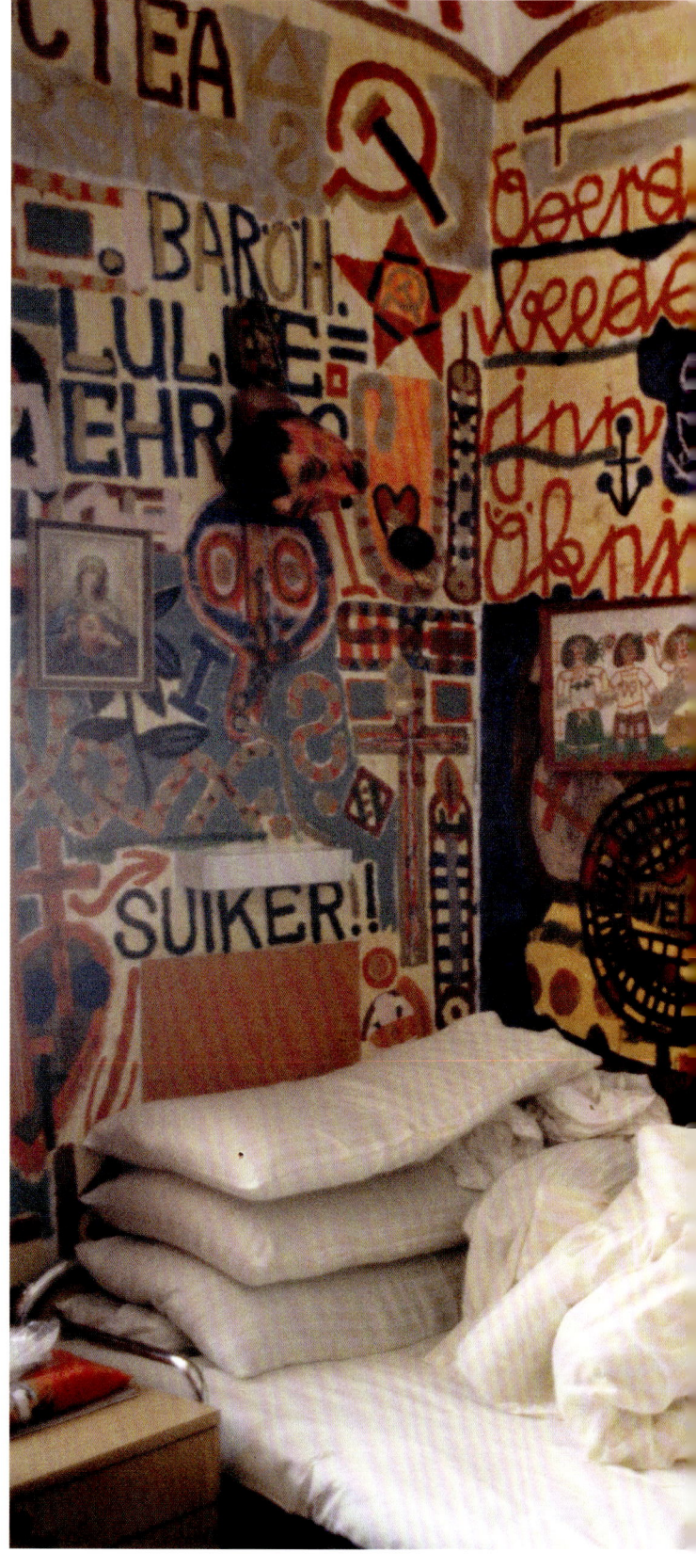

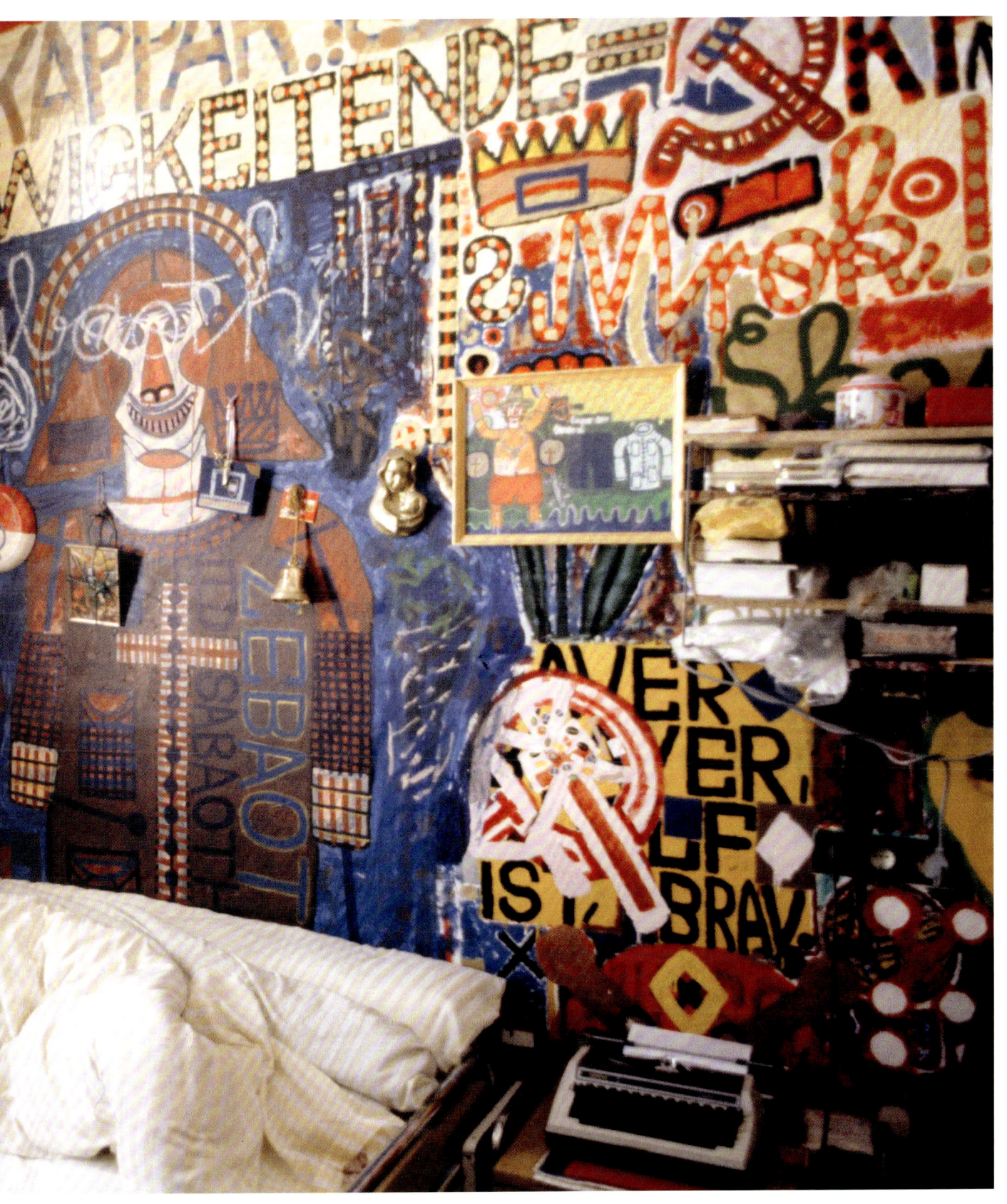

123

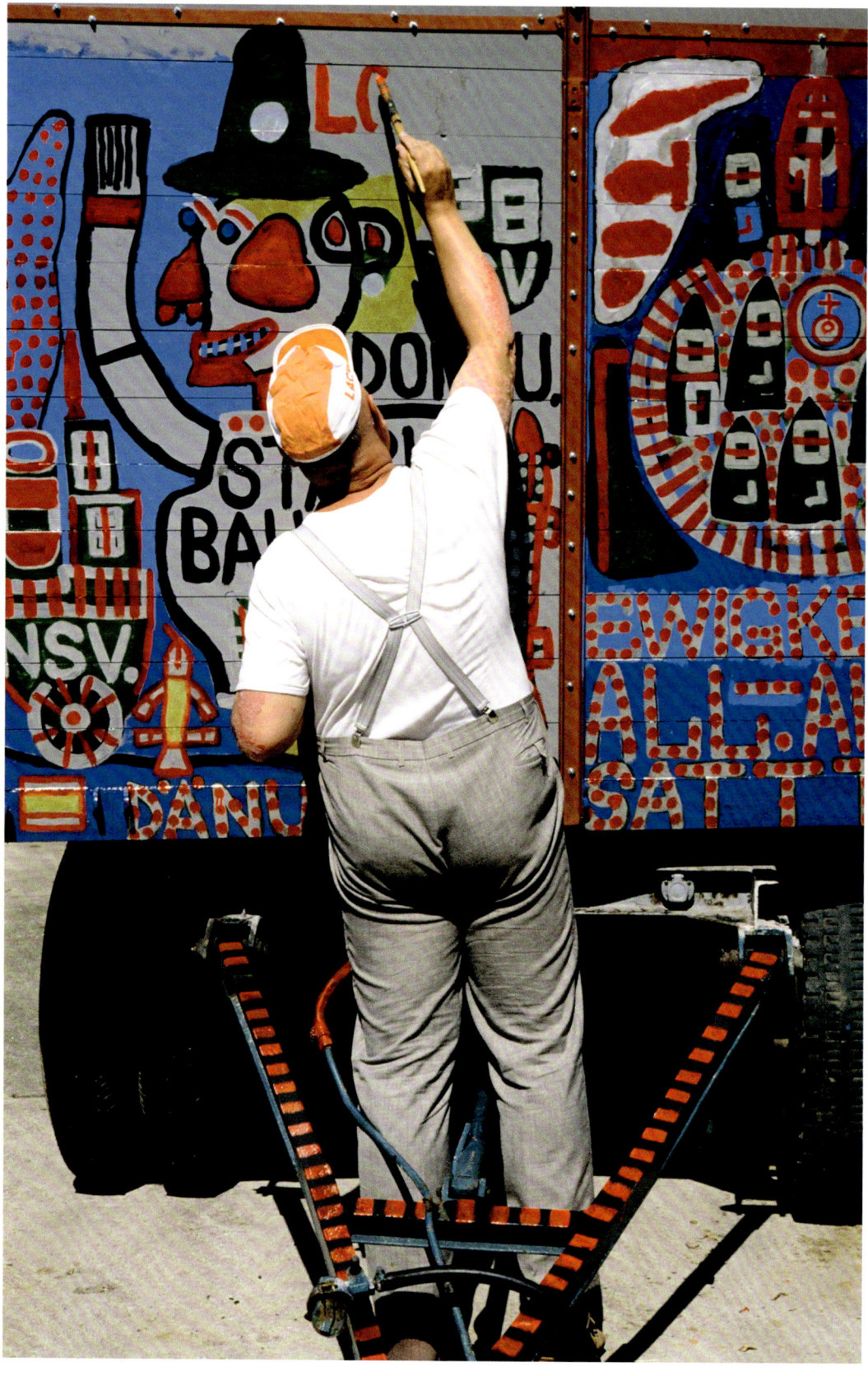

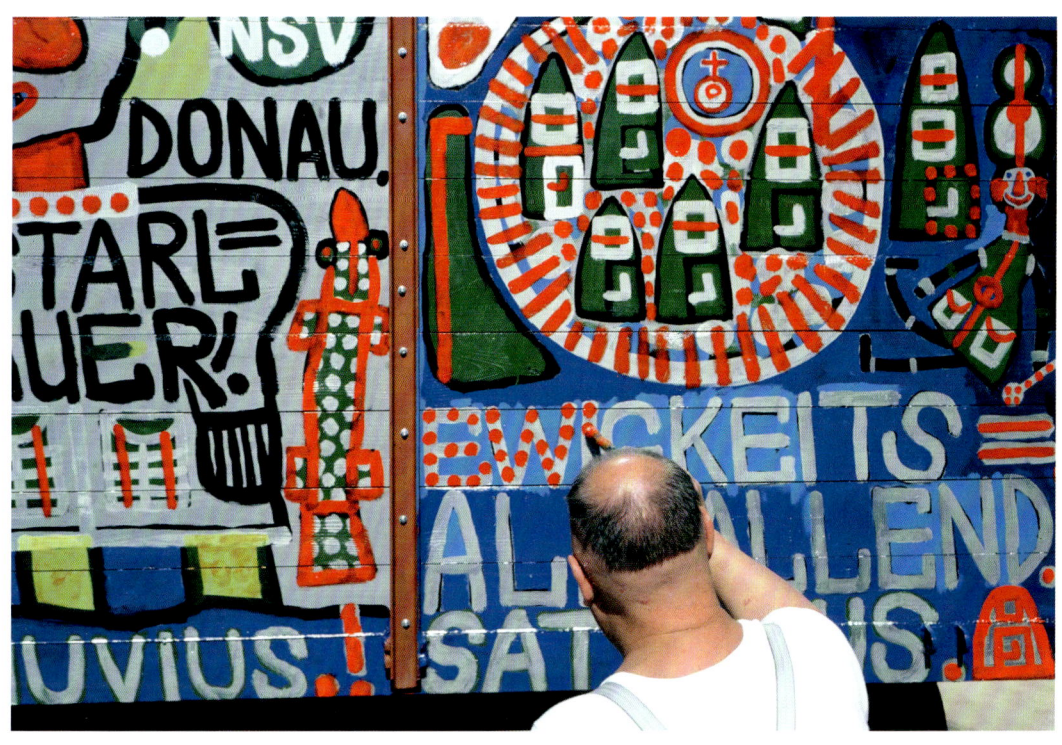

*August Walla at work on the Puzzle Wagon in the garden of the Künstlerhaus in Gugging*

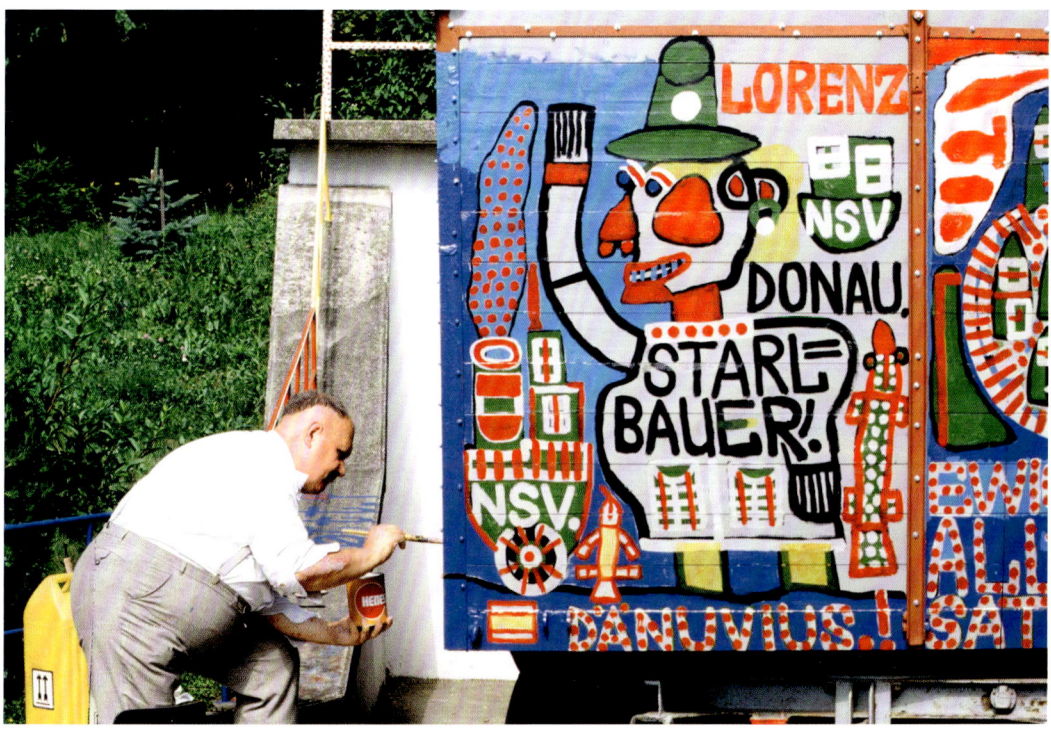

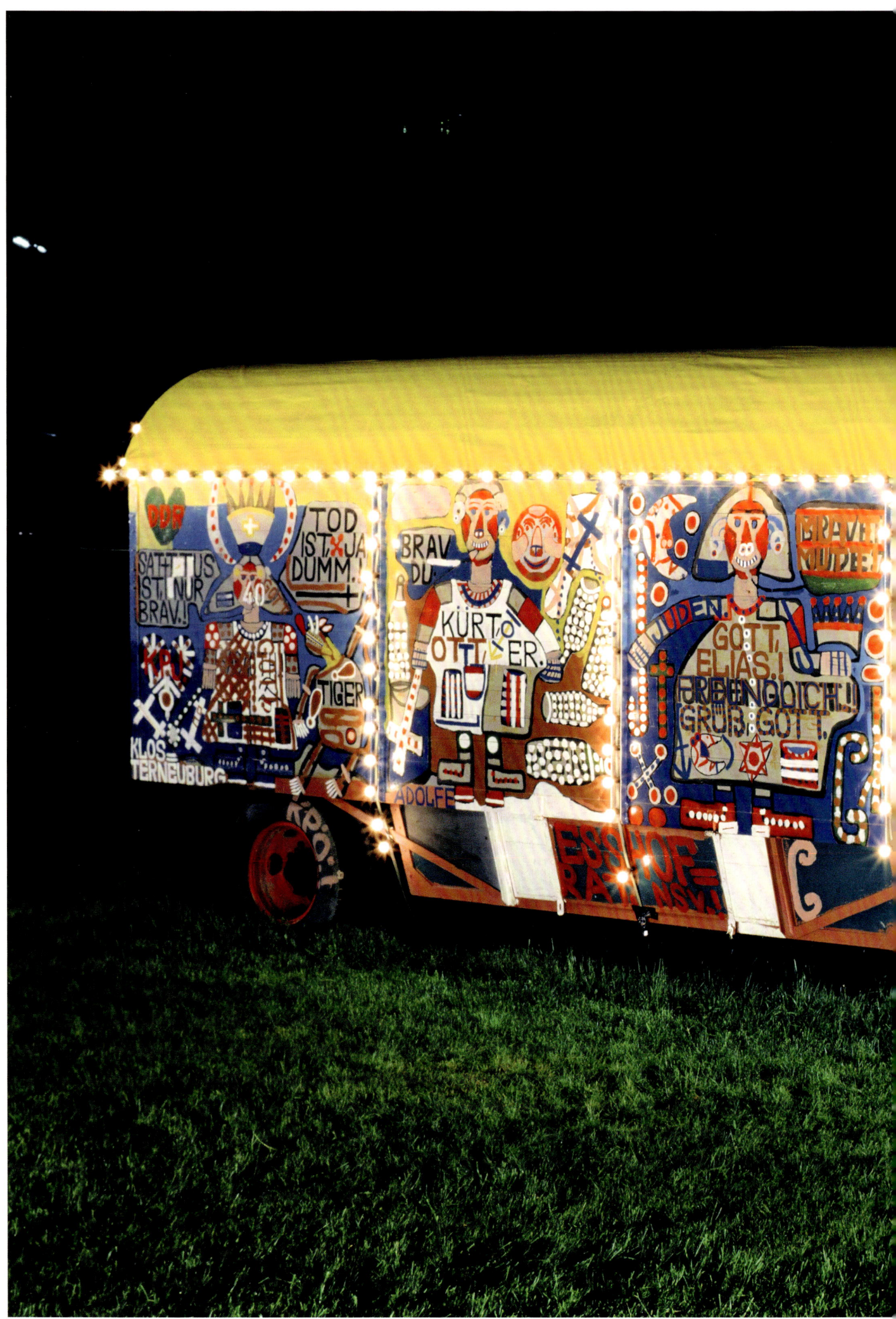

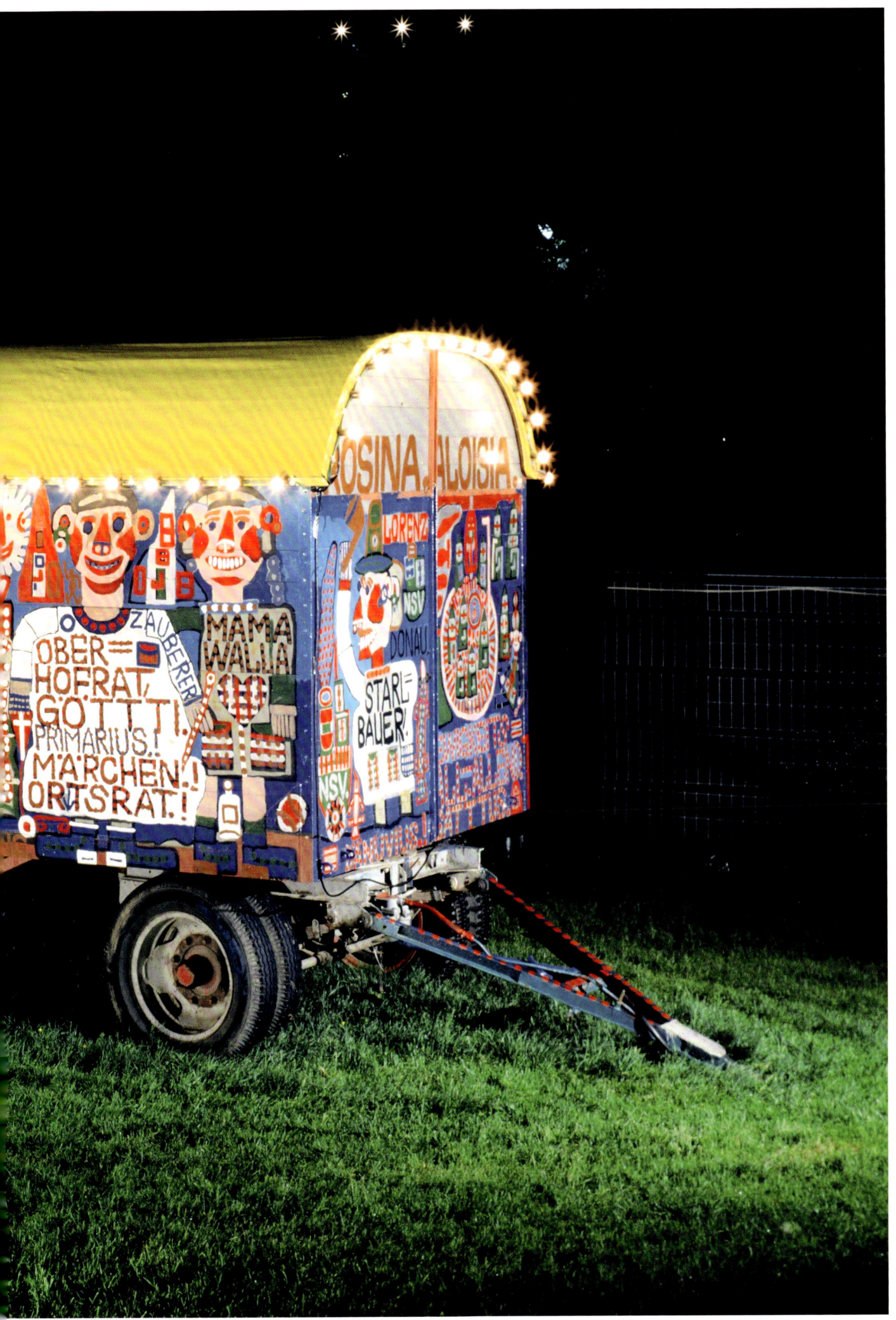

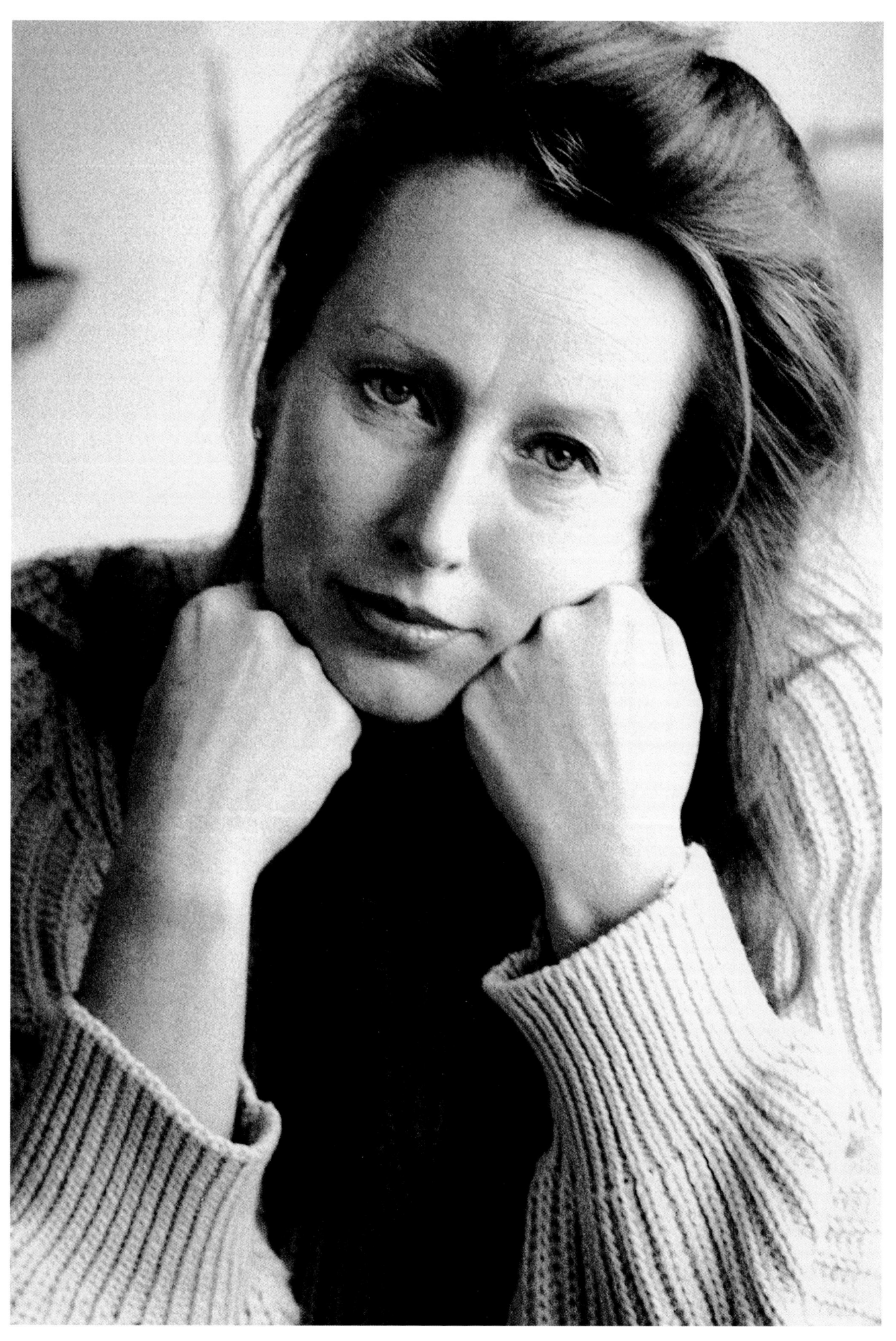

Rebecca Horn

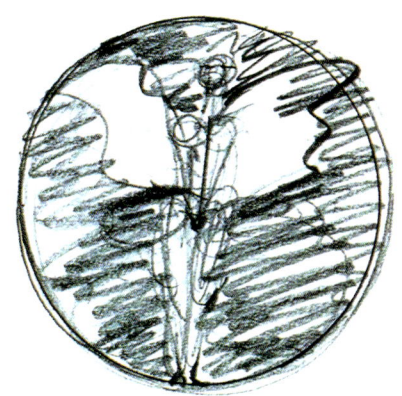

Luna Lunar

Schmetterling motto?
"les Frauchoises"

to

Rebecca Horn

Rebecca Horn

Born: March 24, 1944, in Odenwald, Germany.

Designer, actionist, director, object artist,
makeup artist.

Rebecca Horn designed the **Thermometer of
Lovers** for *Luna Luna*. Those who warm the
instruments with their hands will learn the exact
degree of his or her rapture: loneliness, asceticism,
image, night, skinless, touch, embrace, magic, heart,
body, awaken, tenderness, yearn, wander, wish,
desire, hide, fear, truth, unbearable, mad, perish.

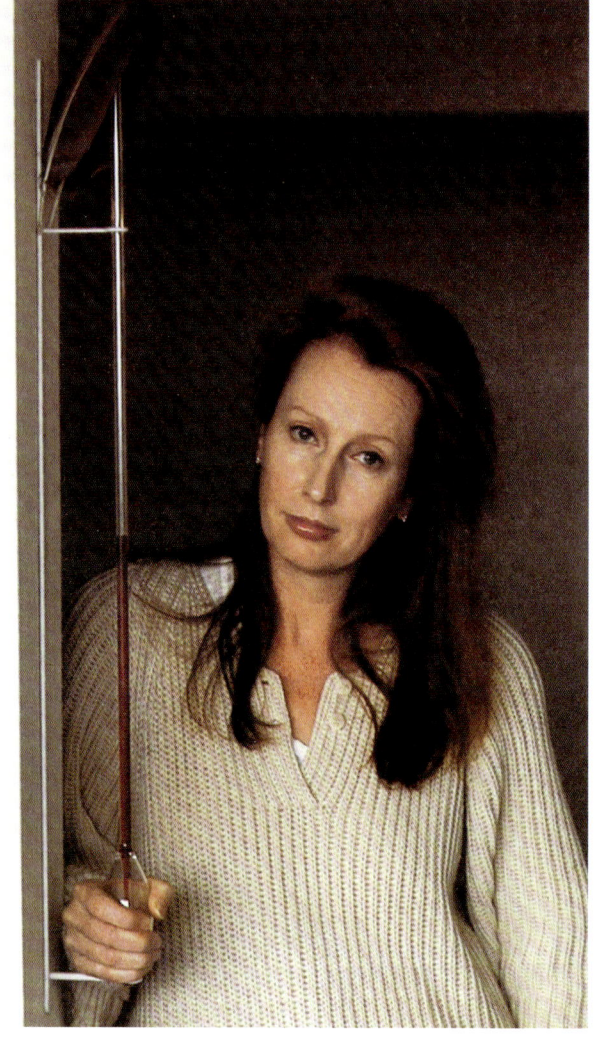

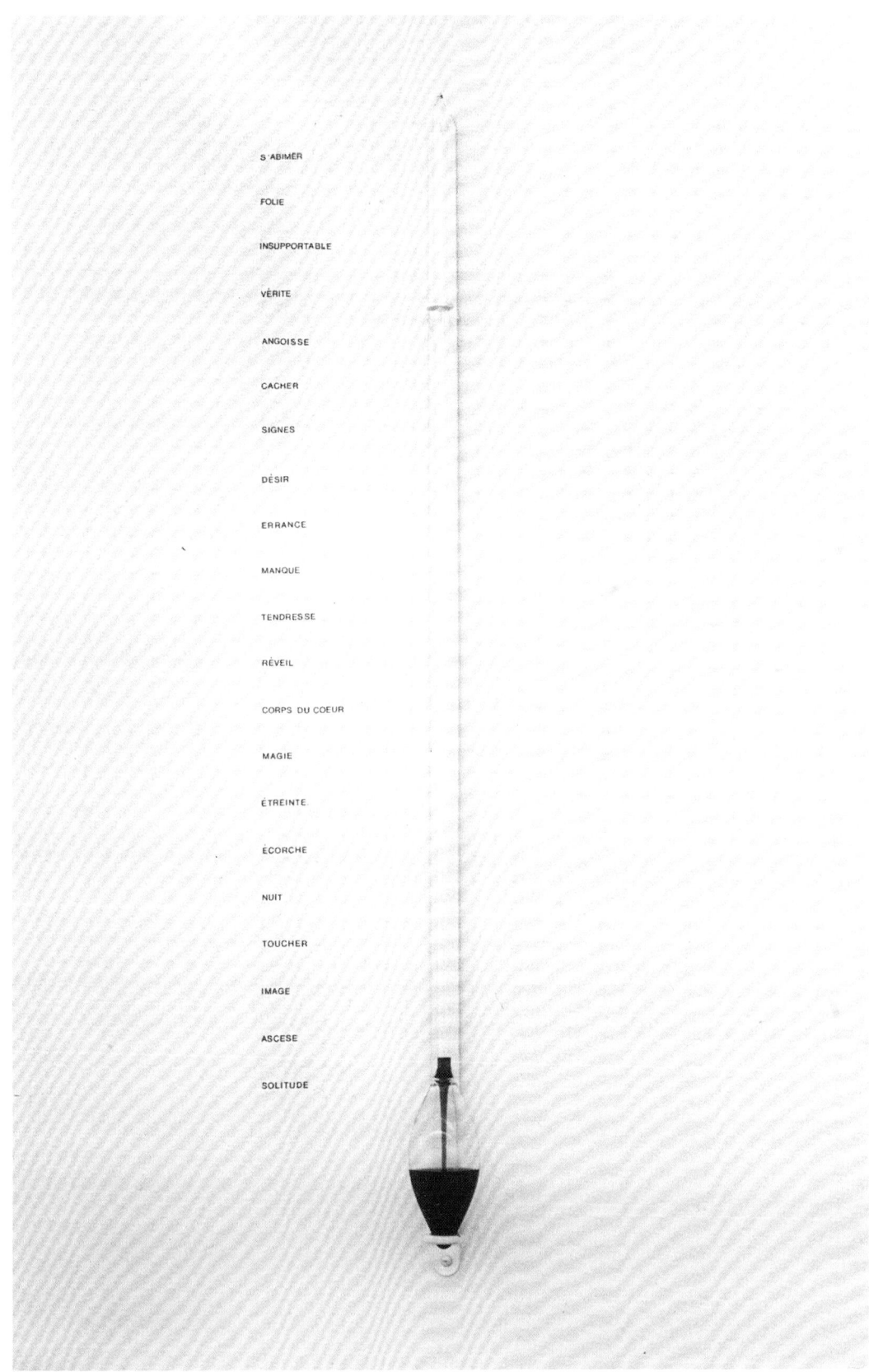

S'ABIMER

FOLIE

INSUPPORTABLE

VÉRITE

ANGOISSE

CACHER

SIGNES

DÉSIR

ERRANCE

MANQUE

TENDRESSE

RÉVEIL

CORPS DU COEUR

MAGIE

ÉTREINTE

ÉCORCHE

NUIT

TOUCHER

IMAGE

ASCÈSE

SOLITUDE

MAGIE
UMARMEN
BERÜHREN
HAUTLOS
NACHT
BILD
ASKESE
EINSAMKEIT

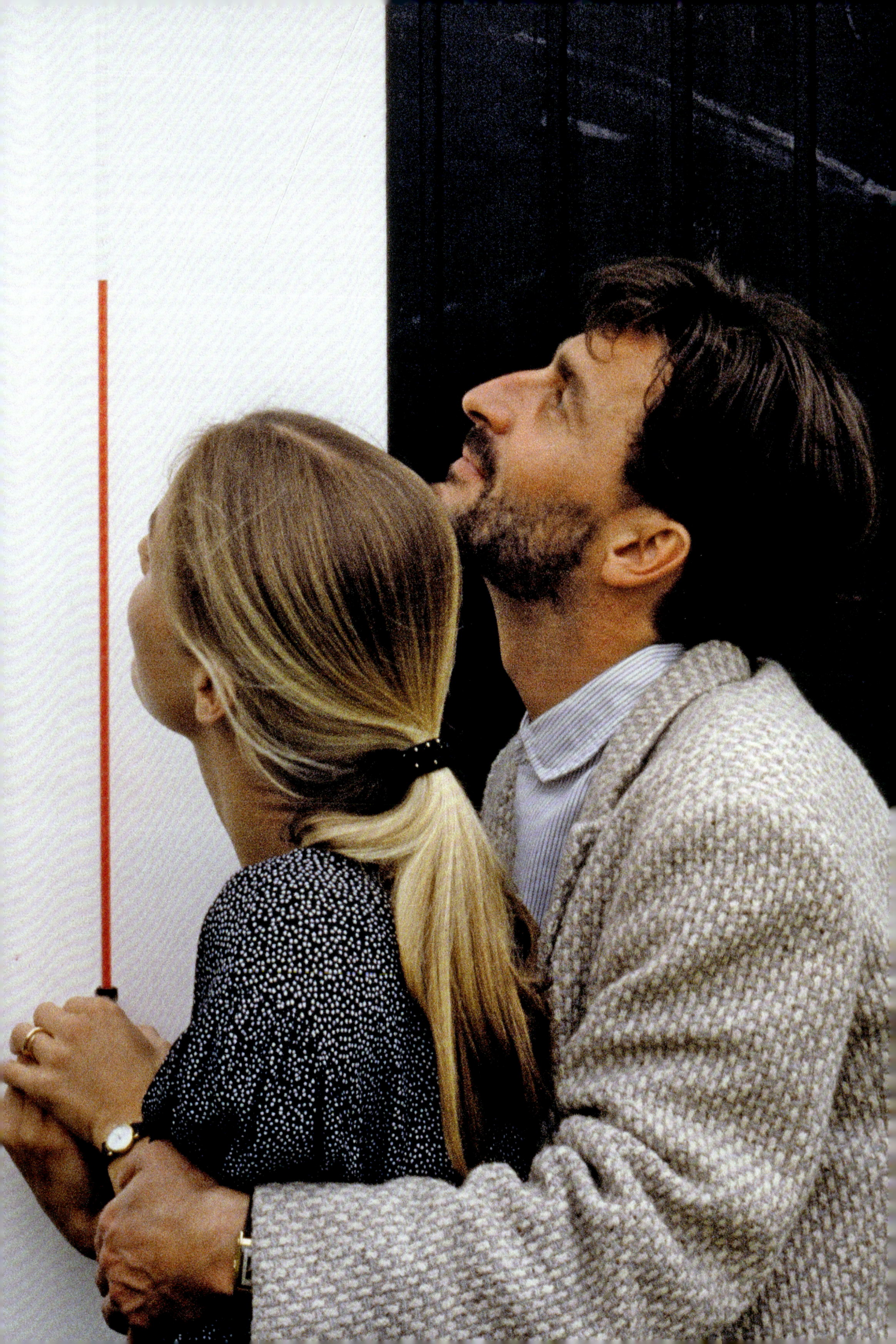

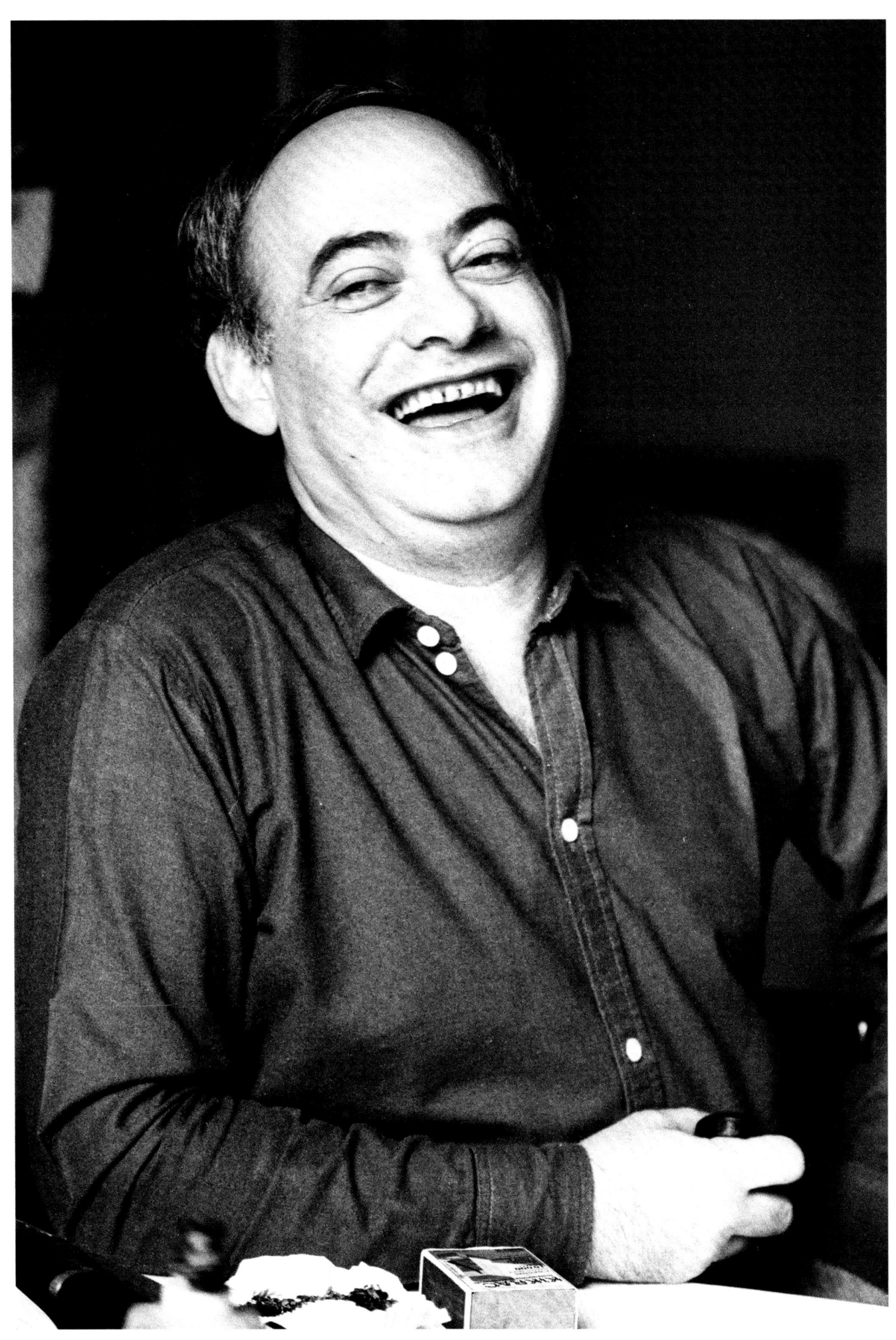

Roland Topor

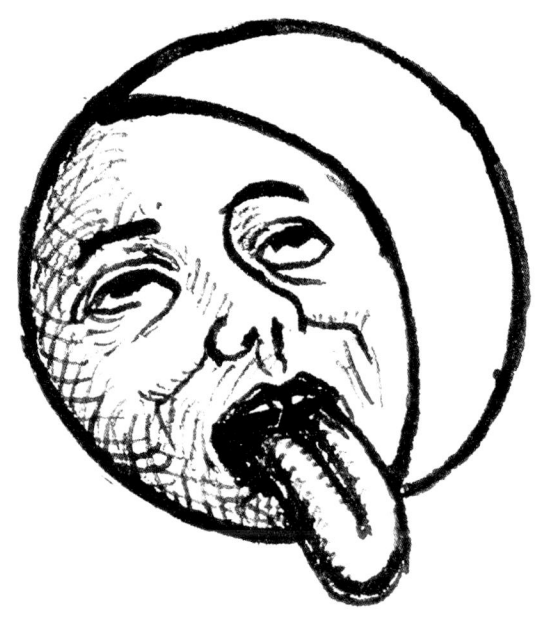

J'espère que les pêcheurs viendront en foule à
luna-luna pour y célébrer le culte des Dieux (pour du beurre)
Roland Topor

Roland Topor

Born: January 7, 1938, in Paris, France.
Died: April 16, 1997, in Paris.

Illustrator, satirist, stage designer, playwright,
novelist, object artist.

Roland Topor designed **Toporrama** for *Luna Luna*,
a school of night stories and bad dreams. The sounds
heard inside the building are the intimate sounds of
mating whales.

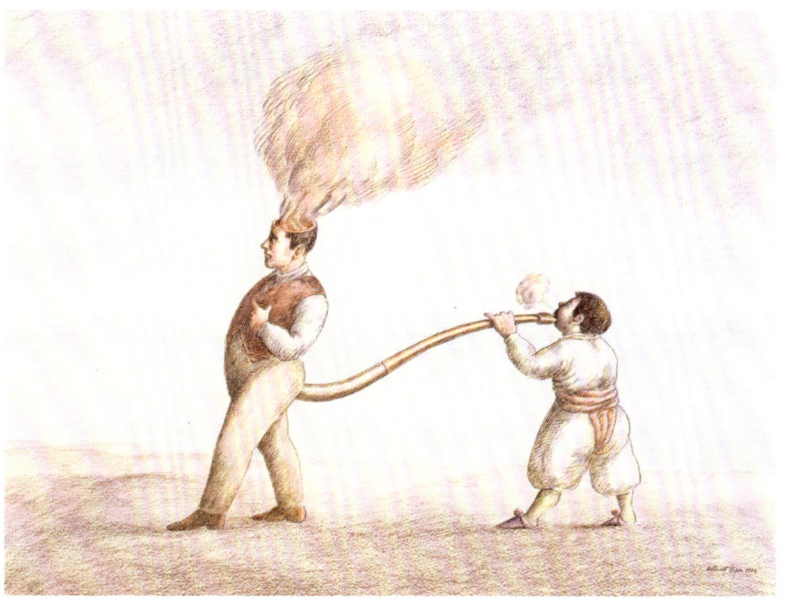

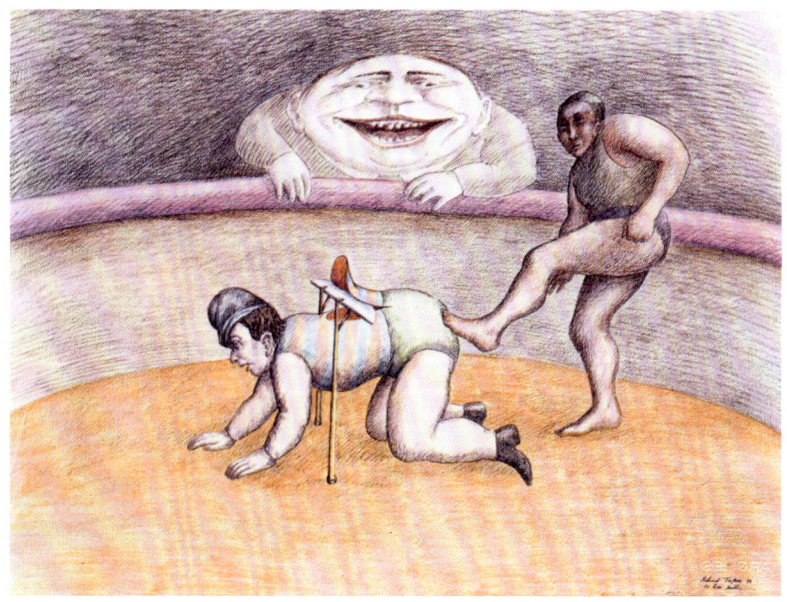

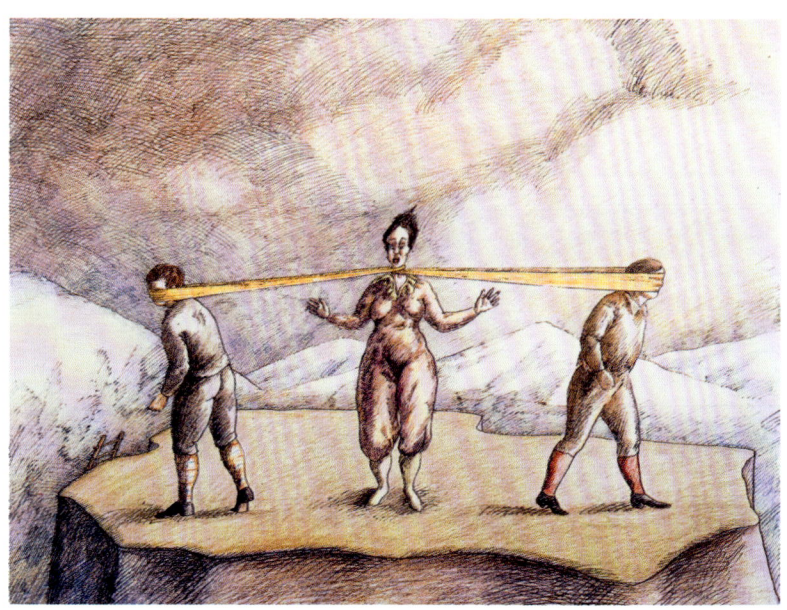

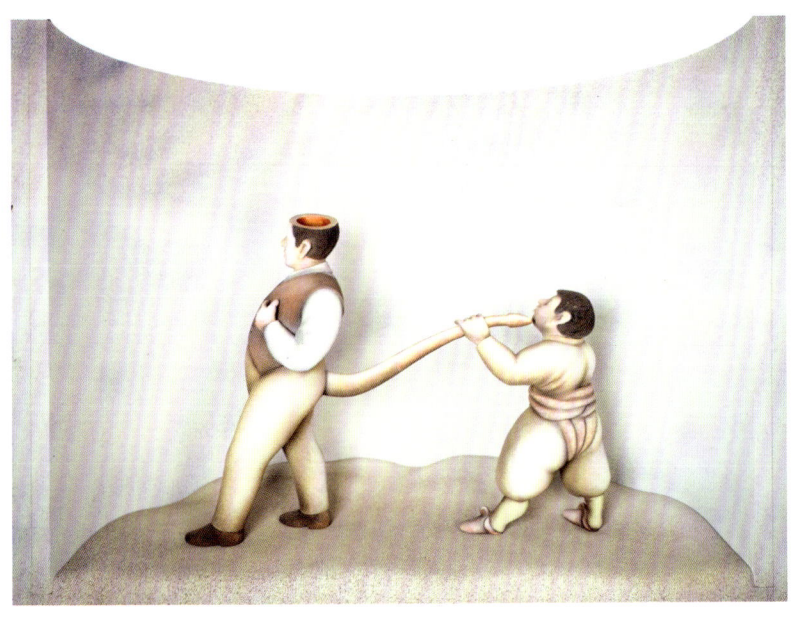

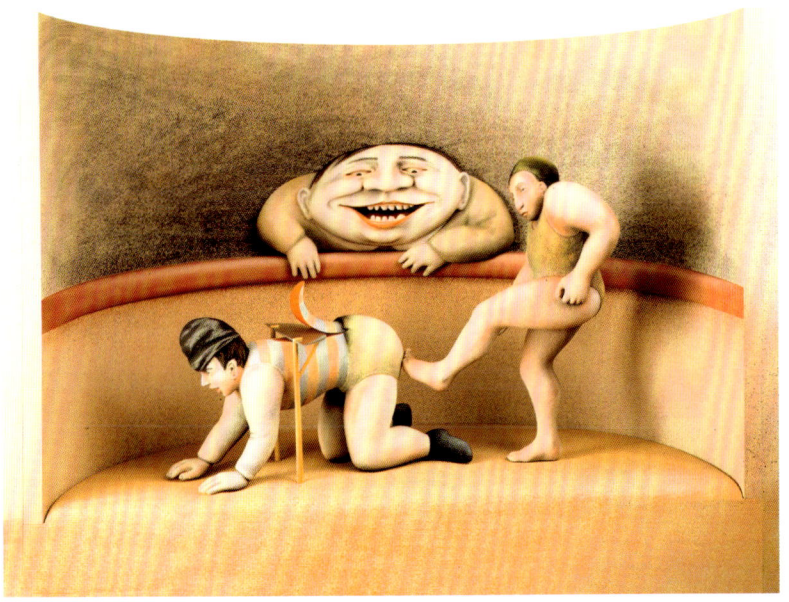

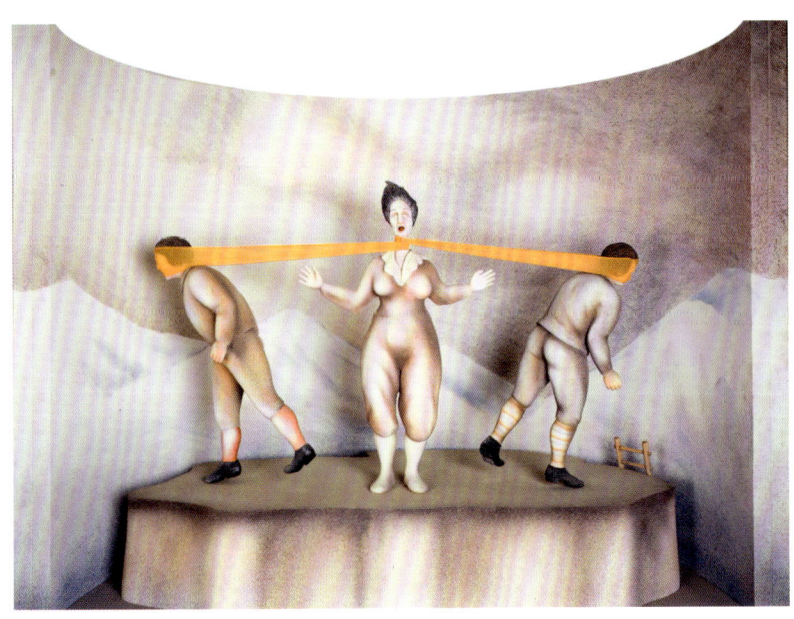

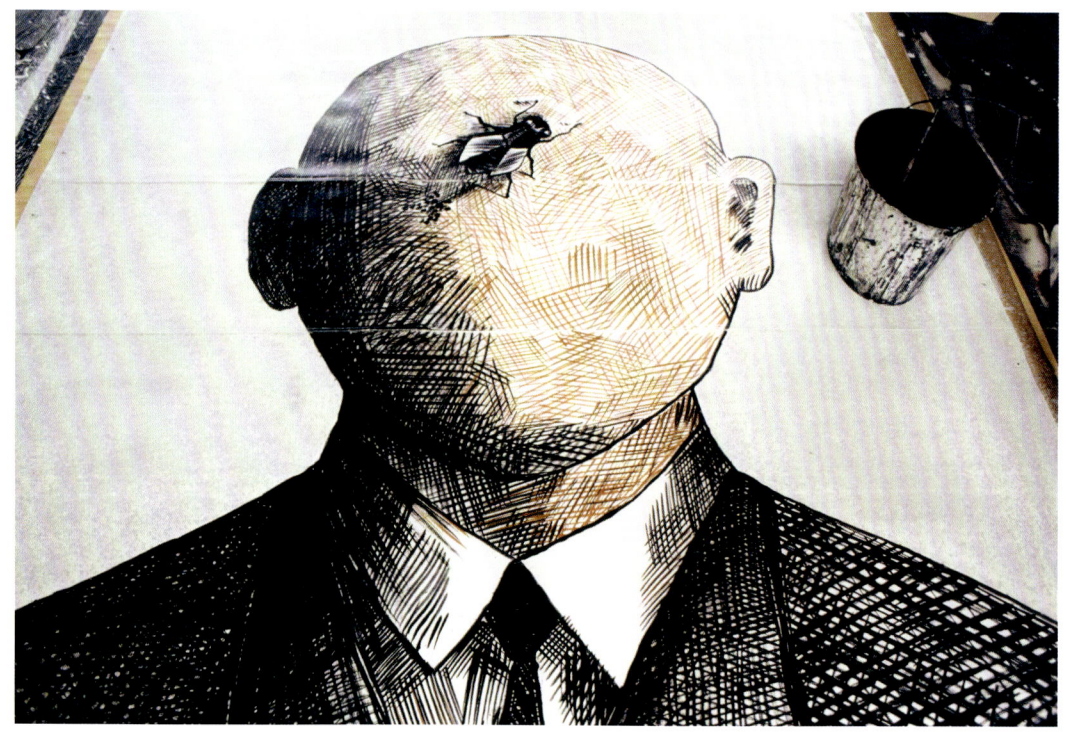

*Vermin*

*The Polonaise*

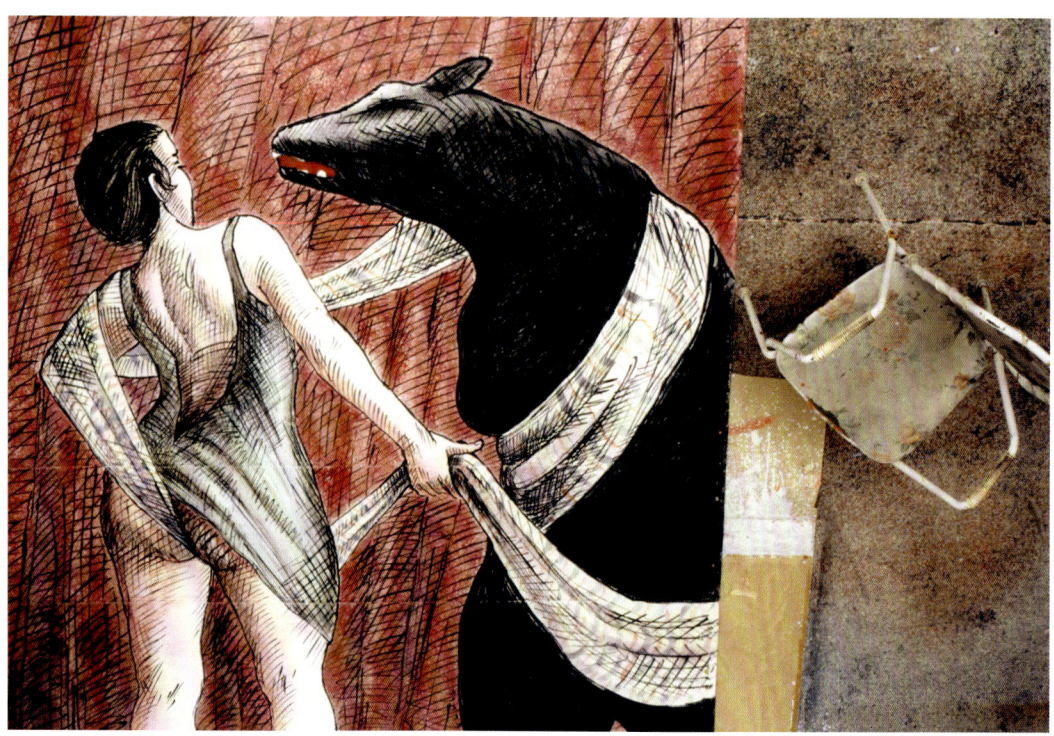

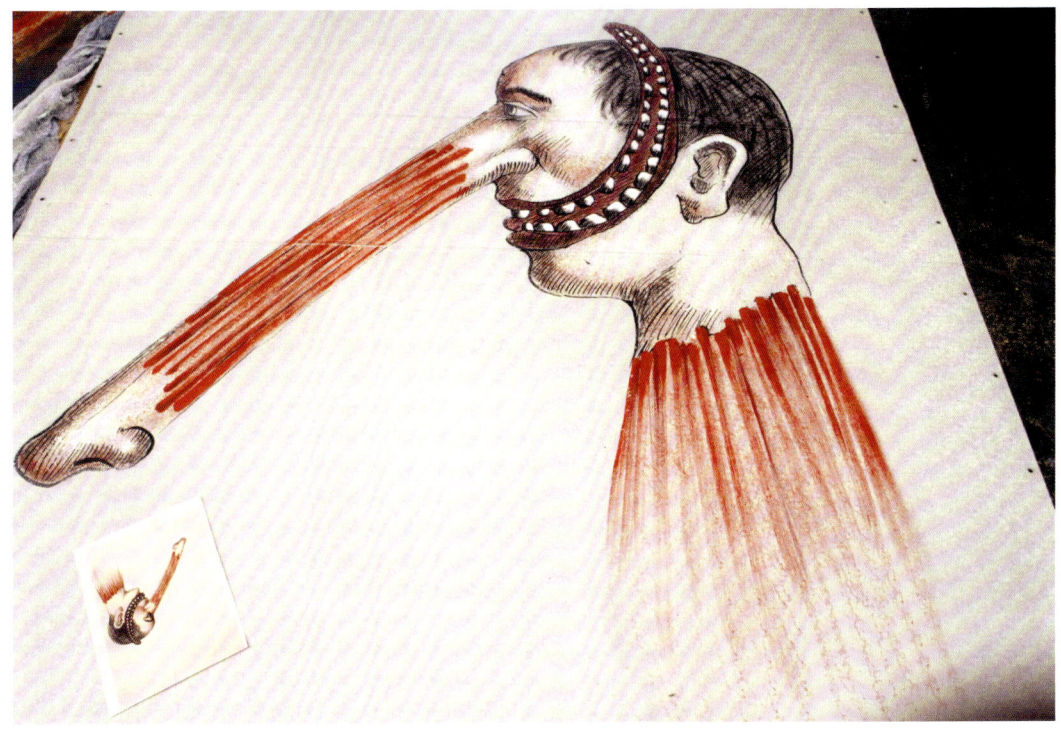

*A fool*

*Happy-End*

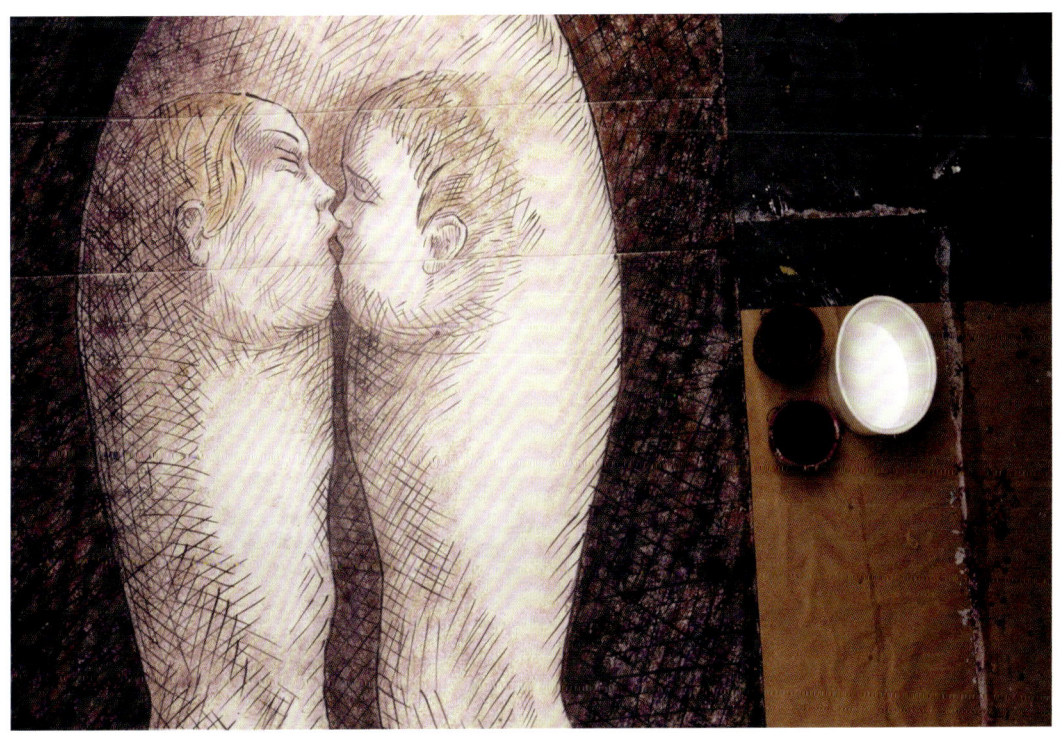

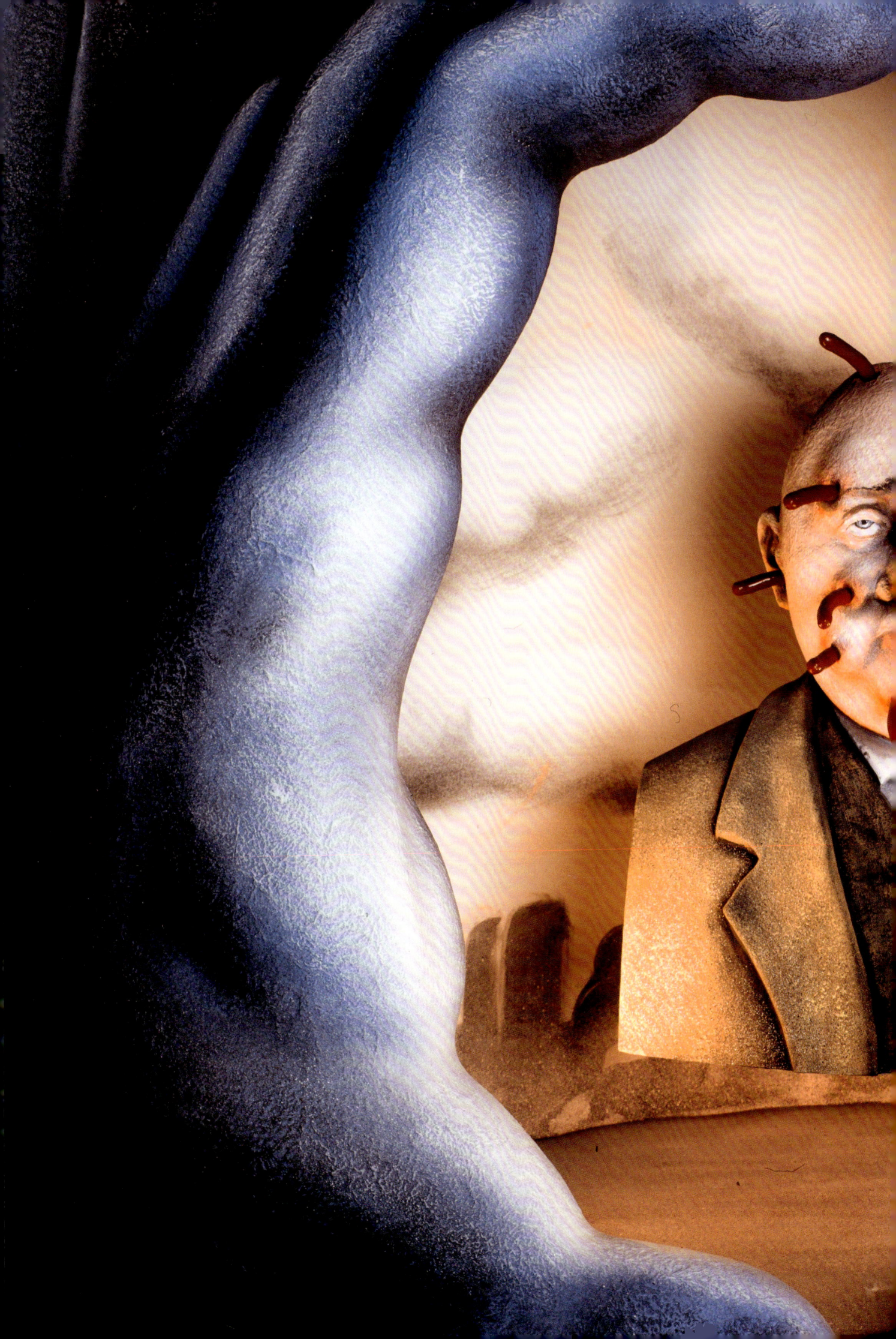

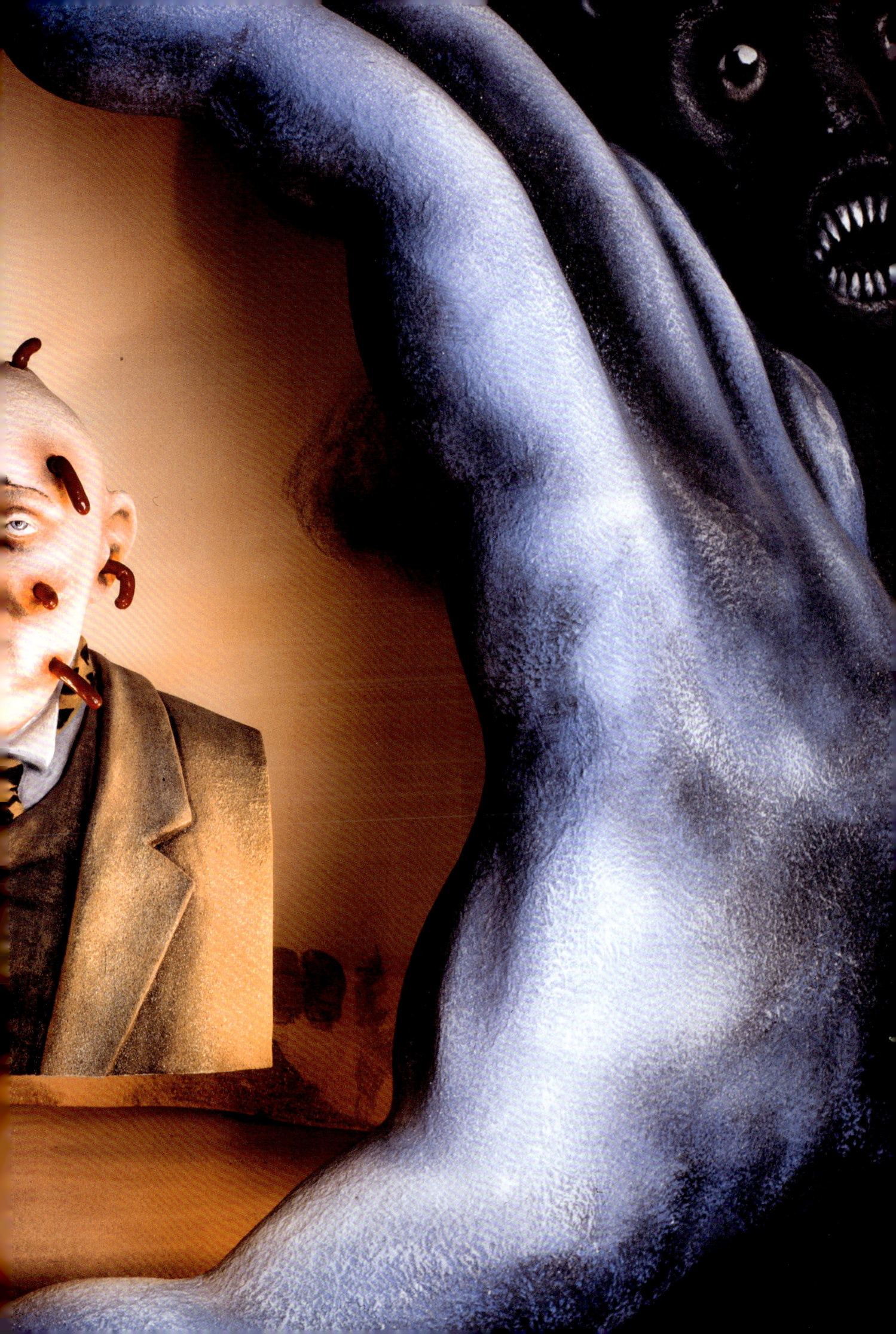

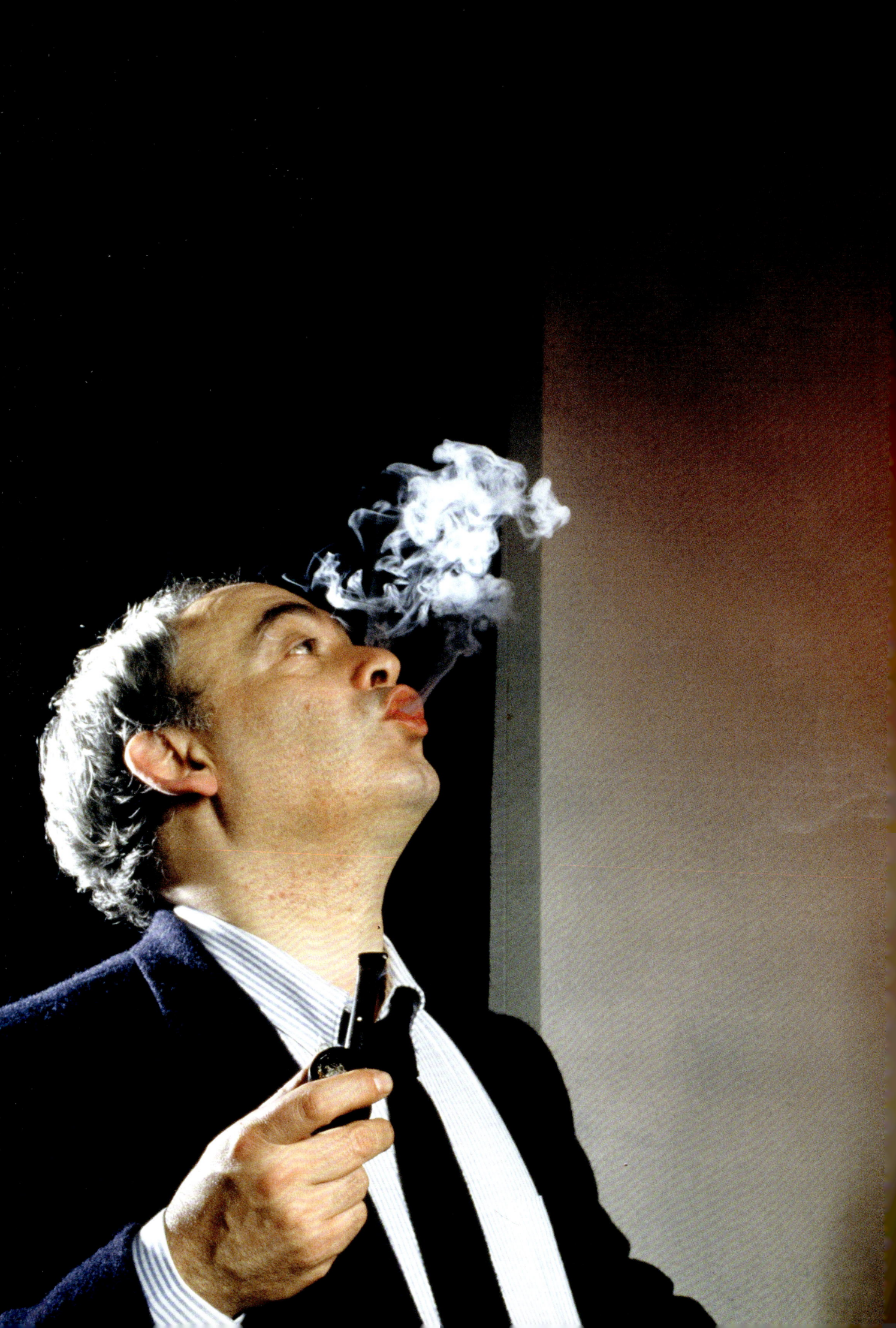

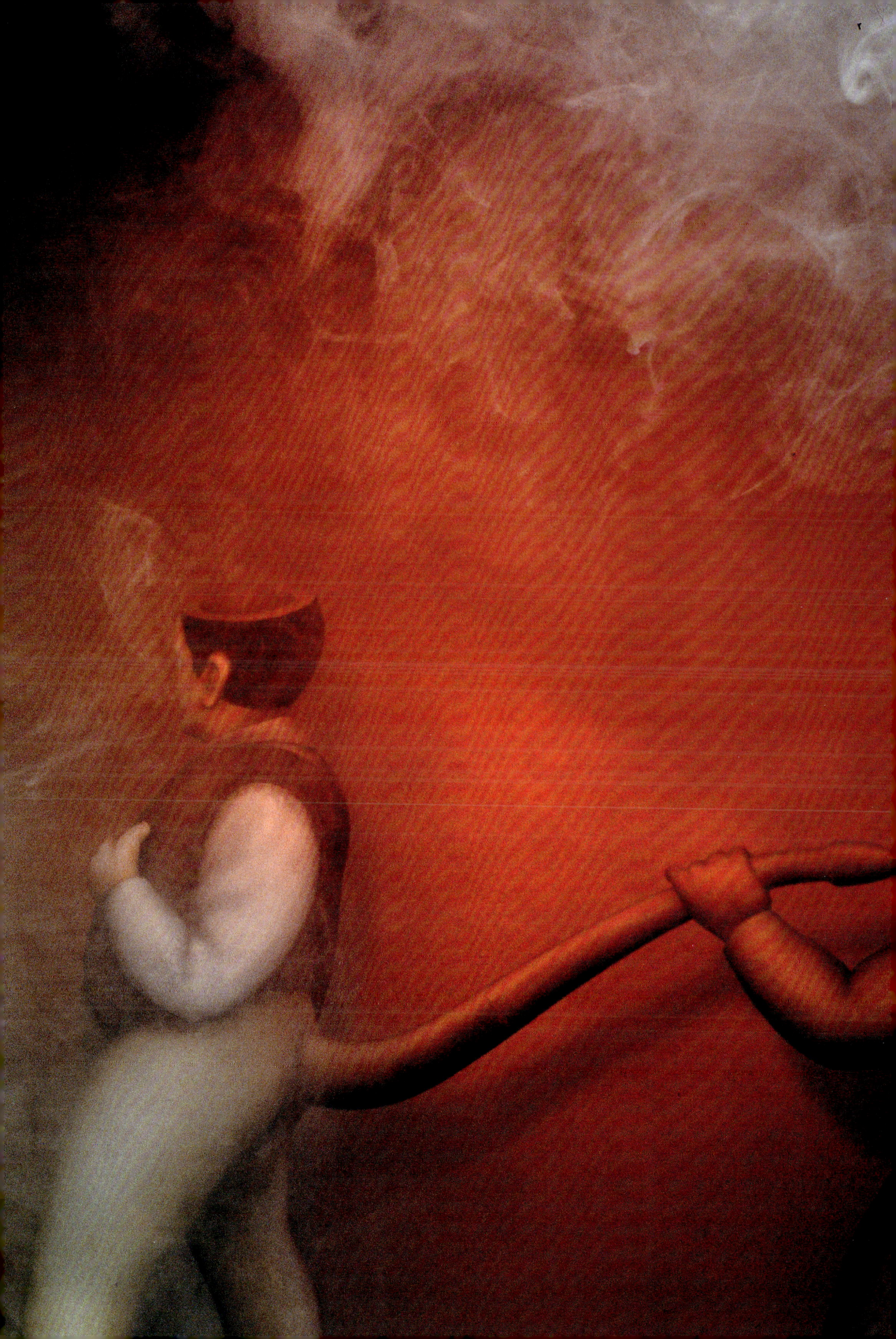

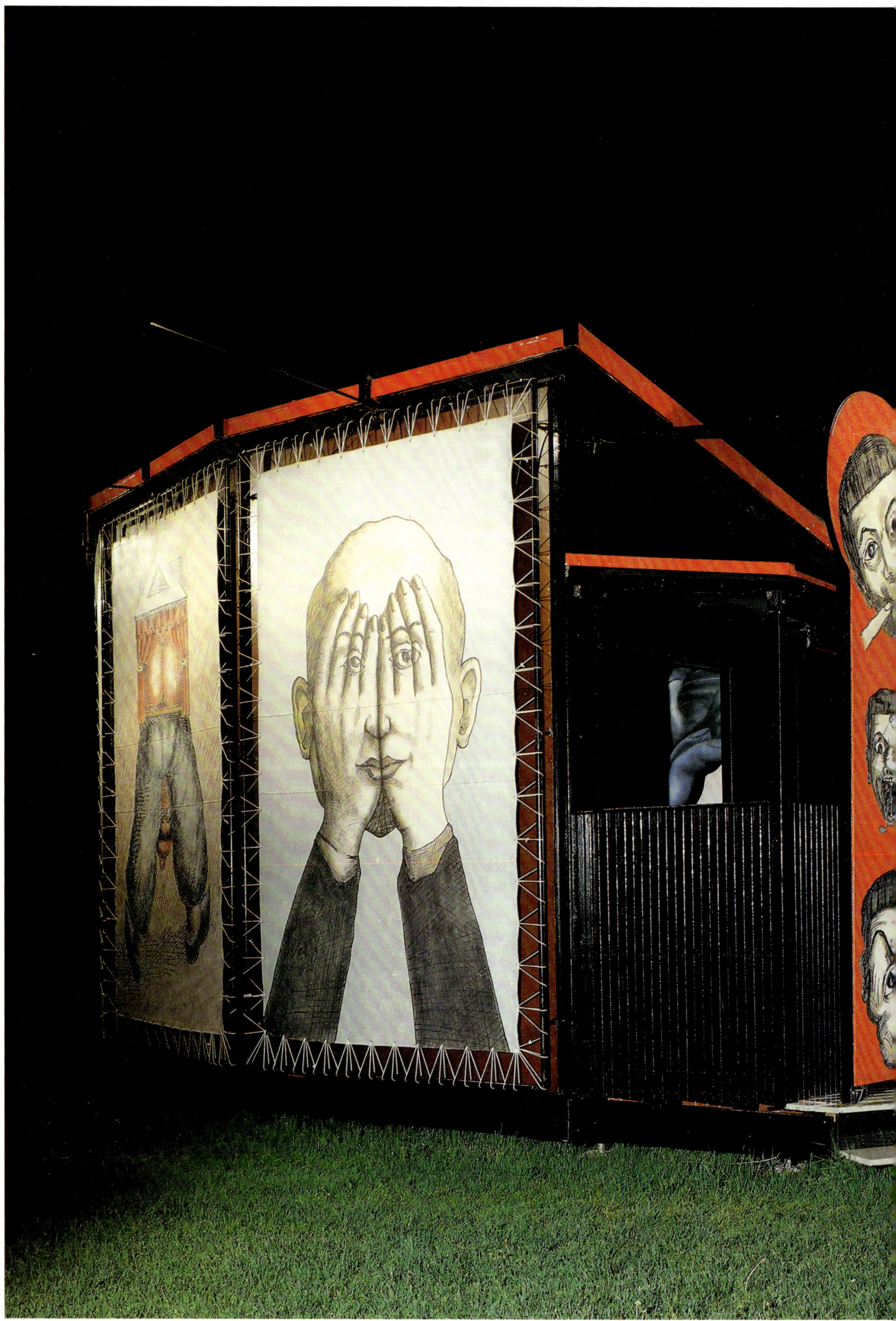

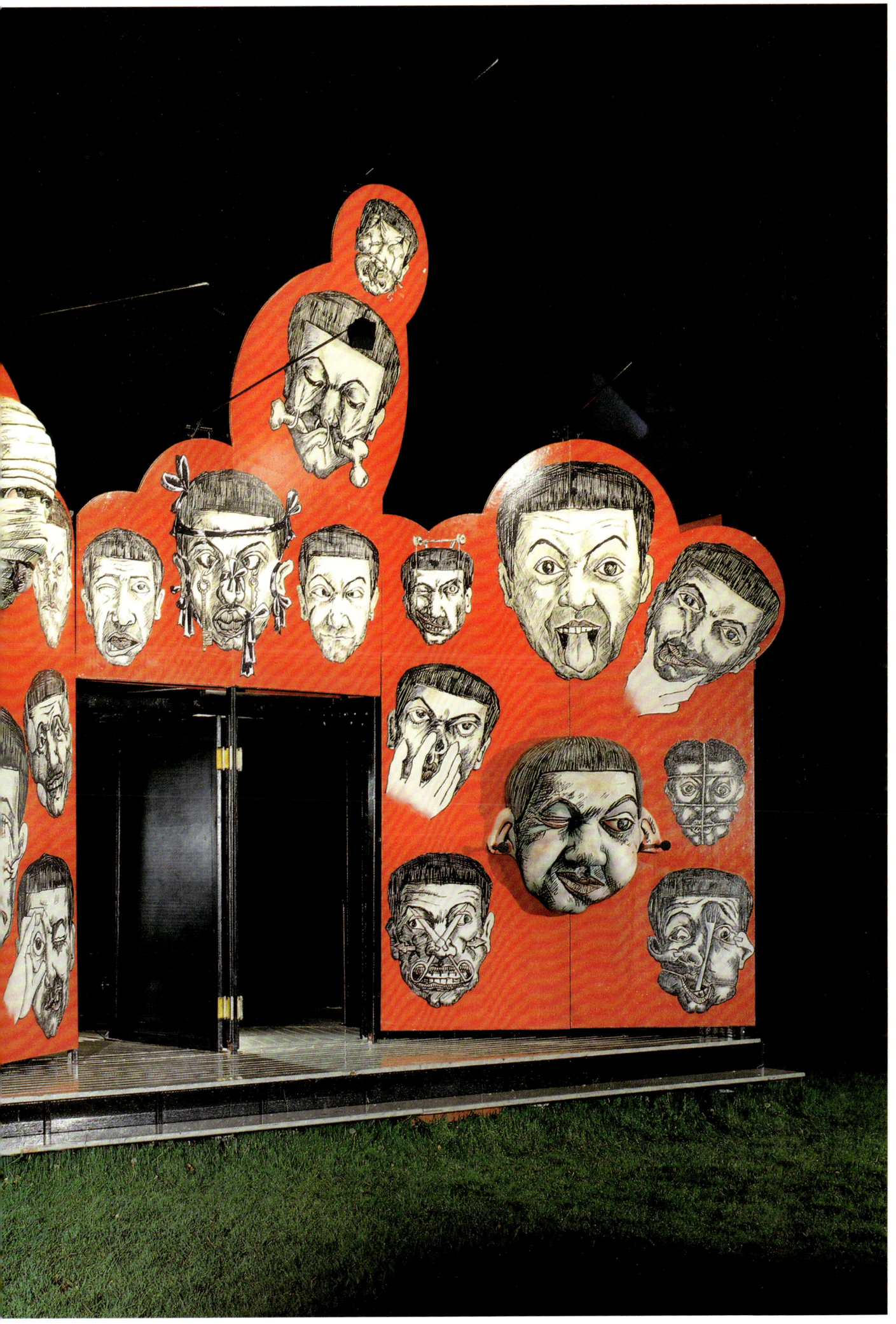

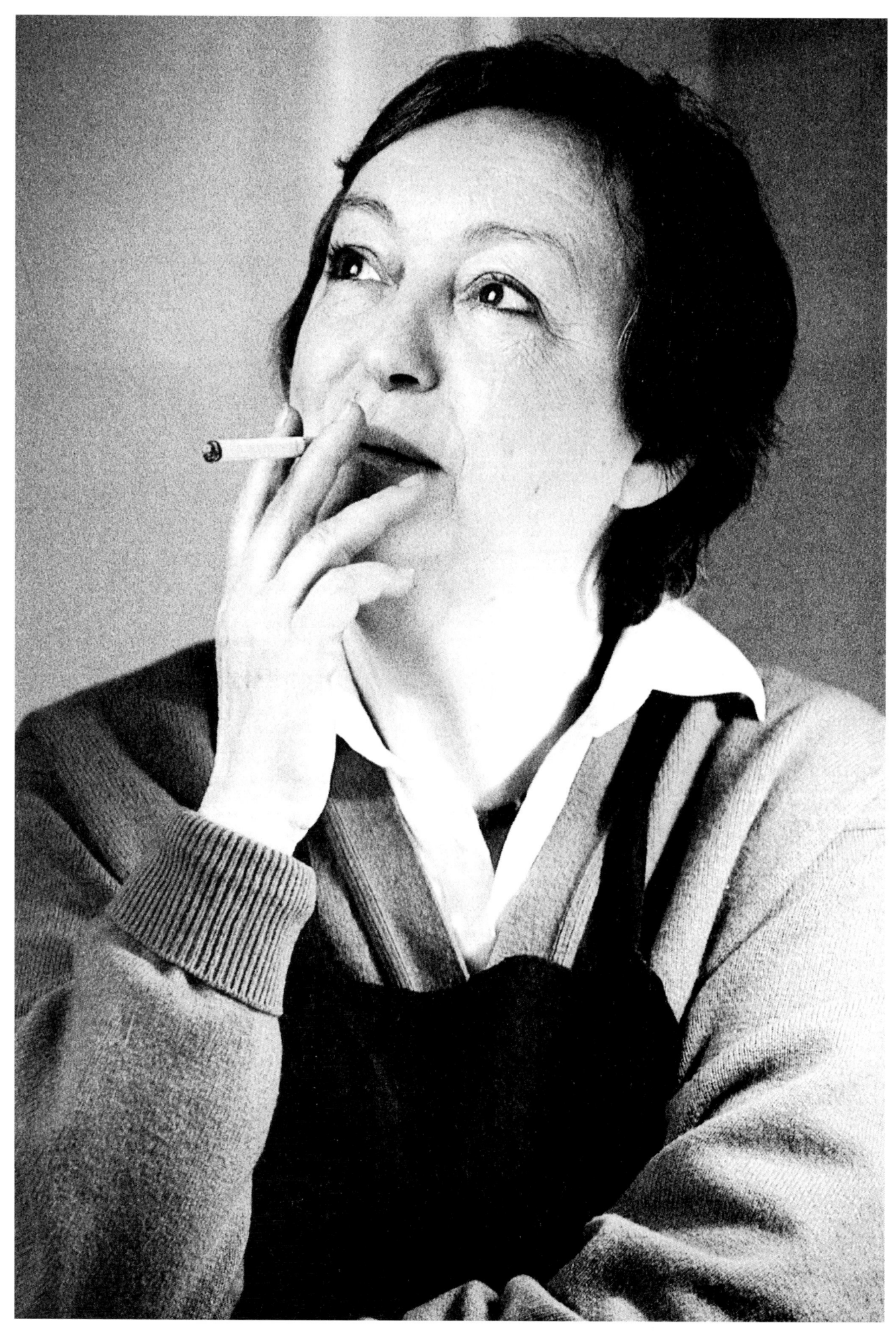

Gertie Fröhlich

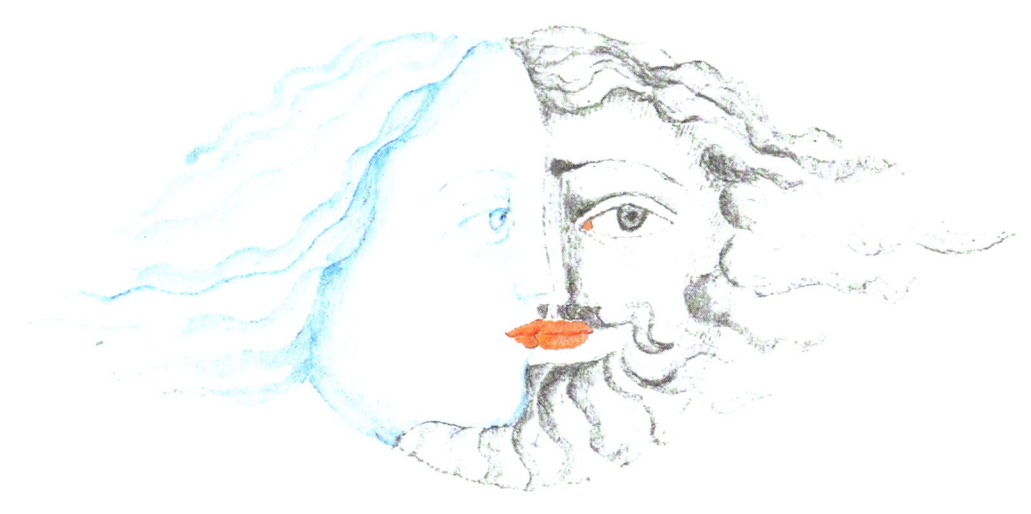

*Luna Luna; ein Kuss von Mond zu Mond*
*gertie fröhlich*

Gertie Fröhlich

Born: June 29, 1930, in Klastor, Czechoslovakia (now Slovakia).
Died: May 17, 2020, in Baden, Austria.

Painter, illustrator, food artist.

Gertie Fröhlich designed food art and a **Gingerbread Booth** for *Luna Luna*; a tumbling Greek temple reveals edible sculptures.

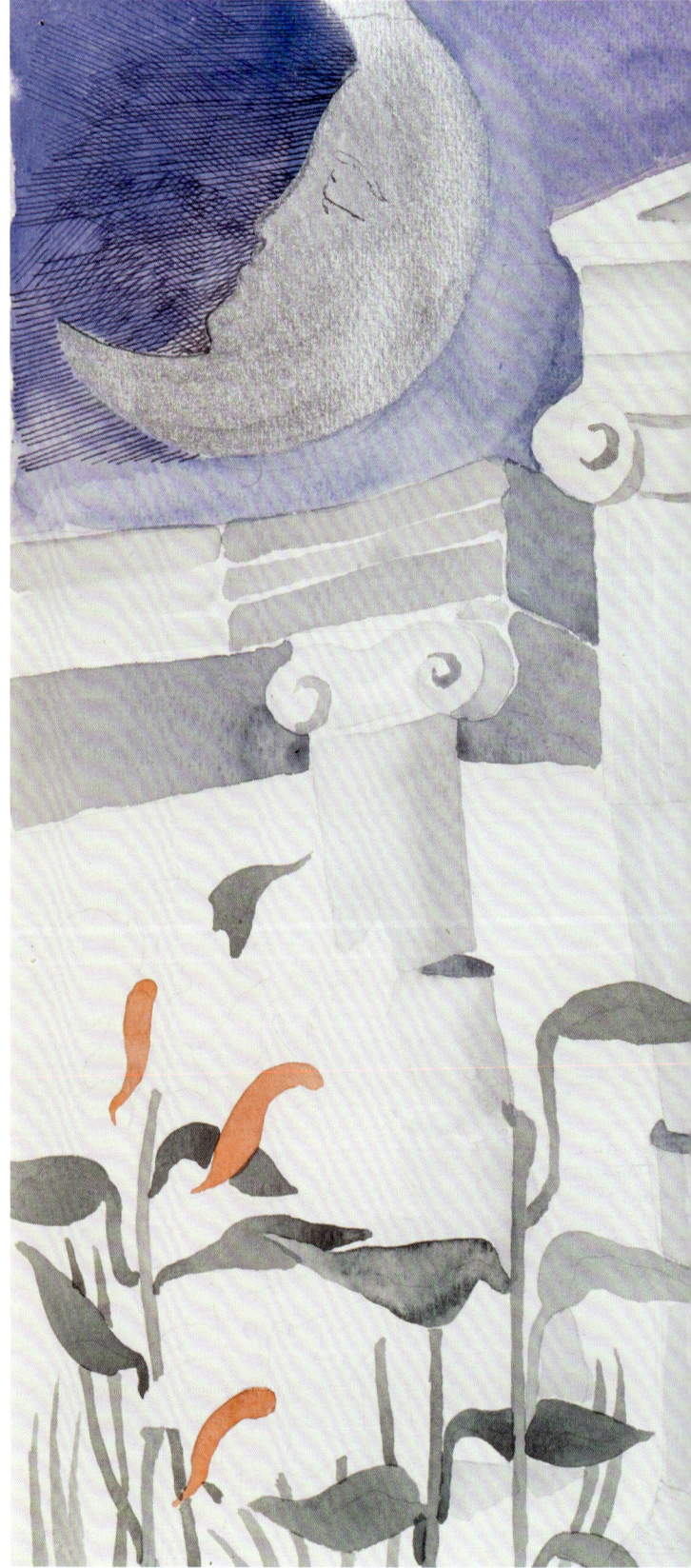

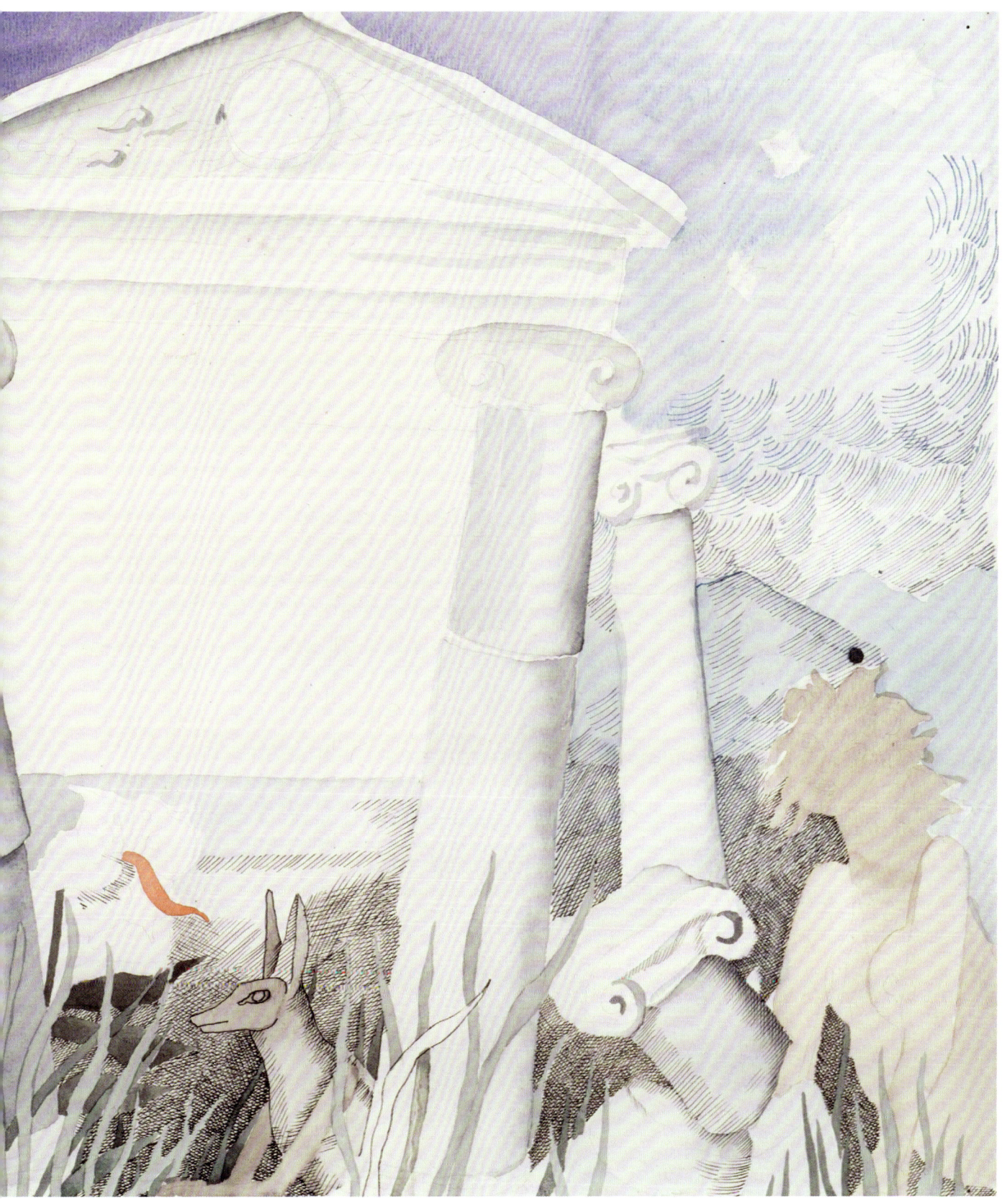

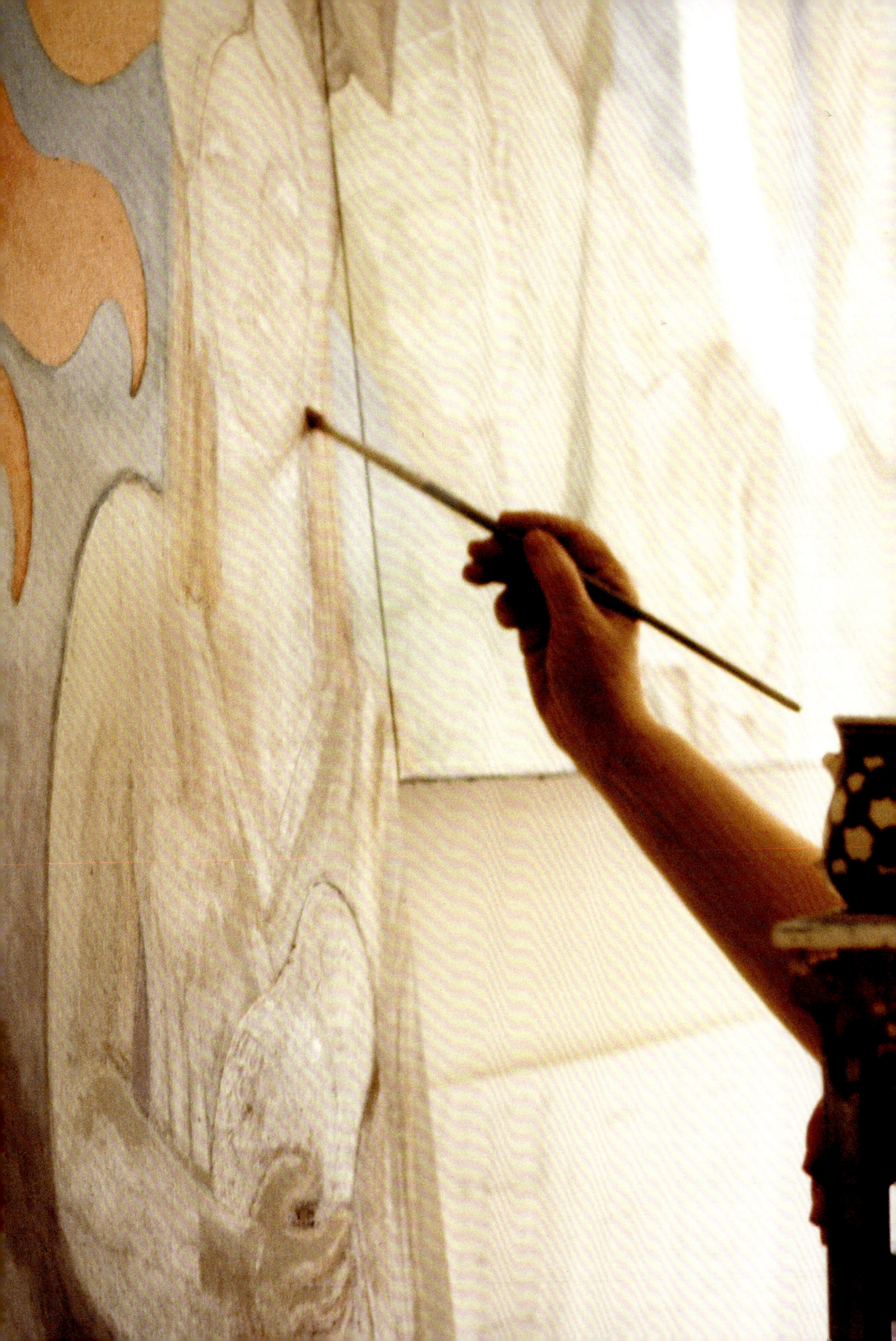

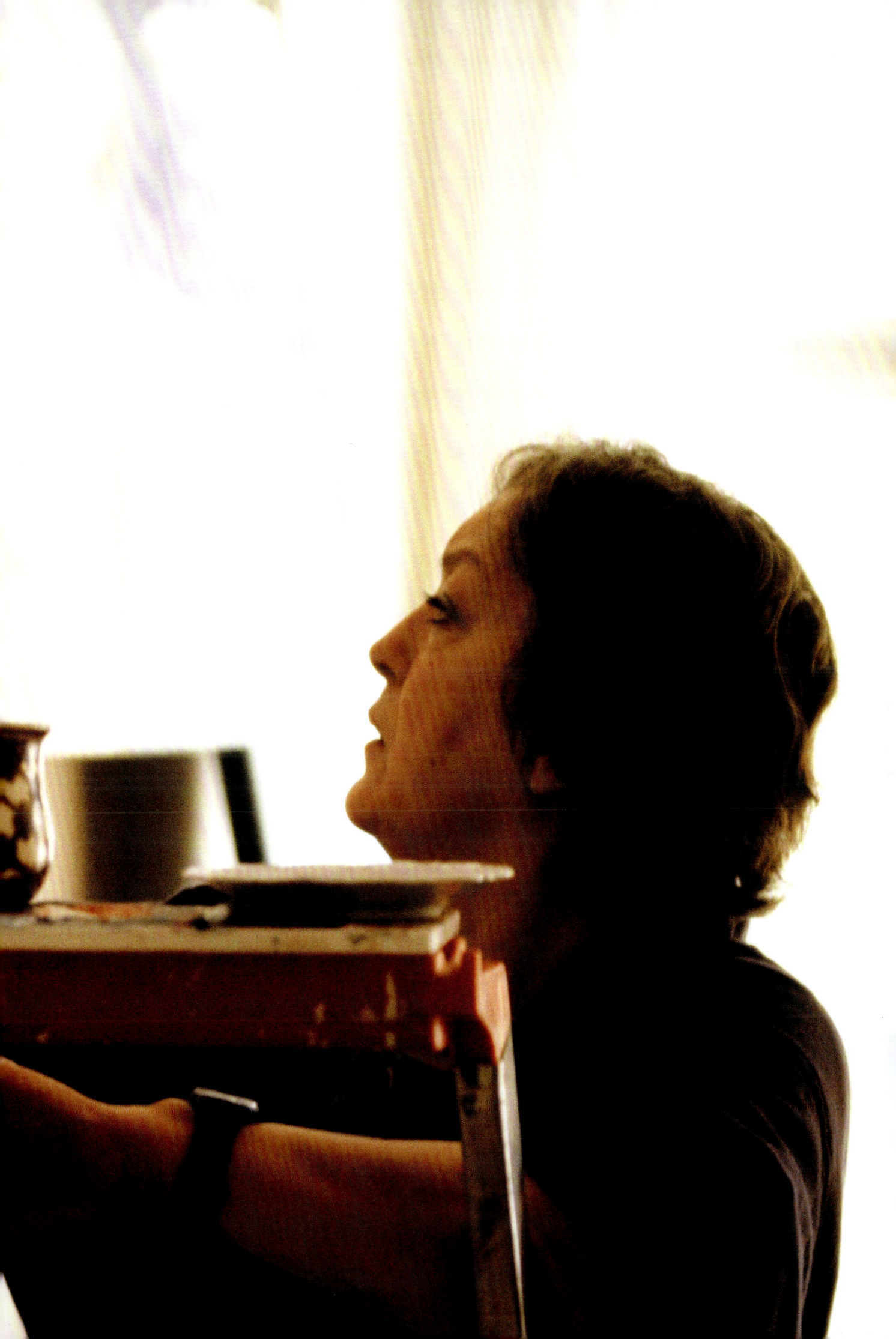

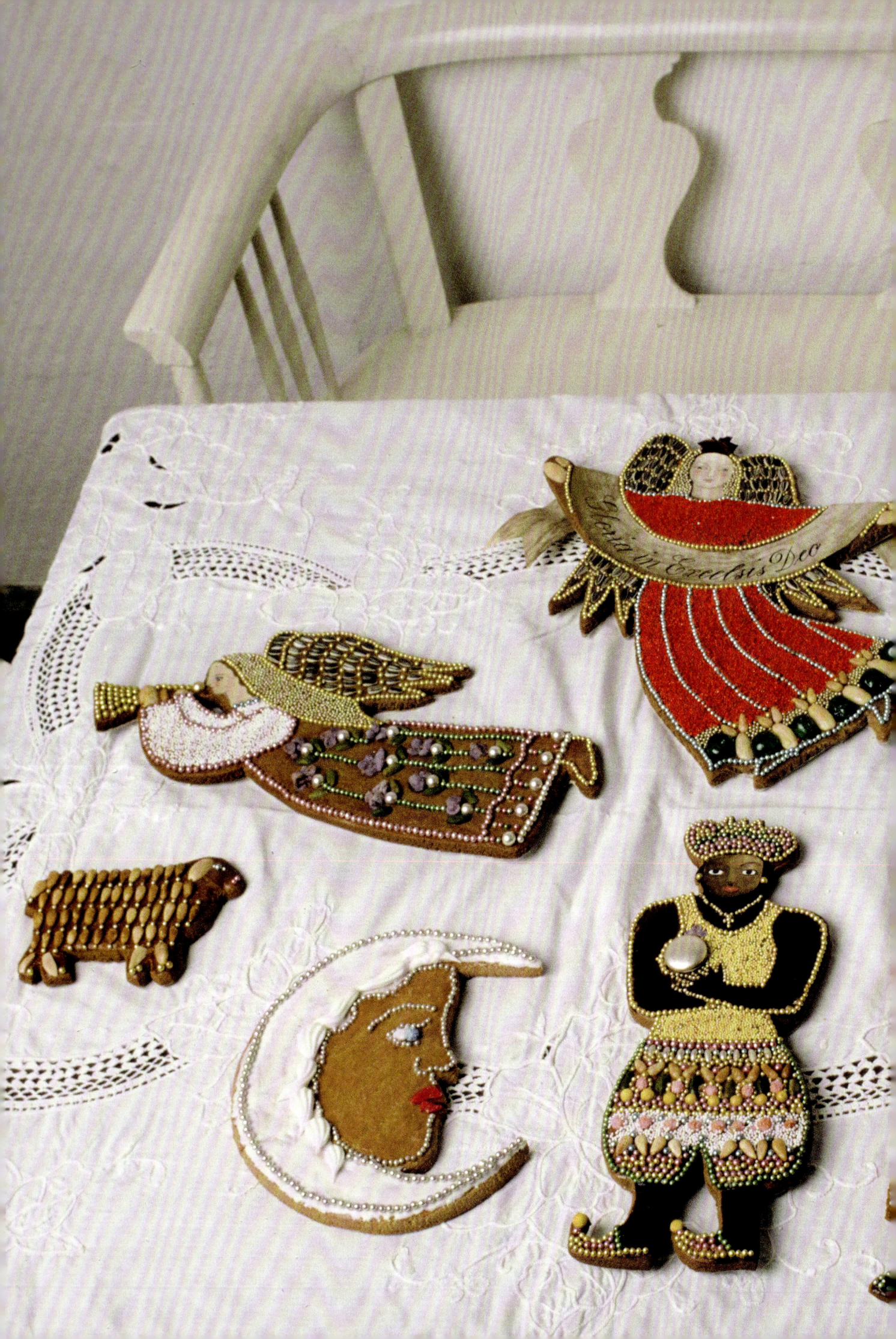

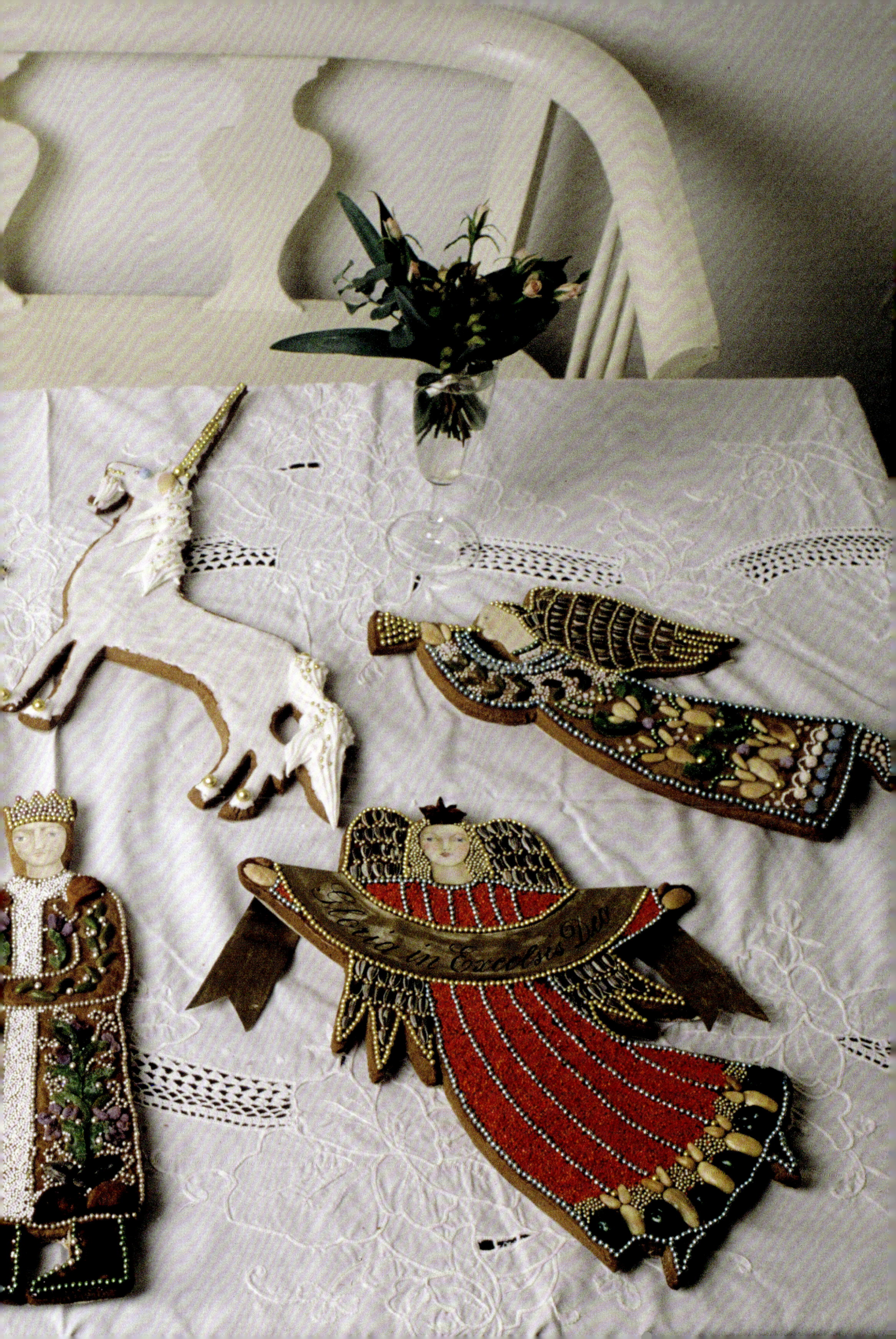

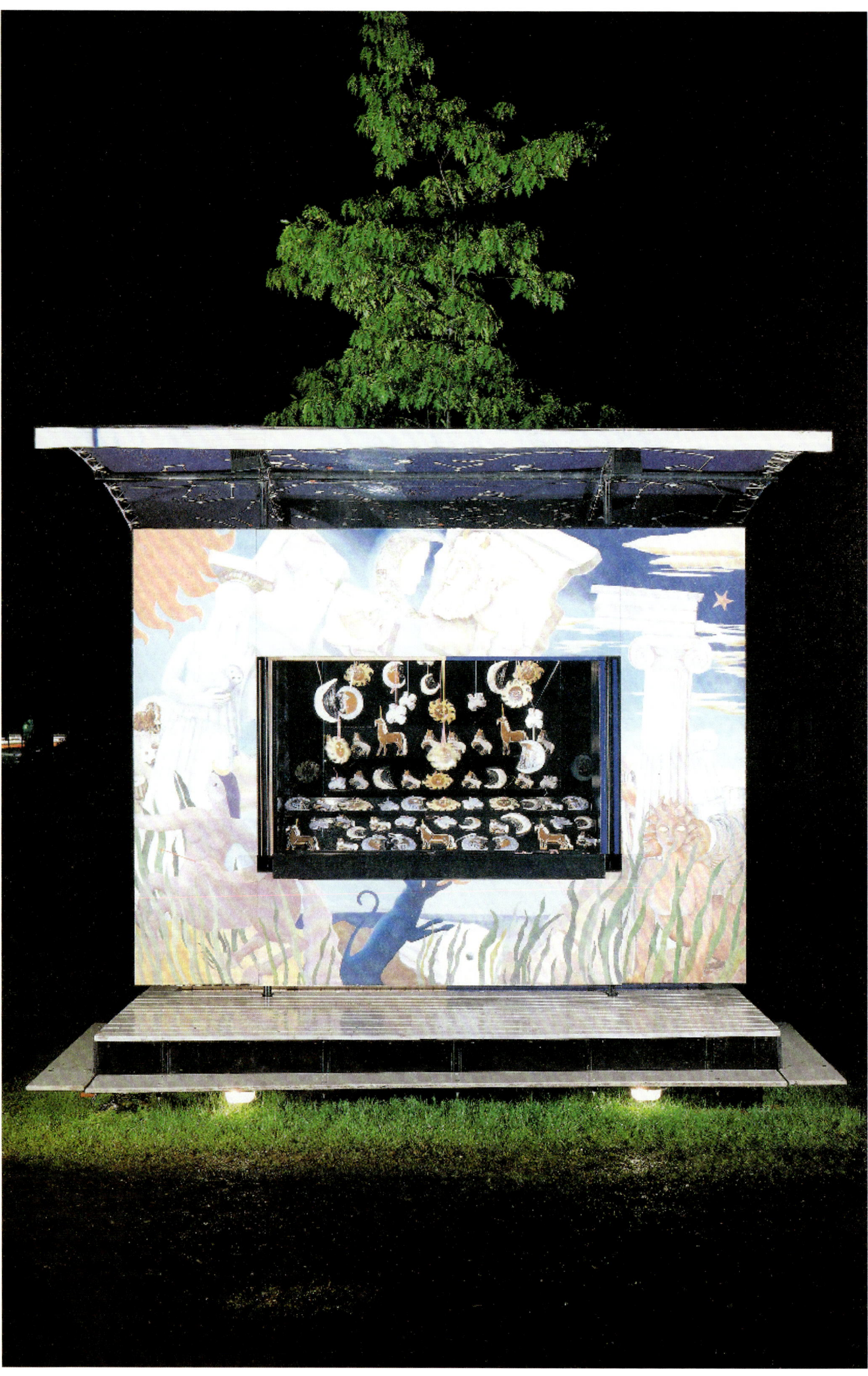

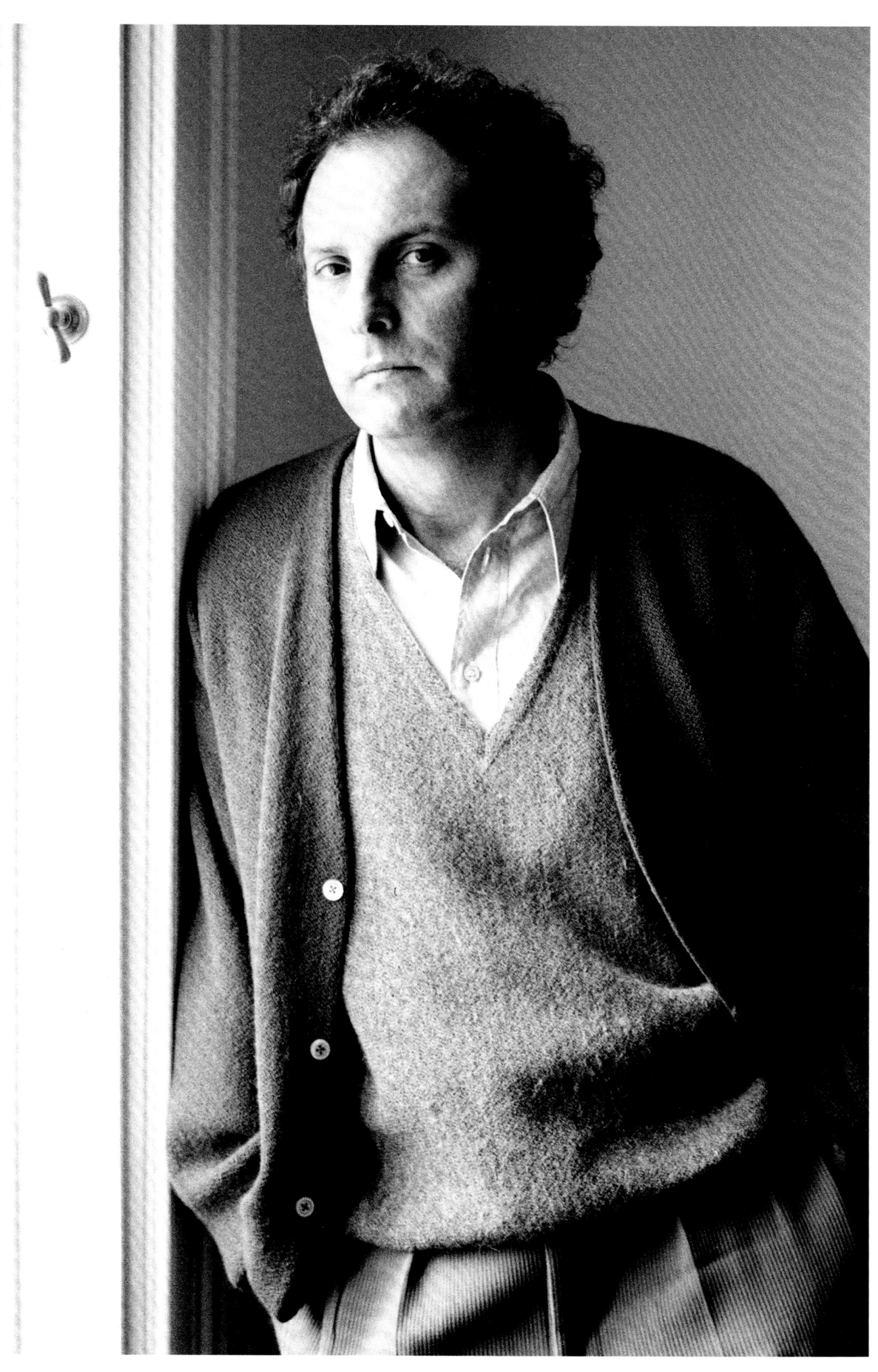

Christian Ludwig Attersee

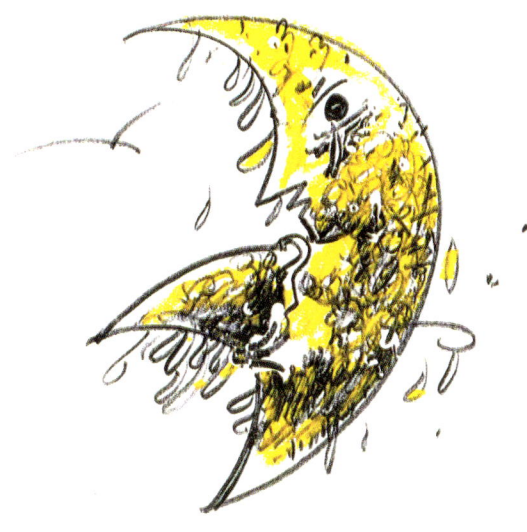

LUNA LUNA, SEIFE FÜRS HERZ,
DIE BESTE

Höllerer

Christian Ludwig Attersee

Born: August 28, 1940, in Bratislava, Czechoslovakia
(now Slovakia).

Painter, illustrator, actionist, inventor, singer,
composer, object designer, poet, stage designer,
filmmaker.

Christian Ludwig Attersee designed **boat swings
with a landscape** for *Luna Luna*. A bizarre
mountain world forms an area where boats move
between painted underwater worlds. The musical
accompaniment is provided by Viennese songs sung
by Willi Forst, Hans Moser, and Paul Hörbiger.

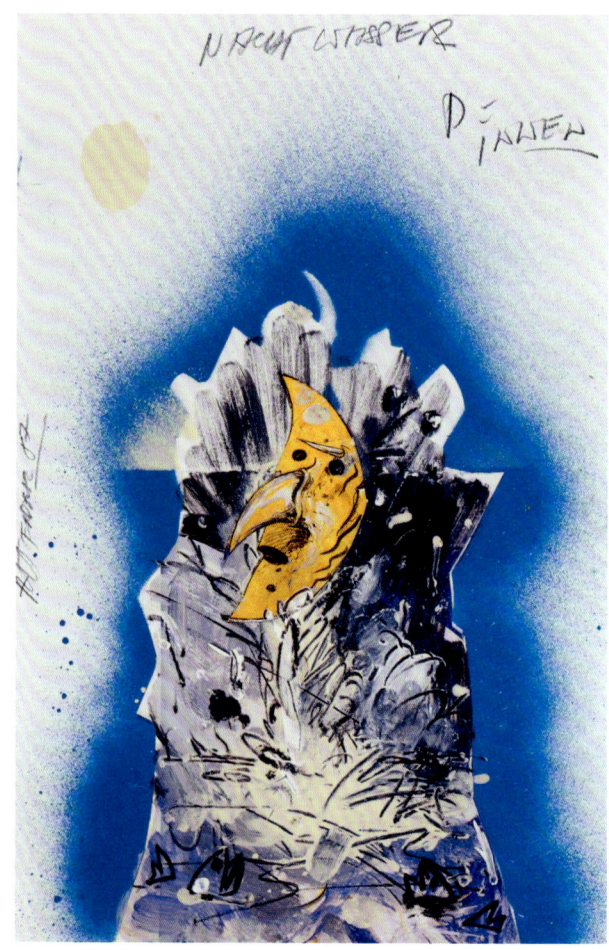

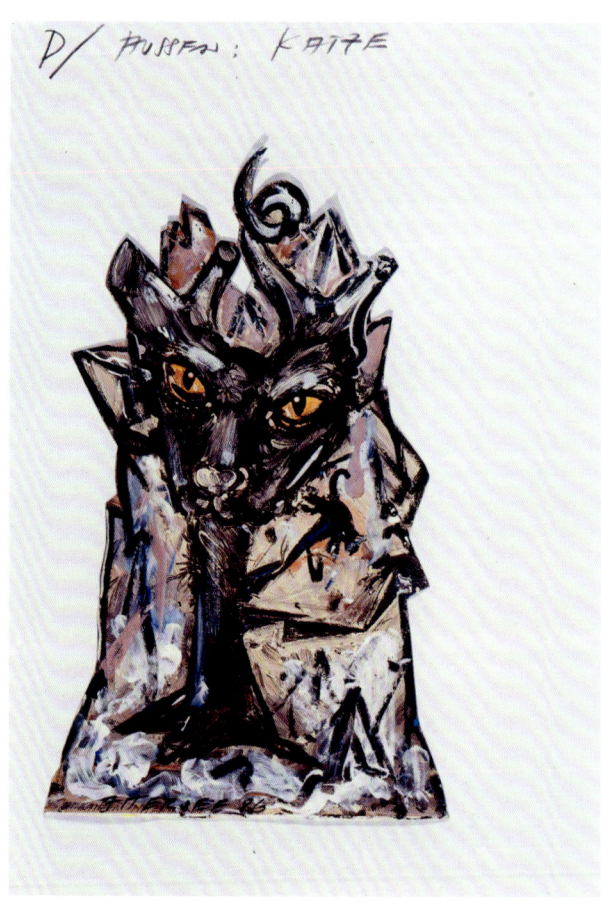

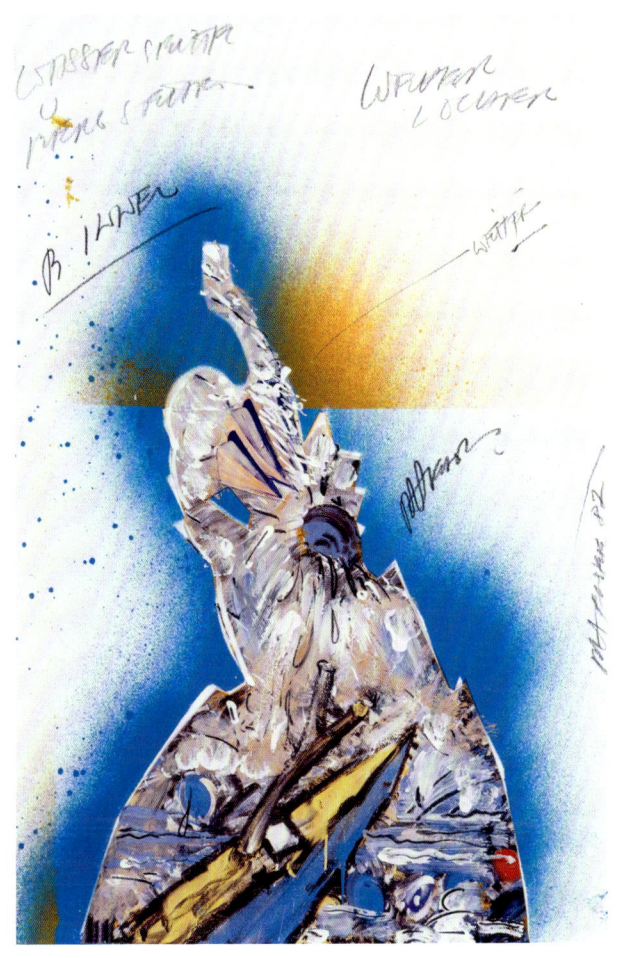

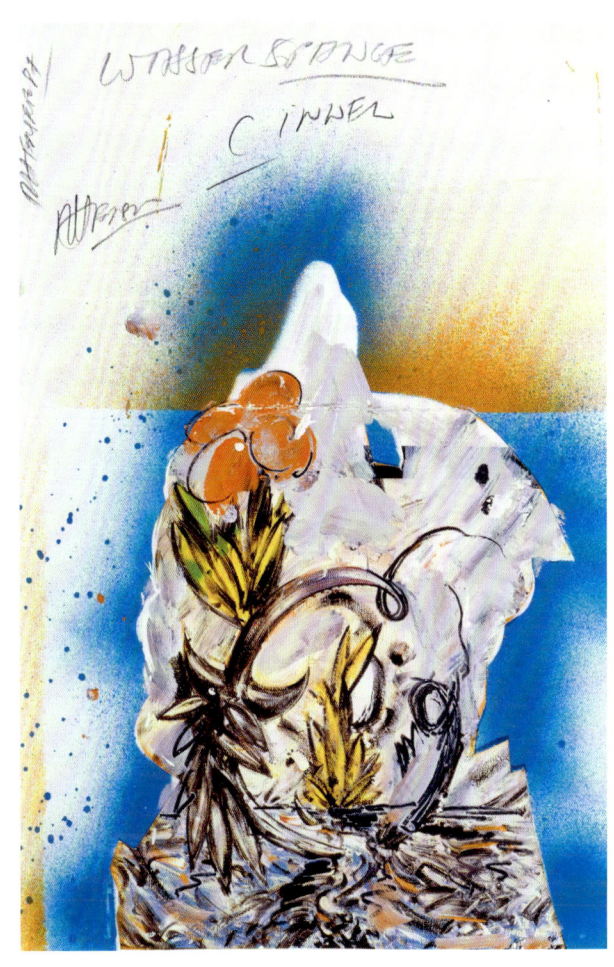

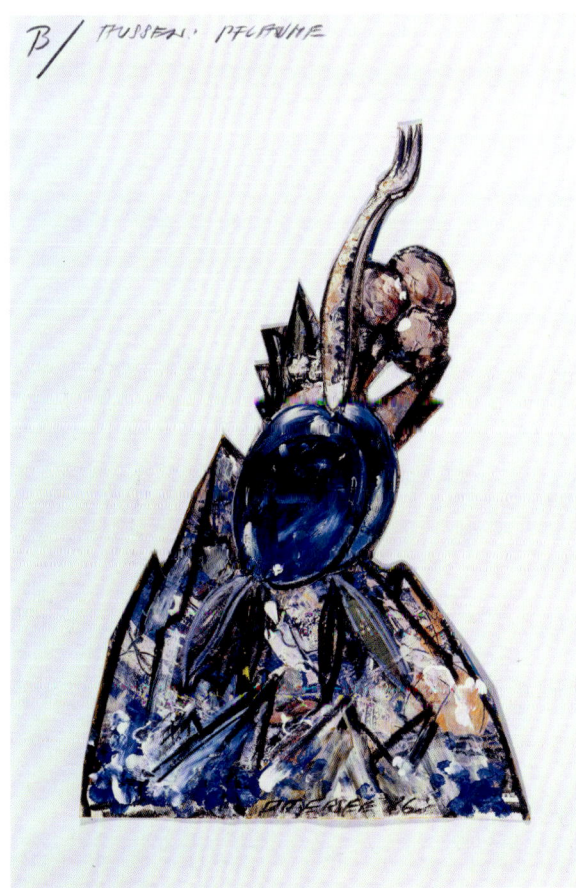

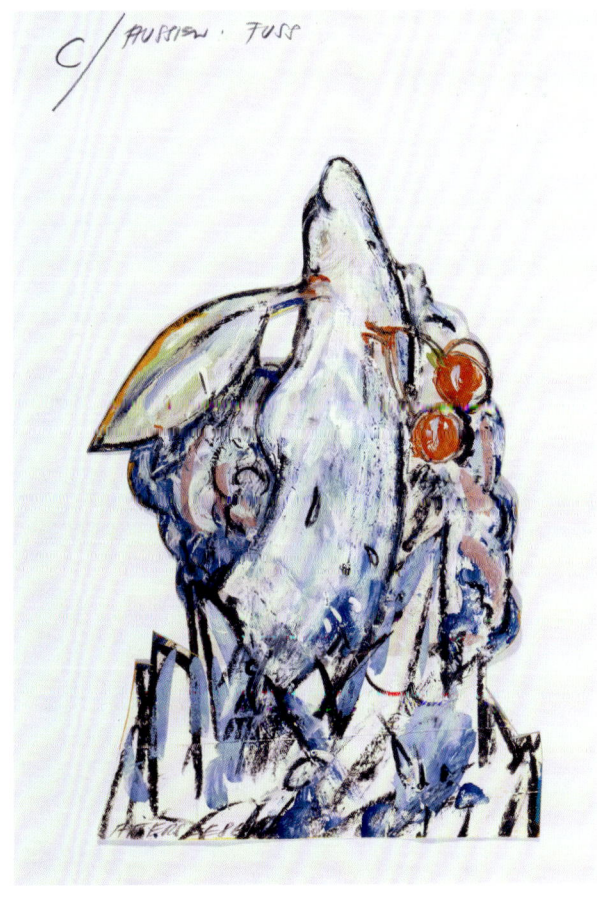

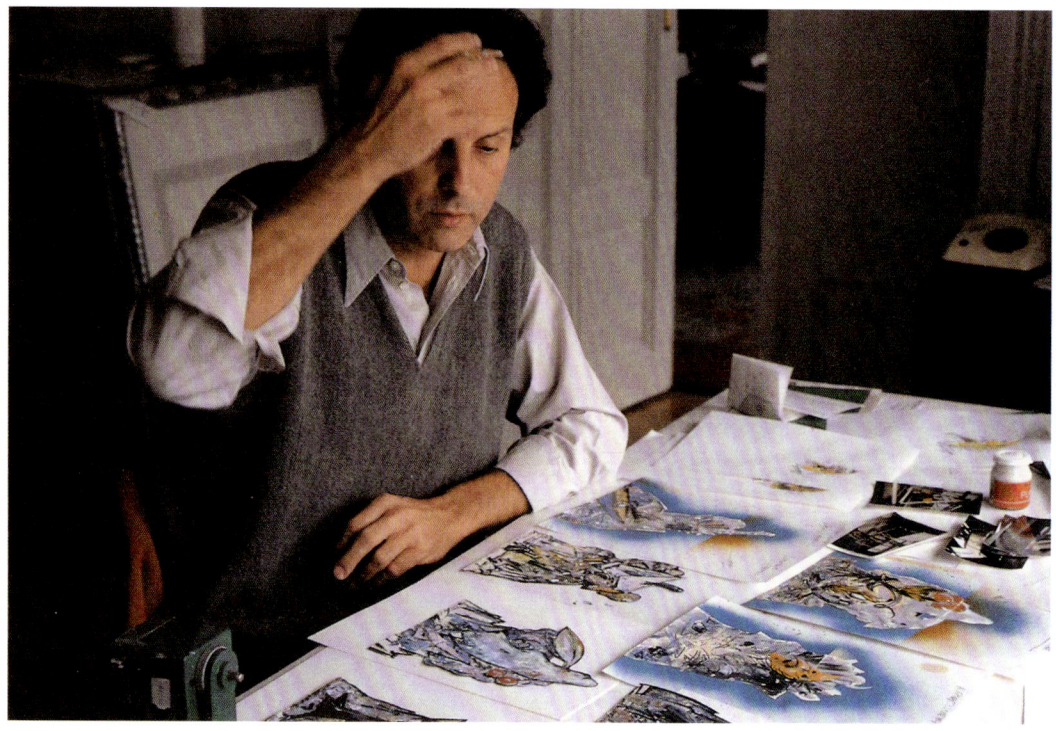

*Christian Ludwig Attersee with the designs for the boat swings …*

*… and drawing the* Luna Luna *moon*

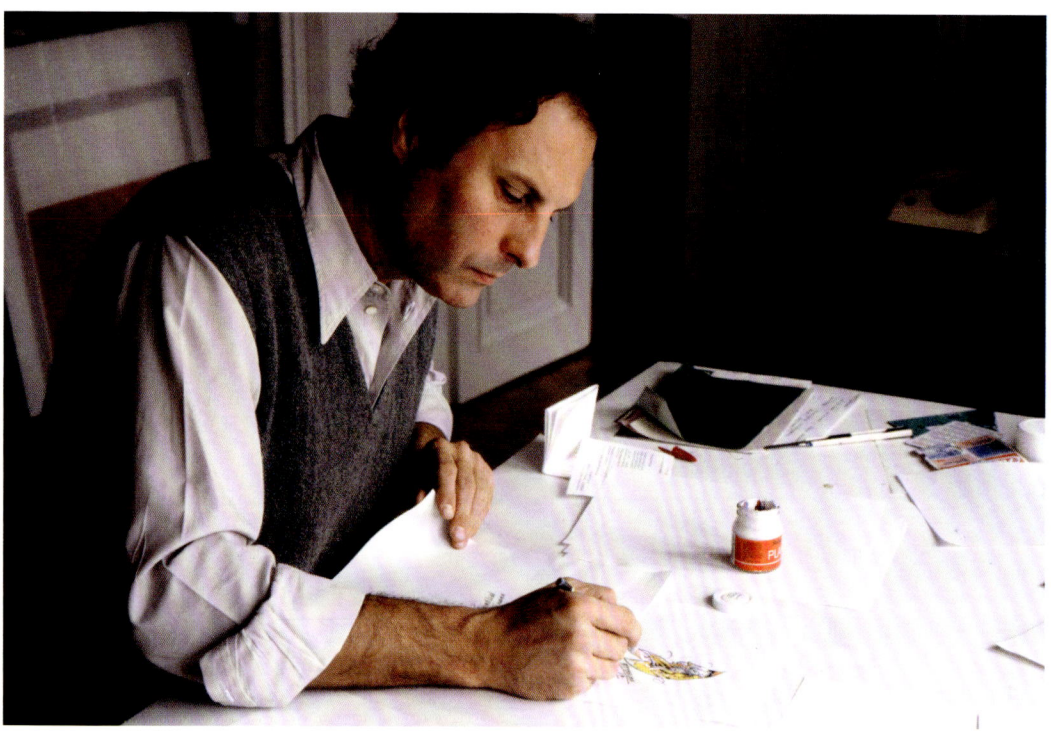

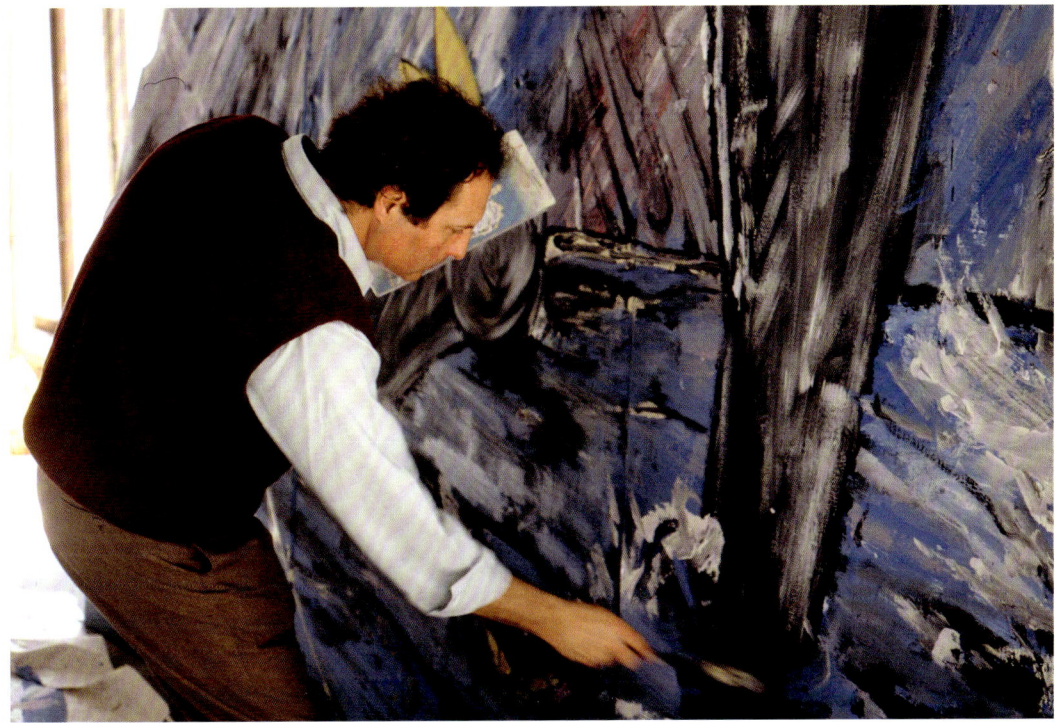

*Christian Ludwig Attersee painting the Water Junction segment …*

*… and signing the finished work*

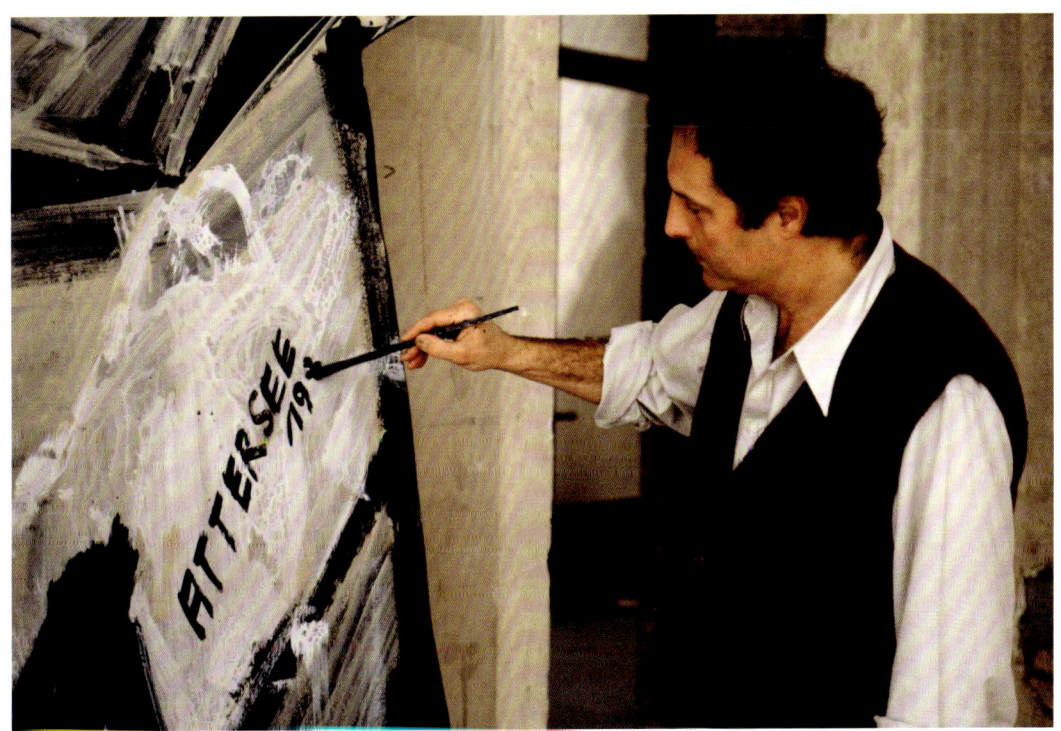

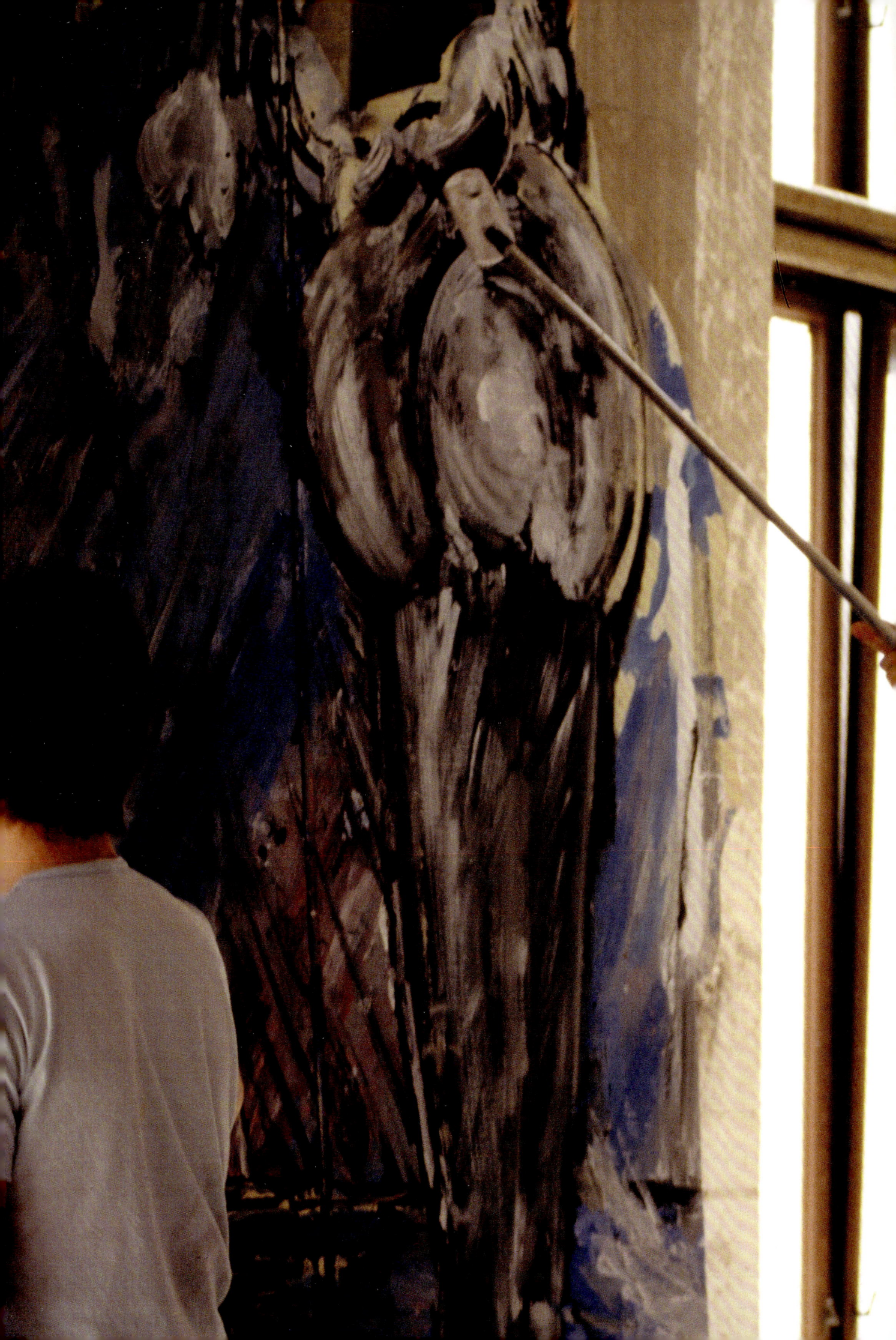

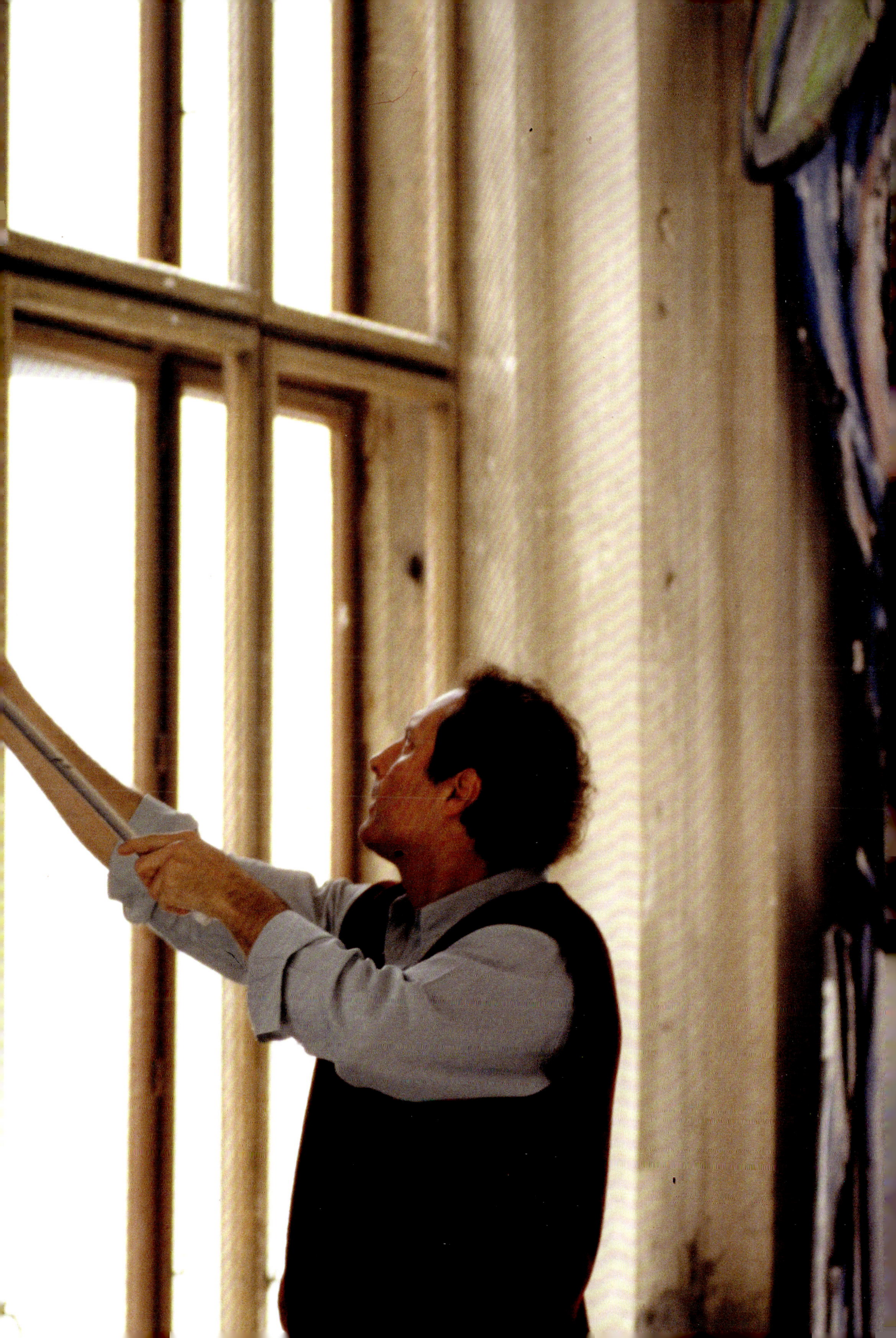

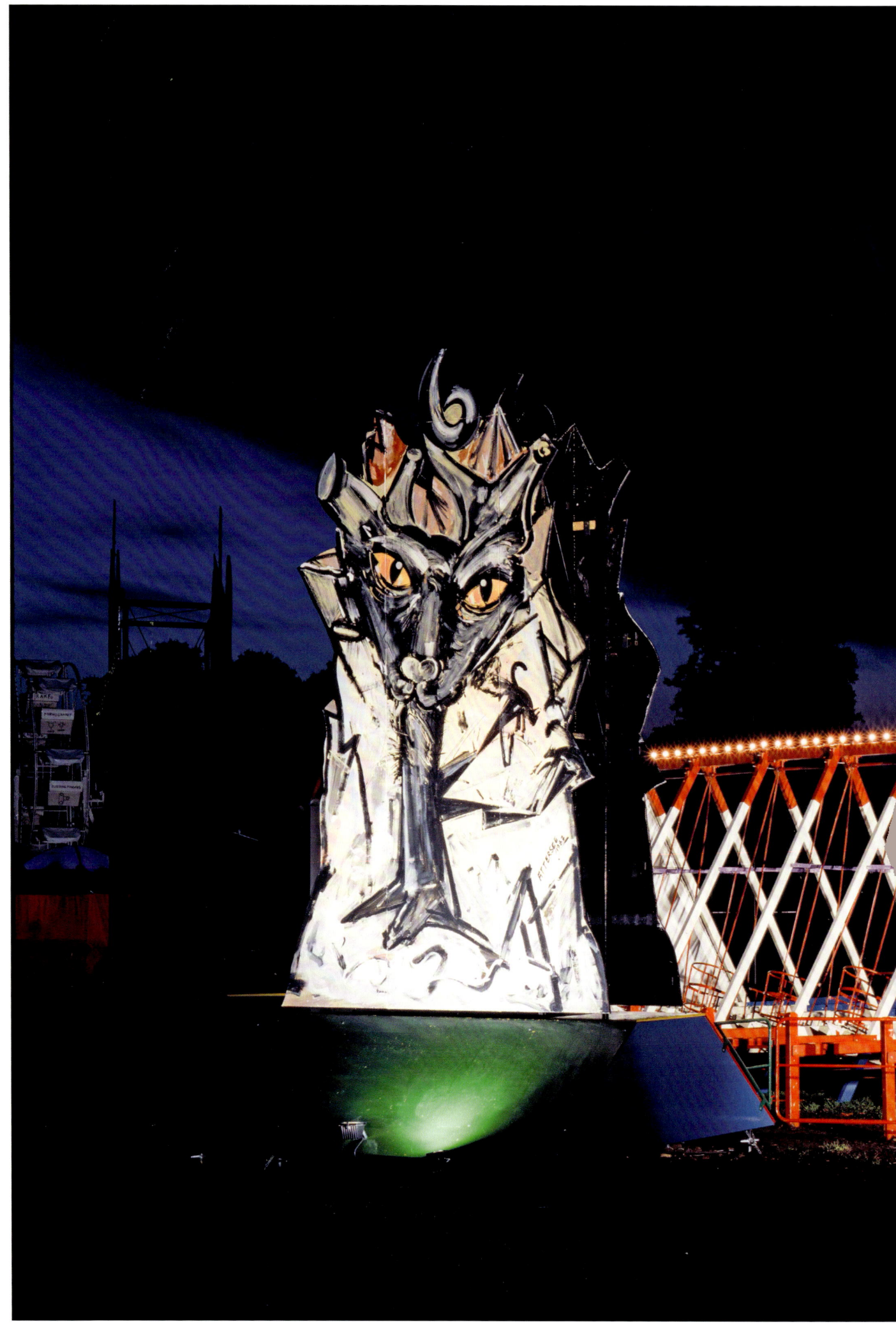

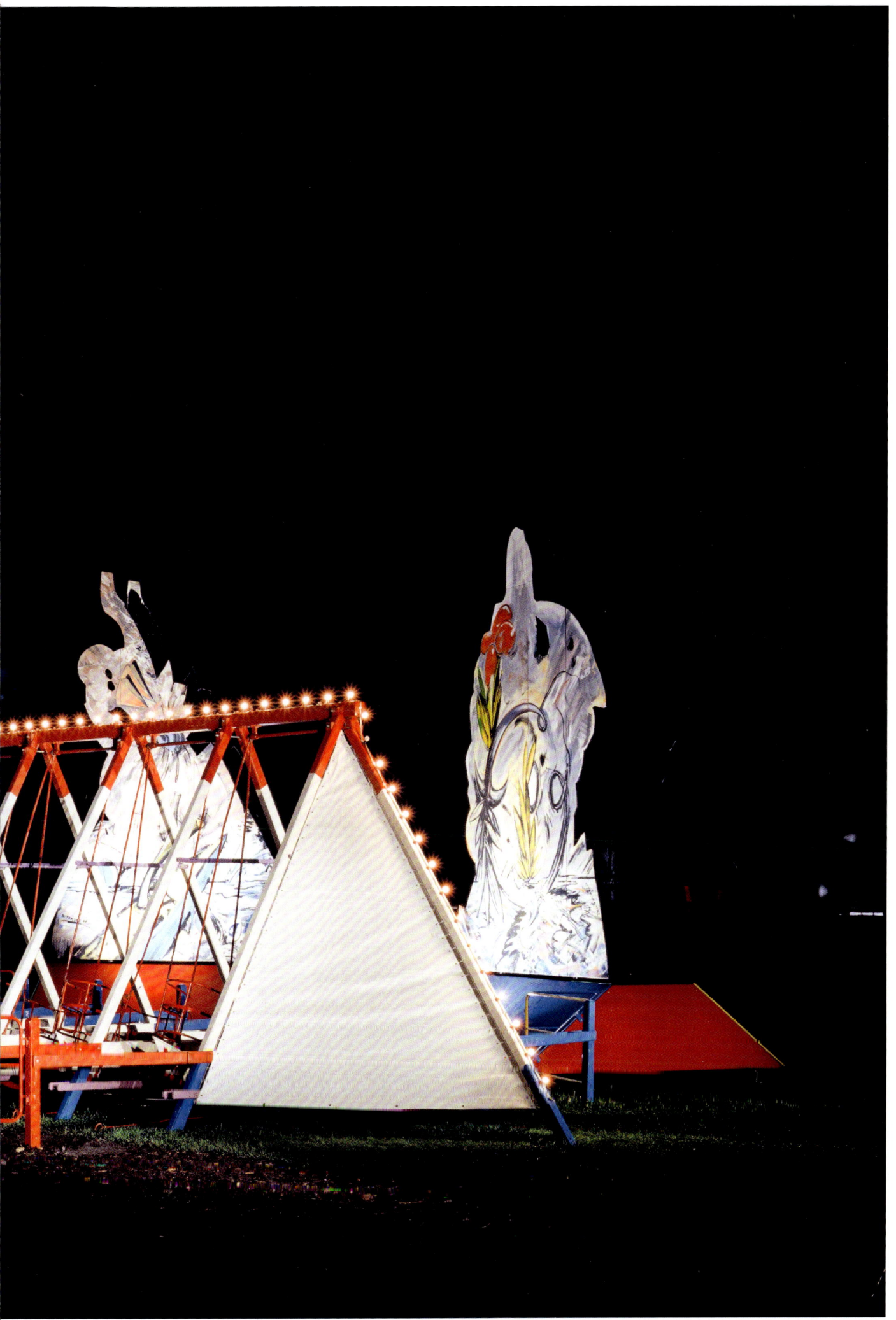

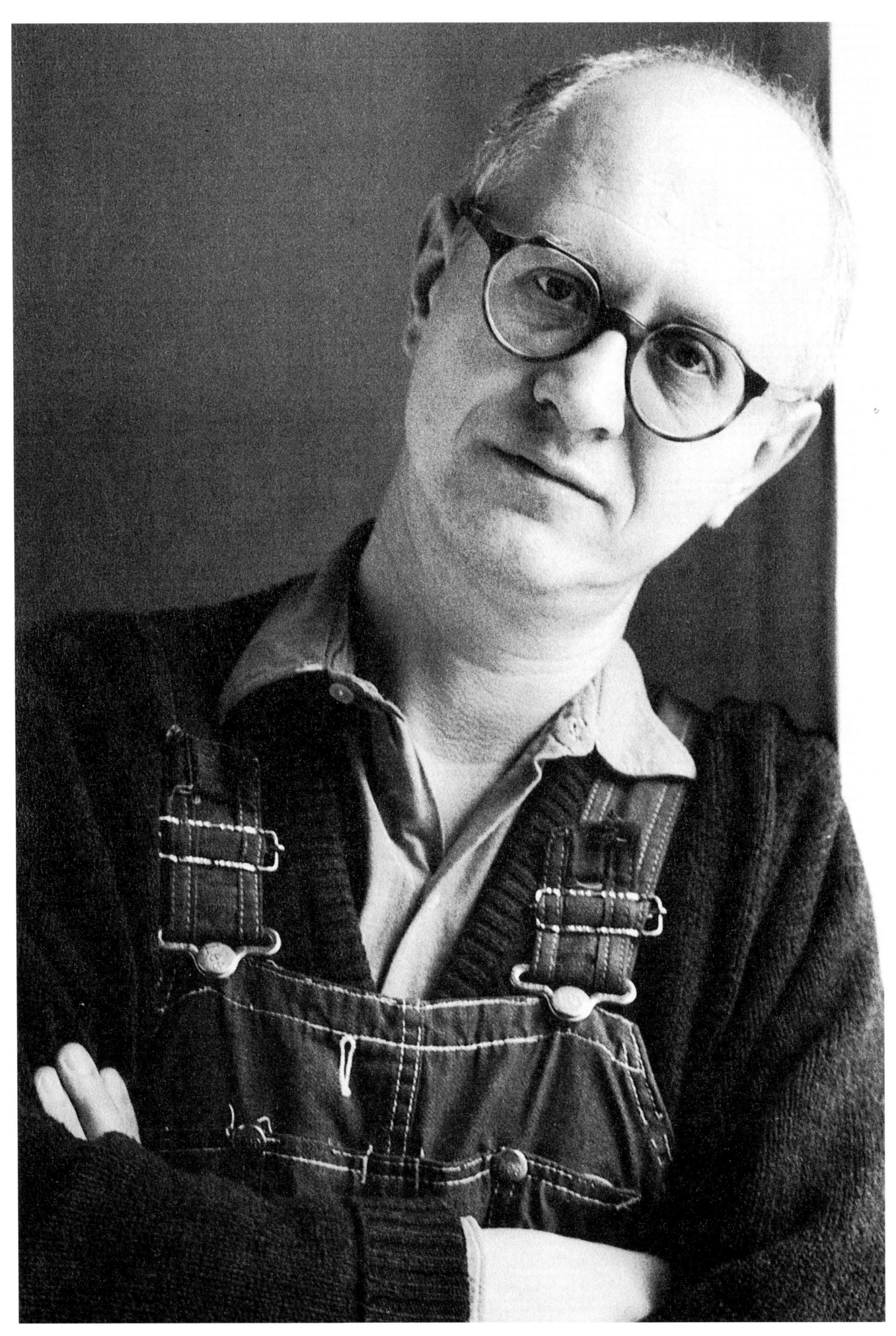

Peter Pongratz

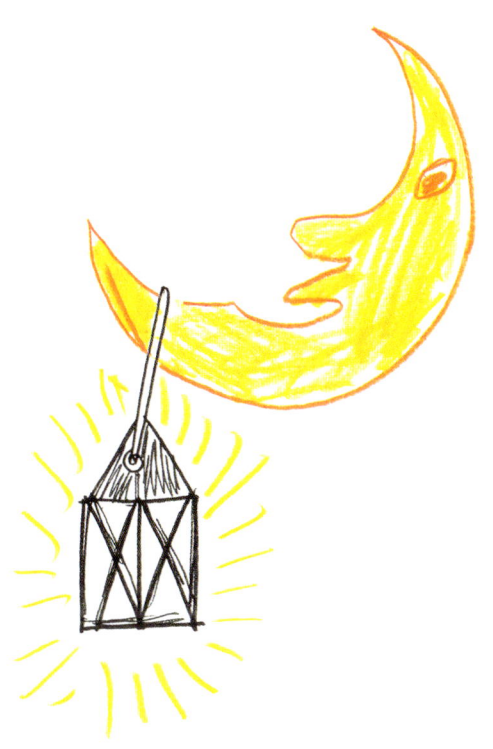

OH' LUNA LUNA WELCH VERGNÜGEN
MICH AN DEIN NÄCHTLICH' KLEID ZU SCHMIEGEN

PETER PONGRATZ

Peter Pongratz

Born: May 22, 1940, in Eisenstadt, Austria.

Painter, sculptor, stage designer, illustrator, inventor, physicist, chemist, biologist, musician.

Peter Pongratz designed a **head-through-the-wall image** for *Luna Luna*. This painting lets visitors take on a different identity, and they can take home a souvenir photo of the moment.

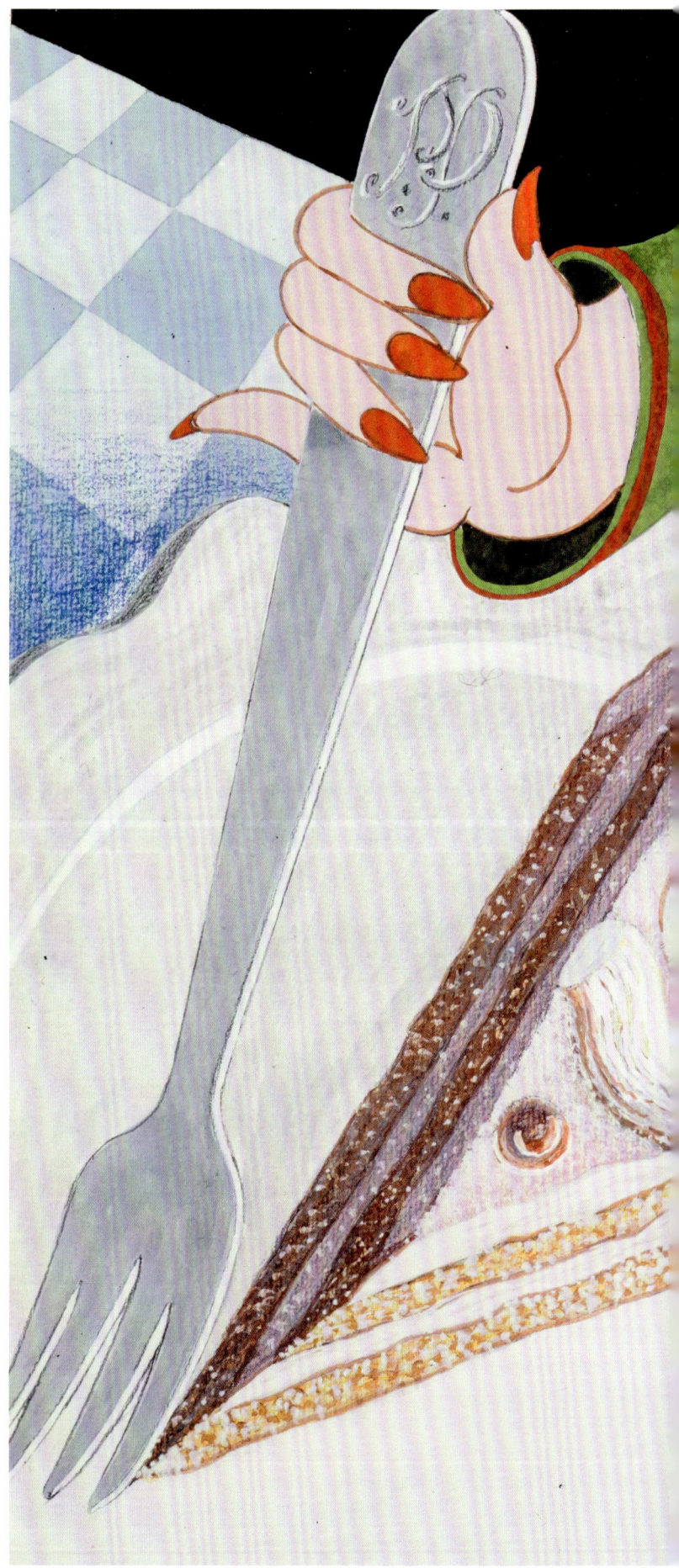

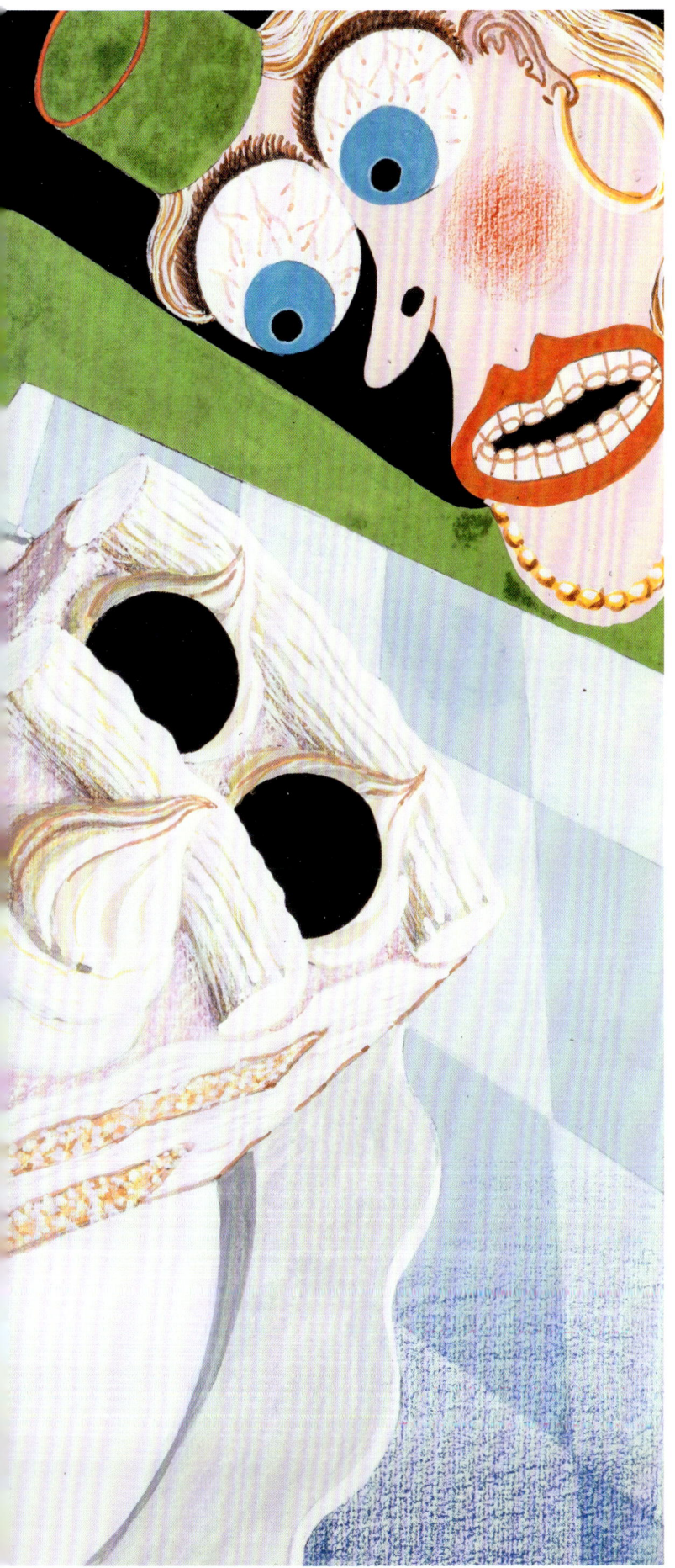

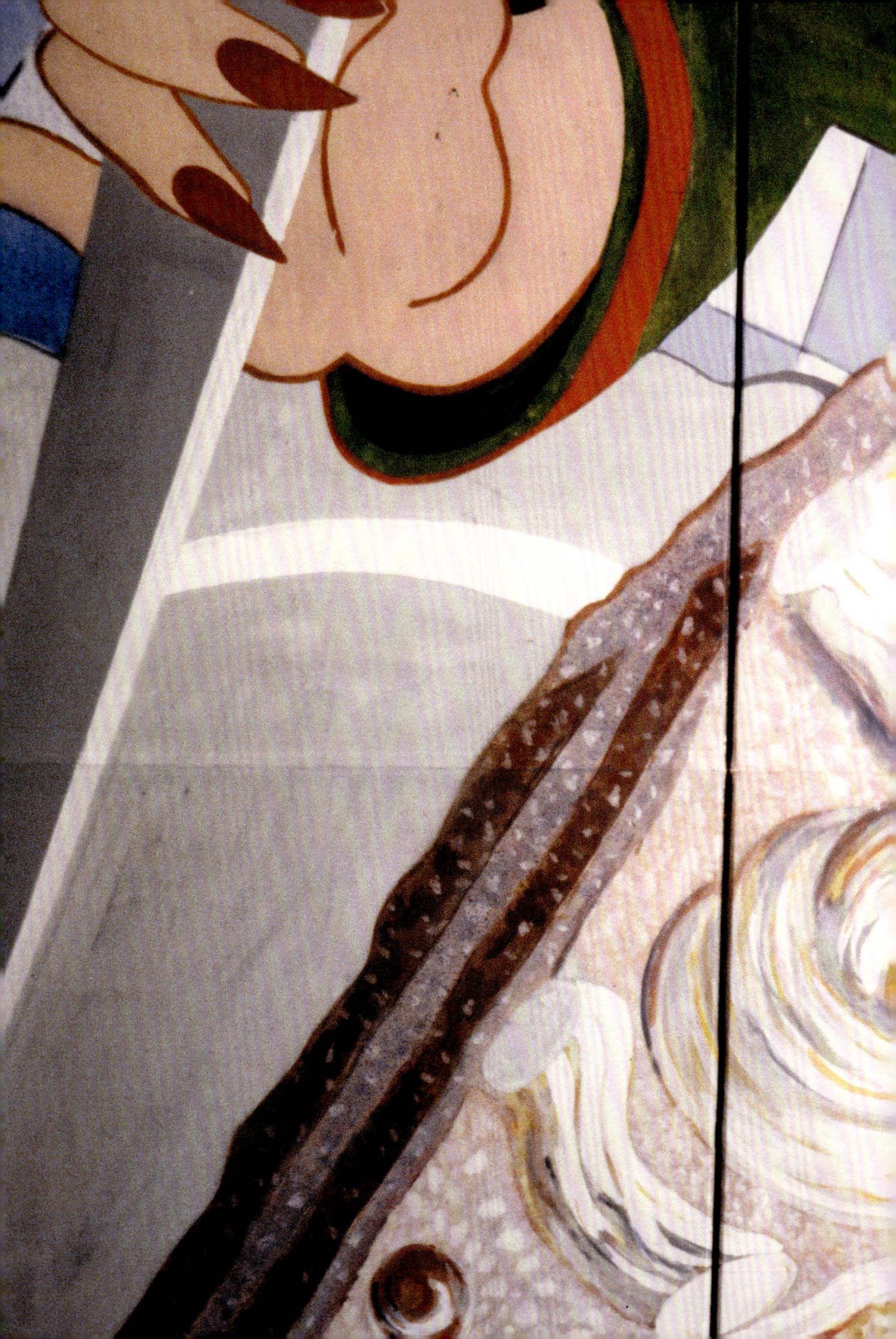

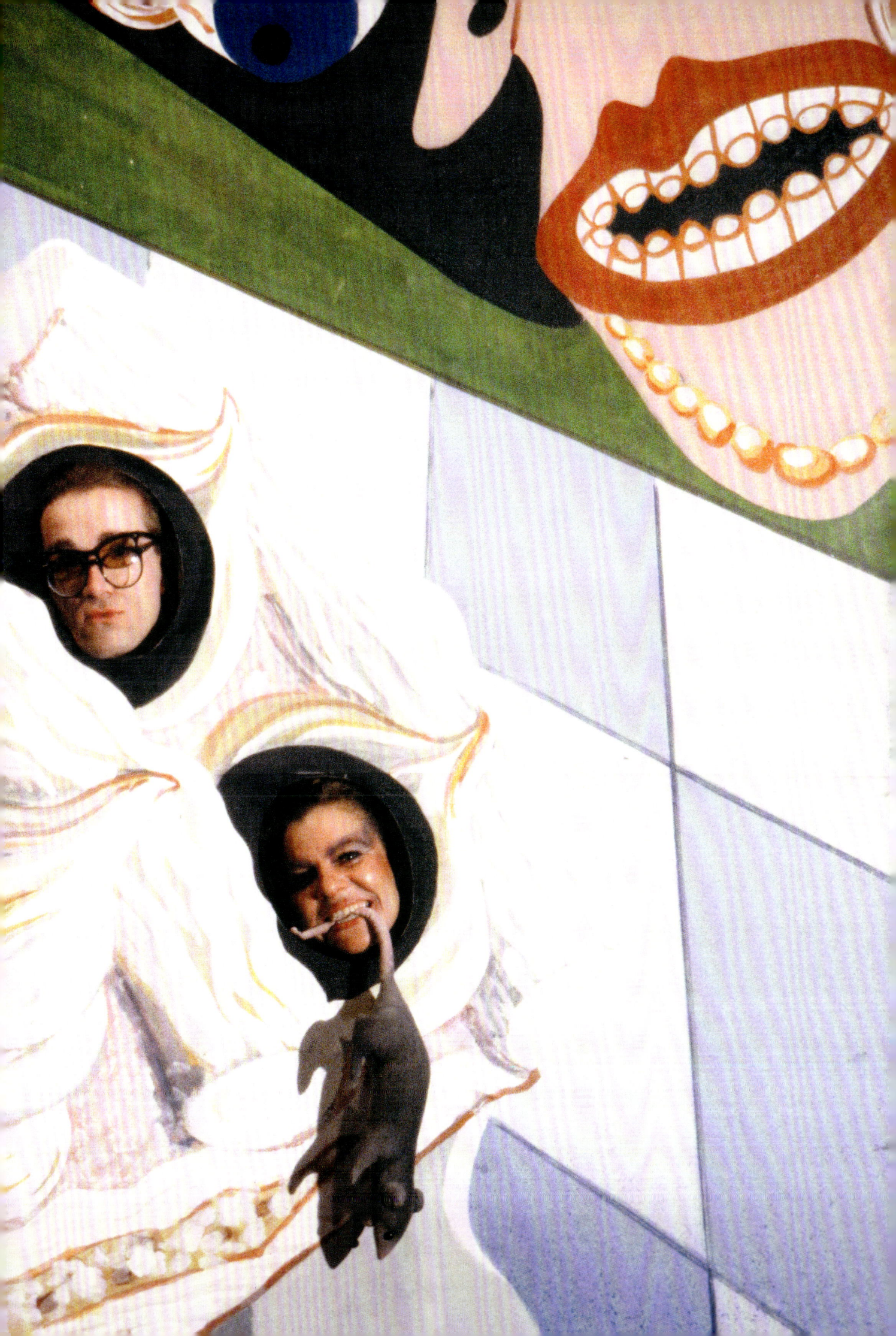

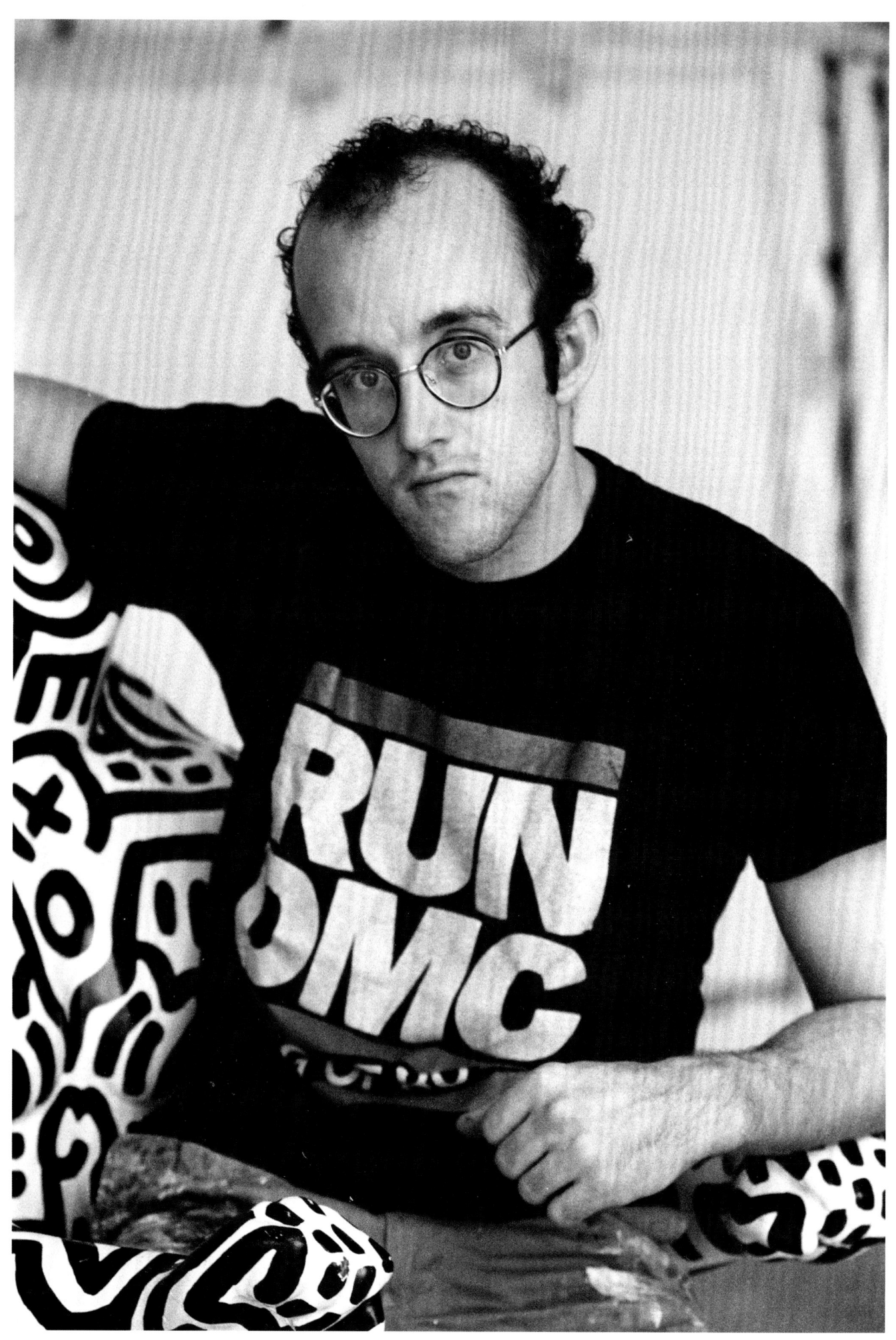

Keith Haring

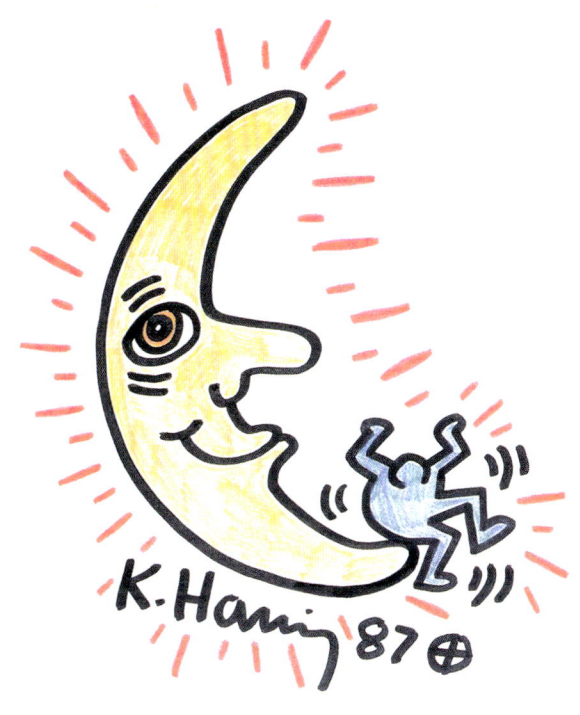

LUNA LUNA IN THE SKY.
WILL YOU MAKE ME LAUGH OR CRY?
K. Haring 1987 NYC ⊕

Keith Haring

Born: May 4, 1958, in Kutztown, Pennsylvania.
Died: February 16, 1990, in New York, New York.

Painter, illustrator, sculptor, actionist.

Keith Haring designed **posters** and a **carousel** for *Luna Luna* with **narrative walls** leading away from it in a star formation.

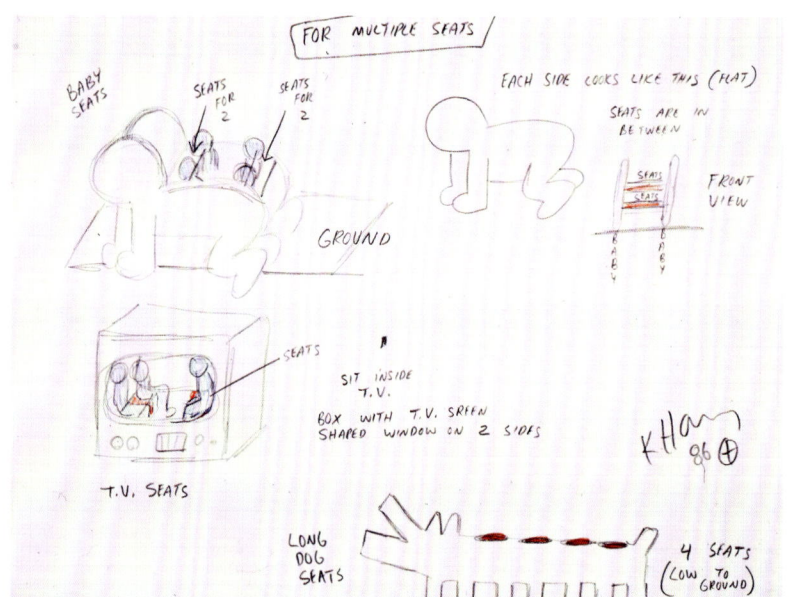

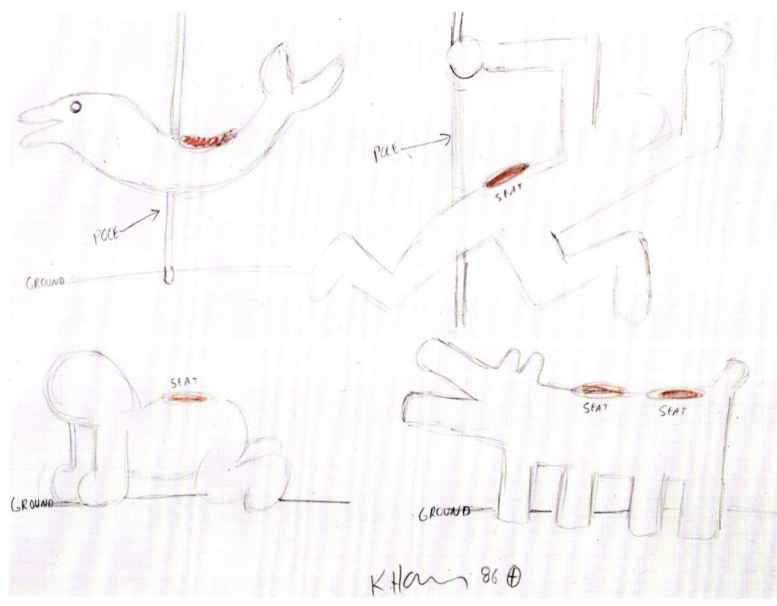

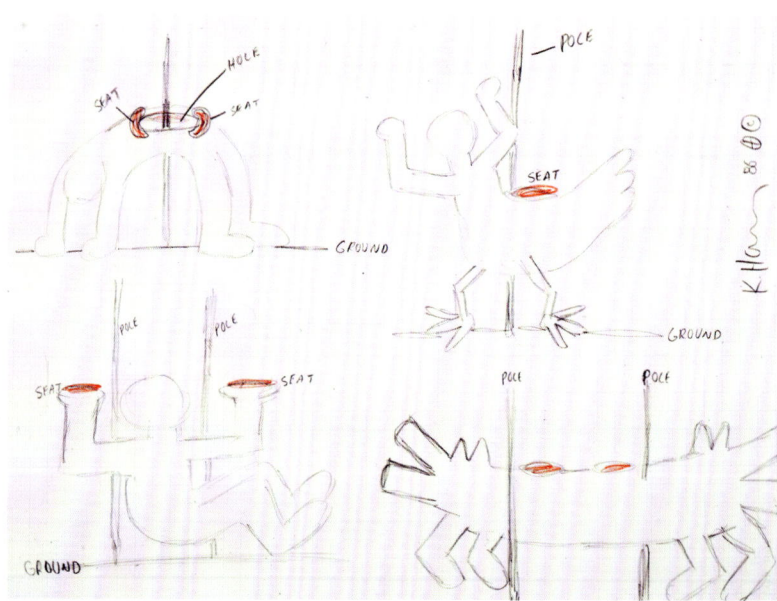

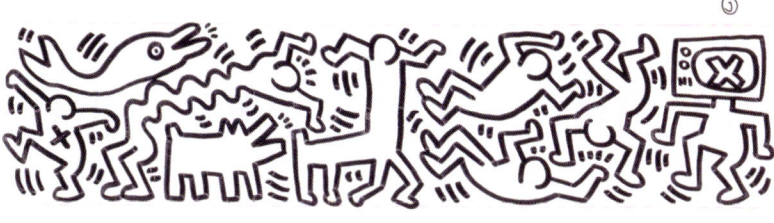

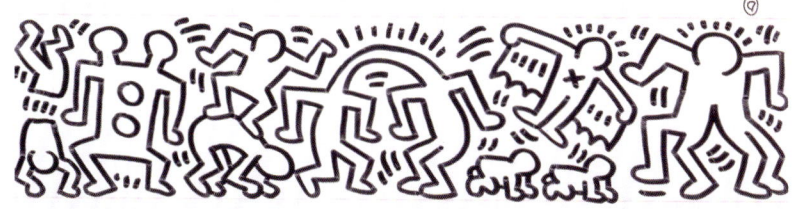

LUNA LUNA DRAWINGS    APRIL 1986  © K. HARING K. Haring ©

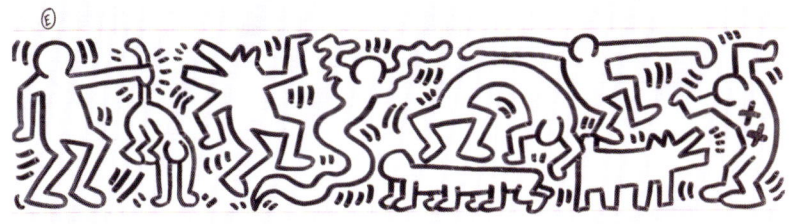

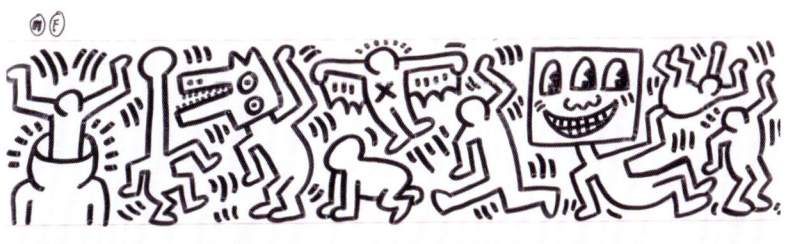

LUNA LUNA DRAWINGS - APRIL 1986  K.Haring ©⊕

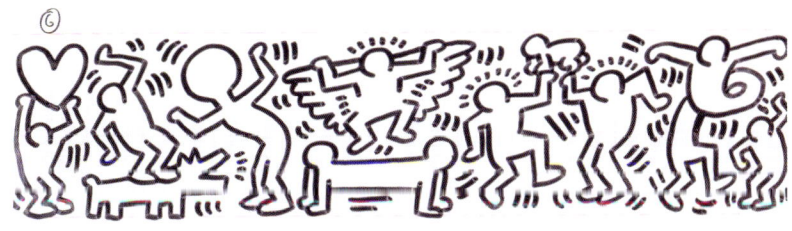

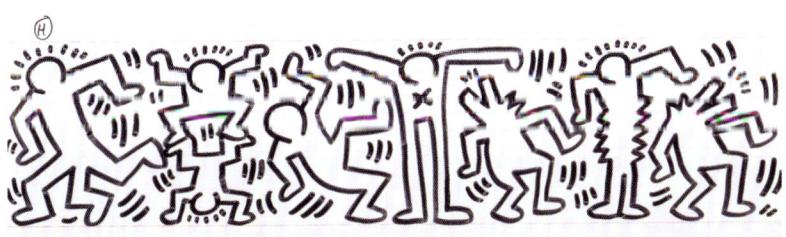

LUNA LUNA DRAWINGS- APRIL 1986 ©K.Haring ⊕

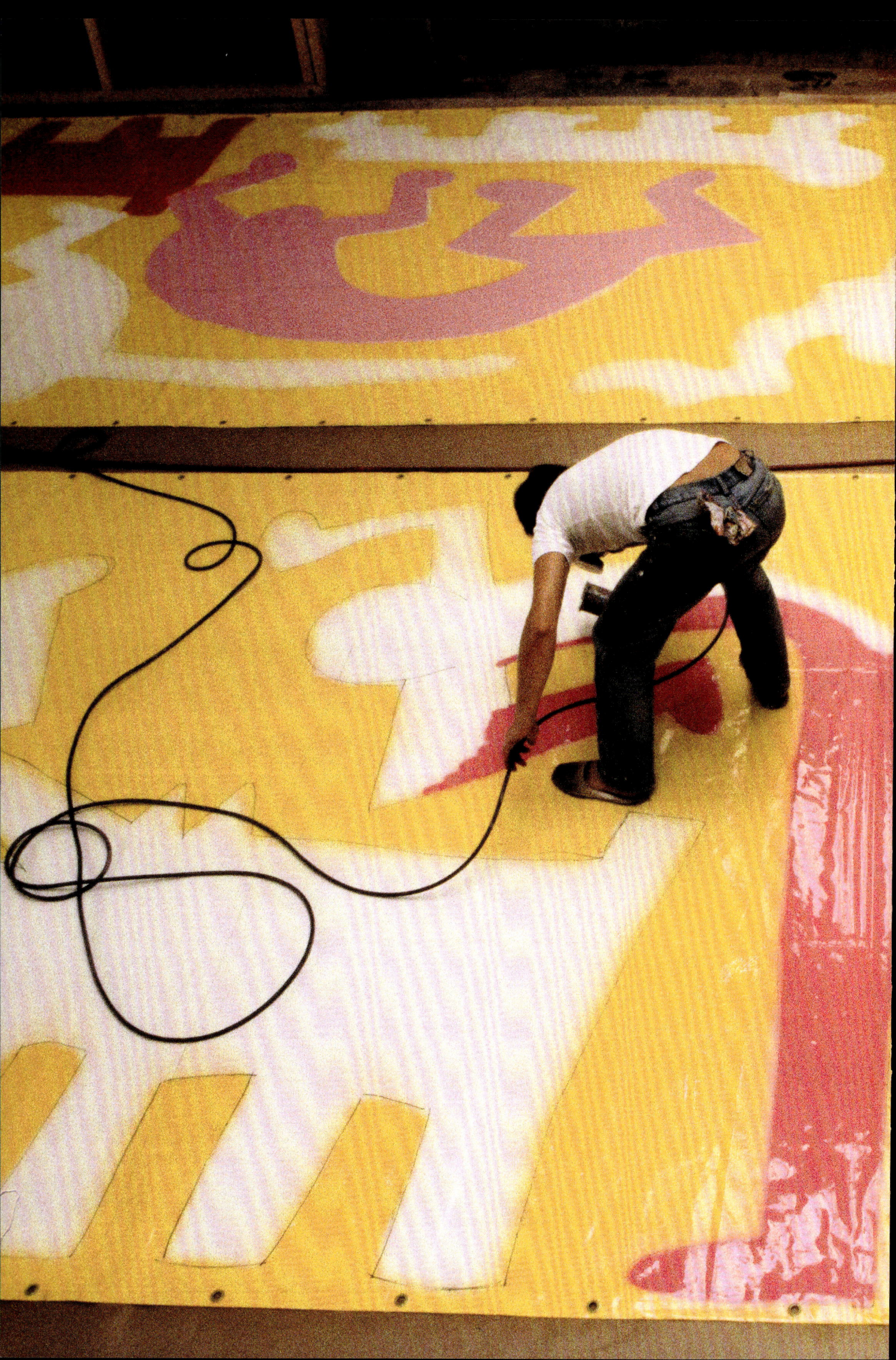

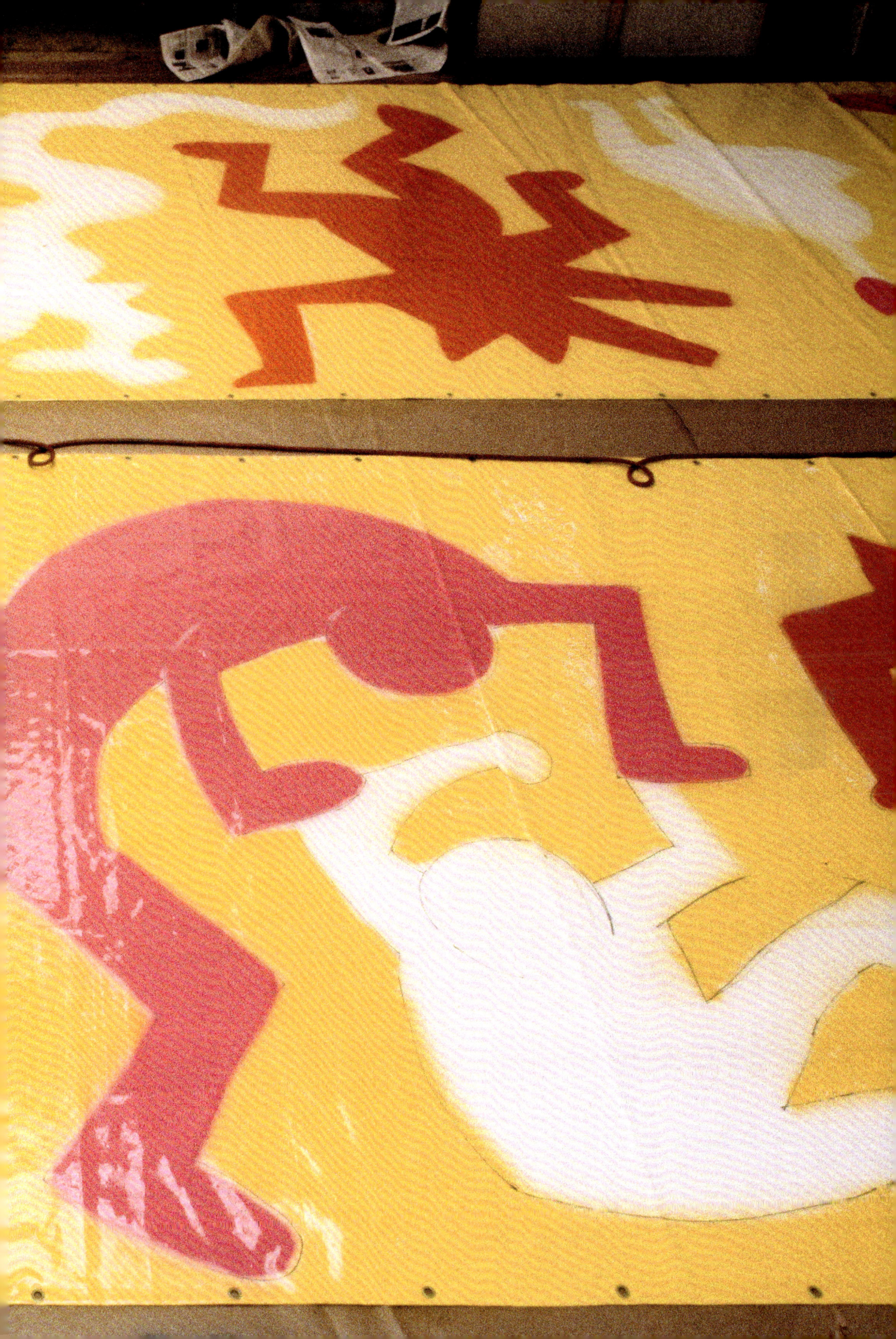

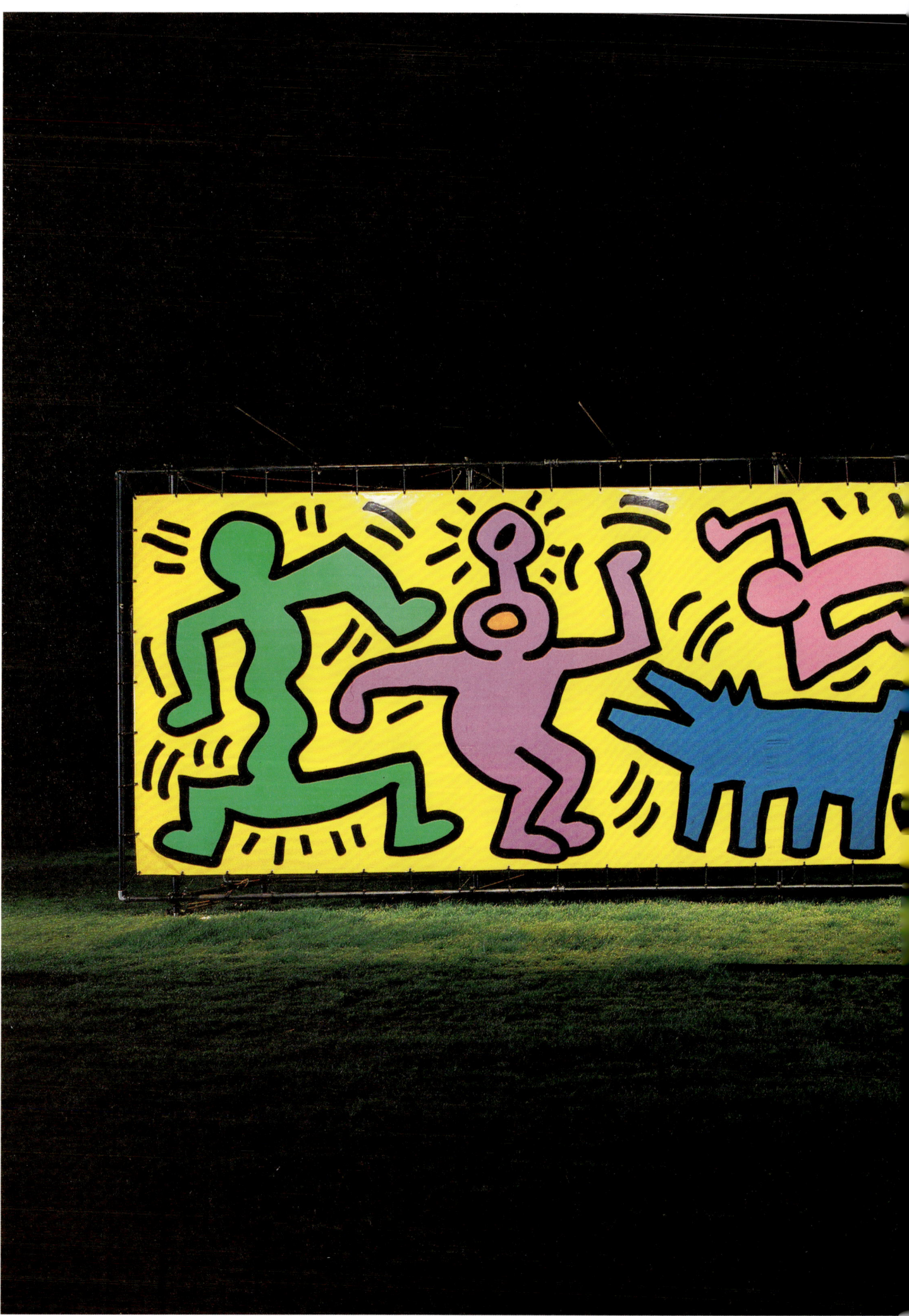

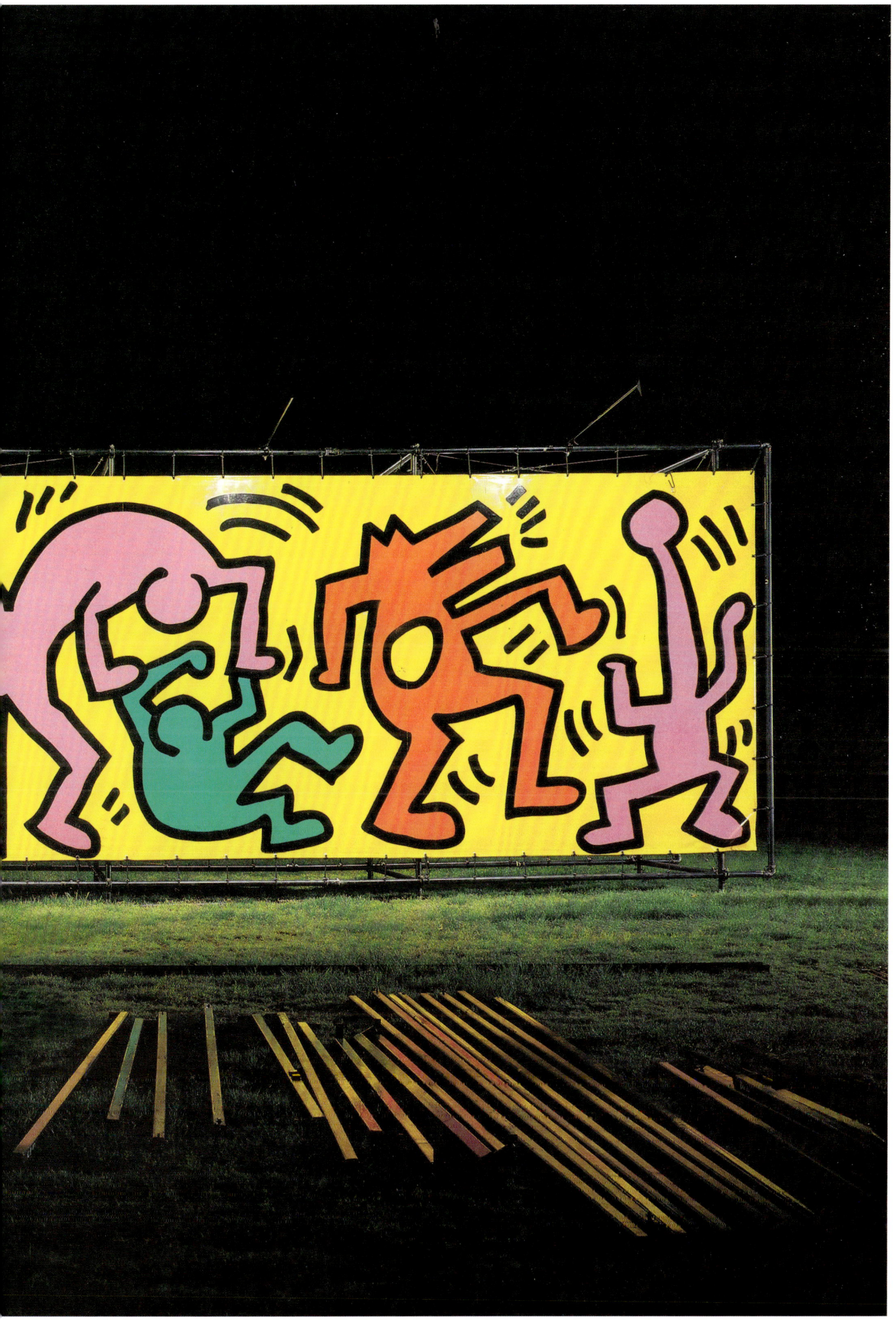

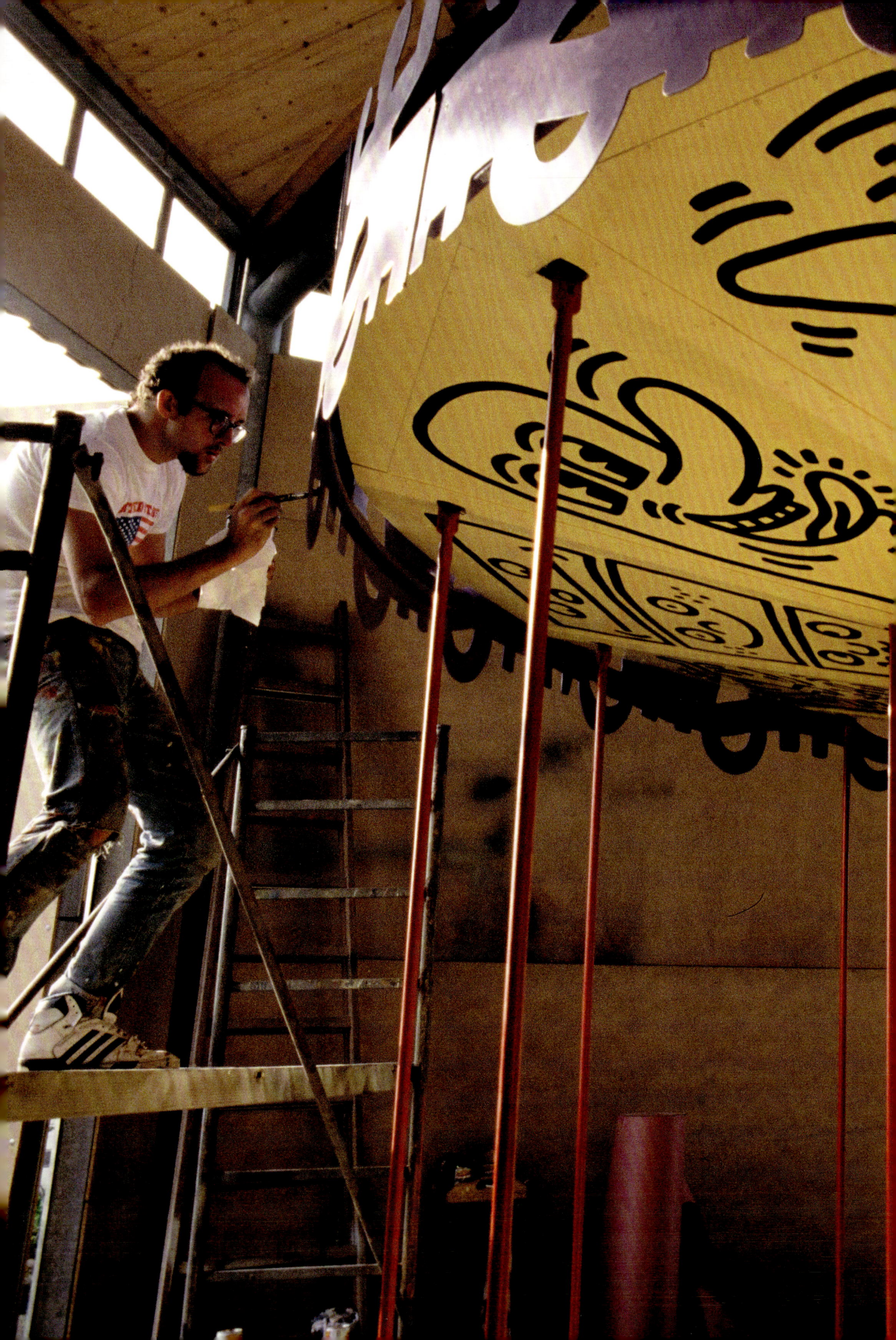

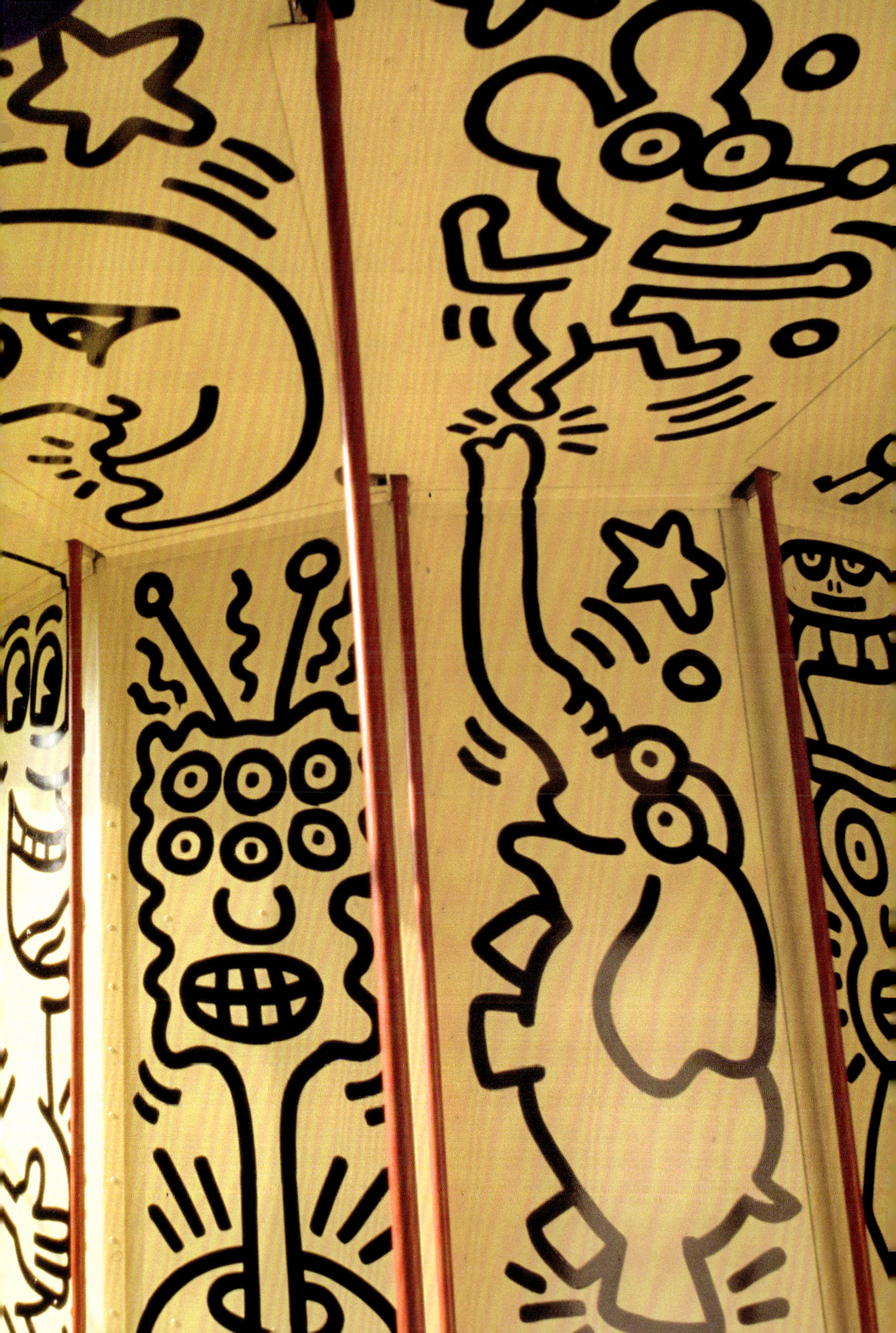

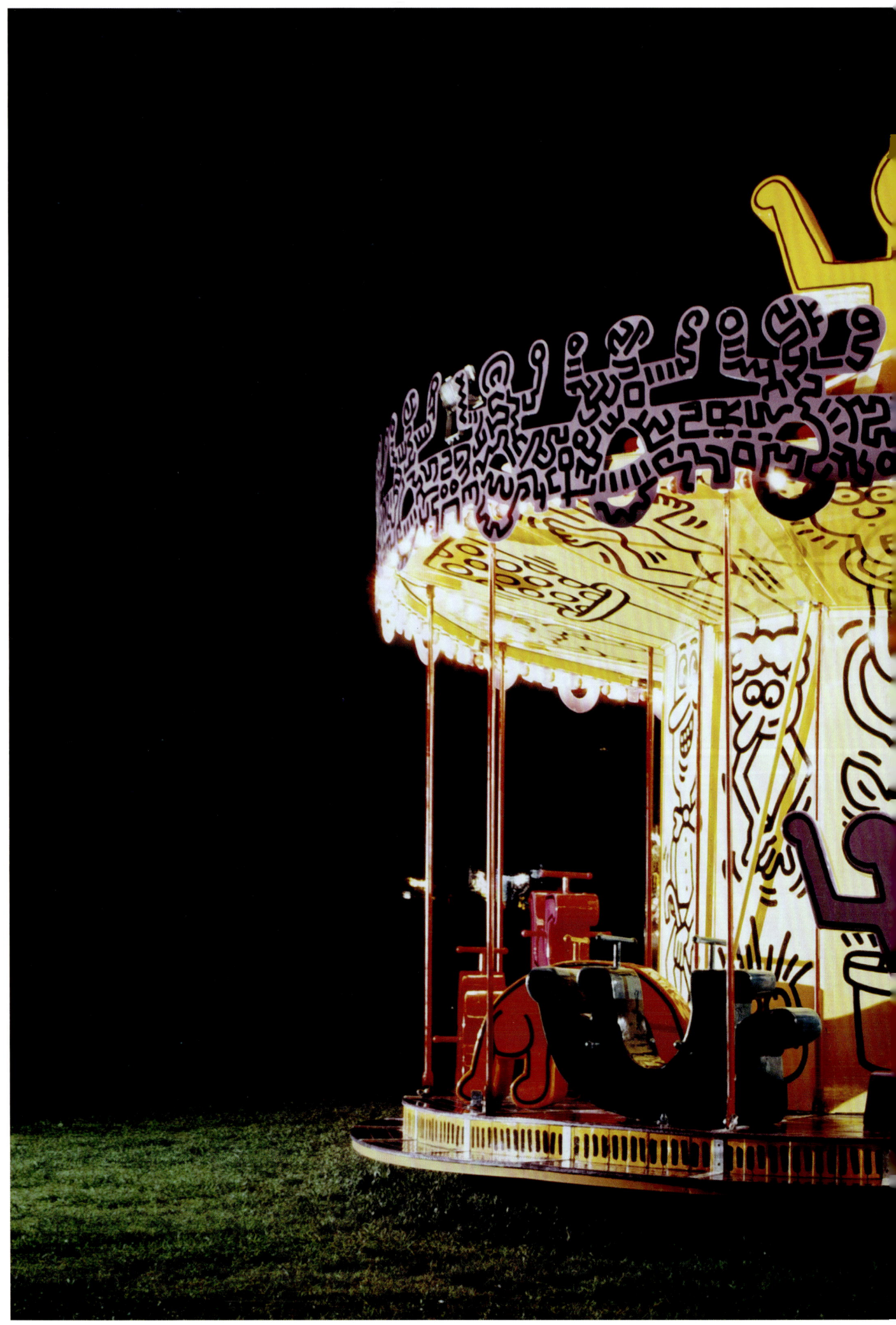

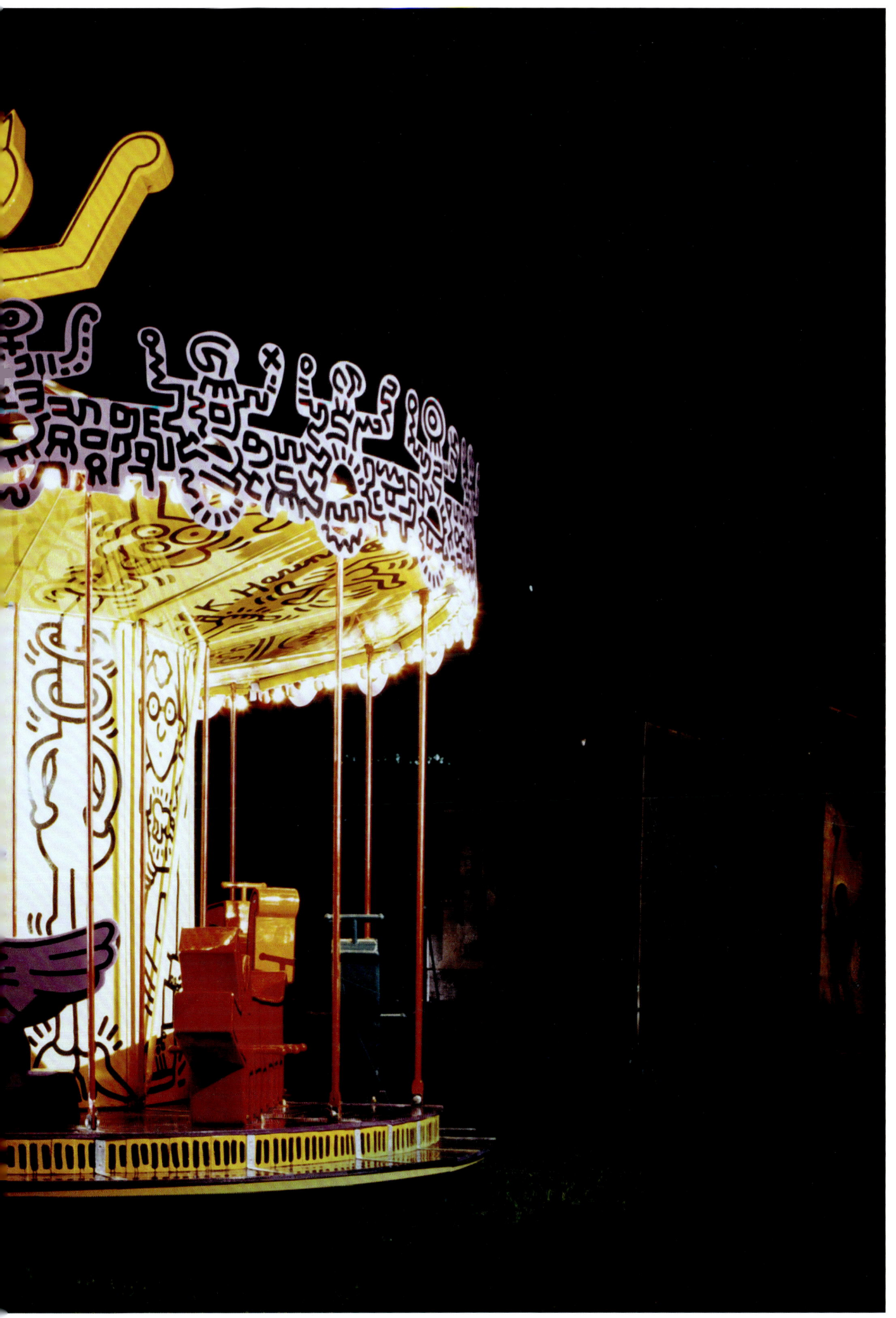

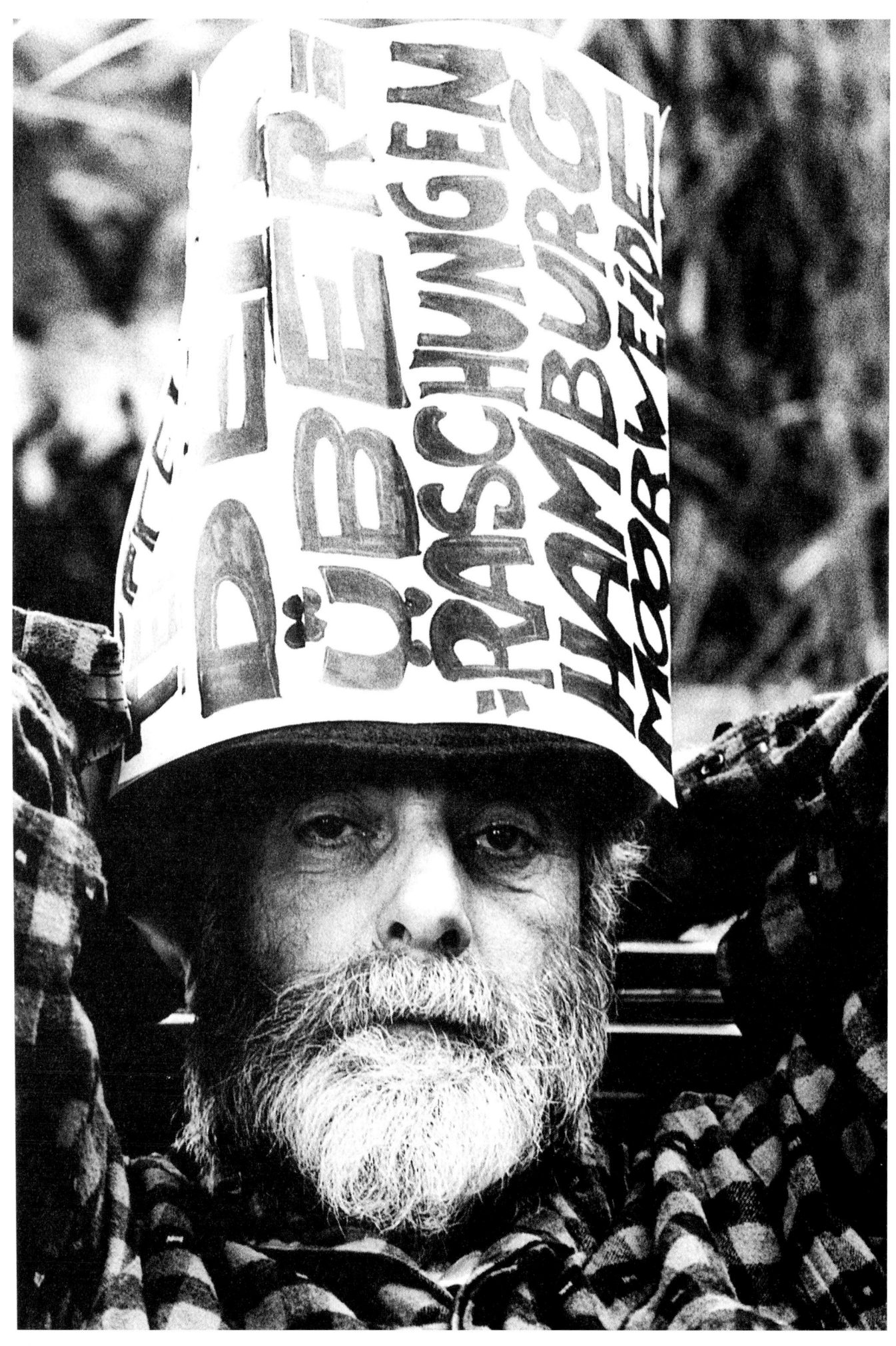

Friedensreich Hundertwasser

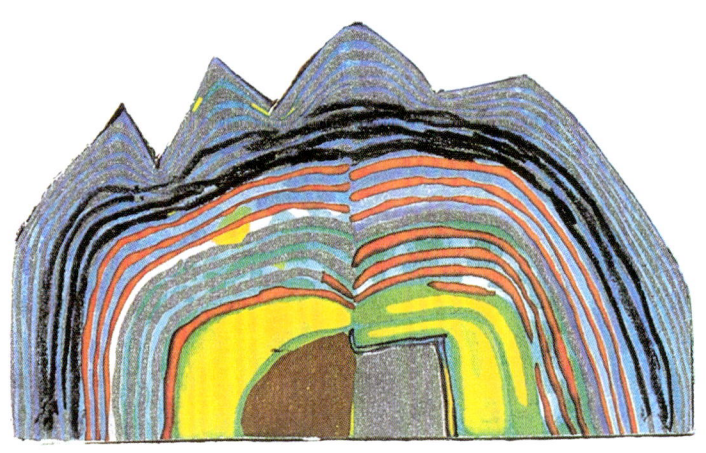

WENN MAN DEM MENSCHEN
SEINE TRÄUME WEGNIMMT
GEHT ER ZUGRUNDE

14. MAI 1987

Friedensreich Hundertwasser

Born: December 15, 1928, in Vienna, Austria.
Died: February 19, 2000, in Queensland, Australia.

Painter, illustrator, actionist, architect, ecologist.

Friedensreich Hundertwasser designed a **poster** for *Luna Luna*.

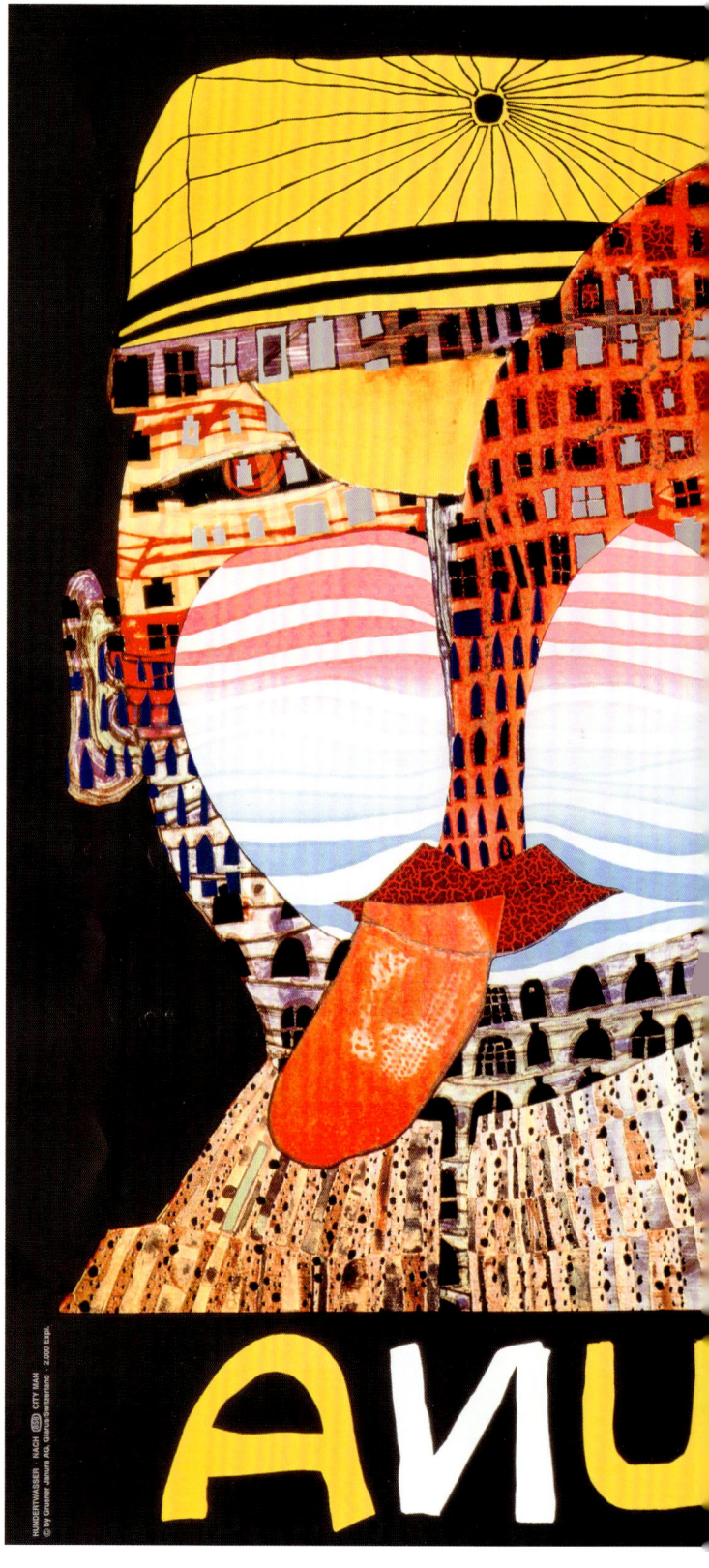

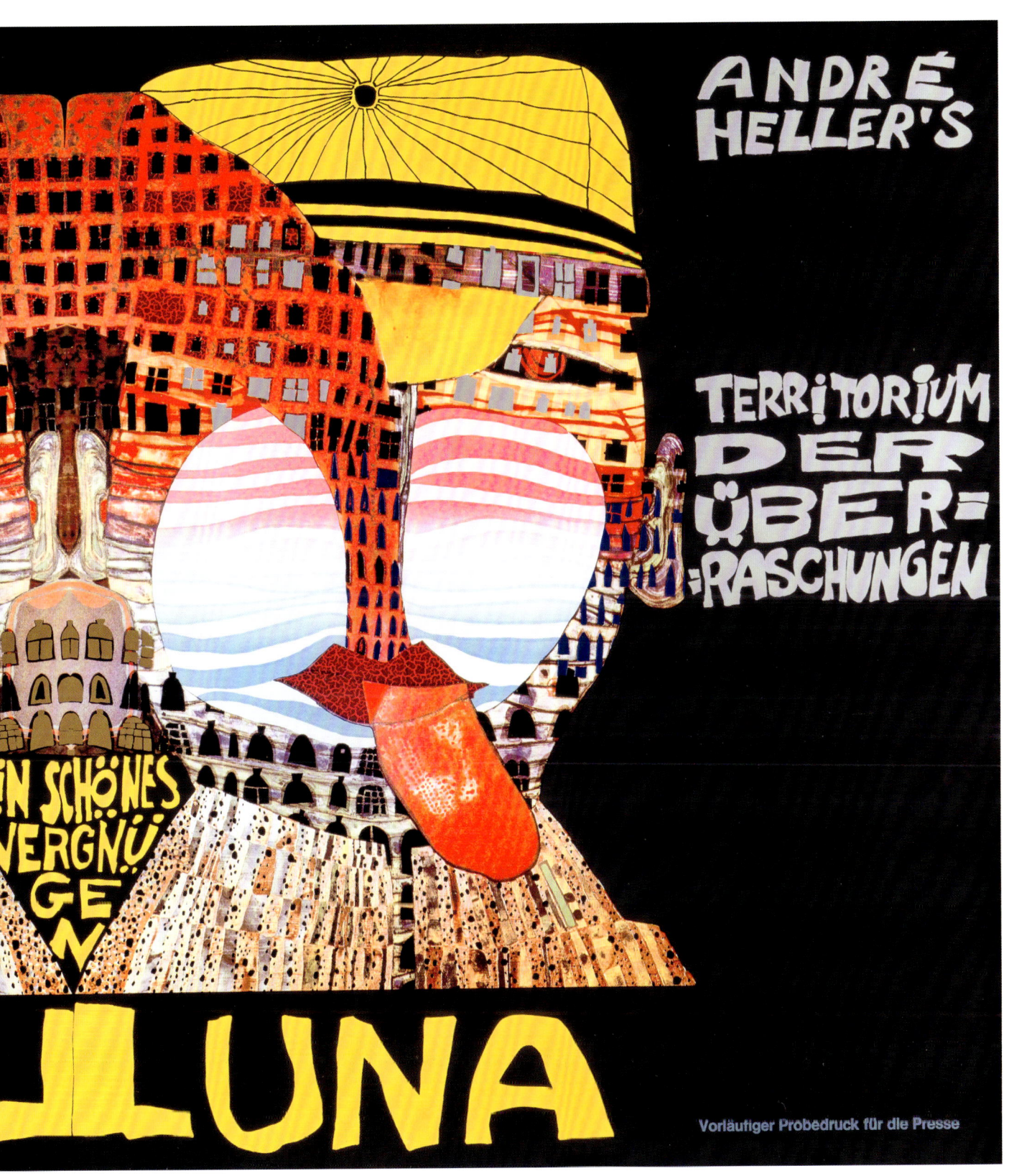

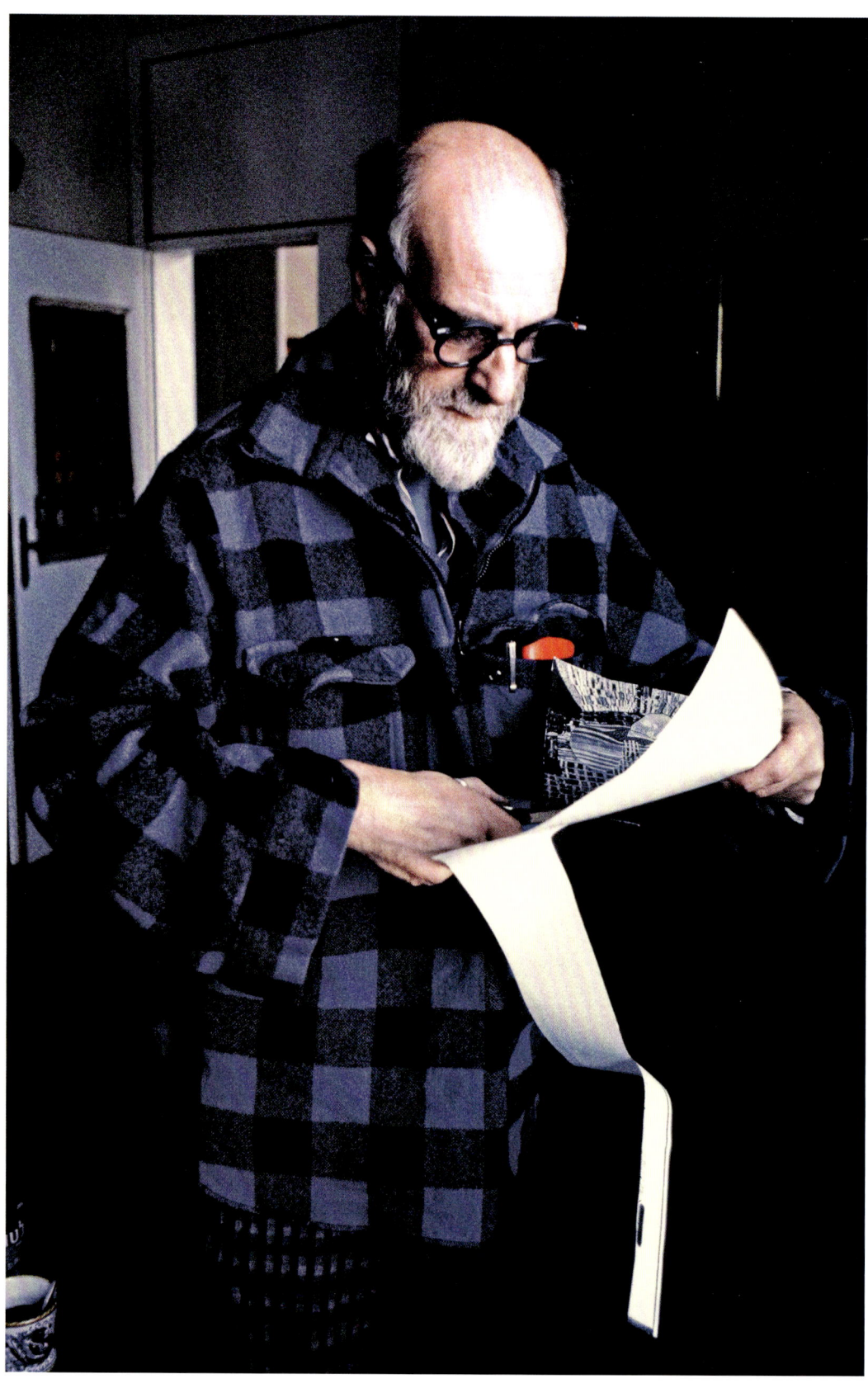

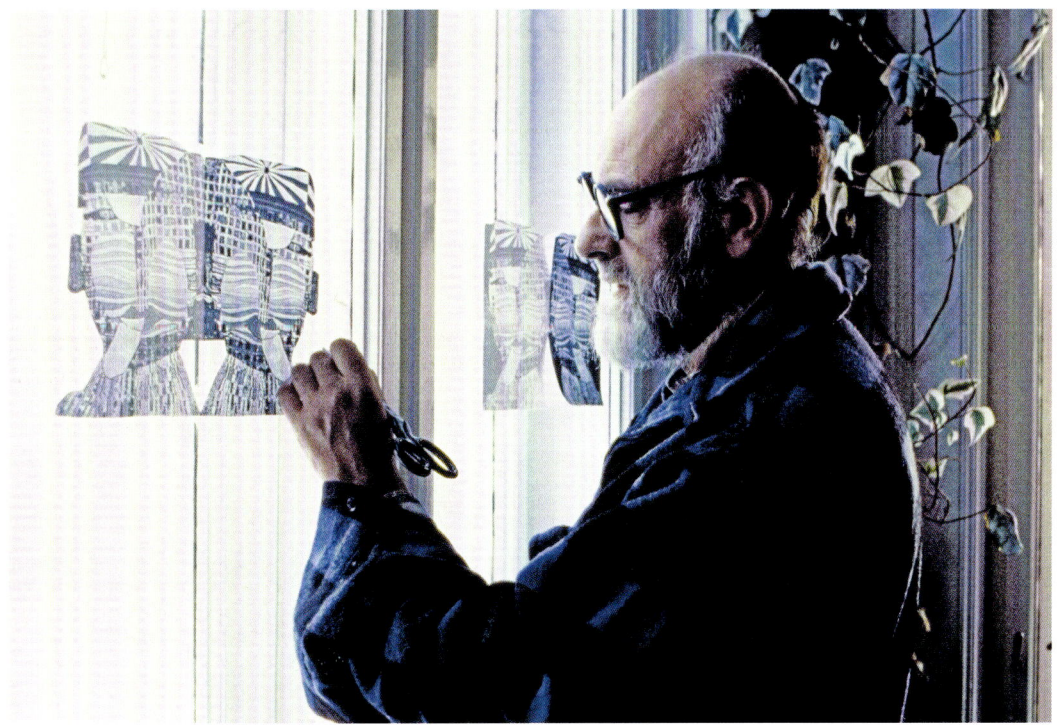

*Friedensreich Hundertwasser designing the two tongue pointers for the poster …*

*… and in his Vienna studio writing the text for the* Luna Luna *book*

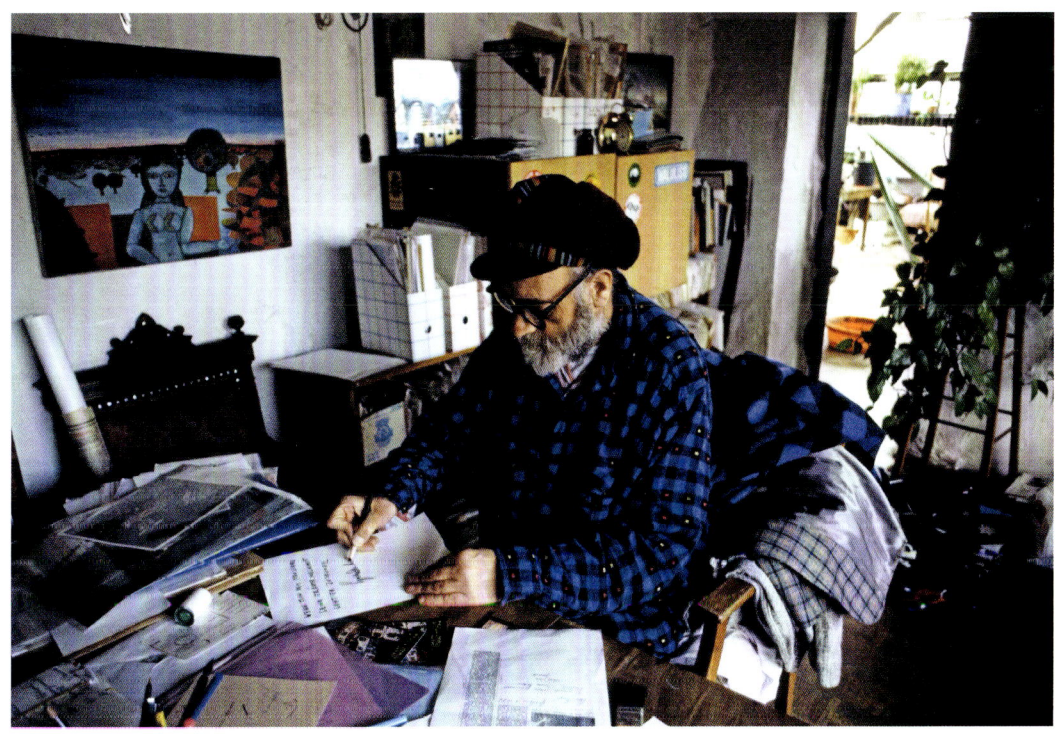

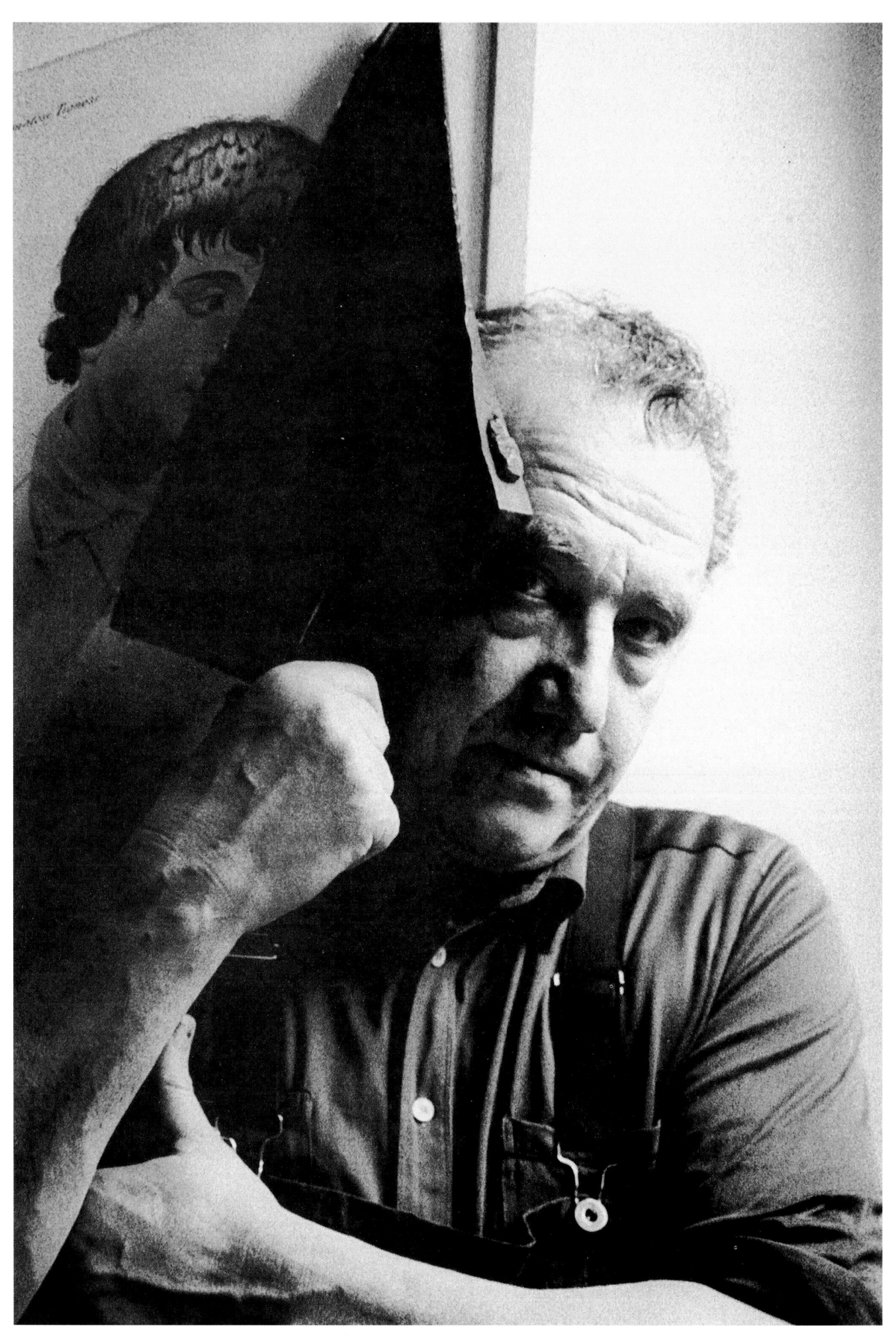

Daniel Spoerri

Daniel Spoerri

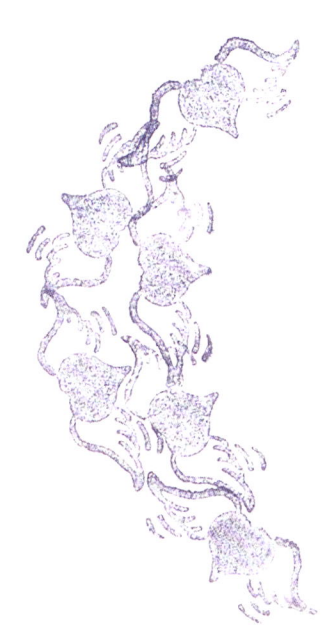

Schaut jeun and in den Mond,
wo der heilige David sitzt
und der Harfe, die er spielt
spreng t eine Saite, so erblindet
ein Mensch.

Daniel Spoerri

Born: March 27, 1930, in Galati, Romania.

Actionist, food artist, object inventor, sculptor, illustrator.

Daniel Spoerri designed the **Excrement Law Firm** for *Luna Luna*. In front of the restroom, there are mock architectures modeled on fascist tastes; in front of them there are three-dimensional victory columns with large piles of excrement steaming on top. Inside the restroom, there are reliefs showing a food scene as a reminder of the bodily origin of the excrement.

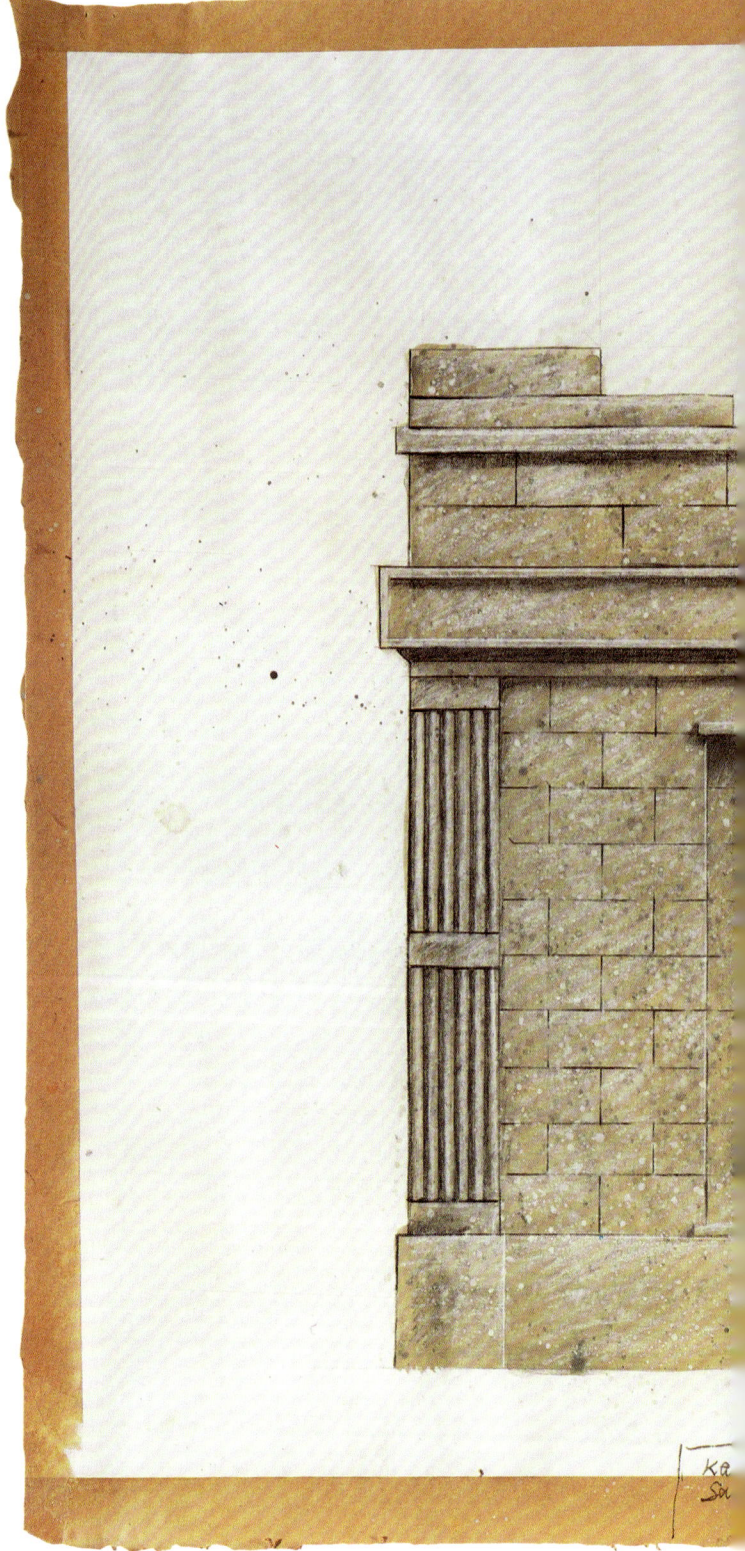

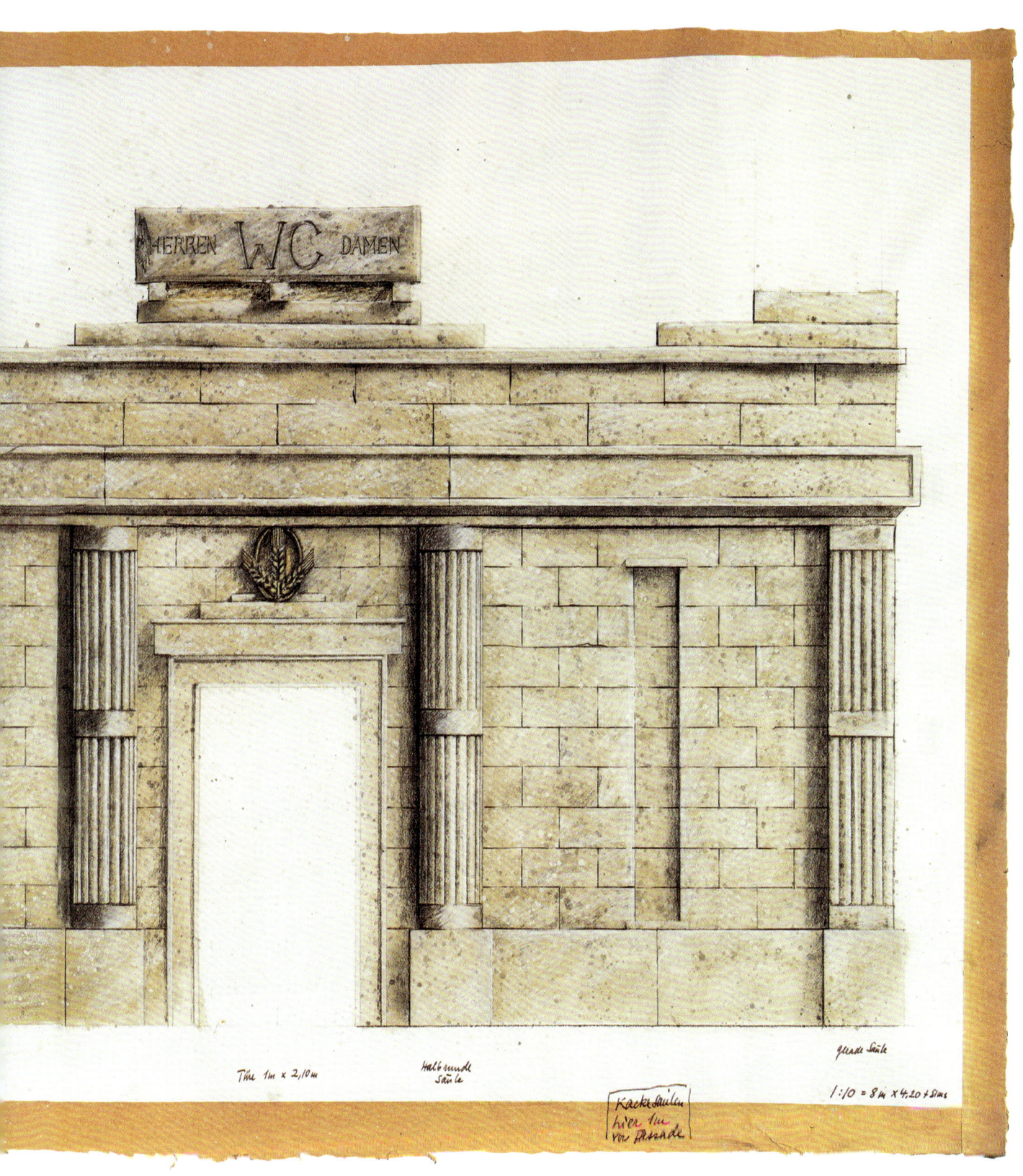

Thre 1m x 2,10m

Halbrunde
Säule

gerade Säule

1:10 = 8m x 4,20 + Sims

Kackesäulen
hier 1m
von Rassade

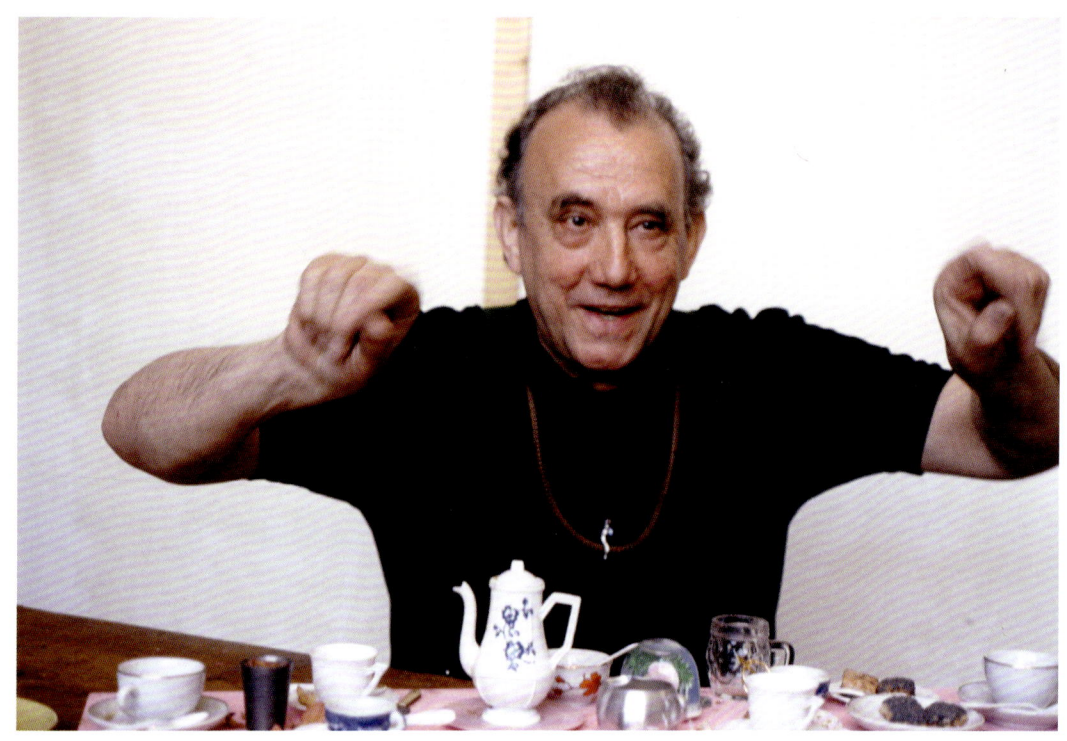

*Daniel Spoerri at work on the reliefs showing food scenes*

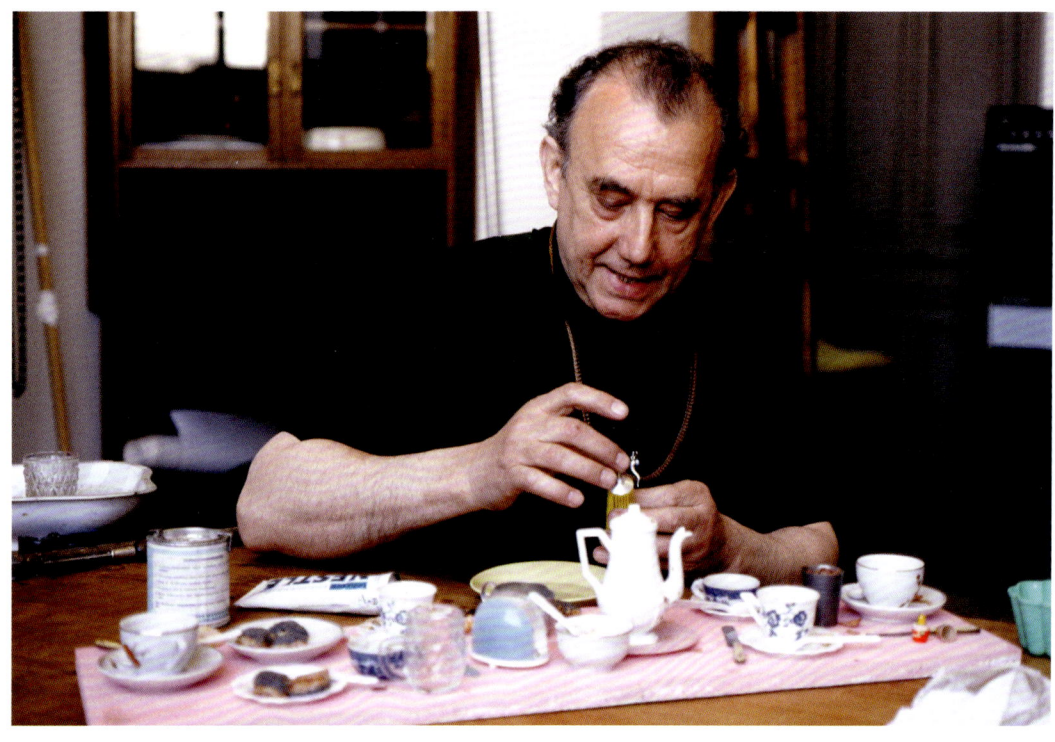

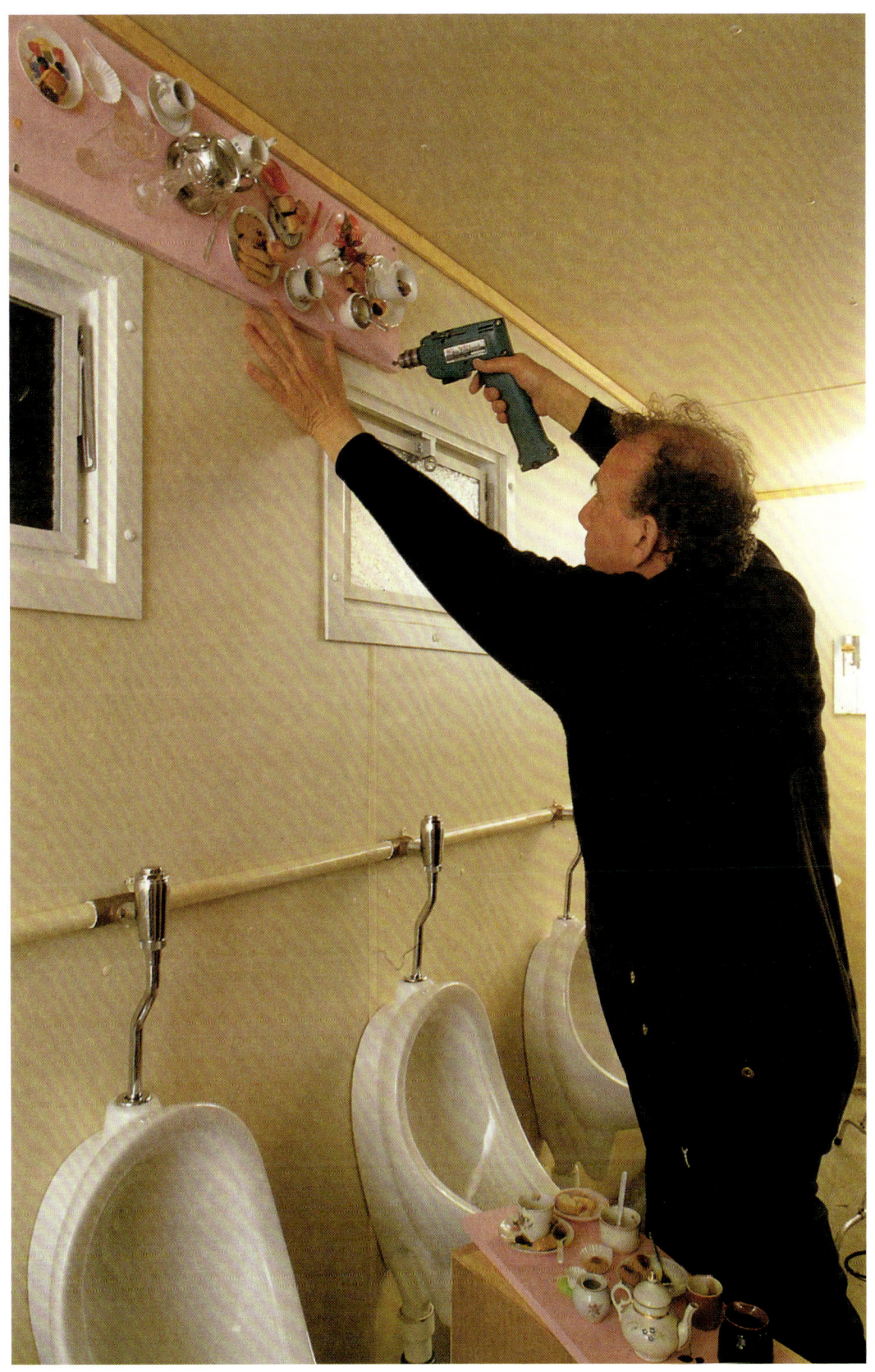

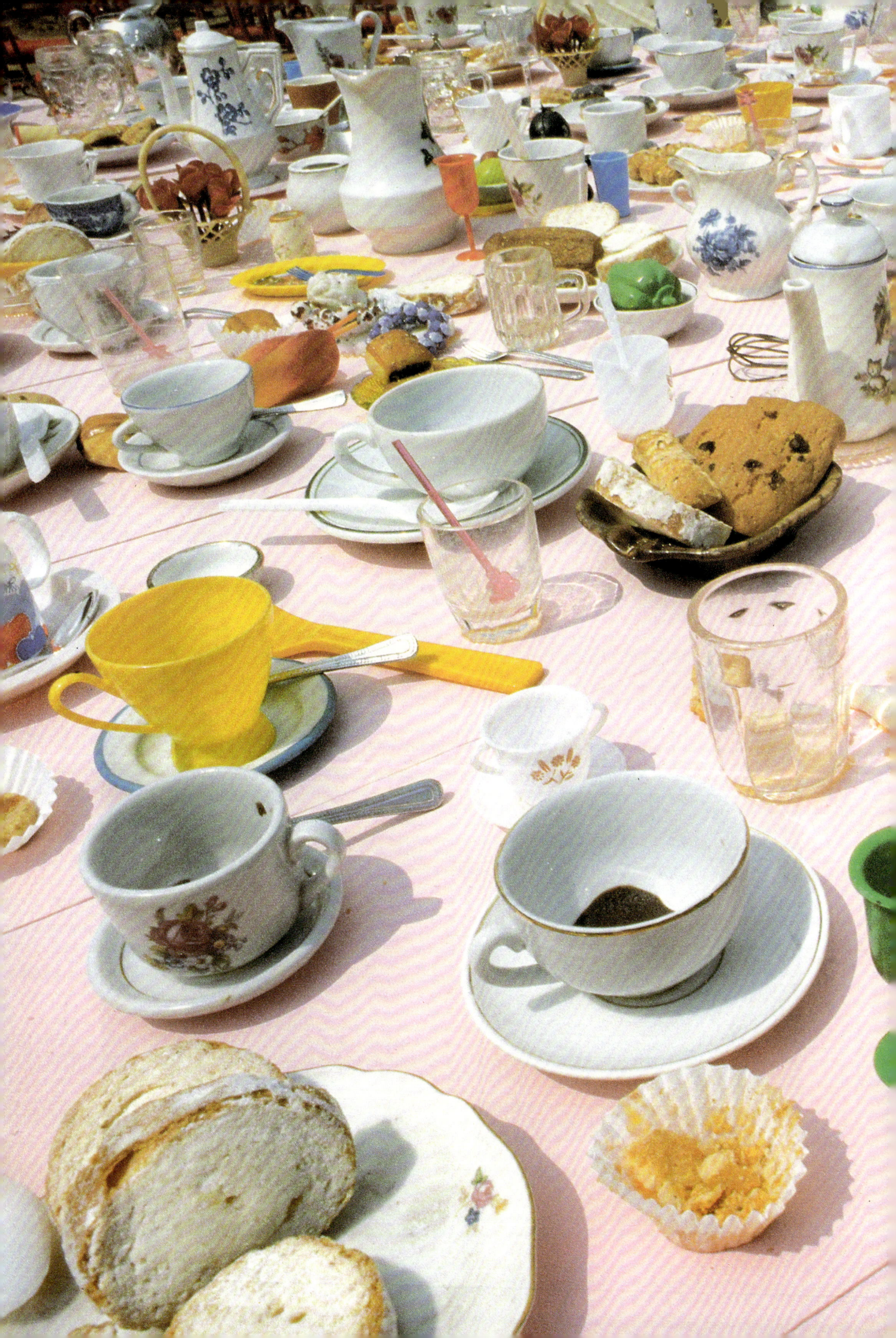

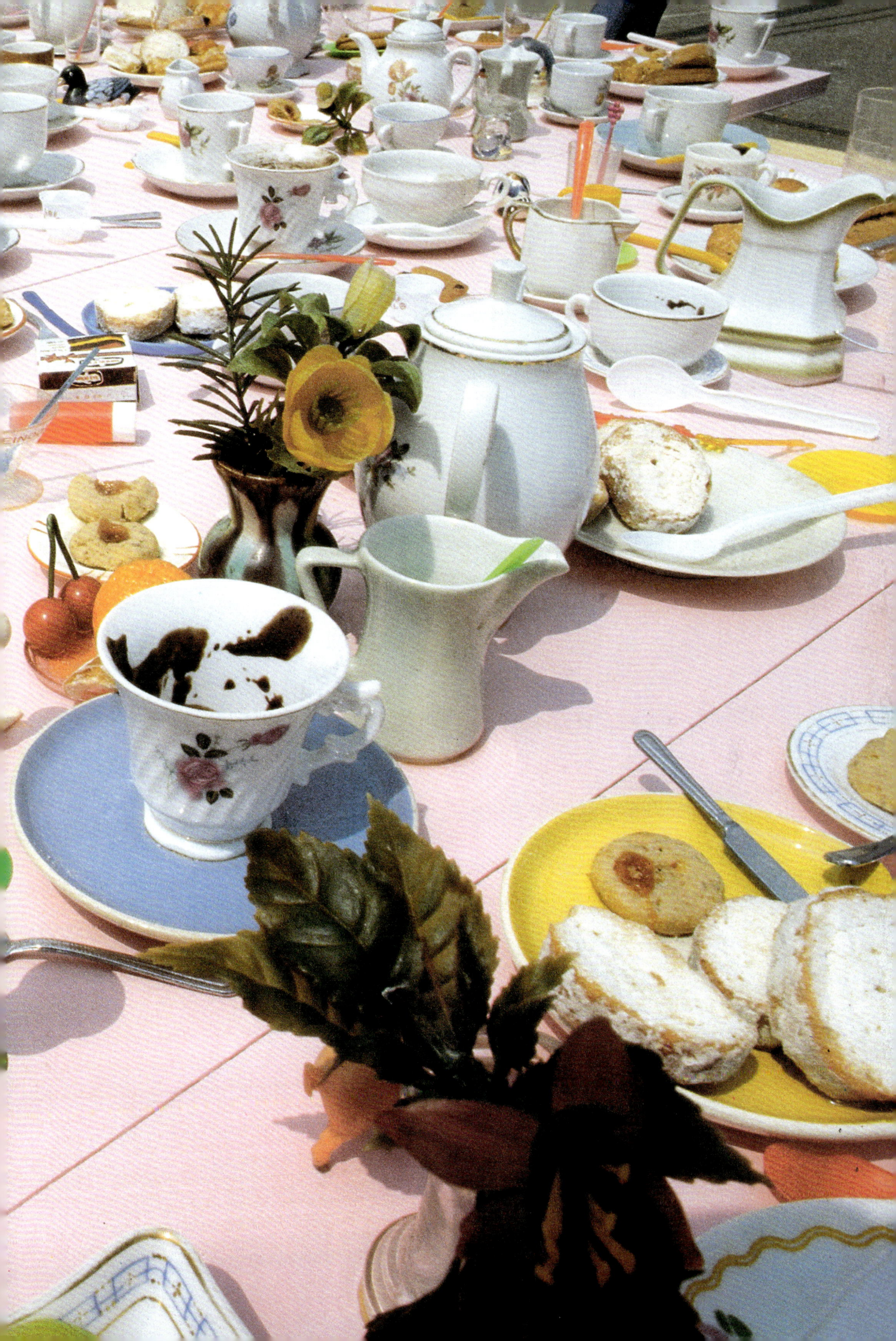

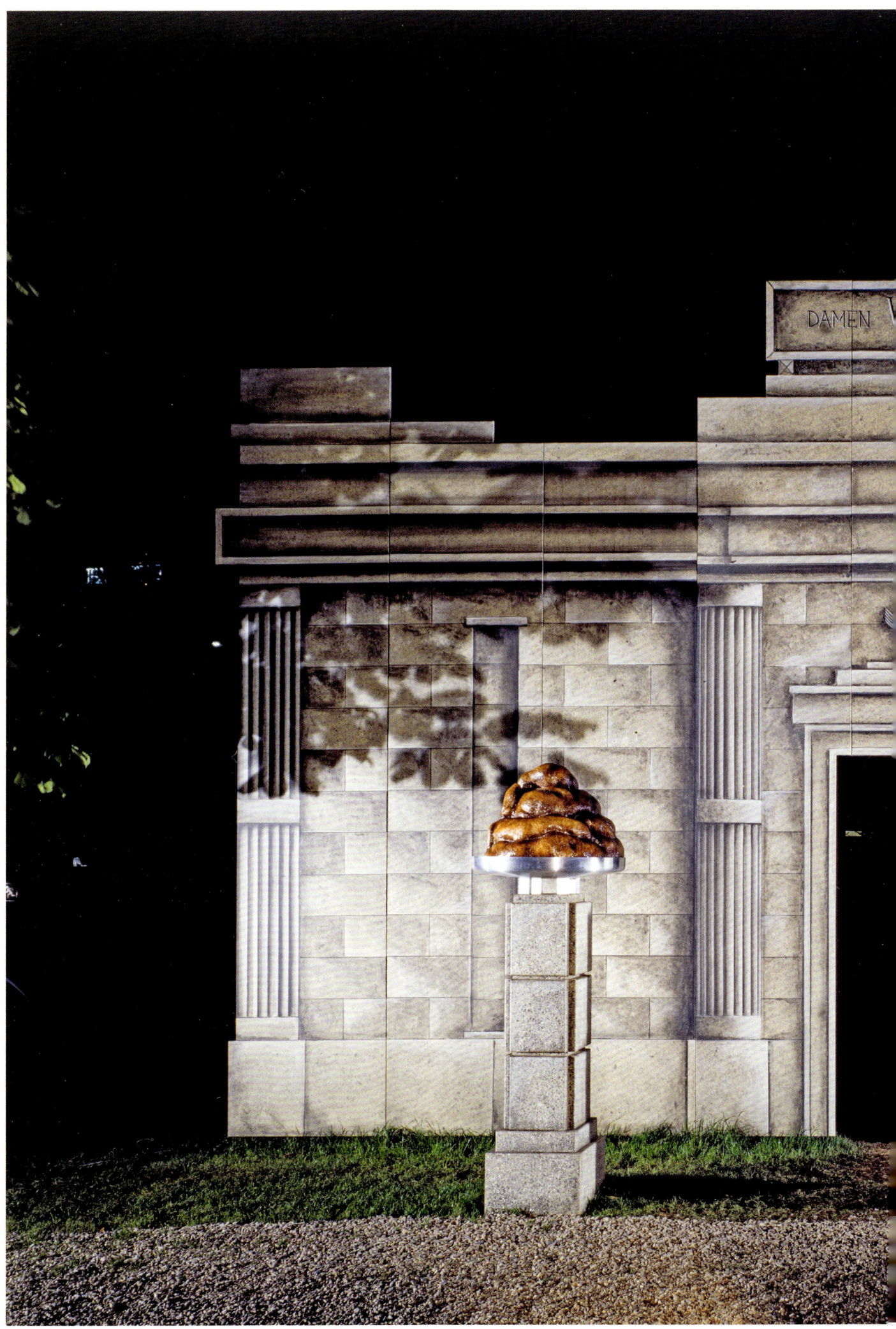

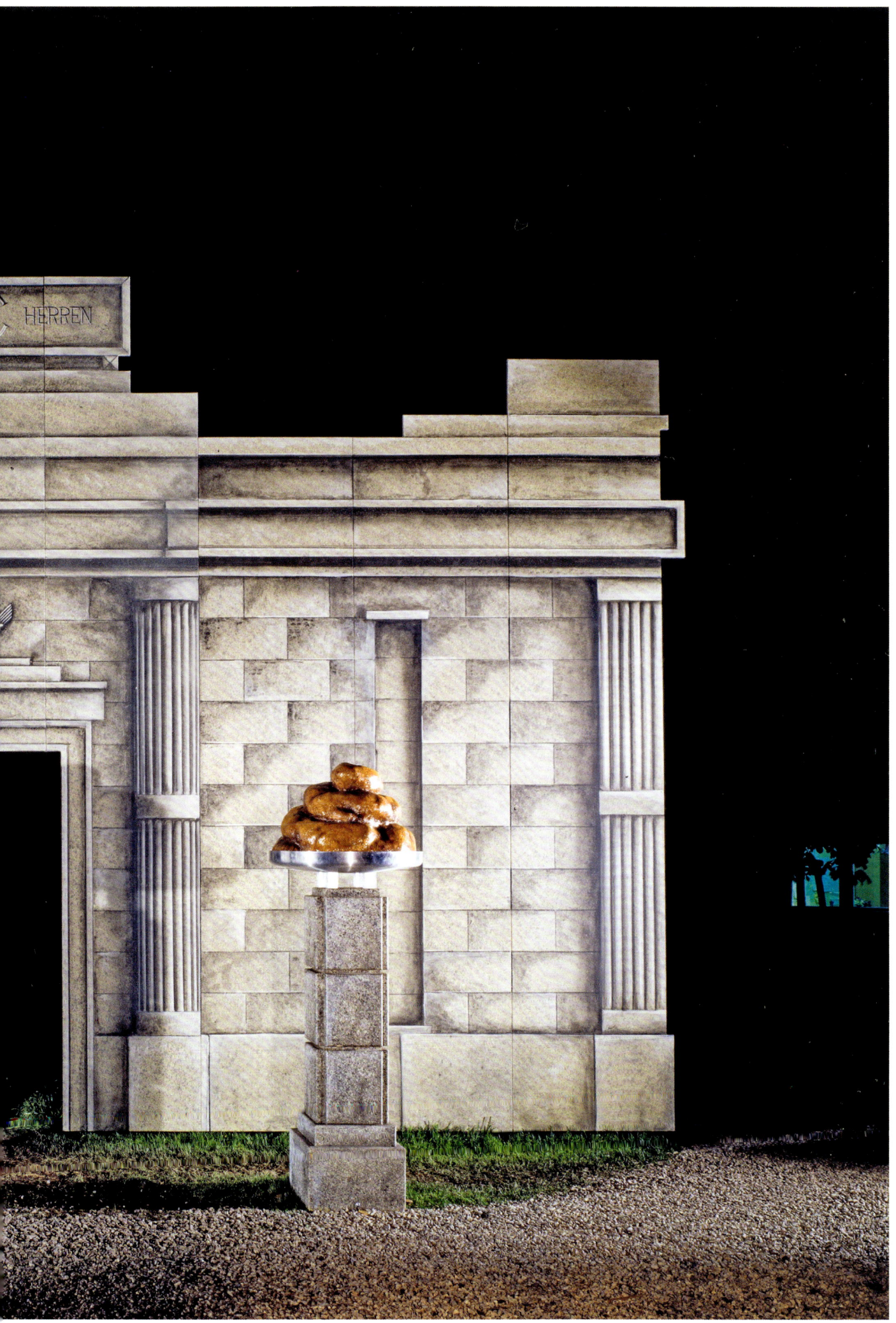

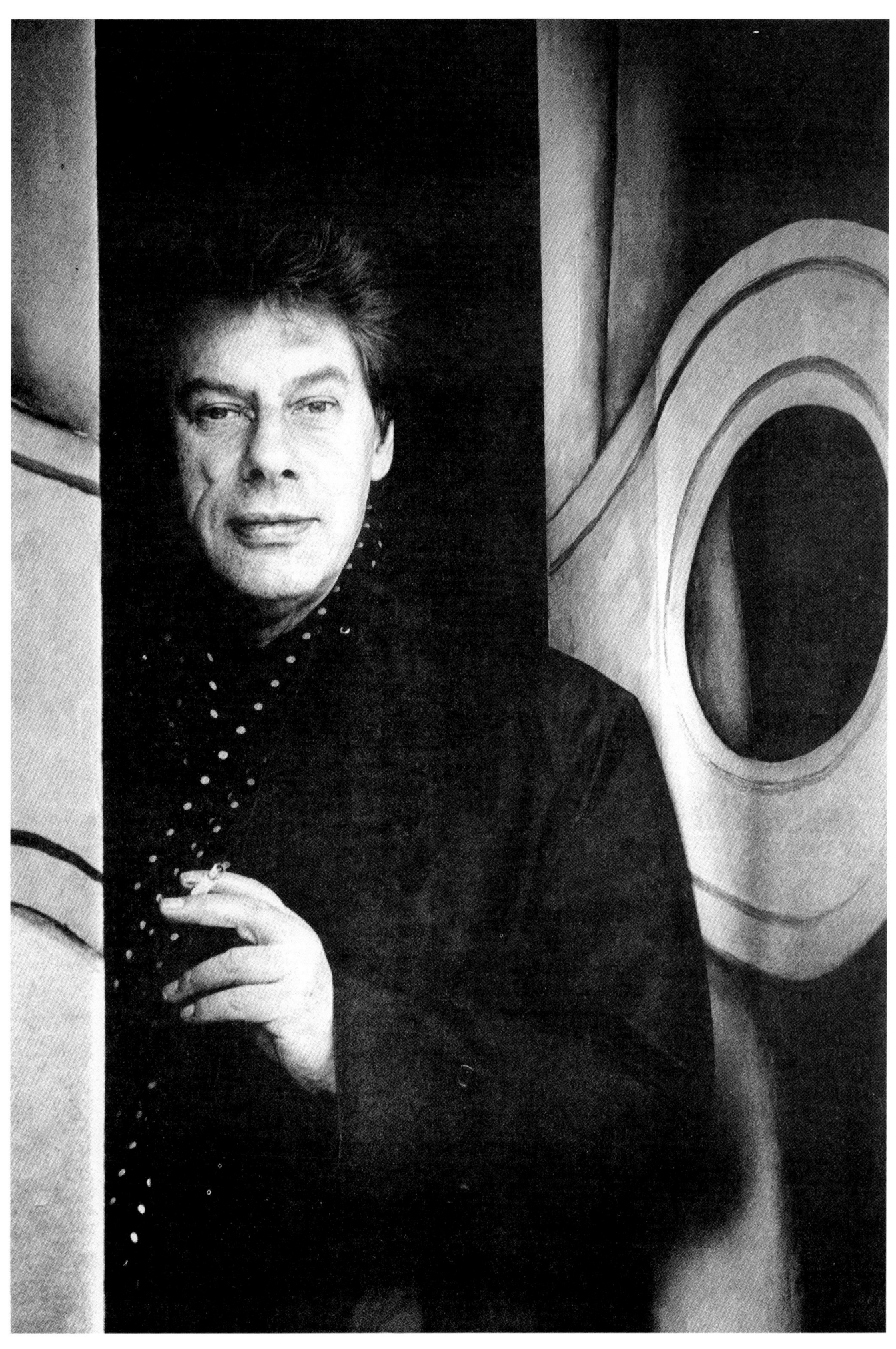

Hubert Aratym

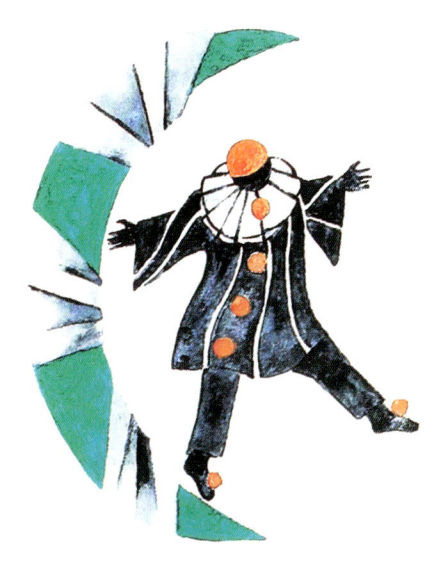

Pierrot Luna Lunaire An Die Hebel Der Macht Des Traums
Zur Endlichen Verwandlung In Die Unendlichkeit Erbittet
Ergebenst ARATYM

Hubert Aratym

Born: January 22, 1926, in Gutenstein, Austria.
Died: February 22, 2000, in Vienna.

Painter.

Hubert Aratym designed a **Transformation Pavilion** for *Luna Luna*. Inside, you can look into the counterworld to see yourself as a beggar, king, harlequin, angel, or whore. The music in this room is by René Clemencic.

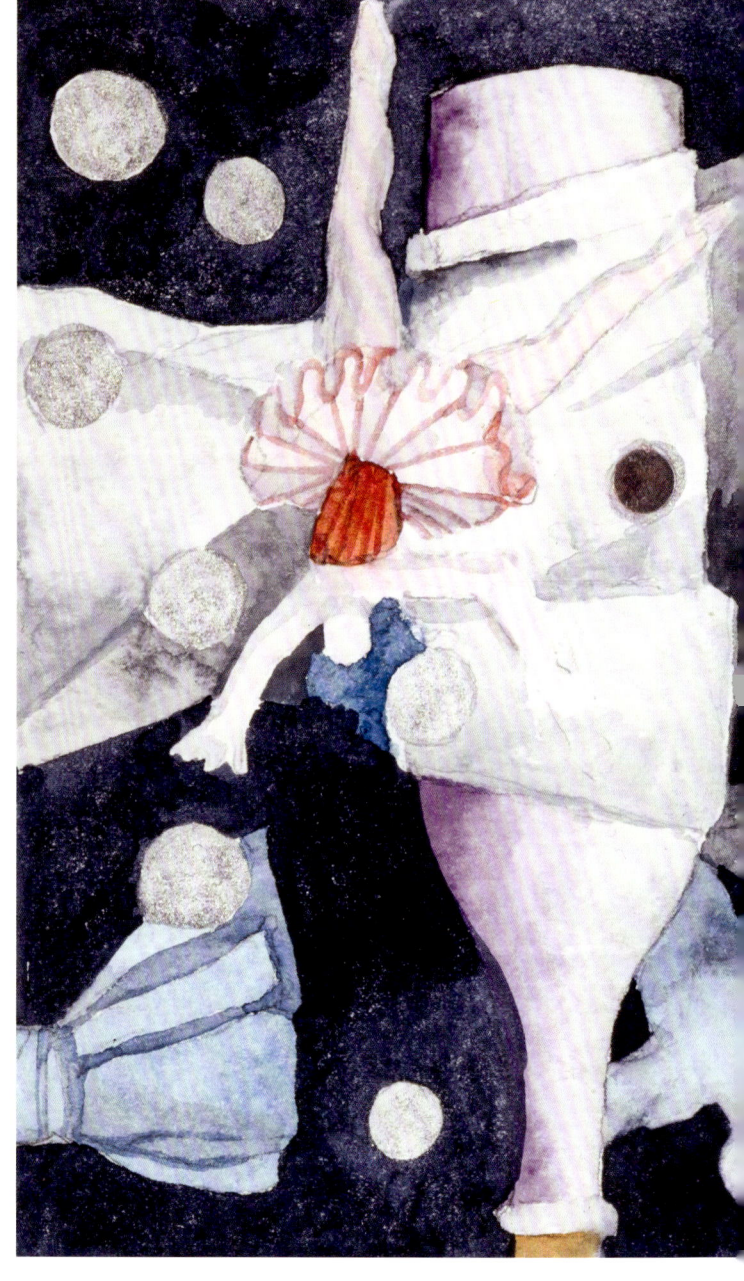

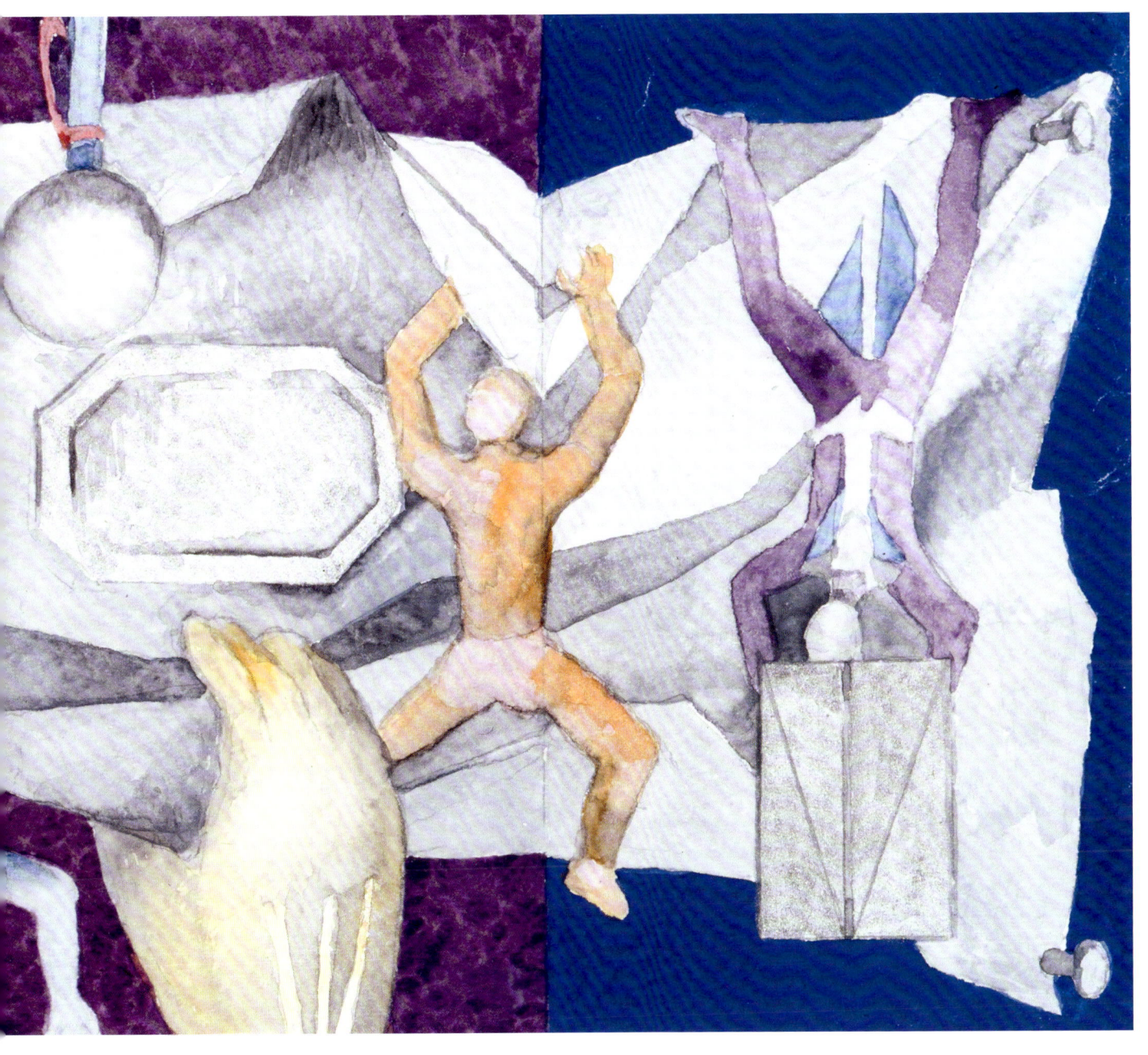

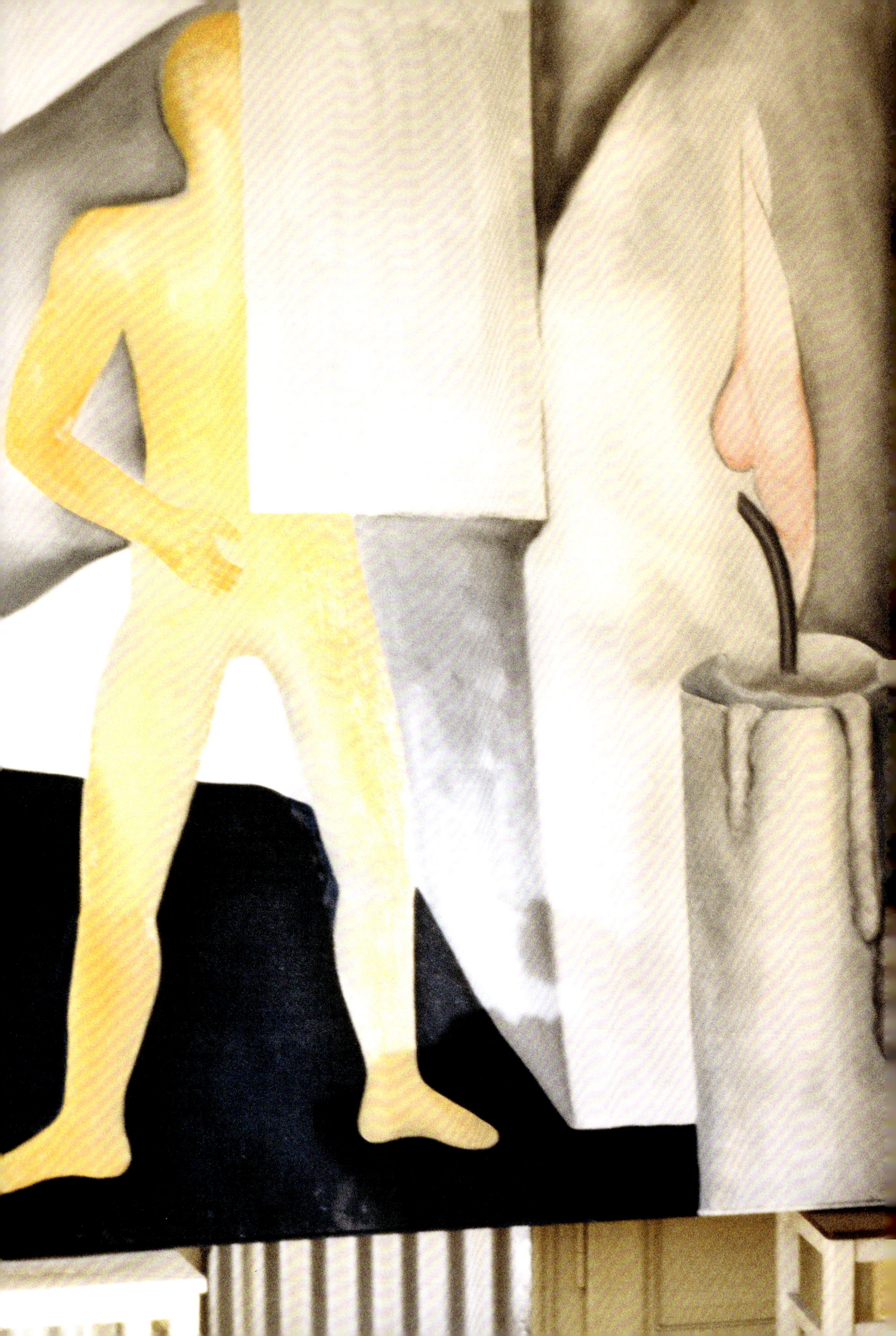

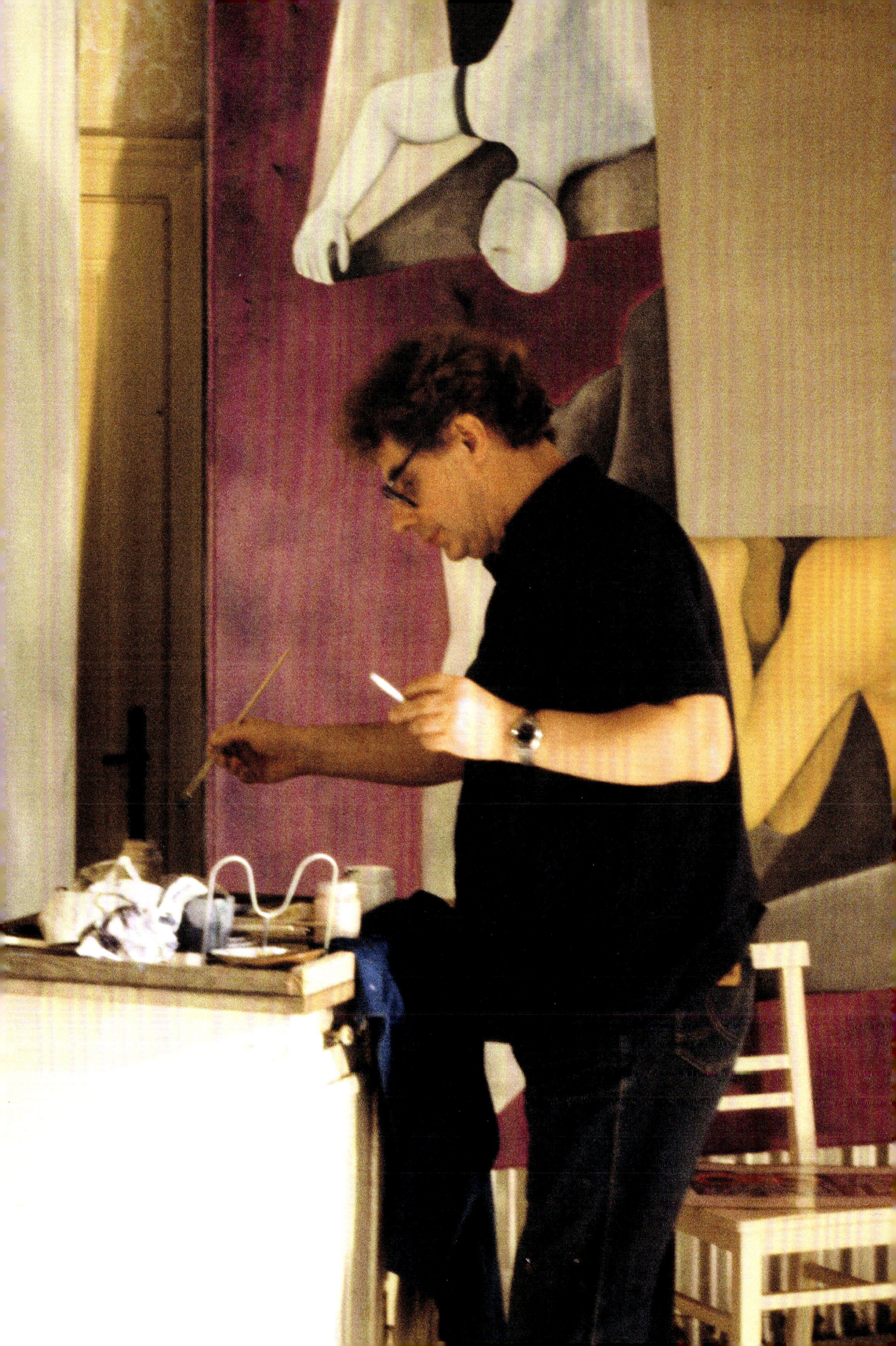

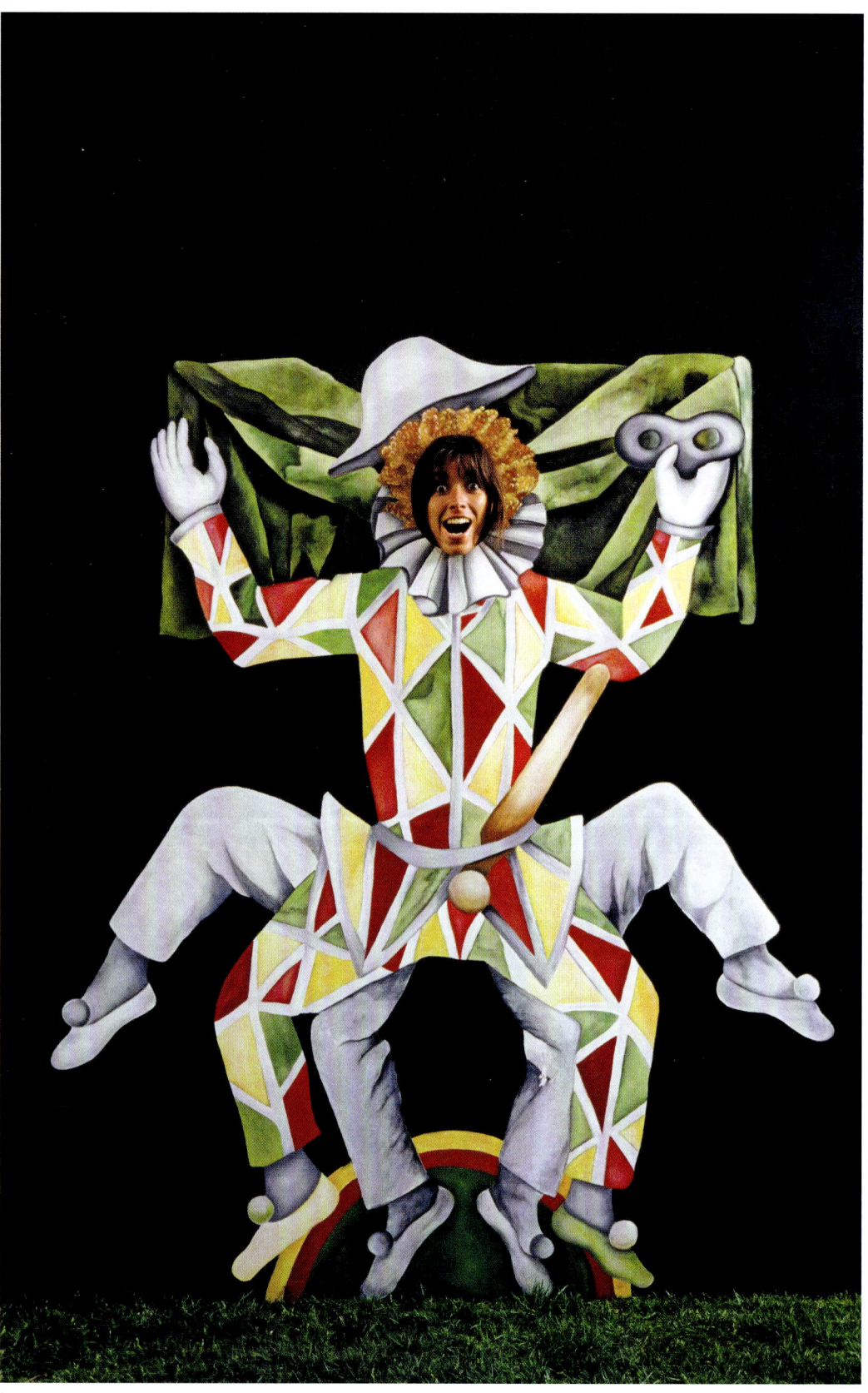

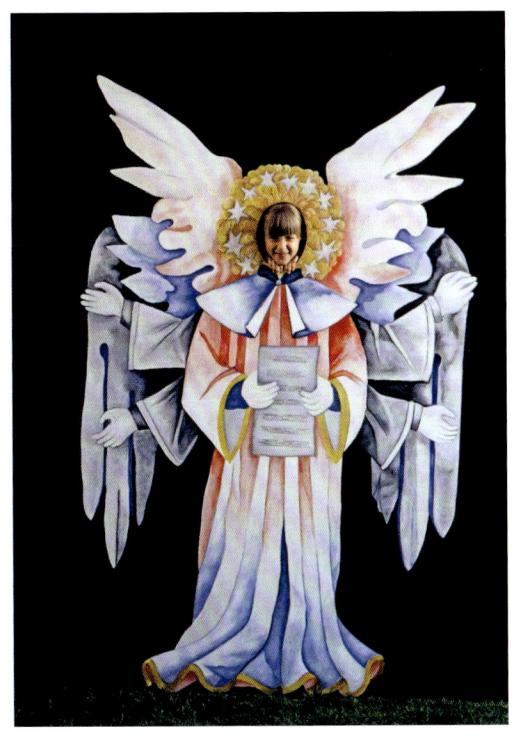
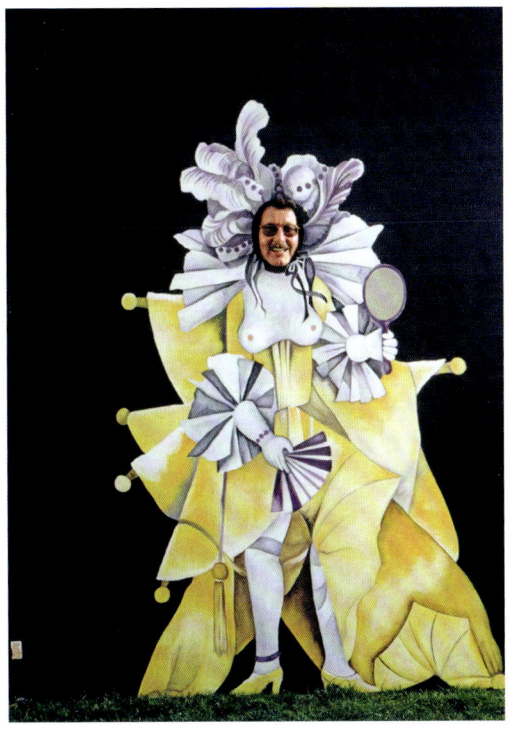

*The transformation figures harlequin, angel, whore, beggar, and king*

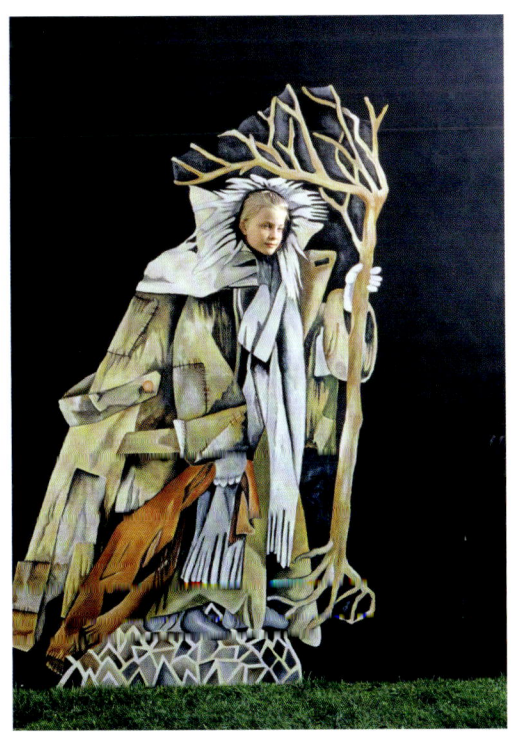
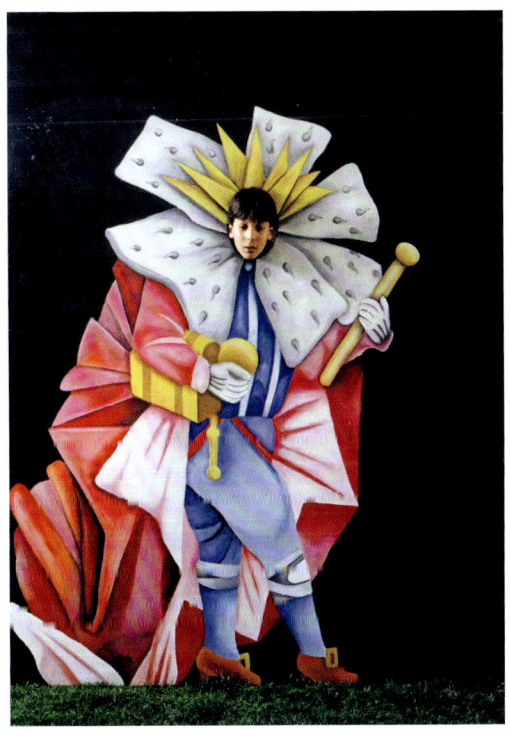

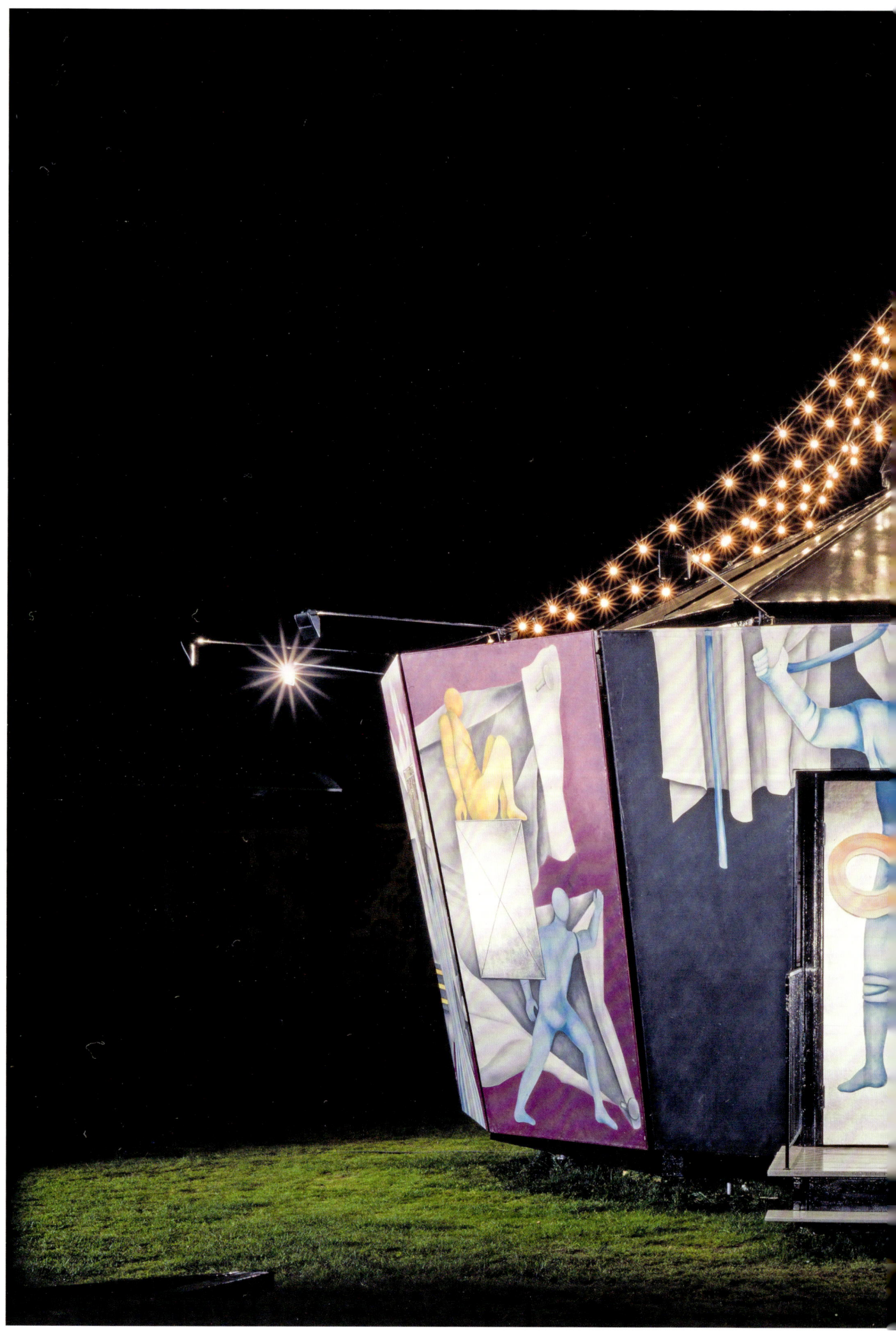

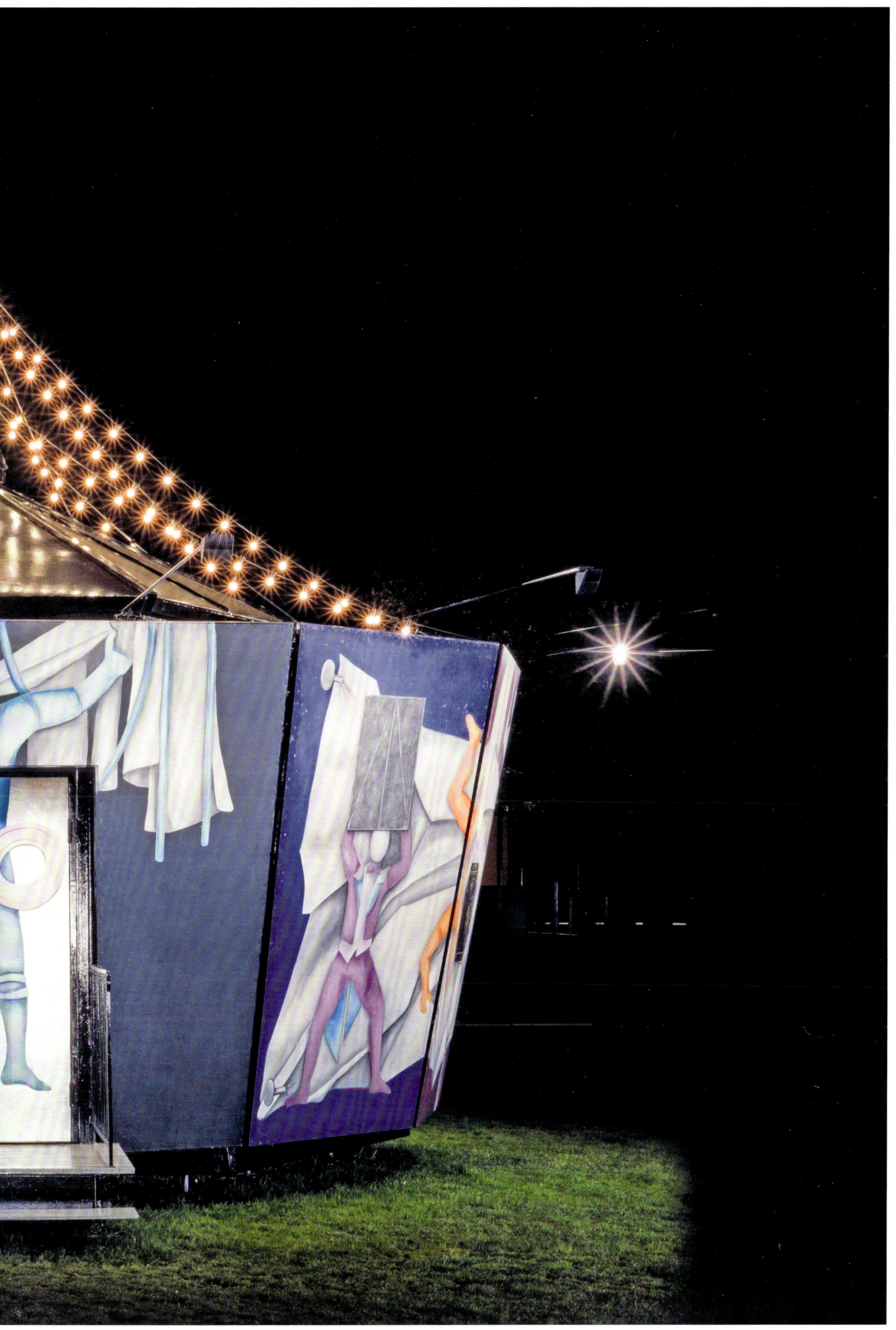

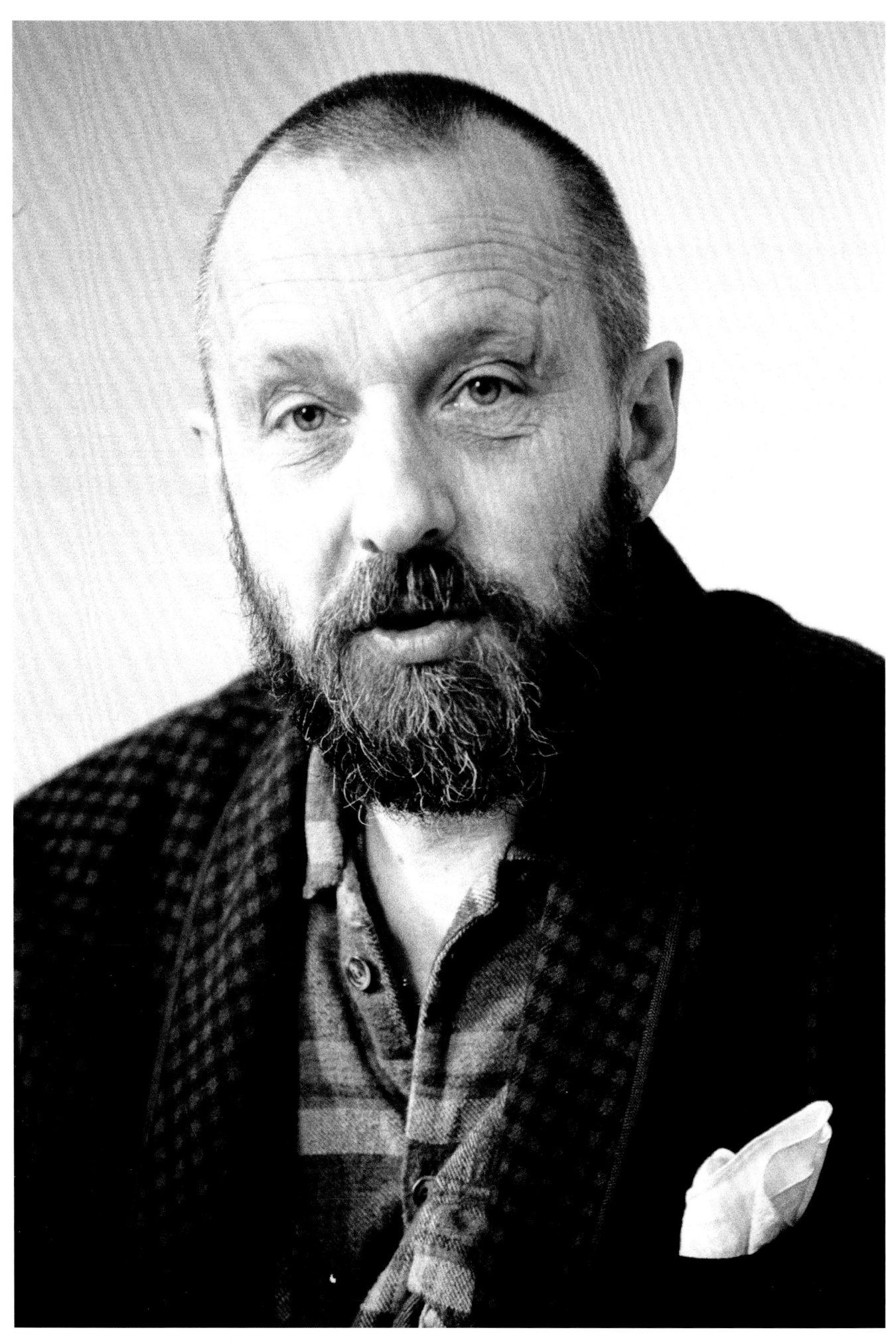

Georg Baselitz

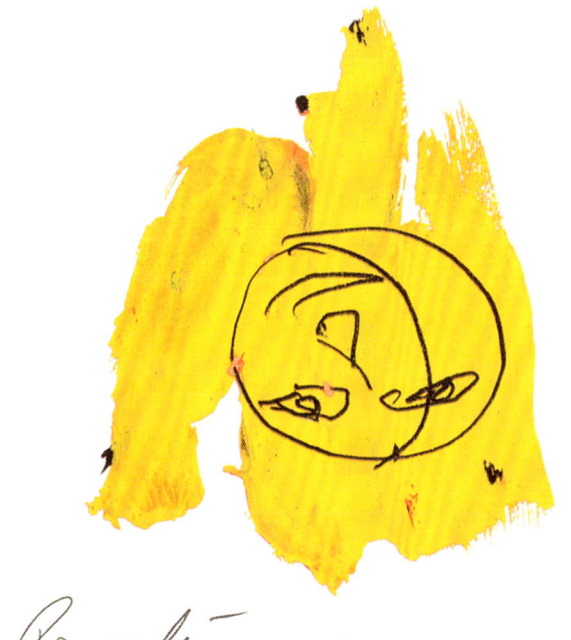

Papaluna-
    ma Luna
Mamaluna
    Luna ma

G. Baselitz 1. IX. 87

Georg Baselitz

Born: January 23, 1938, in Deutschbaselitz, GDR
(East Germany).

Painter, illustrator, sculptor.

Georg Baselitz designed **posters**, **flags**, and the
painting for the **House of Shadows** for *Luna
Luna*. The inner walls of this attraction are
prepared in such a way that any shadow cast on
them remains visible there for 20 seconds and
only then slowly dissipates.

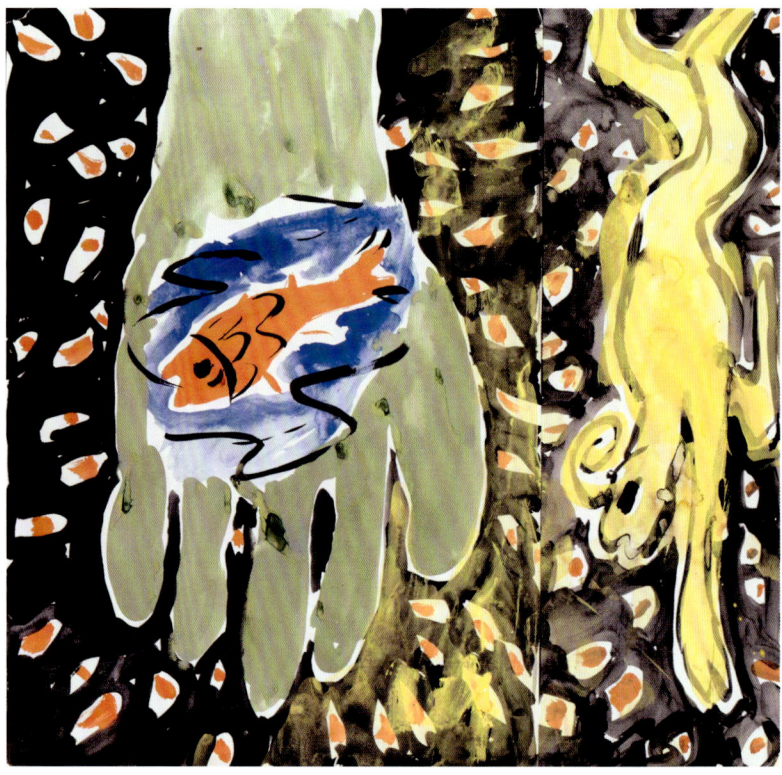

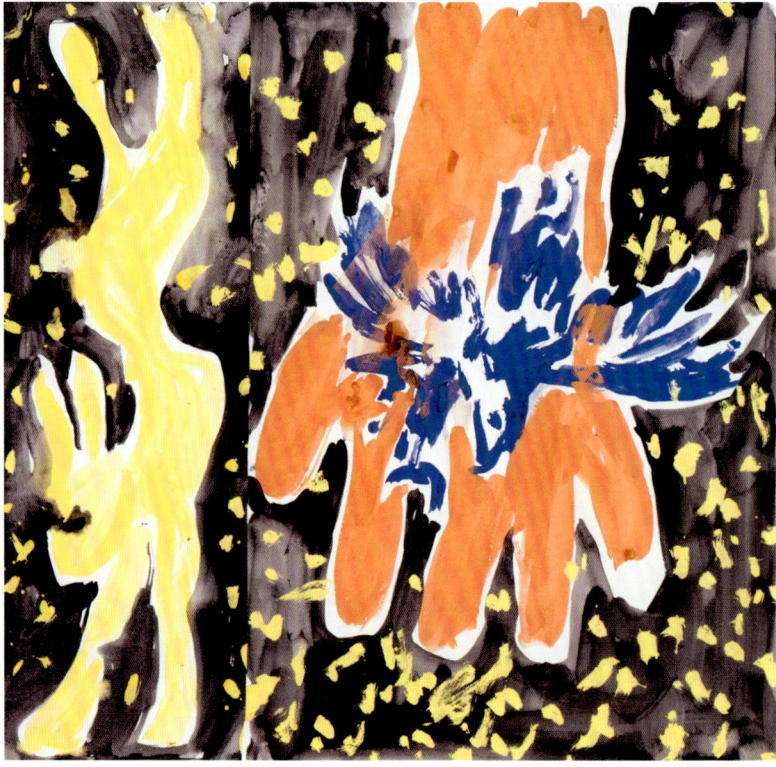

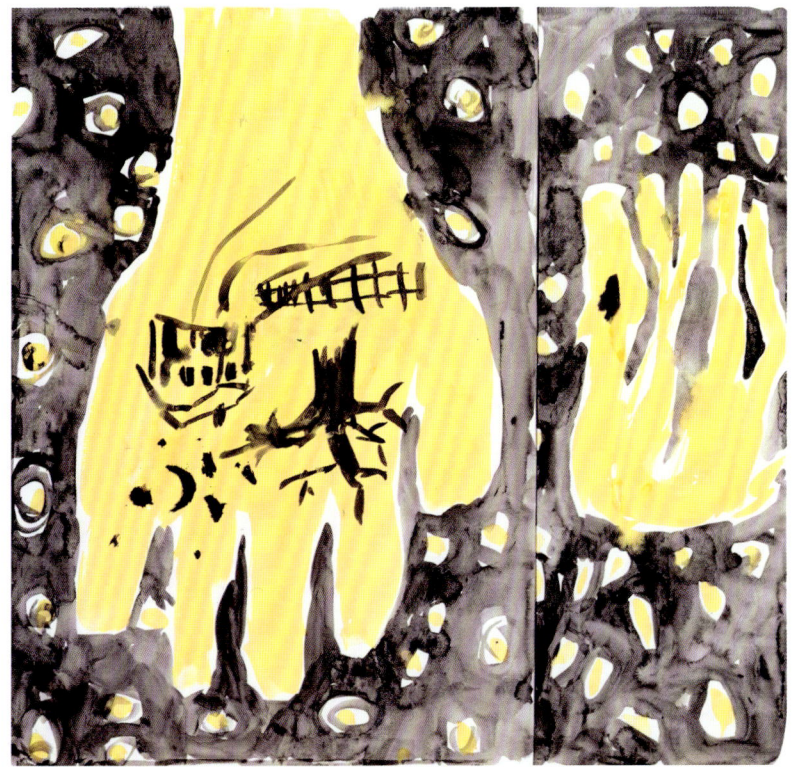

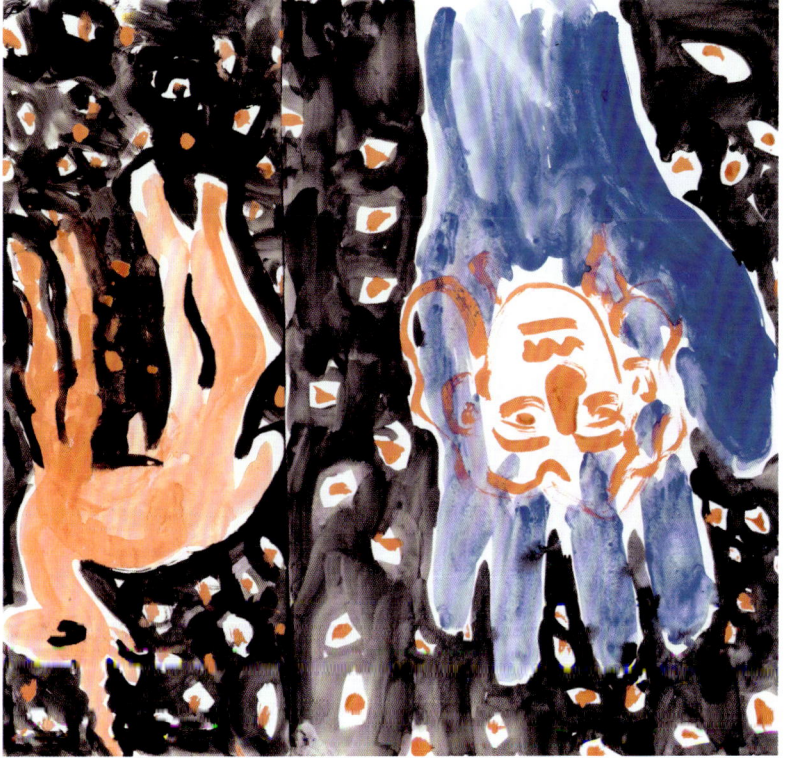

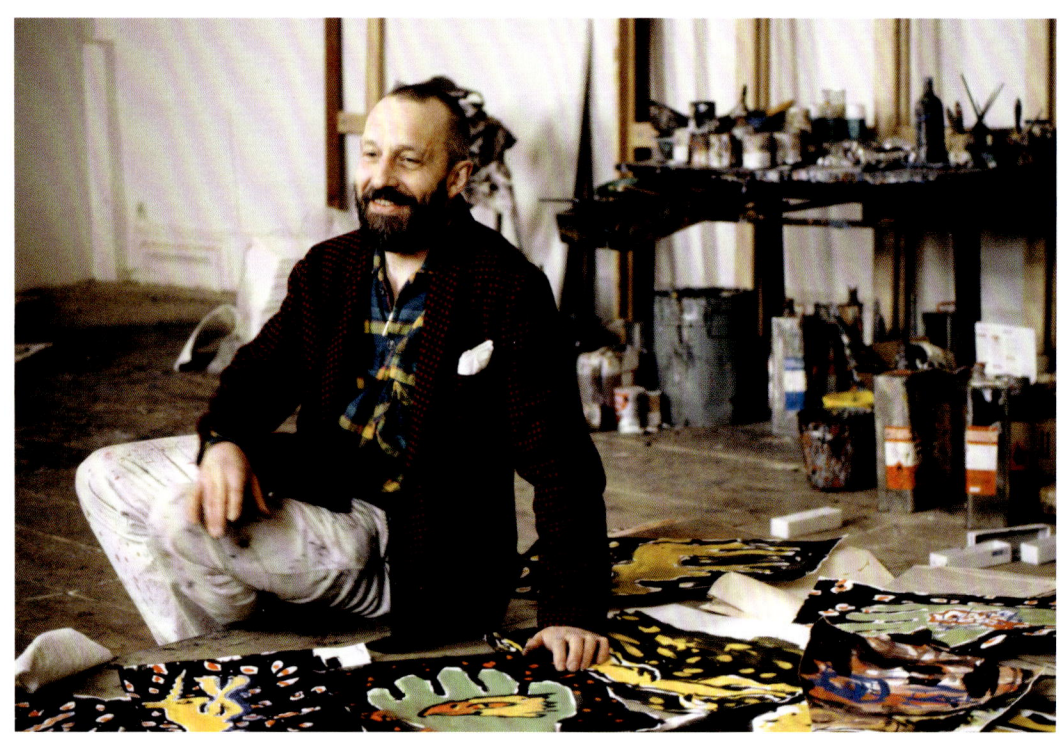

*Georg Baselitz in his studio at Schloss Derneburg, working on the facade designs for the House of Shadows*

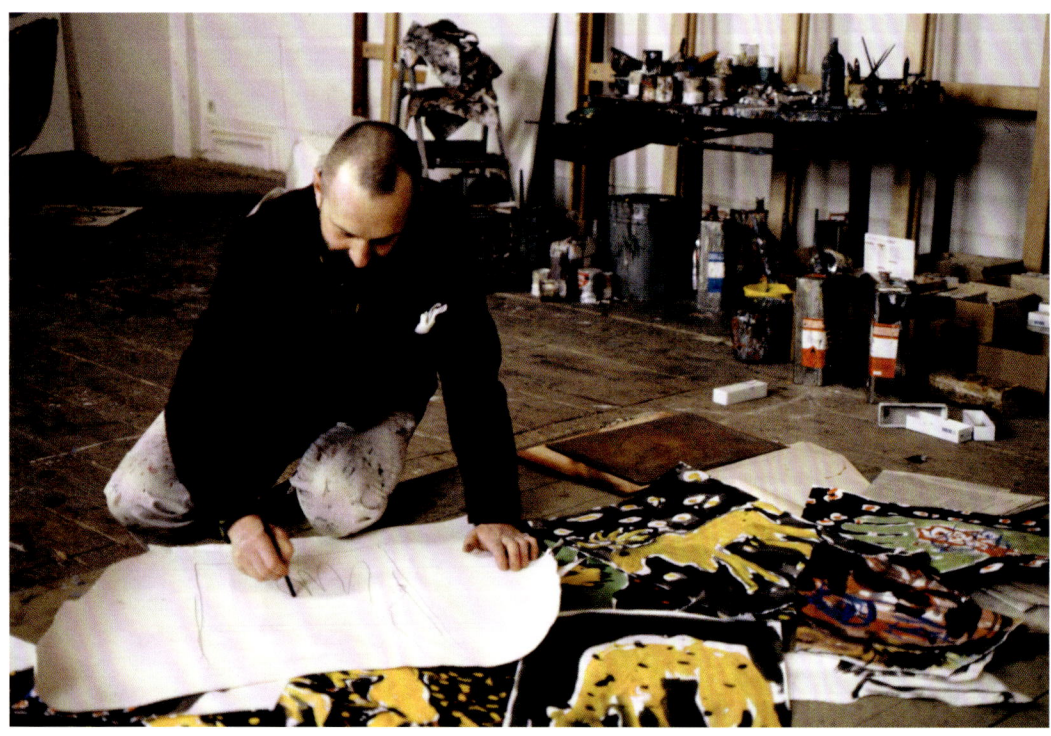

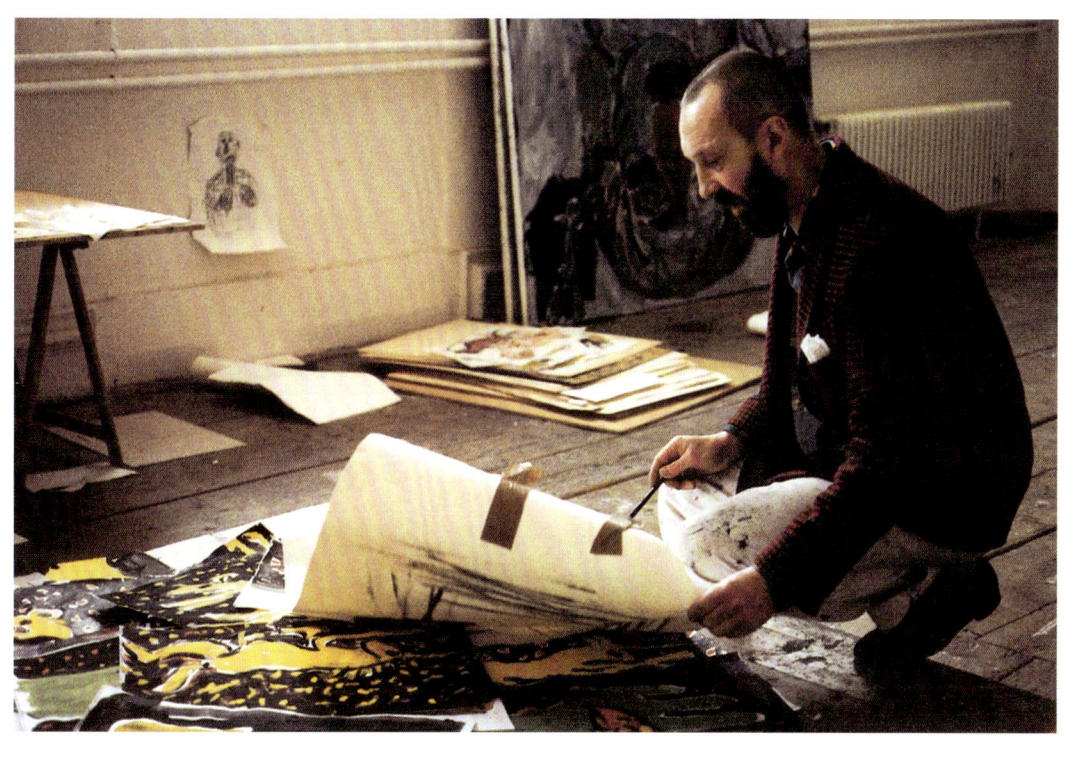

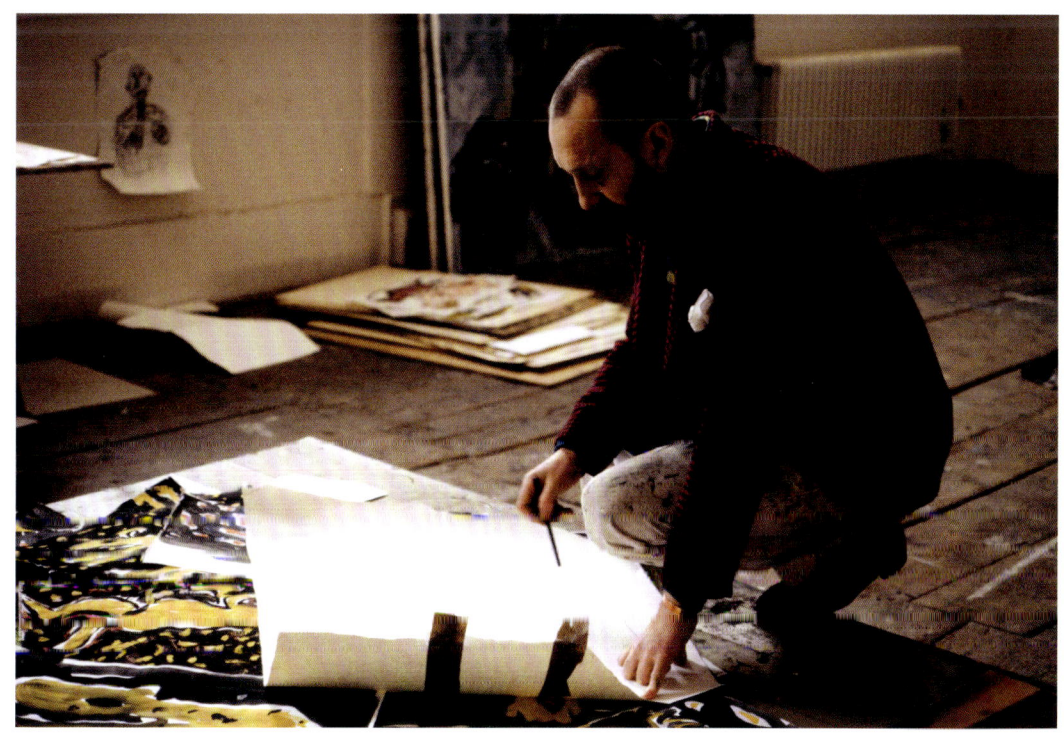

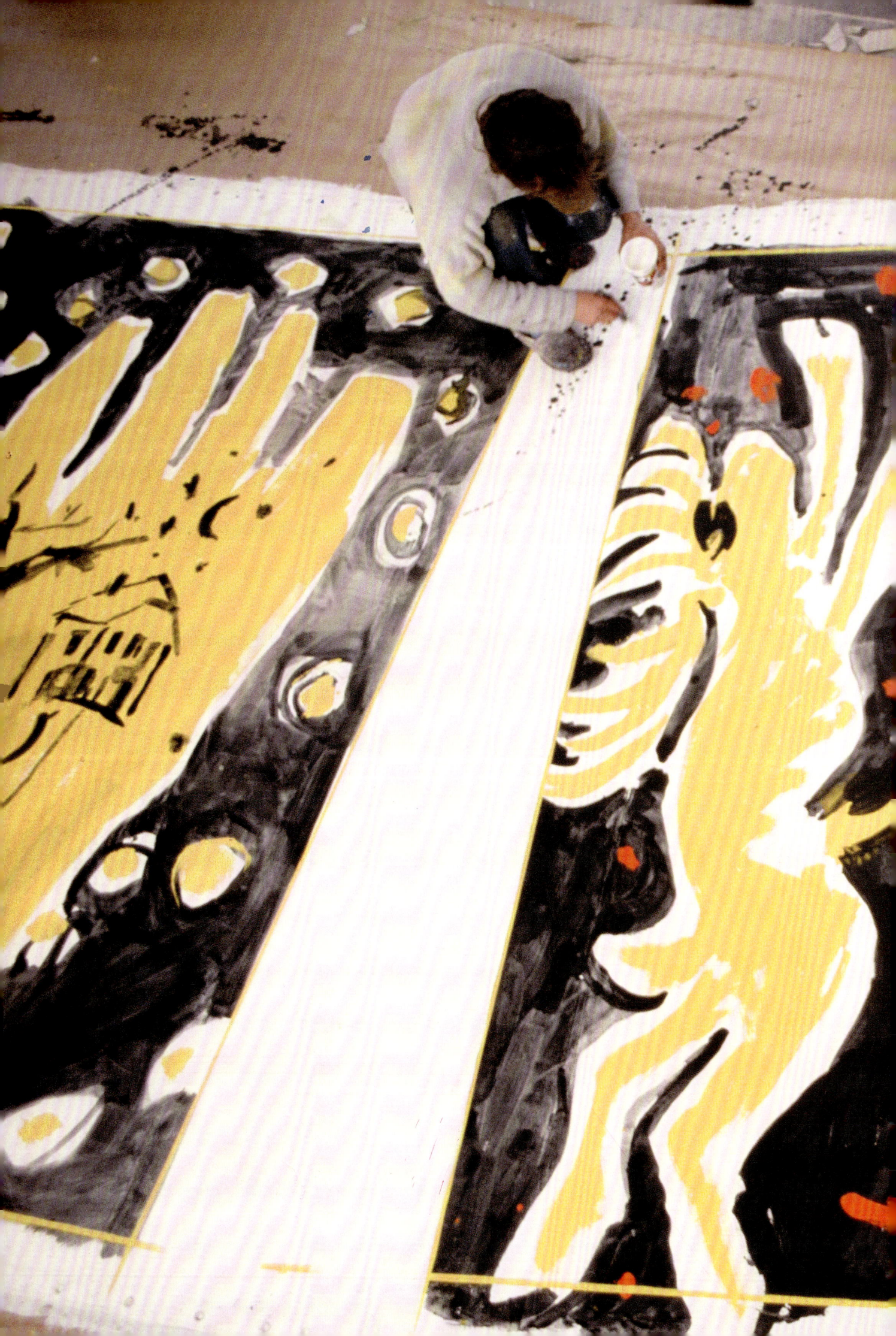

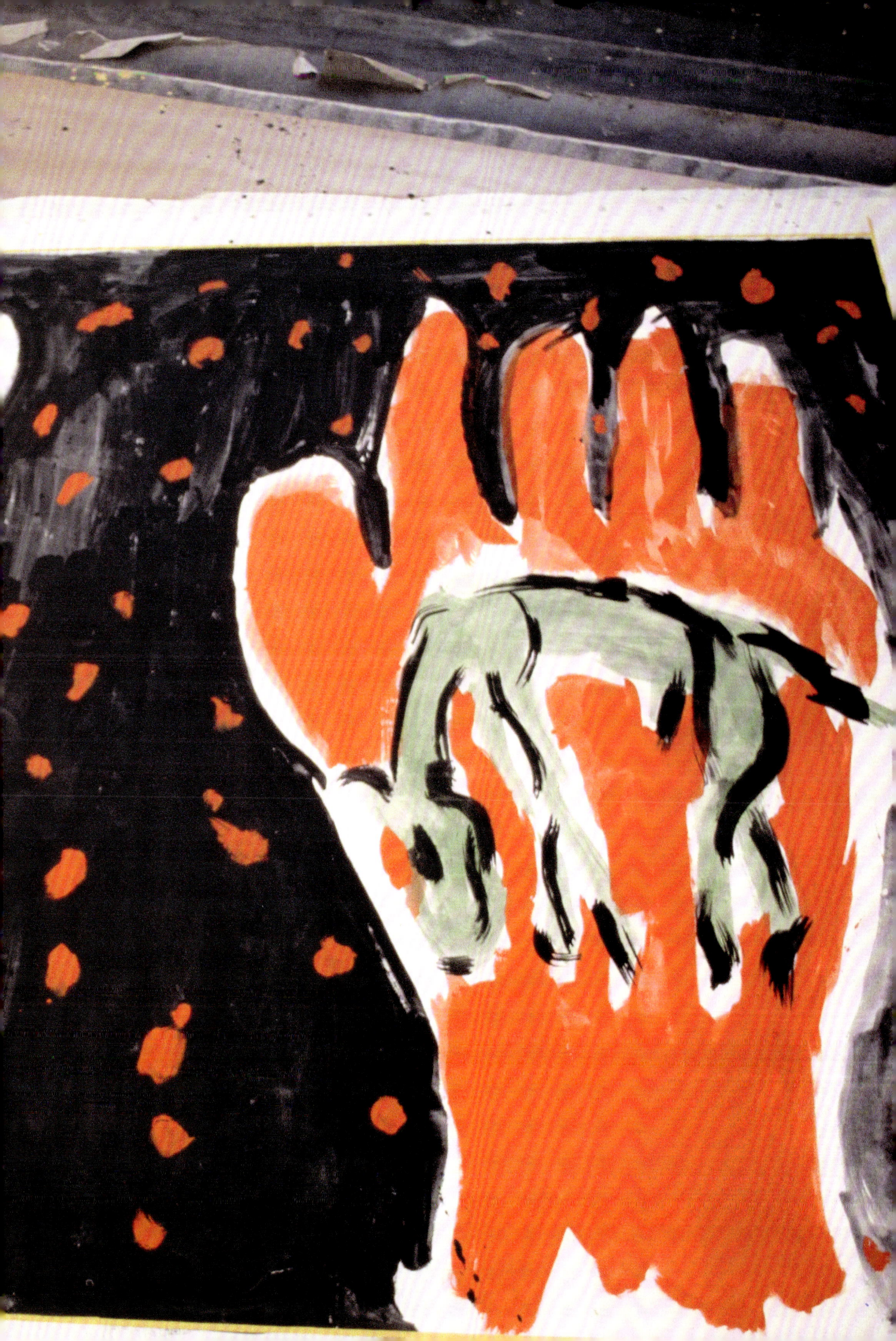

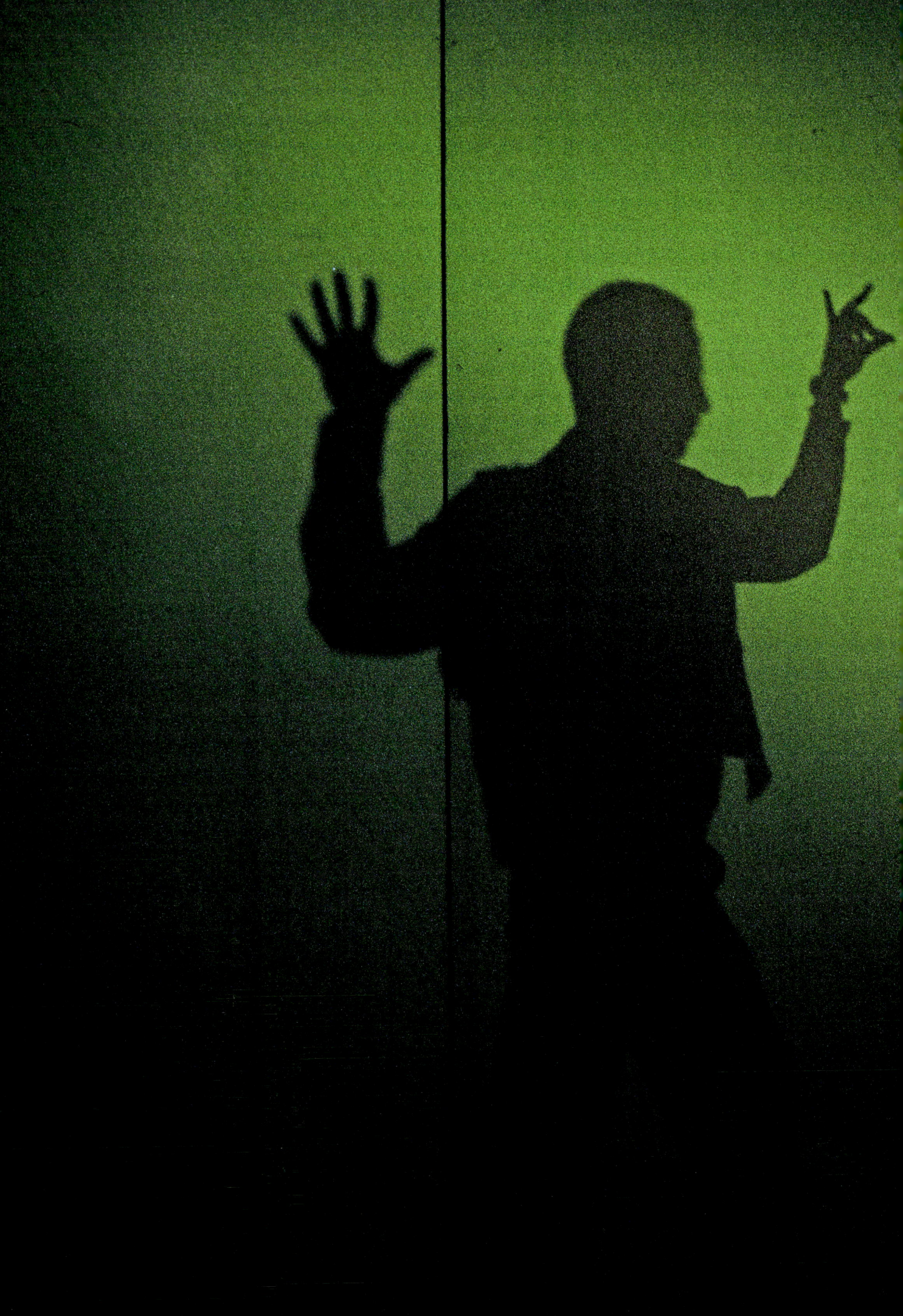

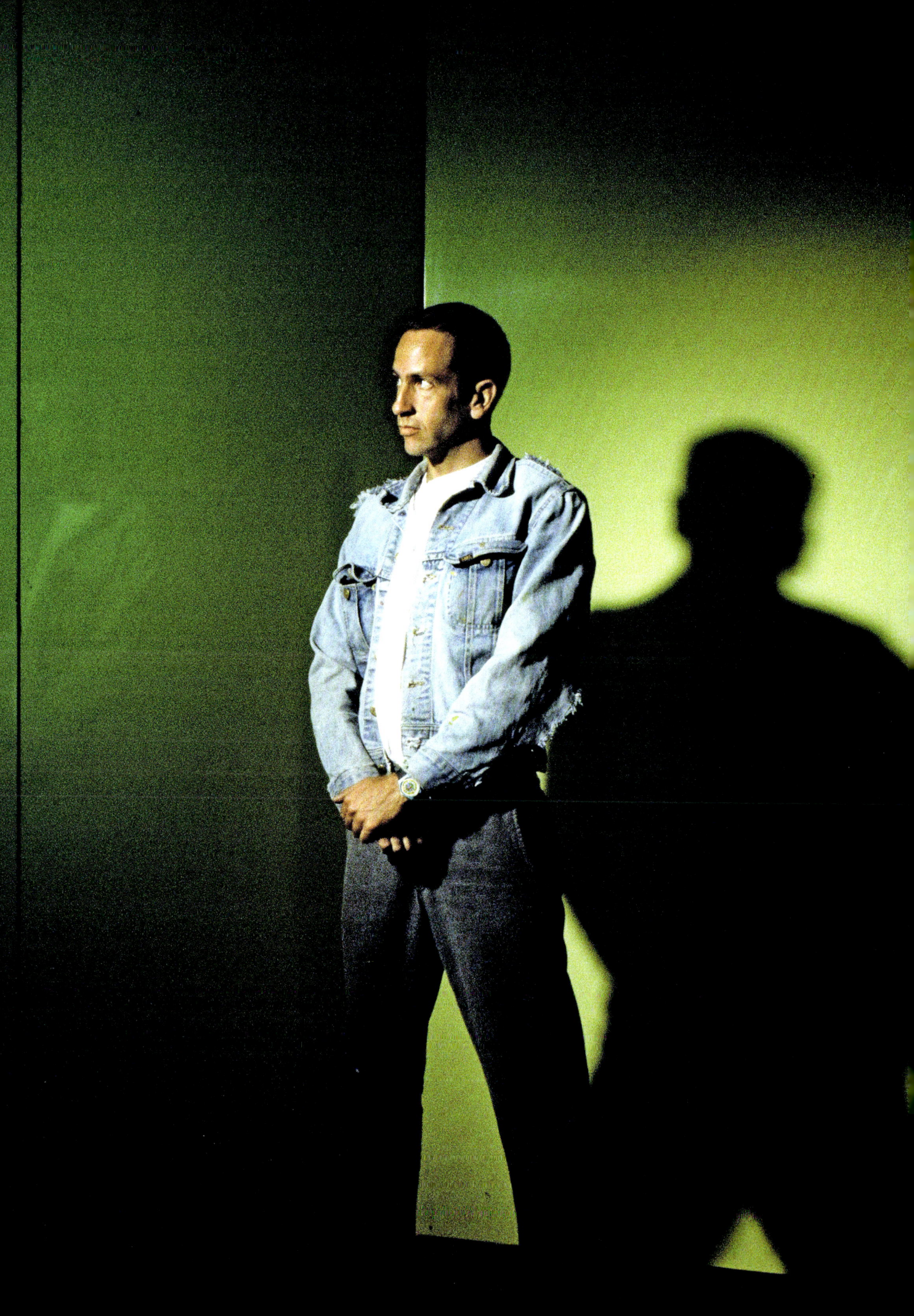

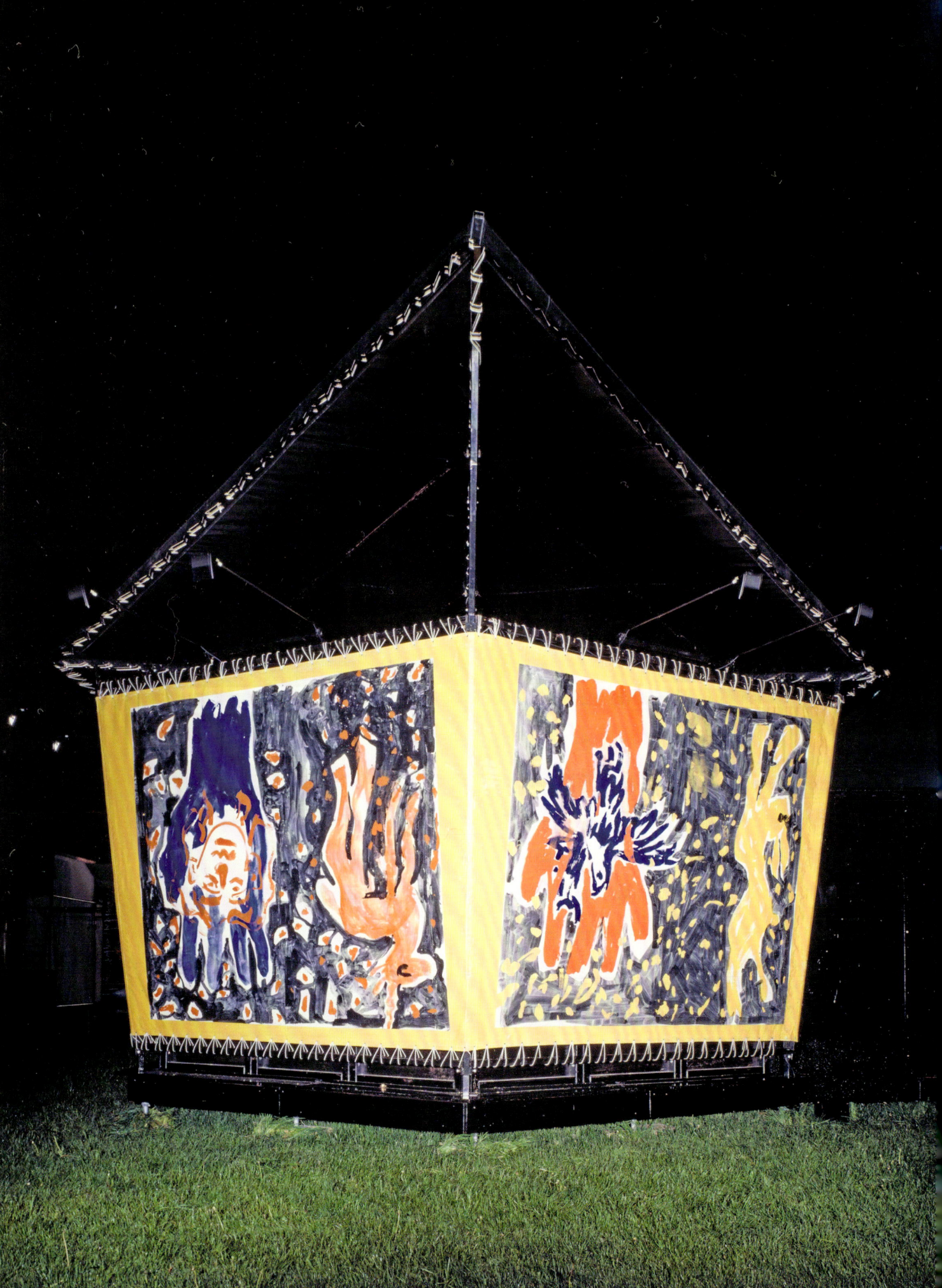

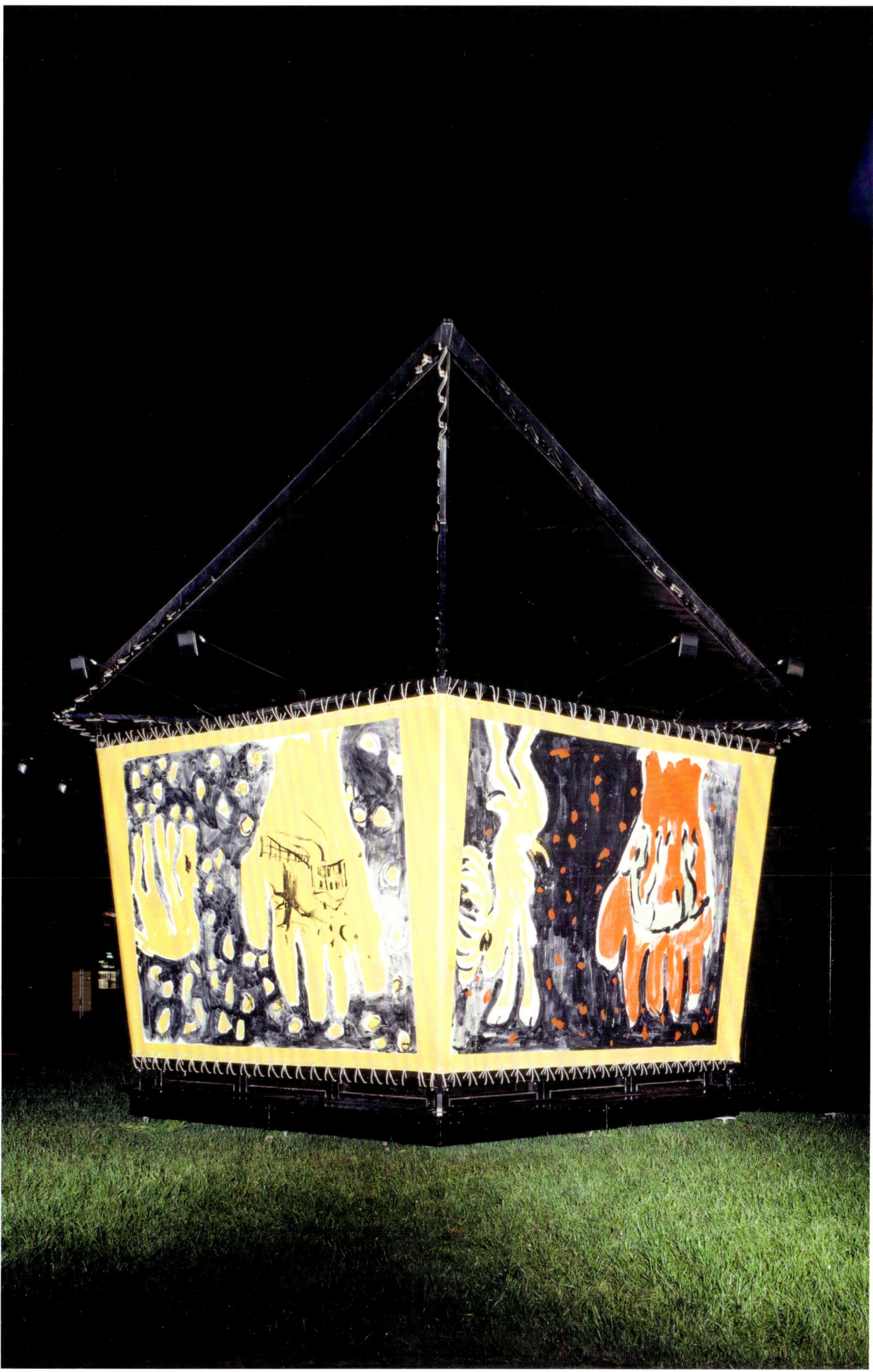

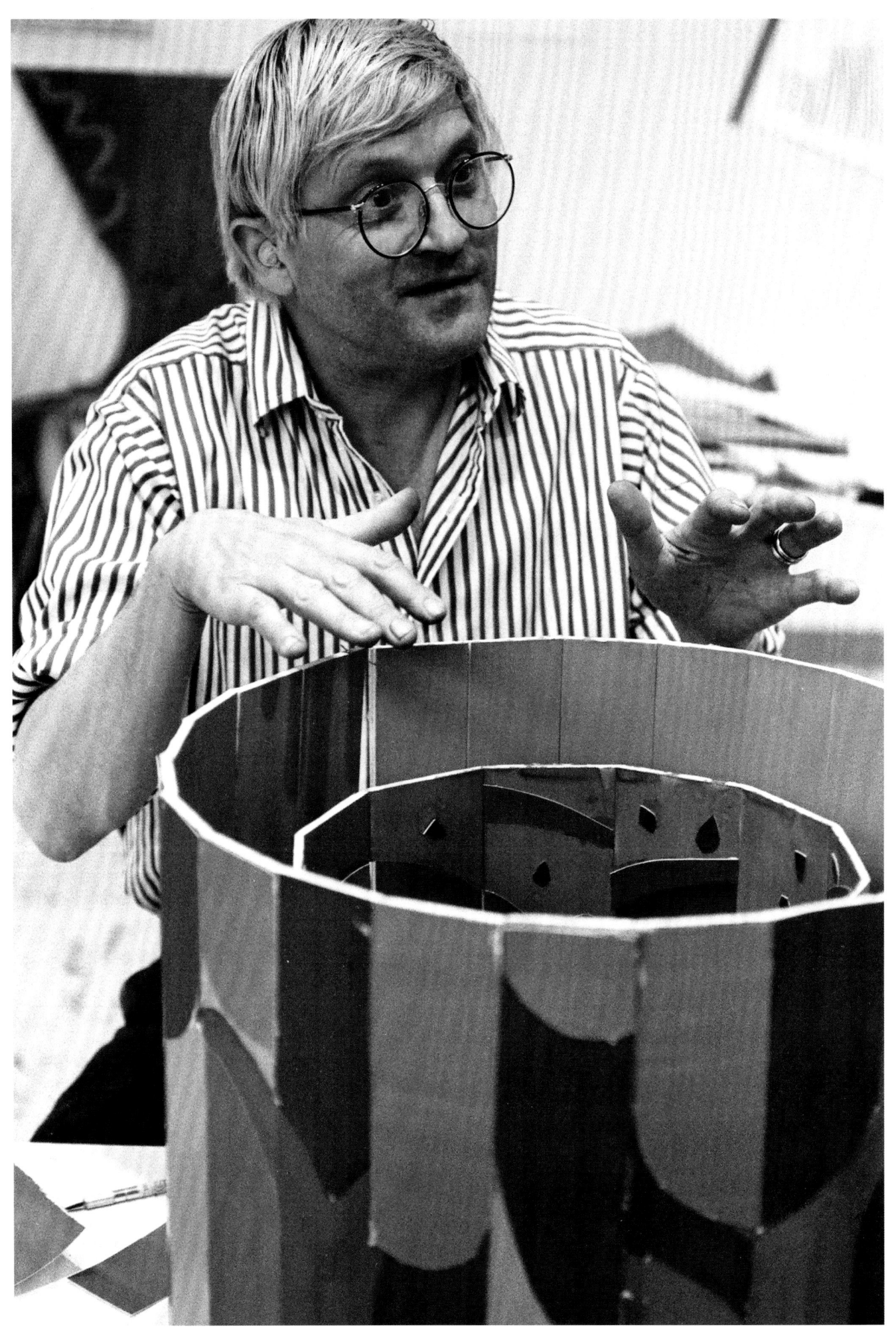

David Hockney

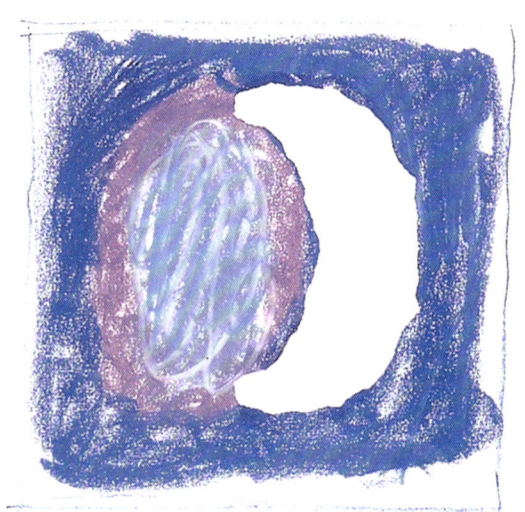

Luna Luna

David Hockney

David Hockney

Born: July 9, 1937, in Bradford, England.

Painter, illustrator, photographer, stage designer.

David Hockney designed the **Enchanted Tree** for
*Luna Luna*, a fairy tale turned into architecture.
It is the story of a symphony orchestra magically
transformed into a sprawling tropical plant.
Music sounds from its foliage day and night.
Compositions are heard by Johann and Joseph
Strauss, played by the Berlin Philharmonic
Orchestra and conducted by Herbert von Karajan.

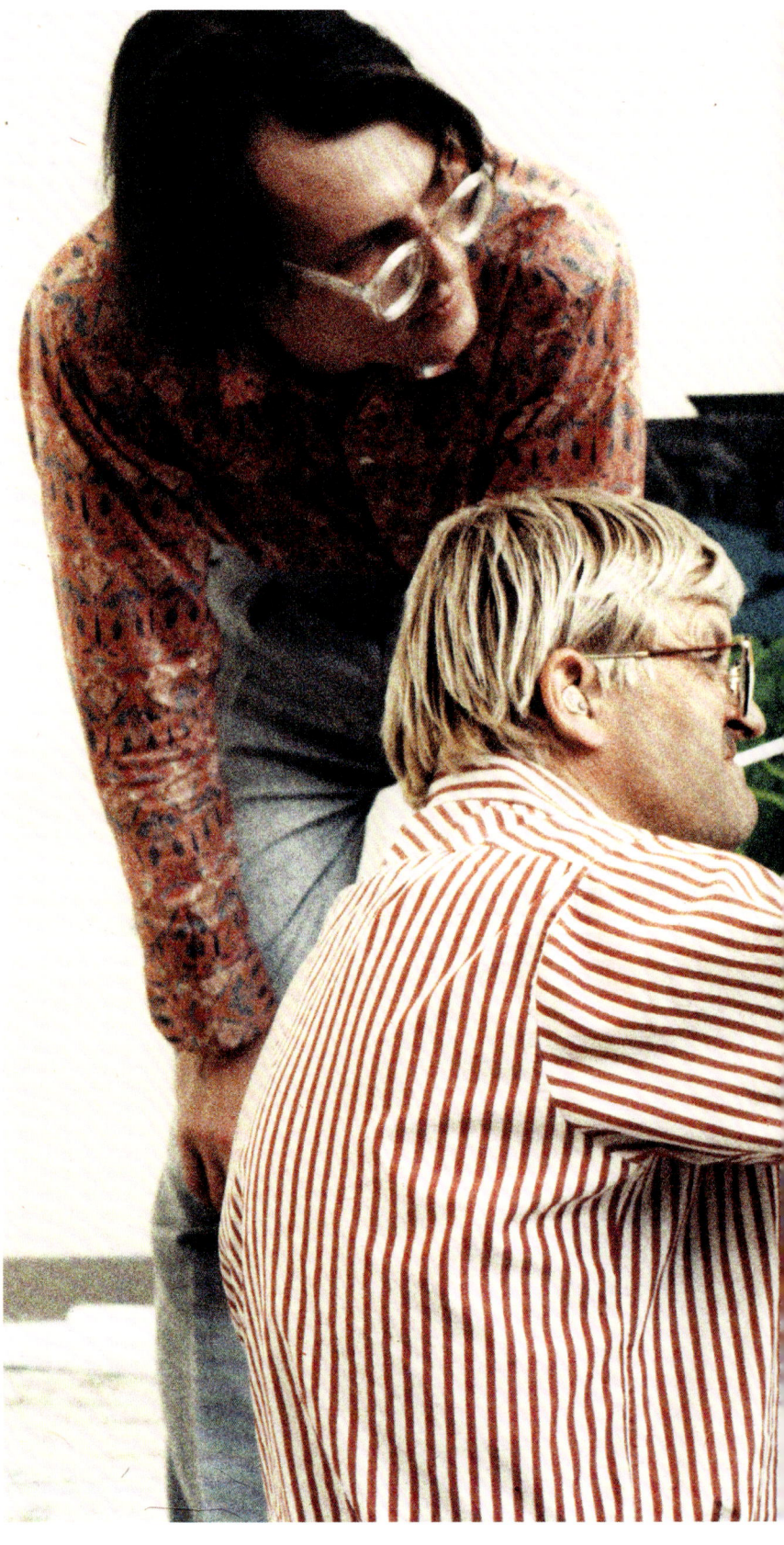

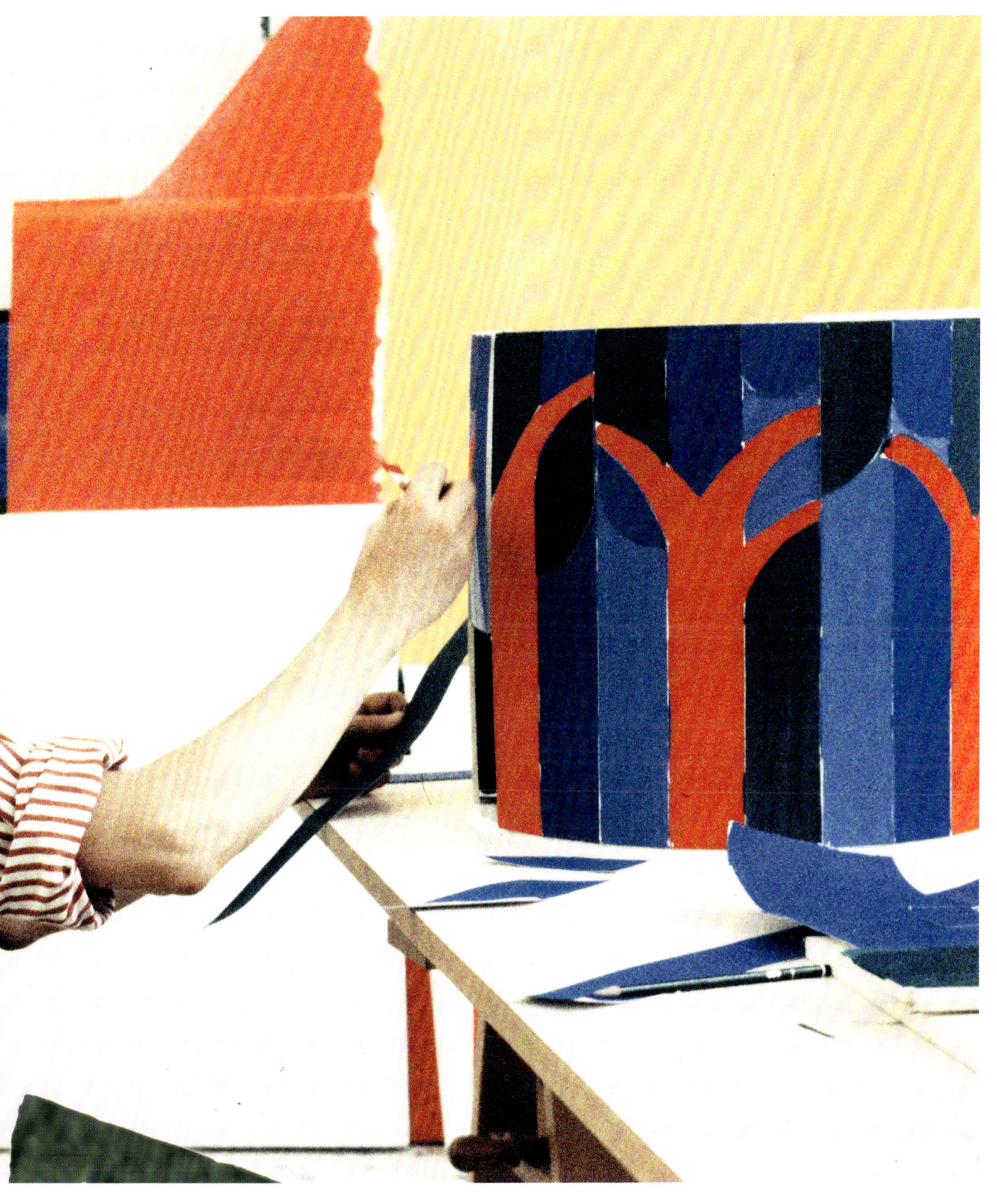

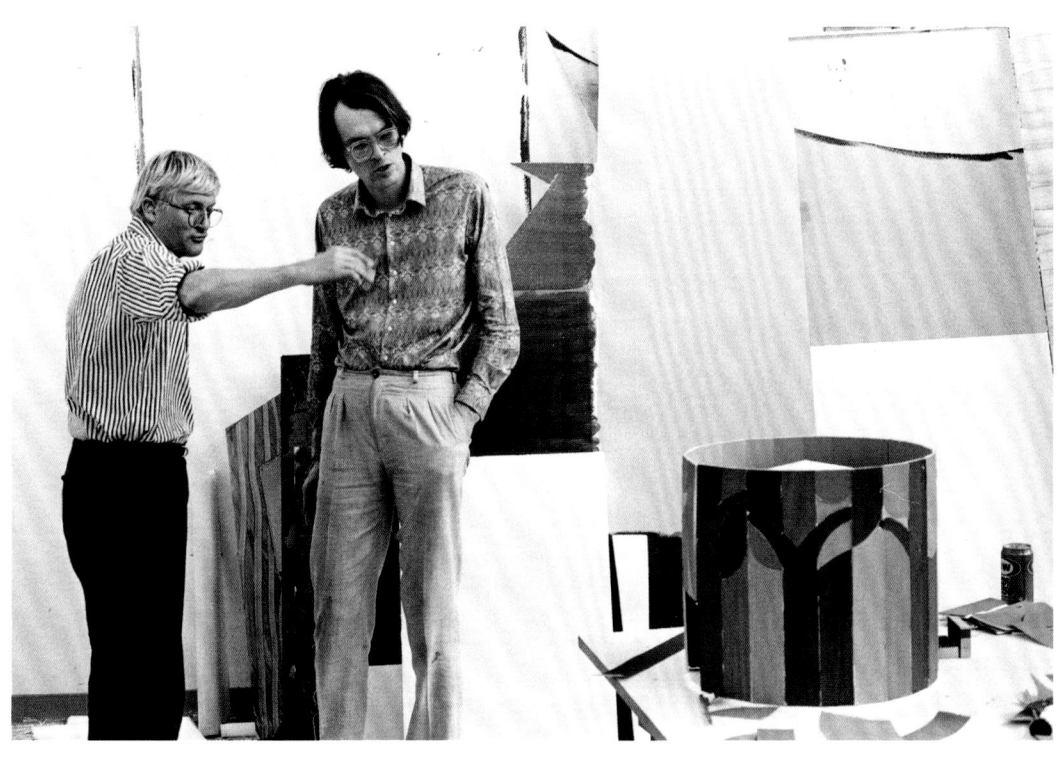

*David Hockney with his assistant building the model for the Enchanted Tree*

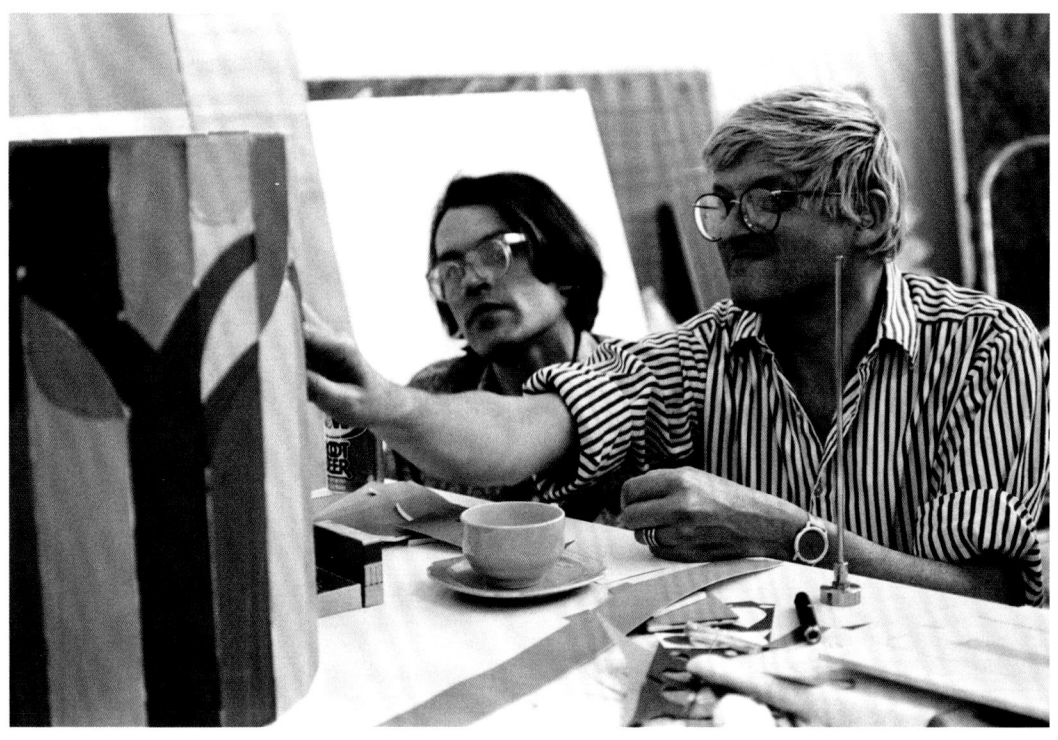

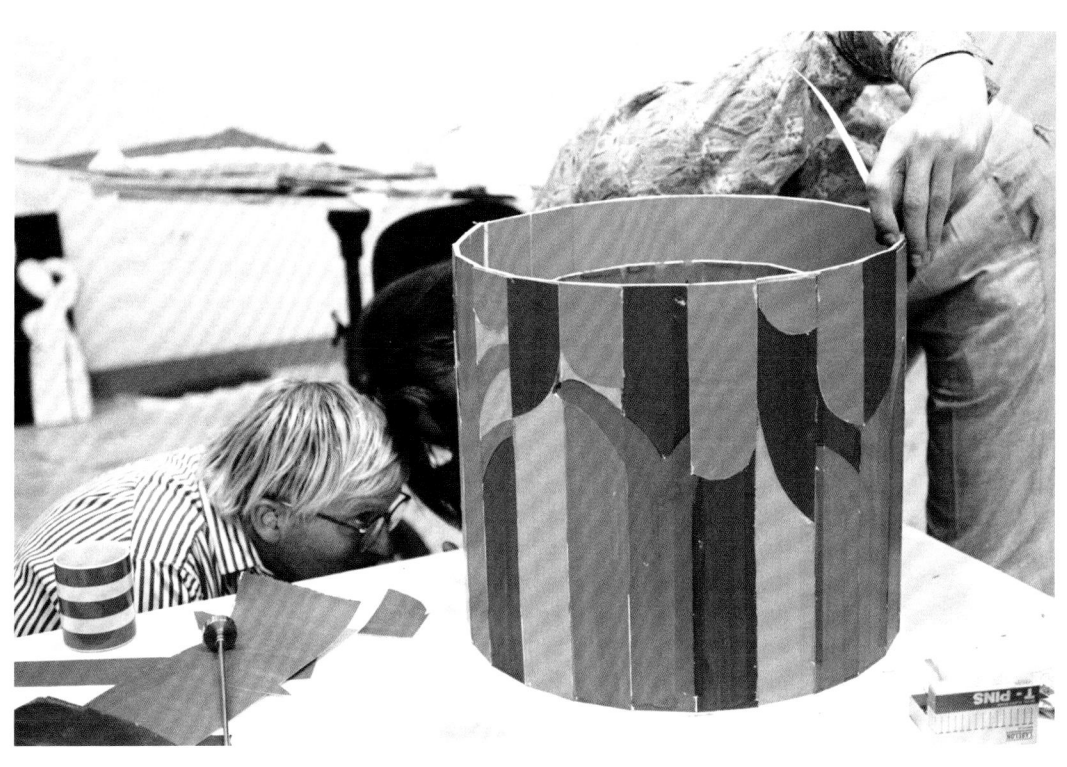

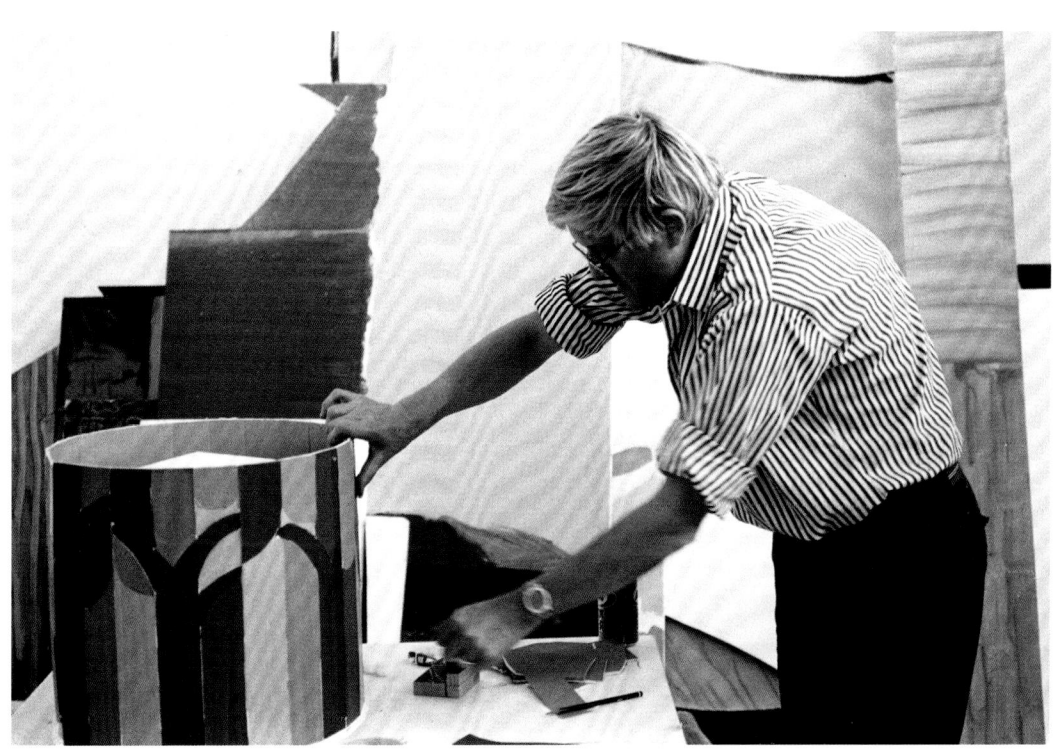

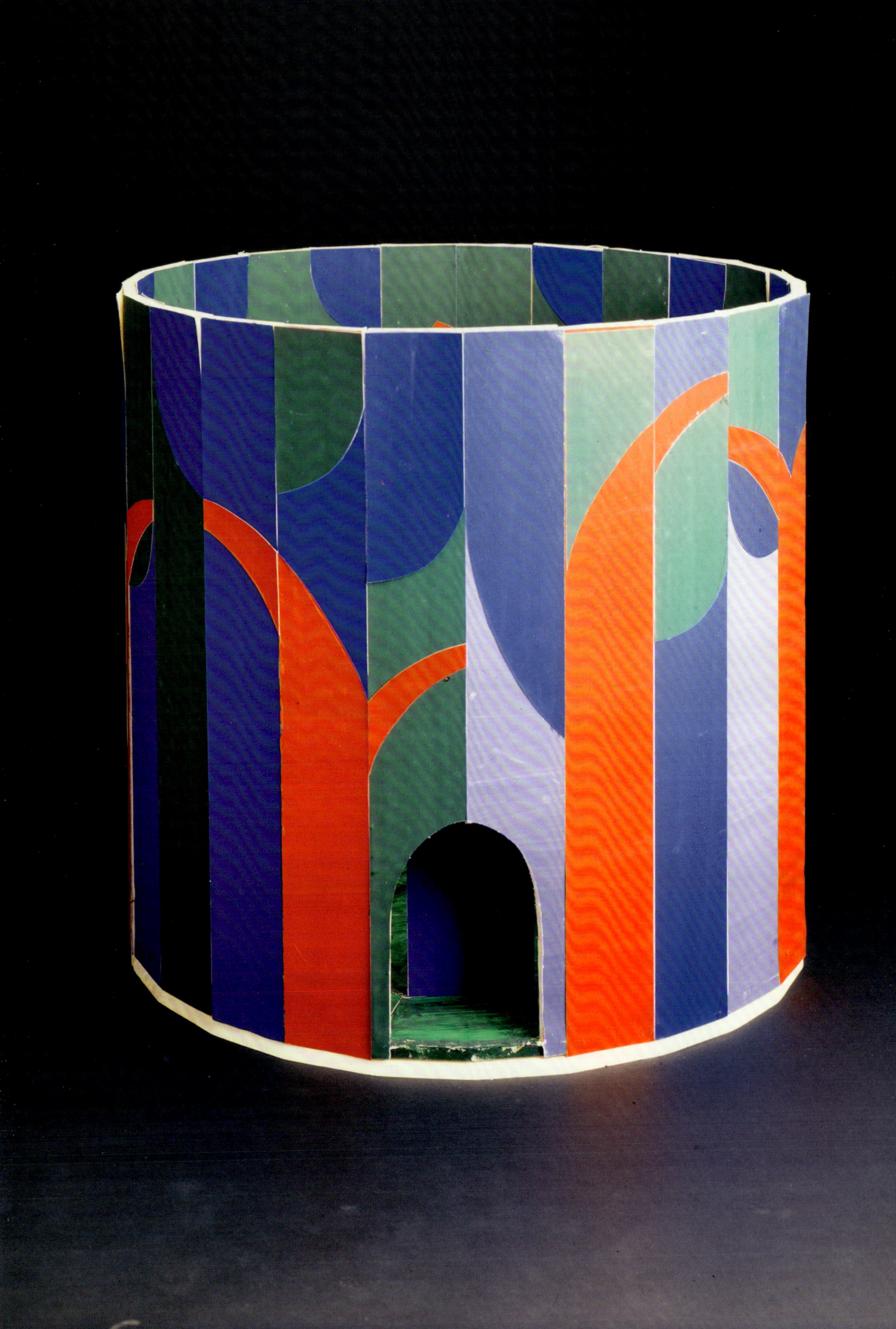

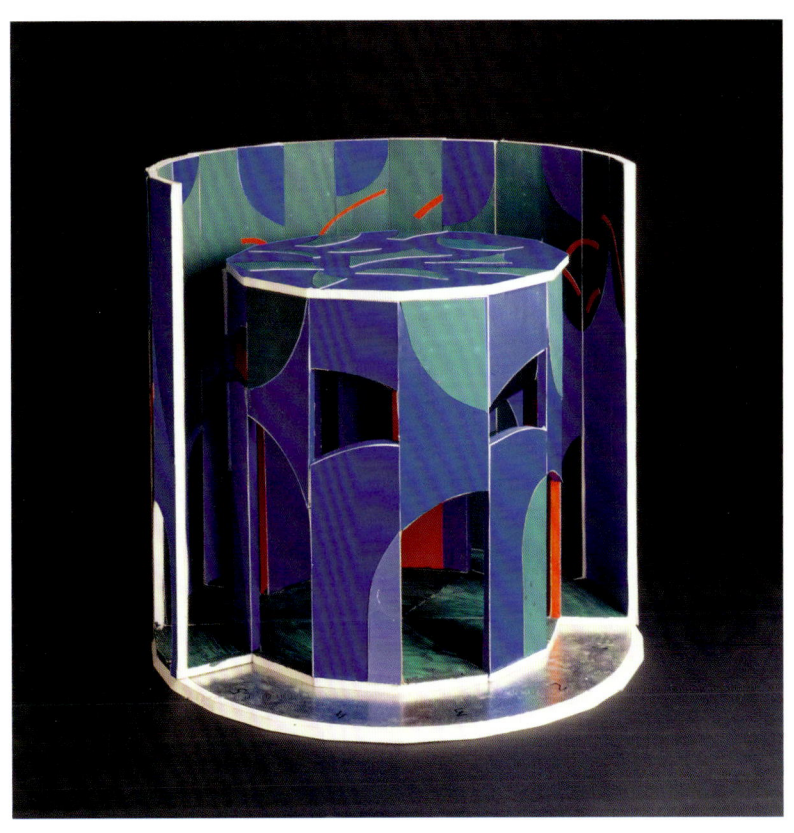

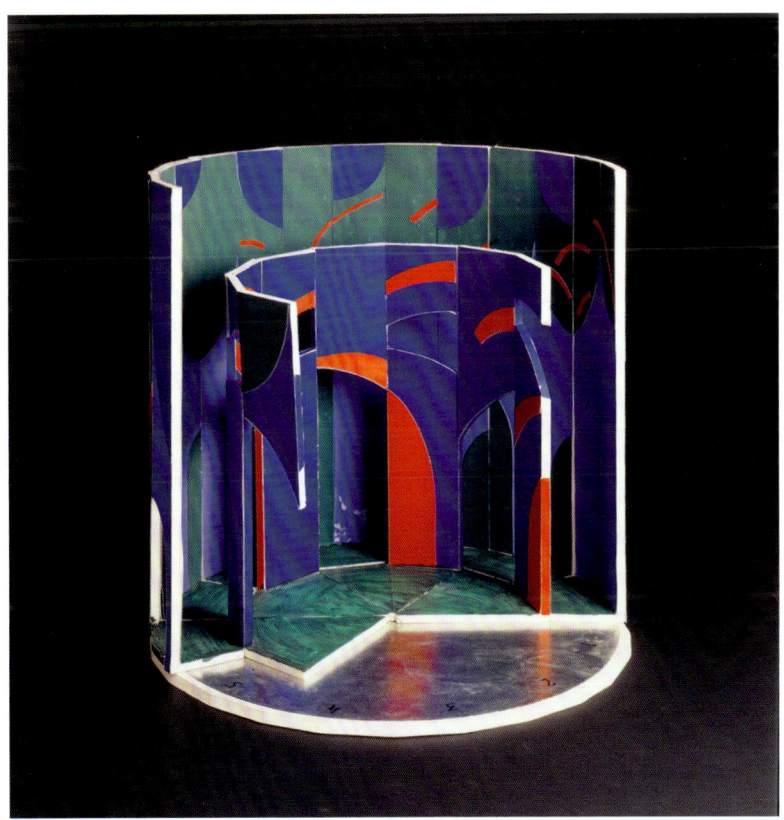

*David Hockney: model for the Enchanted Tree*

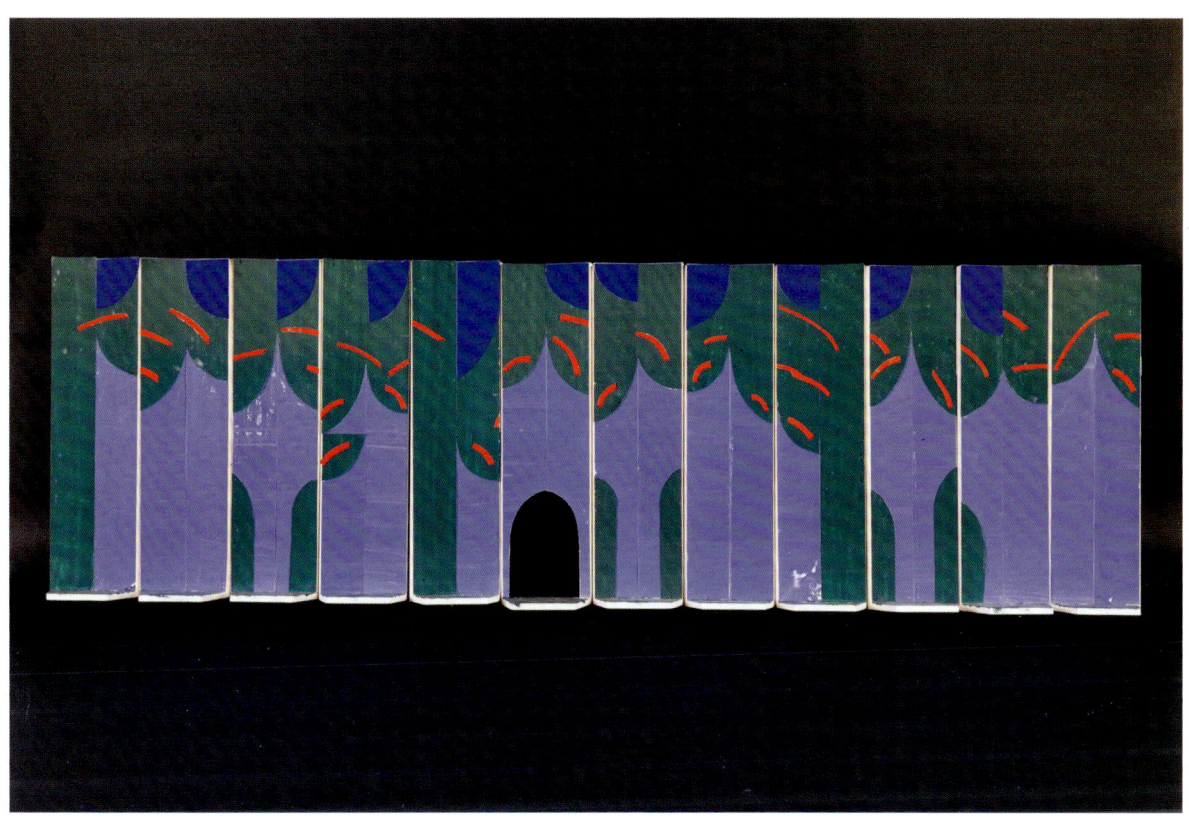

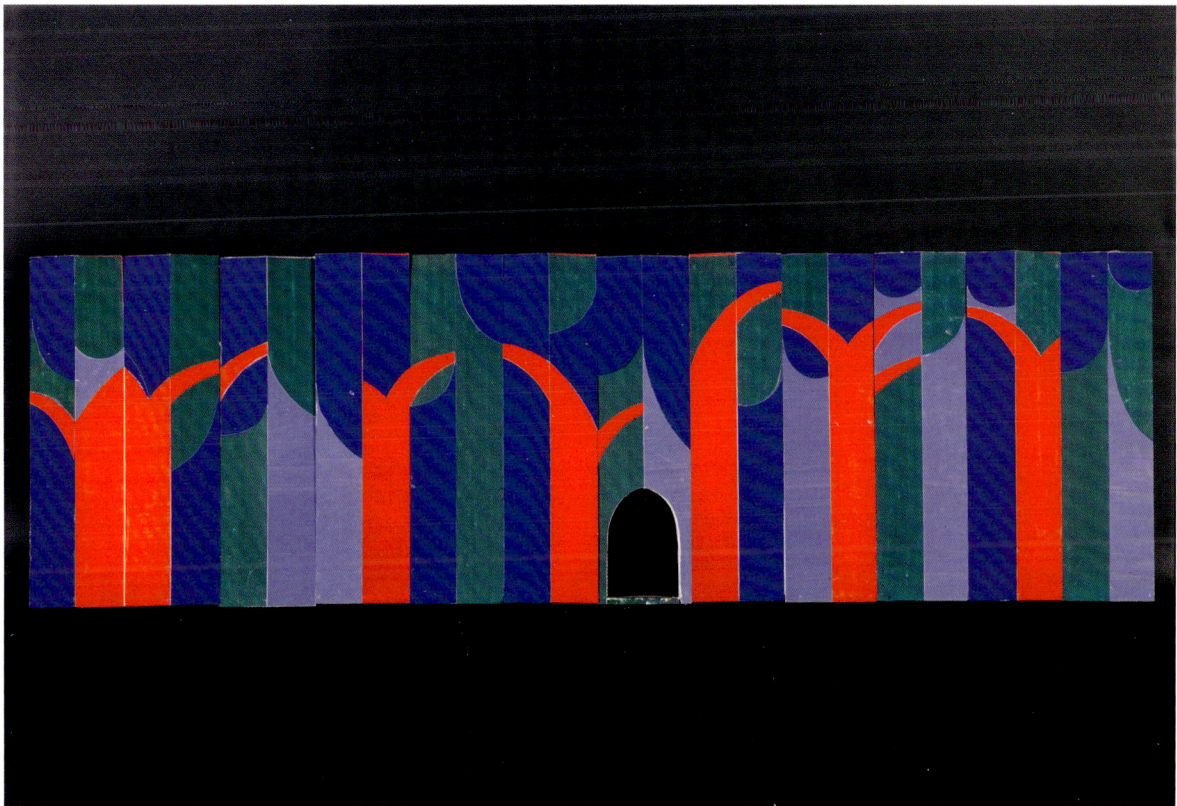

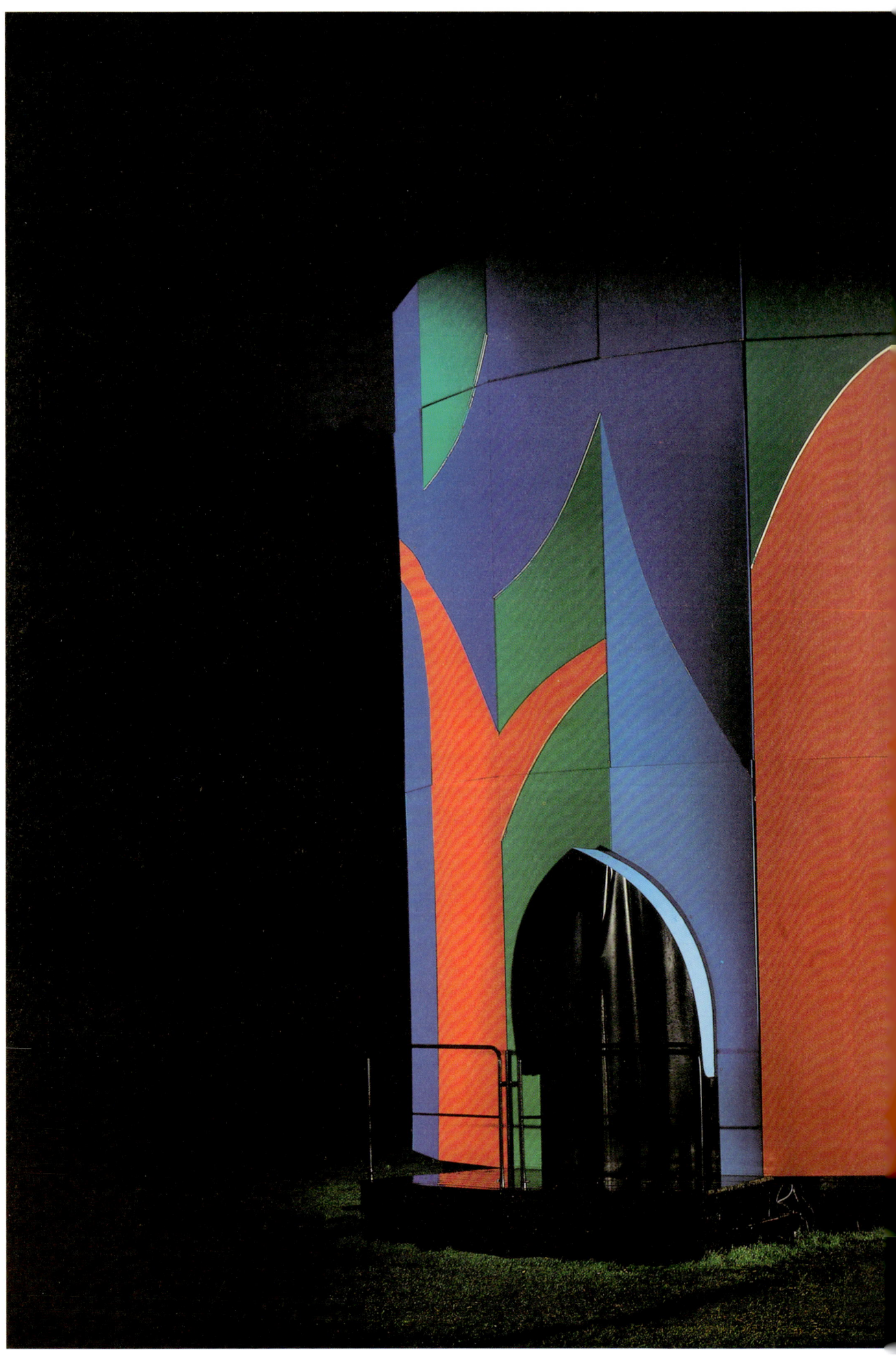

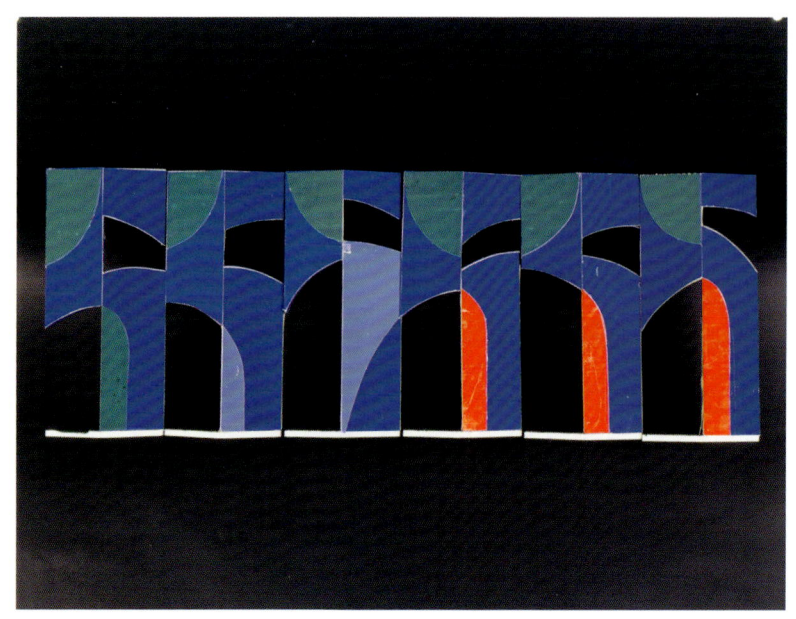

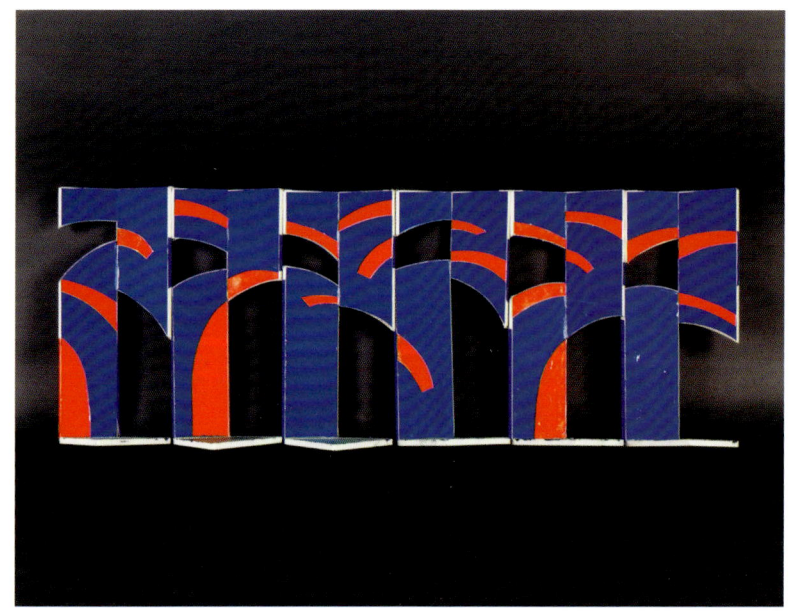

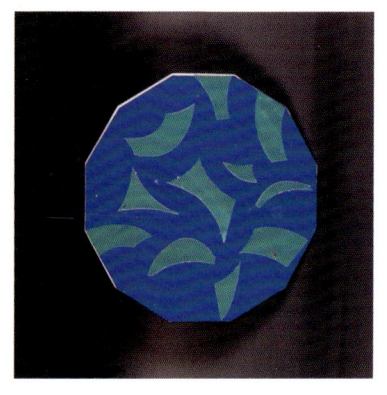 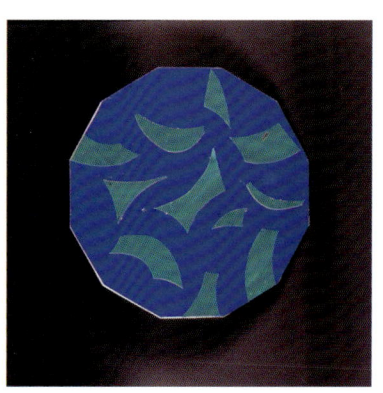

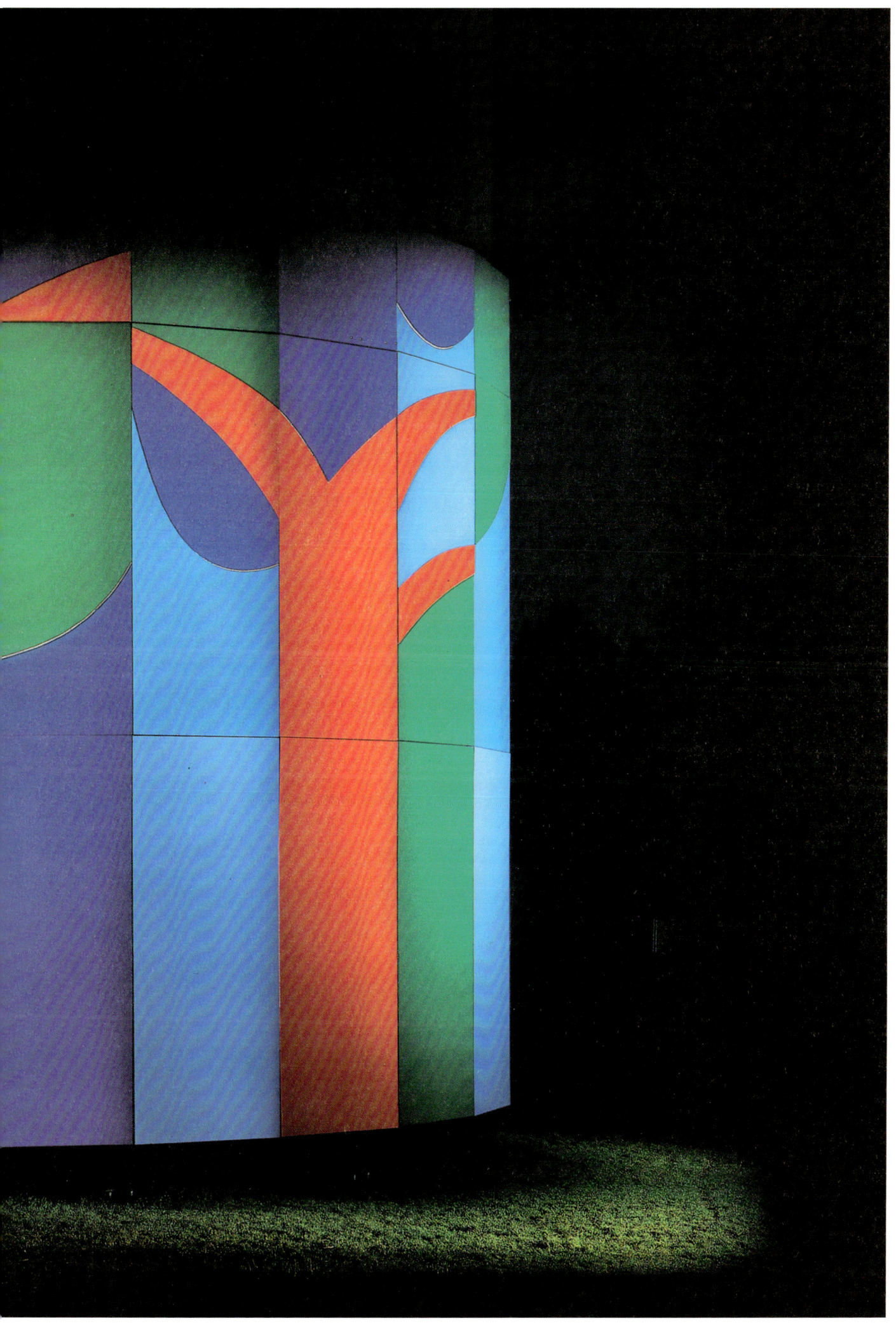

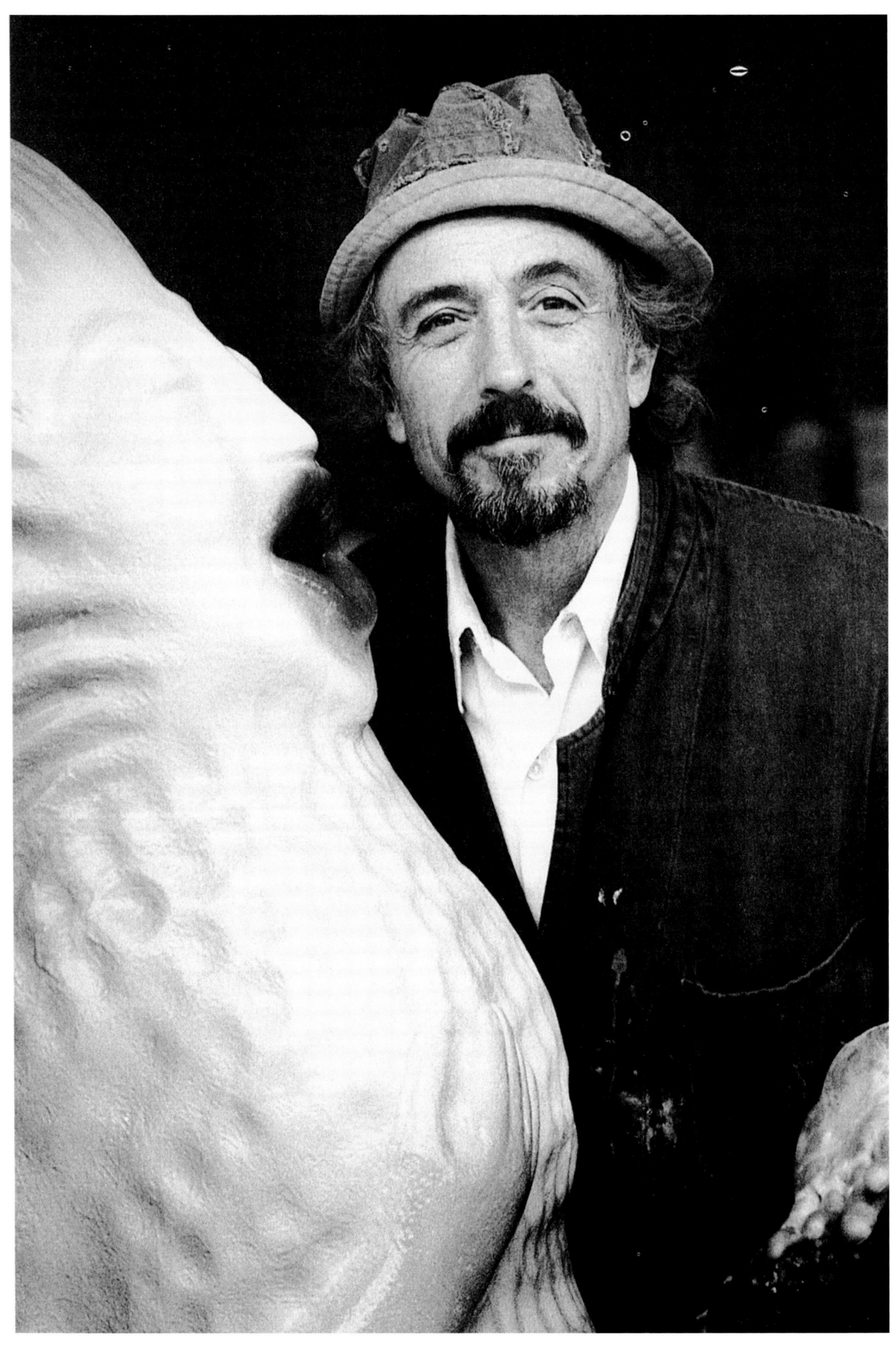

Arik Brauer

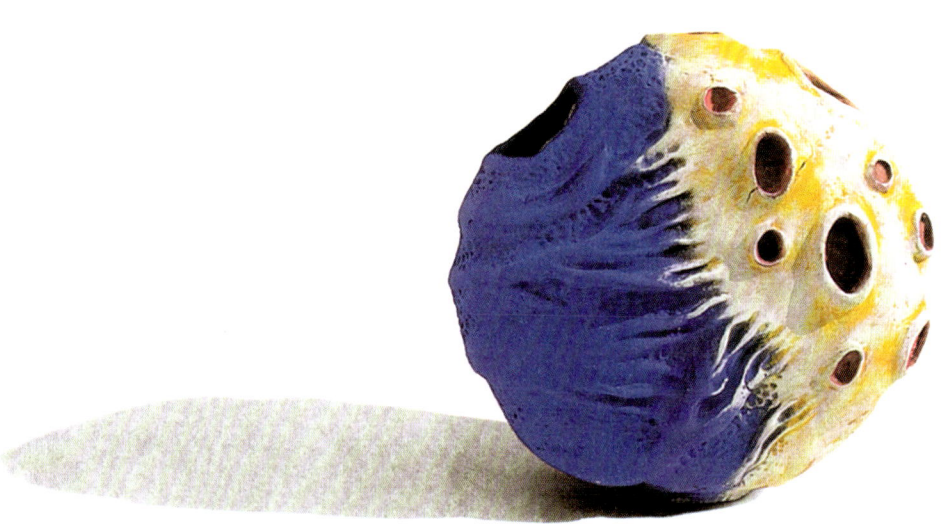

DIE SIEBEN IST DER HALBE MOND DA RASTET JEDER GERN
UND WENN MAN AUS DEM KRATER GUCKST DAM SIEHT MAN SEINEN STERN

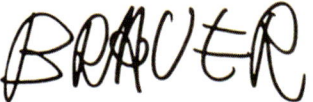

Arik Brauer

Born: January 04, 1929, in Vienna, Austria.
Died: January 24, 2021, in Vienna.

Painter, illustrator, sculptor, stage designer,
architect, singer, composer, writer.

Arik Brauer designed a **carousel** for *Luna Luna*
with eight figures that form a coherent fairy tale.
The **carousel song** is sung by Timna Brauer.

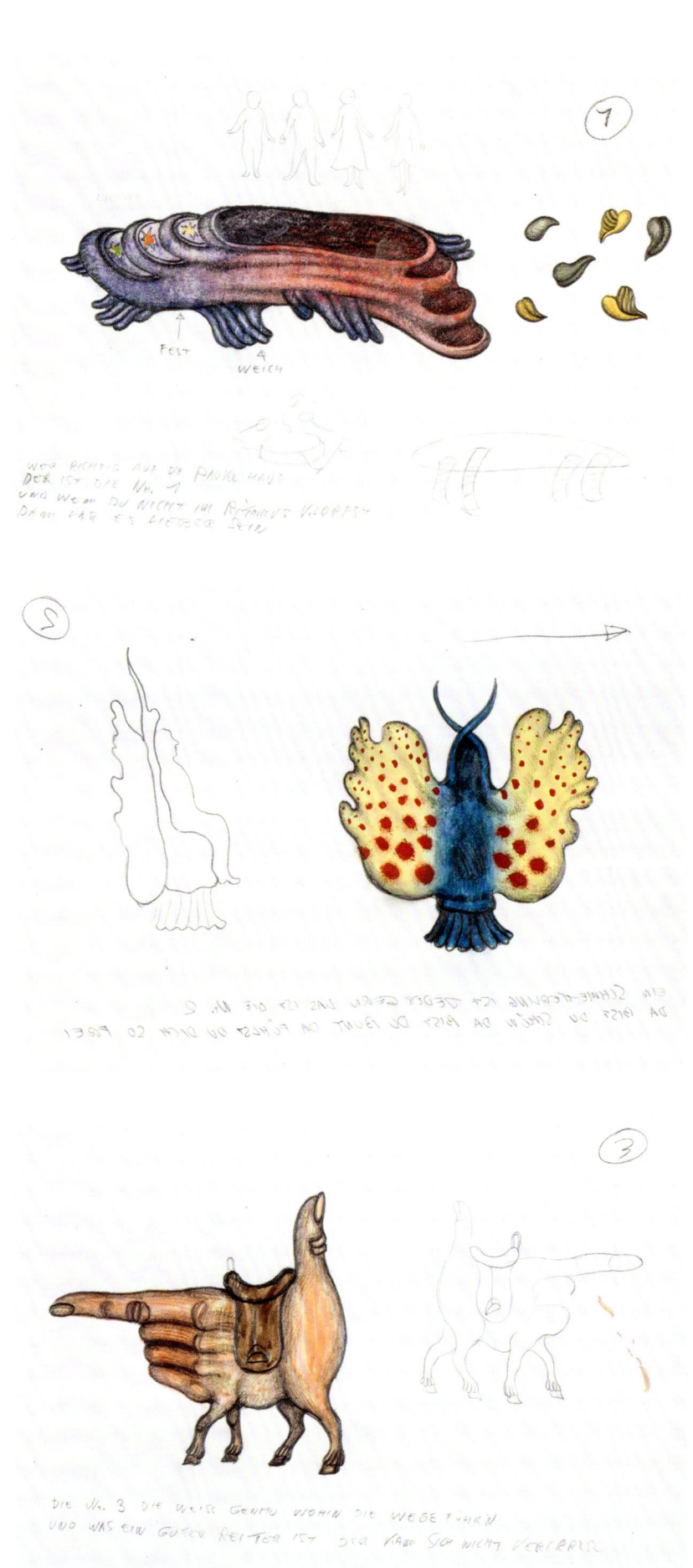

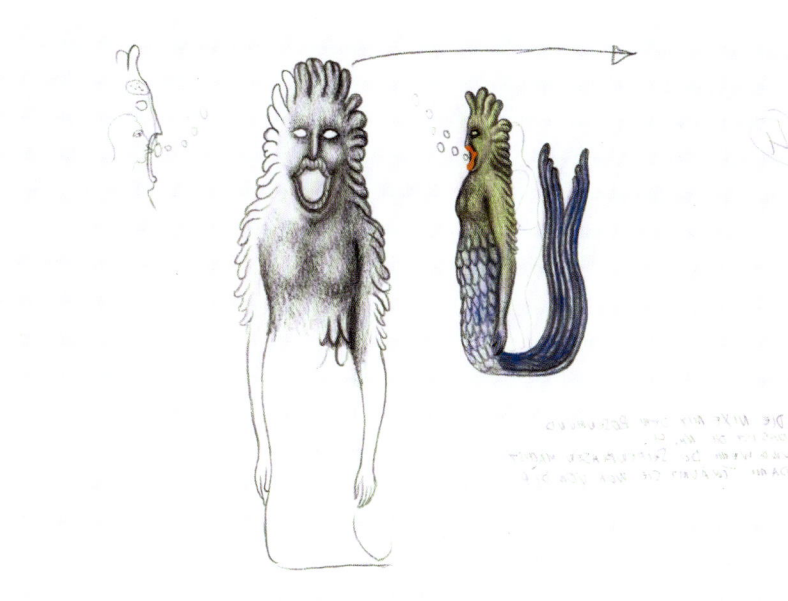

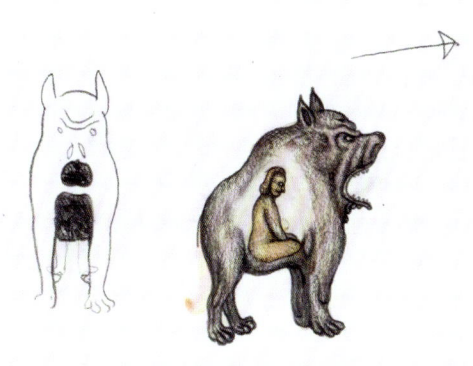

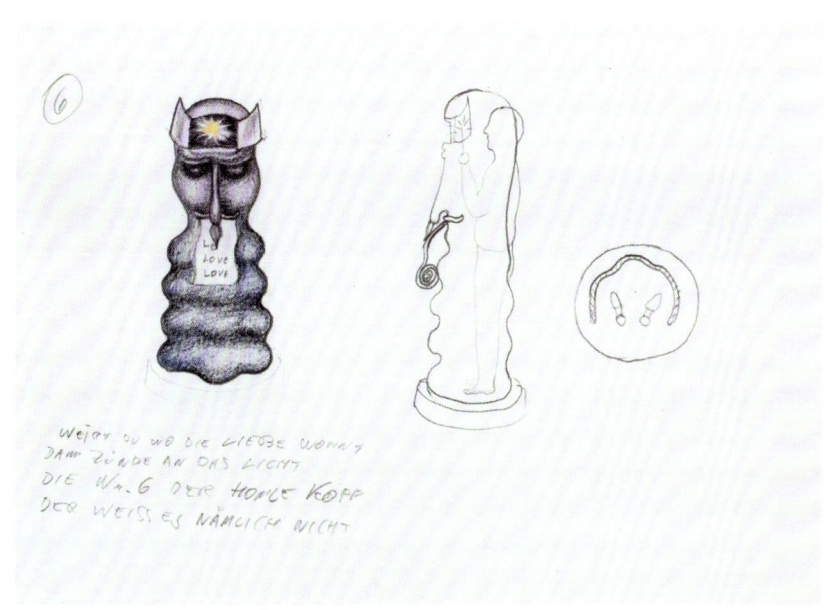

WEIST DU WO DIE LIEBE WOHNT
DANN ZÜNDE AN DAS LICHT
DIE W..G DER HUNDE KOPF
DER WEISS ES NÄMLICH NICHT

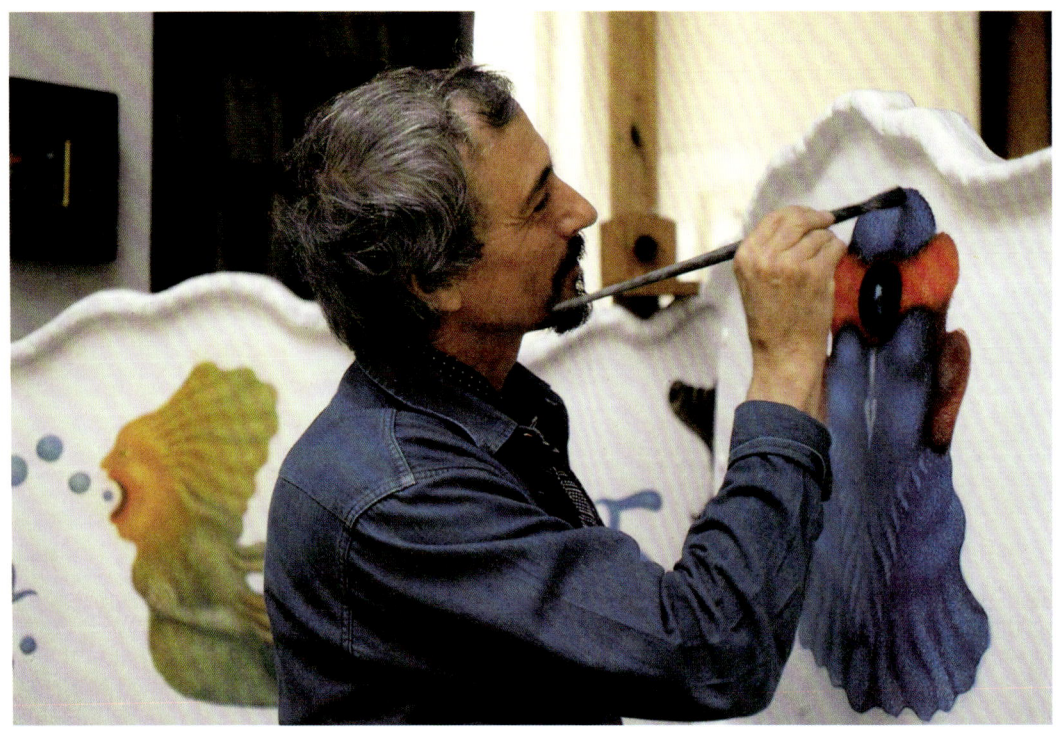

*Arik Brauer painting the cornice for the carousel …*

*… and painting the large moon*

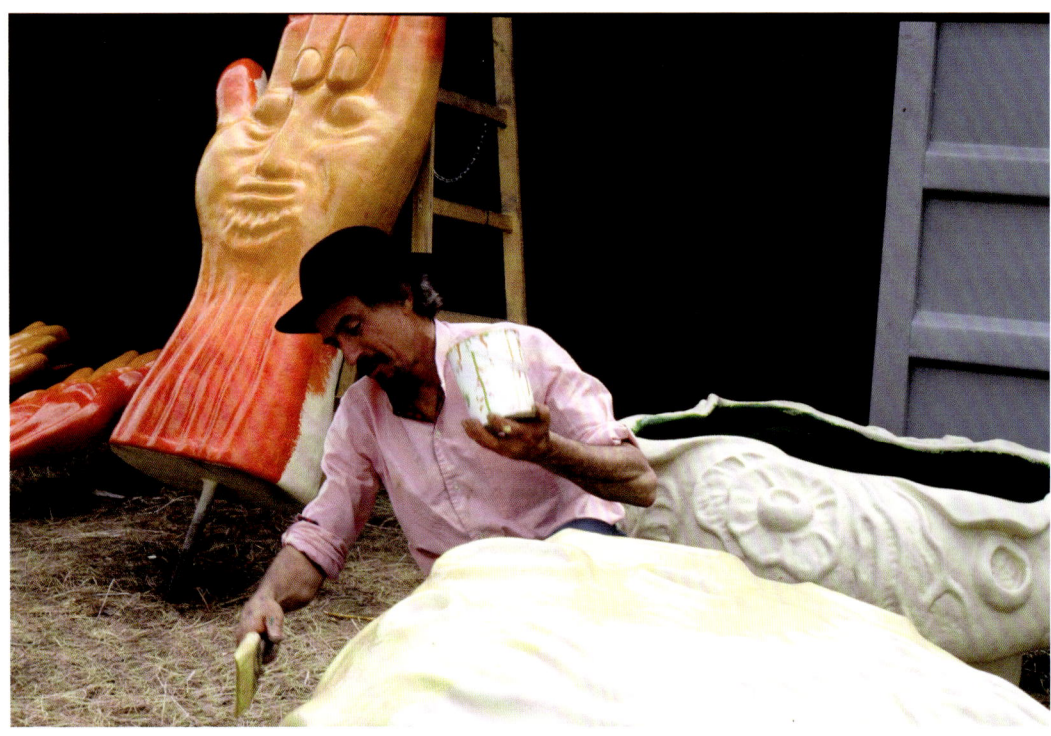

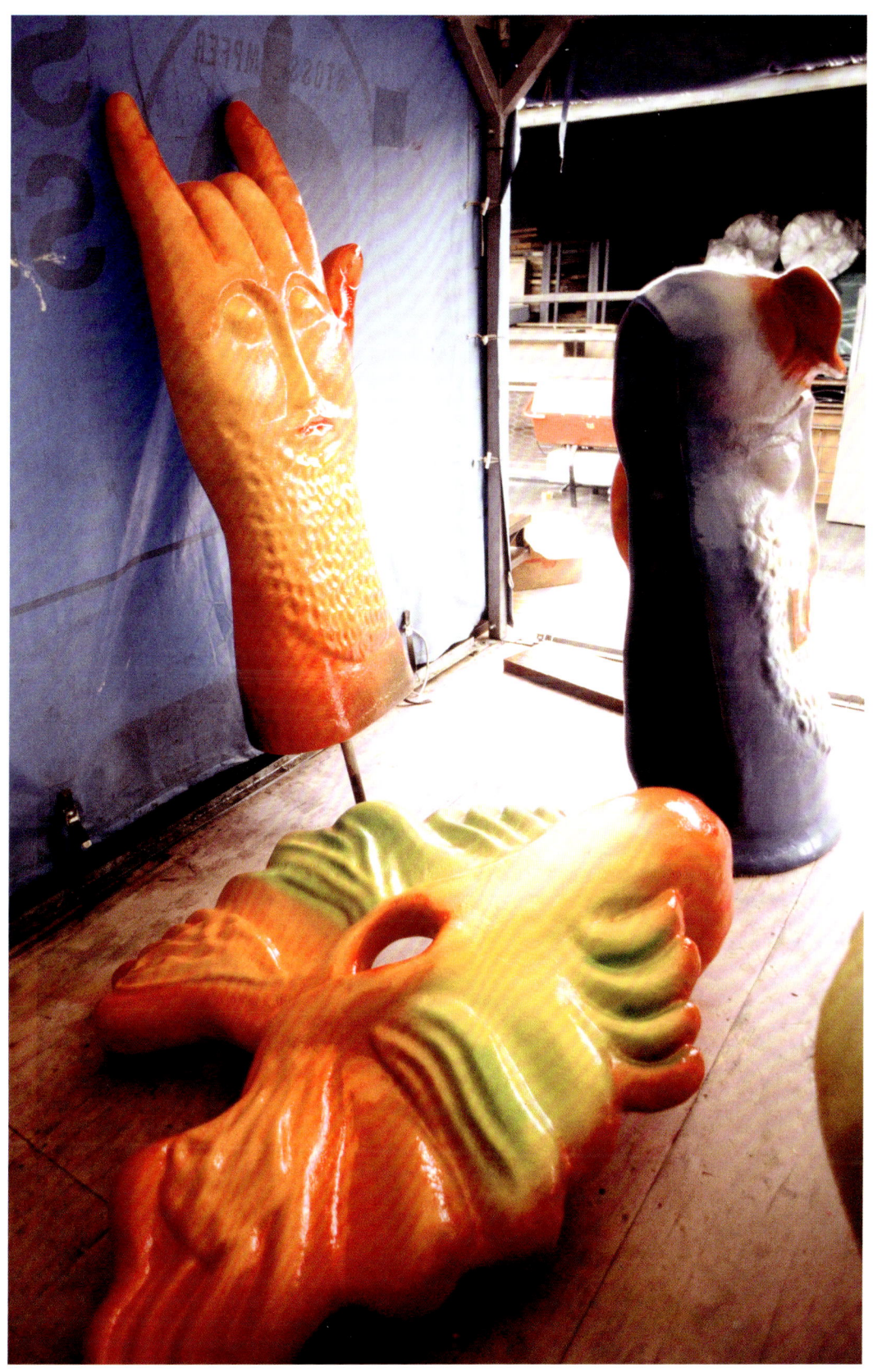

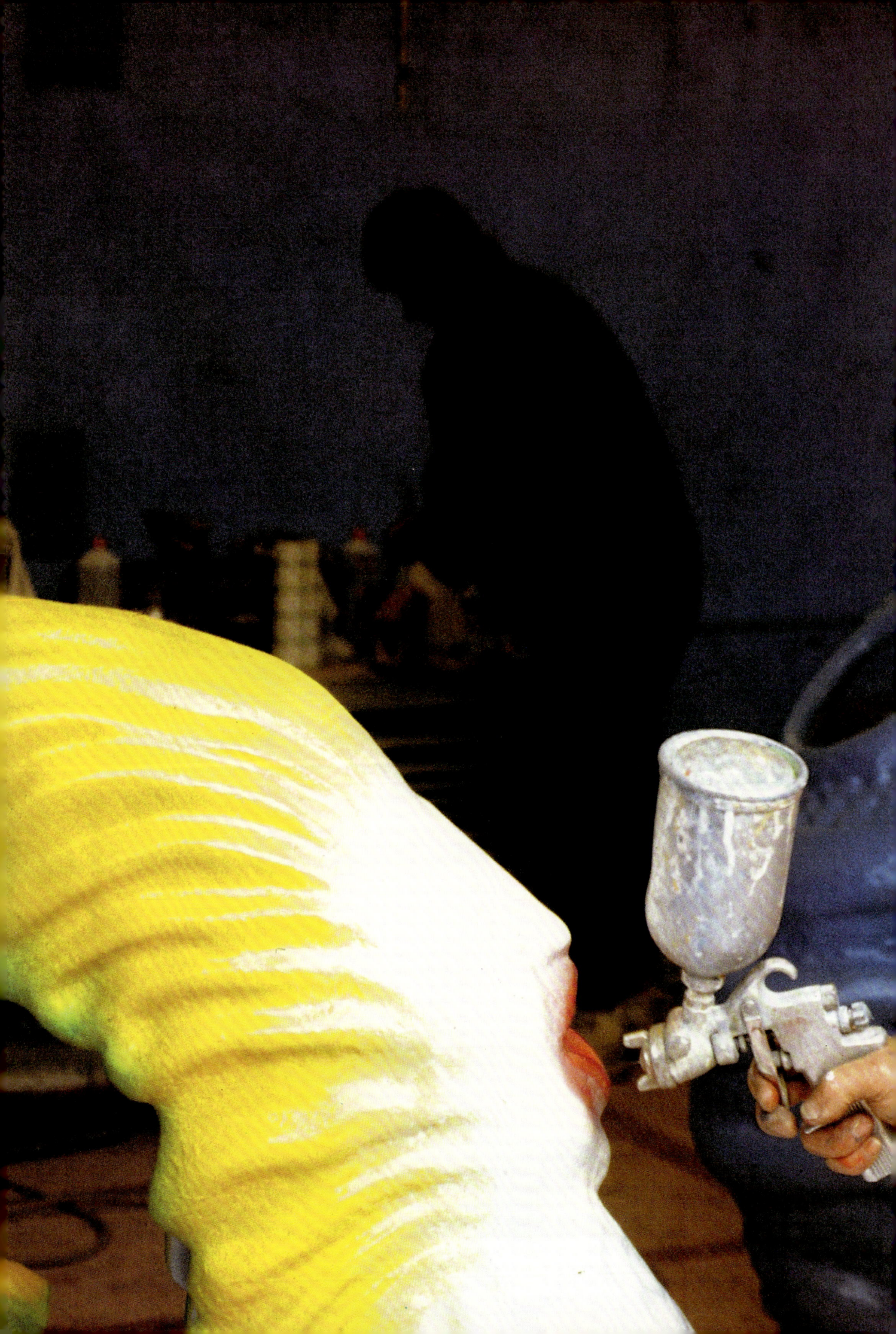

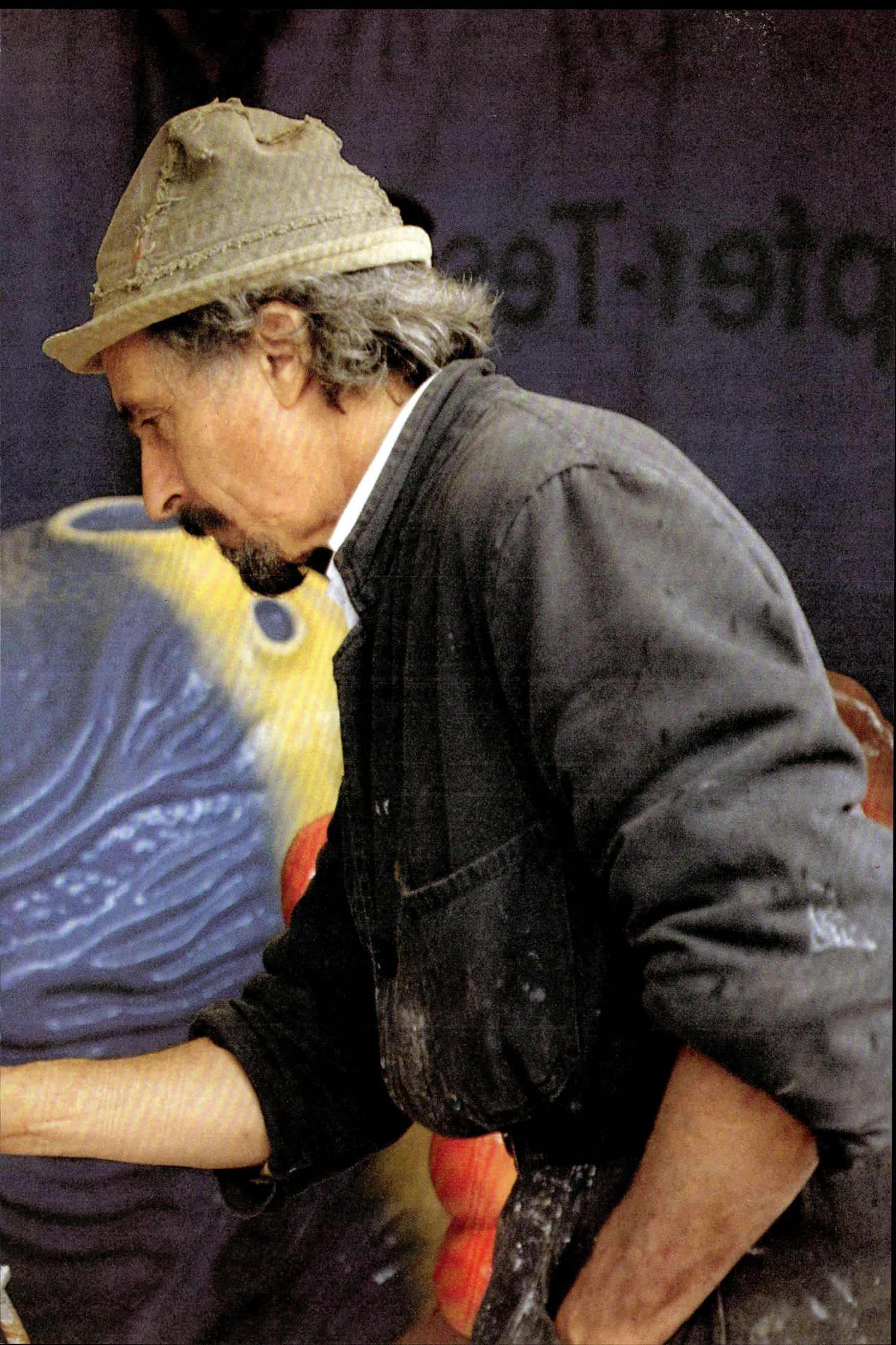

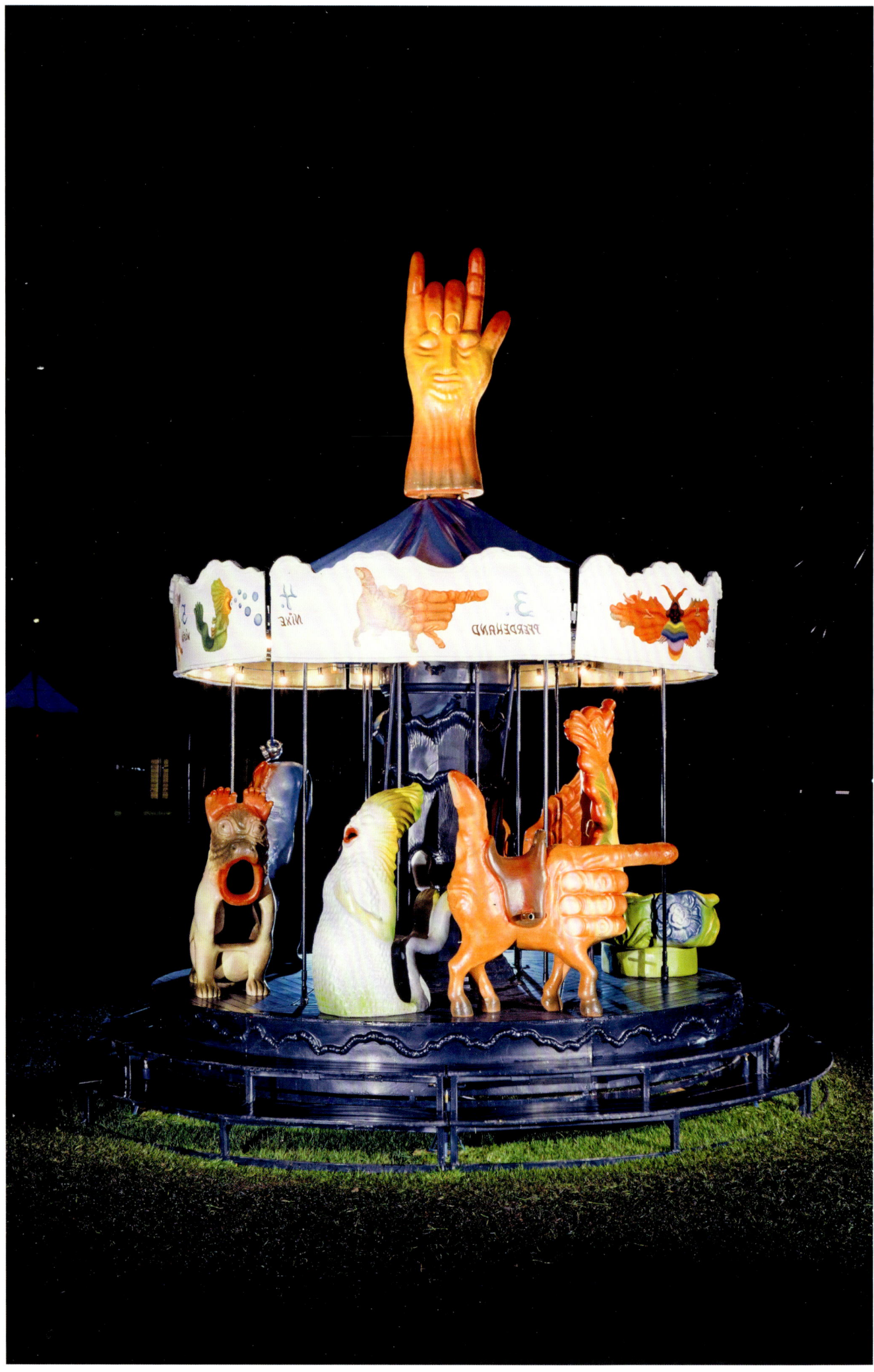

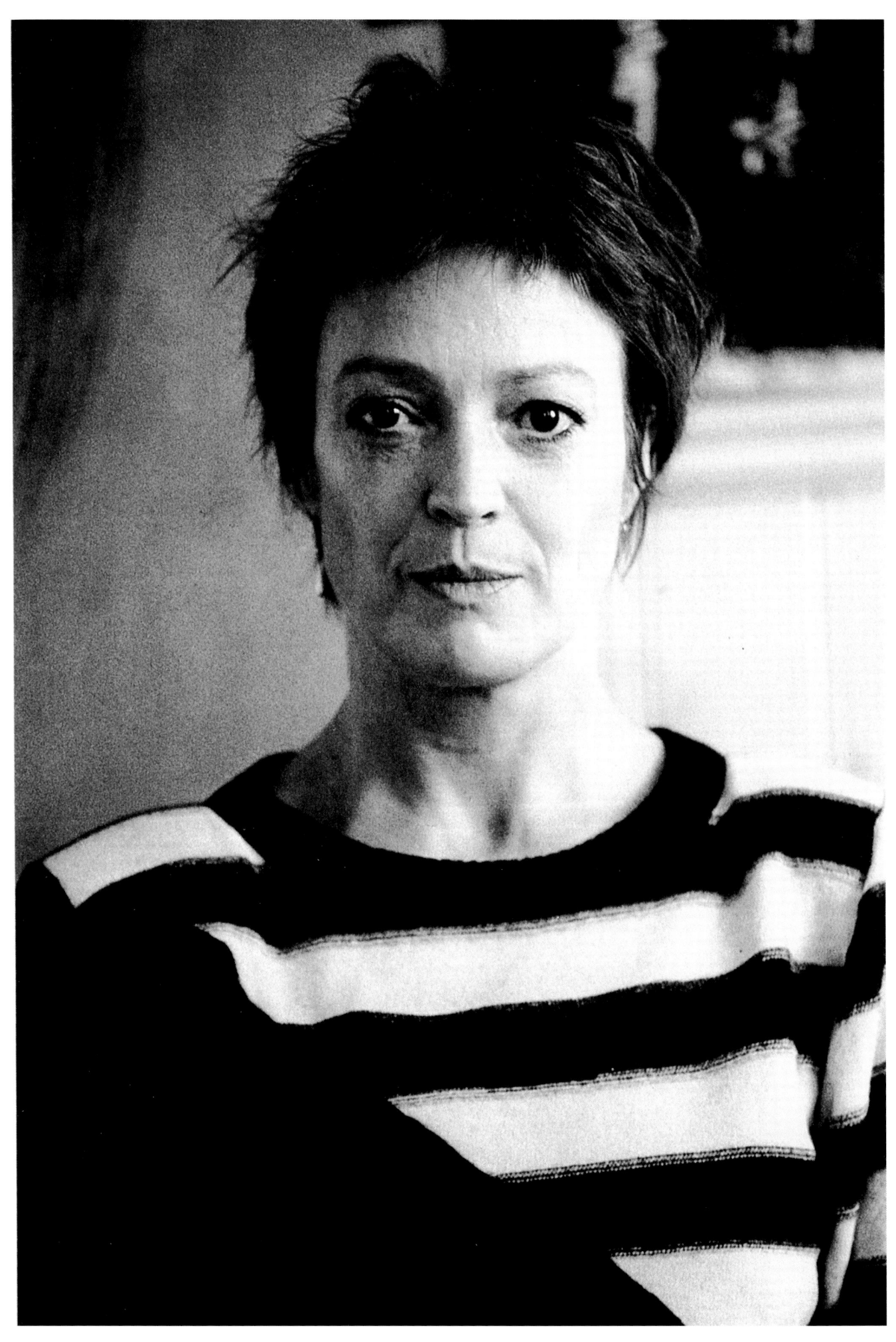

Susanne Schmögner

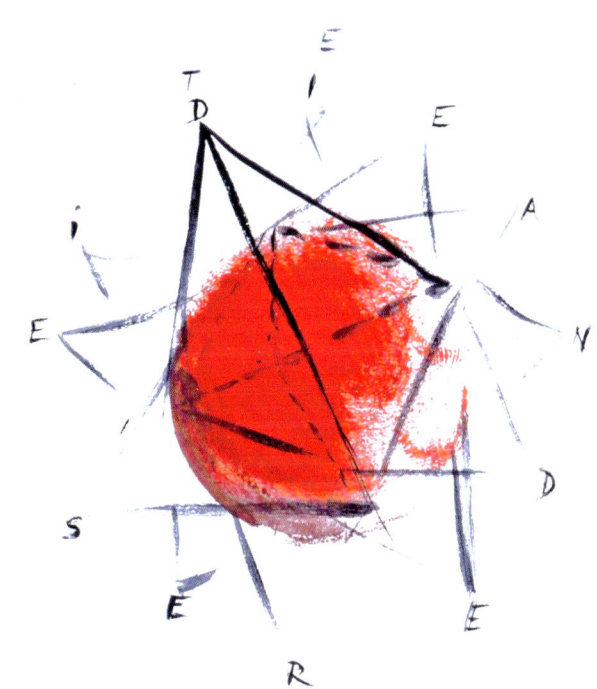

Susanne Schmögner

Born: December 4, 1939, in Vienna, Austria.

Painter, illustrator, stage and costume designer,
makeup artist.

Susanne Schmögner designed a **poster** and a spiral-
shaped **Journey into the Mind** for *Luna Luna*. When
you reach the destination, a sculpture hands you the
poem "Golden Age," by Arthur Rimbaud.

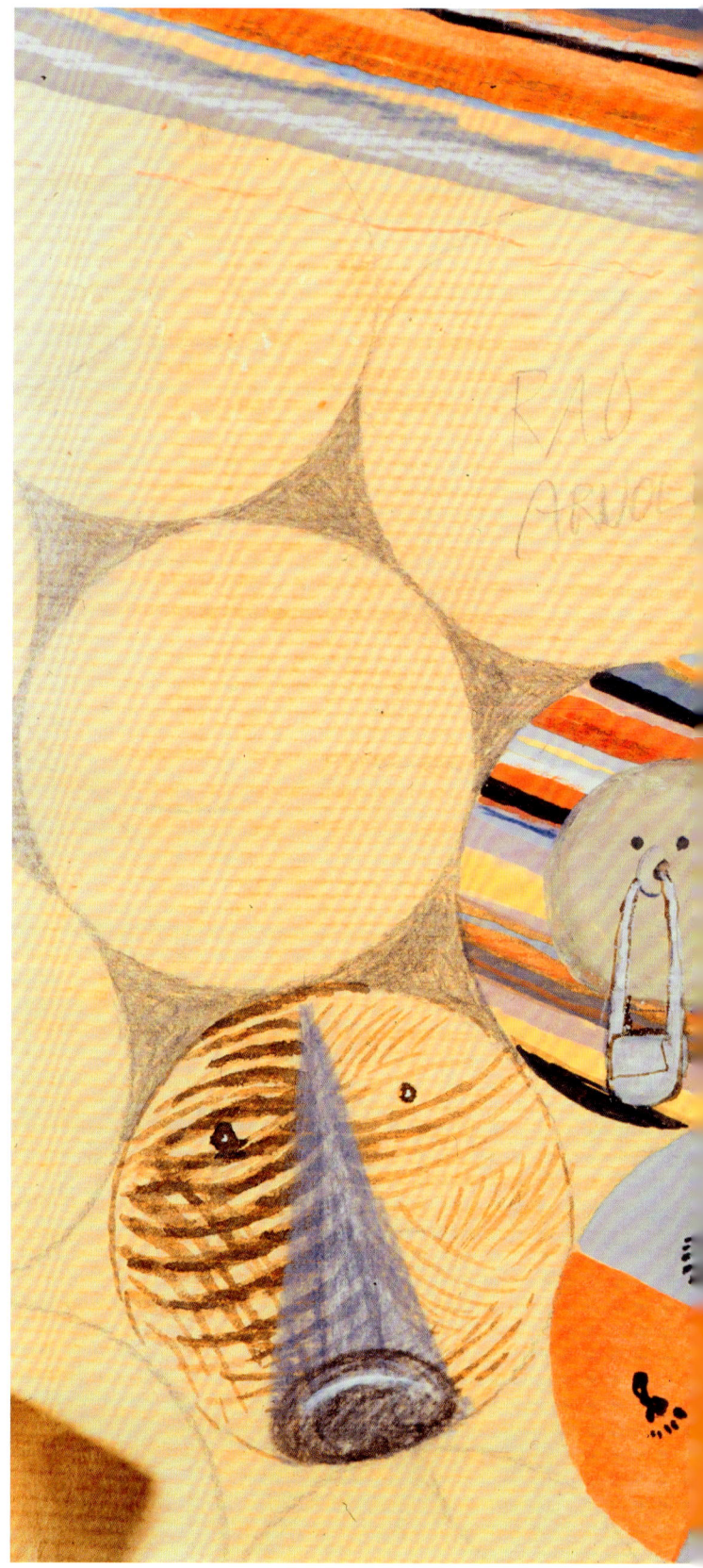

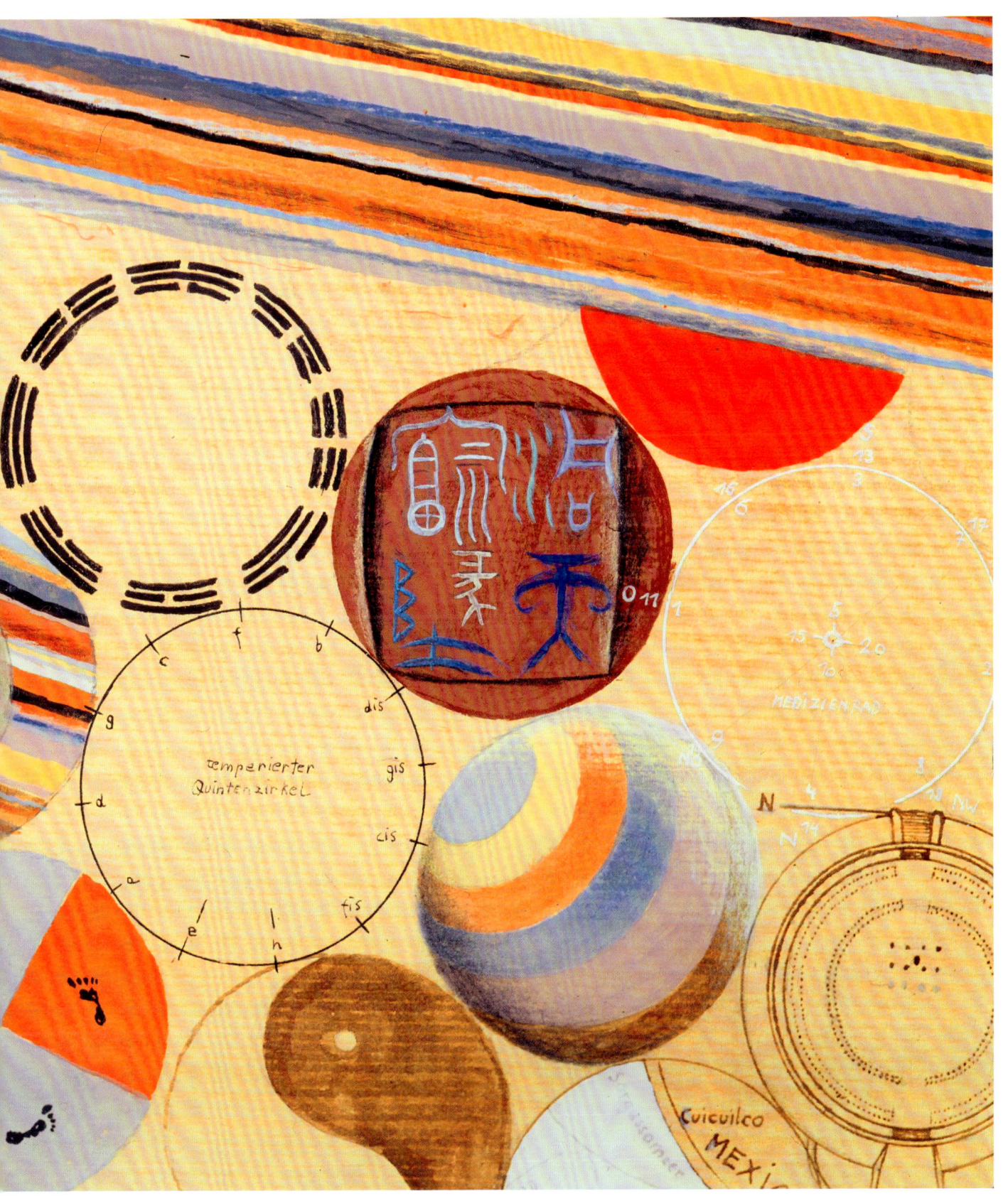

temperierter
Quintenzirkel

MEDIZINRAD

Cuicuilco
MEXI

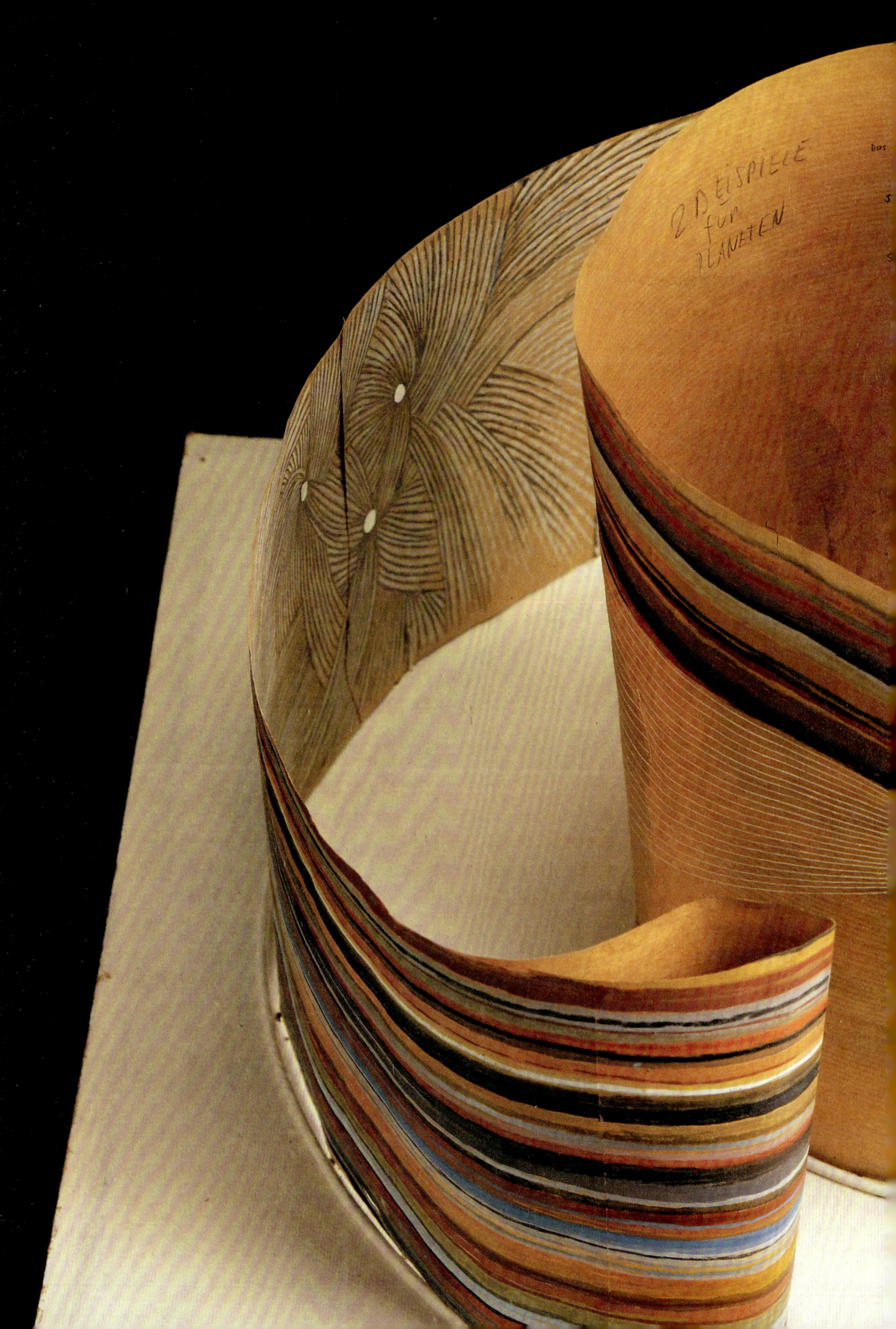

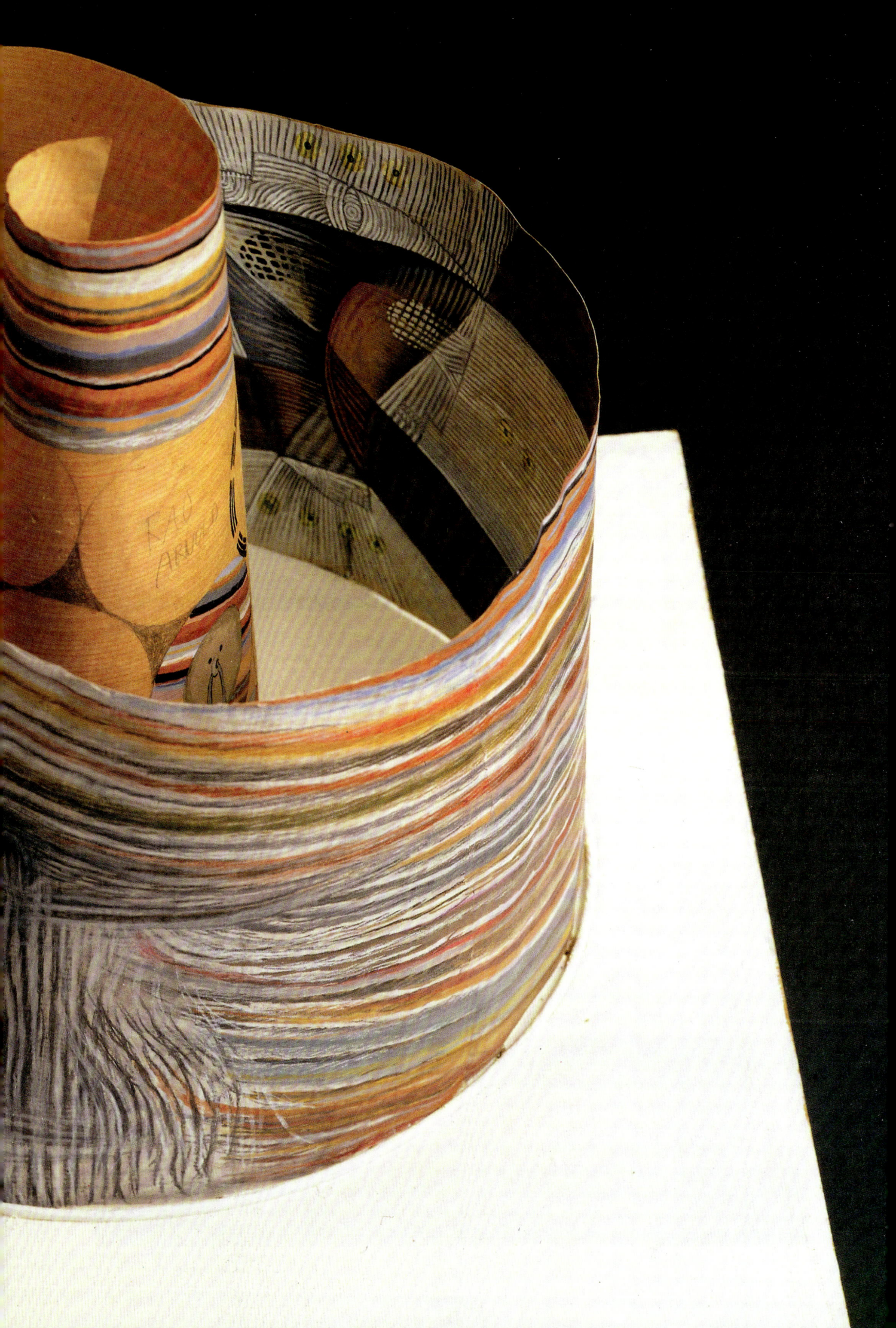

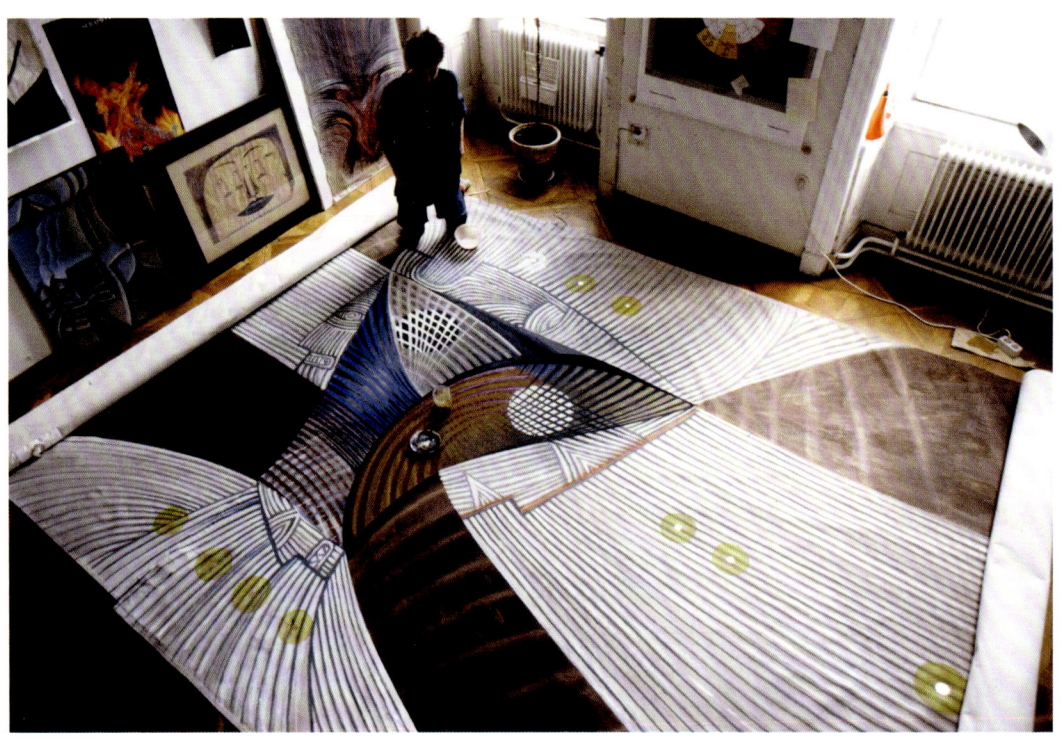

*Susanne Schmögner in her Vienna studio painting the Journey into the Mind*

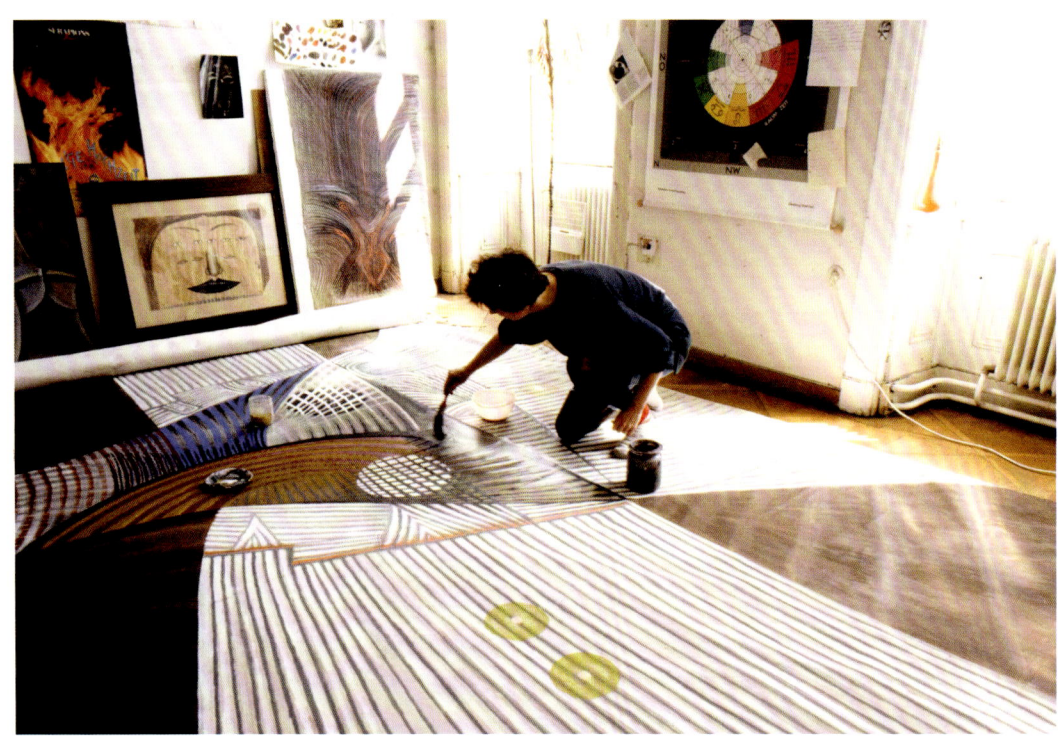

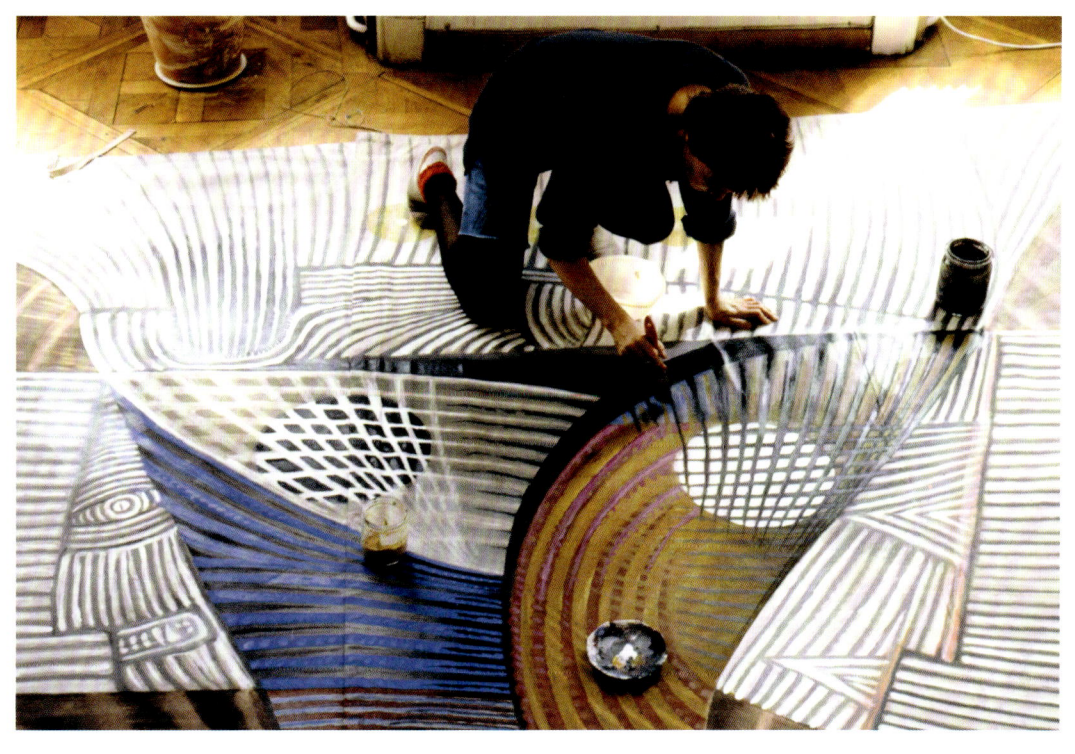

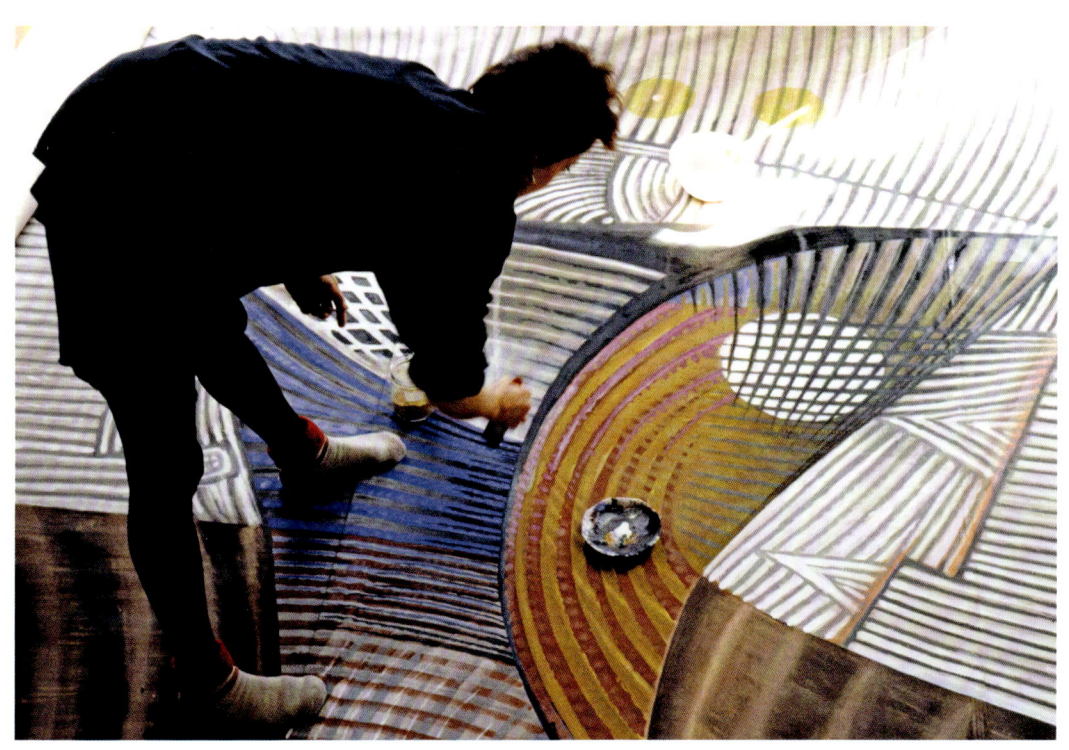

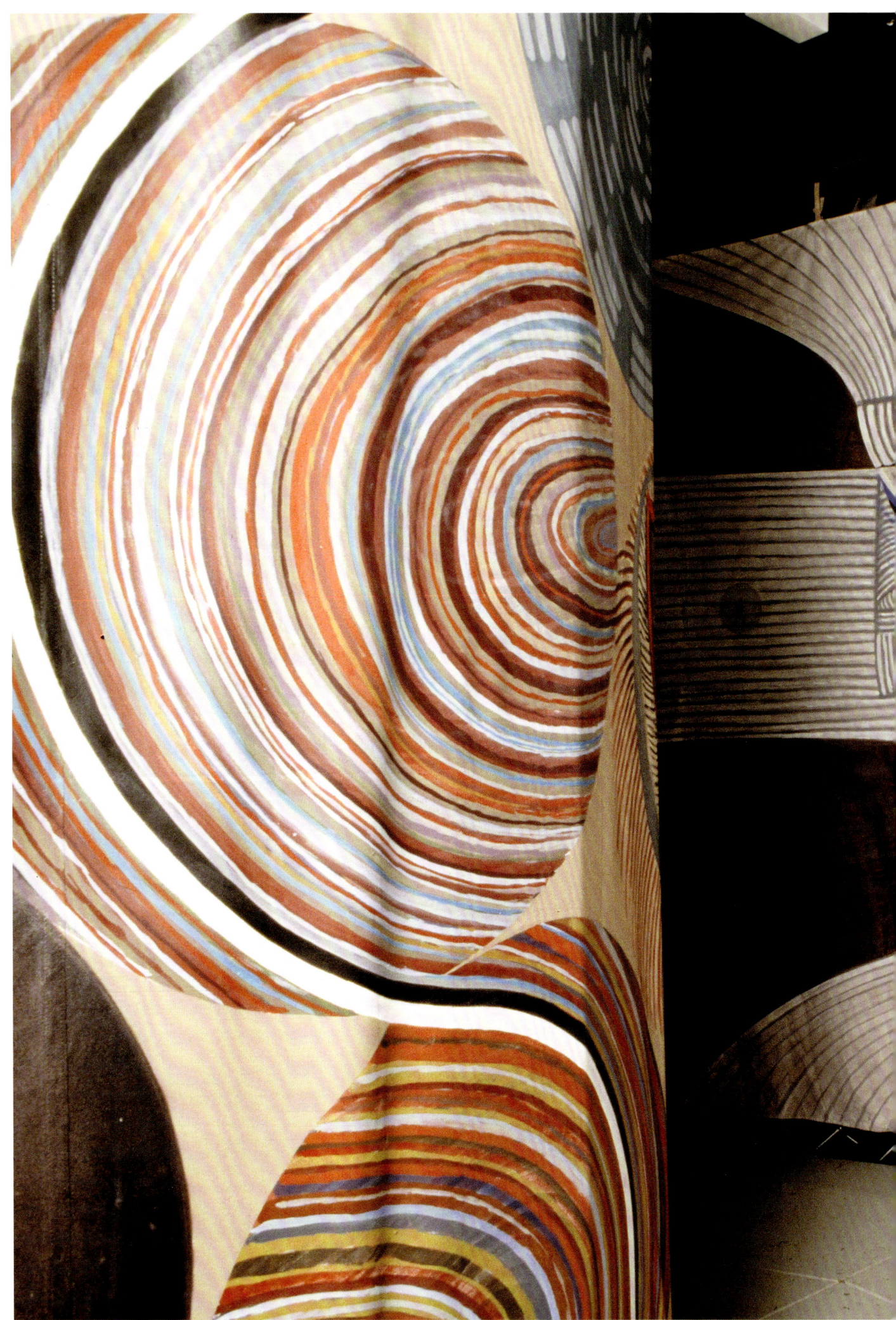

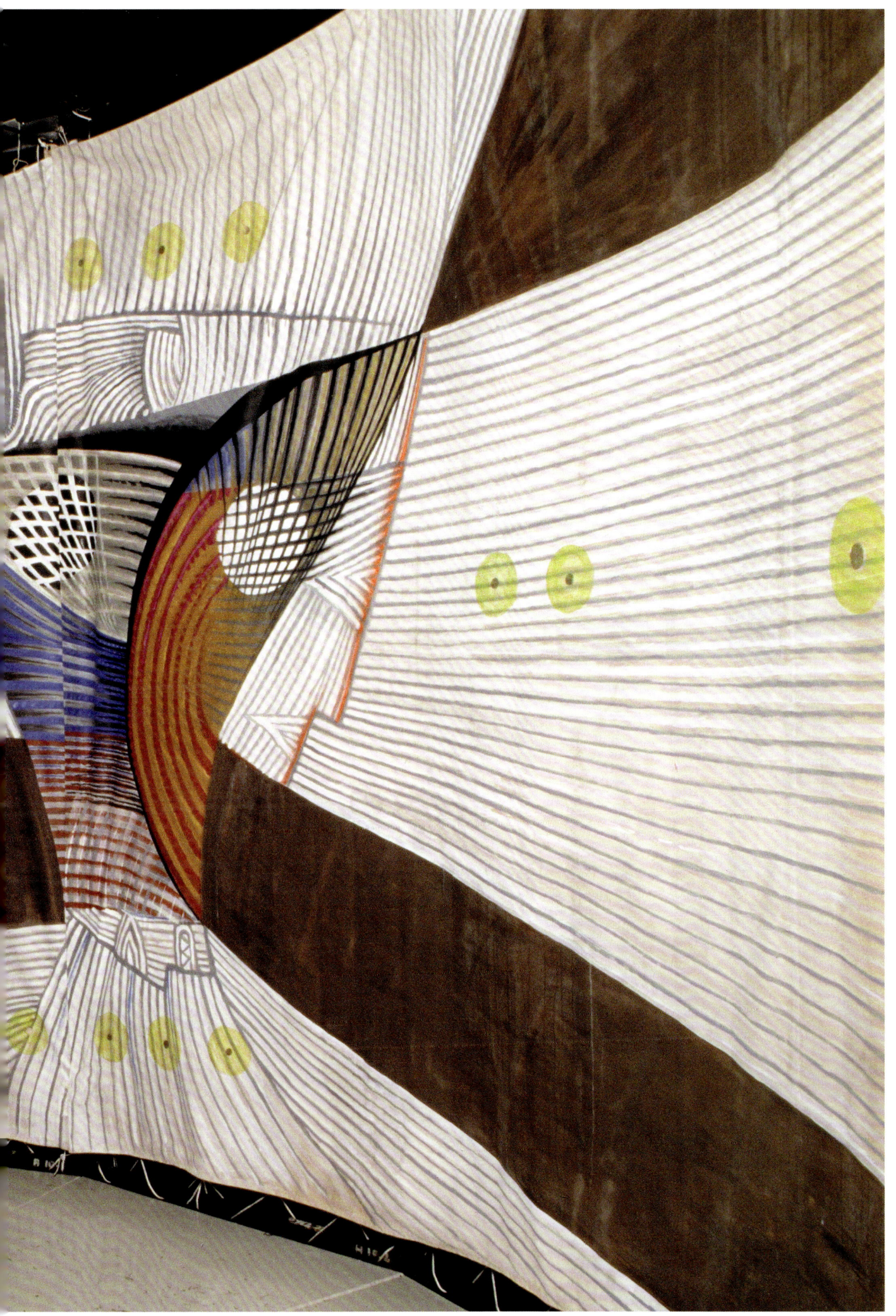

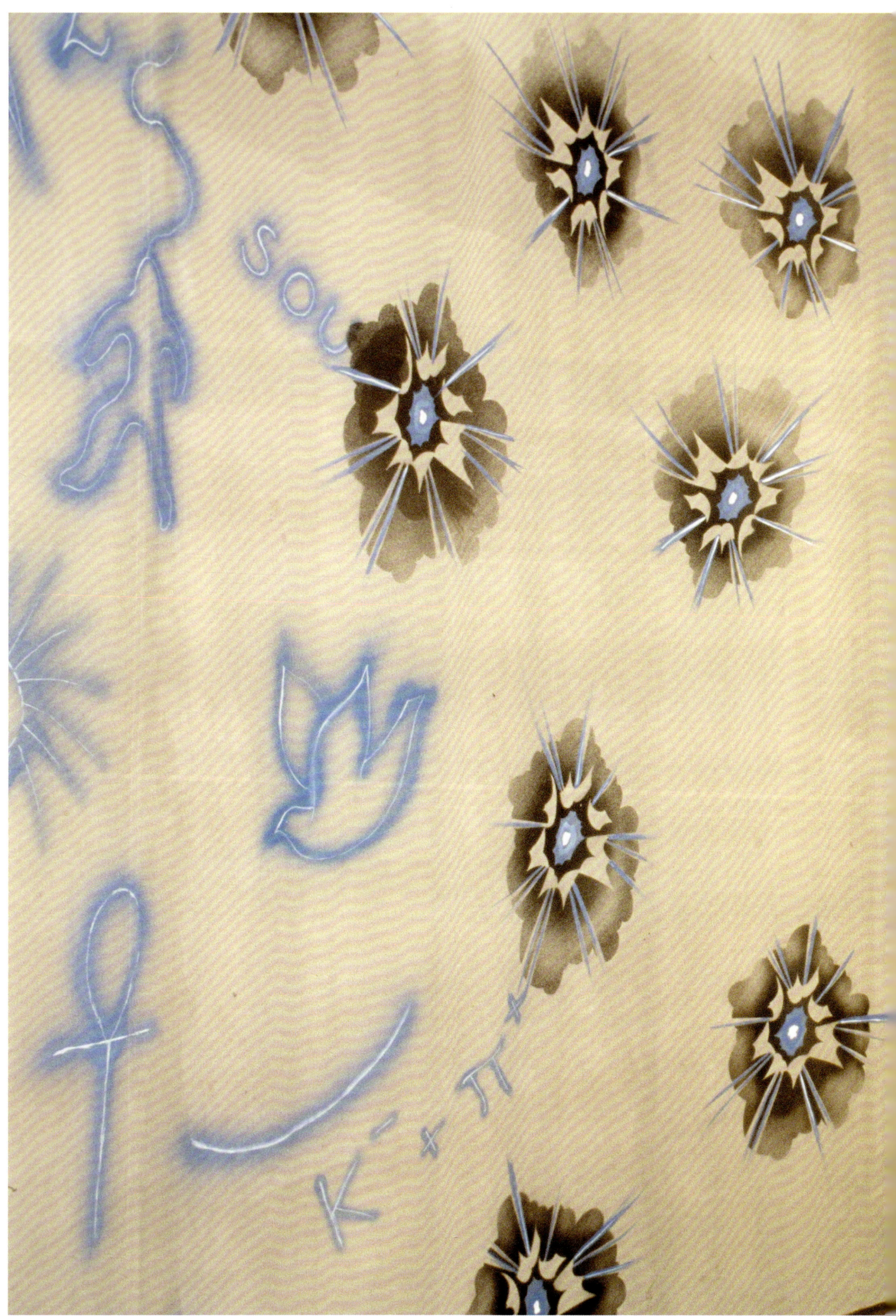

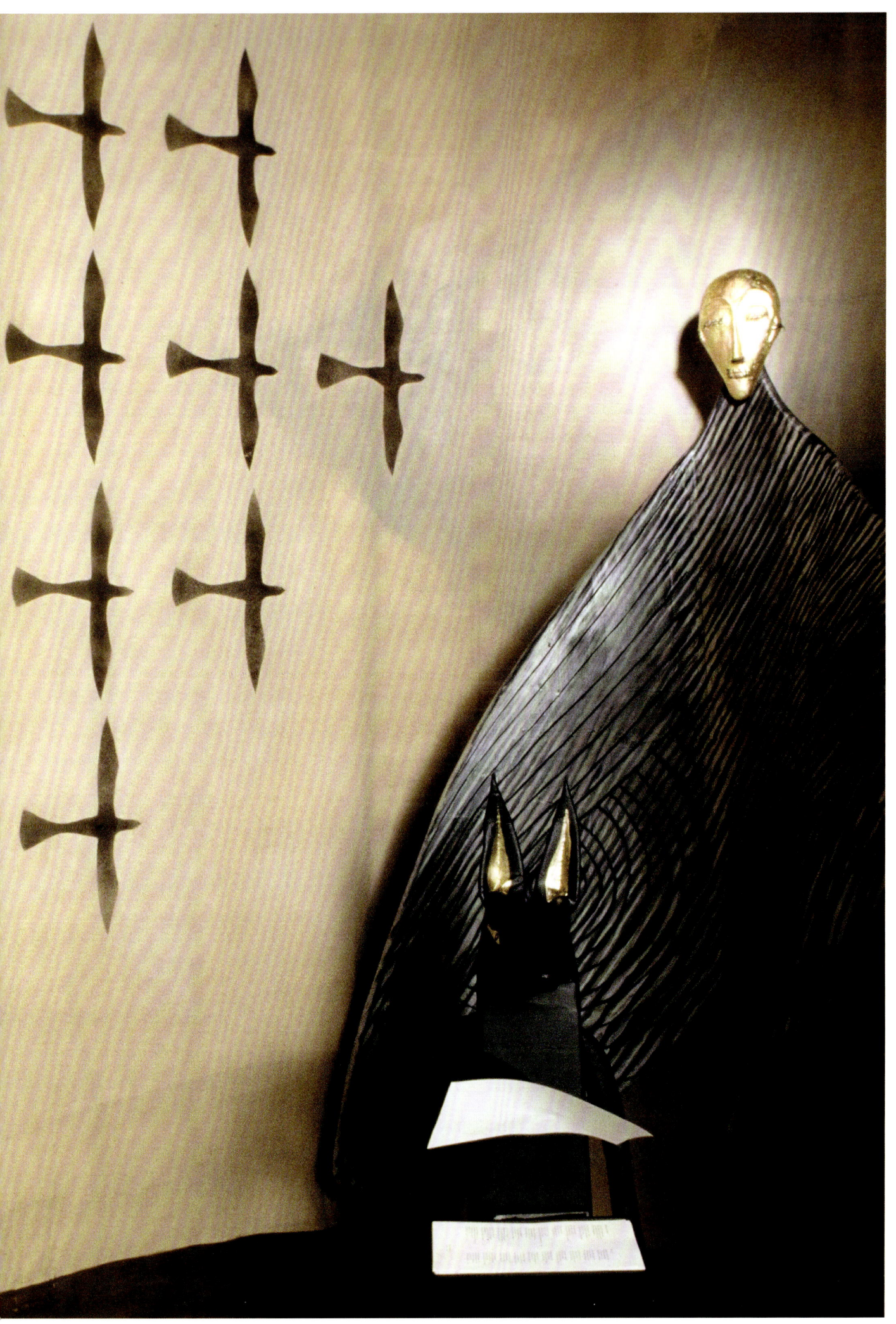

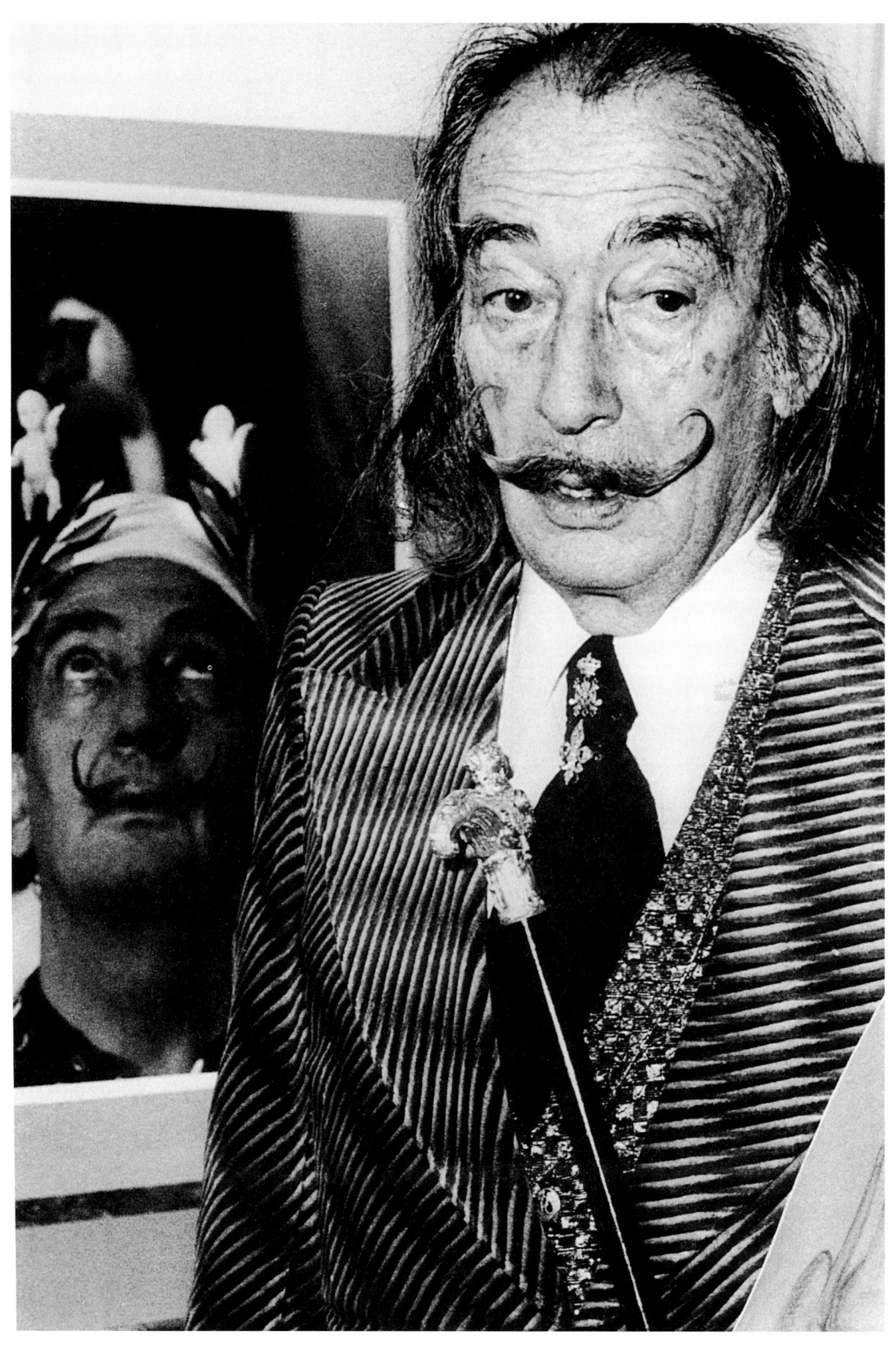

Salvador Dalí

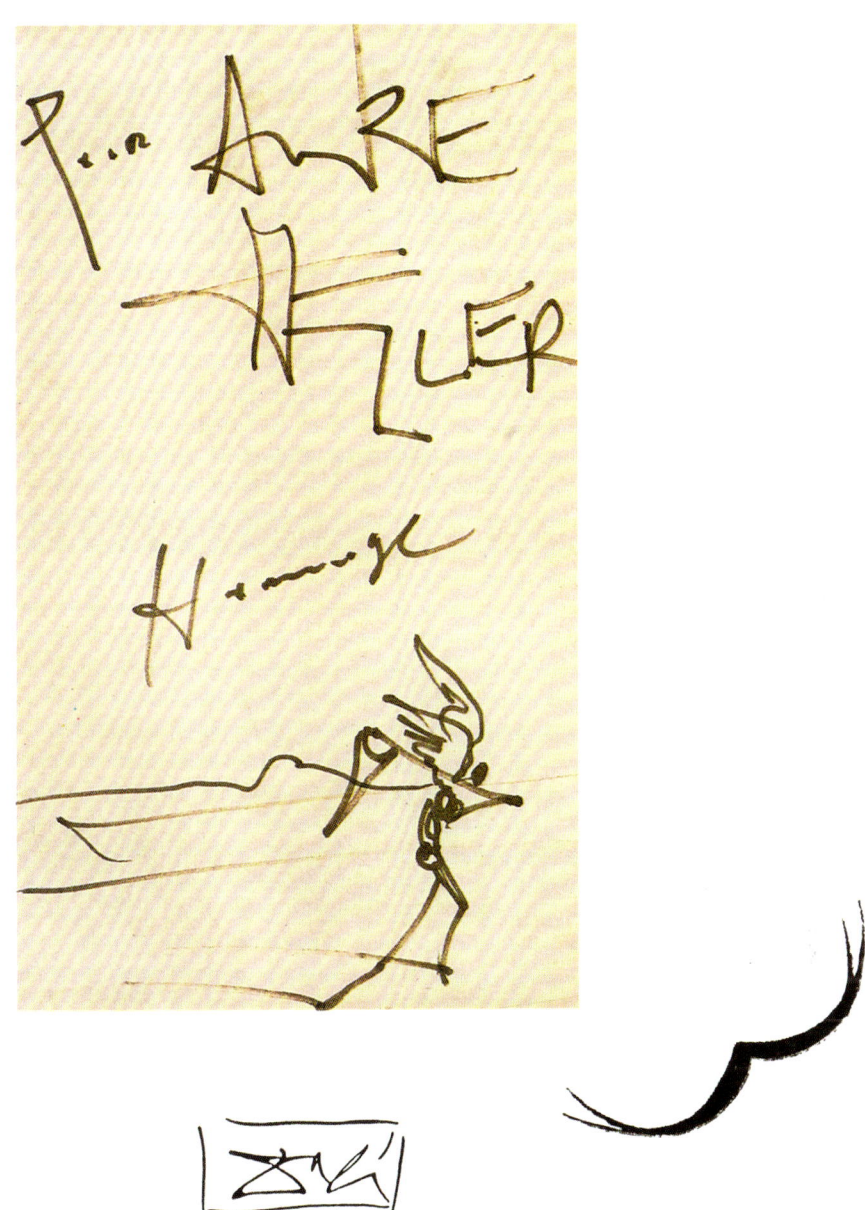

Salvador Dalí

Born: May 11, 1904, in Figueras, Spain.
Died: January 23, 1989, in Figueras.

Painter, graphic artist, poet, filmmaker, sculptor,
designer, actionist, philosopher.

Salvador Dalí designed the **Dalí Dome** for *Luna
Luna*. The building gives the viewer a seemingly
hallucinatory spatial experience. In front of the
mirrored dome is a painted mirrored facade
bordered by a frame of fried eggs and large mirrored
spheres. Dalí also created the designs of the **murals**
in the restaurant depicting Chinese acrobats. The
music was provided by Hubert Bognermayr and
Harold Zuschrader.

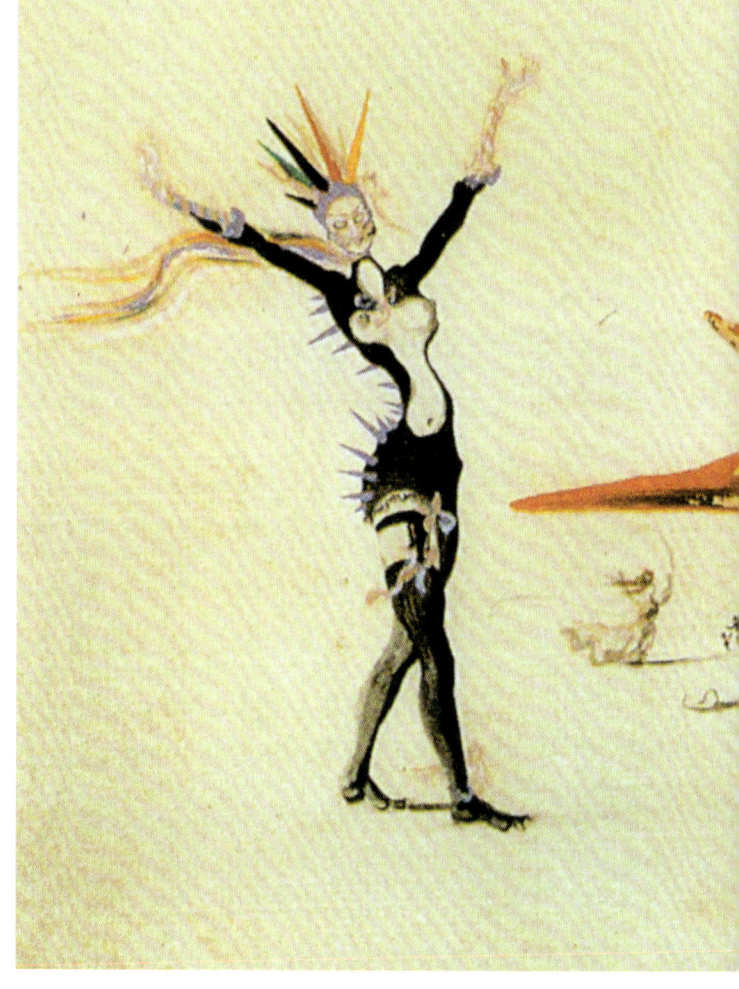

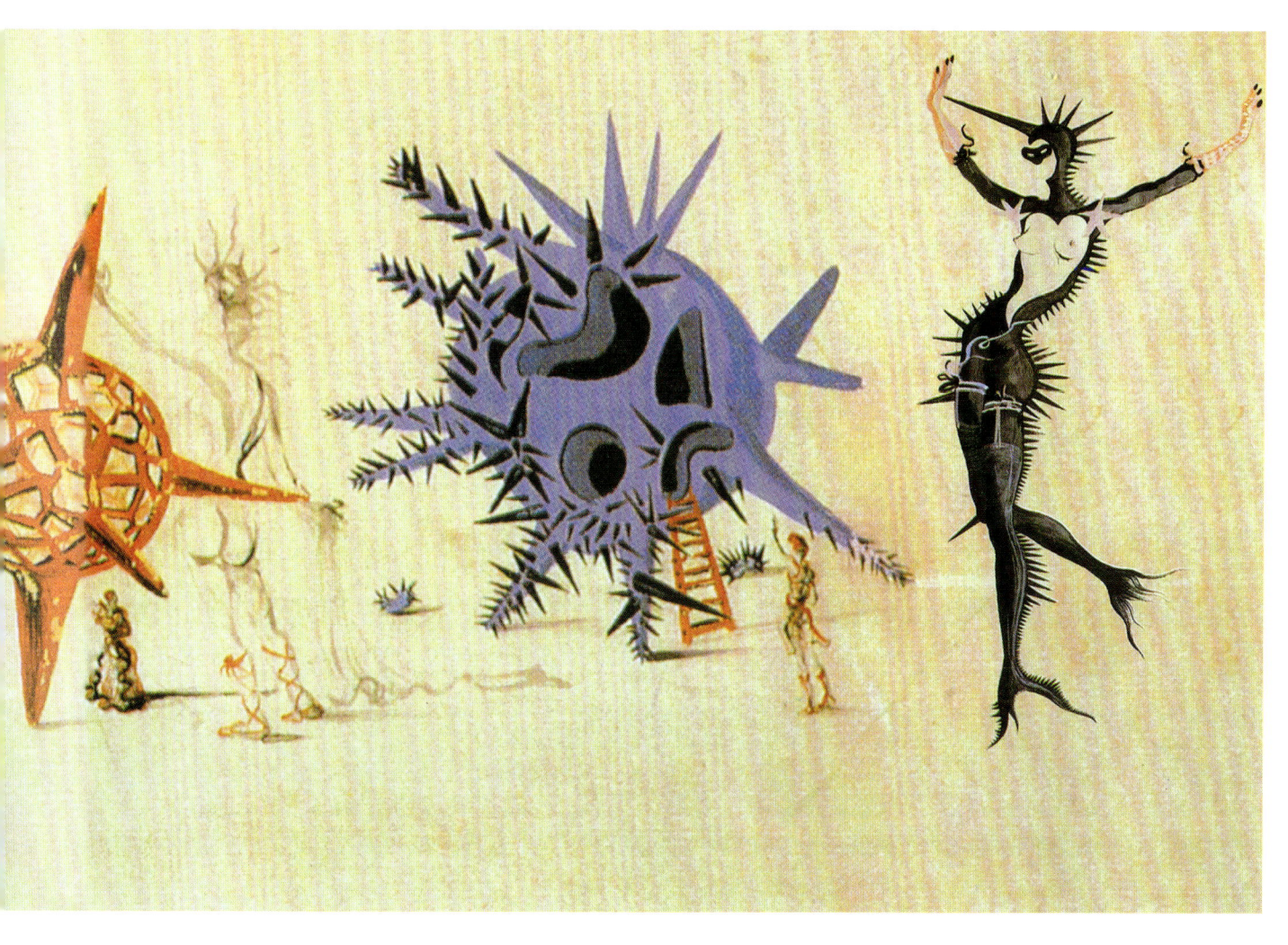

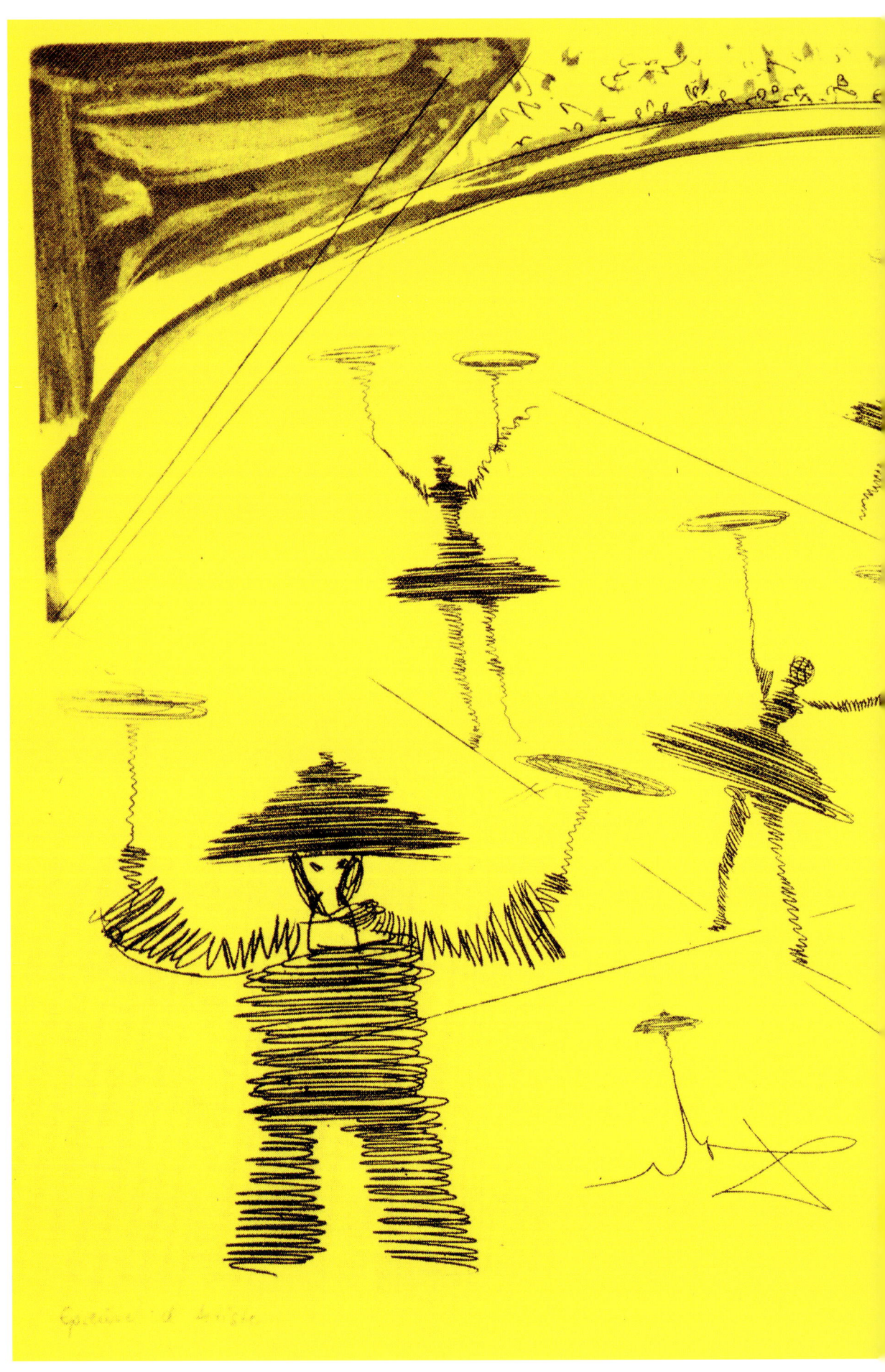

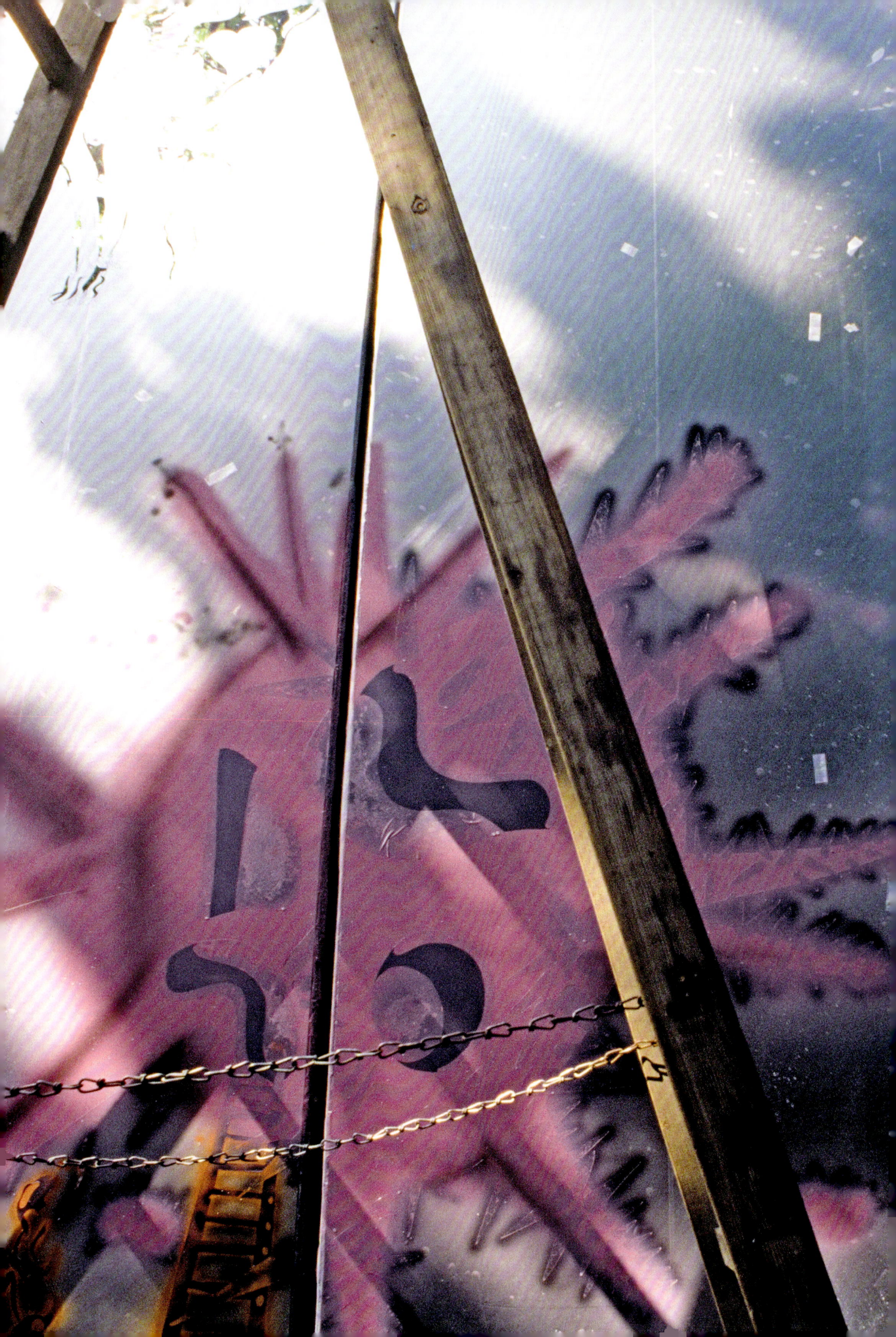

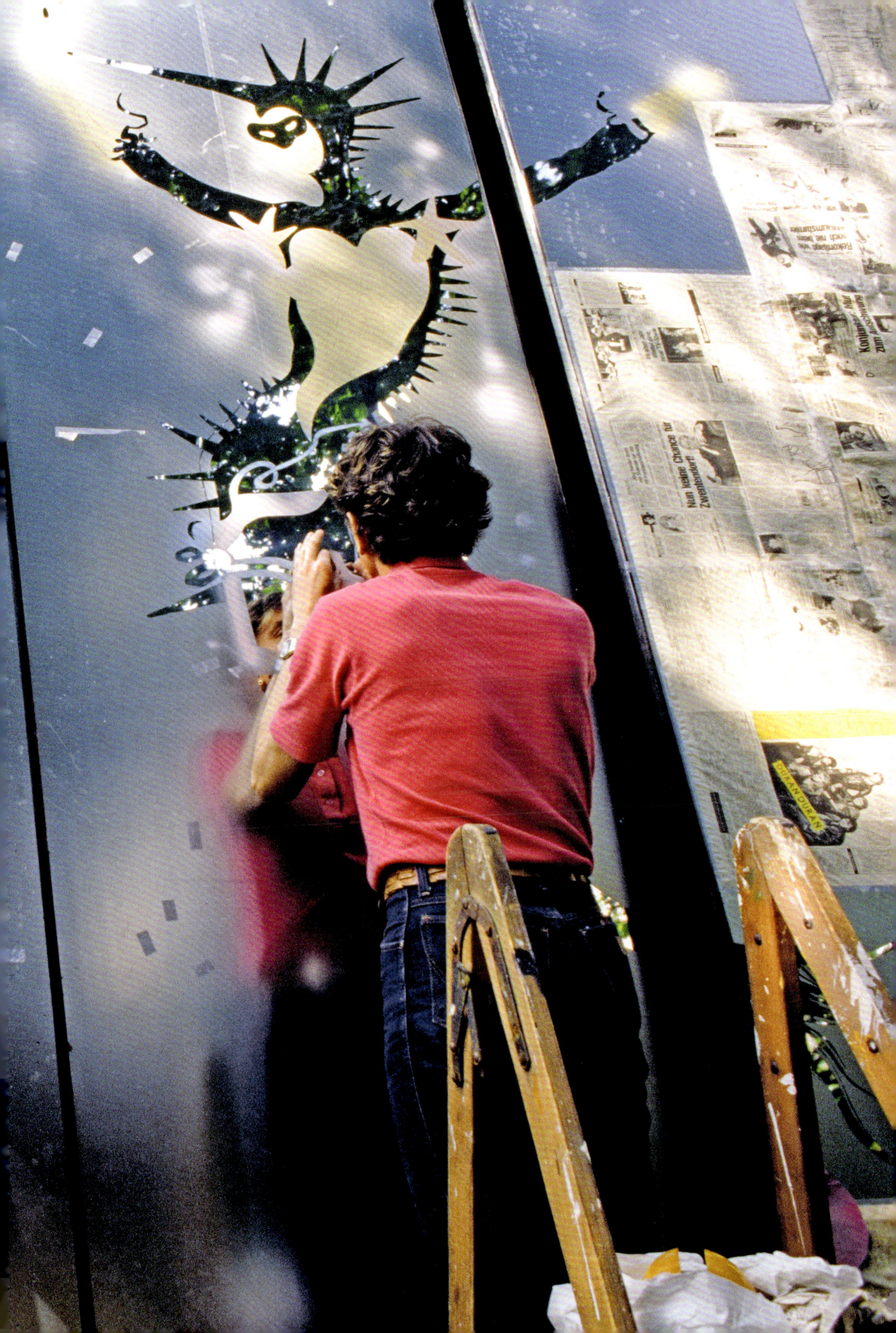

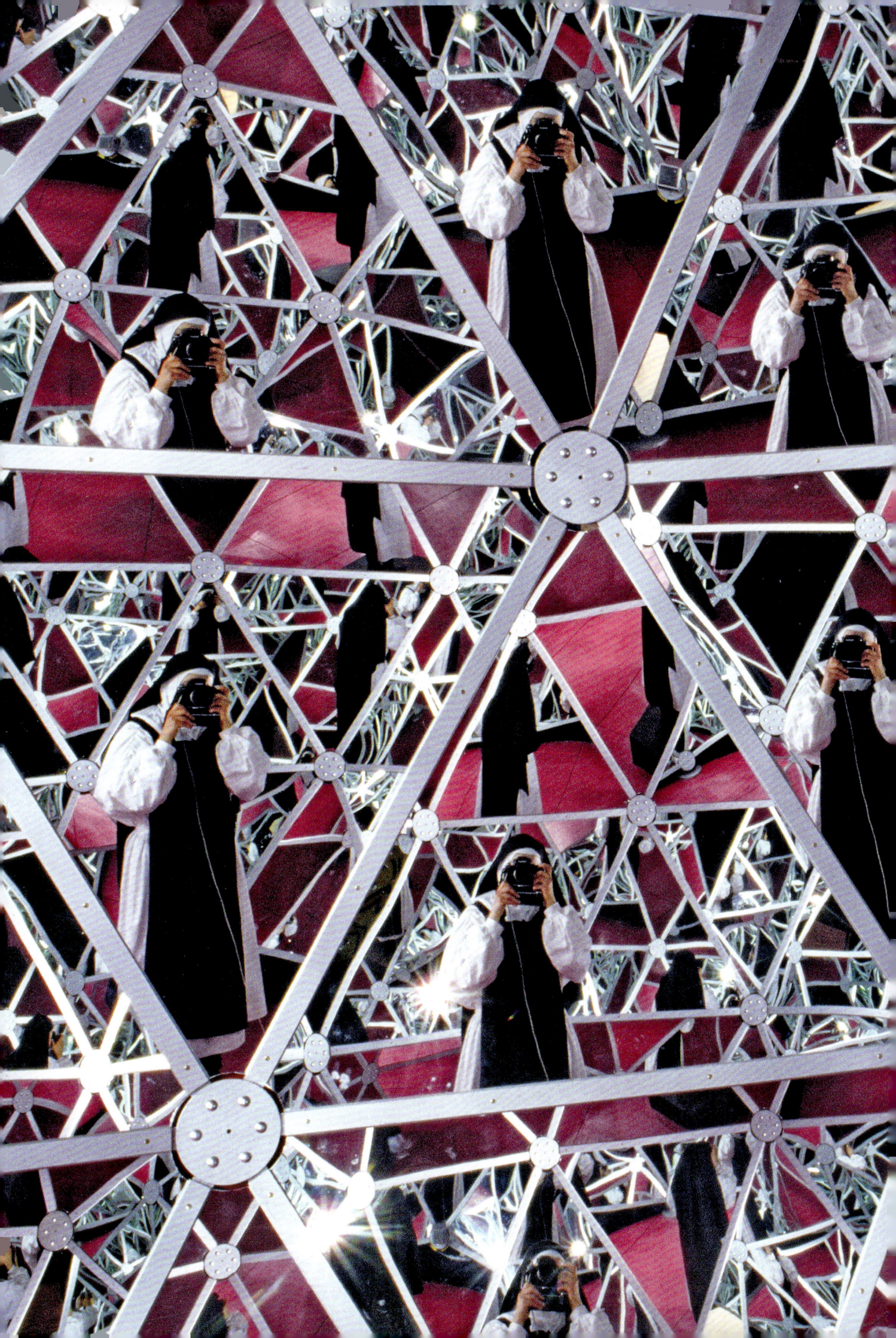

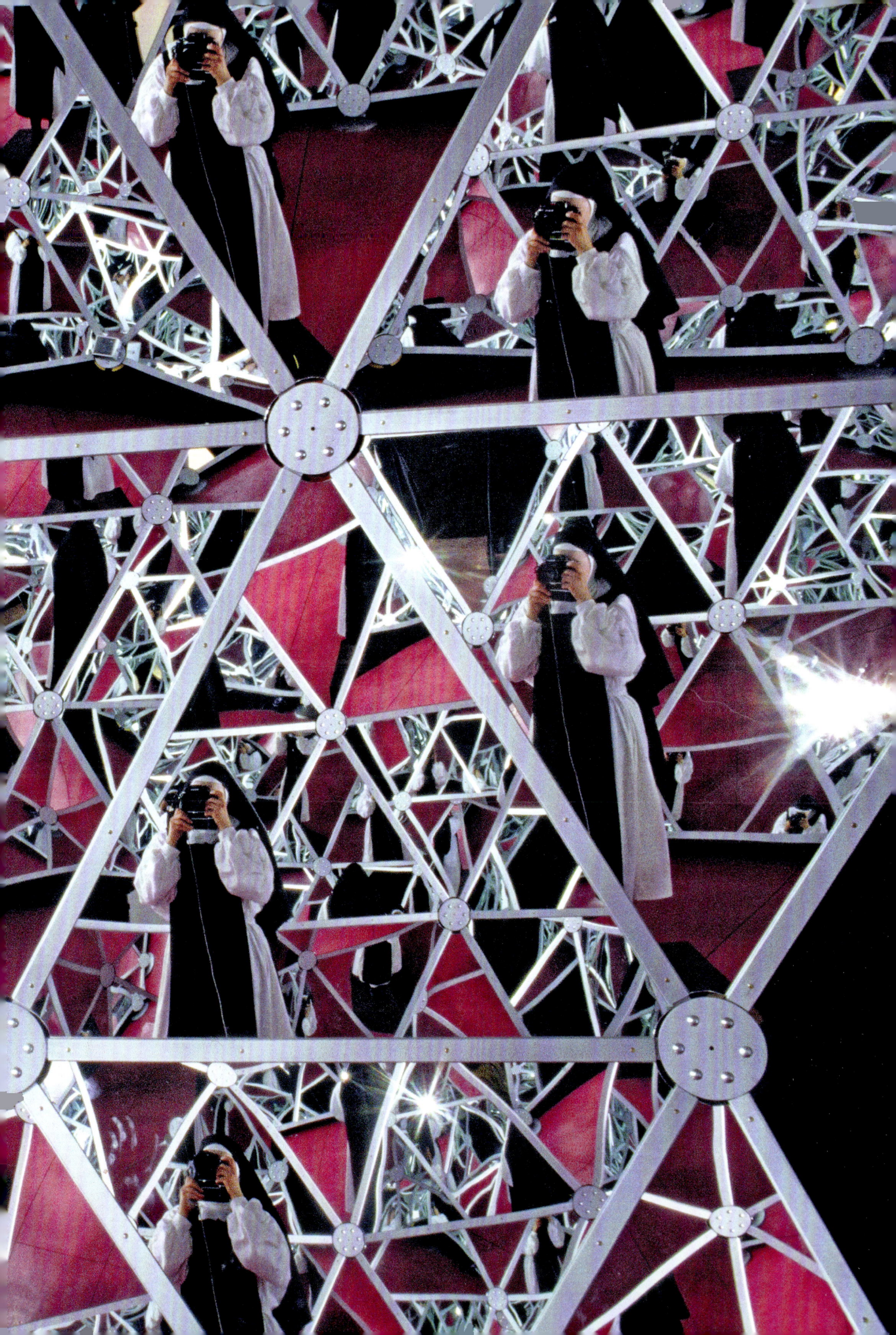

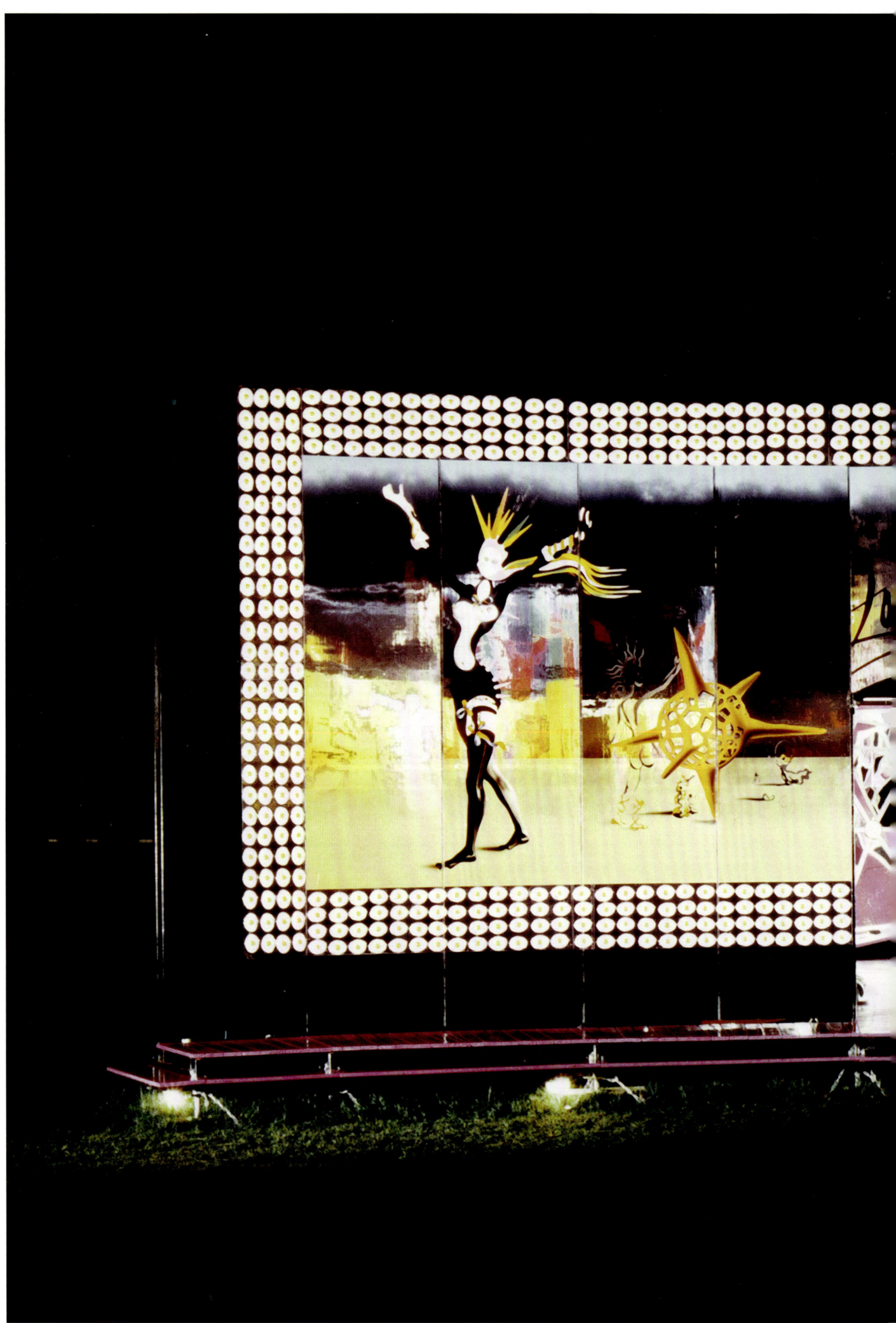

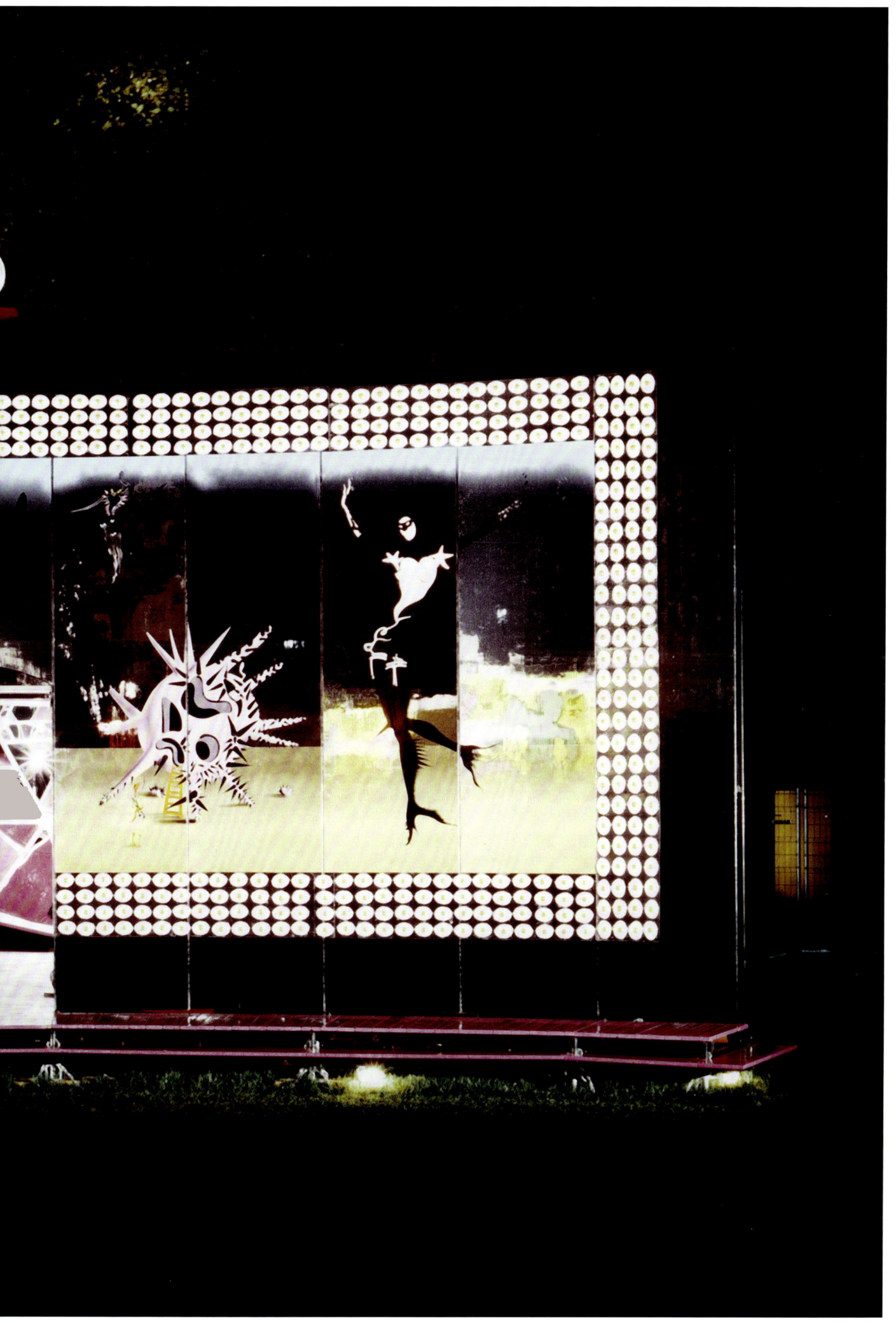

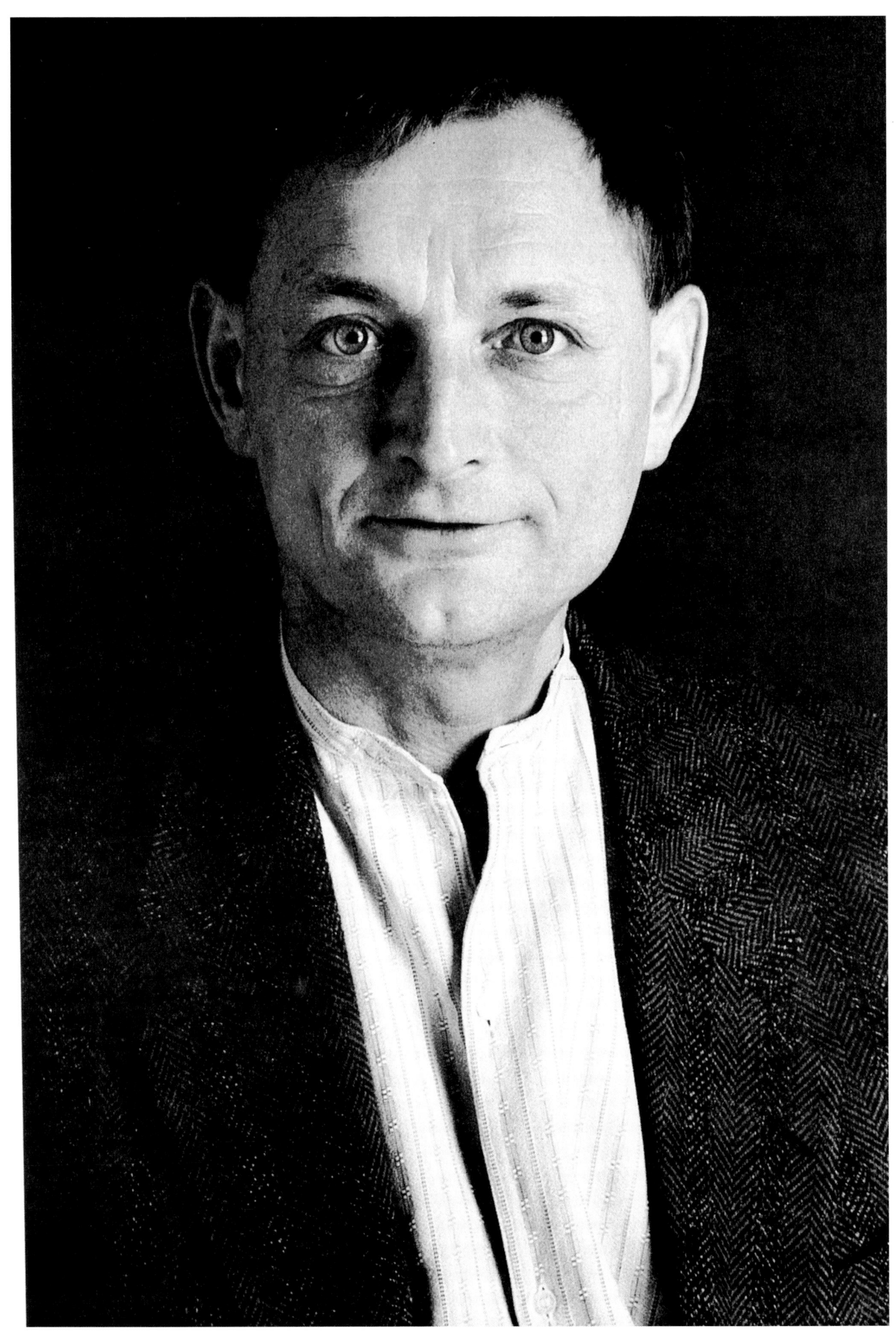

Günter Brus

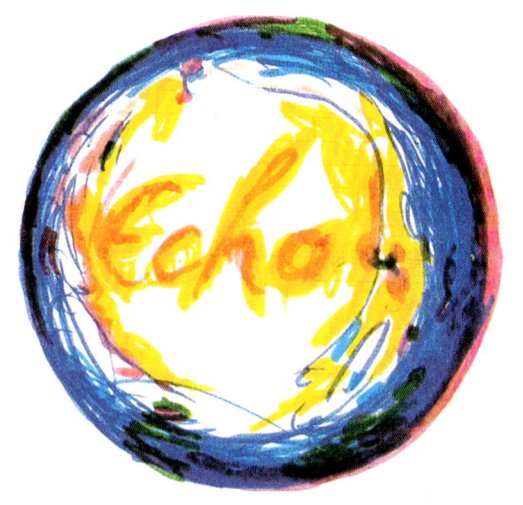

NICHT DAS ZIEL IST EINE REISE WERT,
NUR DER AUSGANGSPUNKT ——
UND DIESER IST EIN WUNDER.

Günter Brus

Born: January 23, 1938, in Ardning, Austria.

Illustrator, actionist, poet.

Günter Brus designed the **Delyrium** for *Luna Luna*, a building that tells of mysterious adventures in the Universe of the Crayons. The accompanying music was written by Hermann Nitsch.

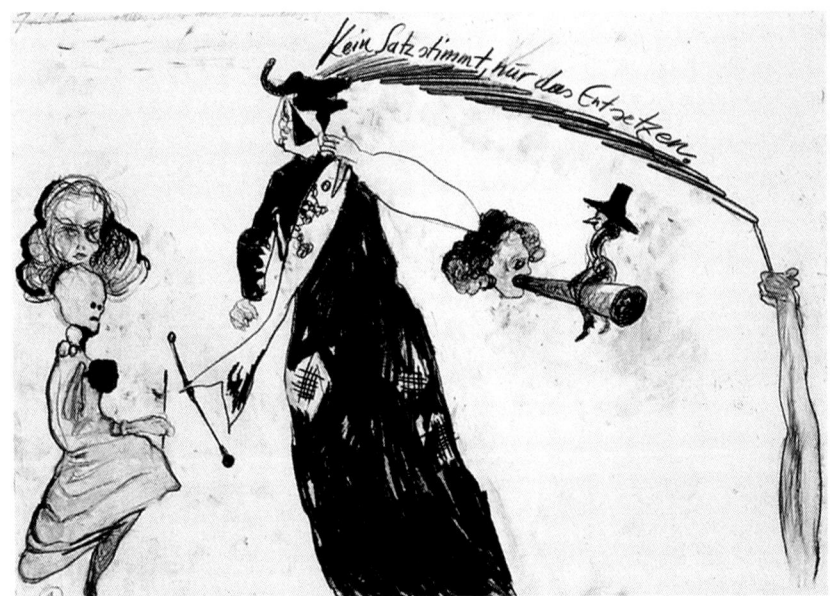

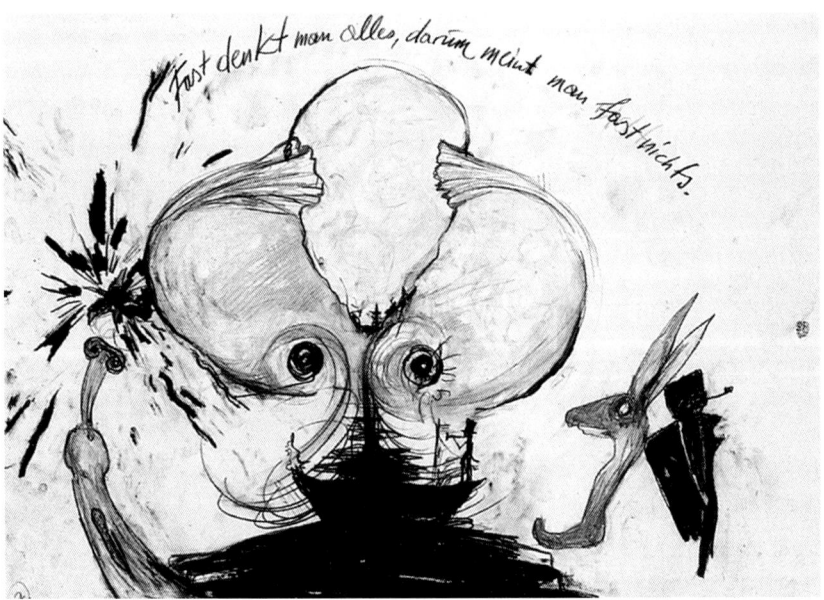

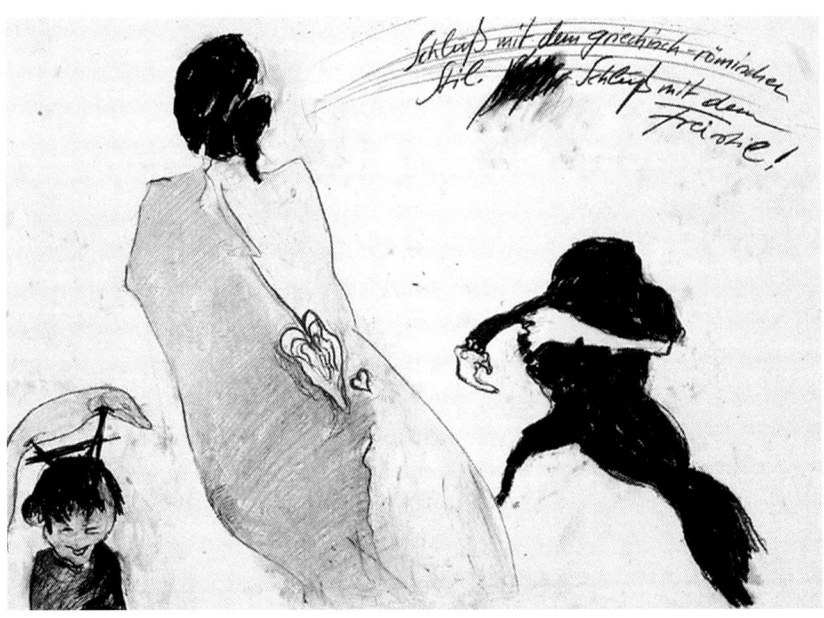

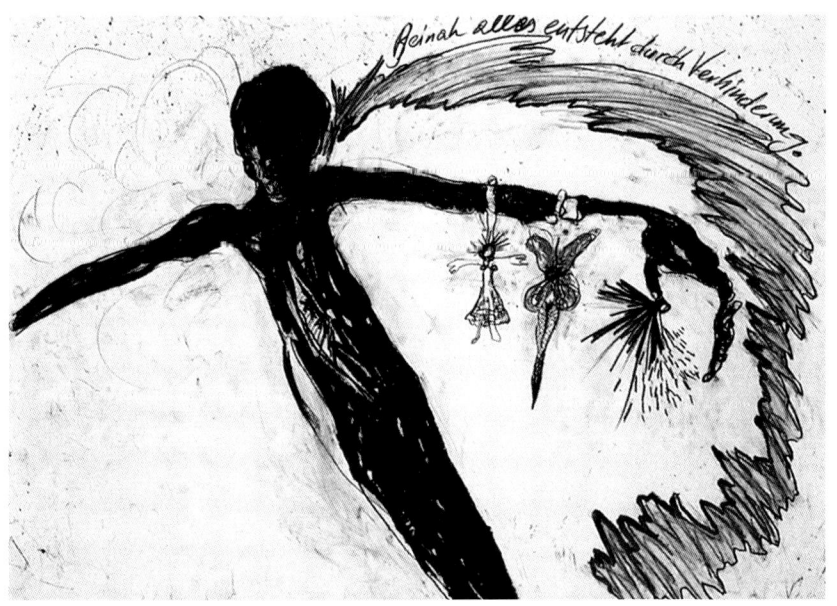

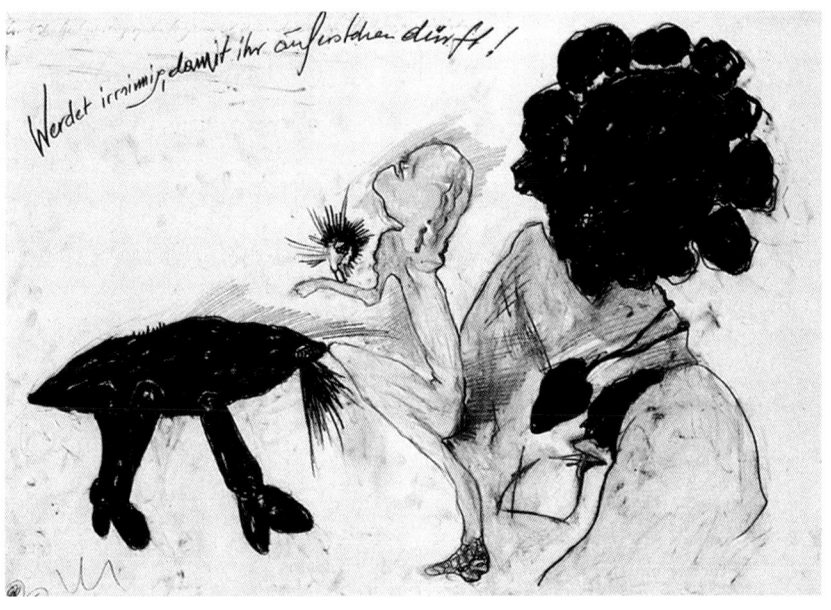

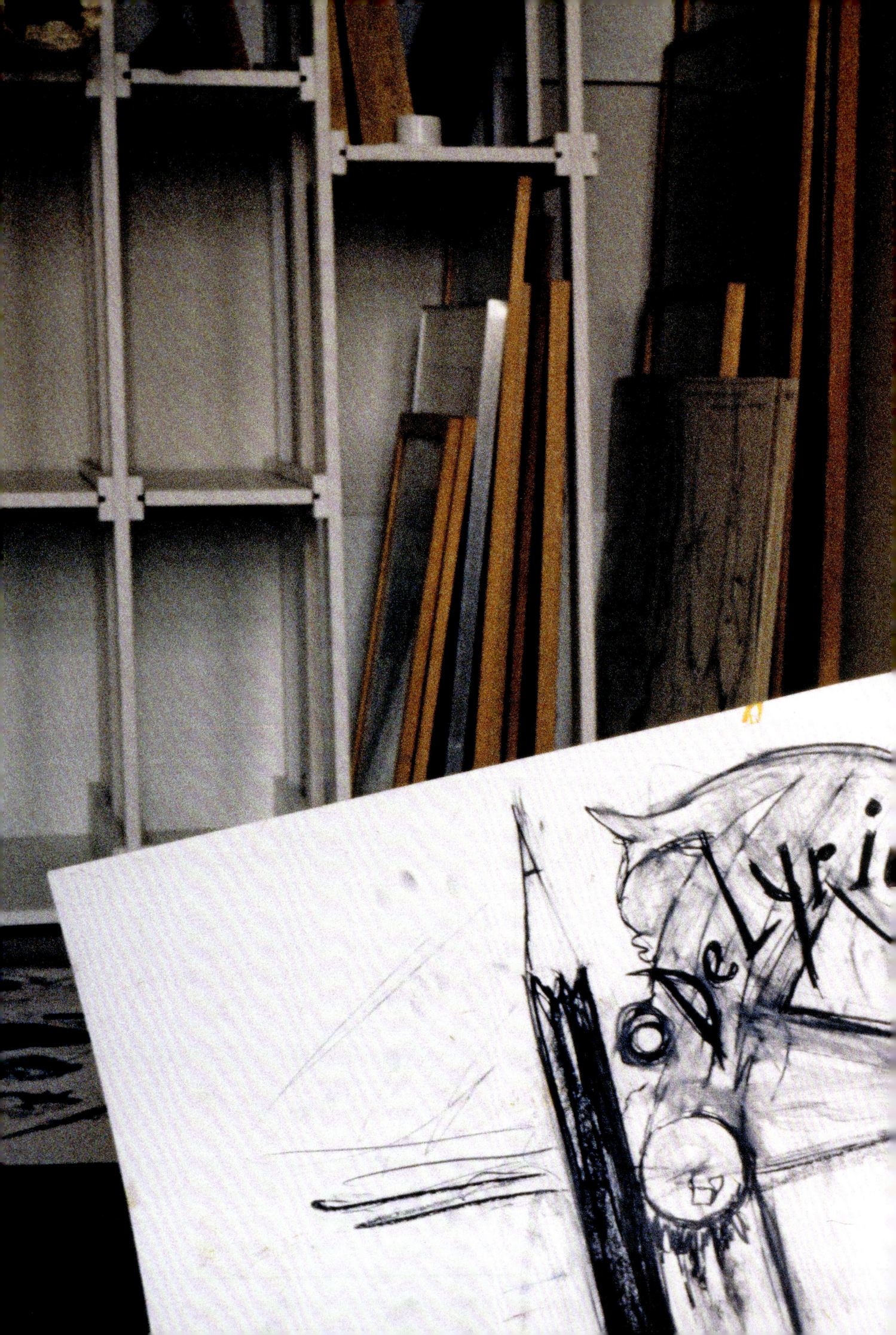

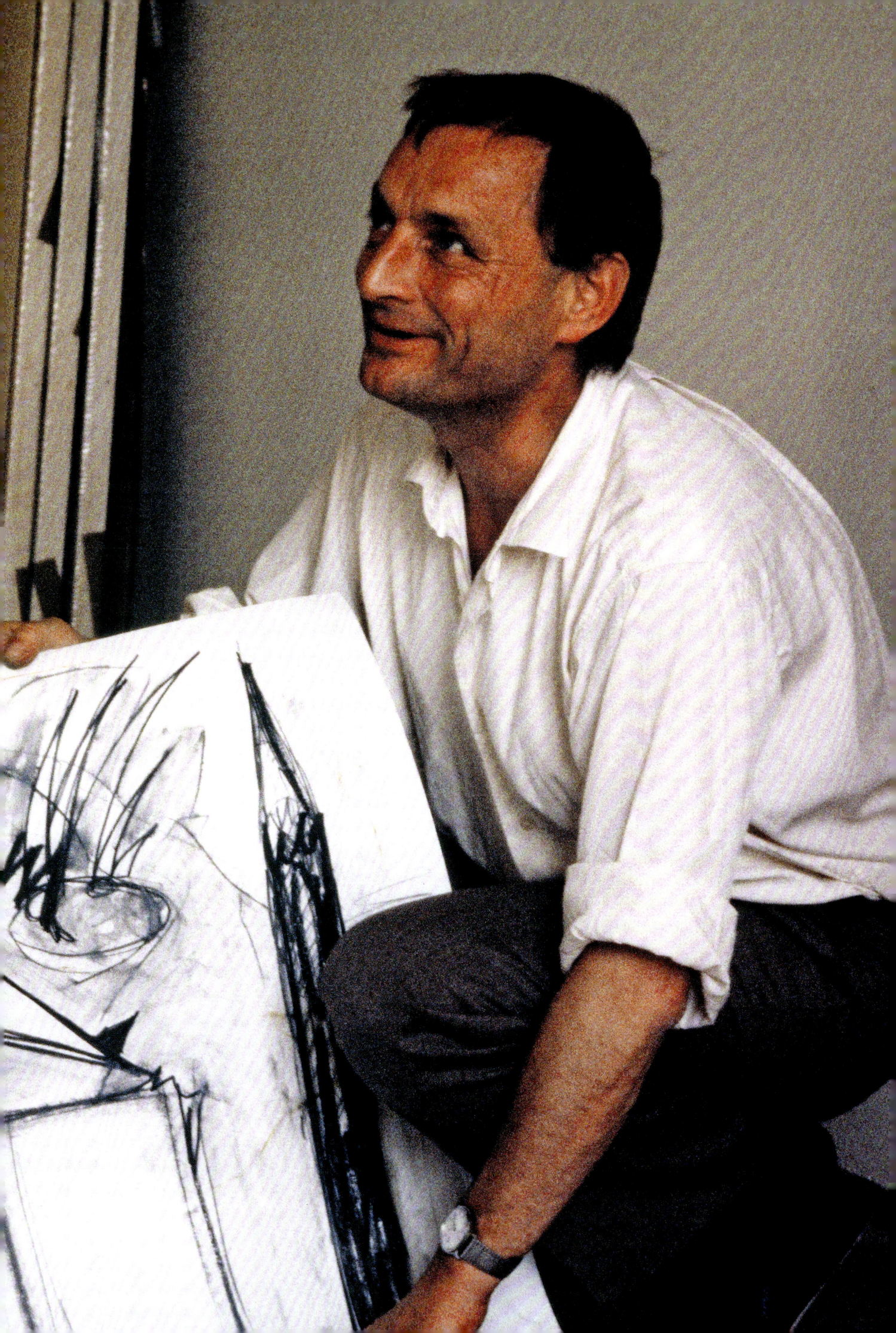

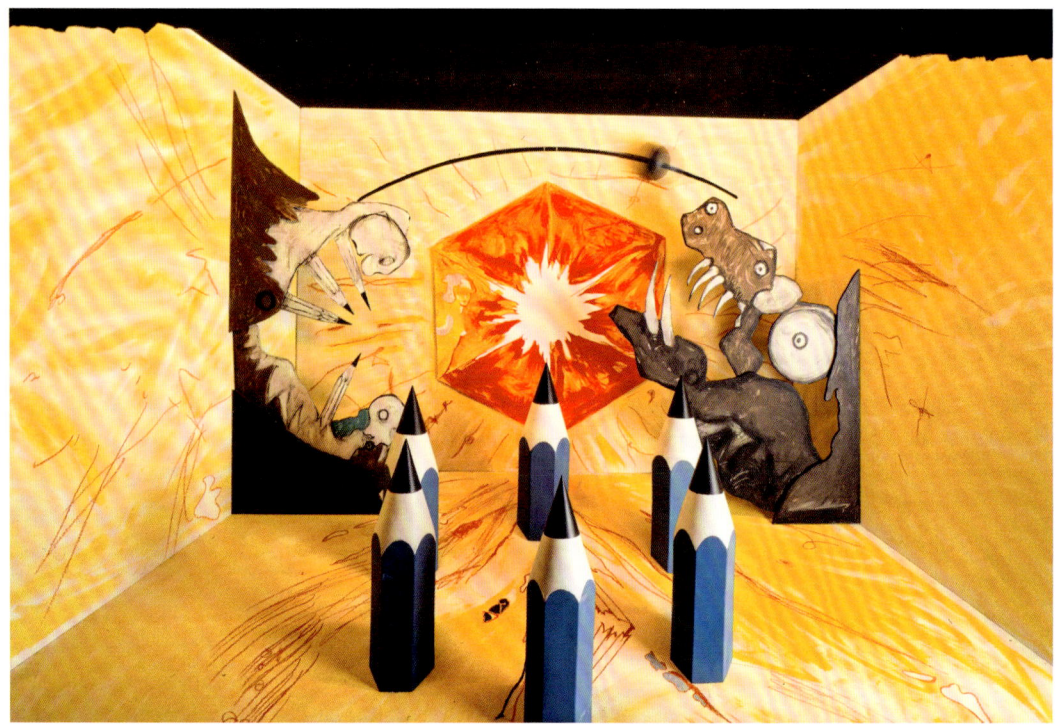

*What is born in the evening can only wander into the night*

*Nightshade in blossom*

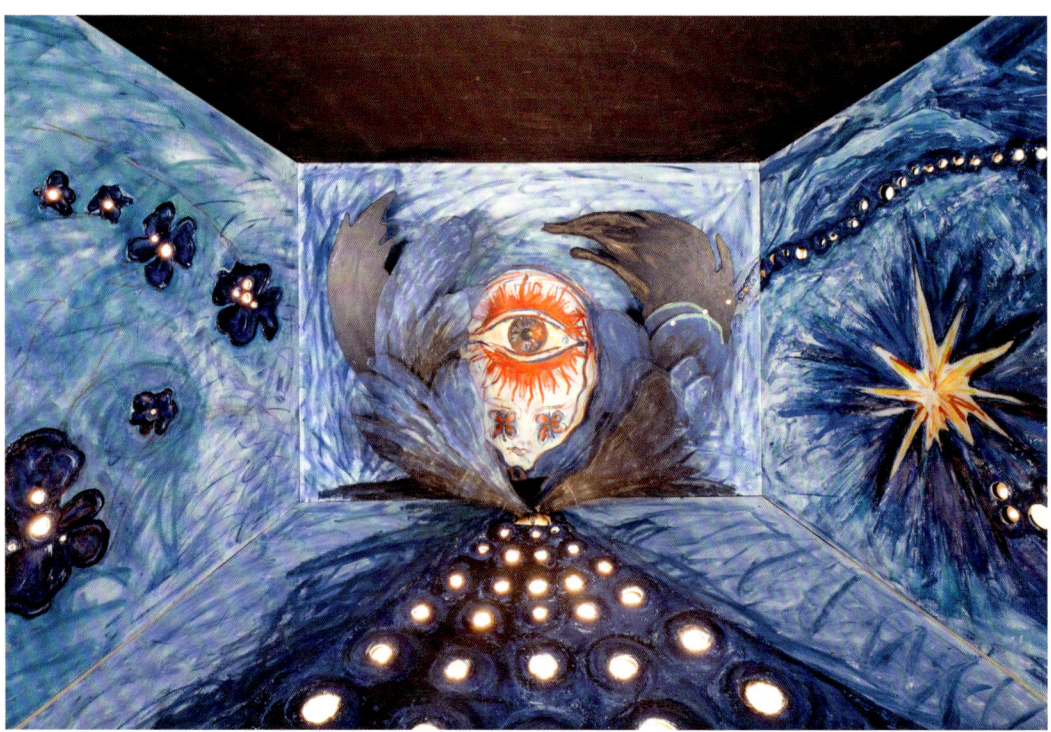

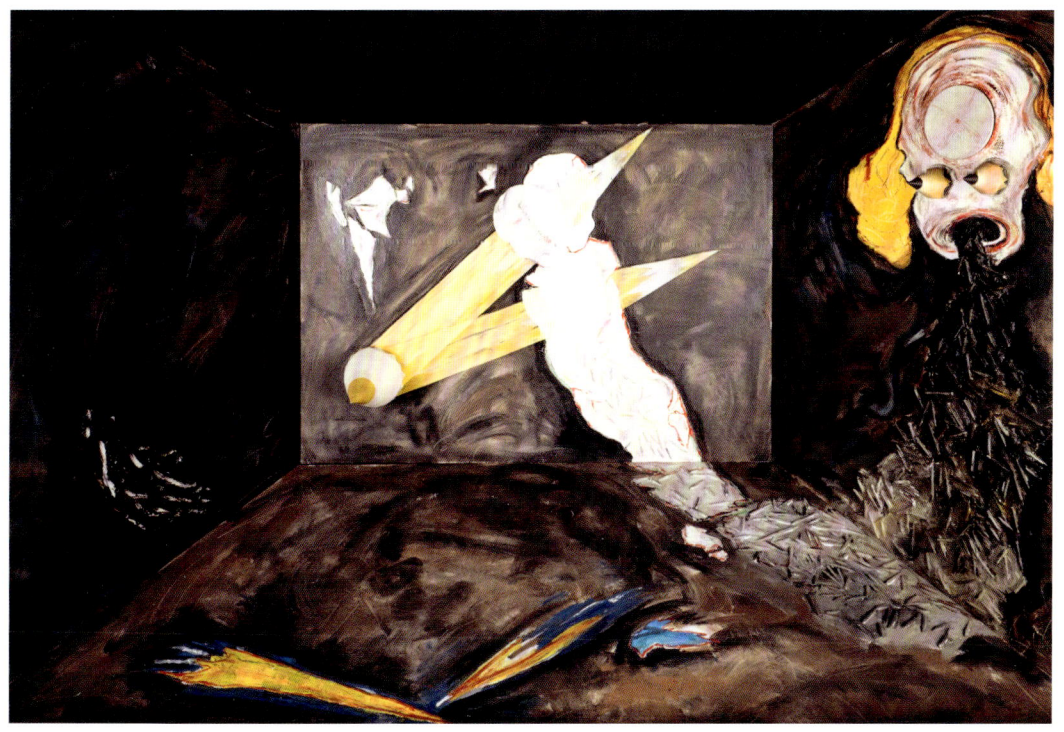

*The assertion decapitates itself*

*Past beings orbit the earth in mourning sleep*

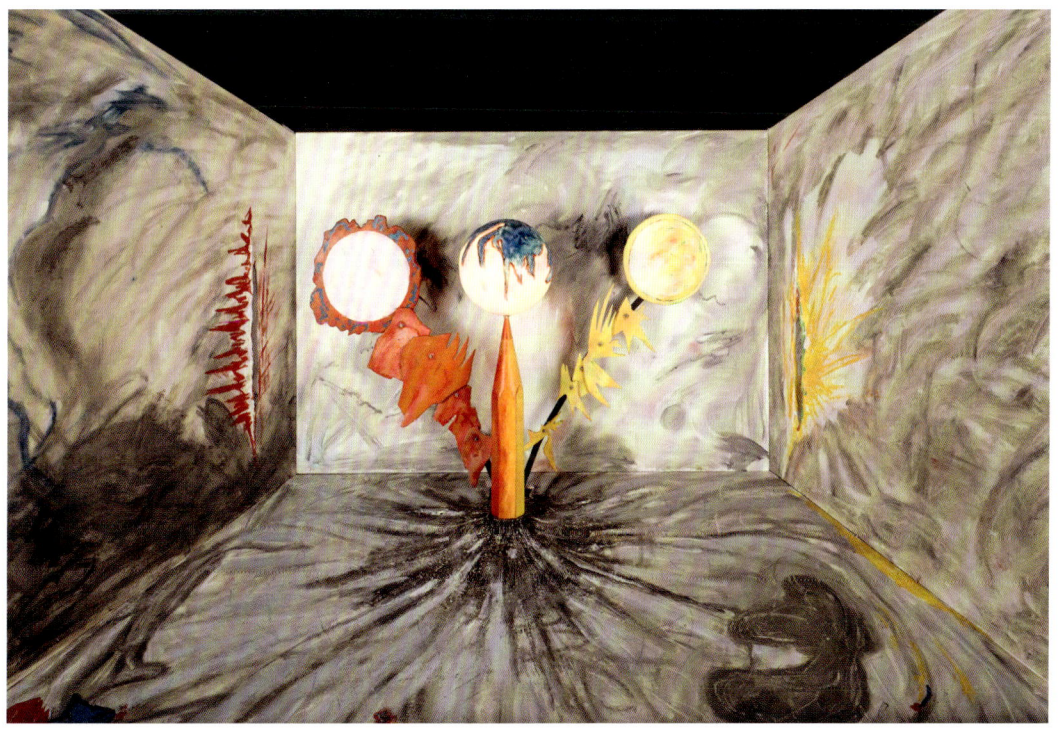

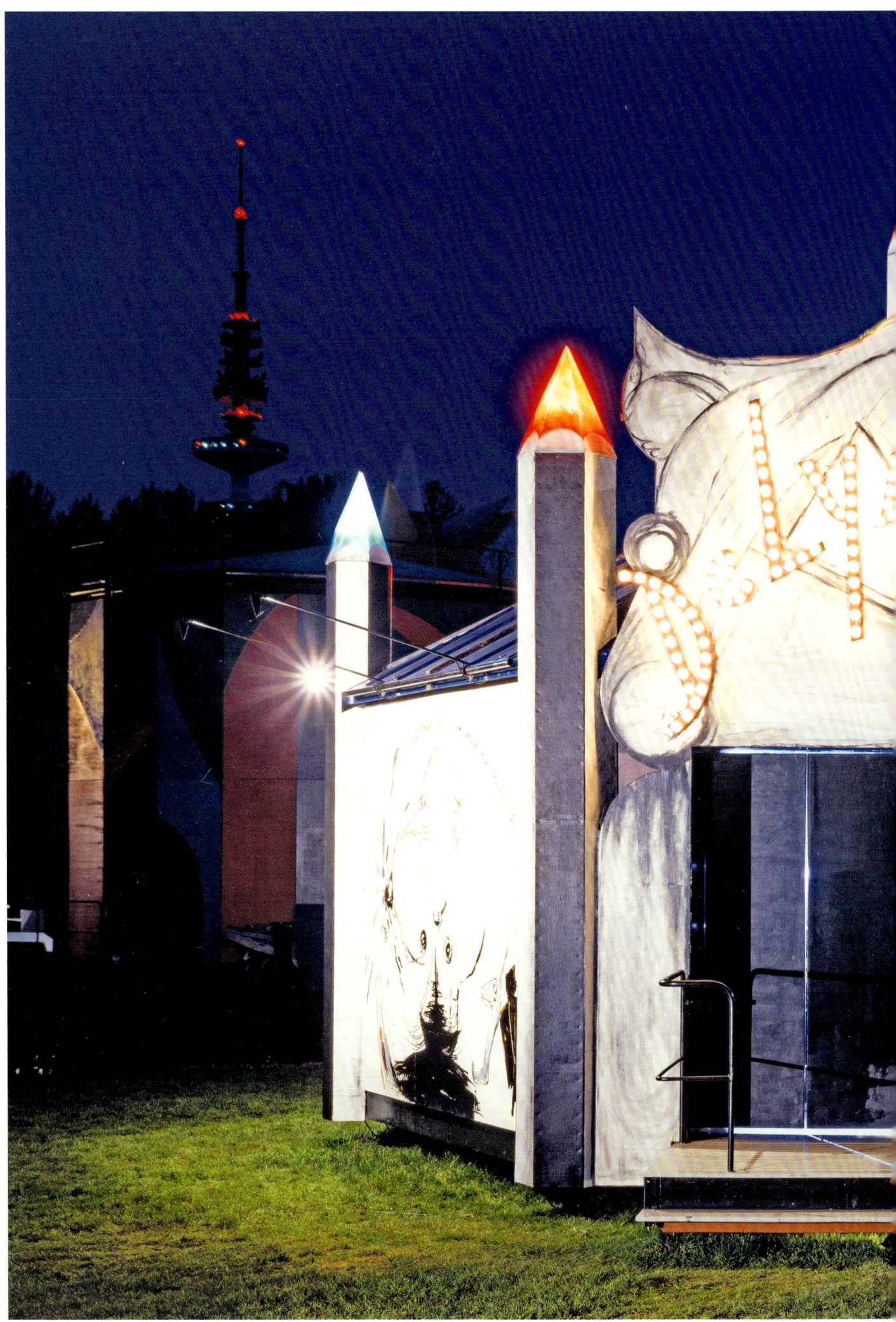

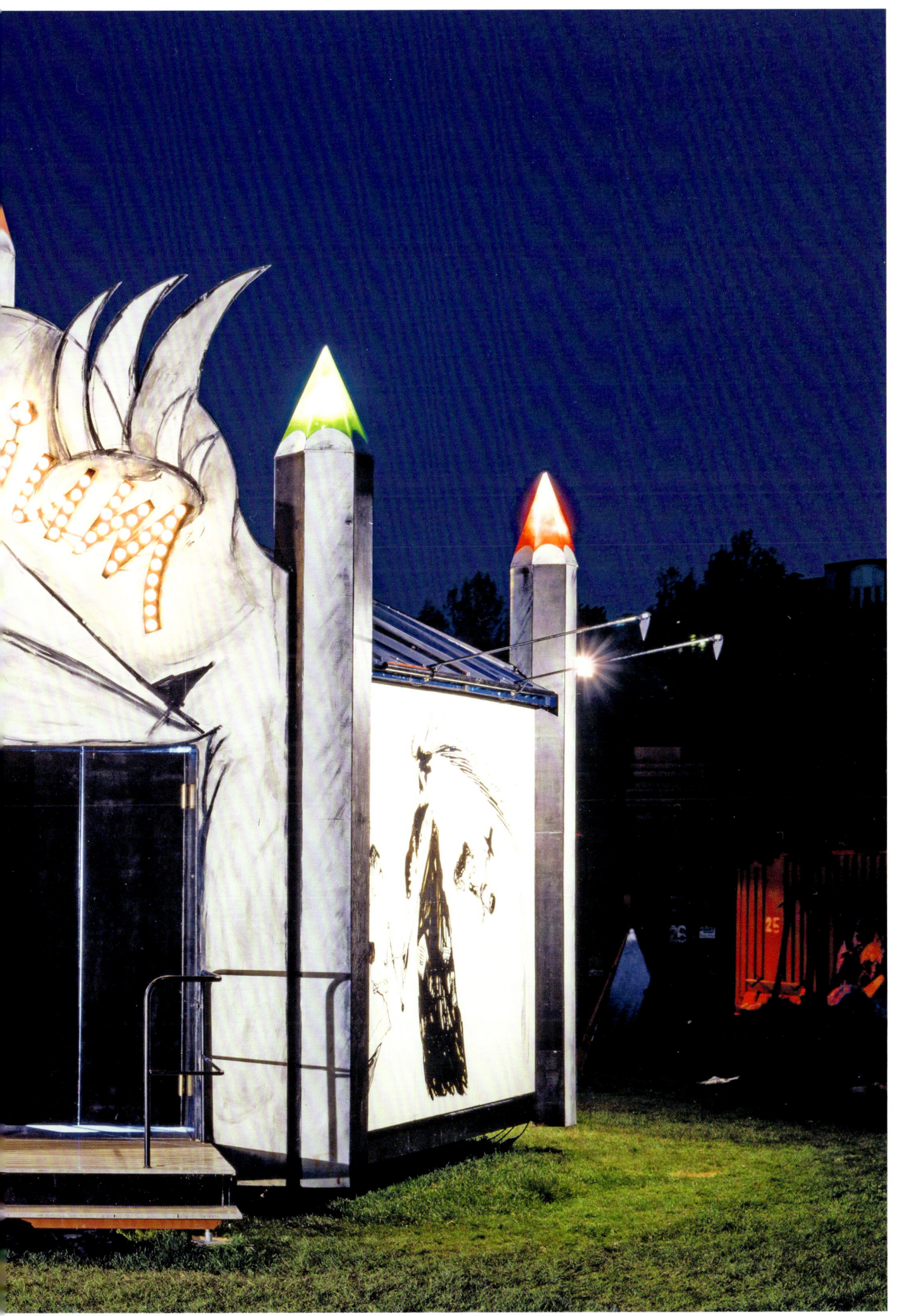

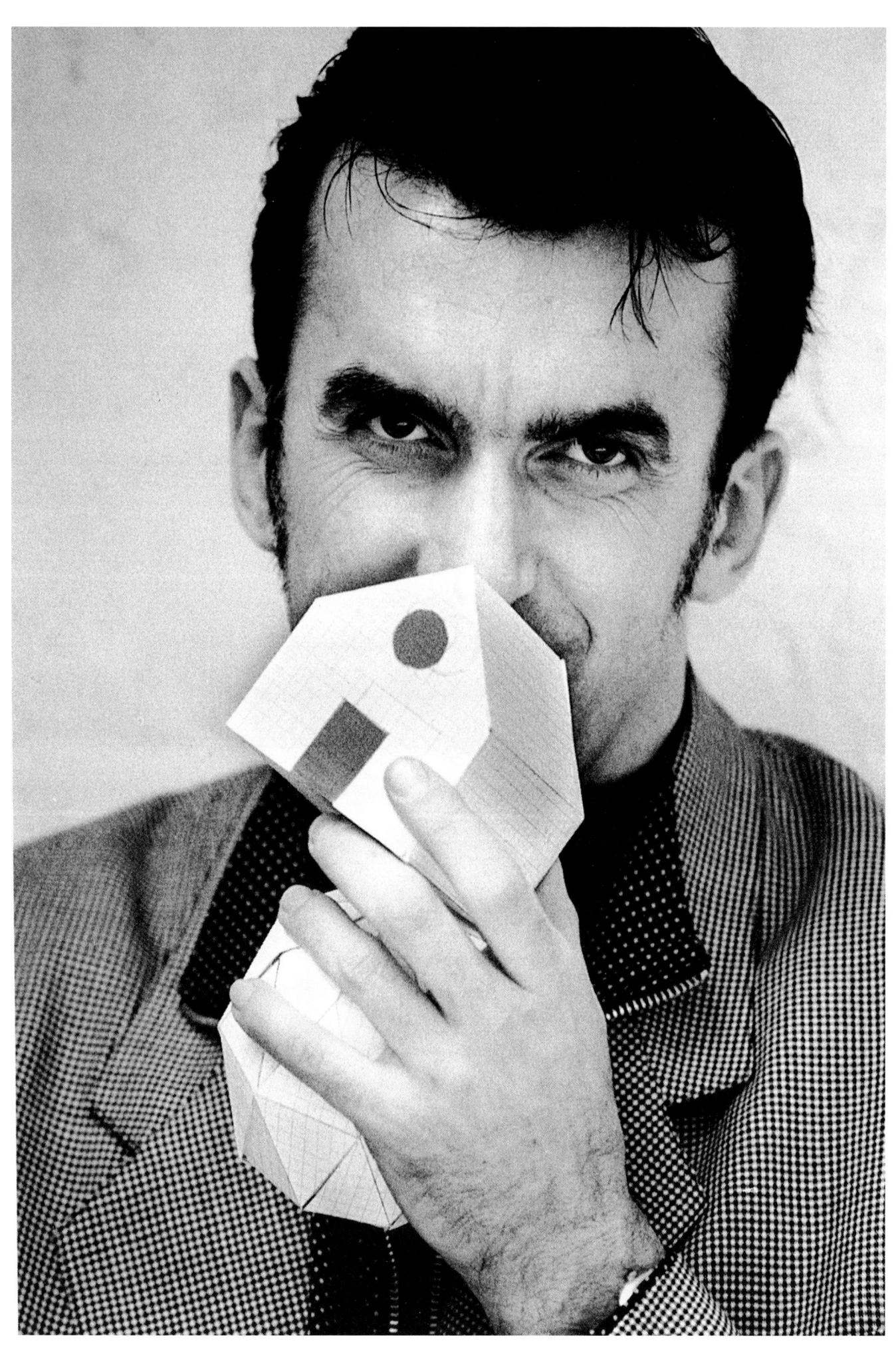

Patrick Raynaud

Comptable des amours, des fêtes et des catastrophes.

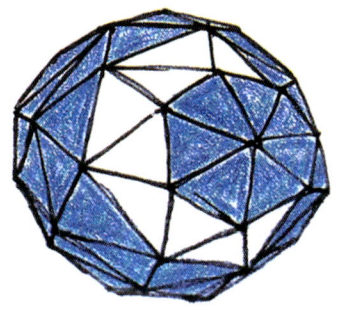

PATRICK RAYNAUD

Patrick Raynaud

Born: April 11, 1946, in Carcassonne, France.

Sculptor, director, illustrator, poet.

Patrick Raynaud designed an **Earthquake Alley** for *Luna Luna* as an exit into the world of everyday horrors.

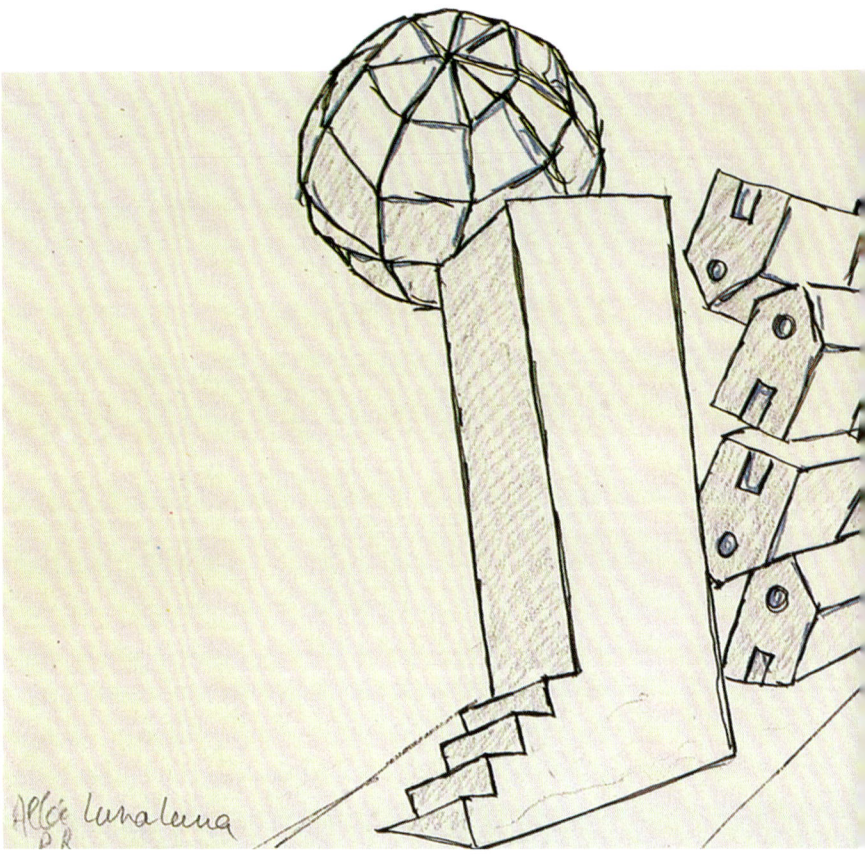

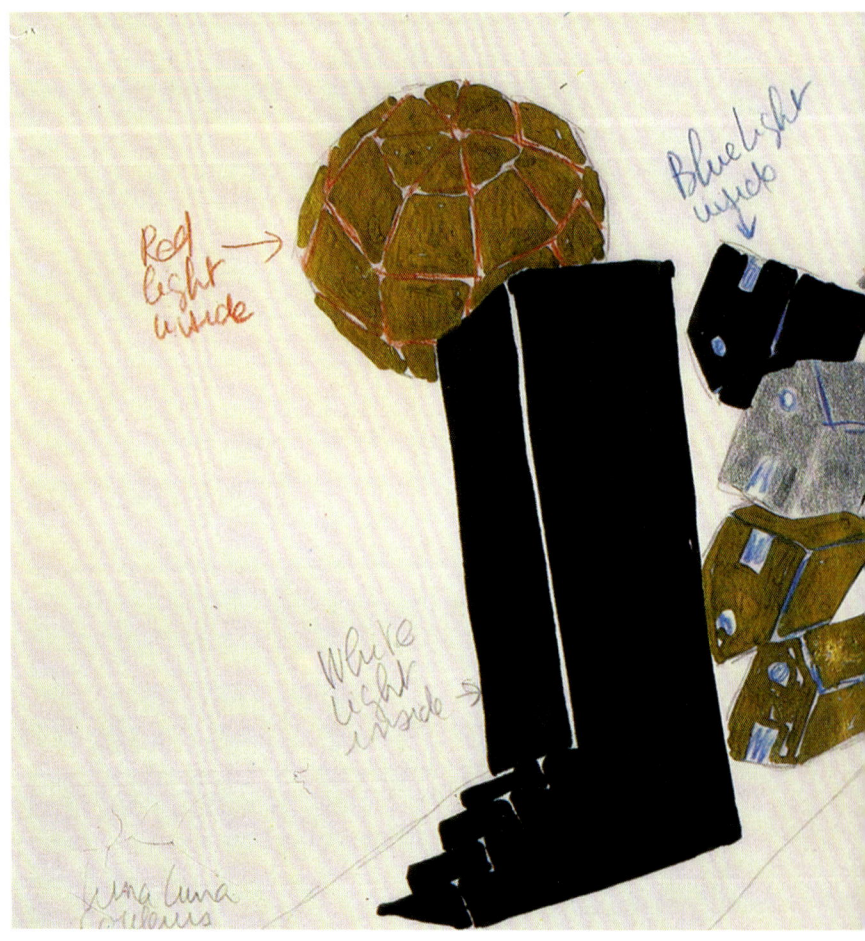

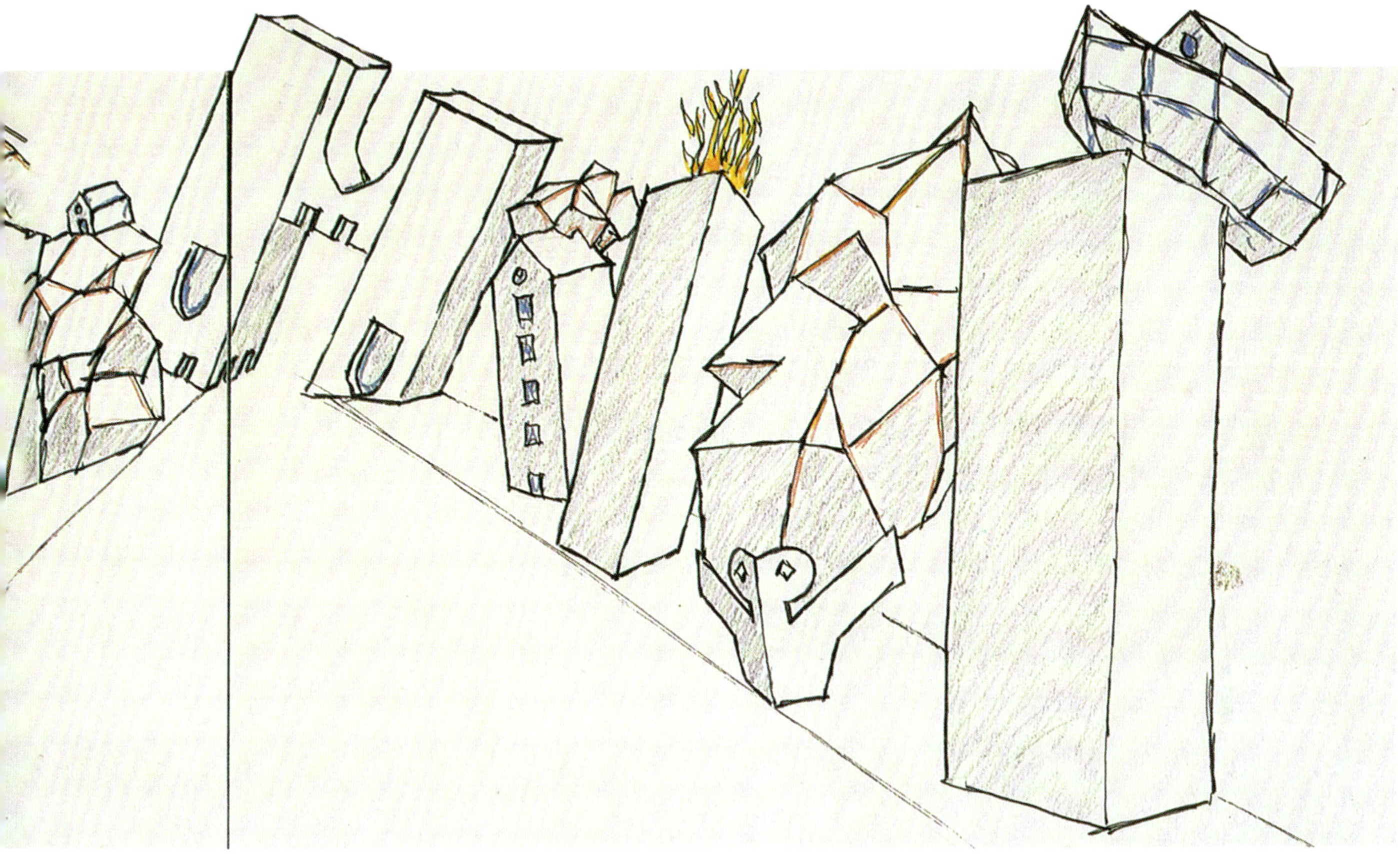

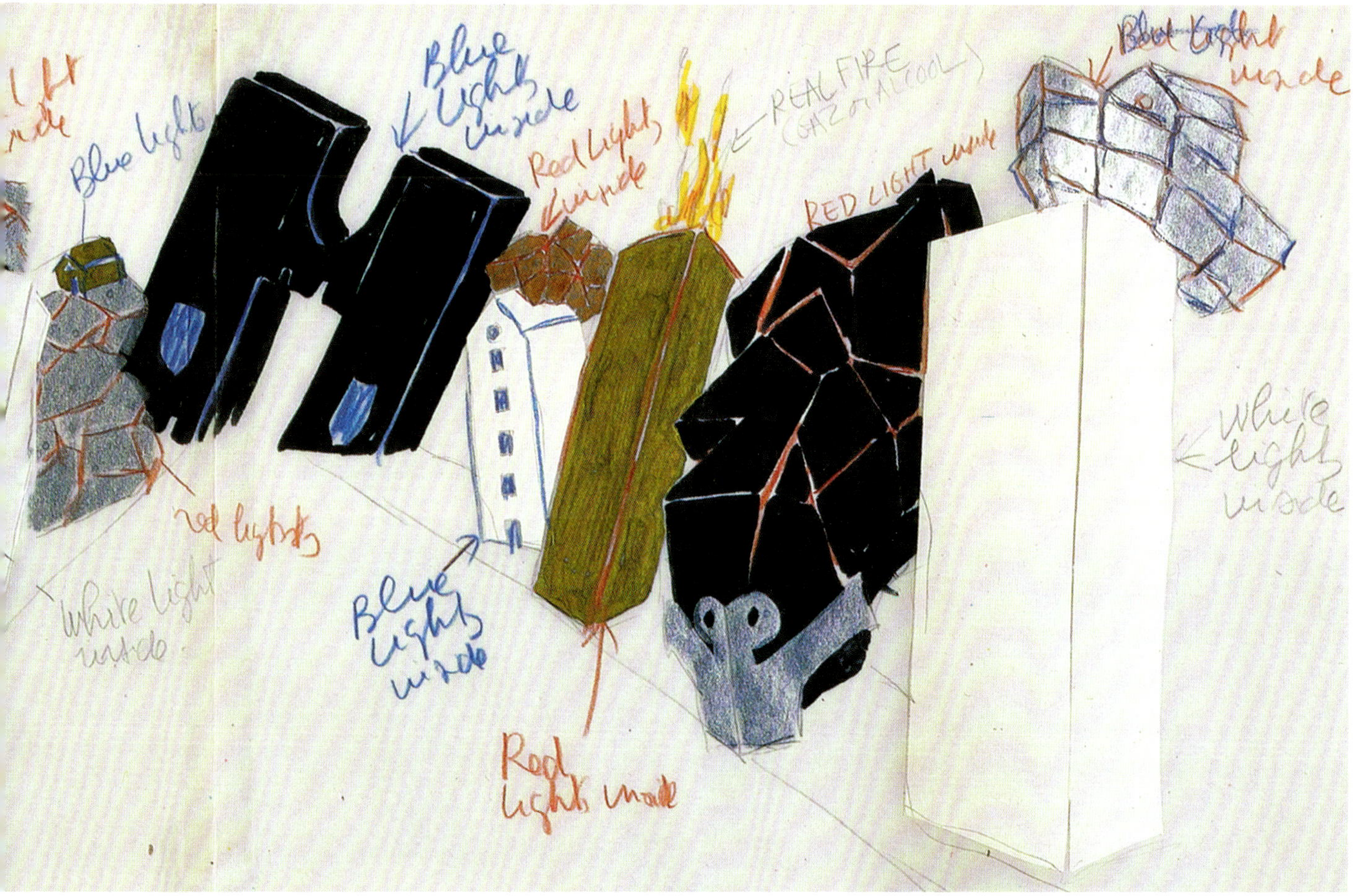

Blue light
Blue Lights inside
Red Lights inside
REAL FIRE (GAZ or ALCOOL)
RED LIGHT inside
Blue Light inside
White light inside
red lights
White light inside
Blue lights inside
Red lights inside

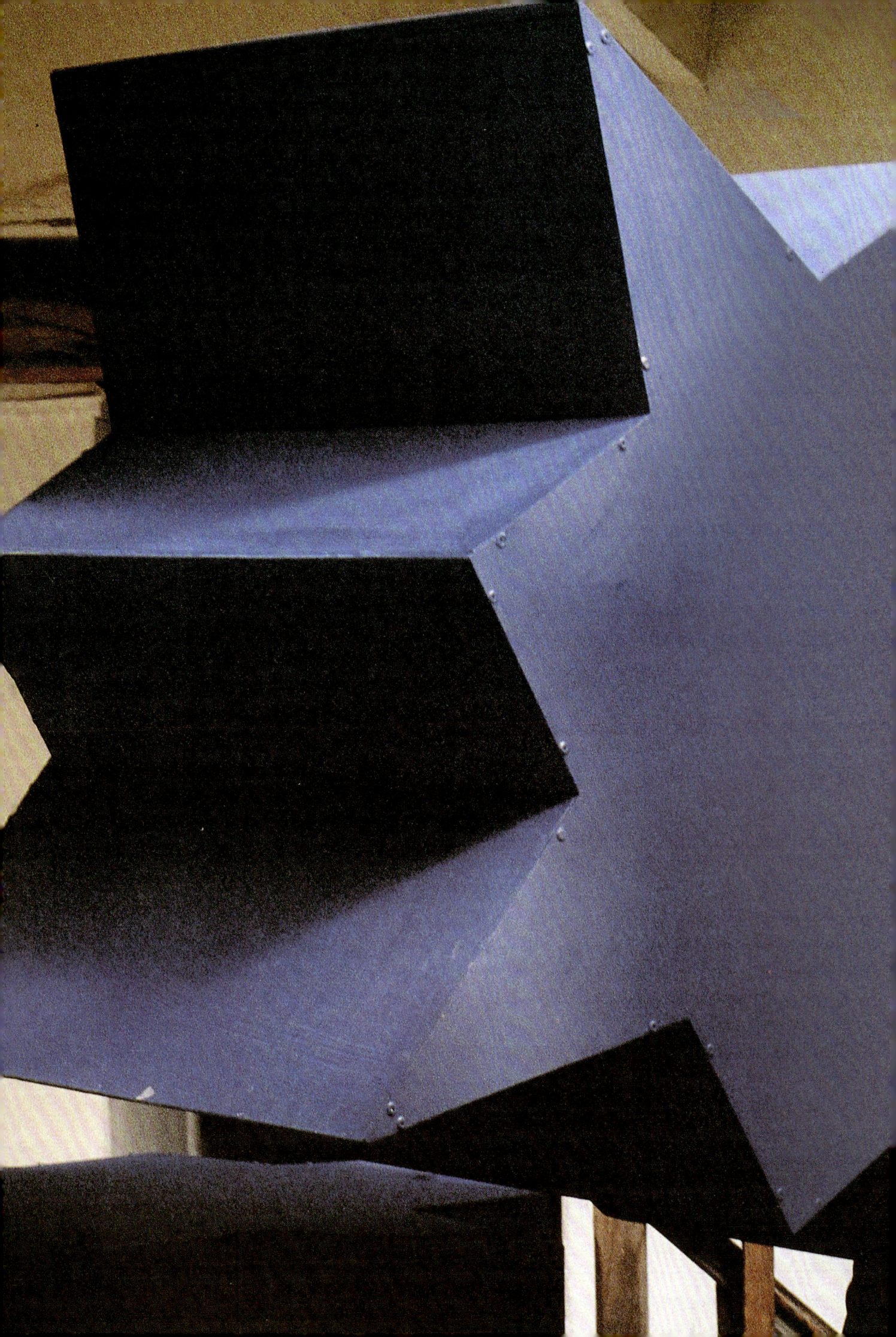

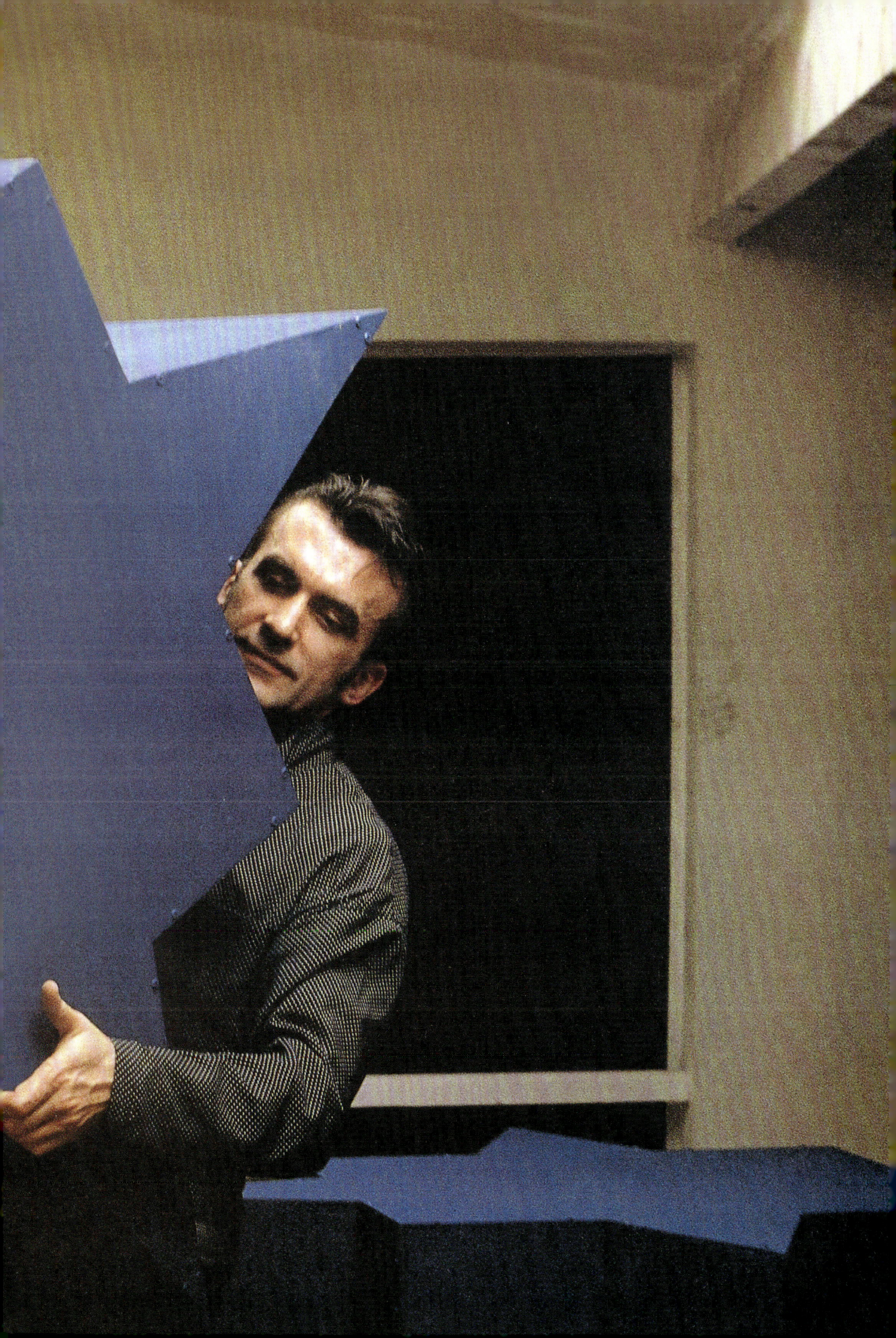

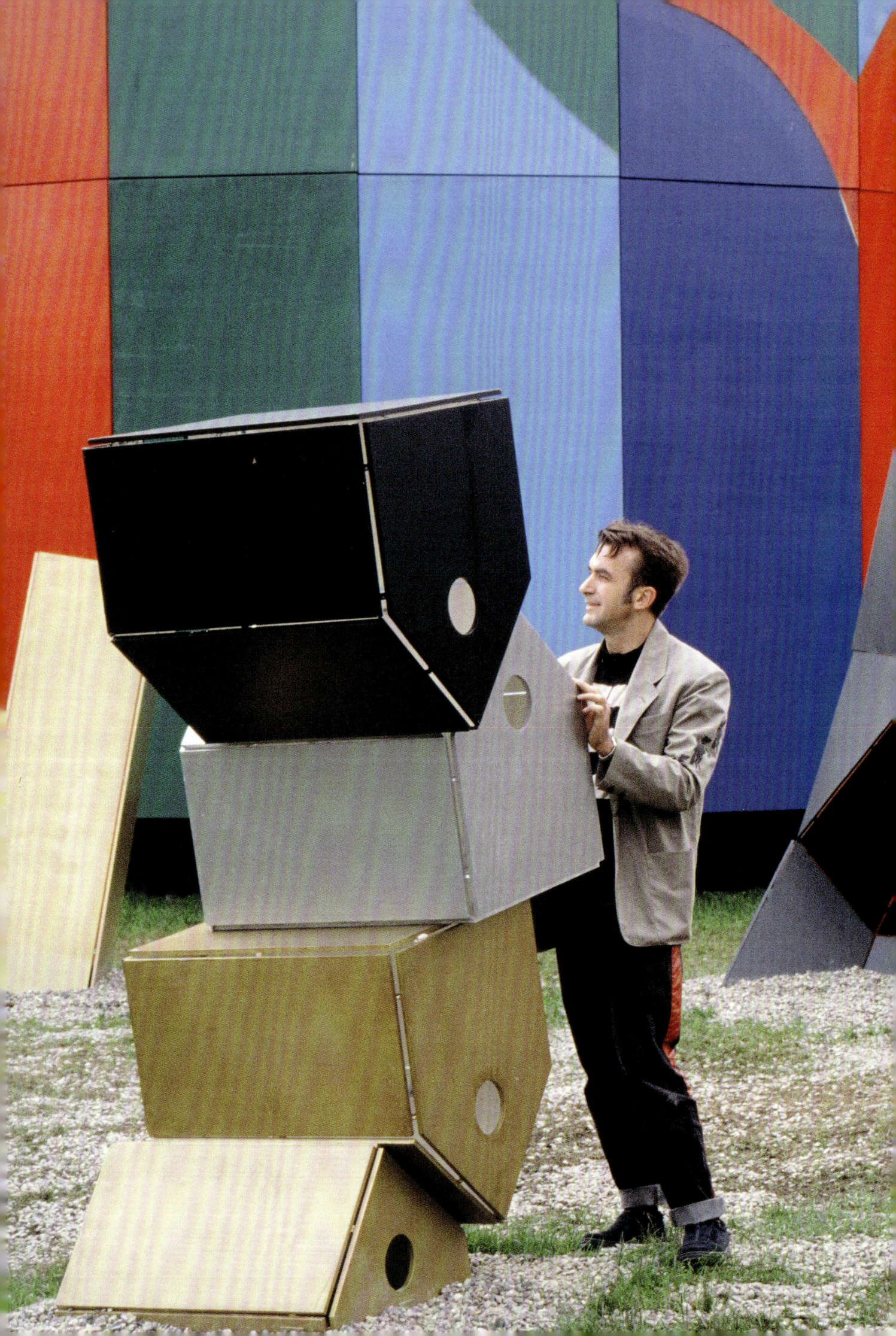

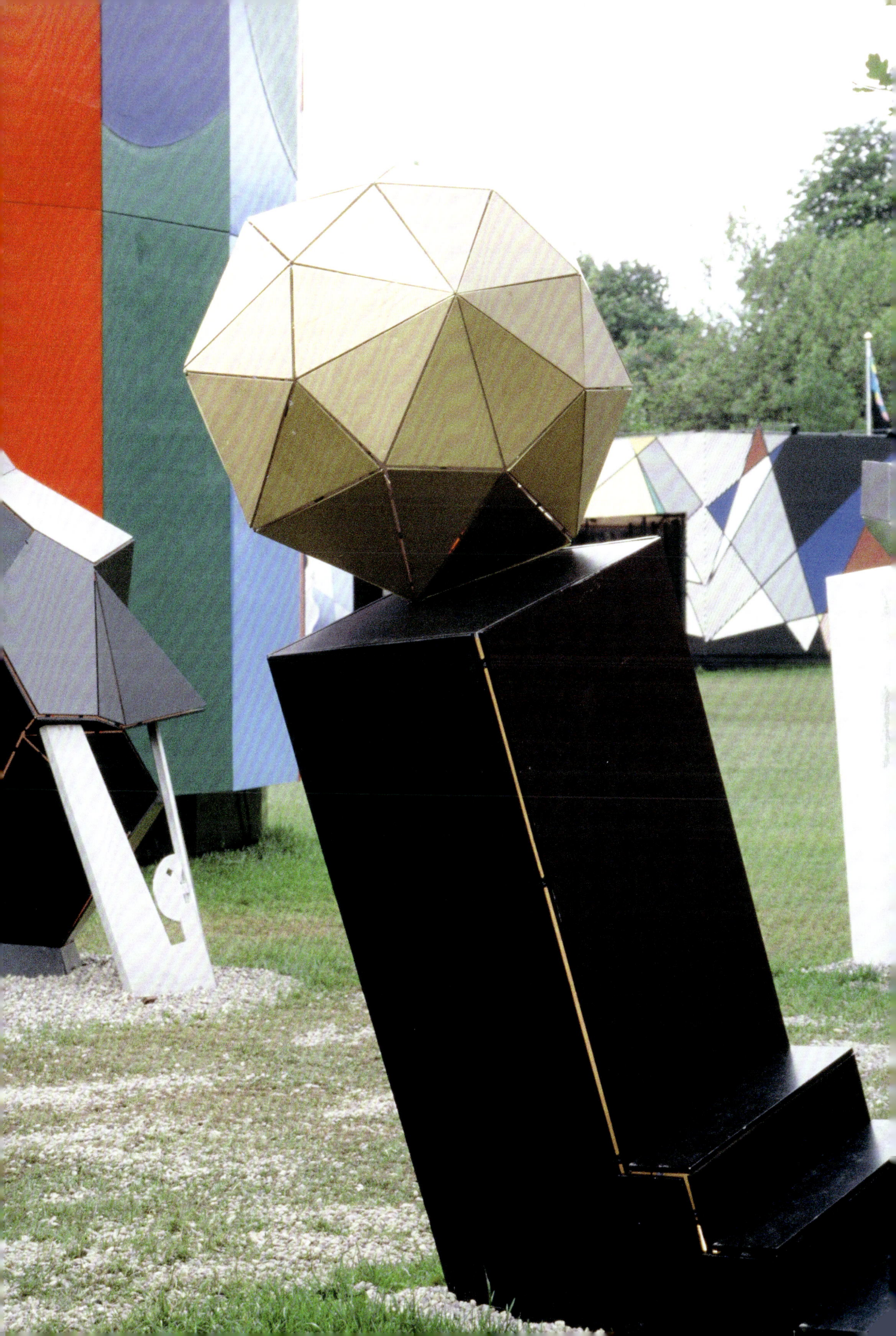

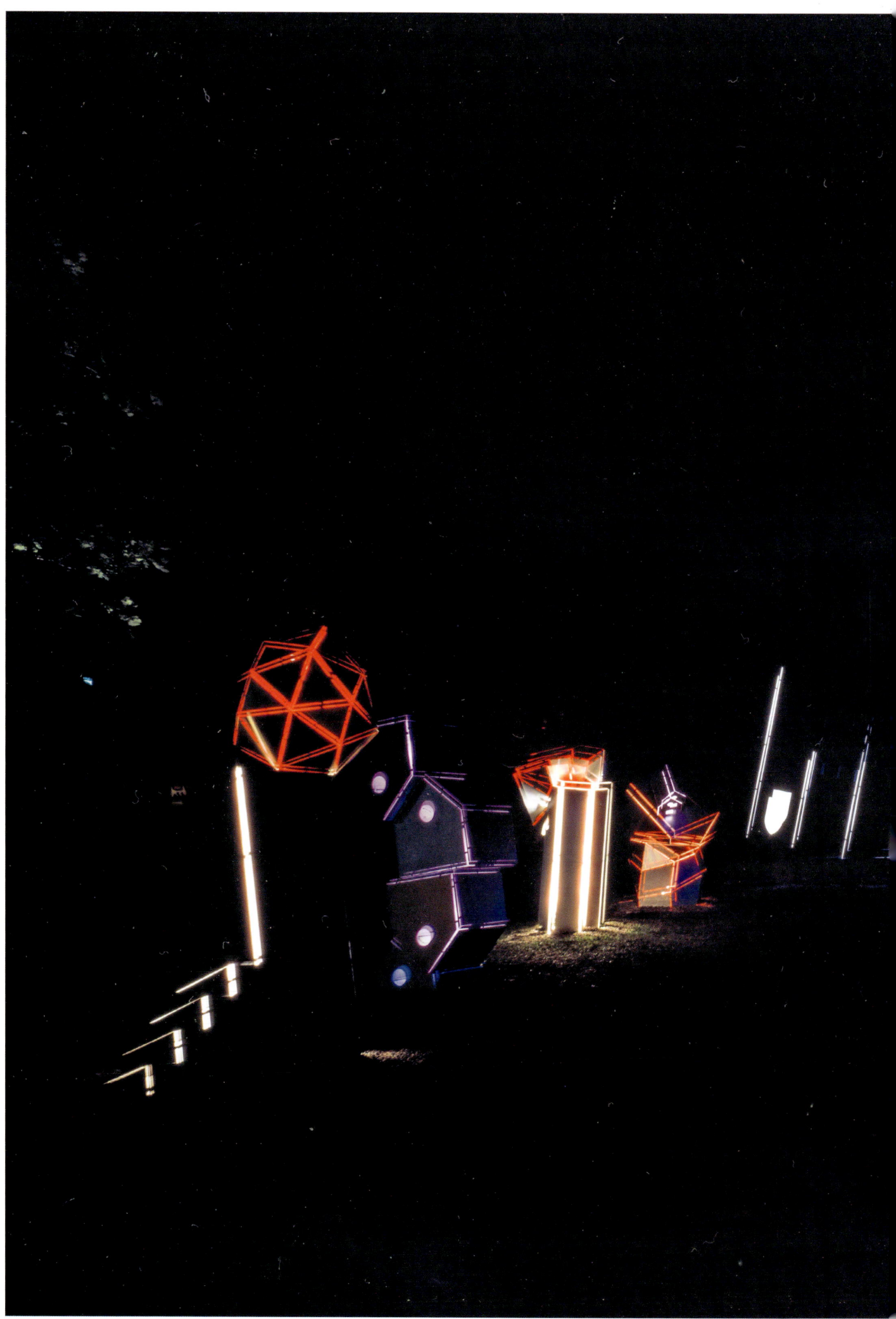

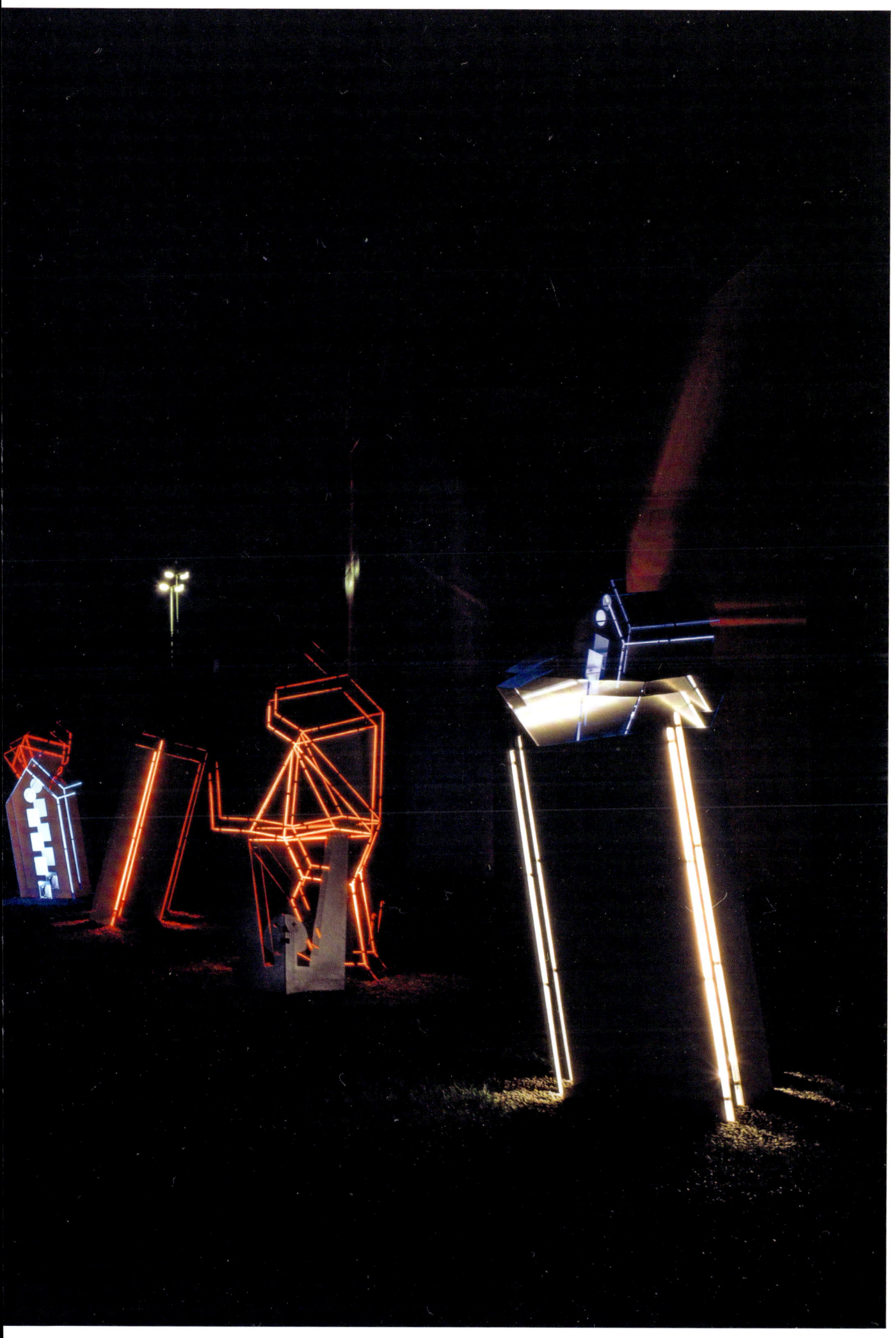

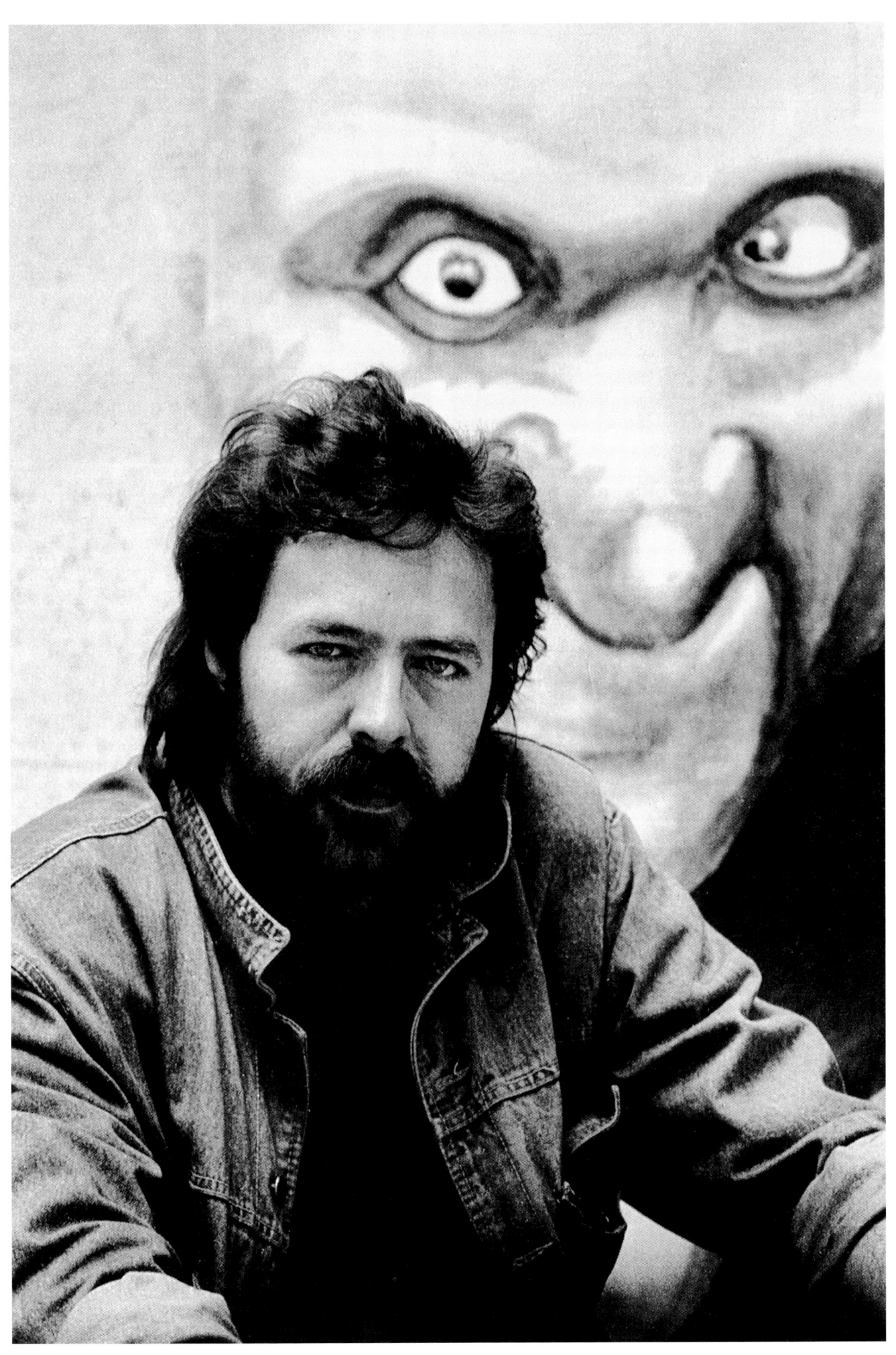

Manfred Deix

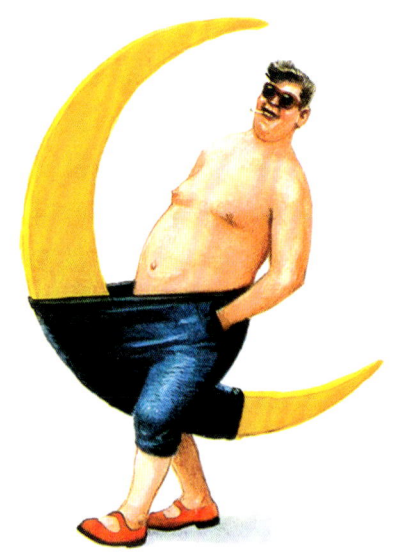

Der FURZ (österr.: SCHAAS) ist lange genug
diskriminiert worden. — Bei LUNA LUNA
wurde ihm endlich ein Palast errichtet.
Da war ich natürlich gerne dabei.

Manfred Dix

Manfred Deix

Born: February 22, 1949, in St. Pölten, Austria.
Died: June 25, 2016, in Klosterneuburg, Austria.

Cartoonist, political satirist.

Manfred Deix designed the facade for the **Palace of the Winds** for *Luna Luna*, a painted glorification of art farting, with its finest pieces being performed on a small stage inside the building.

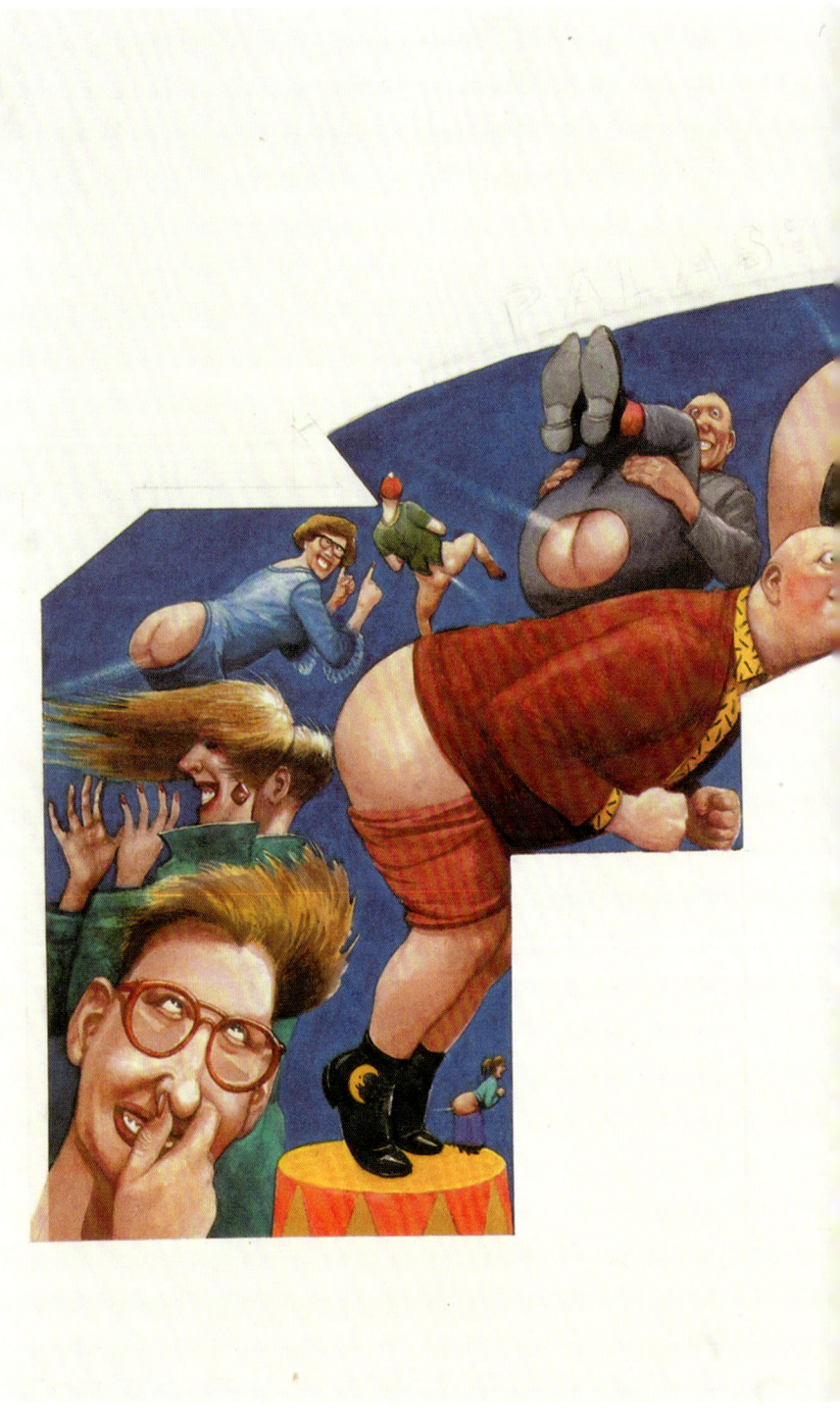

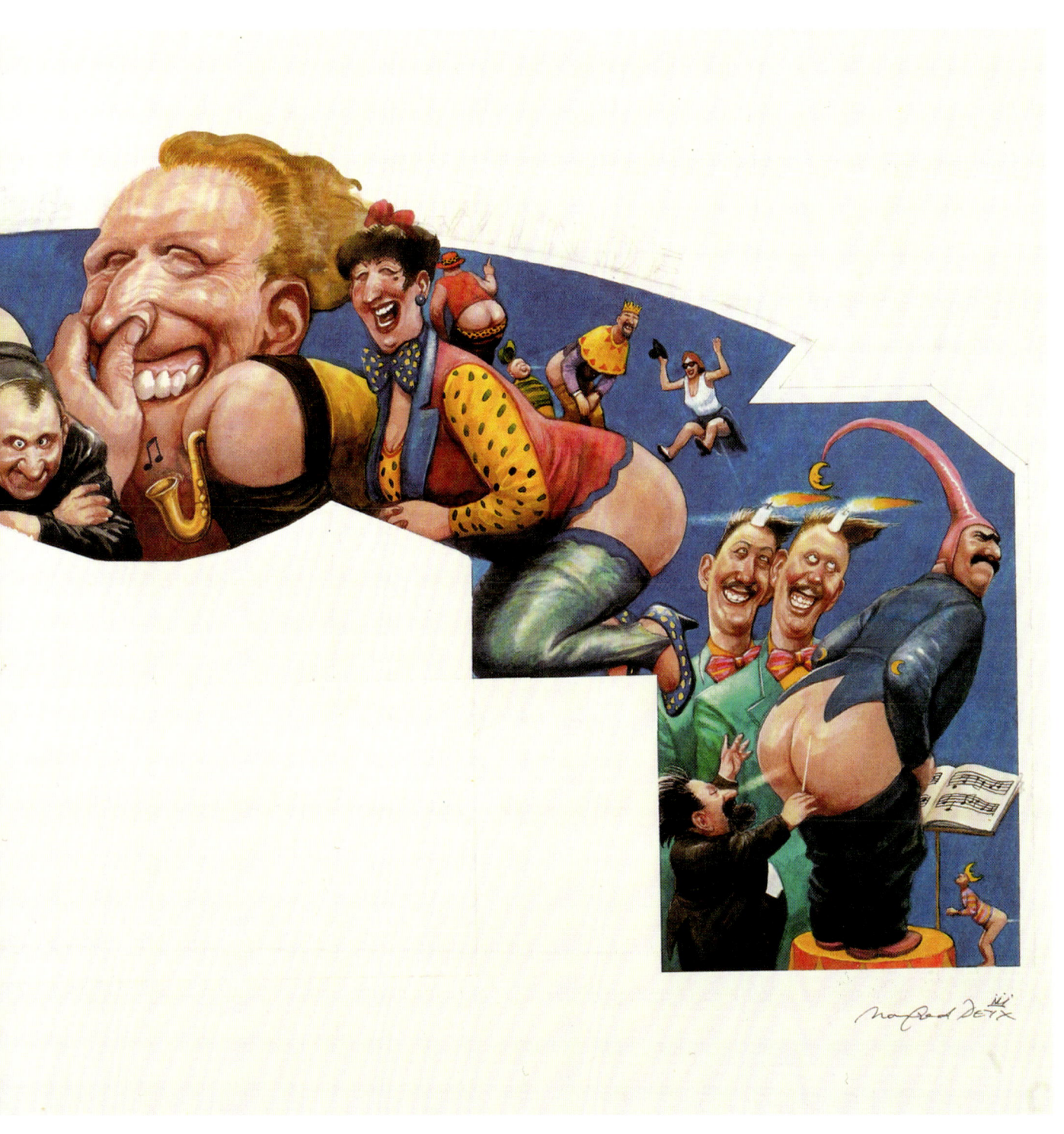

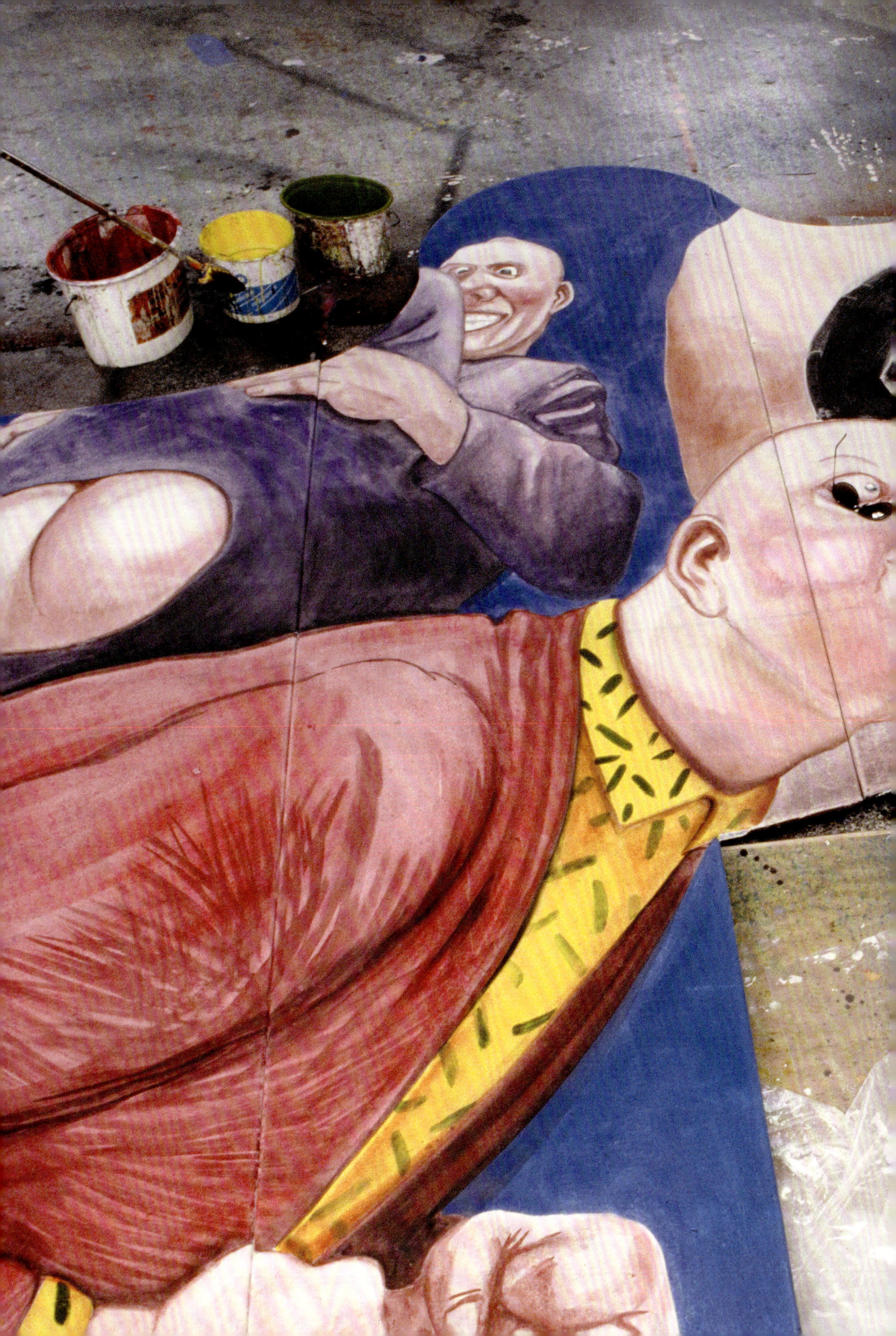

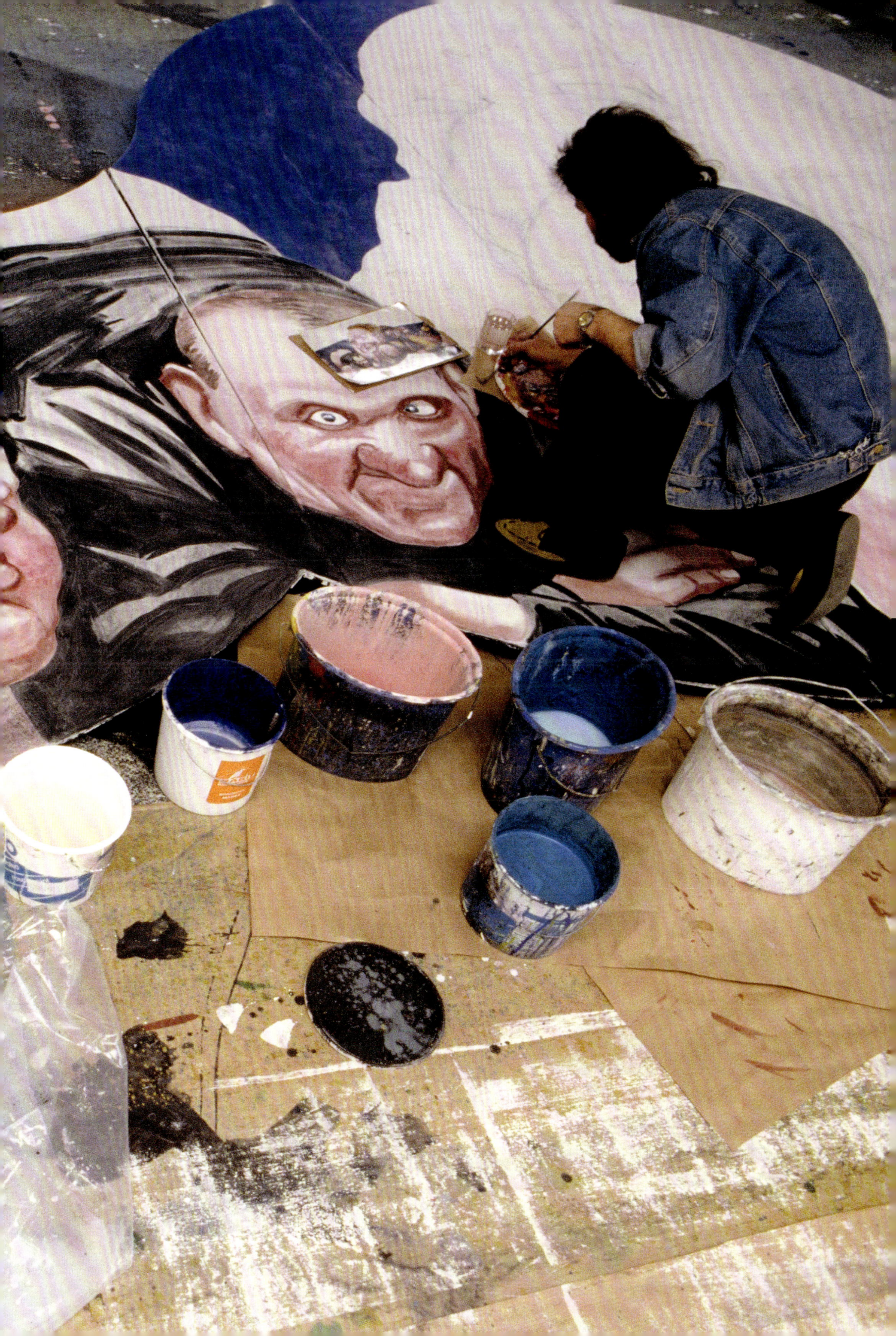

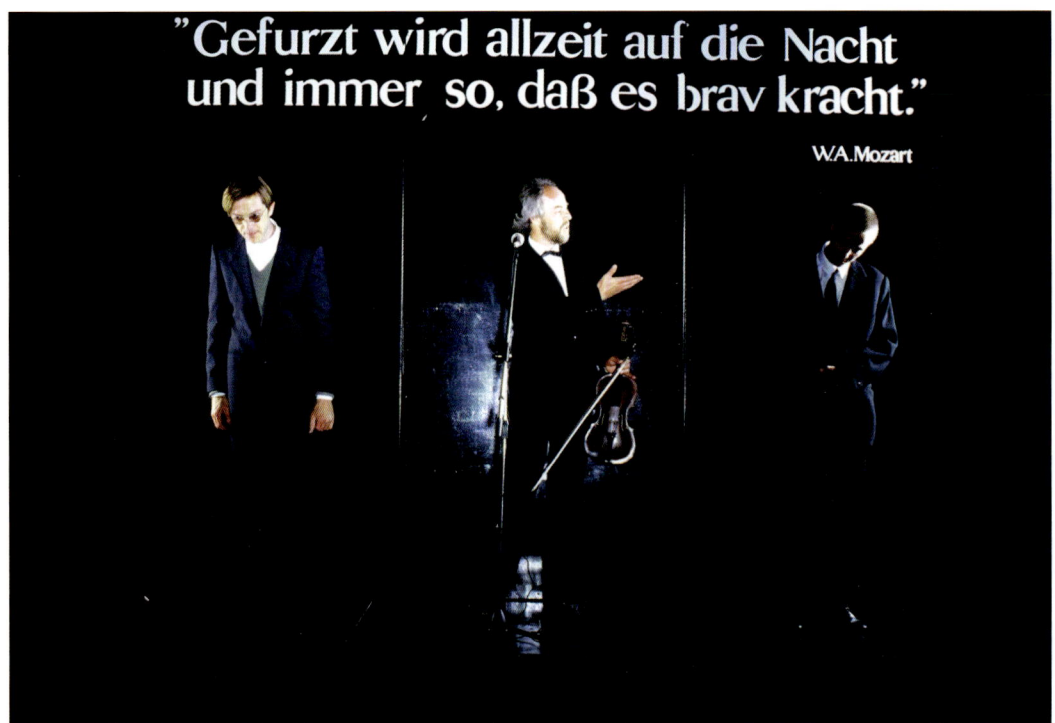

*Presentation of the two art farters by the master of ceremonies*

*Presentation of the instruments*

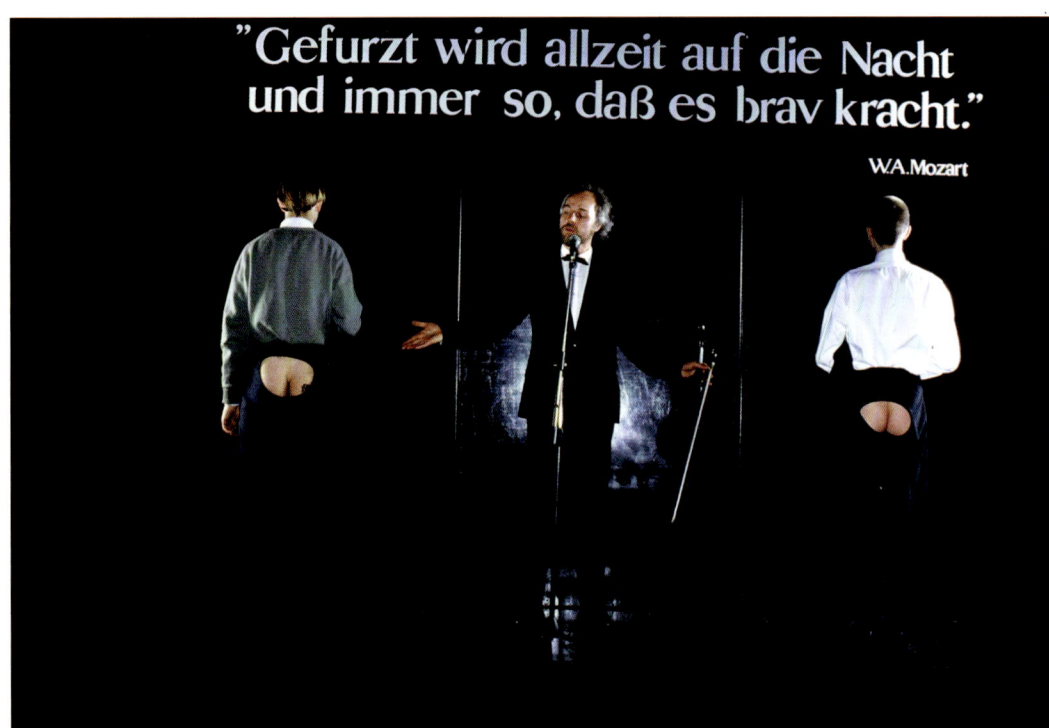

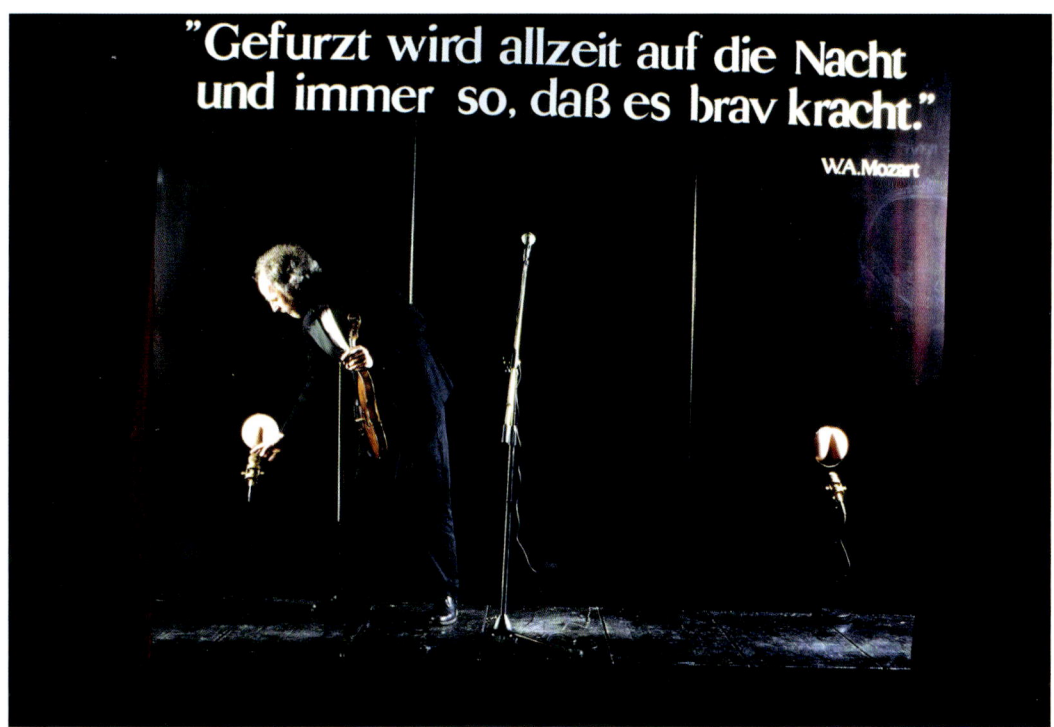

*Technical rehearsal*

*Performance of the "Radetzky March" by Johann Strauss I*

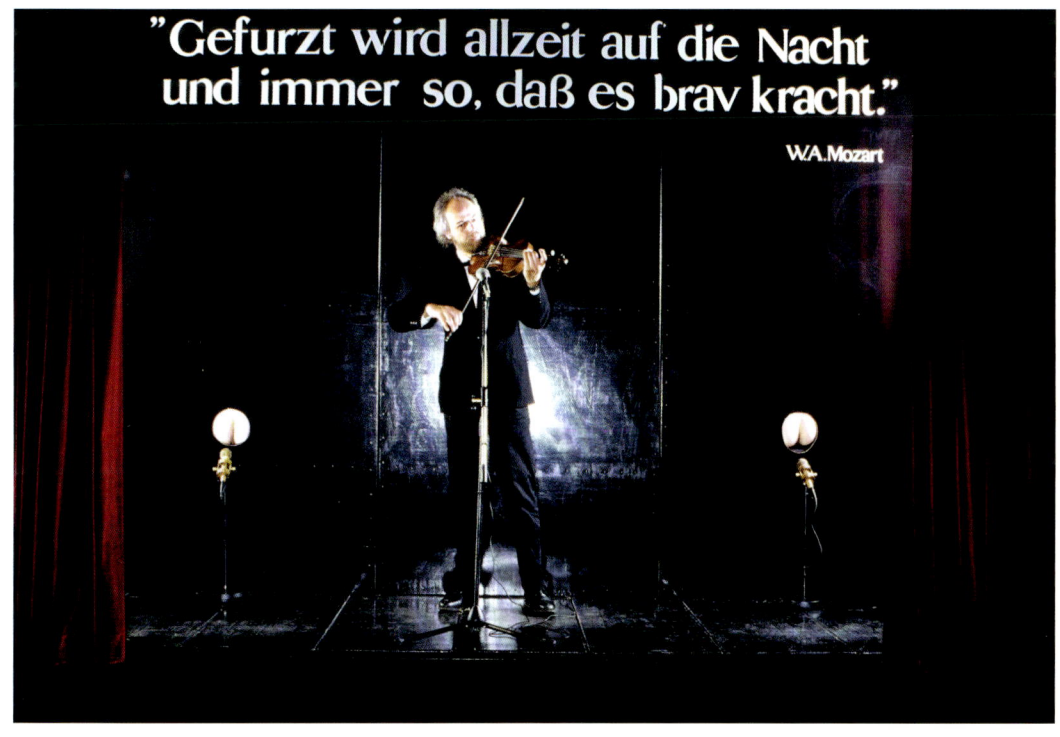

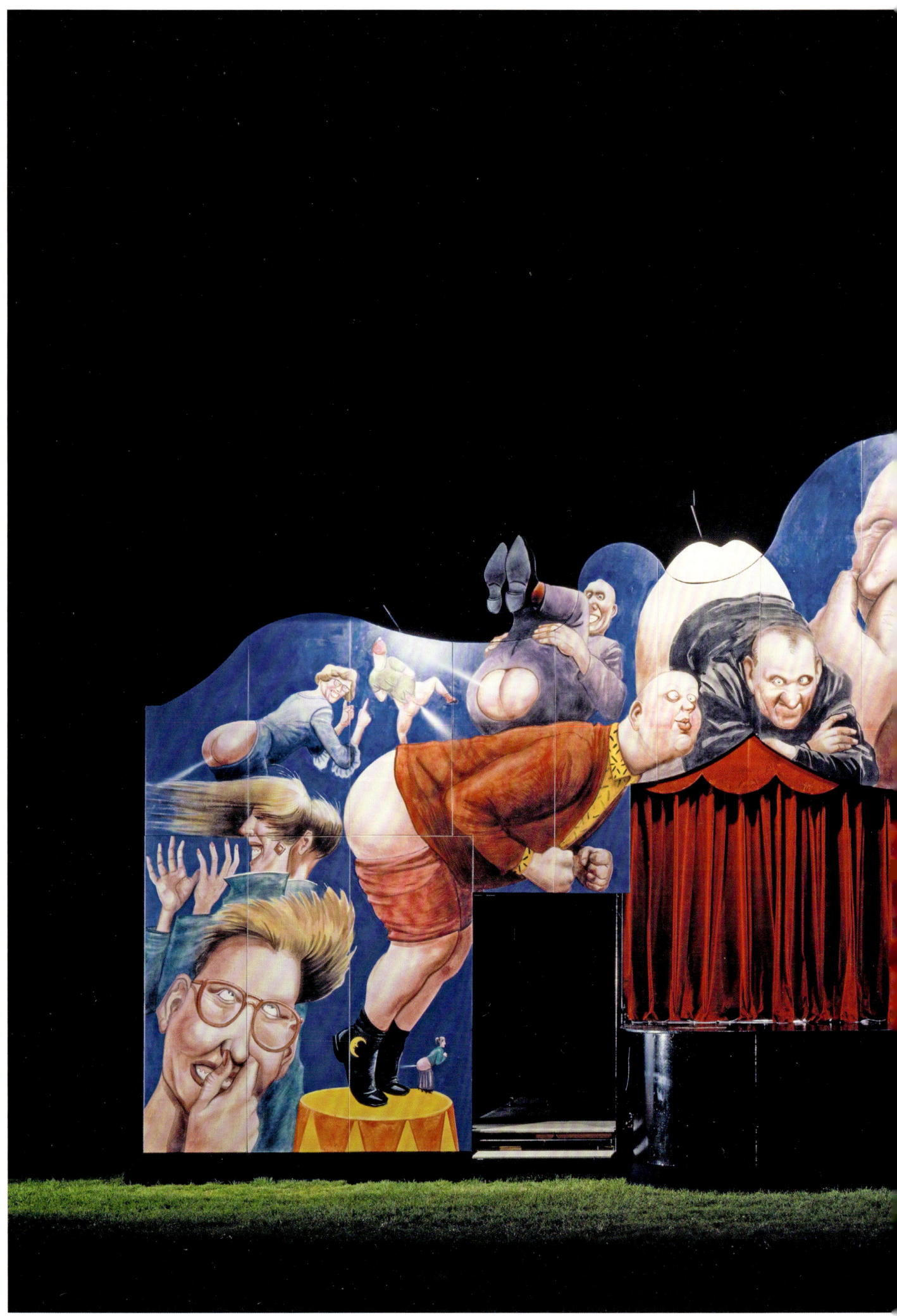

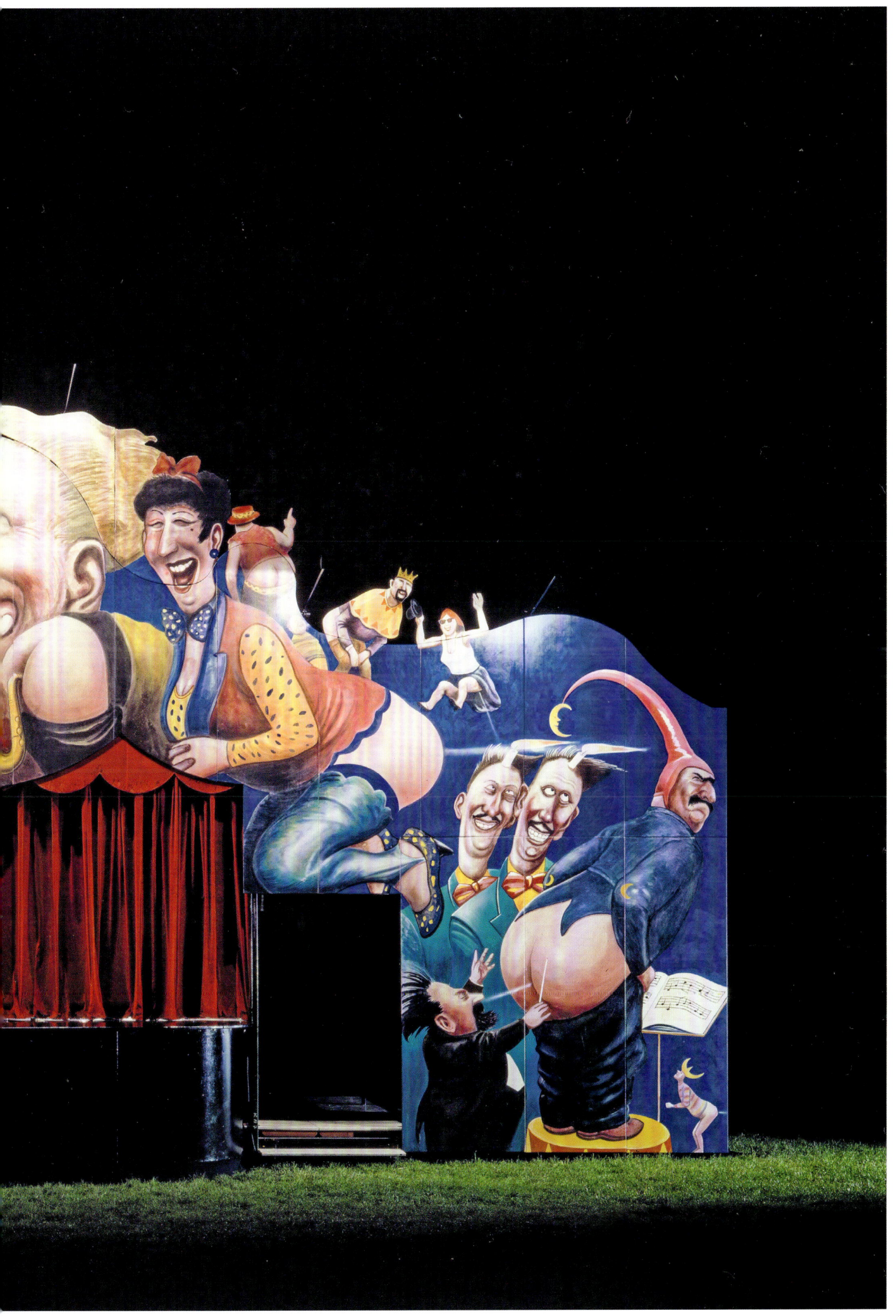

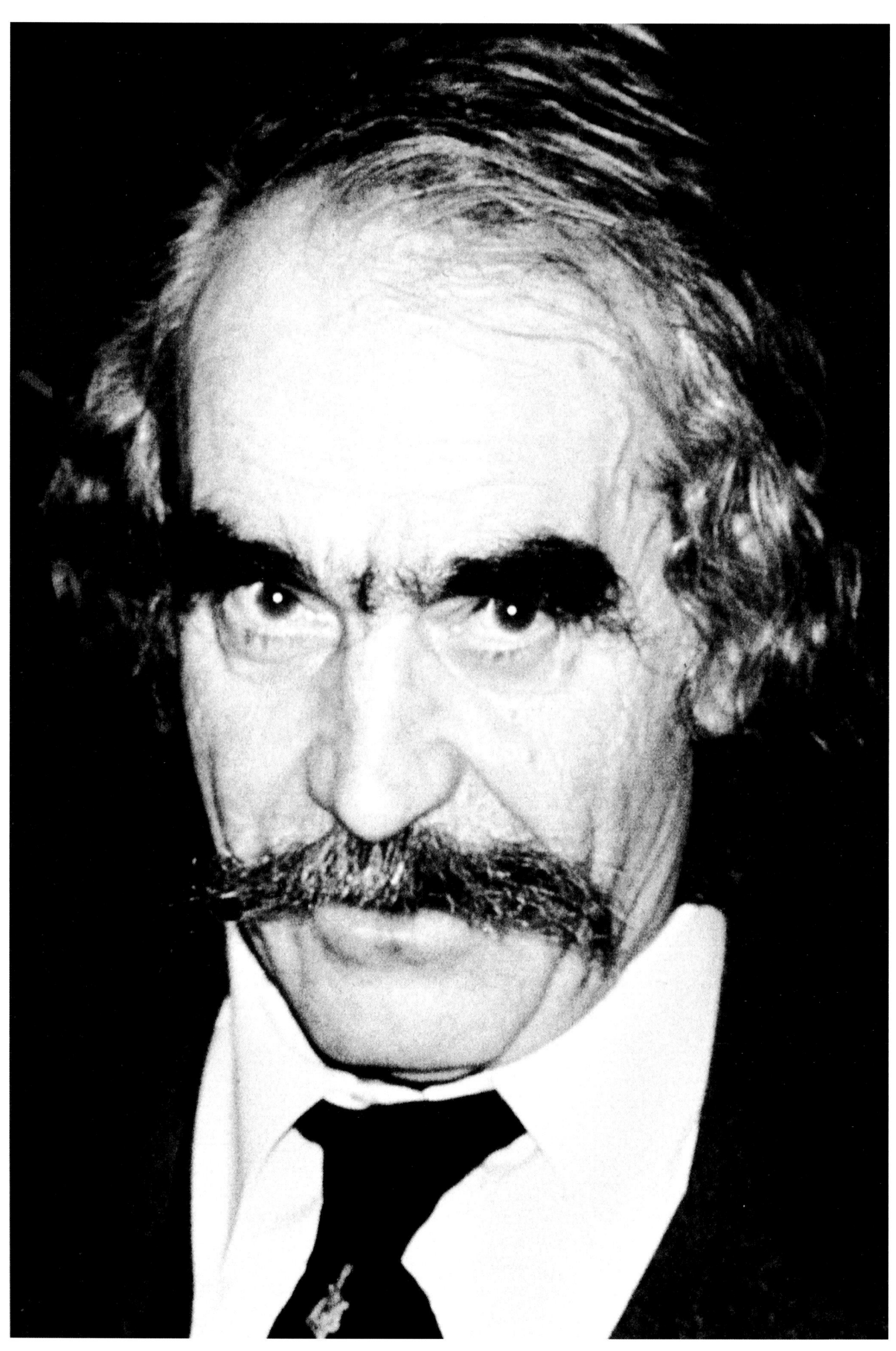

Jean Tinguely

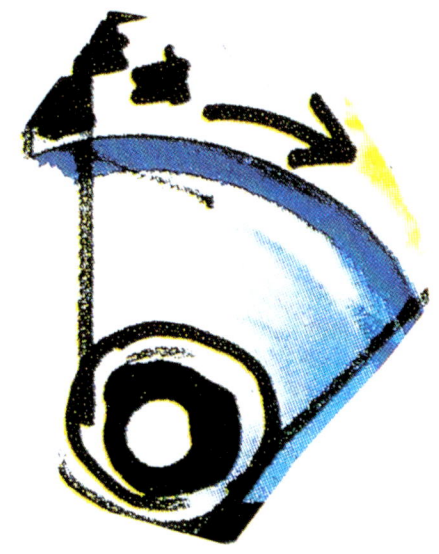

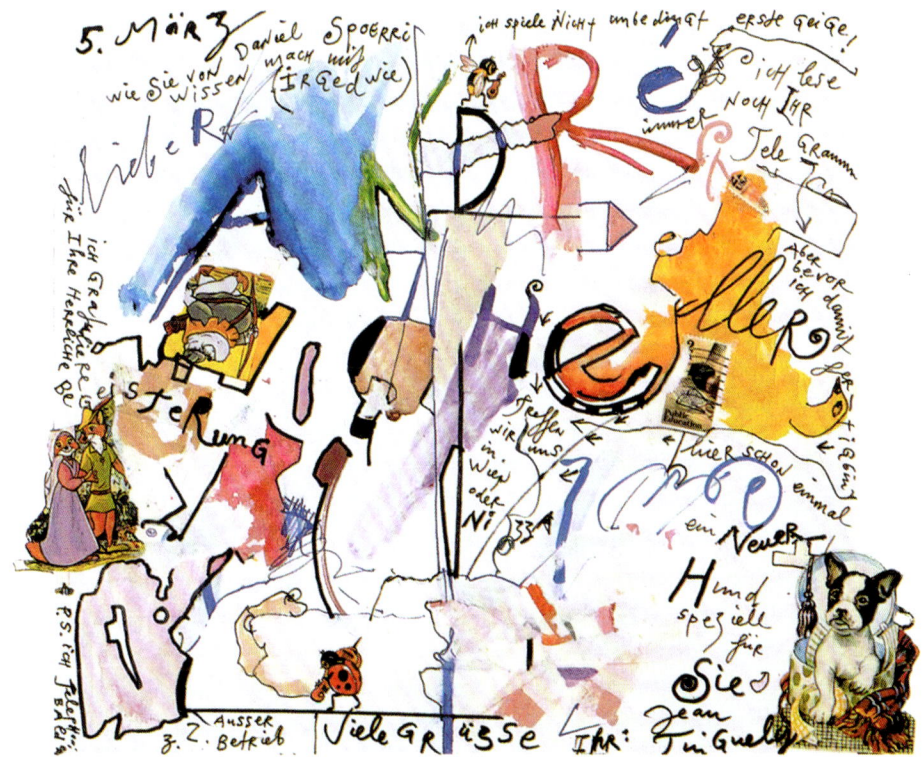

Jean Tinguely

Born: May 22, 1925, in Fribourg, Switzerland.
Died: August 30, 1991, in Bern, Switzerland.

Sculptor, inventor, illustrator.

Jean Tinguely designed a **poster** for *Luna Luna*.

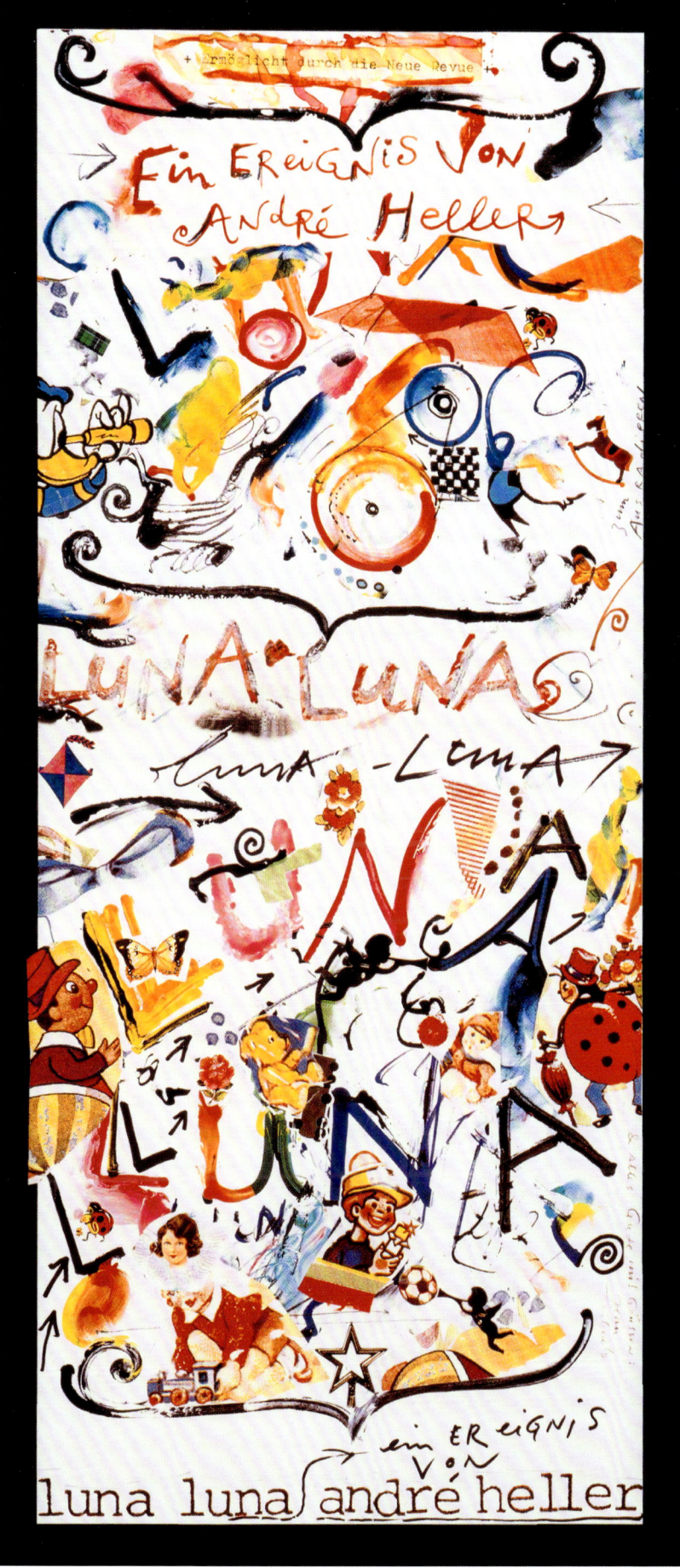

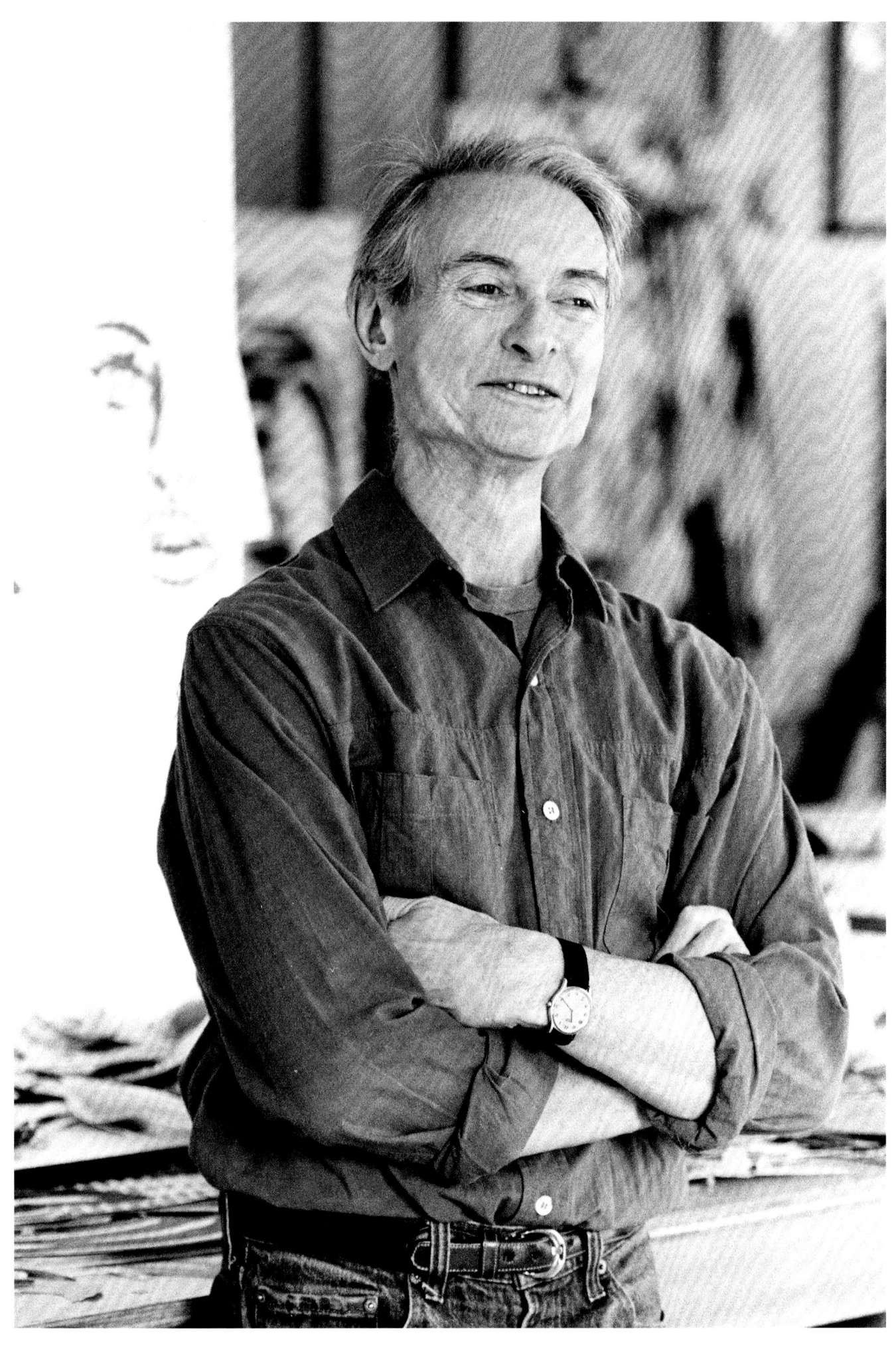

Roy Lichtenstein

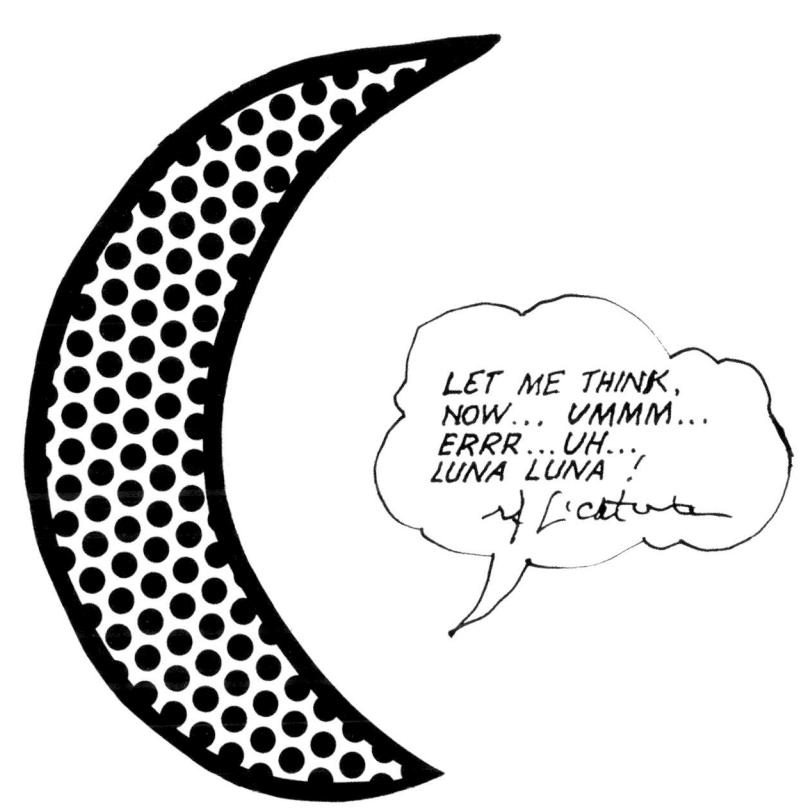

Roy Lichtenstein

Born: October 27, 1923, in New York, New York.
Died: September 29, 1997, in New York, New York.

Painter, illustrator, sculptor.

Roy Lichtenstein designed a **poster** for *Luna Luna* as
well as the **Pavilion of the Glass Labyrinth**.
The music for this attraction was composed
by Philip Glass.

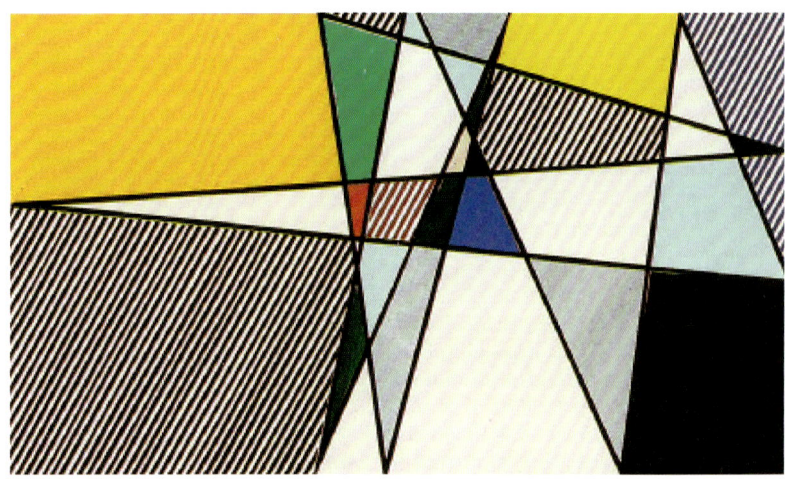

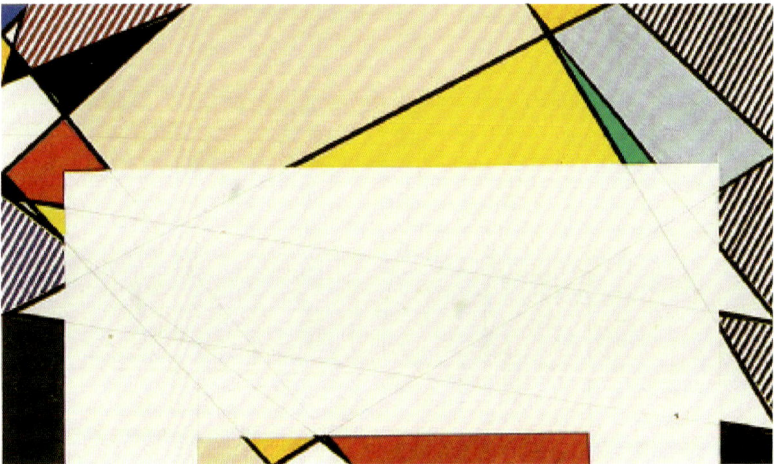

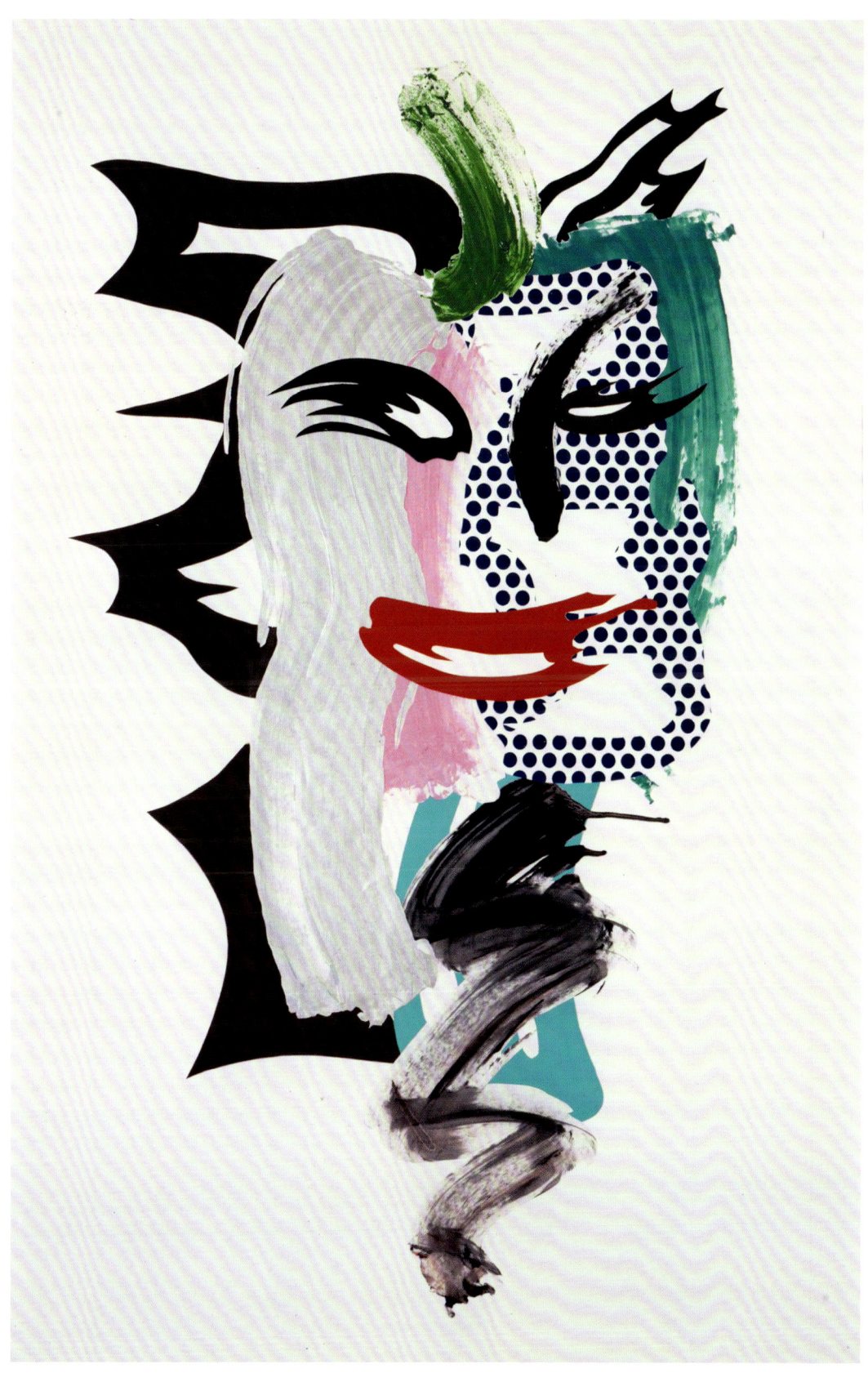

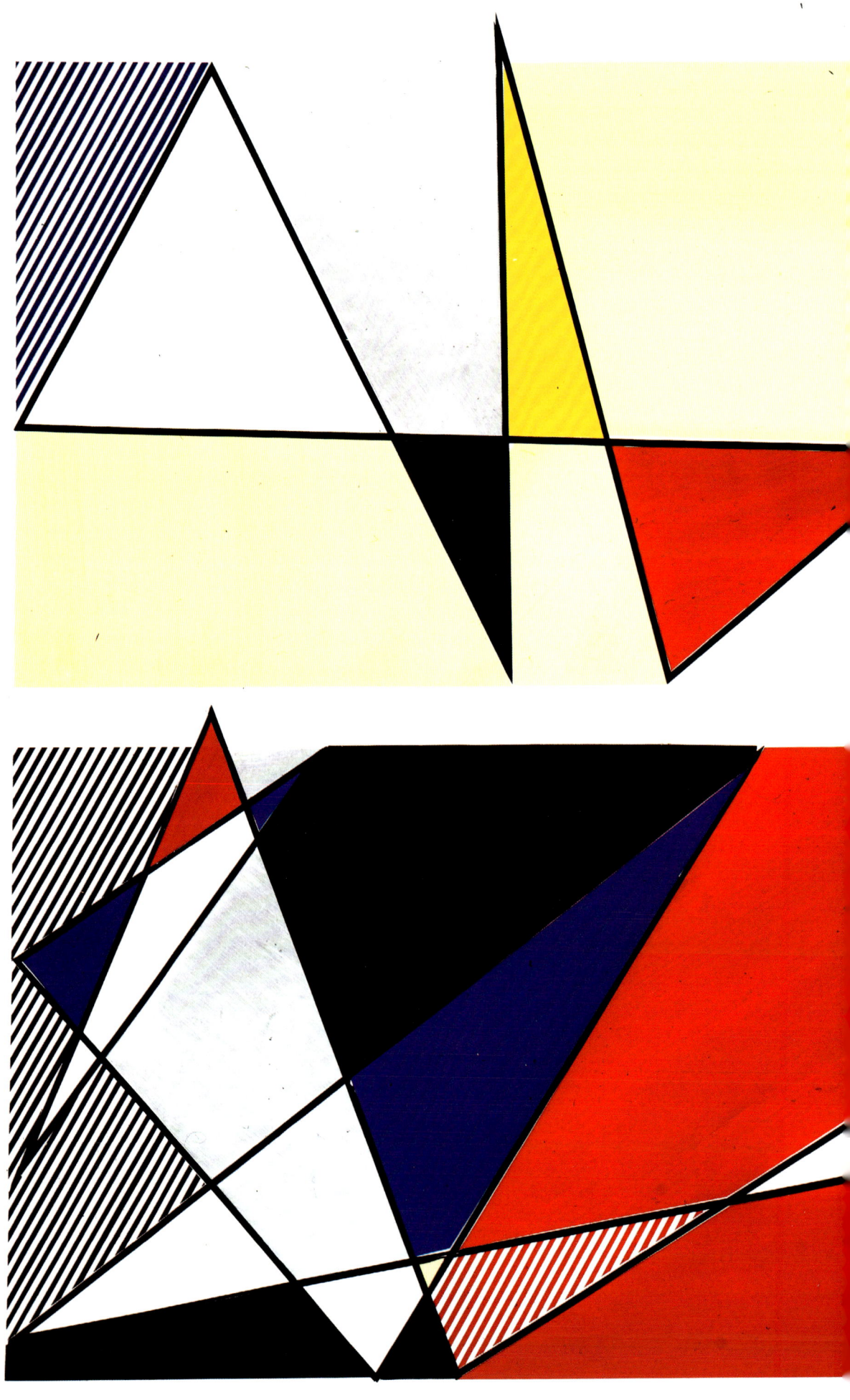

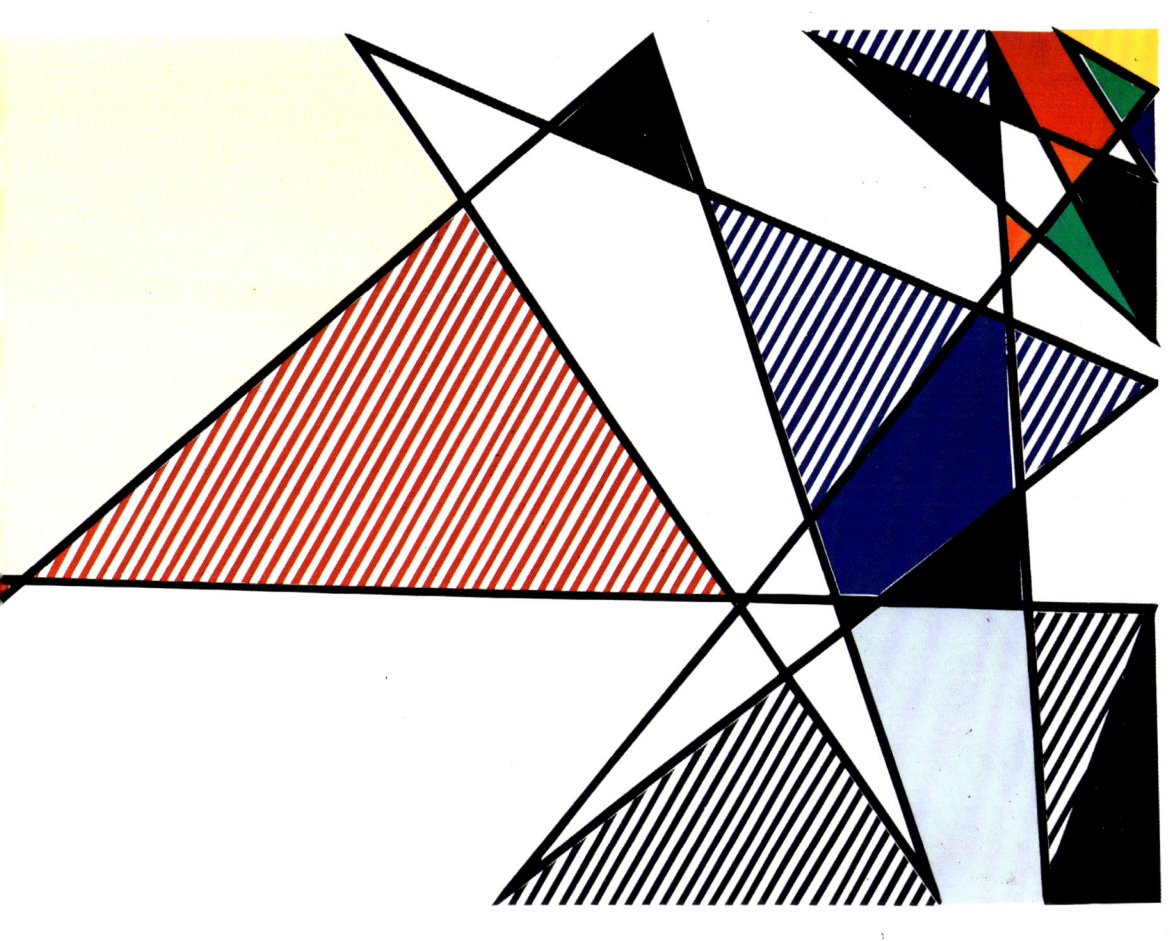

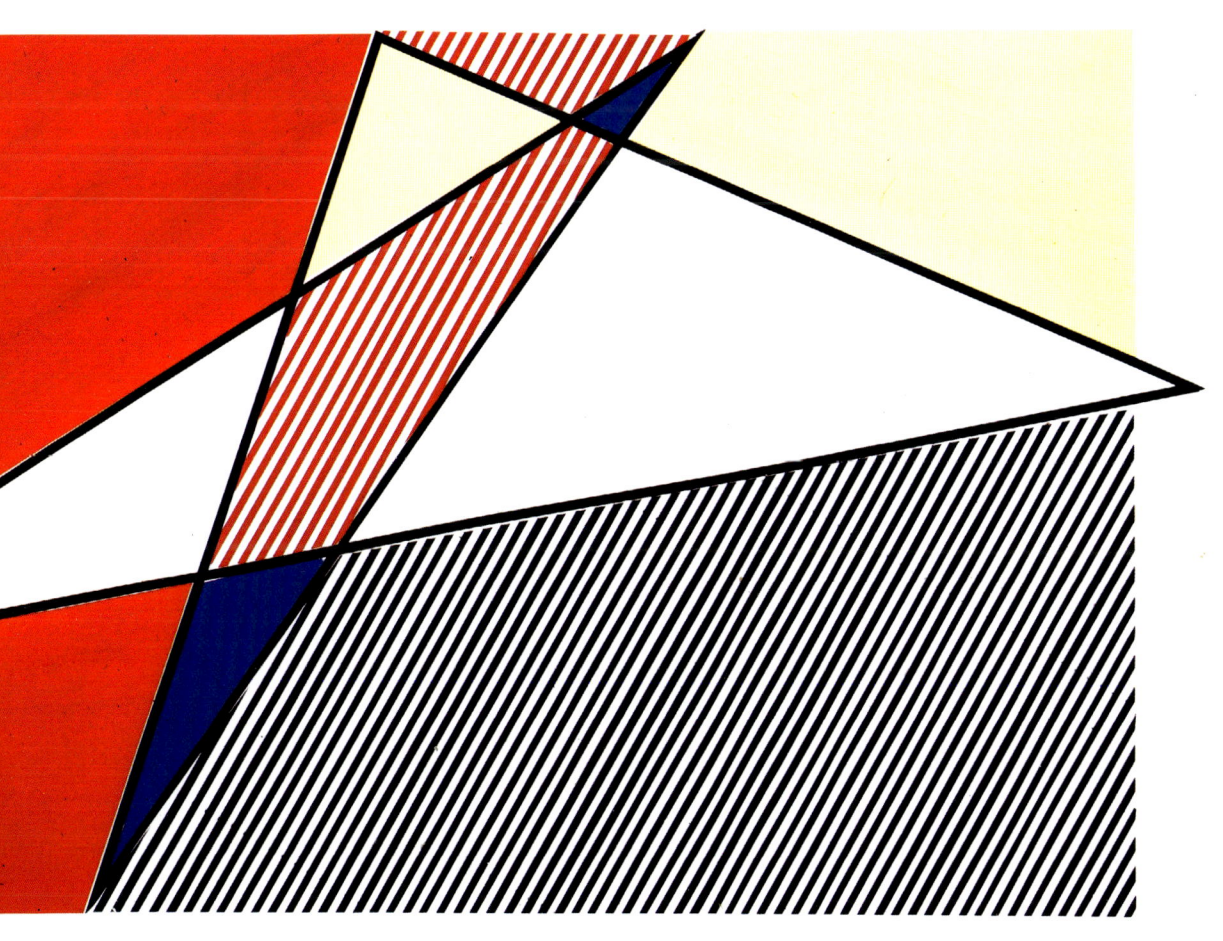

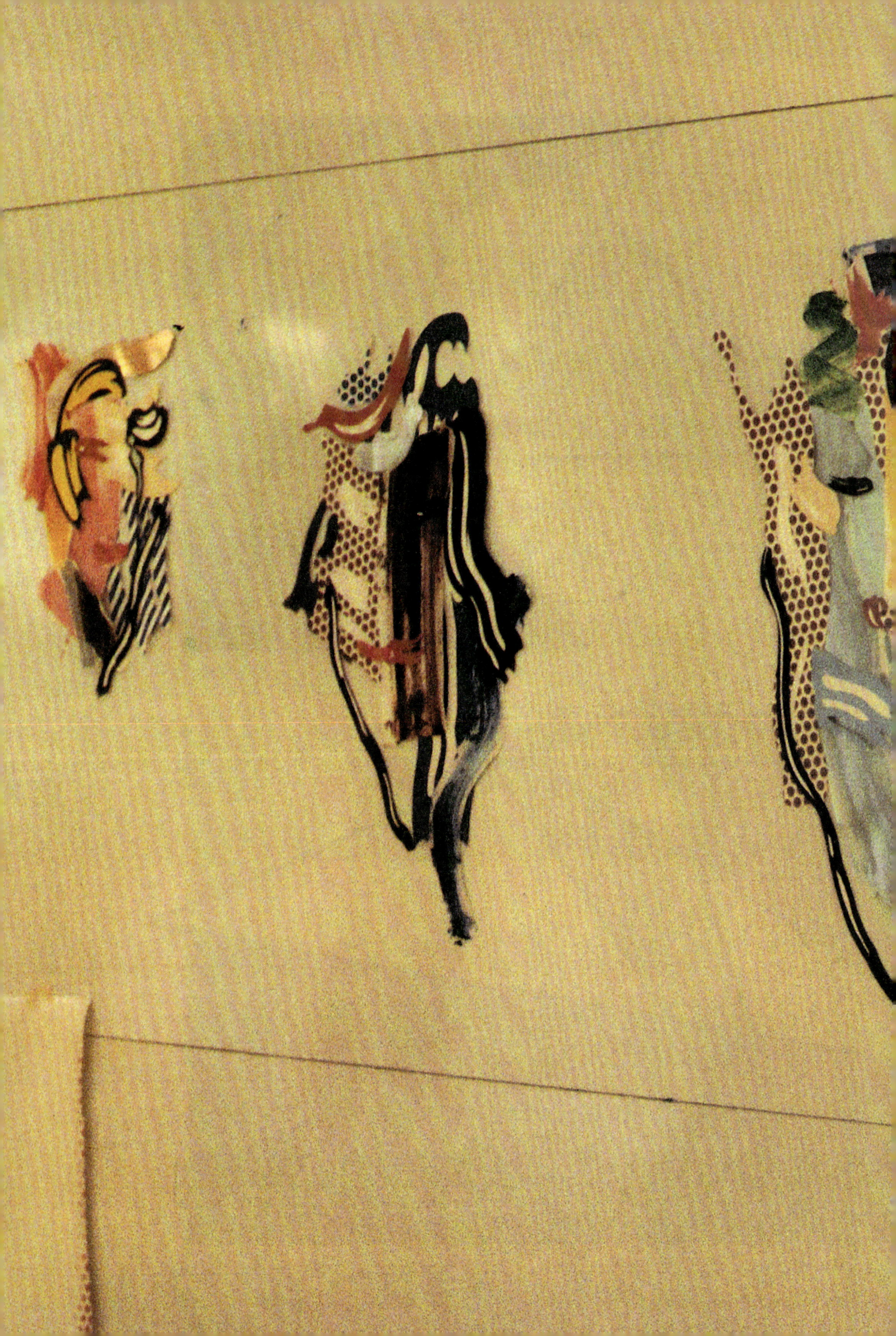

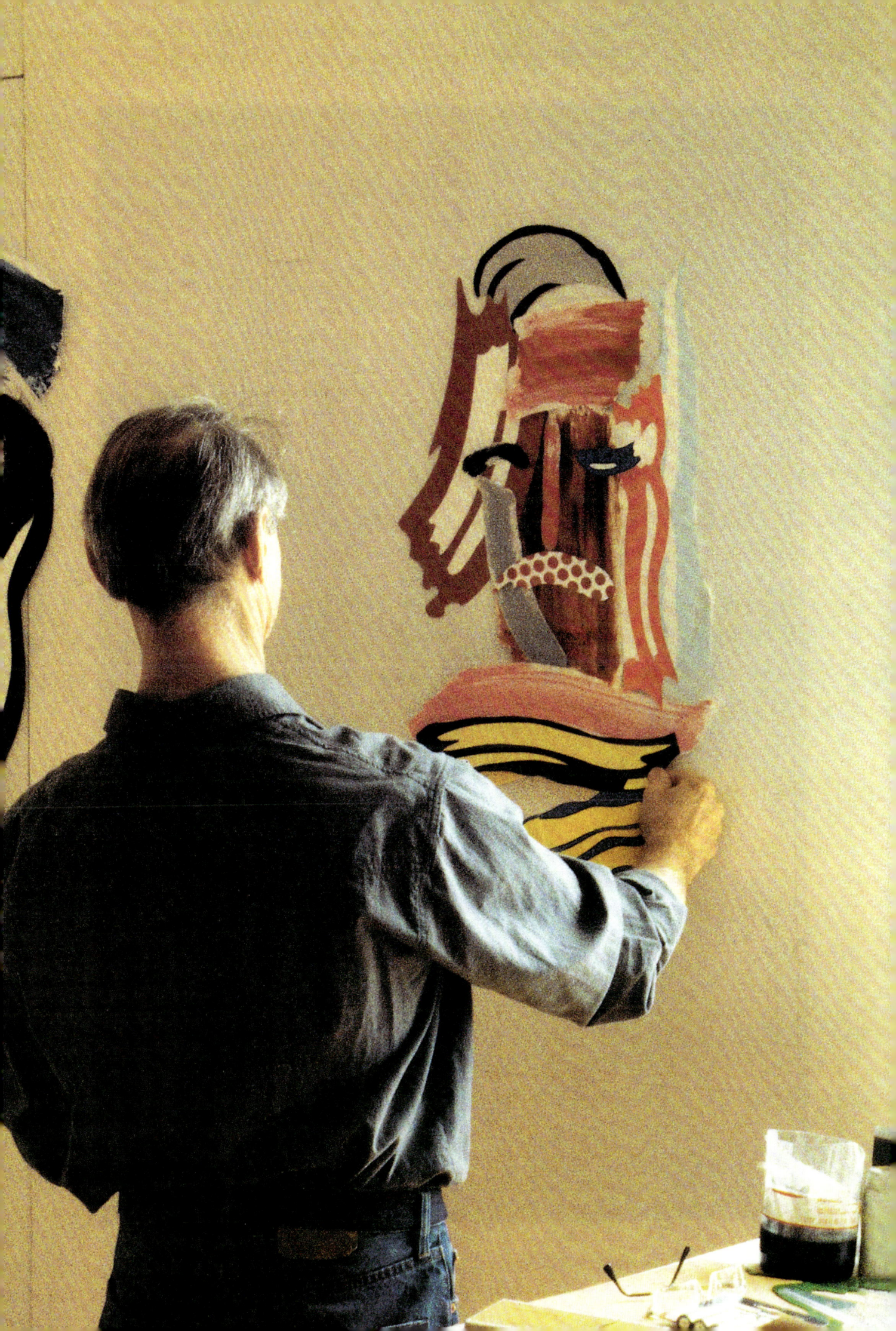

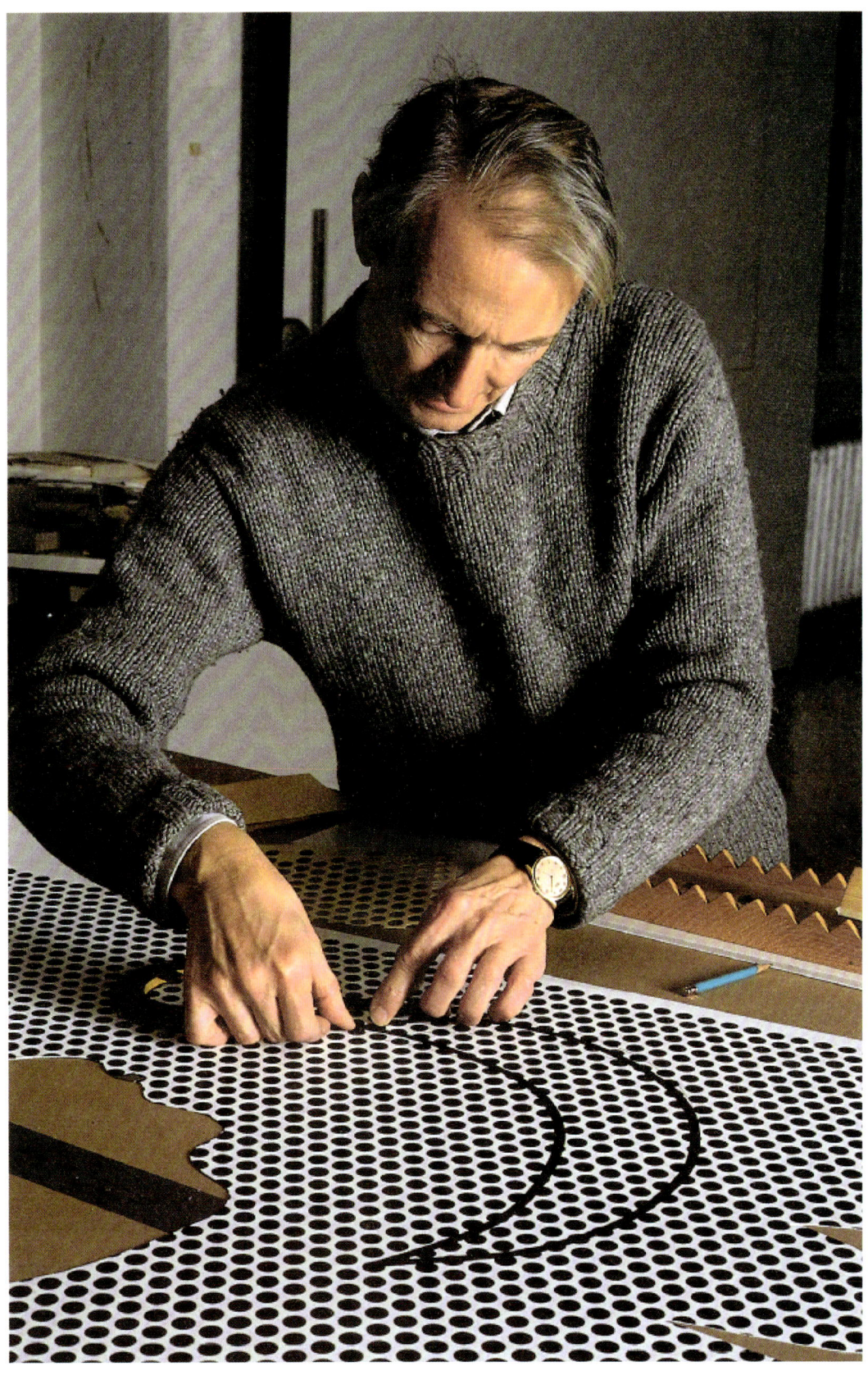

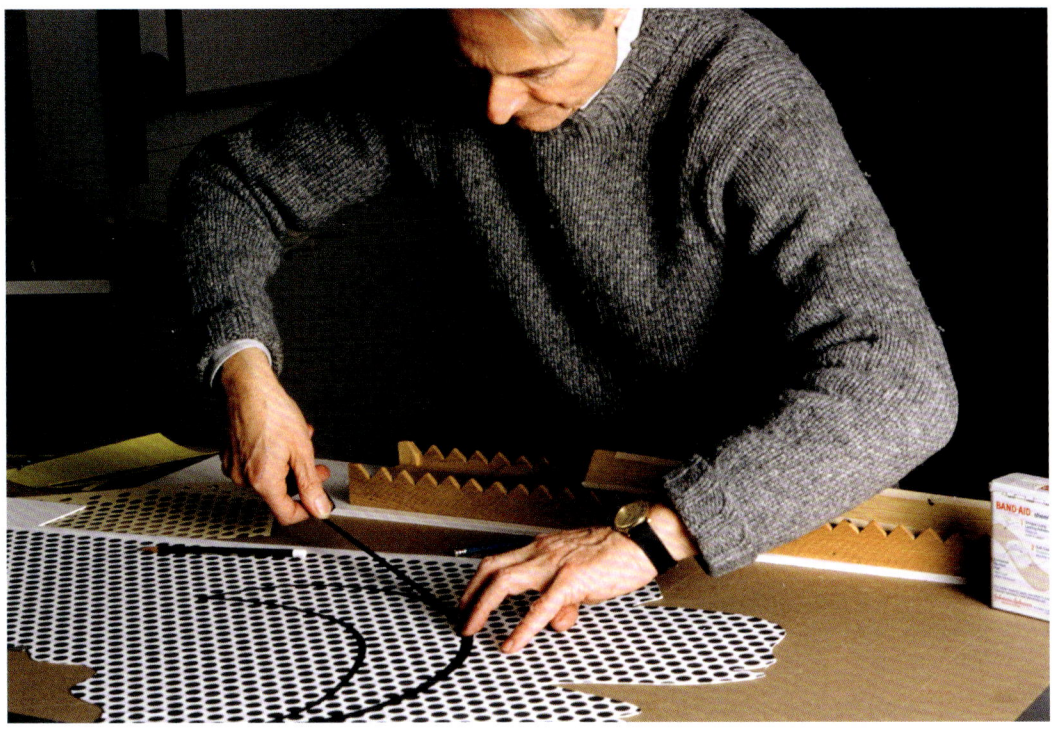

*Roy Lichtenstein at work on the Luna Luna moon in his New York studio*

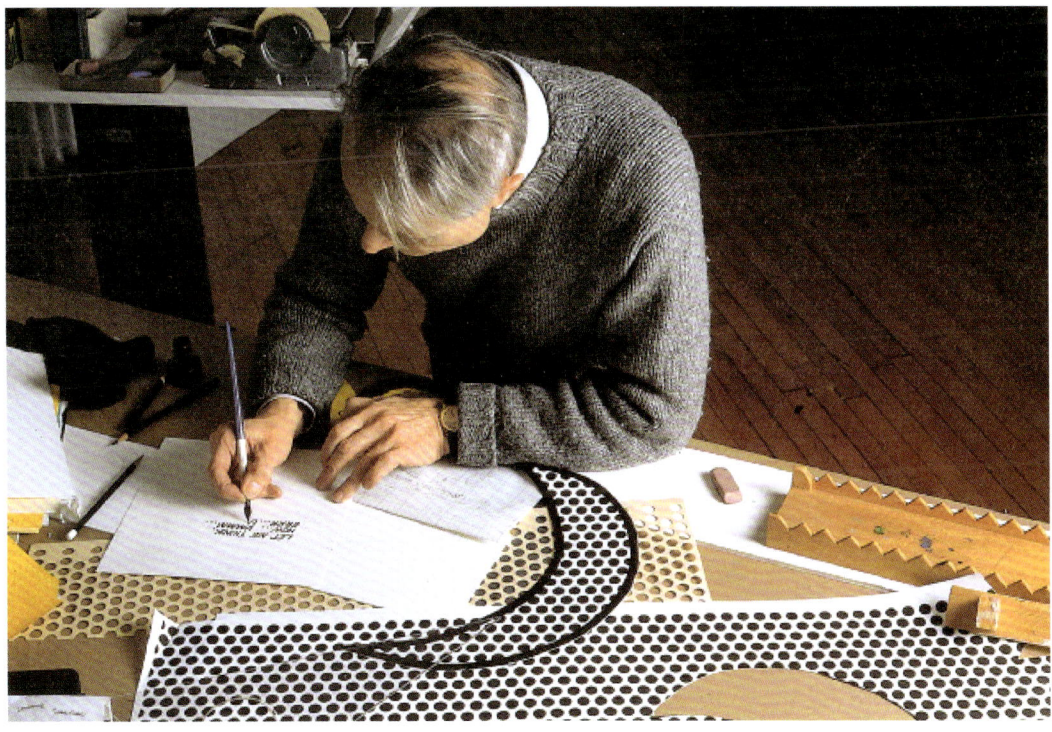

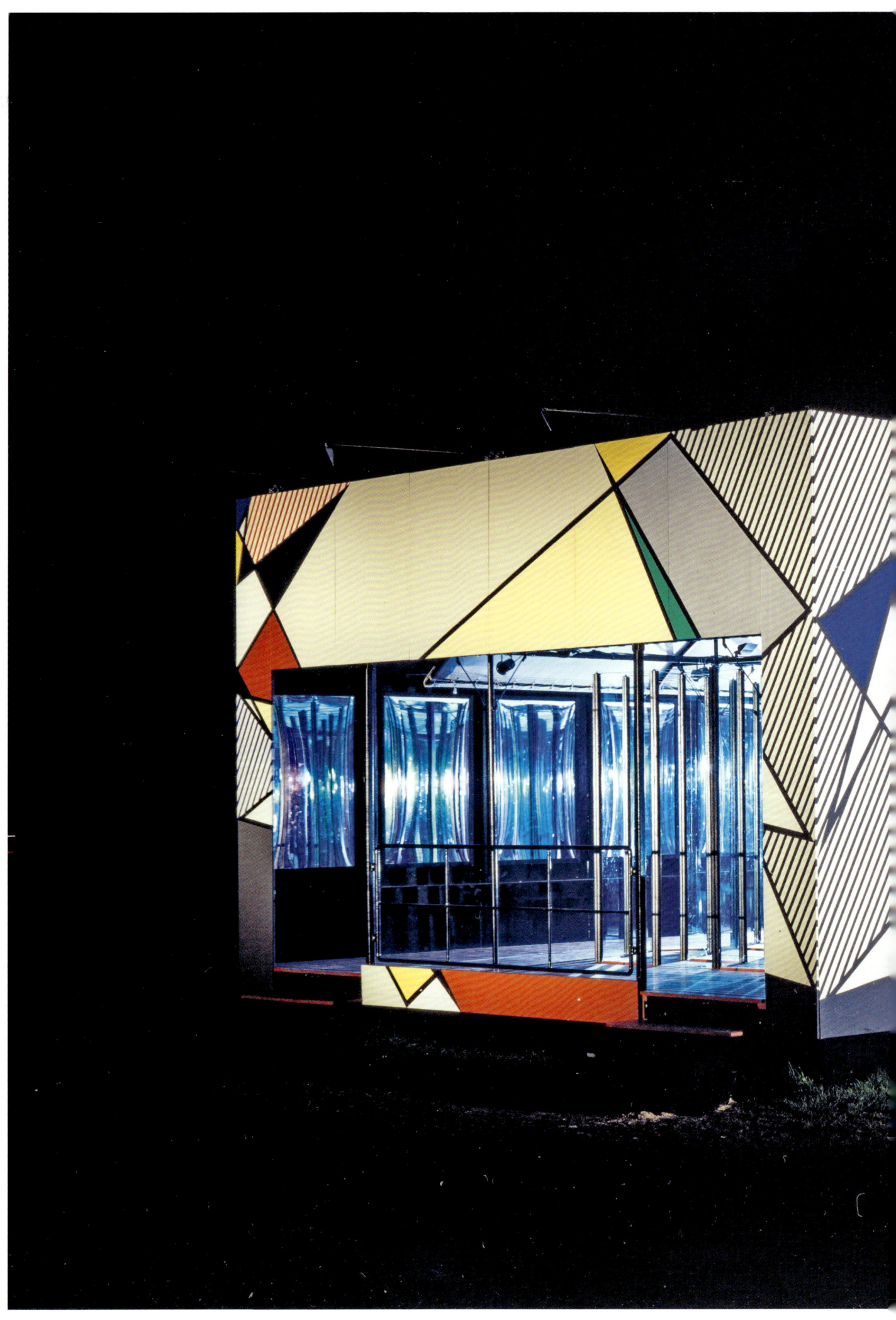

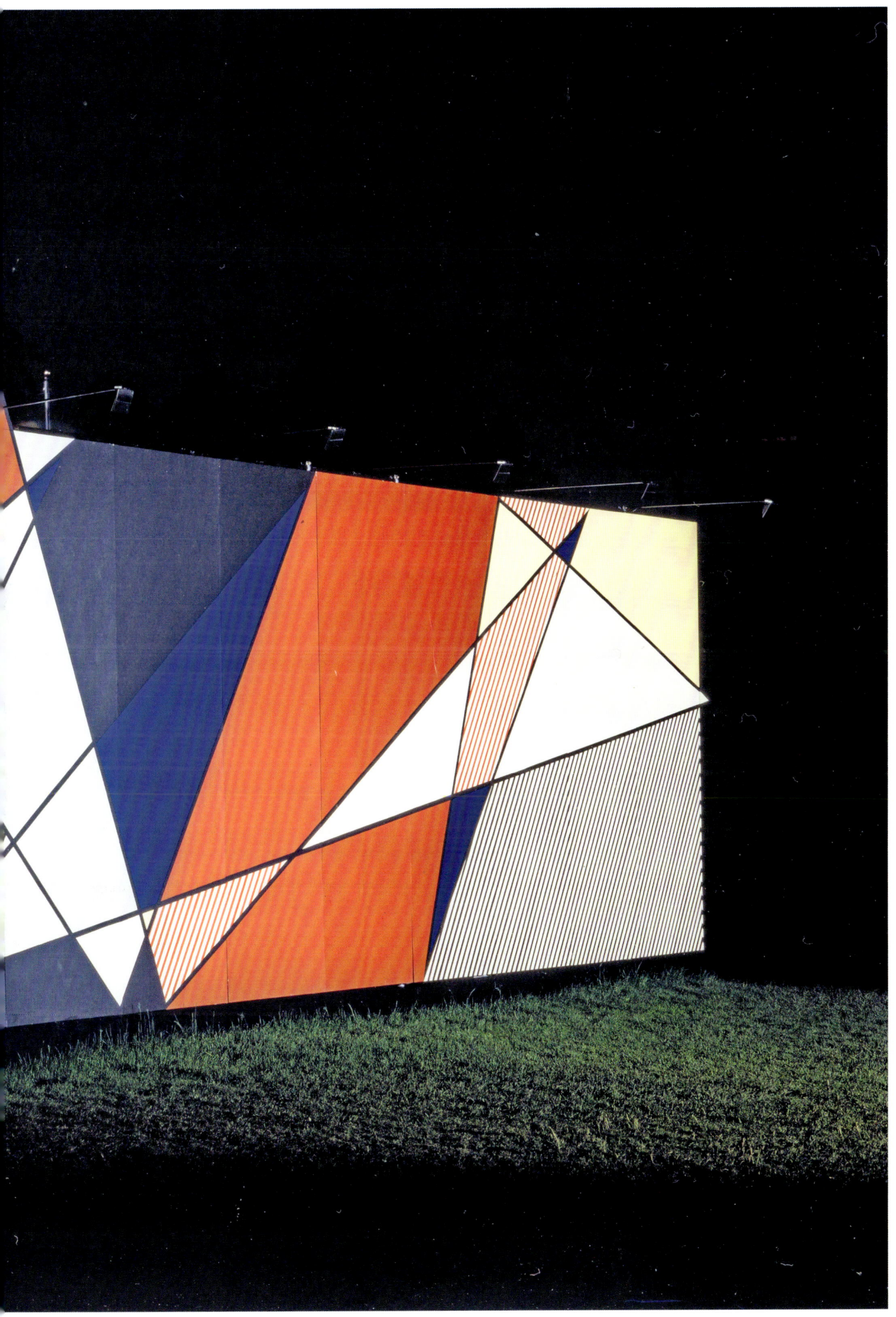

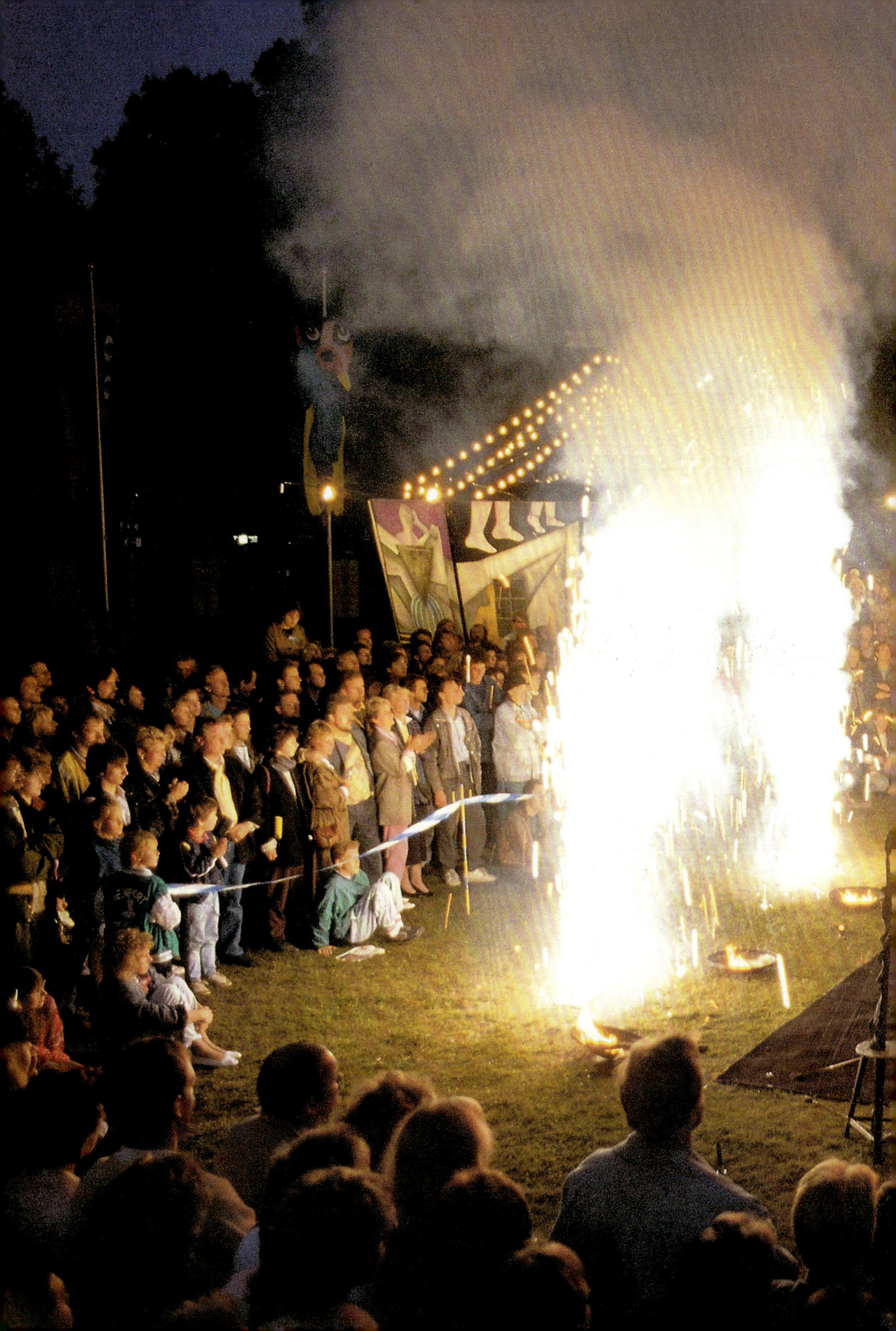

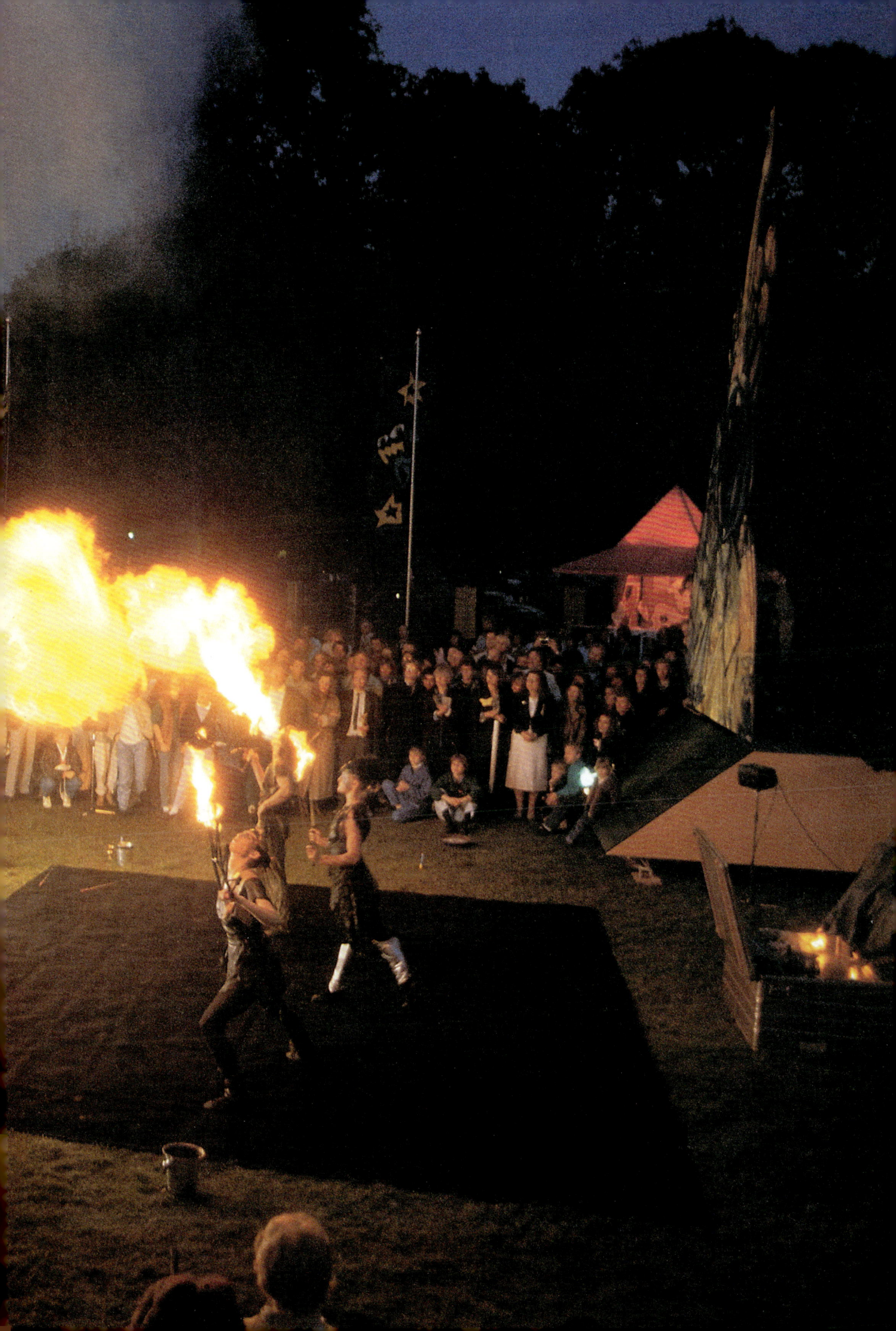

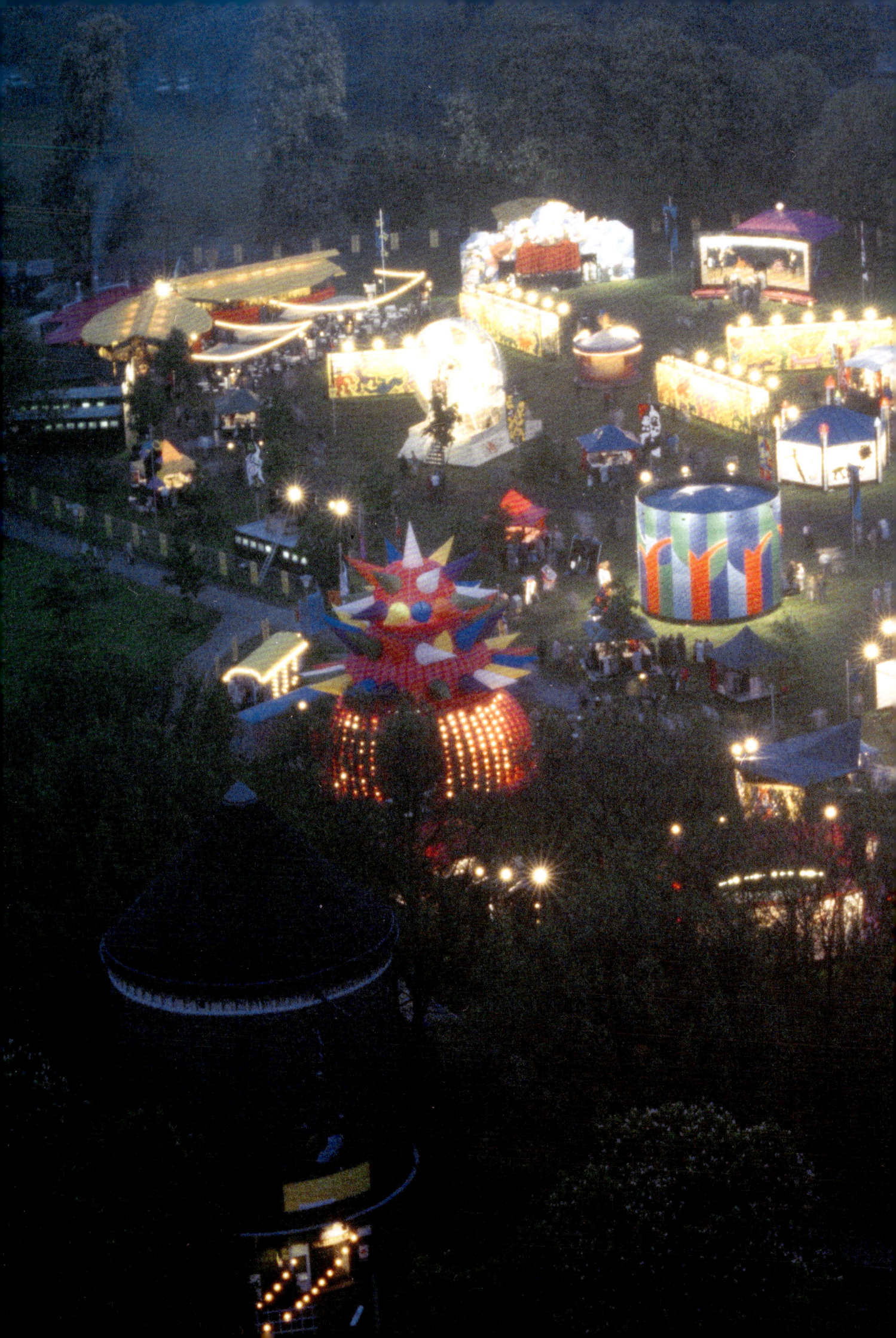

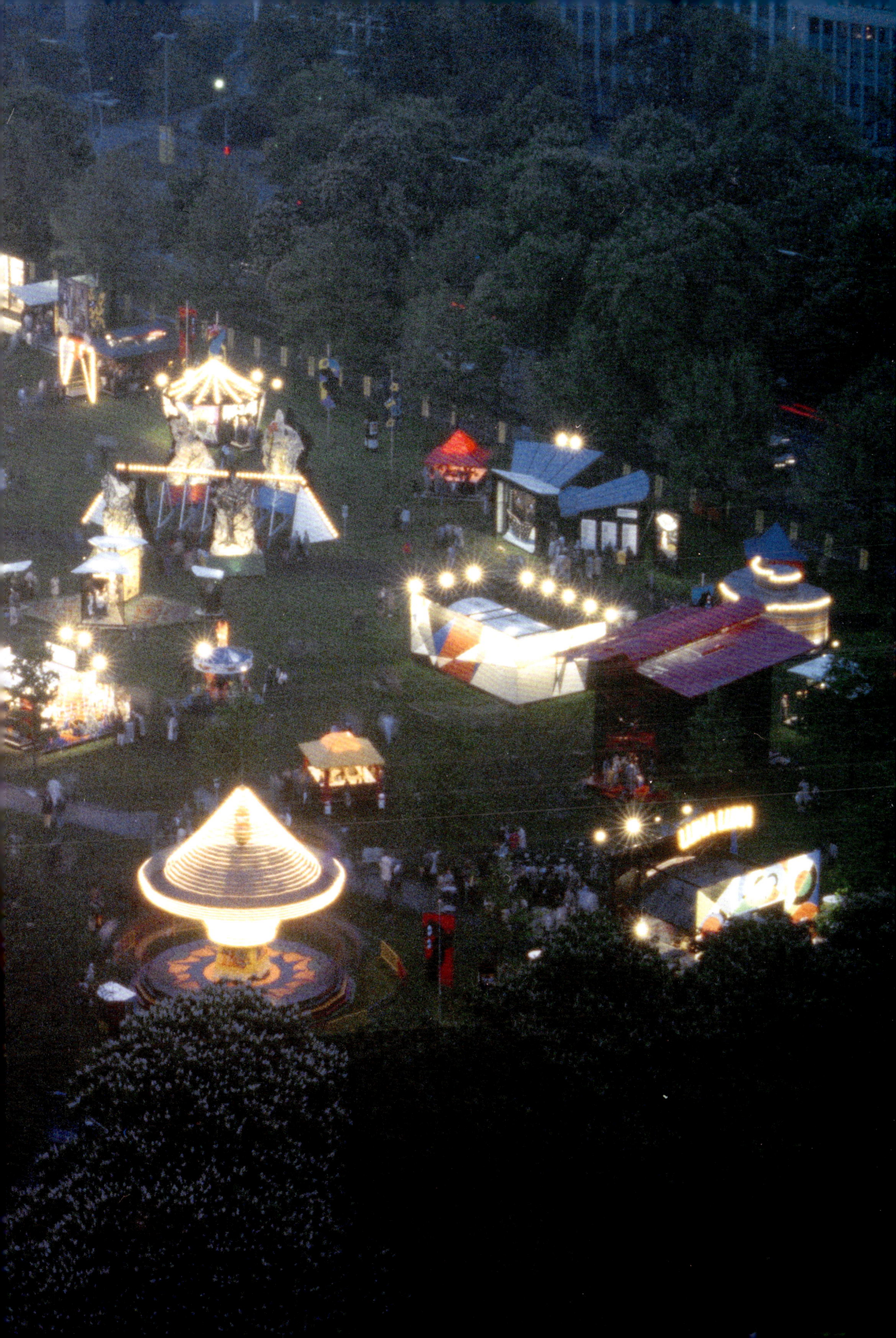

# *Luna Luna—* Made Possible by Neue Revue

## by Richard Mahkor

Editor-in-chief of Neue Revue

A meaningful, fulfilling pleasure combined with creative fun: This is the gift *Neue Revue* sought to give its readers. Fun for all, because the *Illustrierte Neue Revue*, owned by the Heinrich Bauer Verlag in Hamburg, was celebrating its anniversary.

The forty years of *Neue Revue* were an enormous piece of German media history, and the magazine attempted to present an infinite number of events, sensations, trends, and current occurrences as close-up as possible for our readers. It was an exciting and multifaceted pleasure for us journalists, but one in which every step and every decision we made had to be carefully considered.

When André Heller told us about *Luna Luna*, we spontaneously decided to support this sensory art spectacle. From the very beginning, we identified so closely with André Heller's idea that we simply said: "We're doing this! We're going to make *Luna Luna* possible."

This fairground seeks to make art accessible to many more people than before, to derive a pleasurable experience from it: Art and creativity for all, as an international language, as a means of communication that everyone can understand. As a magazine read by millions with a mission to promote understanding among people, we felt challenged by this wonderful idea.

And we wanted to make a dream come true for our readers—the dream of a personal fairground and creatively spent leisure time. *Luna Luna* has given concrete form to a meaningful, eventful, and cheerful leisure activity that involves constant new discovery. This fundamental idea for *Luna Luna* instantly fascinated and excited us.

Important international artists have provided contributions to this fairground project, in which creativity and art are no longer something for an aloof minority but for everyone and anyone. Meet *Luna Luna*—a fantastic revue full of new surprises.

I would like to thank André Heller for his wonderfully realized idea of creating *Luna Luna* for everyone.

# The *Luna Luna* Team

Overall artistic director:
André Heller
Production manager:
Stefan Seigner
Technical director and artistic
collaboration:
Georg Resetschnig
Management of Luna Luna GmbH.:
Gerd Bolls
Dr. Peter Heidenreich
Richard Mahkorn

**Staff at the Heller workshop**
Special tasks:
Doris Seigner
Office manager:
Elfriede Schrammel
Personal assistant to André Heller:
Sushma Lauda
Production assistant:
Matthias Kodric

**Architect**
Marco Ostertag and staff
Martin Prominzer

**Object production**
Helmut Reiter:
Helmut Reiter
Werner Bauer
Wolfgang Bierbaum
Michael Däubl
Josef Heindl
Roland Hofer
Herbert Hoppl
Robert Hradecky
Michael Kowarzik
Robert König
Josef Lutz
Karl Pfeiffer
Alexander Propadalo
Abdul Manan Sattar Poor
Dorel Ion Oanea
Ludwig Schäffer
Josef Schmid
Thomas Schönhofer
Alfred Thuminger
Walter Wagenleitner
Emil Zankl

**Carousel construction and construction
of the special illusions**
Peter Petz:
Hans Peter Hübsch
Walter Lehmann
Georg Bienert
Thomas Bayer
Anton Schwaiger
Michael Braun
Annemarie Weber
The Hausmann brothers
Richard Wehmeyer
Norbert Nassl
Hans Schaffranek

Otto Christa
Ottilie Heugemeier
Geli Kopp
Antonio Baroch-Castelvi
Ulrich Eibel
Anton Meyer
Anni Lindermayer
Wolfgang Jellinek
Uschi Schmidt
Karin Rappel

**Painters' Halls**
Painters' Hall Volksrheater:
Alois Piringer sen.
Alois Piringer jun.
Andreas Piringer
Elisabeth Althaler
Grain Exchange Studio:
Wolfgang Weitzdörfer
Christa Astuy
Adi Frühauf
Josef Havelka
Studio Brighella:
Thomas Frey
Leo May
Gregor Pokorny
Alexandra Reden
Paul Zündel
Elmar Klocker
Studio Princic:
Zak Princic
Anton Sever

**Sculptors**
Bernd Kastl and staff:
Gerold Kubitschek
Kurt Urban
Heinrich Lersch
Christian Jauernik
Annemarie Heigl
Ewald Lang

**Model maker**
Hans Kunitzberger

**Electronics, acoustics, and light**
Kurt Reiter and Reinhold Neuhold

**Technical assistance**
Siegfried Pipirs

**Photo assistance**
Udo Reisinger
Götz Schwan
Andreas Münchbach
Helmut Pichler

**Employees of Luna Luna GmbH, Hamburg**
Hubert Böhle
Wolfgang Bohm
Nicole Brock
Andrea Friedrichs
Eva Menke
Karsten Stodte

**Photo credits:**
Gabriela Brandenstein: p. 24 (top and
bottom left), 27 (bottom left), 30, 54, 78
dpa/Camera Press: p. 254
Alexander Czechatz: p. 16/17

Published on the occasion of the relaunch of *Luna Luna*

Design by Something Special Studios

Phaidon Press Limited
2 Cooperage Yard
London E15 2QR

Phaidon Press Inc.
111 Broadway
New York, NY 10006

phaidon.com

First published 2023
© 2023 Phaidon Press Limited

ISBN 978 1 83866 694 1

A CIP catalogue record for this book is available from the
British Library and the Library of Congress.

Printed in China